ANCIENT INDIA

R. C. MAJUMDAR

MOTILAL BANARSIDASS
Delhi Varanasi Patna Bangalore Madras

First Edition: Varanasi, 1952
Eighth Edition: Delhi, 1977
Reprinted: Delhi, 1982, 1987, 1991

41 U.A., Bungalow Road, Jawahar Nagar, Delhi 110 007

Branches

120 Royapettah High Road, Mylapore, Madras 600 004
16 St. Mark's Road, Bangalore 560 001
Ashok Rajpath, Patna 800 004
Chowk, Varanasi 221 001

ISBN: 81-208-0435-x (Cloth)
ISBN: 81-208-0436-8 (Paper)

Price: **Rs. 150** (Cloth)
Rs. 80 (Paper)

PRINTED IN INDIA
BY JAINENDRA PRAKASH JAIN AT SHRI JAINENDRA PRESS, A-45 NARAINA INDUSTRIAL AREA, PHASE I, NEW DELHI 110 028 AND PUBLISHED BY NARENDRA PRAKASH JAIN FOR MOTILAL BANARSIDASS, BUNGALOW ROAD, JAWAHAR NAGAR, DELHI 110 007

DEDICATED

TO

The Sacred Memory

OF

My Father

HALÁDHAR MAJUMDAR

CONTENTS

LIST OF PLATES

The System of Transliteration

Arranged in order of Indian alphabet.

अ	=	a	ड	=	ḍ
आ	=	ā	ढ	=	ḍh
इ	=	i	ण	=	ṇ
ई	=	ī	त	=	t
उ	=	u	थ	=	th
ऊ	=	ū	द	=	d
ऋ	=	ṛi	ध	=	dh
ए	=	e	न	=	n
ऐ	=	ai	प	=	p
ओ	=	o	फ	=	ph
औ	=	au	ब	=	b
क	=	k	भ	=	bh
ख	=	kh	म	=	m
ग	=	g	य	=	y
घ	=	gh	र	=	r
ङ	=	ṅ	ल	=	l
च	=	ch	व	=	v
छ	=	chh	श	=	ś
ज	=	j	ष	=	sh
झ	=	jh	स	=	s
ञ	=	ñ	ह	=	h
ट	=	ṭ	ं	=	ṁ
ठ	=	ṭh	:	=	ḥ

The System of Transliteration

Arranged in order of English alphabet.

a	=	अ	l	=	ल
ā	=	आ	m	=	म
ai	=	ऐ	ṁ	=	
au	=	औ	n	=	न
b	=	ब	ṇ	=	ण
bh	=	भ	ṅ	=	ङ
ch	=	च	ñ	=	ञ
chh	=	छ	o	=	ओ
d	—	द	p	=	प
d	=	ड	ph	=	फ
dn	—	ध	r	=	र
ḍh	=	ढ	ṛi	=	ऋ
e	=	ए	s	=	स
g	=	ग	ś	=	श
gh	=	घ	sh	=	ष
h	=	ह	t	=	त
ḥ	=	:	ṭ	=	ट
i	=	इ	th	=	थ
ī	=	ई	ṭh	=	ठ
j	=	ज	u	=	उ
jh	=	झ	ū	=	ऊ
k	=	क	v	—	व
kh	=	ख	y	=	य

PREFACE TO THE SECOND EDITION

The first edition of this book has been out of print for a good many years. The second edition has been long delayed because I wanted to revise it thoroughly and bring it up-to-date, and this I could not do so long on account of my various preoccupation and absence from India. In this new edition more details have been added to the history and culture of South India, and some recent publications have been added to the Bibliography.

4 Bepin Pal Road
Calcutta 26.
30 June, 1960.

R. C. Majumdar

PREFACE TO THE FIRST EDITION

This book is a revised and enlarged edition of my "*Outline of Ancient Indian History and Civilisation*" which was published in 1927 and has been out of print since 1938. Constant demands for the book, ever since, showed that the object with which it was written, as explained in the preface, was more than fulfilled. Owing to a variety of circumstances I could not bring out a second edition of the book during the next ten years. When at last I had some leisure to take up the work, I found that the book, in its present form, has, to some extent, outlived its utility, as there are already several other works of the same nature in the field. At the same time I felt the necessity of a book on ancient Indian history and culture of a more advanced type, which would not only serve the needs of general readers but may also be used as a preliminary handbook by more earnest students who require a thorough grasp of the essential facts and features before taking up specialised study in any branch of the subject. Incidentally I also kept in view the requirements of the growing number of candidates for competitive examinations in which ancient Indian history and culture is a prescribed subject. Various personal references to me showed that the competitors keenly feel the absence of a single treatise on the subject such as is available for other periods of Indian history and the history of other countries. The few books that exist, like V. A. Smith's *Early History of India*, are either incomplete (dealing only with the political history) or out of date, and even for a rudimentary knowledge of the subject such students have to go through a large number of books, which they often find it difficult to select and also to procure.

The additions and alterations which were found necessary to meet all these requirements proved to be so considerable that the new book could not, with due propriety, be regarded merely as a revised second edition of the old work. I have therefore adopted a new title for this book, though considerable portions of the old one have been incorporated in it, and the general plan has not been materially altered.

Among the more important additions may be mentioned the chapters on the prehistoric age, including the Indus Valley Civilization, more detailed account of the ancient republican clans and the various mediaeval local dynasties, specially those of the south, and the development of art and colonisation. Important changes, though much less extensive, have been made in chapters dealing with political theory and administrative system, as well as social and economic condition, and an entirely new section on coins has been added. Considerable other modifications and re-arrangements, involving re-grouping of chapters, have been made, and more copious footnotes and fuller bibliography have been added for the guidance of advanced students. On the whole the revision has been a laborious undertaking, and I have spared no pains to make this work useful not only to general readers but also to advanced students and candidates for competitive examinations.

It is hardly necessary to add that in dealing with ancient India I have used the geographical name to denote the whole country and ignored the present political division. But I have adopted some of the new spellings of geographical names introduced in Independent India, such as Gaṅgā and Sindhu, for Ganges and Indus, except where they are used in adjective phrases like 'Indus valley' ; though, due to inadvertence, the old forms and spellings may occur here and there along with the new ones. In writing modern geographical and personal names, no diacritical mark has been used except to indicate long ā.

Hindu University
Banaras.
January, 1952.

R. C. Majumdar

INTRODUCTION

I. Physical Characteristics

India is bounded on the north by the Himālayas and on the south, east, and west by the open sea. On the north-east and on the north-west, ranges of hills connect the main chain of the Himālayas with the sea.

India is thus naturally protected on all sides. It must not be supposed, however, that she was cut off from the rest of the world by these formidable barriers. The Himālaya is the most inaccessible frontier that nature has designed for any country, but even here, there are roads from Tibet to Nepāl that have carried for ages not merely peaceful missionaries of culture and religion, but on rare occasions even formidable hosts of soldiers as well. Besides, there are mountain passes in the north-west which have served for ages as the high road of communication between India and the outer world.

Natural boundaries of India

There are several passes across the Hindu Kush, and the most frequented route on this side of the hill range is the one that runs along the valley of the Kābul river and then descends to Peshāwar, through the Khyber Pass, a winding and narrow defile over 20 miles long. Another well-known route runs from Herāt to Kandahār, and then descends to the Sindhu (Indus) valley through the Bolān Pass. Another road from the west passes along the inhospitable Makrān coast. Apart from invasions and immigrations unrecorded in history, innumerable bands of colonists, merchants, and conquering hosts entered and left India through these passes in historical times ever since the Aryans crossed the Hindu Kush about four thousand years ago.

The north-eastern chains contain a remarkable gap through which the Brahmaputra enters India, and it must have been frequented by people in all ages, though recorded instances are few and far between. The hills further south are covered with dense forests and it is difficult to cross them, but merchants, misssionaries, and sometimes even armed hosts are known to have passed through them.

The sea, too, has never operated as a barrier to the enterprising Aryans. From early times they boldly plied the ocean and came into contact with islands and countries, both far and near. But as the navy in ancient days could hardly ever be a formidable instrument for aggressive purpose, India was practically secure against invasion from the sea. The natural frontiers of India thus gave security, but not immunity from invasions, and while they ensured definite individuality to her people by separating them from the rest of Asia by well-marked boundary lines, they never isolated them from the rest of the world.

Area

Within these frontiers India comprises an area of about fifteen hundred thousand square miles, and is thus equal in extent to the whole of Europe with the exclusion of Russia. Its coast line extends for more than three thousand miles, and its mountain barrier is half that length. Its population numbers nearly four hundred millions.

India, a subcontinent, not a country

The physical features of the country are varied in character—there being inaccessible mountain heights, the highest on the face of the earth, low alluvial plains, high table-lands, wild forests, secluded valleys, as well as arid deserts. It has the hottest plains as well as the coolest hill resorts. The variety in physical characteristics is only equalled by the variety of races, religions and languages, and it may be said, without much exaggeration, that India alone contains greater varieties of each of these than the whole of Europe. India cannot thus be looked upon as a country in the same sense in which we apply the term to modern European countries like France or Germany. It would be more rational to look upon it as a continent and its different provinces as so many countries. The term sub-continent, recently applied to India, is a happy designation, and it will be well to bear in mind the full significance of such a name while reading its history. To give an example, it will be unreasonable to look for that unity in Indian history which the annals of a country like France or Italy afford. Such unity may be expected only in kingdoms like Magadha, Gauḍa, Kośala, Śūrasena (Mathurā), Avanti, and Karṇāṭa, each of which is equal in area and population to many of the European States. The occasional unification of India or a large part of it, under the Mauryas or their successors, should not be likened to processes in the formation of modern European States or of the kingdoms of Egypt, Assyria, Babylonia, and Italy. It should rather be compared to the large but ephemeral empires, established by those ancient States or brought into existence by the imperial ambitions of Charlemagne, Charles V, Louis XIV, and Napoleon.

Modern historians are never tired of emphasising the contrast between the peaceful empire established by the British Rāj and unsuccessful efforts of the ancient Indians in that direction. They conveniently ignore the fact that in speaking of ancient India they are speaking of a period when time and space had not been practically eliminated by the modern discoveries of science. How physical characteristics influence history in this respect may be illustrated by one example. The news of any riot in Southern India would reach the Government at Delhi in less than three minutes and an adequate military force could be despatched in an equal number of days. But if rebellion had occurred in that region in the days of Aśoka, the news would not have reached Pāṭaliputra in less than three months and at least double that period would have been necessary to send a requisite force.

True import of the above

A clear recognition of these factors is of primary importance for a proper understanding of Indian history. Failure to do this has often vitiated the judgment of historians. They have, for example, inferred that the Indians were unenterprising and lacked military skill, because there are no records of their expeditions outside their frontiers. But the fact is ignored that the sub-continent of India, together with Further India, Indo-China and Pacific Islands offered too large a field for their military enterprise to tempt them outside its boundaries. The largest empires ruled over by the Egyptians, the Assyrians, and the Babylonians were less in extent than India, whose political boundaries in ancient times extended up to the Hindu Kush and the Helmand, together with its colonial empire in the east. The Persian and Roman empires, as well as the area over which Alexander gained his meteoric success, are equal to or only a little larger than this Greater India, while the empire of Louis XIV or of Napoleon is insignificant, compared to its whole extent.

As regards the physical characteristics of the interior, the most noteworthy feature is the Central Highlands, a formidable barrier which separates North India

Physical features of the interior

Central Highlands

from the Deccan. It is constituted by two parallel ranges of hills, the Vindhya (including Bhanrer and Kaimur ranges) in the north, and the Sātpurā with the Mahādeo and the Maikal hills in the south, separated by a narrow valley through which flows the Narmadā. This river as well as the hills and dense forests in this region and Chotanagpur made communication extremely difficult, and hence a sharp distinction has always remained between the people of the north and the people of the south. The history of the two portions has also, generally speaking, followed independent courses, though at times they have been brought into contact with each other.

Northern India

The portion north of the Vindhya range contains fertile plains both in the east as well as in the west, with the desert of Rājputāna intervening between the two. The plain on the west of the desert is watered by the Sindhu (Indus) and that on the east by the Gangā (Ganges) system. These two rivers and their tributaries served as easy means of communication and hence their banks were studded from very ancient times with flourishing seats of civilisation. The short space between the desert of Rājputāna and the chains of Himālaya is the only connecting link between these two plains and serves as an admirable defending ground against any army from the west which seeks to penetrate into the interior of Hindusthān. It was no mere accident that several battles which decided the fate of India were fought on the famous fields of Pānipat and Talawāri in this region.

The part of India lying south of the Central Highlands is a triangular peninsula which gradually narrows down almost to a point at Cape Comorin, the southern extremity of India. The two narrow coastal regions from the north-west and north-east, meeting at this point, are known respectively as the Malabar and the Coromandel Coasts. Although there are few good harbours, suitable for modern shipping, on either coast, there are safe anchorages for ships, particularly along the western coast, which served well the purposes of maritime trade to and from India.

The coastal region on the west is a long narrow strip of wet lowlands flanked by a mass of steep and rugged hills, known as the Western Ghats, which rise abruptly to a height of two thousand feet in the north and gradually increasing in height, culminate at the Nilgiris with a peak more than 8,700 ft.

high. Here they are joined by the Eastern Ghats, a lower range of hills similarly running along the eastern coast. Leaving a gap immediately to the south, the Western Ghats continue as far as Cape Comorin, reaching even a greater height of more than 8,800 ft. in Anaimudi peak. This gap stretches about twenty miles from the north to south at a level of about a thousand feet above the sea-level, and affords an easy access from one coast to the other.

Between the Western and the Eastern Ghats lies the broad Deccan Plateau sloping gradually from the west to the east. Its western brink, formed by the Western Ghats, looks like a gigantic wall of enormous height facing the Arabian Sea and running parallel to it at a distance which varies between fifty to hundred miles, though occasionally the margin is narrowed down to five miles or even less. The Eastern Ghats, however, fall down towards the Indian Ocean in gentler slope and the plain between the two is much wider than that on the west. The Krishnā and its tributary the Tungabhadrā divide the tableland into two parts, the Deccan and the South India proper, which have often played separate but important roles in history. The two other important river systems in this region are those of the Godāvarī in the north and the Kāverī in the south.

The fertile plains of India, with easy means of irrigation, made it one of the richest agricultural countries in the world.

The wealth of India

Metallic ores, deposited in the soil, and huge timber forests stimulated industry and manufacture. Large navigable rivers and extensive sea-coasts, studded with good anchorages, developed inland and foreign trade and carried Indian products all over the civilized world. To crown all, gold, jewels, pearls, and various precious stones are found in abundance in the soil. All these factors made India the richest country in the world. The wealth of India became proverbial and tempted greedy invaders from beyond

and its effect.

the mountain passes. The fertility of the soil and the wealth of the country were thus also indirect causes of her downfall and degradation. It has often been alleged that they were also direct causes, inasmuch as they enervated the people and made them an easy prey to foreign invaders. This is, however, not so self-evident as has generally been assumed. Indian soldiers were often distinguished for bravery and hardihood and their defeat is generally to be traced to other causes of a different character.

The wild and sublime beauty of nature, in which India is peculiarly rich, gave a philosophic and poetic turn to the Indian mind, and remarkable progress was made in religion, philosophy, art and literature. But while easy means of livelihood favoured the growth of these elements, the absence of a keen struggle with nature was detrimental to the development of that spirit of inquiry into the mysteries of nature which lead to the growth of positive science. In short, almost all the main peculiarities of intellectual development in India may be explained with reference to its physical environments.

Influence of physical features upon the civilization of the country.

II. Sources of Indian History

One of the gravest defects of Indian culture, which defy rational explanation, is the aversion of Indians to writing history. They applied themselves to all conceivable branches of literature and excelled in many of them, but they never seriously took to the writing of history. It is difficult to accept the view, too often maintained, that the Indians totally lacked the historical sense. This is discredited by the few historical texts, local chronicles like those of Nepāl, Gujarāt, Kāshmir, and other places, and a large number of inscriptions that have come down to us. Still the fact remains that the Indians displayed a strange indifference towards properly recording the public events of their country.

Absence of history

Rudiments of history are indeed preserved in the Purāṇas and the Epics. We find lists of kings and sometimes, though very rarely, their achievements, but it is impossible to arrange them in chronological order without extraneous help. References to historical events and traditions are also scattered in other books, and valuable information is thus obtained from the different branches of literature, both secular and religious, even from such books as the grammatical works of Pāṇini and Patañjali. Biographical works of great historical persons are, of course, of great value, and we are fortunate in possessing a number of them, such as *Harsha-charita* by Bāṇabhaṭṭa, *Vikramāṅkadeva-charita* by Bilhaṇa, *Navasāhasāṅka-charita* of Padmagupta, *Rāma-charita* of Sandhyākara Nandi, *Bhojaprabandha* by Ballāla, *Gauḍavaho* by Vākpatirāja, *Kumārapāla-charita*, both by Jayasiṁha and Hemachandra, *Hammīra-kāvya* of Nayachandra, *Pṛithvīrāja-charita* by Chānd-Bardai, and *Pṛithvīrāja-vijaya* by an anonymous writer. There is only one historical work, properly so called, written by Kalhaṇa in the 12th century A. D. This is *Rājataraṅgiṇī* which deals with the history of Kāshmir from the earliest times up to the date of the composition of that work. It assumes, however, a regular historical form only from the seventh century A. D., the earlier chapters being a medley of confused traditions and fanciful imaginations.

Sources of history : 1. Literature

Like Sanskrit the Tamil literature is also of great value as a source for the history of South India. The literature of the Śaṅgam Age throws much light on the kings and States of the early centuries of the Christian era. Some court poets chose their royal patrons as the heroes of their poems, a good illustration of which is furnished by the *Nandik-Kalambakam*, with the Pallava king Nandivarman III as its hero. There are also a few works of quasi-historical nature such as the *Kaliṅgattupparaṇi* which has as its theme the invasion of Kaliṅga by Kulottuṅga I. Oṭṭakkūttan wrote three works on the three successive kings, Vikrama Chola, Kulottuṅga II, and Rājarāja II.

But although the literary works, both in Sanskrit and Tamil, are of great help in forming an estimate of ancient culture and civilization of India, they do not go far enough in the reconstruction of the history of the country. Our knowledge in this respect was therefore very imperfect till the 19th century, when the genius and patient industry of a number of scholars, mostly European, considerably improved it with the help of evidences of quite a different character. Our present knowledge of Indian history is mainly based on these evidences, and it is therefore necessary to form a correct idea about them.

2. Archaeology

The first in point of importance is the archaeological evidence. It consists of coins, inscriptions, and other monuments of antiquity. The inscriptions, being contemporary records of a reliable character, have helped us most. They have furnished us with the names of kings, sometimes together with their dates and other necessary particulars, and have recorded many important events of history. The coins have preserved the names of additional kings and given us particulars about the locality over which they ruled. The monuments are undying witnesses of the artistic skill of ancient Indians and testify to their wealth and grandeur at different epochs of history. They also give us greater insight into the culture of the people than would be possible from a mere study of literary records. The excavated ruins of Taxila hold out before us a picture of the city-life in ancient India such as no books could give. Sometimes the archaeological excavations reveal unknown epochs of civilization such as that which flourished in the Sindhu (Indus) Valley, to which reference will be made later.

3. Foreigners' accounts.

For a great deal of our knowledge of ancient Indian history we are indebted to the foreigners. India figures in foreign inscriptions, *e.g.*, in those of Darius, and in foreign literature, such as the history of Herodotus. But the most valuable contributions were made by foreigners who came to this country. The Greeks,

The Greeks.

who accompanied Alexander in his Indian campaign or who were subsequently sent as ambassadors to the courts of India, wrote detailed accounts of the country, and although these works are mostly lost, their substance has been preserved in the accounts of later Greek writers. Special reference may be made to the *Indica* of Megasthenes, who lived in the court of Chandragupta Maurya.

Two other important works are the Geography of India written by Ptolemy (about 130 A. D.), and the *Periplus of the Erythraean Sea*, a valuable account of trade and maritime activities in India from the pen of an unknown Greek author who visited India in the second half of first century A. D.

The Chinese.

At a later period, Chinese travellers came to India in large numbers to collect religious books and visit the holy places of Buddhism. Some of them like Fa-hien (5th C. A.D.), Hiuen Tsang (7th C. A. D.) and I-tsing (7th C. A. D.) have recorded very valuable accounts of contemporary India. The Muhammadan traveller, Alberūnī, who accompanied Sultān Mahmūd, made a careful study of the literature, religion, and social institutions of India. His memoir on India is a remarkable product of the age and throws a flood of light on the decadent period of Indian history. The Venetian traveller, Marco Polo, passed through some parts of South India on his way from China to Persia between A. D. 1292 and 1294, and has left a very interesting account of the social manners and customs of South India.

The Muhammadan.

By utilising all these evidences it has been possible to throw some light on the culture and civilization that flourished in India since the third millennium before Christ, and to construct an outline of political history from about the seventh century B. C. to A. D. 1200. No doubt, details remain to be filled in to a large extent, but the success, so far achieved, encourages hope for the future. The chronology of all the royal dynasties, with the sole exception of the Kushāṇas, has been fixed with tolerable certainty; the epochs of Indian eras have been determined; and thus a great deal of spade work has already been accomplished. The following pages are intended to give a brief résumé of the results so far attained, and they will also indicate the directions in which our knowledge is deficient in the extreme.

BOOK I

From the Earliest Times to 600. B. C.

CHAPTER I

The Prehistoric Age—Early Man and His Implements

History is a record of the achievements of man. But, as in other countries, we possess very scanty data about the early human settlers in India. It is now generally held that the earliest traces of human beings in India are found in the Panjāb, in the region between the Sindhu and Jhelum rivers, and belong to the end of the First Inter-Glacial Period and the beginning of the Second Ice Age, i. e., about 500,000 years ago.

Early Man.

This is proved by the discovery of large flakes embedded in boulder-gravels of this period in the Siwalik foot-hills and the plains in N. W. Panjāb, Punch, and Jammu. The continued existence of man in the Second and Third Inter-Glacial as well as in the Fourth Ice Age is similarly proved by the tools and implements—pebble tools, flake, and coral tools—used by him. Their findspots indicate new settlements in Rājputāna, Gujarāt, Upper Narmadā valley, Bengal, Bihār, and Orissa in North India, as well as nearly the whole of Deccan and South India,—in short practically in every part of India except the great Indo-Gangetic plain. It is held by some that "Early Man" in India originated in South India, and migrated towards the Panjāb at the close of the First Ice Age.

The rough stone implements, mainly of quartzite, used by men during this long period, show different varieties and

Paleolithic Age

resemble the paleolithic tools in Europe. This age in India may therefore be called Paleolithic, a term derived from two Greek words meaning old stone (*palaios*=old ; *lithos*=stone). The men of this age belonged to a very primitive stage of civilization. They did not know the use of metals, and had no idea of cultivation. They probably did not even know how to make a fire, and lived on fruits of trees and the animals and fishes which they killed by means of their stone implements. They lived in natural caverns and never constructed houses or tombs of any kind.

The culture which succeeded the Paleolithic is named Mesolithic. Instead of quartzite the men used chalcedony and other silicate varieties such as jasper, chert, and

Mesolithic Age.

bloodstone. The stone implements are, however, extremely small, only about an inch in length, and the technique of making them is also different. These are known as microliths (Gk. *micros*=small) and found all over India. The men who used them were, like their predecessors, primarily hunters and lived on the games of forests. But they also ate wild fruits and used other vegetable products of the forest. Probably, at a later stage, they knew the art of making pottery.

Neolithic Age.

The Mesolithic Age, as the name implies, was really a transitional (Gk. *mesos*=middle) period leading to the next distinctive phase of culture known as Neolithic (Gk. *neo*=new). There was a greater variety of tools than in the preceding ages, and these included celts, adzes, axe-hammers, chisels, mace-heads, pestles, arrow-heads, flakes, saws, burins etc. The material for the stone tools of this age was primarily fine-grained dark-green trap, though diorite, basalt, slate, chlorite, schist, gneiss, sandstone, and quartzite were also occasionally used. Unlike those of the preceding age, these tools, generally speaking, bear unmistakable signs of polish, either all over the body or at the ends. Many of these stone implements were ground, grooved, and polished, till they became highly finished objects of various forms, adapted to diverse purposes. The people who made them belonged to a far advanced state of civilization. They made houses, domesticated animals, and cultivated lands. They knew the use of fire, made potteries, and constructed tombs, some of which have come to light in our days. They seem to have also been acquainted with the elements of the art of painting.[1]

Copper and Bronze Age.

As in the rest of the world, so in India, the Neolithic Age was succeeded by phases of culture distinguished by the use of metals. Copper or bronze (an alloy of copper and tin) was the earliest metal known, and several hoards of axes, swords, daggers, harpoons, and rings made of it have been found, mostly in the Gangā-Yamunā *doāb*. This culture flourished principally in North India, for only a few stray finds of copper or bronze weapons, tools, and

1. This is the general view, but some scholars doubt whether all the rock-paintings, found at different neolithic sites, should be assigned to such an old age.

vessels have so far been recorded in South India. It is generally assumed that the knowledge of iron is characteristic of a distinctly later phase of culture, which is consequently known as the Iron Age. The transition is proved by megalithic monuments i. e., structures made of large blocks of stone (Gk. *megas*=great), such as cromlech, cairns, and menhirs, which are widely distributed all over India. Some of these contain a mixed assortment of polished stone tools, carnelian beads, wheel-made pottery, objects of copper, bronze, and gold, and iron slags. This shows that the change from one cultural phase to another was very gradual, and people did not altogether give up the old material or technique even when they came to know of new ones.

Iron Age.

With the Iron Age, we come to historical period. Until forty years ago, all that we knew of the culture of the Copper or Bronze Age was derived from the finds of tools, weapons, and ornaments. But the archaeological excavations at various sites in Sindh, Panjāb, and Baluchistān have revealed extensive ruins of towns belonging to that age, and hence we know a great deal of this culture which will be described in connection with the Sindhu (Indus) valley civilization.

CHAPTER II

The Prehistoric Age — Race and Culture

1. RACIAL ELEMENTS.

One is naturally anxious to know something of the different peoples who evolved the different cultures described in the preceding chapter. Unfortunately, it is not possible as yet to associate any particular race or group of people with any of them. All that we can do is first of all to ascertain the different types or races of men, and then to correlate, as far as possible, each racial type with a distinctive cultural phase described above.

In order to determine the different races of men that settled in India, it is necessary to analyse the physical features of her existing population. Such an analysis has not yet been properly made; consequently, the results cannot be regarded as very satisfactory, and the scholars hold very different views on the subject. According to the most recent authoritative view, *viz.*, that of Dr. B. S. Guha, no less than six racial elements have contributed to build up the population of India.

Six Racial Elements.

1. The Negrito, immigrant from Africa, is now all but extinct in India. A small group still survives in the Andamans, while traces of this race are found among the Kadars and Palayans of Cochin and Travancore, the Nāgās of Assam, and a few other tribes in India.

2. The Proto-Australoids, who came from the west, form one of the basic elements of Indian population. By admixture with other elements, specially with the Negritos who came before, and the Mongoloids who came after them, they gave rise to Kol or Muṇḍā type, the Mon-Khmer type in Assam, Burma, and Indo-China, and various other primitive types now found in the islands of the Indian Archipelago and those of Melanesia and Polynesia. The speeches of these peoples, scattered in wide areas extending from Kāshmir to Easter Island, belong to the same Family of Languages known as Austric.

3. The Mongoloids are divided into two sub-groups. The Paleo-Mongoloids are represented by tribes living in

Assam, Chittagong Hills, and the Indo-Burmese frontiers. The Tibeto-Mongoloids, a more pronounced and advanced Mongoloid type must have immigrated from Tibet in comparatively later times into Sikkim and Bhutan.

4. The Mediterranean peoples, with different sub-types, all came from the west and spoke the Dravidian language, now represented by Tamil, Telugu, Kannaḍa, and Malayālam.

5. The Alpine, Dinaric, and Armenoid, forming sub-groups of one physical type, probably came from Central Asia. They form main elements in the population of Bengal, Orissa, and Gujarāt, and are also found scattered in other parts of India, including South Indian Peninsula.

6. The Nordic group who spoke the Aryan language, of which the earliest specimen is preserved in the Vedas.

It must be noted that considerable admixture has taken place among these six types of humanity in order to give rise to the present population of India, and none of them is now found in a pure form. Further, all the peoples which resulted from the admixture ultimately adopted one or the other of the four distinct languages, viz., the Austric, the Tibeto-Chinese, the Dravidian, and the Aryan. In other words, the types 1 and 5 have not preserved their own dialects. This very fact, to which other arguments may be added, proves that the people speaking the same language do not necessarily belong to the same race, and vice versa; though, naturally enough, linguistic affinity is, oftener than not, the result of a common racial origin.

It may be surmised that the Negritos belonged to the Paleolithic Age. But it is almost certain that the Proto-Australoids belonged to the Neolithic culture. A study of their language shows that they made rich contributions to the development of material civilization in India. Among various things we owe to them may be mentioned the cultivation of rice and some important vegetables, the manufacture of sugar from the cane, the weaving of cotton cloth, the use of betel-vine, and probably also of turmeric and vermilion in life and ritual, and the practice of counting on the basis of twenty. It has also been suggested that these people were the first to domesticate the elephant, and that the ideas of future life and transmigration, and many mythological and religious stories and notions of later times owe a great deal to them.

2. THE DRAVIDIANS

The Mediterranean peoples are generally, in popular usage, referred to as Dravidians, though properly speaking Dravidian is the name of the language spoken by them and has no ethnic significance. The Dravidian languages now form a solid *bloc* only in the Deccan and South India, but there are good grounds to believe that they were at one time fairly wide-spread all over North India. The Brāhui speech in Baluchistān is the only Dravidian dialect in the north, and may be regarded as the sole surviving fragment of a vast fabric that has perished.

An analysis of the oldest living specimens of the Dravidian language shows that the Mediterranean peoples who spoke them possessed a much higher degree of civilization than the Proto-Australoids whom they partially suppressed. They introduced a city culture as opposed to the village culture of their predecessors, and they developed not only city life but also international trade. They had kings who lived in strong houses and ruled over small States. They probably knew the art of writing, though we are not quite certain about it. They believed in God and built temples for Him. They had laws and customs, and the system of marriage was prevalent among them. They knew most of the metals and planets, made pottery, boats, and ships, and were well acquainted with agriculture, spinning, weaving, and dyeing. They delighted in war and fought with bows, arrows, spears and swords. Many of the Hindu religious ideas and practices, particularly the system of worshipping images of gods with flowers, fruits, leaves, and water, are probably derived from them, and some well-known Hindu divinities may be of Dravidian origin.

Dravidian Culture.

There is a general belief that all the best elements in Hindu religion and culture are derived from the Aryans, and whatever is lowly, degrading, or superstitious in it represents the primitive non-Aryan element mixed up with it. This view is certainly wrong, and we must admit that the Aryan religion, thoughts, and beliefs have been profoundly modified by those of the Proto-Australoids and Dravidians with whom they came into contact in India. Though the extent of their influence is not yet fully known, there is no doubt that they underlie the whole texture of Hindu culture and civilization, and their contribu-

Its influence upon Aryan Culture

tion to it is by no means tiher mean or negligible. In some respects, particularly in material civilization, the Dravidian speaking peoples perhaps excelled the Aryans, and in any case they must be regarded as partners of the Aryans in building up the great structure known as Hinduism.

———

CHAPTER III

The Sindhu (Indus) Valley Civilization

All that has been said above regarding the culture of the early settlers in India is based on what may be described as the linguistic paleontology, i.e., inference derived from a study of the oldest words in their current language. This is at best an indirect and very doubtful process, and cannot in any case supply a comprehensive and detailed picture. But in the absence of any visible memorials which can be definitely associated with these peoples, it is not possible to do anything more. Until about 40 years ago we had no such direct and positive evidence of the history and culture of India before the advent of the Aryans. Their literary works, known as the Vedas, gave us for the first time a comprehensive picture of the social and religious ideas as well as political and economic condition of India. It was inevitable in these circumstances that the history of India should have begun for all practical purposes from this event, and the Aryan culture should have been regarded as the starting point in the delineation of Indian civilization. All this has been changed by an epoch-making discovery in 1922-23 A.D. In that year began the excavations of the ruins at Mohenjo-daro, a big mound situated in the Larkana district in Sindh, which in course of time revealed the remains of successive cities, the earliest of which can be approximately dated about 2700 years before Christ. Further excavations at Harappā in the Montgomery District, W. Pakistan, and various sites in Sindh and Baluchistān have proved the existence of a great civilization in this region which may be described as chalcolithic (Gk. *chalcos*= copper) i.e., combining the characteristics of both Neolithic and Copper Age. This is now generally called the Sindhu (Indus) Valley Civilization, for though it spread far beyond that valley, its most extensive remains have been found at Mohenjo-daro and Harappā, both in the Sindhu Valley, and the largest number of sites, containing traces of it, are also in the same region. The discovery of this civilization has almost revolutionized our conception of Indian history. At a single stroke the antiquity of Indian civilization has been pushed back to 3000 B.C., if

Mohenjo-daro

not earlier still, and India now ranks along with Sumer, Akkad, Babylon, Egypt, and Assyria as a pioneer of human civilization.

It is impossible, within the short scope of this work, to give an adequate account of this ancient civilization in all its bearings, for which the reader may consult the big and monumental volumes on Mohenjo-daro and Harappā referred to in the Bibliography. Here, only a brief outline of its characteristic features must suffice. Unless otherwise stated, the description applies more particularly to Mohenjo-daro.

As noted above, Mohenjo-daro contains the remains of a succession of cities, each built upon the ruins of another, destroyed by the inundation of the Sindhu or other causes. No less than seven different layers have been uncovered so far, and still more ancient ones may yet lie buried under the ground.

Town-planning

Even the extant ruins show remarkable skill in town-planning. The streets, varying in width from 9 to 34 ft., were regularly aligned, sometimes running straight for half a mile. The principal streets were duly oriented to the points of the compass and intersected at right angles, dividing the city into square or rectangular blocks, each of which was divided lengthwise and crosswise by a number of lanes. In the earlier cities the buildings never encroached on these streets and lanes, almost each of which had a public well and lamp-posts at intervals. The city had an elaborate drainage system which opened into great culverts emptying in the river.

Houses

The dwelling houses varied in size from a palatial building to one with two small rooms, showing the quarters of the rich and the poor. They were plain and devoid of architectural embellishments, the aim being to make a house comfortable rather than artistic. Most of the houses had a well, a bathroom and a good system of covered drainage connected with that of the street. All these as well as the main buildings were made of well-made burnt bricks, which have been excellently preserved even to this day and would be considered highly creditable even according to our modern standard. Sun-dried brick was used for foundations, and the roof was flat and made of wood. The rooms were arranged round an open courtyard which was a special feature of the house-planning. Some of the houses had an upper storey with vertical drain pipes indicating additional bath-rooms. The vertical alignment in most of the buildings is marvellously accurate, showing that a plump-bob or a similar instrument was used.

Of the larger buildings, other than dwelling houses, the most remarkable is the Great Bath measuring 180 ft. by 108 ft. The bathing pool, 39 ft. long, 23 ft. wide, and 8 ft. deep, occupies the centre of a quadrangle, surrounded by verandahs with rooms and galleries behind them. A raised platform at each end with a flight of steps gave access to the pool, which could be filled and emptied by means of a vaulted culvert, 6 ft. 6 inches high. Near the Great Bath was a big granary originally 150 ft. by 75 ft. with massive construction and provision of loading-facilities.

Great Bath

The exact nature or object of the other public buildings cannot always be understood. A pillared hall, 80 ft. square, with long corridors and low benches, probably served as an Assembly room. Some other buildings were at first taken to be temples, but this is now regarded to be very doubtful. The largest building at Harappā has been named Great Granary. It measures 169 ft. by 135 ft. and is divided into two blocks, with a passage, 23 ft. wide, between them, each block having six halls with five intervening corridors. Harappā and a few other sites show strong fortifications of which only slight traces have been found at Mohenjo-daro.

The supply of food to the vast population of the city required extensive cultivation, of which some idea may be had by the large number of saddle querns. Specimens of wheat and barley found in the ruins prove that they were not of the wild species and were regularly cultivated. Rice was probably also grown, and the date-palm cultivation is proved by the stones found. In addition to these, the general diet consisted of other fruits, vegetables, milk, fish, and flesh of various animals, including beef, mutton, pork, and poultry.

Food

No actual clothing has come to light, but to judge from the sculptured figures, the usual dress of both men and women consisted of two pieces of cloth ; one resembling a *dhoti* covering the lower part, and an upper garment worn over the left shoulder and under the right arm, so as to leave it free. Men wore long hair, dressed in various ways, and women wore a fan-shaped head-dress which covered the hair (and prevents us from knowing the method of its dressing). Both men and women used various ornaments made of gold, silver, copper and other well-known metals, she ,

Dress

Ornaments

faience with beads of semi-precious stones such as carnelian, steatite, agate, chalcedony, jasper, amazon, lapis lazuli, turquoise, amethyst etc. These were marked by a variety of designs and high technical skill. Men wore fillets, necklaces, finger-rings and armlets, while the women decorated themselves, in addition, with head-dress, ear-rings, bangles, bracelets, girdles, and anklets. Materials for toilet and (vanity ?) cases for holding them, some of which are made of ivory and metal, prove that the ladies at Mohenjo-daro were not probably far behind their sisters of the present day in culture of beauty, and knew the use of collyrium, face-paint, and other cosmetics. Round metal rods for applying cosmetics, lip-sticks, bronze oval mirrors, ivory combs of different shapes, some of which probably decorated the hair, and even small dressing tables have come to light at Mohenjo-daro and other sites.

Furniture and utensils

Furniture and utensils of various kinds and designs indicate a high degree of civilization with centuries of development behind it. Special mention may be made of pottery, sometimes beautifully painted, which supplied numerous vessels for the kitchen ; querns, palettes and jar-stands made of stone ; needles, awls, knives, axes, saws, sickles and fish-hooks made of bronze or copper (the needles and awls also being made of ivory) ; chairs and bed-steads made of wood, stools of wicker-work, and mats of reeds ; lamps of copper, shell and clay ; pottery candle stick indicating the use of candles ; pottery toys for children including whistles, rattles, and clay models of men, women, birds and animals (including those with movable limbs or made to climb up and down by means of a movable cord). Special interest attaches to the toy clay carts, as they are the earliest specimens of wheeled vehicles so far known. Marbles, balls and dice were the favourite games, and among other pastimes may be mentioned hunting, bull-fighting, trapping of birds and fishing. Bullock carts of the common type, with or without a gabled roof, formed the chief conveyance, though a copper specimen found at Harappā resembles the modern *Ekkā* with a canopy. Scales with regular pieces of weight, as well as slips of shell with marks of linear measurements, indicate that regular units of weight and length were in use.

There were numerous and varied types of weapons of war, such as axe, spear, dagger, bow, arrow, mace, sling, and

Weapons

sword, made generally of copper or bronze, as well as shield and scale of armour. Among the tools and implements special importance attaches to toothed saws which were unknown in the ancient world.

Industrial Arts and Crafts

Among industrial arts and crafts, spinning of wool and cotton seems to have been very popular both among the poor and the rich, for the whorls made of cheap as well as costly materials have been found. That the dyeing of the fabrics was well known is proved by the actual find of dyers' vats. Fine wheel-made wares of various shapes and designs show the high development of potter's art.

The representation of ship on a seal indicates maritime activity, and there is enough evidence to show that the peoples of the Sindhu Valley carried on trade not only with other parts of India but also with Sumer and other famous centres of culture in Western Asia, and probably also with Egypt and Crete.

Art

Human and animal figures have been found in large numbers. Some of the animal figures, and specially those engraved on the numerous seals, show a high degree of technical skill and artistic ability. Some of the seals have been regarded as master-pieces of engraver's art. That the artists in the Sindhu Valley excelled in making human figures also. is proved by two small statues discovered at Harappā. For accuracy of anatomical details combined with delineation of feeling and movement, they fully deserve to be ranked as a high class of art. Some European critics have even gone so far as to say that "for pure simplicity and feeling nothing to compare with this masterpiece was produced until the age of Hellas".

Seals

The seals, mentioned above, may be reckoned among the most valuable finds at Mohenjo-daro. They have been found in all the different strata and number more than two thousand. They are usully square or oblong and made of ivory, faience, and steatite. Some of the steatite seals are engraved with figures and some designs which must have been a sort of pictorial writing. Similar inscriptions are found engraved on copper-tablets with human and animal figures. Unfortunately this pictographic script still remains undeciphered, though we have nearly four hundred distinct signs. It is certain, however, that the art of writing was known, though in a rudimentary stage. The writing was generally from right to left, but in a few cases in the opposite direction. Where there was more than one line the direction is *boustrephedon*.

Animals

The figures on the seals are mostly those of animals such as unicorn, bull, elephant, tiger, rhinoceros, the *gharial* and the antelope. The commonest animal is the unicorn with a single protruding horn. There were besides mythical animals of composite nature, trees, and human figures, both male and female. No satisfactory explanation has yet been offered of the nature and object of these seals or the uses to which they were put. This problem cannot be solved until the inscriptions on them are deciphered.

There can be hardly any doubt, however, that some of these seals had a religious significance. Though, in the absence of written texts, we cannot say much of the religious ideas, beliefs, and practices of the people, the seals, images, and the figures enable us to throw some light on the subject.

Mother Goddess

The worship of Female Energy in the shape of Mother Goddess is proved by the discovery of a number of semi-nude female figures, with elaborate head-dress and collar (sometimes with a necklace and cheek-cones), but wearing only a girdle or band round the loins. Such figurines have been found in many other centres of ancient civilization in Western Asia, and the cult of Mother Goddess was very popular among the primitive people everywhere in the world. The scenes depicted on some seals have been taken to represent sacrifices of human beings and animals before this Goddess.

Śiva

Among the male gods the most remarkable figure is that of a deity, seated on a throne with legs crossed in the fashion of a *yogī*. He wears a horned head-dress, a pectoral round the neck, and a number of bangles. He has three faces, though there may be the idea of a fourth, which is, of course, invisible. He sits, with *penis erectus*, surrounded by a number of animals such as tiger, buffalo, and rhinoceros, with a deer under the seat. Many scholars regard him as a representation of God Śiva, for the latter is described as *trimukha* (three-faced), *paśupati* (lord of animals) and *mahāogin* (the great ascetic). They further urge that this god, originally unknown to the Aryans, was later borrowed by them from the people they met in India, a view also held on other grounds long before the discovery of Mohenjo-daro. This view is not, however, shared by all.

The cult of Śiva is proved not only by other seals, with figures of this god, but also by the discovery of a large number of conical and cylindrical stones which can only be regarded as phallic symbols or *liṅgas*, as some of them are only too realistic representations of the same. The worship of *yoni*, or the female symbol of generation, has also been inferred from a number of small stone representations, though the cult seems to have been less popular than that of the *liṅga*.

Liṅga

There are unmistakable representations of the worship of both animals and trees (or the spirit dwelling therein), the unicorn and the *Pipal* tree being regarded as the most sacred. Some have inferred the prevalence of the worship of fire and water also, but the evidence in support of it is very meagre. The representations of *svastika* and the wheel on some seals have been taken to refer to the worship of the sun whose symbols they are supposed to be. The figure of a deity with a hooded cobra over the head shows the prevalence of the Nāga cult.

Worship of trees and animals

Among semi-religious customs, three distinct ways of the disposal of the dead may be inferred from the finds of skeletons and urns. Sometimes the dead body was buried, and furniture and offerings were placed in the grave. Sometimes the dead body was first exposed in order to be devoured by birds and beasts (as is the custom of the Pārsis), and then the bones were collected and placed in an urn with a number of small vessels, balls, beads etc. A third method was to burn the body and then to place the ashes and bones in an urn with a number of objects.

The details given above are sufficient to convey an idea of the general nature of the splendid civilization that flourished at Mohenjo-daro and Harappā. But this civilization was by no means confined to these two cities or even to the area between them. Later explorations have traced its existence at various sites in Sindh from modern Hyderabad to Jacobabad in the north, and two important settlements of this civilization have been located at Chanhu-daro and Amri, about 100 miles respectively to the south-east and south of Mohenjo-

Spread of the civilization

daro. Traces of this culture have also been found in various sites in Western India as far south as the Valley of the Narmadā river, in Western Sindh, and even further west, in Northern and Southern Baluchistān.

The discovery of pictographs, beads, and other objects, exactly similar to those in the Sindhu Valley, proves the influence of this culture, eastward in U. P. and Bihār as far as Pātnā, and northward as far as Ambālā district. Future discoveries may prove its extension almost all over Northern India.

Its influence upon Aryan culture

How such a great culture and civilization could vanish without leaving any trace or even memory behind it, is a problem that cannot be solved at the present state of our knowledge. But it may be regarded as certain that it exercised great influence over the later development of culture and civilization in India in almost all its branches. There is enough evidence to indicate that some of the fundamental conceptions of Hinduism are derived from this culture, and it is not unlikely that the Indian script and punch-marked coins, as well as many arts and crafts in later India, are greatly indebted to the same source. On the whole it is now being gradually realized that the present civilization of India is not merely a development of the Aryan civilization, as has so long been generally held, but that it is a composite product resulting from the fusion of several cultures in which the contribution of the Sindhu Valley Civilization must be regarded as an important factor.

CHAPTER IV

The Aryans

We possess hardly any definite information about the people or peoples who originated and developed the great civilization described in the last chapter. This is the reason why it is named after the region where it flourished.

Authors of the Sindhu Valley Civilization

A scientific examination of the human skeletons and skulls found at Mohenjo-daro shows that the individuals represented by them belonged to four distinct racial types, viz. Proto-Australoid, Mediterranean, Alpinoid, and Mongoloid. But as the number of skeletons examined is very few, we cannot arrive at any definite conclusion about the racial composition of the people at large who built up the culture and civilization described above. There are widely different views on the subject, and we can only briefly refer to a few of them.

Its difference from Vedic culture

The most widely accepted view is that the authors of the Sindhu Valley Civilization were Dravidians, *i.e.*, of the Mediterranean type referred to above. There is no doubt that this civilization closely resembles what we may derive from a study of the later Dravidian languages and the people speaking them. This view would mean that the Sindhu Valley civilization flourished long before the Aryans came into India. Sir John Marshall and others independently arrived at the same conclusion by a comparison of this civilization with that depicted in the Rigveda. The presence of Śiva-image and *liṅga*, the absence of horse, and the worship of icons prove in their opinion that the Sindhu Valley civilization was quite distinct from, and earlier than, the Aryan civilization represented in the Rigveda ; for the latter lays great stress on horses, both in secular and religious life, regards the Śiva-*liṅga* with contempt, and knows no images of gods and goddesses. The importance of Mother Goddess in the former is also a notable distinction, for the female deities play no important part in the Ṛigvedic pantheon. Some scholars, however, do not accept this view. They regard the Vedic civilization as older than the Sindhu Valley civilization, and hold, on the basis of skeletal remains, that the Aryans formed part of the diverse population of Mohenjo-daro.[1]

Relative antiquity of the two

This brings us to the question of the dates of these two civilizations. The discovery of seals of the Sindhu Valley type in Western Asia, in strata of known date, seems to carry their date back to 2500 B. C. Even on other grounds the later settlements of Mohenjo-daro have been referred approximately to the same date. As already seven layers of buildings have come to light at Mohenjo-daro, and probably some still earlier layers remain hidden under the sub-soil water, we must allow a pretty long time for the growth and development of this civilization. This, according to the generally accepted view, may, therefore, be approximately referred to the period 3000-2500 B.C. There is, however, a tendency among modern scholars to push down this date by about 500 years.

On the other hand, in the opinion of the majority of competent scholars, the Ṛigveda could not possibly be older than 2000 to 1500 B. C.[2] Although this text must have been composed after, possibly long after, the Aryan immigration into India, still that event can hardly be placed much earlier than 2500 to 2000 B. C. From this point of view also the Sindhu Valley civilization probably flourished before the Aryans migrated to India.

Without being dogmatic in any way, and fully admitting that no definite or final conclusion is possible at the present state of our knowledge, we may provisionally accept the view that the Sindhu Valley civilization represents the Dravidian culture, and its authors belonged to the racial type commonly referred to as Dravidian. On this basis the history of this period may be hypothetically reconstructed somewhat as follows:

The Aryans

About five thousand years ago, or even somewhat earlier, a new race of Mediterranean type entered India from the West and occupied large parts of India (including Baluchistān). This people, who later came to be called Dravidians from the name of their common language, developed a high degree of civilization and founded many important cities. About 2000 B. C., or a few centuries later, a new race of fair complexion, speaking Aryan

1. Cf. *ABORI*, XVIII. 385-95
2. The date of Ṛigveda has been discussed in Chapter V.

language, and generally, though not correctly, designated as Aryans or Indo-Aryans, gradually advanced from the north-west, across the Hindu Kush mountains, and entered India through Afghānistān. The Dravidians naturally resisted the new-comers with all their might, and a fierce and protracted struggle ensued. It was not merely a struggle between two nationalities, but a conflict between two types of civilization. The Dravidians had to fight for their very existence, and there are several passages in the Ṛigveda which indicate the severity of the struggle. But all in vain. History has repeatedly shown that the peoples, born and brought up for generations in the genial soil of India, are no match for the fresh hardy mountaineers of the north-western regions who poured into the country at irregular intervals. The Dravidians proved no exception to the rule. They put up a brave fight, and laid down their lives in hundreds and thousands on various battle-fields, but ultimately had to succumb to the attacks of the invaders. The Aryans destroyed their castles and cities, burnt their houses, and reduced a large number of them to slaves.

Their struggle with the Dravidians.

The hard-won victory enabled the Aryans gradually to occupy the whole of the Panjāb, and ultimately to conquer the greater part of Northern India. The vanquished natives, the Dravidians as well as the remnants of their predecessors, mostly submitted to them, and became the Dāsas; but large bodies of Dravidians found shelter in the south, and their descendants still use the languages known as Tamil, Telugu, Kannaḍa, and Malayālam. Some of the other tribes retreated towards the north, south, and east, and maintained a precarious existence in hills and forests. Their descendants, the Kols, Bhils, Gonds, and many Himālayan tribes, are still to be found in the fastnesses to which their ancestors were driven by the Aryans about four thousand years ago.

The Aryans, who thus obtained a footing on Indian soil, had a previous history. They belonged to a very ancient stock of the human race, and lived for a long period with the forefathers of the Greek, the Roman, the German, the English, the Dutch, the Scandinavian, the Spanish, the French, the Russian, and the Bulgarian nations. This is best shown by the fact, that some words, denoting essential ideas of a civilized man, are still used in

The origin of the Aryans

common by their descendants, although removed from one another by hundreds of miles and thousands of years. Thus the Sanskrit words *pitar* and *mātar* are essentially the same as *pater* and *mater* in Latin, *patér* and *métér* in Greek, *father* and *mother* in English, and *vater* and *mutter* in German, all denoting the most notable of the earliest notions of mankind viz., that of the parents. The community of language has led many scholars to suppose that the Aryans, who conquered India, belonged to what may be called the parent stock of the many nations named above, famed in the ancient and the modern world. This is not, however, a very logical conclusion, for the community of language does not necessarily prove the community of blood. The Bengali language, for example, is now spoken by people of diverse races. The only certain conclusion, therefore, is that the forefathers of all these nations lived for long in close intimacy at a certain region. The locality of this region and the time when the different groups of people separated, are alike uncertain and subjects of a keen and protracted controversy.[1] The general view is, that they lived somewhere in Central Asia or South Russia. But some would place them still further north, in the Arctic regions, while others locate them in the area now occupied by Austria, Hungary, and Bohemia.

Anyhow one or more of these groups separated from the rest, and proceeded towards India. In course of time, some of them settled in the province now known as Persia, and deve loped a civilization of which distinct traces are still to be seen among their descendants, the Parsis of the present day. The remaining clans crossed the Hindu Kush and occupied the Panjāb after driving away the Dravidians as has already been narrated.

1. A vast literature has grown up on the question of the original home of the Aryans, their migration and cognate questions. The earlier views on this subject are summarised in Muir's "Original Sanskrit Texts", Vol, II. Chap. II. For the modern views, Cf. articles on 'Aryan' and 'Indo-European Language' in Encyclopaedia Britannica, Camb. Hist., Ch. III, and the references given there. The most important evidence recently brought to light is that of the Boghaz-köi inscription, dating from about 1400 B. C., which contains the names of familiar Vedic deities, Indra, Varuṇa, and the great twin brethren, the Nāsatyas. The importance of this inscription for fixing the antiquity of Vedic culture is indeed very great. Unfortunately the scholars are not unanimous in accepting the view that the gods mentioned above represent Vedic deities, thereby carrying the beginning of Vedic civilization to a date much anterior to 1400 B. C.; cf. Camb. Hist. pp. 72-3. p. 320 fn (2). For a recent discussion of the whole problem, cf. *The History and Culture of the Indian People*, Vol. I, Chapters X, XI.

In conclusion it must be mentioned that some Indian scholars do not accept the view that the Aryans came from outside. They regard them as indigenous people of India, some sections of whom gradually migrated to the different parts of Asia and Europe. The Greeks, Romans and other peoples, speaking Aryan languages, were the descendants either of these peoples or of others upon whom they imposed their language by conquest or more peaceful means.[1] This view, however, presents too many difficulties and is not accepted by many Indians or anybody outside India.

---

1. K. M. Munshi—*The Glory that was Gurjaradesa*, Part I, Section II. *The History and Culture of the Indian People*, Vol. I, pp., 215. ff.

CHAPTER V

The Vedas

Before proceeding with the history of the Aryans in India, it will be well to give a short account of the Vedas, their sacred literature, as practically everything we know about them is derived from this source alone. But even apart from this, there are other reasons why we should give a prominent place to the Vedas. They form the oldest literary works not only of the Indo-Aryans, but of the entire Aryan group known as the Indo-Germans, and, as such, occupy a very distinguished place in the history of the world-literature. Besides, for more than three thousand years, the Vedas have been looked upon as revealed words of God by millions of Hindus, and have formed the basis of their culture and religion amid continual changes and successive developments.

The Vedic Literature

The word "VEDA" means "knowledge", "knowledge *par excellence*, *i.e.*, the sacred, spiritual knowledge." It does not signify either any individual literary work as the "Koran," or even a collection of definite number of books arranged at a particular time, such as the Bible or the Tripiṭaka. It is a mass of literature which had grown up in course of many centuries and was orally handed down from generation to generation. It consists of three successive classes of literary productions, to each of which belonged a number of single works, some of which still exist, but many have completely disappeared.

These three classes are :—

I. The Saṁhitās or Mantras. As the name signifies, these are collections of hymns, prayers, charms, litanies, and sacrificial formulas.

II. The Brāhmaṇas. These are massive prose texts which contain "speculation on the meaning of the hymns, give precepts for their application, relate stories of their origin in connection with that of sacrificial rites, and explain the secret meaning of the latter. In short, they form a kind of primitive theology and philosophy of the Brāhmaṇas."

III. The Āraṇyakas and Upanishads. These are partly included in the Brāhmaṇas or attached thereto, and partly exist as separate works. They embody philosophical meditations of the hermits and ascetics on soul, God, world, and man.

A large number of Saṁhitās must have existed among the different schools of priests and singers. But many of them are only different recensions of one and the same Saṁhitā. There are, however, four Saṁhitās, which are notably different from one another, and each of which has reached us in several recensions. These are :—

1. The Ṛigveda Saṁhitā—A collection of hymns.

2. The Atharvaveda Saṁhitā—A collection of spells and charms.

3. The Sāmaveda Saṁhitā—A collection of songs mostly taken from the Ṛigveda.

4. The Yajurveda Saṁhitā—A collection of sacrificial formulas. (There are two distinct forms of this Saṁhitā *viz.*, the Saṁhitās of the Black Yajurveda and the Saṁhitās of the White-Yajurveda.

These four Saṁhitās have formed the basis of four different Vedas, and every work belonging to the second and third classes of Vedic literature *viz.*, the Brāhmaṇas, the Āraṇyakas and the Upanishads, is attached to one or other of these Saṁhitās, and is said to belong to that particular Veda. There are thus not only Saṁhitās, but Brāhmaṇas, Āraṇyakas, and Upanishads of the Ṛigveda, and the same thing holds good with regard to the other three Vedas. Every single work of this vast literature belongs to the category of Veda, and the authors of these works are always referred to as '*Ṛishis*' or sages. Sometimes, the names of these *Ṛishis* or sages denoted not so much an individual as a group, and thus the hymns attributed to Viśvāmitra, for example, were probably composed not by a single individual of that name, but by various members of his family or school. It may be noted that women and people of the lowest classes of society are mentioned as composers of some of these hymns.

Although the hymns are attributed to these *Ṛishis*, pious Hindus have always laid stress upon their divine origin. They maintain that these hymns were merely revealed to the sages and not composed by them. Thus the Vedas are called *apaurusheya* (not made by man), and *nitya* (existing in all eternity) while the *Ṛishis*,

The Authorhip of the Vedic Literature

or sacred poets to whom they are ascribed, are known as *mantradrashṭā*, *i.e.*, inspired seers who saw or received the *mantra* by sight directly from the Supreme Creator. These ideas about the sanctity of the Vedas have ever formed the cardinal doctrines of Hinduism, and no religious sect that refuses to subscribe to them can have any legitimate place within its fold.

Besides the revealed literature, described above, to which alone the name Veda may be properly applied, there is another class of works which, strictly speaking, belong to the Vedic literature, but which cannot claim to be ranked in that category, as its authorship is ascribed to human beings. These are called Sūtras or Vedāṅgas.

Vedāṅgas

There are altogether six Vedāṅgas. This does not mean six distinct books or treatises, but merely six subjects, 'the study of which was necessary either for the reading, the understanding, or the proper sacrificial employment of the Veda.' These six subjects are Śikshā (pronunciation), Chhandas (metre), Vyākaraṇa (grammar), Nirukta (explanation of words), Jyotisha (astronomy), and Kalpa (ceremonial). 'The first two are considered necessary for reading the Veda, the two next, for understanding it, and the last two for employing it at sacrifices.'

These topics were originally dealt with in the Brāhmaṇas and Āraṇyakas, but, later on, separate text books were written on each of them. These texts were written in a very peculiar style. They consisted of a series of extremely concise formulas called Sūtras, which in point of brevity may almost be compared to Algebraic formulas. From this fact the texts are also called Sūtras. These were, however, mostly composed in later periods and will be dealt with in a later chapter.

The Upavedas

What has been said of the Vedāṅgas applies equally well to another class of literature, called the Upavedas or subsidiary Vedas, dealing with secular subjects such as medical science (*Āyurveda*), military science (*Dhanurveda*), music (*Gandharvaveda*), art, architecture and analogous subjects.

Detailed account of the Vedic Literature.

Having given a general description of the Vedic literature, we may now proceed to give a short account of the more important individual works, the composition of which may be roughly placed during the period under review.

I. The Ṛigveda.

A. The Saṁhitās. Of the various Saṁhitās of the Ṛigveda, only one has reached us, *viz.*, that belonging to the Śākala School. It contains 1028 (according to some 1017) *sūktas* (hymns), divided into ten *maṇḍalas* and again in eight *ashṭakas*. This Saṁhitā is the earliest work in the Vedic literature, but its different portions must have been composed at different ages, and put together at a subsequent date. The oldest hymns occur in *maṇḍalas* 2-7, each of which is ascribed to a family of priests, *viz.* Gṛitsamada, Viśvāmitra, Vāmadeva, Atri, Bharadvāja, and Vasishṭha. The ninth *maṇḍala* is a collection of all the hymns addressed to Soma which were originally included in the other *maṇḍalas*. The first and tenth *maṇḍalas* are the latest additions, although they contain many old passages. The Saṁhitā contains hymns addressed to various deities. An idea of their poetical beauty and general nature may be gathered from the specimens given at the end of Chapter VI. Besides, the Saṁhitā throws a flood of light on the early life of the Aryans, which will be discussed in detail in Chapter VI.

B. The Brāhmaṇas. There are two Brāhmaṇas belonging to the Ṛigveda; The first, the Aitareya Brāhmaṇa, is traditionally regarded as the work of Mahidāsa Aitareya. It deals principally with the great Soma sacrifices and the different ceremonies of royal inauguration. The second, the Kaushītaki or Śāṅkhāyana Brāhmaṇa, deals not only with the Soma but also with various other sacrifices.

C. The Āraṇyakas and Upanishads. To the Aitareya Brāhmaṇa belongs the Aitareya Āraṇyaka, which includes the Aitareya Upanishad. The Kaushītaki Brāhmaṇa contains Kaushītaki Āraṇyaka, a portion of which is known as the Kaushītaki Upanishad.

II. The Atharvaveda.

A. The Saṁhitā is known to us in two recensions, the Śaunakīya and Paippalāda, but the latter is very imperfectly known. The Śaunakīya recension contains 731 (according to some 760) hymns, divided into 20 books. The last two or three books seem to be later additions. The Saṁhitā contains many verses which occur in the Ṛigveda. It deals mostly with charms, magic, and spells, by which one could overcome demons and enemies, win over friends, and gain worldly successes. For this reason the Saṁhitā was not included in the Vedic literature for a long time. It preserves many old popular cults and superstitions.

B. No ancient work of the Brāhmaṇa class, belonging to Atharvaveda, is known. The Gopatha Brāhmaṇa, although classed as a Brāhmaṇa, really belongs to the Vedāṅga literature, and is a very late work.

C. There are three Upanishads, *viz*.

(1) The Muṇḍaka Upanishad.

(2) The Praśna Upanishad.

(3) The Māṇḍukya Upanishad.

All these are comparatively late works.

III. The Sāmaveda.

A. The Purāṇas refer to thousand Saṁhitās of the Sāmaveda. But only one has reached us in three recensions, *viz*., the Kauthuma current in Gujarāt, the Jaiminīya in the Carnatic, and the Rāṇāyaṇīya in the Marāṭhā country. It consists of a collection of hymns, which were sung by a particular class of priests, called Udgātar, at the Soma sacrifices. These hymns are 1810, or omitting the repetitions, 1549 in number, but all of them, with the exception of 75, are taken from the Saṁhitā of the Ṛigveda. The 75 verses, which are not found in that Saṁhitā, occur partly in other Saṁhitās, and partly in different Brāhmaṇas or other works on ritual. These texts were, however, merely used for the melody, which was all-important for the followers of the Sāmaveda. Thus while the Sāmaveda is very important for the history of Indian music, and throws interesting light on the growth or sacrificial ceremonies, its value as a literary work is practically nil.

B. Brāhmaṇas.

(1) The Tāṇḍya-mahā-Brāhmaṇa, also called Pañchaviṁśa (*i.e.* consisting of twenty-five chapters), is one of the oldest and most important of Brāhmaṇas. It contains many old legends, and includes the *Vrātyastoma*, a ceremony by which people of non-Aryan stock could be admitted into the Aryan family.

(2) The Shaḍviṁśa Brāhmaṇa (the twenty-sixth Brāhmaṇa) is merely a supplement to Pañchaviṁśa Brāhmaṇa. The last portion of this forms what is known as 'Adbhuta Brāhmaṇa', a Vedāṅga-text dealing with omens and supernatural things.

(3) The Jaiminīya Brāhmaṇa—very little is at present known of this book.

C. Āraṇyakas and Upanishads.

(1) The Chhāndogya Upanishad, the first part of which is merely an Āraṇyaka, belongs to a Brāhmaṇa of the Sāmaveda, probably the Tāṇḍya-mahā-Brāhmaṇa.

(2) The Jaiminīya-Upanishad-Brāhmaṇa is an Āraṇyaka of the Jaiminīya or Talavakāra school of Sāmaveda, and a part of it forms the Kena-Upanishad, also called the Talavakāra Upanishad.

IV. The Yajurveda

A. Saṁhitās.

The grammarian Patañjali speaks of the 101 schools of Yajurveda. At present, however, only the following five are known. Of these the first four belong to the Black Yajurveda and the last to the White-Yajurveda.

1. The Kāṭhaka Saṁhitā of the Kaṭha school.
2. The Kapishṭhala-Kaṭha Saṁhitā—known only in fragments.
3. The Maitrāyaṇī Saṁhitā, *i.e.*, the Saṁhitā of the Maitrāyaṇīya school.
4. The Taittirīya Saṁhitā, *i. e.*, the Saṁhitā of the Taittirīya school.
5. The Vājasaneyi Saṁhitā, known in two recensions of the Kāṇva and Mādhyandina schools.

The principal distinction between the White and the Black-Yajurveda consists in the fact, that while the Vājasaneyi Saṁhitā, belonging to the former, contains only the hymns *i. e.*, the prayers and sacrificial formulas, the *Saṁhitās* of the Black-Yajurveda contain, in addition, the prose commentaries which should properly be relegated to the Brāhmaṇa portion. It seems that the Black-Yajurveda belongs to an earlier period, when the Saṁhitā and the Brāhmaṇa portions were mixed up together, and that it is only at a later time, that necessity was felt of separating the two as had probably already been done in the case of the other Vedas.

The Vājasaneyi Saṁhitā consists of forty chapters, and about two thousand verses, including repetitions. It consists of hymns, many of which are borrowed from the Ṛigveda and the Atharvaveda, as well as sacrificial formulas in prose. As the Sāmavedā Saṁhitā contains only those hymns which were sung by the Udgātar priests, so the Yajurveda Saṁhitā consists only of texts which were to be recited by the Adhvaryu priests in connection with the more important sacrifices.

B. The Brāhmaṇas.

(1) The Taittirīya Brāhmaṇa belongs to the Black-Yajurveda. As has been already pointed out, the Black-Yajurveda Saṁhitās contain both Saṁhitā and Brāhmaṇa. The Taittirīya Brāhmaṇa therefore contains only later additions to the Taittirīya Saṁhitā.

(2) The Śatapatha Brāhmaṇa belonging to the White-Yajurveda is the most voluminous, and, at the same time, the most important of all the Brāhmaṇas. Like the Vājasaneyi Saṁhitā, of which it is a commentary, it occurs in two recensions, the Kāṇva and the Mādhyandina. The Śatapatha Brāhmaṇa is a very important source of information, not only about the sacrificial ceremonies of ancient India, but also about her theology and philosophy, as well as her thoughts, ideas, manners and customs.

C. Āraṇyakas and Upanishads.

(1) The Taittirīya Āraṇyaka is practically a continuation of the Taittirīya Brāhmaṇa. Its concluding portion constitutes the Taittirīya Upanishad and the Mahā-Nārāyaṇa Upanishad, the last one being a comparatively late work.

(2) The first portion of the fourteenth book of Śatapatha Brāhmaṇa really constitutes an Āraṇyaka, while the last portion of the same book constitutes the famous Bṛihadāraṇyaka Upanishad.

(3) The Kāṭhaka Upanishad, belonging to Black-Yajurveda.

(4) The Īśa Upanishad forms the concluding chapter of the Vājasaneyi Saṁhitā.

(5) The Śvetāśvatara Upanishad, belonging to the Black-Yajurveda.

(6) The Maitrāyaṇīya Upanishad, belonging to the Black-Yajurveda, is a late work.

Antiquity of the Ṛigveda

Of all the books noticed above, the Saṁhitā of the Ṛigveda is the earliest. It must have been finally arranged in its present form long before the Saṁhitās of the other Vedas, so far as they are independent of the Ṛigveda, began to be composed as such. Again, the composition of the Saṁhitās of the Sāma, Yaju, and Atharva-veda must have preceded the prose Brāhmaṇical texts. It is probable, however, that the final arrangement of the Yajurveda and the Atharvaveda Saṁhitās took place at a time when the

Brāhmaṇa literature had already commenced to take shape, so that the latest portion of the former is sometimes contemporary with the oldest portion of the latter.

So far the conclusions are easy to draw, and, on the whole, reliable, but when we try to fix the time of these different compositions, our difficulty at once commences.

The Age of the Vedas

The date of the Vedic literature has formed the subject of a keen and protracted controversy. Max Müller, who first dealt with the question in a critical manner, started from the well-known fact that some of the Upanishads were older than the Buddha (c. 500 B. C.). He then counted backwards, assigning a minimum period of 200 years to the development of each distinct stage of Vedic literature mentioned above, and came to the conclusion that the hymns of the Ṛigveda must have been composed before 1200-1000 B. C. He was, however, loath to lay down any positive date for its composition, and expressly remarked that the question, whether this date should be fixed as 1000, 1500, 2000 or 3000 years before Christ, can never be solved. As Winternitz observes, later scholars have, without offering any new argument, regarded 1200-1000 B. C., which was merely looked upon by Max Müller as *terminus ad quem*, as the date of the composition of the Ṛik Saṁhitā.

This date is, however, supported on entirely different grounds by some other scholars who proceed on the assumption that the languages of the Ṛigveda and the Avesta must be assigned approximately to the same age. From a comparison of the language of the Avesta with that of the old Persian Inscriptions of the 6th century B. C., they conclude, on the analogy of similar linguistic developments of known dates, that the Avesta, and therefore also the Ṛigveda in its present form, was composed about 1000 B. C. On the other hand, scholars like Jacobi and Tilak have, on astronomical grounds, referred the date of the Ṛik Saṁhitā to a much higher antiquity than was contemplated by Max Müller. Thus Tilak refers some Vedic texts to a period as far back as 6000 B. C. According to Jacobi, the Vedic civilization flourished between 4500 and 2500 B. C., and the Saṁhitās were composed during the latter half of the period.

The present position about this question may be summed up in the following lines of Winternitz, a great authority on this subject : "The available evidence merely proves, that the Vedic period extends from an unknown past, say X, to 500 B. C., none of the dates 1200-500 B. C., 1500-500 B. C., and 2000-500 B. C., which are usually assumed, being justified by facts. Only it may be added, as a result of recent researches, that 800 B. C. should probably be substituted for 500 B. C., and that the unknown date X more probably falls in the third rather than in the second, millennium before Christ."[1]

Origin and antiquity of the art of writing

The discussion of Vedic literature naturally leads to the cognate subject, the antiquity of the art of writing. Scholars have almost unanimously held the view, that the art of writing was unknown in the period when the Saṁhitās and the Brāhmaṇas were composed. The great Vedic scholar Max Müller even went so far as to assert, that the art of writing was unknown to the Indians before the fourth century B. C. But these views have since been abandoned, and most scholars now agree in referring the introduction of writing in India to seventh century B. C. They also hold that the ancient Indian alphabet, called '*Brāhmī lipi*', was derived from Semitic alphabets, although there is difference of opinion as to the particular Semitic race from which the Indians borrowed this knowledge of writing. The generally accepted view is that of Bühler, who maintained that the Indian alphabet was derived from the earliest Phoenician alphabet which was in use in the 9th century B. C.

The European views on this subject have been challenged by some Indian scholars, notably by Prof. D. R. Bhandarkar. He maintains on the ground of internal evidence that the art of writing was known to the Indians as early as the time of the Ṛigveda, and derives the *Brāhmī* alphabet from alphabetic signs found on prehistoric potteries dug out of the Hyderabad cairns.

The discovery of the seals at Mohenjo-daro with pictorial writing (p. 24) has put an altogether new complexion on the whole subject. It may now be regarded as very probable, if not almost certain, that the old Indian alphabet was derived from the pictographic script current in the Sindhu Valley. Unfortunately we cannot trace its development during the long period of more than 2000 years which elapsed before we

1. Winternitz Vol. I. P. 258

come across the first actual specimen of the *Brāhmī lipi* in the third or fourth century B. C.

The scholars, who hold that the art of writing was unknown in the Vedic period, are naturally forced to the conclusion, that the whole Vedic literature was preserved by oral tradition only. To those who look upon this as incredible, the following lines of Max Müller would serve as a reply :

"It is of little avail in researches of this kind to say that such a thing is impossible. We can form no opinion of the powers of memory in a state of society so different from ours as the Indian Parishads are from our Universities...Even at the present day, when manuscripts are neither scarce nor expensive, the young Brāhmaṇas who learn the songs of the Veda and the Brāhmaṇas and the Sūtras, invariably learn them from oral tradition, and know them by heart. They spend year after year under the guidance of their teacher, learning a little, day after day, repeating what they have learnt as part of their daily devotion, until at last they have mastered their subject and are able to become teachers in turn.

"How then was the Veda learnt ? It was learnt by every Brāhmaṇa during twelve years of his studentship (forty-eight years in the case of those who did not wish to marry). The Prātiśākhya gives us a glimpse into the lecture rooms of the Brāhmanic colleges...The pupils embrace their master, and say "Sir, read." The master gravely says '*om*' *i. e.*, 'Yes.' He then begins to say a *praśna* (a question) which consists of three verses. In order that no word may escape the attention of his pupils, he pronounces all with the high accent, and repeats certain words twice.

"After the *Guru* (teacher) has pronounced a group of words, consisting of three or sometimes (in long compounds) of more words, the first pupil repeats the first word, and when anything is to be explained, the teacher stops him and says: "Sir." After it has been explained by the pupil who is at the head of the class, the permission to continue is given with the words "Well, Sir." After the words of the teacher have thus been repeated by one, the next pupil has to apply to him with the word, "Sir"... After a section of three verses has thus been gone through, all the pupils have to rehearse it again and again."

CHAPTER VI

Early Aryan Society

The sacred literature, of which a short account has been given in the last chapter, covers a period, roughly speaking, of about 1400 years. For, although, as noted above, it is impossible to assign precise dates, the period 2000 to 600 B. C. may be looked upon as a fair approximation. For the history of the Aryans during this period, we are almost solely dependent upon these books, and when carefully studied, they furnish a valuable account of the life led by the Aryans during these 1400 years.

The Saṁhitā of the Rigveda, being earliest literary production of the Aryans, reveals to us the earliest phase of Aryan life, and we proceed to give a short sketch of its essential features.

The Home of the Aryans

First, as to the home of the Aryans. The valleys of the river Sindhu and its tributaries, and of the Sarasvatī[1] and the Drishadvatī, formed their earliest settlements in India proper. Although they were thus mainly confined to the province now called the Panjāb, their outer settlements reached further eastward,—to the banks of the Gaṅgā and the Yamunā. On the other hand, some Aryan tribes still lingered on the western side of the Sindhu on the banks of the Kābul, the Swat, the Kurram and the Gomal rivers.

The Aryans had given up their nomadic habit, and lived in fixed dwelling houses. These were made of wood and bamboo, and did not differ much from those in Indian villages at the present day. Only we sometimes hear of 'removable houses built of wood, which could be taken in parts and re-fixed at different sites.'

Within these homes, the Aryans developed a healthy family life, the prototype of what we see around us to-day. It rested upon the sacred tie of marriage, and 'the old Aryans

1. The river Sarasvatī, which was looked upon as very sacred by the Aryans, flowed through the territory now belonging to Patiala Raj, but has been completely lost in the sands.

Family life

knew of no more tender relation than that between husband and wife'. The wife, though subject to her husband, was the mistress of the household, and had authorities over farm-labourers and slaves. Her importance is sufficiently indicated by the fact, that she participated with her husband in all religious ceremonies, and we read how, in early dawn, the loving couple, with harmonious mind and in fitting words, sends up their prayers to the gods above. There was no *purdah* system. The women spoke to the people gathered at the husband's house, and went to feasts and general sacrifices, gaily decorated and decked with ornaments. They were fully attentive to their household duties, and we have a refreshing picture in the Ṛigveda as to how they rose at early hours, set the household servants at work, and made themselves active, 'singing songs while working'. Their education was not neglected, and some ladies like Viśvavārā, Apālā, and Ghoshā even composed *mantras* and rose to the rank of *Ṛishis*.

Ghoshā grew up in the houses of her parents, and was not married. Generally, the girls were married after attaining the age of puberty. There were hardly any restrictions about marriage and both boys and girls enjoyed considerable freedom in choosing their partners in life. A very interesting hymn of the Rigveda (X. 85) gives us some idea of the oldest marriage ritual in India.

Besides the wife or wives (for polygamy was not unknown), the parents, brothers, and sisters formed the other important members of an Aryan family. It was characterised by sweet and affectionate relation between its members, which forms such a distintctive feature of the Hindu society, and have been so fascinatingly described in later times in immortal works like the Rāmāyaṇa and the Mahābhārata.

The family was patriarchal, and theoretically the parents had absolute control over children. An extreme instance of family discipline is furnished by the case of Ṛijrāśva who was deprived of his sight as a punishment by his father.

The family served as the foundation of the State. A number of families, bound together by real or supposed ties of kindred, formed a clan, several clans formed a district, and a number of these districts composed a tribe, the highest political unit. Various tribes are mentioned in the Ṛigveda, such as the Bharatas,

Political organisation

Matsyas, Krivis, Tṛitsus and the well-known group of five tribes *viz.*, the Turvaśas, Yadus, Pūrus, Druhyus and Anus.

The organisation of the tribal State was varied in character. Hereditary monarchy was the normal form of government, but sometimes we hear of election of king. In some States there was a sort of oligarchy, several members of the royal family exercising the power in common. Some tribes again had a democratic organisation and their chiefs were elected by the assembled people.

The kingdom was, generally speaking, small in extent. But various passages in the Ṛigveda indicate a king's supremacy over other kings and his great wealth. King Kaśu, for example, made a gift of ten kings to a *Ṛishi*, and many kings are said to have made rich presents to the priests consisting of cows, thousands in number, horses, chariots, gold, dresses, and female slaves. The word *samrāṭ*, which in later days meant an emperor, as well as an expression meaning the ruler of the whole world (*viśvasya bhuvanasya rājā*) occur in the Ṛigveda. In any case, the king was not always a petty tribal chief. Sometimes he occupied a position of great dignity, markedly distinguished from that of the people. He was anointed king by a formal ceremony, wore gorgeous robes, and lived in a house much bigger and more gaily decorated than a common building.

The King

He led the tribe in war and considered the protection of life and property of his subjects as his most sacred duty. In return they voluntarily gave him *bali* (tribute or offering). The conquered hostile tribes were also forced to pay tribute. The king was not, however, the owner of the land.

The king administered justice with the assistance of *Purohita* (priest) and probably also other advisers. Theft, burglary, robbery, and cattle-lifting were the principal crimes. The common punishment was to tie the criminal to a stake. The system of wergeld (*vairadeya*) was in force and we come across the epithet *śatadāya i. e.*, one the price of whose blood was one hundred (cows or coins).

Among the royal officials, the *Purohita*, *Senānī* (general) and the *Grāmaṇī* (headman of the village) were the most important. We hear also of *Dūtas* (envoy) and spies (*spaś*). There must have been many others of whom we do not know anything.

Officials

Great prominence is given in the Ṛigveda to two popular

Popular Assemblies

assemblies called *sabhā* and *samiti* which seem to have formed an essential feature of the government. We possess no definite information about the composition of either or the distinction between the two. Most probably the *samiti*, which mainly dealt with the political business, included the common people, while the *sabhā*, less political in character, was a more select body of the aristocrats. The larger number of passages which refer to them leave no doubt that they wielded great power and authority in administration, and worked as great checks to the exercise of arbitrary power by the king. Political affairs were freely discussed in these bodies, and debates ran high, everyone wishing to convert others to his faith. But all the same, their ideal was a harmonious activity of the different members of the assembly, and this is beautifully set forth in the concluding hymn of the Rigveda :

"Assemble, speak together, let your minds be all of one accord. The place is common, common the assembly, common the mind, so be their thought united. A common purpose do I lay before you. One and the same be your resolve, and be your minds of one accord. United be the thoughts of all that all may happily agree."

When the serious business of the assembly was over, the *sabhā* or assembly-hall was converted into a club-house, where

Food and Drink.

the people ate and drank, talking merrily all the while. Both animal and vegetable foods were taken by the Aryans. Not only fish, birds, goats, and rams, but horses, buffaloes, and even bulls were slaughtered for their food. Rice, barley, bean and sesamum formed the chief vegetable food-stuff, and they ate not only boiled rice but also bread and cakes made of flour. Milk and its various preparations, such as *ghee*, butter and curd, together with fruits, vegetables, sugar-cane, and various parts of the lotus plant formed favourite commodities of food and drink.

It would be a mistake to suppose, however, that the Vedic Aryans quenched their thirst by milk and water alone. They used stronger drinks, the chief among which were *surā*, a brandy made from corn and barley, and the juice of Soma plant. To such an extent were they addicted to the last, that they even raised it to the position of a god.

Normally the people wore one lower and one

Dress

upper garment, though an under-garment came

to be used in the age of the Later Vedic Saṁhitās. There are, however, references to many special kinds of clothing, such as those worn by the bride or the female dancers. Garments were sometimes made of wool and skin and were of different colours. Several kinds of ornaments, both of gold and precious stones, were worn by men as well as women, both of whom also oiled and combed their hair, which was plaited or braided. The men kept beard and moustache, but sometimes also shaved them.

Agriculture naturally formed the chief occupation of the people. They ploughed the field, as cultivators do to-day, by means of a pair of oxen bound to the yoke, and irrigation and other subsidiary processes have practically continued unaltered for the last three or four thousand years.

Occupations

The later Saṃhitās, however, refer to large and heavy ploughs drawn by six, eight, twelve, and even twenty-four oxen. The people had not yet passed beyond the pastoral stage and hence cows and bullocks formed their chief wealth. Much attention was naturally devoted to cattle-rearing, and many a singer represent the cows as the sum of all good which Indra has created for our enjoyment.

Among other important occupations, the first place must be given to weaving both in cotton and wool, which supplied cloths and garments to the people. It is noteworthy, that as in later days, both men and women were engaged in this work, as well as in the subsidiary processes of dyeing and embroidery. Next came the carpenter who constructed houses, and supplied household utensils and furniture. They also built chariots, carts, boats, and ships. Many of them were skilled in wood-carving, and produced delicate artistic cups. Then there were blacksmiths who supplied various necessaries of life, from the fine needles and razors to the sickles, ploughshares, spears, and swords. Goldsmiths worked in gold and jewels, and ministered to the fashions of the gay and the rich. The leather-workers tanned leather, and made various articles out of it, such as bow-strings and casks for holding liquor.

Last, but not the least in importance, come the physician and the priest. The former not only cured diseases by means of the 'healing virtues of plants,' but also chased away evil spirits which sometimes possessed a man. The latter composed hymns, taught the boys how to learn them by rote, and served as the priests of kings, nobles, and common people.

The Caste System

Members of the same family took to different arts, crafts, and trades. This is well illustrated in a hymn (IX. 112) where the author says:

"A bard I am, my father a leech,
And my mother is a grinder of corn,
Diverse in means, but all wishing wealth,
Equally we strive for cattle."

It is clear therefore that there was freedom and mobility of labour, and the idea of hereditary trades and occupations had not yet developed in society.

Two of the professions, *viz.*, those of priests and warriors, naturally occupied higher position than the rest, and those who followed them came to be known as *Brāhmaṇas* and *Rājanyas* (later, *Kshatriyas*), as distinguished from the *Viś* or Aryan people at large, who were consequently known as *Vaiśyas*. But like the other professions, those of the Brāhmaṇas and Kshatriyas, too, were not exclusive and hereditary, and they did not even probably form regular and distinct classes at the beginning. While the homogeneity of the Aryan society was thus fully preserved, there was a real distinction between the Aryans and the aborigines who had submitted to them. Most of them served the Aryans as menials or followed low arts and crafts, though some of them probably occupied a more dignified position by virtue of their learning or former status in their society. They were collectively known as *Dāsas* or *Śūdras* and occupied a lower rank in society than the Aryans.

A late hymn (X. 90) of the Ṛigveda, known as Purusha-sūkta, says that when the gods divided Purusha (the primeval giant or creator), "the Brāhmaṇa was his mouth ; the Rājanya was made his arms ; the being (called) the Vaiśya was his thighs ; the Śūdra sprang from his feet". This is the only hymn in that vast collection, known as the Ṛigveda, in which occur the names Rājanya, Vaiśya, and Śūdra, and the term Brāhmaṇa also occurs very rarely. It would thus appear that towards the very end of the Ṛigvedic period the distinction between the four classes had just begun to take shape, foreshadowing the development of the caste system in future. Such class distinctions were also known among the Iranians and other ancient peoples, though the caste system never developed among them. How and why the social development followed a different course among the Indo-Aryans will be explained in the next chapter.

Some scholars are, however, of opinion that the Brāhmaṇas and Kshatriyas had become hereditary, and the essential features of the caste system were already developed in the age of the Rigveda. But this view does not appear to be very likely, as not only Brāhmaṇa, but even the term Kshatriya occurs very seldom in the Ṛigveda.

In view of the widely accepted current belief, based on later Brāhmaṇical literature, that the Brāhmaṇas, Kshatriyas, Vaiśyas, and Śūdras issued respectively from the mouth, arms, thighs, and feet of the creator, it is significant that according to the Purusha-sūkta, the earliest Vedic hymn on the subject, the first three castes were identical with, not sprung from, those parts of his body. The distinction between the two is a vital one. The former implies membership of the same organism and therefore equality in status, while the latter is a deliberate attempt to introduce gradations in rank according to place of origin. Thus the advocates of the later social changes sought to derive support by wrongly interpreting the mythical conception in their favour.

Trade.

There were trade and maritime activity ; navigation was not confined to the streams of the Panjāb, for the Aryans seem to have boldly ventured out into the open sea. There was probably commercial intercourse with Babylon and other countries in Western Asia.

Exchange.

Coined money or something like it, *viz.*, a piece of metal with a recognised unit of value, was probably known, but it had a restricted use. The ordinary transactions were carried on by means of barter, *i.e.*, exchange of one thing for another. Cows formed an important standard of valuation ; in other words, things were usually valued at the worth of so many cows.

War.

The usual equanimity of the society was no doubt disturbed by occasional wars. Reference has already been made to the fight between Aryans and the original settlers of the country. This must have been constantly going on as the Aryans advanced further and further into the interior. But the Aryan tribes also not infrequently fought with one another. We hear, for instance, that king Sudās of the Tṛitsu tribe, in alliance with the Bharatas, fought with a confederacy of ten kings, and gained a complete victory.

Army.

The main elements of the army were charioteers and infantry, and their weapons chiefly consisted of bows, arrows, spears, lances, and slings. The soldiers were arranged according to the clans and districts to which they belonged, and were protected by helmet and coat of mail.

Amusements.

On the whole, people led a merry, easy-going life. Men and women enjoyed themselves in festive assemblies with music and dance. Gambling houses were very common, and men whiled away their time in dice and drinking. Of manly games, chariot-racing and hunting seem to have been the most prominent.

Sense of morality.

It must not be supposed, however, that the people were light-hearted, and lacked the sense of duty or morality. The Vedic hymns "give evidence of an exalted and comprehensive morality." They condemn those who, with food in store, harden their hearts against the needy[1], and praise the bounty of others, who give unto the beggar what he wants, or minister to the physical comforts of the feeble. Hospitality to guests is repeatedly enjoined, while prayers are offered to the gods to hurl destruction upon thieves, robbers, and those guilty of telling lies. Sorcery, witchcraft, seductions, and adultery are denounced as criminal, and they acknowledge no wicked divinities, nor any mean and harmful practices. On the other hand, minstrels fervently prayed to Agni to urge them on to 'holy thought', and to Varuṇa, to loosen the bonds of sin committed by them,—the bonds above, between and under—so that they could stand without reproach before Aditi.

Religion.

The Vedic minstrels thus gave due weight to duties other than those of multiplying offerings to the gods and the punctilious observance of religious rituals, although it must be admitted that their religion was pre-eminently ritualistic, and the worship of gods was looked upon as the first duty of man.

Prayer.

The Vedic worship meant primarily only oblation and prayer. The recitation of sacred, but stereotyped, texts was yet unknown; on the contrary, a great value was attached to the novelty of the hymns. The ascetic practices had not yet probably had any importance in the ceremony, which merely consisted of sacrifice, along with

1. Cf. the hymn on liberality quoted at the end of this chapter.

devout prayers. These prayers have been handed down to us in the shape of hymns, and a few specimens will be quoted at the end of this chapter.

Sacrifice.

As to the sacrifice itself, we do not know much in detail, but it appears that the offerings, consisting of ordinary food and drink, were thrown into the fire, in order that they might reach the gods. Animals like horses, rams, buffaloes, bulls, and even cows were also sometimes sacrificed. But although the process of sacrifice was simple enough, the theory about it was quite a complex one, as the object and necessity of sacrifice were often regarded from radically different points of view. Thus it was sometimes looked upon as a bargain between God and man ; the man has necessities which can only be, and actually are, provided by the bounty of God, and, in return, man offers food and drink to quench His thirst, and satisfy His hunger. Sometimes this idea of give-and-take is entirely dropped, and sacrifice becomes an act of thanks-giving, mingled with affection and gratitude, to the gods, for the benefits already received from them, and expected in future. But, above all, there was a mystic air about the sacrifice. It was somehow associated with the supreme energy which keeps the universe in order. Without it there would be no day and night, no harvest and rain, because the gods would lose the power of sending them. Nay, even the gods themselves, as well as the universe, are said to have owed their origin to an act of sacrifice, without which everything would again be in a state of chaos. Proceeding on this line of symbolism, the whole system of nature came to be looked upon as a vast and perennial sacrifice. The lightning and the sun were looked upon as its sacred flame, thunder as the hymn, the rains and rivers as the libations, and the gods and the celestial apparitions, as the priests. Whatever we might think of these mystic fancies, no one can fail to be struck with the grandeur and sublime beauty of the conception.

The Vedic Deities.

The gods, to whom the sacrifice was offered, formed a motley group of varied and complex character. It is true that almost everything in nature, which impressed the imagination, or was supposed to be possessed of the power of doing good or evil, received the

1. Barth - *The Religion of India*, p. 37.

homage and worship of the old Aryans. But these were of minor importance, compared to the personal divinities to whom the Vedic hymns were generally addressed. These personal divinities were mostly deified representatives of the phenomena or agencies of nature, and were endowed with human passions and instincts. The true origin of these gods is often betrayed by their names and attributes, such as 'Dyaus' (the Heaven), 'Pṛithvī' (the earth), 'Sūrya' (the Sun), 'Ushas' (the dawn), 'Agni' (the fire), and 'Soma' (the plant of that name).

Usually, the natural phenomena, out of which these gods arose, pass into the shade amid a variety of attributes superimposed upon them; so much so, that in some cases the origin of these gods is altogether obscured. Thus Agni and Soma, while clearly retaining their physical characters, are credited with mystic powers, by virtue of which they kindle the sun and the stars, render water fertile, and make the plants and all the seeds of the earth spring up and grow. In Indra, on the other hand, the physical characteristics are practically hidden under the superimposed attributes. He is primarily the thunder-god, but a host of fanciful myths have gathered round him. On the whole, he appears as the ideal Aryan chief, leading his followers to victory against the unbelievers, *i.e.*, non-Aryan inhabitants of India.

It would be impossible to refer to even the prominent Vedic gods in detail. Various attempts have been made to classify them. The earliest, and perhaps the best, classification is that of Yāska, "founded on the natural bases which they represent." It places the gods mainly in three categories, according as they represent some phenomena in earth, atmosphere, or heaven. We have thus (1) the *terrestrial gods*, such as Pṛithvī, Agni, Bṛihaspati (Prayer), and Soma; (2) the *atmospheric gods*, such as Indra, Rudra (probably lightning), Maruts, Vāyu (wind), and Parjanya ; and (3) *celestial gods*, such as Dyaus, Varuṇa (vault of Heaven), Ushas (dawn), Aśvins (probably the twilight and morning stars), and Sūrya, Mitra, Savitṛi and Vishṇu, all associated with the most glorious phenomenon of nature, *viz.*, the Sun.

There was no hierarchy among the host of Vedic gods. It is true that some gods figure more prominently in the Vedic hymns than others. Indra, for example, is invoked in about one-fourth of the total hymns of the Ṛigveda. But still there was no recognised chief among them, like the Greek Zeus, the position of supremacy being ascribed to different gods, at different times ; by their worshippers. The true sentiment of the Vedic Aryans in this respect is indicated as follows in one of the hymns: 'Not one of you, ye gods, is small, none of you is a feeble child : All of you, verily, are great.' Reference is, however, sometimes made, even in the Vedic hymns, to "the mighty and the lesser, the younger and the elder gods." Gods, who are sometimes said to rule over others, are elsewhere described to be dependent upon them, and such contradictory statements are by no means infrequent. Sometimes one god was identified with others, and the process went on, till they arrived at the grand monotheistic doctrine, viz., 'That the gods are one and the same, only the sages describe them differently.'

In concluding this short sketch of the Aryans, we cannot but refer to the pious, lofty, and poetic sentiments which are still preserved in their hymns. The following examples are calculated to give some idea, not only of the characteristics of some of their principal gods, but also of their philosophic insight and ethical conceptions. The first three poems give a metrical sketch of the three principal Vedic deities, Indra, Agni and Ushas. They are not literal translations of any particular Vedic hymn, but combine in one picture the most salient and characteristic points in the representations of the deities which are contained in the hymns.' Special reference may be made to the last, as the hymns to the Ushas (1; 84) have preserved to us fine specimens of real poetry, distinguished alike by lyric beauty and love of nature. This feature is also prominent in the hymn to Parjanya (V.83) which contains a fine realistic description of storm, thunder, and rain.

The last four poems are metrical renderings of select Vedic hymns. The first is a fine poetic description of the most glorious phenomenon of nature, the Sun. The hymn addressed to Varuṇa is a "beautiful description of the divine omniscience", and the relation between God and man. The third is a fine example of the lofty philosophic speculations of the Vedic Ṛishis foreshadowing the doctrines of the Upanishads. The last one contains a passionate appeal to the rich to feed the hungry and to share his wealth with the poor. It is a remarkable hymn which recalls to our mind the modern conception of socialistic or welfare state.

I. INDRA

(A METRICAL SKETCH)

(1) *Indra's Greatness.*

What poet now, what sage of old,
The greatness of that god hath told,
Who from his body vast gave birth
To father Sky and mother Earth;
Who hung the heavens in empty space,
And gave the earth a stable base;
Who framed and lighted up the sun,
And made a path for him to run;
Whose power transcendent, since their birth
Asunder holds the heaven and earth,
As chariot-wheels are kept apart
By axles framed by workmen's art?
In greatness who with Him can vie,
Who fills the earth, the air, the sky,
Whose presence unperceived extends
Beyond the world's remotest ends?
A hundred earths, if such there be,
A hundred skies fall short of thee;
A thousand sun would not outshine
The effulgence of thy light divine.
The worlds, which mortals boundless deem,
To thee but as a handful seem.
Thou, Indra, art without a peer
On earth, or yonder heavenly sphere.
Thee, god, such matchless powers adorn,
That thou without a foe wast born.
Thou art the universal lord,
By gods revered, by men adored.
Should all the other gods conspire,
They could not frustrate thy desire.
The circling years, which wear away
All else, to thee bring no decay;
Thou bloomest on in youthful force,
While countless ages run their course.
Unvexed by cares, or fears, or strife,
In bliss serene flows on thy life.

(Muir—*Original Sanskrit Texts*, Vol. V., p. 135)

(2) *Indra's conflict with Vṛittra.*

Who is it that, without alarm,

Defies the might of Indra's arm ;
That stands and sees without dismay
The approaching Maruts' dread array ;
That does not shun, in wild affright,
The terrors of deadly fight ?
'Tis Vṛittra*, he whose magic powers
From earth withhold the genial showers,
Of mortal men the foe malign,
And rival of the race divine,
Whose demon hosts from age to age
With Indra war unceasing wage,
Who, times unnumbered, crushed and slain,
Is ever newly born again,
And evermore renews the strife
In which again he forfeits life.
Perched on a steep aerial height,
Shone Vṛittra's stately fortress bright.
Upon the wall, in martial mood,
The bold gigantic demon stood,
Confiding in his magic arts,
And armed with store of fiery darts.
And then was seen a dreadful sight,
When god and demon met in fight.
His sharpest missiles Vṛittra shot,
His thunderbolts and lightnings hot
He hurled as thick as rain.
The god his fiercest rage defied,
His blunted weapons glanced aside,
At Indra launched in vain.
When thus he long had vainly toiled,
When all his weapons had recoiled,
His final efforts had been foiled,
And all his force consumed—,
In gloomy and despairing mood
The baffled demon helpless stood,
And knew his end was doomed.
The lightnings then began to flash,
The direful thunderbolts to crash,
By Indra proudly hurled.

* The demon who personifies drought, and is also called Śushṇa and Ahi.

The gods themselves with awe were stilled
And stood aghast, and terror filled
The universal world.
Even Tvashṭri sage, whose master-hand
Had forged the bolts his art had planned,
Who well their temper knew,—
Quailed when he heard the dreadful clang
That through the quivering welkin rang,
As o'er the sky they flew.
And who the arrowy shower could stand,
Discharged by Indra's red right hand,—
The thunderbolts with hundred joints,
The iron shafts with thousand points,
Which blaze and hiss athwart the sky,
Swift to their mark unerring fly,
And lay the proudest foemen low,
With sudden and resistless blow,
Whose very sound can put to flight
The fools who dare the Thunderer's might ?
And soon the knell of Vṛittra's doom
Was sounded by the clang and boom
Of Indra's iron shower ;
Pierced, cloven, crushed, with horrid yell.
The dying demon headlong fell
Down from his cloud-built tower.
Now bound by Śushaṇa's spell no more,
The clouds discharge their liquid store ;
The rivers swell, and sea-ward sweep
Their turbid torrents broad and deep.
The peasant views, with deep delight
And thankful heart, the auspicious sight.
His leafless fields, so sere and sad,
Will soon with waving crops be clad,
And mother Earth, now brown and bare,
A robe of brilliant green will wear.
And now the clouds disperse, the blue
Of heaven once more comes forth to view.
The sun shines out, all nature smiles,
Redeemed from Vṛittra's power and wiles ;
The gods, with gratulations meet,
And loud acclaim, the victor greet ;
While Indra's mortal votaries sing

The praises of their friends and king.
The frogs, too, dormant long, awake,
And floating on the brimming lake,
In loud responsive croak unite,
And swell the chorus of delight.

(Muir—*Original Sanskrit Texts,* Vol. V, p. 133)

II. AGNI.

(A Metrical Sketch)

Great Agni, though thine essence be but one,
Thy forms are three; as fire thou blazest here,
As lightning flashest in the atmosphere,
In heaven thou flamest as the golden sun.

It was in heaven thou hadst thy primal birth ;
By art of sage skilled in sacred lore
Thou wast drawn down to human hearths of yore,
And thou abid'st a denizen of earth.

Sprung from the mystic pair,[1] by priestly hands
In wedlock joined, forth flashes Agni bright ;
But,—o ye Heavens and Earth, I tell you right,—
The unnatural child devours the parent brands.

But Agni is god : we must not deem
That he can err, or dare to reprehend
His acts, which far our reason's grasp transcend :
He best can judge what deeds a god beseem.

And yet this orphaned god himself survives :
Although his hapless mother soon expires,
And cannot nurse the babe, as babe requires,—
Great Agni, wondrous infant, grows and thrives.

Smoke-bannered Agni, god with crackling voice
And flaming hair, when thou dost pierce the gloom
At early morn, and all the world illume,
Both Heaven and Earth and gods and men rejoice.

In every home thou art a welcome guest ;
The household's tutelary lord; a son,
A father, mother, brother, all in one;
A friend by whom thy faithful friends are blest.

1. The two pieces of fuel by the attrition on which fire is produced and which are represented as husband and wife.

A swift-winged messenger, thou callest down
From heaven, to crowd our hearths, the race divine,
To taste our food, our hymns to hear, benign,
And all our fondest aspirations crown.

Thou, Agni, art our priest, divinely wise,
In holy science versed ; thy skill detects
The faults that mar our rites, mistakes corrects,
And all our acts completes and sanctifies.

Thou art the cord that stretches to the skies,
The bridge that spans the chasm, profound and vast,
Dividing Earth from Heaven, o'er which at last
The good shall safely pass to Paradise.

But when, great god, thine awful anger glows,
And thou revealest thy destroying force,
All creatures flee before thy furious course,
As hosts are chased by overpowering foes.

Thou levellest all thou touchest; forests vast
Thou shear'st like beards which barber's razor shaves,
Thy wind-driven flames roar loud as ocean-waves
And all thy track is black when thou hast past.

But thou, great Agni, dost not always wear
That direful form ; thou rather lov'st to shine
Upon our hearths with milder flame benign,
And cheer the homes where thou art nursed with care.

Yes, thou delightest all those men to bless,
Who toil, unwearied, to supply the food
Which thou so lovest, logs of well-dried wood,
And heaps of butter bring, –they favourite mess.

Though I no cow possess, and have no store
Of butter,—nor an axe fresh wood to cleave,
Thou, gracious god, wilt my poor gift receive,–
These few dry sticks I bring ; I have no more.

Preserve us, lord, thy faithful servants save
From all the ills by which our bliss is marred ;
Tower like an iron wall our homes to guard,
And all the boons bestow our hearts can crave.

And when away our brief existence wanes,
When we at length our earthly homes must quit,
And our freed souls to worlds unknown shall flit,
Do thou deal gently with our cold remains ;

And then thy gracious form assuming, guide
Our unborn part across the dark abyss
Aloft to realms serene of light and bliss,
Where righteous men among the gods abide.

(Muir—*Original Sanskrit Texts*, Vol. V, p. 221).

III. USHAS.

(A Metrical Sketch.)

Hail, Ushas, daughter of the sky,
Who, borne upon thy shining car
By ruddy steeds from realms afar,
And ever lightening, drawest nigh :—

Thou sweetly smilest, goddess fair,
Disclosing all thy youthful grace,
Thy bosom bright, thy radiant face,
And lustre of thy golden hair ;—

(So shines a fond and winning bride,
Who robes her form in brilliant guise,
And to her lord's admiring eyes
Displays her charms with conscious pride ;—

Or virgin by her mother decked,
Who, glorying in her beauty, shews
In every glance, her power she knows
All eyes to fix, all hearts subject ;—

Or actress, who by skill in song
And dance, and graceful gestures light,
And many-coloured vestures bright,
Enchants the eager, gazing throng ;—

Or maid who, wont her limbs to lave
In some cool stream among the woods,
Where never vulgar eye intrudes,
Emerges fairer from the wave) ;—

But closely by the amorous sun
  Pursued, and vanquished in the race,
  Thou soon art locked in his embrace,
And with him blendest into one.

Fair Ushas, though through years untold
  Thou hast lived on, yet thou art born
  Anew on each succeeding morn,
And so thou art both young and old.

As in thy fated ceaseless course
  Thou risest on us day by day,
  Thou wearest all our lives away
With silent, ever-wasting, force.

Their round our generations run :
  The old depart, and in their place
  Springs ever up a younger race,
Whilst thou, immortal, lookest on.

All those who watched for thee of old
  Are gone, and now 't is we who gaze
  On thy approach ; in future days
Shall other men thy beams behold.

But 't is not thoughts so grave and sad
  Alone that thou dost with thee bring,
  A shadow o'er our hearts to fling ;
Thy beams returning make us glad.

Thy sister, sad and sombre Night
  With stars that in the blue expanse
  Like sleepless eyes mysterious glance,
At thy approach is quenched in light ;—

And earthly forms, till now concealed
  Behind her veil of dusky hue,
  Once more come sharply out to view,
By thine illuming glow revealed.

Thou art the life of all that lives,
  The breath of all that breathes ; the sight
  Of thee makes every countenance bright,
New strength to every spirit gives.

When thou dost pierce the murky gloom,
Birds flutter forth from every brake,
All sleepers as from death awake,
And men their myriad tasks resume.

Some, prosperous, wake in listless mood,
And others every nerve to strain
The goal of power or wealth to gain,
Or what they deem the highest good.

But some to holier thoughts aspire,
In hymns the race celestial praise,
And light, on human hearths to blaze,
The heaven-born sacrificial Fire.

And not alone do bard and priest
Awake ;—the gods thy power confess
By starting into consciousness
When thy first rays suffuse the east ;

And hasting downward from the sky,
They visit men devout and good,
Consume their consecrated food,
And all their longings satisfy.

Bright goddess, let thy genial rays
To us bring stores of envied wealth
In kine and steeds, and sons, with health,
And joy of heart, and length of days.

Muir—(*Original Sanskrit Texts*, Vol. V, p. 196)

IV. SUN.

(A Vedic Hymn.)

1. By lustrous heralds led on high,
The omniscient Sun ascends the sky,
His glory drawing every eye.

2. All-seeing Sun, the stars so bright,
Which gleamed throughout the sombre night,
Now scared, like thieves, slink fast away,
Quenched by the splendour of thy ray.

3. Thy beams to men thy presence shew ;
Like blazing fires they seem to glow.

4. Conspicuous, rapid, source of light,
Thou makest all the welkin bright.

5. In sight of gods, and mortal eyes,
In sight of heaven thou scal'st the skies.
6. Bright god, thou scann'st with searching ken
The doings all of busy men.
7. Thou stridest o'er the sky ; thy rays
Create, and measure out, our days;
Thine eye all living things surveys.
8. 9. Seven lucid mares thy chariot bear,
Self-yoked, athwart the fields of air,
Bright Sūrya, god with flaming hair.
10. That glow above the darkness we
Beholding, upward soar to thee,
For there among the gods thy light
Supreme is seen, divinely bright.

(Translation of Ṛigveda 1, 50
Muir—*Original Sanskrit Texts*, Vol V. p. 160. f, n.)

VARUNA.

(A Vedic Hymn)

The mighty Lord on high, our deeds, as if at hand, espies :
The gods know all men do, though men would fain their deeds disguise.
Whoever stands, whoever moves, or steals from place to place,
Or hides him in his secret cell,—the gods his movements trace.
Wherever two together plot, and deem they are alone,
King Varuṇa is there, a third, and all their schemes are known.
This earth is his, to him belong those vast and boundless skies;
Both seas within him rest, and yet in that small pool he lies.
Whoever far beyond the sky should think his way to wing,
He could not there elude the grasp of Varuṇa the king.
His spies descending from the skies glide all this world around,
Their thousand eyes all-scanning sweep to earth's remotest bound.
Whate'er exists in heaven and earth, whate'er beyond the skies,
Before the eyes of Varuṇa, the king, unfolded lies.
The ceaseless winkings all he counts of every mortal's eyes :
He wields this universal frame, as gamester throws his dice.
Those knotted nooses which thou fling'st, o god, the bad to snare,—
All liars let them overtake, but all the truthful spare.

(Translation of Atharvaveda, Book IV, 16.
Muir—*Original Sanskrit Texts*, Vol V, p, 64 f, n.)

V. CREATION HYMN.

Nor Aught nor Nought existed ; yon bright sky
Wast not, nor heaven's broad woof outstretched above.
What covered all ? what sheltered ? what concealed ?
Was it the water's fathomless abyss ?
There was not death—yet was there nought immortal,
There was no confine betwixt day and night ;
The only One breathed breathless by itself,
Other than It there nothing since has been.
Darkness there was, and all at first was veiled
In gloom profound—an ocean without light—
The germ that still lay covered in the husk
Burst forth, one nature, from the fervent heat.
Then first came love upon it, the new spring
Of mind—yea, poets in their hearts discerned,
Pondering, this bond between created things
And uncreated. Comes this spark from earth
Piercing and all-pervading, or from heaven ?
Then seeds were sown, and mighty powers arose—
Nature below, and power and will above—
Who knows the secret ? who proclaimed it here,
Whence, whence this manifold creation sprang ?
The Gods themselves came later into being—
Who knows from whence this great creation sprang ?
He from whom all this great creation came,
Whether His will created or was mute,
The most High Seer that is in highest heaven,
He knows it—or perchance even He knows not.

(Rigveda, X, 129, Translated by Max Müller in *Chips from a German Workshop*, Vol. I, p. 78.

VI. HYMN ON LIBERALITY

1. The Gods have not ordained hunger to be our death: even to the well-fed man comes death in varied shape.

   The riches of the liberal never waste away, while he who will not give finds none to comfort him.

2. The man with food in store who, when the needy comes in miserable case begging for bread to eat,

   Hardens his heart against him—even when of old he did him service—finds not one to comfort him.

3. Bounteous is he who gives unto the beggar who comes to him in want of food and feeble.
Success attends him in the shout of battle. He makes a friend of him in future troubles.

4. No friend is he who to his friend and comrade who comes imploring food, will offer nothing.
Let him depart—no home is that to rest in—,and rather seek a stranger to support him.

5. Let the rich satisfy the poor implorer, and bend his eye upon a longer pathway.
Riches come now to one, now to another, and like the wheels of cars are ever rolling.

6. The foolish man wins food with fruitless labour; that food—I speak the truth—shall be his ruin.
He feeds no trusty friend, no man to love him. All guilt is he who eats with no partaker.

7. The ploughshare ploughing makes the food that feeds us, and with its feet cuts through the path it follows.
Better the speaking than the silent Brahman : the liberal friend outvalues him who gives not.

(Rigveda. X. 117. Trānslated by R.T.H. Griffith)

CHAPTER VII

Later Vedic Period—Political History

During the period represented by the later Vedic literature which, roughly speaking, comes down to about 600 B. C., some remarkable changes came over the Aryans in India. The first and foremost of these was their gradual expansion towards the east and south.[1] We have seen that the main Aryan settlements, in the earlier period, were on the banks of the rivers of the Panjāb, although their outlying colonies reached as far as the Gaṅgā. During the period represented by the Later Saṁhitās and the Brāhmaṇas, however, they continued their progress, and well-nigh covered the whole of Northern India, from the Himālaya to the Vindhyas. The spread of the Aryans over the whole of India was completed before 400 B.C., and was probably due to a variety of causes, the most important of which were, no doubt, the military conquest and the missionary propaganda. The earlier inhabitants either resigned themselves to the fate of the Śūdras, or were pushed back still further, and Northern India was almost completely Aryanised. Of the new Aryan kingdoms in the east, the most important were those of the Kurus, Pañchālas, Kāśis, Kośalas and Videhas.

Extension of Aryan Settlements

For a long time the Vindhya Range denoted roughly the southern limit of the extent of Aryan settlements. Their gradual

1. The assumption that the Aryans of the Panjāb gradually spread further east is not unanimously accepted. Some hold the theory of a second Aryan immigration into the valley of the Gaṅgā, through Gilgit and Chitral. Others are of opinion that while the early Aryan immigrations into the Panjāb "were no mere incursions of armies but gradual progressive movements of whole tribes, the waves of tribal migration were impeded about the longitude of Sirhind and the Indo-Aryan influence far thereast was due rather to warlike or peaceful penetration than to the wholesale encroachment of multitudes." Both these theories are mere hypotheses to explain the undeniable ethnic and linguistic differences prevailing between the different parts of Northern India.

Cf. 1. *Camb. Hist. Ind.* I. pp. 43 ff;

2. R. P. Chanda, *Indo-Aryan Races*;

3. Muir's *Original Sanskrit Texts* Vol. II, Chap. III

progress over the Deccan into South India cannot be clearly traced. There are, however, good grounds to believe that this southern movement began during the period of the Brāhmaṇa literature, about 1000 B. C., and went on steadily until the Aryans reached the southernmost extremity of the Peninsula in or some time before the fourth century B. C. The grammarian, Kātyāyana, who flourished in the fourth century B. C., knew the countries of the extreme south such as Pāṇḍya, Chola and Kerala, and these are also referred to in the inscriptions of Aśoka. But the Aryan conquest and colonisation in the south was not as complete as in the north. Pre-Aryan language, and, to a certain extent, l manners and customs, survived the Aryan penetration, specially in the region south of the Krishnā river.

With the progress of the Aryans in Northern India, their centre of civilization, too, was shifted towards the east. The bank of the Sarasvatī was now regarded as the most sacred spot, and witnessed the performance of many a sacrifice of great sanctity and importance. The territory between this holy river and the Gaṅgā came to be the seat of the orthodox Aryan civilization, and nothing is more indicative of the change that had taken place, than that the people of this region should look down upon the Aryans of the Panjāb as of impure descent, and imperfect in manners and customs.

Growth of Powerful States.

The progress of the Aryans was followed by other important consequences. The old tribal organization was gradually strengthened and consolidated, and led in many instances to the growth of powerful territorial States. Many of the famous tribes of the earlier period passed into oblivion, and new ones took their place. Thus the far-famed Bharatas, Pūrus, Tṛitsus and Turvasas of old were now fast disappearing or rather merging into new peoples like the Kurus and the Pañchālas, whose names do not occur in the Ṛigvedic hymns, but who now began to play the most conspicuous role. The political life became more keen and the struggle for supremacy among different States was of frequent occurrence. Already the ideal of universal empire loomed large in the political horizon, and it is difficult to maintain that it was never actually realized in practice to any considerable extent. The references to *Aśvamedha* and *Rājasūya* sacrifices are too frequent in literature to be dismissed as mere fiction, and those rulers who per-

Imperialism in ancient India.

formed either of them had, as their immediate and only object, the establishment of imperial sway over a number of other States. We may readily believe that political India was already exhibiting those characteristic features which have ever distinguished it in historical times, *viz.* a congeries of States, fighting for supremacy, and yielding at times to the irresistible force of a mighty empire-builder.

A few concrete instances may be noted. The *Śatapatha Brāhmaṇa* refers to two Bharata kings, Bharata Dauḥshanti and Śatānīka Sātrājita, as having performed the *Aśvamedha* sacrifice. They advanced as far as the Gaṅgā and the Yamunā, and conquered the Kāśis in the east, and the Sātvatas in the west. The same Brāhmaṇa refers to an old *gāthā* which says: "The greatness of the Bharatas neither the men before nor those after them attained." The *Śatapatha Brāhmaṇa* further refers to *Aśvamedha* sacrifices performed by Para, the Kośala king; Purukutsa, the Aikshvāka king; Marutta Āvikshita, the Āyogava king; Kraivya and Soṇa Sātrāsāha, the Pāñchāla kings; Dhvasan Dvaitavana, the king of the Matsyas; and Ṛishabha Yājñatura, the king of the Śviknas.

Again, the *Aitareya Brāhmaṇa* refers specifically to no less than twelve kings who, being inaugurated with the Mahābhisheka ceremony, "went everywhere, conquering the earth, up to its ends, and sacrificed the sacrificial horse." Three of these kings are identical with those in the *Śatapatha Brāhmaṇa* list.

It is against the background of this struggle for supremacy that we have to study the political history of the period. Unfortunately very little of it that may be regarded even as tolerably certain is known to us. There were no doubt genuine traditions about kings and royal dynasties from the earliest period, but in course of transmission through thousands of years, the texts containing them were mostly lost, and even those that have been preserved have suffered to such an extent by way of additions and alterations, that it is at present almost impossible to reconcile them with one another. Mr. Pargiter, who went more deeply into this branch of study than any other scholar, prepared an outline of political history of this period on the basis of these early traditions.[1] His views have

Political history.

Pargiter's view.

1. *Ancient Indian Historical Tradition* (1922).

been challenged by other scholars, but their reconstruction of the history of the period is not less open to criticism. It may be readily admitted that none of these hypotheses can be regarded as historical, and considering the material at our disposal, we could hardly expect otherwise. Pargiter's theory cannot be regarded as very satisfactory, and some of his views are open to serious objections. But as a first bold attempt to reconstruct the framework of the early political history of India, its importance cannot be over-estimated. We therefore give below a summary of his main conclusions.

The mythical king Manu.

Tradition naturally begins with myth, and so all the early dynasties that ruled in India are derived from a primaeval king Manu Vaivasvata. Manu had nine sons and a daughter, among whom the whole of India was divided. Ikshvāku, the eldest son, obtained Madhyadeśa, and was the progenitor of the solar race or dynasty, with its capital at Ayodhyā. From Ikshvāku's son Nimi (or Nemi) sprang the dynasty that reigned in Videha, with its capital at Mithilā, which is said to have been named after his son Mithi.

The dynasty of Purūravas

Ilā, the daughter of Manu, had a son, called Purūravas Aila, who got the kingdom of Pratishṭhāna (Allahabad). This kingdom rapidly developed, and members of this family carved out independent principalities at Kānyakubja (or Kanauj) and Banaras. Yayāti, the son of Nahusha, and the great-grandson of Purūravas, was a renowned conqueror. He extended his kingdom widely, and was reckoned a *Samrāj* (emperor). He divided his empire among his five sons, Yadu, Turvaśu, Druhyu, Anu and Pūru, each of whom became the founder of a long line of kings. Pūru, the youngest son, got the ancestral property, and Yadu's realm lay in the country watered by the rivers Chambal, Betwa, and Ken. At a later period, Yadu's descendants increased and divided into two great branches, 'the Haihayas' and 'the Yādavas'. The Yādava branch established a great kingdom by extending its sway over neighbouring countries. They defeated the Pauravas (descendants of Pūru), and drove the Druhyus into the Panjāb.

The kingdom of Ayodhyā then rose to very great eminence under Yuvanāśva II, and especially his son Mandhātā. The

Mandhātā. latter was a famous king, a *Samrāj* (emperor) and extended his sway very widely. He overran the Paurava and Kānyakubja kingdoms, and defeated the Druhyus. The Druhyu king Gāndhāra retired to the north-west, and gave his name to the Gāndhāra country. It is also probable that Mandhātā or his sons carried their arms south to the river Narmadā.

The supremacy of Ayodhyā soon waned, and the Haihayas became the dominant power. One of their kings traversed the prostrate Paurava kingdom, and conquered Kāśi. The most famous king of this dynasty was Arjuna, son of Kṛitavirya. He extended his conquests from the mout of the Narmadā as far as the Himālayas, and raised the Haihaya power to pre-eminence during his long reign.

The Haihayas.

The principal Brāhmaṇas, who dwelt in the lower region of the Narmadā, were the Bhārgavas. They were ill-treated by the Haihaya kings, and fled into Madhyadeśa. The famous Ṛishi Ṛichika Aurva, who was chief among them, married a daughter of Gādhi, king of Kānyakubja. The issue of the marriage was Jamadagni, who married a princess of Ayodhyā. Gādhi's son Viśvaratha became the Brāhmaṇa Viśvāmitra.

At the end of his long reign Arjuna came into collision with Jamadagni, and ki led him. The latter's son Rāma took up the fight, and was supported by the princes of Ayodhyā and Kānyakubja, who were allied to him by marriage, and who would naturally have opposed the dangerous raids of the Haihayas. With their help Rāma killed Arjuna, and punished the Haihayas.

Jamadagni and Arjuna.

But although th e Haihayas received a set-back, they grew in power, and their dominions stretched from the gulf of Cambay to Gaṅgā-Yamunā Doab, and thence to Banaras. They overthrew the kingdoms of Ayodhyā and Kānyakubja, and many other kingdoms in the north-west, with the co-operatio of various foreign tribes. The king of Ayodhyā, driven from his throne, took refuge in the forest, and died there, leaving a child Sagara. Sagara, on reaching manhood, defeated the Haihayas, and regained Ayodhyā. He extended his campaign, crushed the Haihayas in their own territories, and subdued all the other enemies in North India. India was thus saved from age-long struggles and depredations, bringing ruin and carnage in their train.

Sagara.

When Sagara established his empire over Northern India, the only noticeable kingdoms that survived were the Videha, Vaiśāli[1] and Ānava (descendants of Anu) kingdoms in the east, Kāśi in Madhyadeśa, and the Yādava kingdoms in Vidarbha, and on the Chambal. After the death of Sagara, the over-

Minor States.

thrown dynasties appear to have generally recovered themselves, and the Yādavas of Vidarbha seem to have extended their authority northward over the Haihaya territory. Vidarbha, after whom the province was named, had a grandson, Chedi, who founded the dynasty of Chaidya kings in Chedi, the country lying along the south bank of the Yamunā. The Ānava kingdom in the east, the nucleus of which was Aṅga, became divided up into five kingdoms, said to have been named after king Bali's sons, Aṅga, Vaṅga, Kaliṅga, Suhma, and Puṇḍra. The capital of Aṅga was Mālinī, and its name was changed afterwards to Champā or Champāvatī (Bhāgalpur) after king Champa.

The Paurava realm had been overthrown in Mandhātā's time, but, after Sagara's death, it was re-established by Dush-

The Pauravas.

yanta. Dushyanta's son by Śakuntalā was the famous and pious Bharata. Their territory, however, appears to have been shifted to the northern portion of the Gaṅga-Yamunā Doab, for Pratishṭhāna is no longer mentioned, and the district was included in the Vatsa realm. Bharata was a great monarch with a wide sway, and his successors, were the famous Bharatas. Bharata's fifth successor Hastin made Hastināpura his capital. Under Hastin and his successors the Paurava dynasty extended its sway over Pañchāla and other neighbouring realms.

In the meantime Ayodhyā again rose to prominence under Sagara's great-grandson Bhagīratha, and the latter's successors.

Kingdom of Ayodhyā.

But after the reign of Kalmāshapāda, who killed the sons of his priest Vasiṣṭha, troublesome period ensued, and the kingdom was divided among two rival lines. The internal dissensionscont inued for six or seven generations, until Dilīpa II re-established the single monarchy. The kingdom of Ayodhyā, which now acquired the name of Kośala, rose to prominence under Dilīpa II and

1. This name is given in anticipation to the foundation of the city by a later king named Viśāla.

his successors Raghu, Aja, Daśaratha, and Rāma. After them Ayodhyā ceased to play any prominent part in history.

The Yādavas.

About this time the Yādavas rose to power. For a long time their territory was divided into a number of small kingdoms, but the famous king Madhu consolidated them, and his territory is alleged to have extended from Gujarāt to the Yamunā. His descendants were the Madhus or Mādhavas. But the large Yādava kingdom was again divided among Sātvata's four sons, of whom Andhaka and Vṛishṇi became the founders of important ruling dynasties. Andhaka reigned at Mathurā, the chief Yādava capital, and Vṛishṇi reigned probably at Dvārakā in Gujarāt.

The Kurus

About this time the kingdom of North Pañchāla rose to great power, and the famous king Sudāsa established its pre-eminence by driving out the Paurava king of Hastināpura, and defeating a confederacy of hostile kings. But not long afterwards the table was turned. The Pauravas not only recovered Hastināpura, but conquered North Pañchāla, and under the famous king Kuru, their sway extended beyond Prayāga. Kuru gave his name to Kurukshetra, and to Kurujāṅgala, which adjoined it on the east and in which Hastināpura lay. His successors were called the Kurus or the Kauravas, a name that was extended also to the people.

Jarāsandha.

Vasu, a descendant of Kuru, conquered the kingdom of Chedi, and extended his conquests as far as Magadha in the east, and Matsya in the north-west. He divided the kingdom among his five sons. Bṛihadratha, the eldest, took Magadha, with Girivraja as his capital, and founded the famous Bārhadratha dynasty there. Jarāsandha was one of the most famous kings of this dynasty, and extended his kingdom as far as Mathurā, where Kaṁsa, the Yādava king, acknowledged him as overlord. Kaṁsa, relying on his favour, tyrannised over his own subjects, and was killed by Kṛishṇa. This roused Jarāsandha's wrath against Kṛishṇa and the Bhojas of Mathurā. For a long time they resisted him, but feeling their position there insecure, they migrated in a body to Gujarāt, and established themselves in Dvārakā, where Kṛishṇa ultimately obtained the lordship.

In the meantime the Kauravas had again become prominent under Pratīpa and his successor Śāntanu. Śāntanu's grandsons were Dhṛitarāshṭra and Pāṇḍu. Dhṛitarāshṭra had many

The Kauravas and the Pāṇḍavas.

sons, Duryodhana and others, who, as the elder branch, were called the Kauravas. Pāṇḍu had five sons, Yudhishṭhira and others, who were known as the Pāṇḍavas. Pāṇḍu died early, and there was intense jealousy between the cousins. The young Pāṇḍavas received the small principality of Indraprastha (Delhi) as their share of the Kaurava territory, but being ambitious they, with Kṛishṇa's help, killed Jarāsandha, their common enemy. They were banished for fourteen years as the penalty of losing at dice, and, at the end of that time, re-claimed their principality; but Duryodhana refused all terms, and they appealed to arms. They were aided by the Matsyas, Chedis, Kārushas, Kāśis, south Pañchālas, western Magadhas, and the western Yādavas from Gujarāt and Surāshṭra; and on Duryodhana's side were all the Panjāb nations and all the other kingdoms of Northern India, and the north of the Deccan.

The great battle, fought in the famous field of Kurukshetra, ended in the victory of the Pāṇḍavas, with the slaughter of nearly all the kings and princes who took part in it. It was the famous Bhārata War. Yudhishṭhira became the undisputed king of the Kurus, and reigned at Hastināpura. The great statesman Vāsudeva Kṛishṇa had conceived the bold idea of uniting all the warring States of India into an empire, and it was thus realized in practice for some time. A few years later, the Yādavas of Gujarāt were ruined by fratricidal strife, and Kṛishṇa died. Yudhishṭhira then abdicated, and retired to forest with his brothers, leaving Arjuna's grandson Parīkshit II on the throne.

Here ends the hypothetical reconstruction of history by Pargiter (and other scholars). From this point onwards we have a firmer grasp of the main events of political history and can also arrange them roughly in a chronological system.

Although the Mahābhārata was composed at a later period, the central event of the epic, *viz.*, the struggle between the Kauravas and the Pāṇḍavas described above, may be regarded as historical. This Great War, the echo of which persists down to our own time, may be approximately dated at about 1000 B.C. It must have caused a tremendous sensation, comparable to the late great wars in Europe, for the ancient writers are unanimous in their view that it ushered in a new epoch (the Kali Yuga or Dark Age) in the history of India.

The battle of Kurukshetra left the Pāṇḍavas the supreme political power in India. The Purāṇas name thirty kings of this dynasty, called Paurava, beginning from Arjuna's grandson Parīkshit II.

Parīkshit and his son Janamejaya are famous figures in the Mahābhārata, and the latter is one of the twelve universal sovereigns mentioned in the *Aitareya Brāhmaṇa.* During the reign of Nichakshu, fourth in descent from Janamejaya, the city of Hastināpura was washed away by the Gaṅgā, and other calamities befell the Kuru kingdom. The capital was then transferred to Kauśāmbī, but the Kuru kingdom steadily declined from that time. No detail is known of any of the succeeding Pauravas, till we come to the twenty-sixth king Udayana, whose history will be dealt with in a later chapter.

The contemporary, and probably allied, dynasty of the Aikshvākus ruled in Kośala with Ayodhyā as their capital.

Other contemporary kingdoms.

Twenty-four kings ruled in this line, but our detailed knowledge begins from the time of Prasenajit, a contemporary of Udayana, of whom more will be heard hereafter. At the time of the Great War, the Bārhadrathas were ruling in Magadha. They were descendants of the famous Jarāsandha. Sixteen kings of this dynasty ruled at Giribraja (Rājagṛiha) after the Great War, when the dynasty was overthrown.

In addition to the above, other ruling dynasties flourished in different parts of India, during the period that followed the Great War. Of these, the kingdoms of Kāśi and Videha rose to great eminence and among others may be mentioned the Pāñchālas, the Haihayas, the Kaliṅgas, and the Śūrasenas.

Thus the supremacy which the Pāṇḍavas gained by the Great War must have been shortlived. During the six hundred years that followed, India must have presented the same political condition, out of which she was rescued by the genius of Kṛishṇa and the prowess of Arjuna. The next great empire that we know of was built up by Mahāpadma Nanda, and if any flourished during the interval, its memory has been completely lost.

CHAPTER VIII

Later Vedic Period—Political Theory and Administrative System.

Side by side with the growth of territorial States and the ideal of imperialism, we find also the clear beginnings of political speculations during the period under review. But as our only source of information is sacerdotal literature, we naturally find the theories often presented in a theological garb. It does not, however, require much ingenuity to deduce secular ideas from what is discussed or propounded in connection with the gods.

The origin of sovereignty, for example, is discussed in relation to gods. It is said in the *Aitareya Brāhmaṇa* (I. 1. 14) that gods and demons fought with one another, but the gods were defeated, whereupon they said : "It is because we have no king that the demons defeat us ; so let us elect a king". They elected a king and through his help obtained complete victory over the demons. Again, the same Brāhmaṇa (VIII. 4.12) tells us that the gods installed Indra as king as they agreed, after discussion among themselves, that he was "among the gods the most vigorous, the most strong, the most valiant, the most perfect who carries out best any work (to be done)." In these passages one cannot fail to notice a rational theory of the origin of kingship which may be defined as the election, by common consent, of a person who is regarded as the most suitable for carrying on the business of the State, in general, or in a particular emergency such as a great war. Side by side with this view, we also find the enunciation of the divine origin of kingship. The *Taittirīya Brāhmaṇa* (II. 2, 10. 1-2), for example, describes how Indra, "though occupying a low rank among the gods, was created their king by Prajāpati."

Origin of kingship.

It is interesting to note that both these ideas of the origin of kingship. *viz.* election and divine creation, are discussed in detail in later political literature of India. A further development of the theory is the view, that there was originally a state of nature, in which might alone was right, and in order to establish law and order the people elected (or God created) a king, who promised to secure life and property on condition of receiving a tribute from the people. This is analogous to the theory of contract enunciated by Locke in the 18th century. This theory, too, is foreshadowed, though not clearly enunciated, in a mystic passage in *Śatapatha Brāhmaṇa* (XI. 1. 6. 24) : "Whenever there is drought, then the stronger seizes upon the weaker, for the waters are the law".

The passages quoted above demonstrate that even in those remote days there was a scientific spirit of inquiry into the origin of political institutions, and an attempt to answer the most pertinent question : "How is it that the king who is one rules over so many subjects"? In this the Brāhmaṇa literature clearly anticipates more detailed discussion in the Epics and Arthaśāstras (texts on polity) of a later age. Most European writers readily take for granted that such a spirit of inquiry was foreign to oriental intellect. One of them writes : "To the early Eastern mind, the fact that a thing existed was sufficient of itself to show its right to be. Thus was effectually excluded all possibility of inquiries as to the relative perfection, or justification for the existence of *de facto* social and political institutions"[1]. The speculations about the origin of kingship and the caste system (p. 48) are sufficient to refute this view. It must be admitted, however, that though we find a promising beginning, so far as this inquisitive mood is concerned, during the later Vedic period, it was not logically carried out, at least as much as we could desire, in the succeeding ages.

Imperialism

Reference has been made above (p. 66) to the imperialist ideas of the period, sanctified, or symbolised, by ceremonies like Aśvamedha, Rājasūya etc. New political terms were coined to suit the new ideas. The *Aitareya Brāhmaṇa* applies the terms *samrāṭ*, *bhoja*, *virāṭ*, and *rājan* to the rulers respectively of the east, south, north, and the middle country, and reserves the terms *ekarāṭ* and *sārvabhauma* for those who had conquered the kings in four directions. The details of the Rājasūya ceremony also contain symbolical representation of the imperial powers of the ruler who performs it.

The increase in the royal power, due to the growth of large territorial States, is duly reflected in the enlarged entourage of

1. Willoughby – *Political Theories of the Ancient World*, p. 14.

Officials.

the king. We hear of new officials such as *Sūta* (charioteer), *Saṁgrahītṛi* (treasurer), *Akshāvāpa* (superintendent of dicing), *Takshan* (carpenter), *Rathakāra* (chariot-maker), *Kshattṛi* (chamberlain) and several others whose exact functions cannot be ascertained. These officers, as well as the *Purohita*, *Senānī* and *Grāmaṇī* were known as Ratnins (jewels) and their importance is testified to by the fact that in course of the Rājasūya ceremony the king had to visit, on successive days, the houses of these officials and make offerings to the gods. Everything indicates that the administrative machinery was highly organized and became an efficient instrument for ruling over large kingdoms. It also seems that the high royal officials formed a sort of aristocracy which rivalled, if not replaced, the order of nobility by birth.

Growth of Royal Power

The splendour and majesty of the king found expression n new theories about his power and dignity. Thus the *Śatapatha Brāhmaṇa*[1] lays down that by means of certain rites performed in the Rājasūya sacrifice "the king becomes not only exempt from punishment but also the lord of the law". But such highly exaggerated doctrines can hardly be taken as reflecting the general view of the age, far less the actual state of things. It is directly opposed to the conception of Dharma or Sacred Law which sustains the world, and to which all, including the king, are subject. It has been all along stressed by the political thinkers of India, that this Sacred Law was to be interpreted by the sages, and the king must abide by, and give effect to, it. Indeed this fundamental principle may be recognised as the keystone of the political thought of India in all ages. It is also important to note that both the later Saṁhitās and Brāhmaṇas refer to kings who were driven away by the people. The Sṛiñjayas expelled their king Dushṭarītu Pauṁsāyana, who could claim at least ten generations of royal descent[2]. The *Tāṇḍya Brāhmaṇa* (VI. 6. 5.) describes a specific sacrifice which was performed by the subjects to destroy the king.

The liberal spirit of the age is reflected in the following advice which, according to the White Yajurveda, was tendered by the priest to the king at the coronation ceromony : "As a

1. V. 3. 3. 9; 4. 4. 7.
2. *Sat., Br.*, XII, 9. 3. 1.

Coronation Oath. ruler, from this day onwards, judge the strong and the weak impartially and fairly. Strive unceasingly to do good to the people, and above all, protect the country from all calamities". Reference may also be made to the coronation oath taken by the king which includes the following :

> 'Between e nigh t I am born and the night I die, whatever good I might have done, my heaven, my life and my progeny may I be deprived of, if I oppress (injure) you'.

Thus while the growth of royal power was an undeniable fact, there is no reason to suppose that there was an undiluted autocracy, the so-called oriental despotism, either in theory or in practice. The election of kings by the people is referred to in the Atharvaveda which also lays stress (III. 4) on the necessity of concord between the king and the electors. The later Saṁhitās and Brāhmaṇas also contain references to the *sabhā* and *samiti* which show that they continued to exercise an effective authority over the king. It is interesting to note that the *Śatapatha Brāhmaṇa* refers to these two popular assemblies as 'twin daughters of Prajāpati', ascribing to them the same divine origin as it does to the king. Thus even theoretically the monarchy and the popular assemblies were, as divine institutions, placed on the same footing.

—·—

CHAPTER IX.

Later Vedic Period—Social and Religious Condition.

The gradual political evolution was by no means the most important factor in the history of the Aryans during the later Vedic period. Changes of far greater significance were gradually taking place in their society and religion.

The obscurity of the Vedic language.

One fact, which contributed more than anything else to this development, and which indeed supplies a key to all the subsequent changes, is the growing obscurity of the language of the hymns. For languages, like human beings, have their rise, growth, and decay, and here, as in other domains of nature, "the old order changeth yielding place to new'. The language of the old Vedic hymns was no longer understood by the common people, and a special training was required to master them. The consequences of this natural phenomenon were great and far-reaching.

Its consequences.

In the first place, need was felt of a class of men, who had special instruction in the old Vedic texts, and thus arose the professional Brāhmaṇa class, destined to develop into a rigid caste at no distant date. Secondly, the Vedic hymns came to be regarded as a Canonical book, to which it was impossible to add, and the religion thus assumed a more or less stereotyped form.

As a matter of fact, the theology of the later Vedic literature did not essentially differ from the theology of the hymns. Although some new deities had arisen, and some of the old ones had passed into oblivion, the change in the pantheon as a whole could not be said to be very striking, in view of the number of years that had passed.

Change of religious spirit.

But although the theology remained more or less the same, the religious spirit underwent a great change. The charming appreciation of all that is good and sublime in nature, leading to outburst of individual enthusiasm in inspiring stanzas addressed to various divinities,—all these were now things of the past. The creative age was succeeded by one of criticism, and inspiration had yielded to rigid formalism. We hear no more of those simple ceremonials of worship, breathing a sense of healthy and intimate relation between God and man. Instead, we find the energy of the priestly class directed to a number of ceremonies, which they developed in endless details, and to which they attached the most fanciful and mystic significance. Indeed the priestly class now devoted their whole attention to find out the hidden and mystic meaning of the rites and ceremonies. These ceremonies comprehend both domestic rites as well as great sacrifices, and form a body of rituals, probably the most stupendous and complex which has ever been elaborated by man. The domestic rites embrace the whole course of a man's life, from his conception in the mother's womb up to his death, or rather beyond it, as several ceremonies refer to the departed souls. The following conventional list of forty *saṁskāras* or sacraments, finally drawn up at a later period, but reflecting conditions of an earlier age, will not only explain the general nature of these rites and ceremonies, but also throw a flood of light on the manners and customs of the period.

Elaborate Rituals.

The Forty Saṁskāras

1. Garbhādhāna—Ceremony to cause conception.
2. Puṁsavana—Ceremony to secure the birth of a male child. It consisted in pounding a Soma stalk, or some other plant, and then sprinkling it into the right nostril of the would-be mother, with four Vedic verses.
3. Sīmantonnayana—The parting of the pregnant wife's hair by the husband with a porcupine's quill after due oblations and sacrifices, and offering prayers to Vishṇu to take care of the womb.
4. Jātakarman—Ceremony for the new-born child.
5. Nāmakaraṇa—Ceremony of naming the ehild.
6. Annaprāśana—The first feeding of the child with solid food in the sixth month. The father gave the child goat's flesh, if he was desirous of nourishment, flesh of partridge, if desirous of holy lustre, fish, if desirous of swiftness, boiled rice with *ghee*, if

desirous of splendour,--such food mixed with curds honey and *ghee*, the father gave to the child to eat, after making oblations to the gods with vedic verses.

7. Chūḍākarman—The tonsure of the child's head.
8. Upanayana—Initiation. By this ceremony the child enters upon the *Brahmacharya* or the austere life of a student. A passage in the *Śatapatha Brāhmaṇa* (XI. 3. 3. 1-7) shows that all the essential features of this ceremony which are elaborated in the later Gṛihya Sūtras were already present in this period.

9-12. The four vows, differently named in different *Sūtras* which were undertaken for studying the different portions of the Vedic literature.

13. Samāvartana—The ceremony on the completion of studentship. The student pays a fee to his teacher, cuts his hair, beard and the nails, takes his bath, and returns home.
14. Sahadharmachāriṇī-saṁyoga— The taking of helpmate for the fulfilment of the religious duties—in other words,

Marriage—After the student-career is over, that of the householder begins. The first duty of the householder is to marry a girl of equal rank, who has no t belonged to another man, is younger than himself, and is outside certain degrees of relationship, both on his father's and mother's side.

Eight different kinds of marriage were in vogue :—

(a) If the father gives his daughter, dressed in two garments and decked with ornaments, to aperson, possessing sacred learning, of virtuous conduct, who has relatives and good disposition, that is a *Brāhma* wedding.

(b) The *Prājāpatya* wedding is similar to the above, but the marriage formula used is : "Fulfil your duties conjointly". Although the wives, married according to other rites, shared the duties of the husband, the *Prājāpatya* marriage laid particular stress on this aspect of marriage, and the husband could not take to any other *Āśrama*, or marry another wife, owing to the formula used.

(c) At the *Ārsha* wedding, the bridegroom presents a cow and a bull to the guardians of the girl.

(d) If the bride is given, decked with ornaments, to a priest, who duly officiates at a sacrifice, during the course of its performance, it is called a *Daiva* marriage.

(e) The spontaneous union with a willing maiden is called a *Gāndharva* wedding.

(f) If those, who have authority over a female, are propitiated by money, that is an *Āsura* wedding.

(g) If a bride is taken by force, that is a *Rākshasa* wedding.

(h) If a man abducts a female, while deprived of consciousness, that is a *Paiśāçha* wedding.

The first four of the above were unanimously held to be lawful. The fifth and the sixth were valid, only in the opinion of some. The last two were always regarded as blameworthy.

15-19. Pañcha-Mahāyajñas. The five great daily sacrifices to the gods, manes, men, goblins and Brahman. 'Teaching (and studying) is the sacrifice (offered) to Brahman, the (offerings of water and food called) Tarpaṇa, the sacrifice offered to the manes, the burnt oblation, the sacrifice offered to the gods, the Bali offering, the sacrifice offered to the Bhūtas (goblins), and the hospitable reception of guests, that offered to men.' These are to be regularly performed every day by the householder.

20-26. The seven kinds of Pākayajñas (or small sacrifices) *viz.*, the Ashṭakā, the Śrāvaṇī, the Āgrahāyaṇī, the Chaitrī, the Āśvayujī, the Pārvaṇa and the Śrāddha.

The Ashṭakās are sacrifices offered on the eighth day of the dark halves of the four months from 'Kārtika to Māgha". The Śrāvaṇī is offered on the full moon day of Śrāvaṇa, the Āgrahāyaṇī, on the forteenth or on the full moon day of Agrahāyaṇa, the Chaitrī, on the full moon day of Chaitra, and the Āśvayujī on the full moon day of the month of Āśvina. Pārvaṇa is offered on the new and full moon days. The Śrāddha is one of the most important domestic rites. It is the monthly funeral offering to the manes on the new moon days.

27-33. The seven kinds of Haviryajñas.

34-40. The seven kinds of Somayajñas.

The Haviryajñas, as well as the Somayajñas, are more highly developed rituals than those described above, and are treated in detail in the Srauta-sūtras. The essential point in both is the kindling of at least three sacred fires, to which offerings of cakes, grain, milk, honey etc., are made. In the case of Somayajñas, the additional offering of Soma, of course, forms an essential part, and most of them were characterised by the killing of animals. There was another important distinction between these and the other rituals (Nos. 1—26), which are described in the Gṛihya-sūtras. In these Śrauta rituals, the priests play the most prominent part, whereas, in the Gṛihya rituals, the essential duties are performed by the householder himself.

The seven kinds of Haviyrajñas are :—

1. The Agnyādheya—The establishment of the sacred fires, three or more in number. It was the bounden duty of every householder to set up these sacrificial fires in his house. These fire-places served the purposes of temples where god was worshipped.
2. The Agnihotra—Daily oblation in the three sacred fires.
3. The Darśa-paurṇamāsas—Yajñas of the full and new moon.
4. The Āgrayaṇa—The oblation of the first fruits of the harvest.
5. The Chāturmāsyas—Yajñas at the beginning of each of the three seasons.
6. The Nirūḍhapaśubandha—The animal-sacrifice, effected separately, not as an integral part of another ceremony.
7. The Sautrāmaṇī—The essence of this is the offering of *surā* (wine) to the Aśvins and Sarasvatī. It was usually an epilogue to the Somayajñas, its object being to cure persons who had drunk too much Soma therein.

The seven kinds of Somayajñas are :—

The Agnishṭoma or Jyotir-agnishṭoma, the Atyagnishṭoma the Ukthya, the Shoḍaśin, the Vājapeya, the Atirātra, and the Aptoryāma. All these were more or less different forms of the Agnishṭoma, and varied only in the number of victims and some details.

The actual ceremony of the Agnishṭoma lasted for only one day in which the Soma was pressed thrice, in the morning, midday and in the evening, and cattle were offered to Agni. But the ceremony was preceded by a long period of *dīkshā* or consecration, sometimes extending for a year, during which the sacrificer and his wife lived an austere life in two adjacent huts, built for the purpose. One of the most interesting features of this ceremony was the purchase of the Soma plant, which was brought on a cart, and solemnly received as a guest.

There were many other sacrifices besides those mentioned in the above list. It is not necessary to enumerate these, but four of them deserve special notice. The first is the Vrātya-Stoma. It consisted of four rites, by means of which persons outside the pale of Brahmanic fold were admitted into the orthodox society. The existence of this sacrifice conclusively proves that the Hindu society in old days was not so rigid as at present, and opened its doors to all persons.

Vrātya-Stoma.

The next two ceremonies to be described, *viz.*, the Rājasūya and Aśvamedha, have obtained a wide celebrity.

The Rājasūya was a ceremony for the consecration of a king. Like Agnishṭoma it lasted for a day in which Soma was pressed and other ceremonies performed, preceded by a long period extending to a year, in which the various preliminary rites were celebrated. The principal officers of the State took part in the ceremony, and the king, in his State-dress, received from the priest a bow and arrow, and declared himself king. He performed various acts symbolising his conquests in all directions, and was then anointed by a priest, a kinsman, a Kshatriya and a Vaiśya.

Rājasūya.

In the Aśvamedha ceremony, a horse, duly consecrated and protected by warriors, was let loose, along with 100 other horses, to move about at its own free will as a challenge to other kings. Then, for about a year, the king, accompanied by his queen, with the maids-in-waiting and high officials, performed daily sacrifices, in course of which the legends of the king's ancestors were recited. After the year was over, the horse was brought back, and the king was consecrated. The horse was anointed by the queens, and various ceremonies were gone through. It was then killed and its flesh roasted.

Aśvamedha.

There can be no doubt that both the Rājasūya and Aśvamedha ceremonies could only be performed by powerful sovereigns, and were usually regarded as a visible symbol of their supremacy over other kings. In order to emphasise this aspect, the subordinate kings were sometimes made to perform menial services in these sacrifices, particularly in the Rājasūya.

More efficacious than the Aśvamedha, but far more dreadful, was the Purushamedha, in which a human being was sacrificed instead of a horse. The ceremonies performed were very similar in the two cases. As the horse was let loose for about a year, the human victim was allowed to enjoy himself for the same period, during which all his wishes were satisfied. The queen behaved with the human victim exactly as she did with the horse in the Aśvamedha sacrifice.

Purushamedha.

These rites and ceremonies were not, however, the only means of attaining success in this world, or bliss in heaven. Shortly, there developed the idea of *tapas* or self-mortification as leading to the same or even more important results. *Tapas* means meditation, accompanied by physical tortures. These took various forms, such as remaining in the same posture for months and years, living on the least quantity of food, standing in the sun in summer, and in the cold in winter, lying on iron spikes, and various other similar performances, testifying to the perfect control over physical body. Men retired into solitude, and exercised all these ascetic practices under the belief, that they would thereby not only gain heaven, but also develop "mystic, extra-ordinary and superhuman faculties." Thus *tapas* was substituted for sacrifice to a considerable extent in the religious outlook of the age.

Tapas.

While elaborate rites, ceremonies, and ascetic practices had been taking the place of the simple religious worship of the good old time, an intellectual section of the people was more and more urged on by the conviction, that bliss and salvation were attainable only by true knowledge. They did not altogether discard rites, ceremonies, and austerities, but relegated them to a minor position, and laid down the doctrine, that 'he who knows God, attains to God, nay, he is God.' Such philosophic speculation was of course no new thing, for its germs are traceable even in the Ṛgveda, and a distinction between *Karma-kāṇḍa* and *Jñāna-kāṇḍa*, *i.e.* between rituals and knowledge, was always recognised in the Vedas. But it is only towards the close of the Vedic period, that these philosophic speculations were systematised and incorporated in the revealed literature, and thereby assumed an important position.

Philosophic speculations.

The general body of early philosophical treatises is known by the name of Upanishad. The number of Upanishads known to us is exceedingly large, about 200 in number, but many of them belong to very late times. The oldest Upanishads like the Bṛhadāraṇyaka and the Chhāndogya, however, go back to a period anterior to 600 B.C., and contain bold speculations about the eternal problems of human thought concerning God, man, and the universe. There was no doubt some sort of antagonism between the devotees of the ritual and the philosophers, and it is not without significance that the Kshatriyas distinguished themselves in the domain of pure thought. The Brāhmaṇas were the sole authorities in questions affecting rites and ceremonies, but in philosophical speculations, the had rivals in the Kshatriyas, and sometimes even took lessons from them.

Upanishads

It is impossible to deal in detail with the philosophic speculations of the Upanishads, which are justly regarded as the most important contribution of India towards the world's stock of spiritual thought. They give evidence of a rare intellectual attainment which has won the rapturous praise of the learned world. The great philosopher Schopenhauer was so much carried away by the perusal of a Latin translation of the Persian translation of the Upanishads, that he broke out in the following rapturous applause :

"From every sentence deep, original and sublime thoughts arise, and the whole is pervaded by a high and holy and earnest spirit. Indian air surrounds us, and original thoughts of kindred spirits. And oh, how thoroughly is the mind here washed clean of all early engrafted Jewish superstitions, and of all philosophy that cringes before those superstitions ! In the whole world there is no study, except that of the originals, so beneficial and so elevating as that of the Oupnekhat (Upanishad). It has been the solace of my life, it will be the solace of my death !"[1]

This may be considered as somewhat extravagant, but even the sober Max Müller held that "the earliest of these philosophical treatises will always maintain a place in the literature of the world, among the most astounding productions of the human mind in any age and in any country."[2]

The Egyptians and the Indians were both faced with the common problem of death. "Had all ended for the man with the moment in which he had ceased to breathe ?" was their

1. *SBE* 1, p. lxi.
2. *Ibid*, p. lxvii.

common enquiry, and to prevent such a horrible thing, their common endeavour. Yet the one found the true solution in the mighty Pyramids, containing the embalmed bodies, while the other was led to evolve the immortal Upanishads. This contrast is interesting and instructive, and not only indicates the true character of Indian civilization, but its superiority to all that preceded it.

The four Āśramas.

At the close of the period we are dealing with, there were thus developing, side by side, a stupendous system of rites and observances, a curious method of self-torture, and highly elaborate philosophical speculations into the mysteries of the universe. The life of an ancient Indian, swayed by these cross-currents, may be best realised from a study of what is technically called the 'four Orders' or Āśramas. These four Orders are, that of the student, that of the householder, that of the ascetic, and that of the hermit in the woods. After the ordinary course of training at the teacher's house was over, every man had to make a choice of his further career out of these four.

He might choose the first, and devote his whole life to study. He had then to live at his teacher's house until his death, and follow the course of strict discipline prescribed for a student. He had to lead a chaste life of strict virtue, maintaining proper control over all his organs, and avoiding all luxuries and pleasures of life.

If he chose the second, he had to return from his teacher's house, after his study was over, in order to marry, and maintain a household. His chief duty was to study the Vedas, maintain a fire, and perform the different rites and ceremonies noted above.

Or he might adopt the third, and go forth as an ascetic from his teacher's house. He was to live without a fire, without a house, without pleasures, without protection. Remaining silent, and uttering speech only on the occasion of the daily recitation of the Vedas, begging so much food only in the village as will sustain his life, he had to wander about, neither caring for this world nor for heaven. He had to wear clothes thrown away by others as useless, or he might even go naked, though this last practice was not much countenanced. Indifferent towards all creatures whether they do him an injury or a kindness, without undertaking anything for this world and the next, he was to seek the Ātman or Self ; in other words, he had to consecrate his whole life to philosophic meditation. No doubt, it was to this type of men that we owe the development of philosophy.

Fourtlhly, one might, after finishing his studies, adopt the life of a hermit in the woods. A hermit was to live in the forest, in order to practise austerities. He maintained a fire, and performed the five great daily sacrifices referred to above. He could enter a village, and dressed himself in garments made of bark and skins. At first he had to live on roots, fruits, leaves and grass, then on whatever became detatched spontaneously, next on water, and lastly on nothing.

Although any one of these four Orders was open to a student who had a course of training at his teacher's house, he could follow even two or more of them if he chose. Thus he might live as a householder for some time, and then take to the life of an ascetic or a hermit at a fairly advanced age. There are reasons to believe that this was the course more often followed. We even hear of kings retiring to forest towards the close of their lives.

The organisation of the four Orders is a unique feature of Indian society. Though the historian is mostly concerned with one of them alone, *viz.* that of the householder, he cannot ignore the influence that the other three must have exercised upon it. The presence of a band of pious selfless seekers after knowledge and spiritual truth leading to salvation must have improved the moral tone of the society as a whole. Many of them, again, although generally aloof from worldly affairs, lived too close to society not to help it with constant advice, and, if necessary, by occasional intervention. The laws and regulations, for example, were codified by them, and tyrannical kings had not infrequently to tremble before their terrible wrath. Many instances are on record, in which the sages intervened to put an end to a tyrant's career.

The Caste System.

Another important change in this period was the evolution of that unique social institution, called caste. As mentioned above (p. 48), at first the Aryans formed a homogeneous mass of people, but gradually two classes of men gained a position of honour and distinction. A primitive people naturally looks with awe and reverence upon those who possess a knowledge of sacred literature and religious ceremonies, as well as upon those who wield political authority. Thus the Brāhmaṇas and the Kshatriyas emerged as the two leading classes out of the general mass of population, now known as the Vaiśyas.

Whether these distinctions took a definite shape when the Ṛgveda was written, it is difficult to say. The probability is, that in the early Vedic period the only real distinction was between the white-skinned Aryans and the black-skinned Dāsas or Śūdras, as the aborigines, conquered by the Aryans, and incorporated in their society, came to be called. It is only in the later Vedic period, when the obscurity of the Vedic texts required a professional class of interpreters, that a definite class of Brāhmaṇas arose. At the same time, the extension of the Aryans increased the importance of the military leaders, who established political powers in various directions, and a distinct Kshatriya class was evolved.

The Vaiśyas, as the remaining Aryans now came to be called, were no doubt much superior to the Śūdras, but their position was steadily deteriorating. A passage in Aitareya Brāhmaṇa even goes so far as to say that a Vaiśya "is to be lived on by another and to be oppressed at will", indicating thereby their absolute dependence on the two upper classes.

But although the society was divided into four classes, there was no rigid caste system as yet. There is nothing to show that none but the son of a Brāhmaṇa could belong to that class. Many passages indicate that the knowledge of Vedic texts and religious ceremonies was looked upon as the primary qualification, and heredity counted for little, in the recognition of a person as Brāhmaṇa. Rules were indeed laid down in the Sūtra period, that nobody should serve as a priest who could not prove his descent from three generations of Ṛishis. But these very rules prove distinctly, that the unbroken descent in a Brāhmaṇa line was yet an ideal, and not an actuality. They further indicate a deliberate attempt towards making the system more and more rigid. There is enough evidence to show that the caste was not solely determined by the accident of birth, and the professions normally laid down for the different castes were never scrupulously followed in practice. As to the other essentials of caste, the prohibition of interdining among the different classes was not even thought of, and intermarriage between different classes was in vogue. The marriage of the three upper classes with the Śūdras was indeed looked upon with disfavour, but it was not positively forbidden.

Absence of rigidity.

Lastly, the Brāhmaṇas had not yet attained an unquestioned position of supremacy, the Kshatriyas having successfully contested it for long.

The contrast between the 'Ārya' and the 'Śūdra,' however, came to be more and more accentuated during the later part of the Vedic period. It was claimed that the Śūdras had no right to approach the sacred fire, i.e. perform sacrifice, or to read the sacred texts, although many passages in early texts clearly admit these rights. The Śūdras were further denied the rite of burning the dead body, although old texts even go so far as to lay down the measurements for the tumulus of a Śūdra. Further, as has just been mentioned, marriage with the Śūdra gradually came to be looked upon with disfavour. These were portents of evil days for the Śūdras, but as yet there was no question of relegating them to a position of abject humiliation, such as has since been their fate.

Śūdras.

The Kshatriyas pushed the Aryan colonies into remote and unknown lands, the Brāhmaṇas elaborated and spread the Aryan culture into the newly conquered regions and even far beyond, while the Vaiśyas and the Śūdras ministered to the growing needs of a wealthy people, fast developing a life of ease and luxury, by means of trade, commerce, manufacture, cultivation and various other arts and crafts.

The general position of women changed for the worse. They lost the right to the *Upanayana* ceremony, and all their sacraments, excluding marriage, were performed without the recitation of Vedic mantras.

Position of women.

As in the earlier period, the marriage of women normally took place after puberty. Polygamy certainly prevailed, and the following hymn in the Atharvaveda (V. 17.8) clearly refers to polyandry and inter-marriage:

> Even though there were ten non-Brāhmaṇa
> previous husbands of a woman,
> The Brāhmaṇa alone becomes her husband
> if he seizes her hand.

Theoretically the wife was still accorded a very high position. Thus the *Śatapatha Brāhmaṇa* (V. 2.1.10) says that she is half her husband and completes him. But there are unerring signs that her status and dignity were lowered a great deal during this period. Thus many of the religious ceremonies, formerly left to the wife, were now performed by priests. She was not allowed to attend the political assemblies. A submissive wife who would keep her mouth shut and dine after her husband is now held up as the ideal. The birth of a daughter was most unwelcome; for she was regarded as a source of misery and a son alone was the saviour of the family.

The women were taught to dance and to sing, and various kinds of musical instruments such as drums, flutes, lyre or harp, cymbals, and lutes of various kinds are mentioned. But some women were highly learned. In spite of the gradual deterioration in their position it is gratifying to find that even in the latest Vedic age represented by the Upanishads, women maintained a high position even in the learned world. Two very interesting incidents, described in the *Bṛihadāraṇyakopanishad*, may be referred to in this connection.

The great king Janaka of Videha once performed a sacrifice at which the most learned Brāhmaṇas, including those from Kuru and Pañchāla countries, were present. Janaka wished to know, which of those Brāhmaṇas was the best read. So he enclosed a thousand cows, and ten *pādas* of gold were fastened to each pair of horns. And then Janaka spoke to the assembled Brāhmaṇas: "Let the wisest among you drive away these cows." Yājñavalkya, the great philosopher, asked his pupil to drive them away. Then the other Brāhmaṇas became very angry, and one after another, they plied Yājñavalkya with questions. Yājñavalkya silenced them all. One of his interlocutors was the venerable lady Gārgī Vāchaknavī. She stood up in the midst of the assembly, and held a philosophic discussion with the great Yājñavalkya, till the latter remarked : "O Gārgī, do not ask too much, lest thy head should fall off. Thou askest too much about a deity, about which we are not to ask too much." Gārgī stopped for the moment, but some time after she rose again, and began with the proud remark : "Venerable Brāhmaṇas, I shall ask him two questions. If he will answer them, none of you, I think, will defeat him in any argument concerning Brahman." The questions were asked and Yājñavalkya answered them.[1]

The second incident is also connected with Yājñavalkya. "Maitreyī", said he, addressing his wife, "verily I am going away from this my house into the forest. Let me make a settlement between thee and that Kātyāyanī, my other wife."

1. *SBE*, Vol. XV, pp. 121 ff.

Maitreyī said: "My Lord, if this whole earth, full of wealth, belonged to me, tell me, should I be immortal by it ?" 'No' replied Yājñavalkya. And Maitreyī said: 'What should I do with that by which I do not become immortal? What my Lord knoweth of immortality, tell that to me.'

Yājñavalkya replied: "Thou who art truly dear to me, thou speakest dear words. Come, sit down, I will explain it to thee, and mark well what I say." Then followed one of the most abstruse philosophical dissertations about the Universal Self, and its relation to the Individual.[1]

These two incidents eloquently testify to the high position, learning, and mental equipment of women in ancient India, to which it would be difficult to find a parallel in the history of the world.

But these two gifted ladies did not stand alone, for there are many references to women teachers, possessing high spiritual knowledge. Even later literature refers to *Brahmavādinīs*, a class of women who devoted their whole lives to study and spiritual meditation. All these offer a striking contrast to the later age, such as that represented by the *Manu-saṁhitā* when a woman was forbidden to study Vedic literature.

Education.

Such a highly developed intellectual life, as well as the vast mass of Vedic literature, presupposes a well-planned system of education. As noted above, the *Upanayana* was the religious ceremony by which a boy was initiated into the life of a student and handed over to a *guru* or preceptor. Henceforth he had to live in the house of the *guru* and lead the chaste life of a *Brahmachārin*, whose principal duties were study and service to the teacher. The latter included even gathering fuel, tending cows, and begging alms. There was no system of public schools as at the present day, but the student got a thorough moral and intellectual training by his constant association with his *guru*. The students got free boarding and lodging at his house, and in return did personal service to him and paid fees (*dakshiṇā*) at the completion of their study, though sometimes sons of wealthy parents probably gave regular fees even before.

There were many great centres of Vedic learning under famous teachers, and these forerunners of what were later known

1. *SBE,* Vol. XV, pp. 108 ff.

as Sūtra-charaṇas are mainly responsible for the different Vedic schools with various redactions of Vedic texts. The story of Gārgī quoted above shows that highly philosophical debates in learned assemblies formed a distinct feature of the educational system of those days.

The chief subjects of study were undoubtedly the Vedic texts, including Itihāsa and Purāṇa (old historical traditions), as well as Brahmavidyā (philosophy and spiritual knowledge) and the subjects included in the Vedāṅgas mentioned above (p. 35). But other and more secular branches of study were not neglected. The Upanishads contain several lists of subjects which must have formed the regular curriculum of study These included dialectics (*vākovākya*), mathematics (*rāśi*), chronology (*nidhi*), military science, science of snakes, knowledge of portents, and several others whose exact scope or nature cannot be asçertained, such as *pitrya*, *devavidyā*, *bhūta-vidyā* and *devajana-vidyā*, which evidently related to gods and earthly elements. Ethics (*ekāyana*) also formed a subject of study, and high moral training leading to the formation of character and development of personality formed the backbone of the educational system. The students were taught both by precepts and examples of the *guru* (teacher).

BOOK II

From c. 600 B. C. to c. 300 A. D.

CHAPTER I

Political History from the Sixth to the Fourth Century B. C.

1. *Foundation of the Magadha Empire*

Indian history assumes a more or less definite shape towards the close of the seventh century B. C. There was no paramount power in Northern India at this period, but the whole country was divided into a number of independent States. The literary works of the 4th century B. C. give the number of important States as sixteen, but in all probability the actual number exceeded this conventional figure. Some of the States were monarchical, but others had republican or oligarchic constitution. The four important royal dynasties that stand out prominently at this period, are the Haryaṅkas in Magadha, the Aikshvākus in Kośala, the Pauravas in Vatsa (Kauśāmbī), and the Pradyotas in Avanti[1]. It is interesting to note that the kingdom of Kuru-Pañchāla, Kāśī and Matsya, celebrated in the *Mahābhārata*, continued at this period, although they ranked as minor powers. Of the non-monarchical States we hear mostly of the Vṛijis of Mithilā, the Śākyas of Kapilavastu, and the Mallas of Pāvā and Kuśinagara. The Vṛijis formed a confederacy of eight different clans, the most prominent of which were the Lichchhavis, who had their capital at Vaiśālī.

The sixteen States

There were matrimonial alliances between many of these States, but that did not prevent the outbreak of hostility among them. Each of the four important royal dynasties, mentioned above, tried to establish its supremacy, and aggrandise itself at the cost of minor States. We hear, for example, that Pradyota, king of Avanti, fought with Udayana, king of Kauśāmbī, although the latter was his son-in-law, and at another time he threatened Rājagṛiha, the capital of Magadha. Prasenajit, king of Kośala, was already master of Kāśī, and his son afterwards conquered

1. Haryaṅka is the name of a new dynasty founded in Magadha by Bimbisāra after overthrowing the Bārhadrathas. The Pradyotas are so called after the founder Pradyota. The other two are old royal dynasties (pp. 68-70).

the Śākya State of Kapilavastu. Again, Bimbisāra, king of Magadha, annexed Aṅga, and his son Ajātaśatru conquered the Lichchhavis of Vaiśālī. All these kings—Pradyota, Udayana, Bimbisāra and Prasenajit—flourished in the second half of the sixth century B. C.

At the beginning of the fifth century B. C. the Pauravas and the Pradyotas seem to have retired from the contest for supremacy, which was thus left to be fought out between the Haryaṅkas of Magadha, and the Aikshvākus of Kośala. A fierce and protracted struggle ensued between Prasenajit and Ajātaśatru, and although the results were indecisive for a long time, victory ultimately inclined to the Magadha kingdom. Henceforth Magadha stands out as the supreme power in Northern India, a position which was ultimately destined to convert her into the greatest empire that India has ever seen. Ajātaśatru, who had seized the throne by murdering his father, thus became the founder of the supremacy of Magadha. He died about 475 B. C., and was succeeded by Udayī[1], to whom tradition ascribes the foundation of Pāṭaliputra, the new capital of the Magadha kingdom. From remote times, described in epic literature, Rājagṛiha, now represented by the ruins at Rājgir in the Patna District, served as the capital of the Magadha kingdom. While Ajātaśatru was fighting against the Lichchhavis he built, as a defensive measure, a fortress at Pāṭaligrāma, a village at the junction of the Gaṅgā and the Sone. In course of time, the strategic importance of the place must have attracted the attention of the statesmen of Magadha, aud Udayī evidently thought it a more suitable capital for his kingdom, which had lately extended its boundaries in all directions.

Rise of Magadha

According to the Buddhist tradition Udayī and his three successors were all parricides. So the people got disgusted and elected as king Śiśunāga, the minister of the last of the parricides. The Purāṇas, however, take Śiśunāga to be the founder of the royal line to which Bimbisāra belonged, and hence calls it the Śaiśunāga Dynasty. In any case, the statement in the Purāṇa that Śiśunāga destroyed the power of the Pradyotas seems to be true.

Śisunāga

1. According to the Purāṇas Ajātaśatru was succeeded by Darśaka, but the Buddhist tradition, which seems to be more reliable, has been followed.

Kālasoka, the son and successor of Siśunāga, was assassinated by a man of low origin—barber according to some accounts—named Mahāpadma Nanda, who succeeded to the throne, and founded a new dynasty known as the Nanda. Mahāpadma seems to have been a great military genius. He defeated and destroyed the far-famed Kshatriya families, such as the Pauravas, the Aikshvākus, and the Pradyotas, who were ruling in Kauśāmbī, Kośala and Avanti, and established an empire which included the greater part of Northern India excluding Kāshmīr, Panjāb and Sindh. Thus did the work begun by Bimbisāra and Ajātaśatru make triumphant progress.

Nanda Dynasty

2. *Invasion of Alexander*

The western borderland of India comprising the Panjāb, Sindh and Afghānistān seems to have been lacking in political power and prestige during this period. Of the sixteen traditional States mentioned in Indian literature, only two, Kāmboja and Gandhāra, may be placed in this outlying region. It appears to have been divided into two dozen or more independent principalities, some of which were ruled by kings, while others had democratic or oligarchic constitution They were not infrequently at war with one another, and thus offered an easy prey to foreign invaders.

The Panjāb

The powerful Achaemenian Emperors of Persia naturally cast their longing eyes towards this region, and it is probable that Cyrus (558-530 B. C.) subjugated a number of tribes living to the south of the Hindu Kush mountains. It was not, however, till the reign of Darius (522-486 B. C.) that we have positive evidence of the extension of Achaemenian rule in India proper. Two later inscriptions of this monarch dated between 518 and 515 B. C., but not an earlier one dated two years before, mention Hi(n)du as a part of his dominion. The exact connotation of this term is not known, but it certainly comprised some territory to the east of the Sindhu, which Darius must have conquered about 518 B. C. Herodotus, the Greek historian, tells us that in 517 B. C. Darius sent a naval expedition under Scylax to explore the valley of the Sindhu river. We further learn from the same source that the Indian dominion formed the twentieth Satrapy of the empire of Darius, but contributed a third of its entire

Persian conquest of Indian borderland

revenue in gold dust which amounted to over a million pounds sterling.

How long the Persian domination lasted in India is not definitely known. Its continuance up to about 330 B. C. is generally presumed on the ground that the Indian soldiers formed part of the Achaemenian army that conquered Greece in the time of Xerxes (486-465 B. C.) and fought against Alexander at Gaugamela in 330 B. C. But this is by no means a sure conclusion, as the Indians might have joined the army as mercenary soldiers This seems to be the more probable, as on the later occasion the Indian contingents are expressly mentioned as having fought under Satraps of other provinces. This shows that there were perhaps no Persian Satraps in India at that time.

The defeat of the Achaemenian king Darius III at Gaugamela in the hands of Alexander profoundly affected the course of Indian history. Alexander pursued the fugitive king and overran the whole of Persian dominions in the east as far as the Jaxartes. He then returned, re-crossed the Hindu Kush, and advanced against India in May, 327 B. C. The king of Takshaśilā (Taxilā, near Rawalpindi in the Panjāb) offered to help Alexander, and thus followed in the footsteps of those Greek princelings and statesmen who, in the preceding century, joined the Achaemenian Emperors and betrayed the interests of Hellas in order to secure personal gain or safety. But though one or two Indian princes followed the ignoble example of Taxilā, most of the numerous kings and republican or oligarchic tribes in Afghānistān, Panjāb and Sindh opposed a brave resistance, though in vain. These petty chieftains and tribes were, of course, no match for the seasoned troops of Alexander. But though they knew they had no chance of success they refused to submit without a fight. The Greek writers have paid well-deserved tribute to the bravery and patriotism of a large number of them, though their own countrymen have kept no record of their heroic deeds and their very names have been forgotten. Alexander's triumphant march over the dead bodies of thousands of such heroes and patriots is no doubt a brilliant episode in the history of Greece, but indirectly it also sheds lustre on India for the fearlessness of death and the love of freedom shown by her sons. Among those who acquired undying fame by their heroic conduct only a few may be mentioned here, but the Greek annals are full of them.

Alexander crosses the Hindu Kush

Indian resistance

Alexander sent a part of his army along the Kābul river under two of his best generals. They were opposed by the chief of Pushkalāvatī (Charsaddā near Peshāwar) who defended his capital for thirty days till he fell fighting. Alexander himself led the other division of the army in the valleys of the Kunār, Panjkorā, and Swāt rivers in order to secure his flank. He was opposed by the hilly tribes whom the Greeks called Aspasioi and Assakenoi, problably a corruption of Asvakas. They held out in their citadels and offered stubborn resistance. While attacking one of these, Alexander himself received a wound, and in retaliation he put the whole population to the sword. When the king of the Assakenoi fell fighting his army was led by the queen, whose example induced the entire womanhood of the locality to join this struggle for-freedom. After a brave resistance for several days Massaga, the capital city, capitulated. A body of mercenary troops, 7000 in number, who had distinguished themselves in the fight, were granted their lives by a special agreement which Alexander concluded with them, but at night they were surrounded and butchered to a man. This massacre has been condemned even by the Greek writers. The capture of Aornus, the strongest citadel of the Assakenoi, is described by the Greek writers at great length, and is regarded by them almost as the greatest military feat of Alexander in his Indian campaign.

The Assakenoi

Aornus

Having thus subdued the Assakenoi and some other tribes, Alexander joined his other division which had in the meanwhile reached the Sindhu and built a bridge of boats at Ohind, 16 miles above Attock. Alexander crossed with his whole army and halted at Taxilā. He then invited the neighbouring chiefs to come and offer submission. The most powerful among them was the ruler of a kingdom between the Jhelum and the Chenab whom the Greeks call Porus, probably a corruption of Paurava. When he was summoned by Alexander's envoys to meet the great Emperor he proudly replied that he would undoubtedly do so, but at his own frontiers and in arms. Alexander made elaborate preparations to fight against him and the way in which the Greek writers describe the campaign shows that it taxed the resources and ingenuity of Alexander to the utmost. Yet it must be remembered that Porus was a ruler of a small territory, perhaps not bigger than a modern district in the Punjāb.

Porus

Porus fought bravely, and, with nine wounds on his body, was led a captive before Alexander. The latter asked him how he should like to be treated. "Like a king" came the proud and prompt reply. Alexander secured the alliance of this brave chief by restoring his kingdom and adding to it the territories of "15 republican tribes with their 5000 cities and villages without number," and the kingdom of Porus II between the Chenab and the Ravī, all of which he conquered later. In course of his advance to the next river Beas he had to fight hard with the Kathaioi (Kaṭhas?) whose casualties amounted to 17,000 killed and 70,000 captured.

Alexander's Retreat

Alexander's advance was arrested on the bank of the Beas, for his soldiers mutinied and refused to proceed further (end of July 326 B.C.). Whether this insubordination of the soldiers was due merely to war-weariness, as represented by the Greek writers, or at least partly to the fear inspired by the mighty empire of the Nandas which lay beyond the river, it is difficult to say. It is interesting to note, however, that in course of their reply to Alexander's arguments the troops laid great stress on the calamity that would befall the whole army if Alexander met with accident in course of the campaign.

Mālavas and other tribes

Whatever may be the real reason, Alexander had to bow to the decision of his mutinous soldiers. He went back along the road by which he came till he reached the Jhelum river. Then he sailed down the river with a part of his army in 1000 boats, while troops marched along its either bank to protect him. Near the confluence of this river with the Chenab he had to fight with a confederacy of republican tribes led by the Malloi (Mālavas) and the Oxydrakai (Kshudrakas). All the towns of the Mālavas became citadels of resistance. In one of them the Brāhmaṇas, 5000 in number, left the pen for the sword and died fighting, only a few being taken prisoners. While taking another town by assault Alexander was severely wounded, and when it was captured, his infuriated soldiers killed everybody they found within irrespective of age and sex. Another tribe, the Agalassoi (Arjunāyanas?) also fought with great valour, and when one of their towns was captured by Alexander all the citizens, numbering 20,000, after a heroic resistance, threw themselves into the fire with their wives and children. This is the first recorded *Jauhar* ceremony in Indian history—the precursor of many terrible repetitions in later days.

The Brāhmaṇas

When two kings, Musicanus (king of the Mūsṇikas ?) and Oxycanus, in the lower Sindhu valley, submitted to Alexander, they were denounced as traitors by the Brāhmaṇas who urged the people to oppose foreign invaders as part of their *dharma* (religion). The kings revoked their submission and fought, but were put to the sword along with the Brāhmaṇas. In September 325 B.C. Alexander reached Patala, where the Sindhu was divided into two branches before reaching the sea, and began his homeward journey. He proceeded with his army by land, but sent the ships under Nearchus with instructions to bring them along the coast into the Persian Gulf as far as the mouth of the Euphrates.

Death of Alexander

Alexander reached Susa in Persia in 324 B. C. and died there the next year. He had made arrangements for the administration of the conquered territories and put several Satraps in charge of different parts. But some conquered tribes rebelled and there were other troubles even before he left India. After his death the whole system collapsed within a short time.

Reflections on Alexander's invasion

The invasion of Alexander the Great has been recorded in minute details by the Greek historians who naturally felt elated at the triumphant progress of their hero over unknown lands and seas. From the Indian point of view, its importance lies in the fact that it opened up a free intercourse between India and the western countries which was big with future consequences. For the rest there was nothing to distinguish his raid in Indian history. It can hardly be called a great military success as the only military achievements to his credit were the conquest of petty tribes and States by instalments. He never approached even within a measurable distance of what may be called the citadel of Indian military strength, and the exertions he had to make against Porus, the ruler of a small district between the Jhelum and the Chenab, do not certainly favour the hypothesis that he would have found it an easy task to subdue the mighty Nanda empire. Taking everything into consideration, a modern historian, unprejudiced by the halo of Greek name, may perhaps be excused for the belief, that the majority of Greek writers did not tell the whole truth when they represented the retreat of Alexander as solely due to the unwillingness of his soldiers to proceed any further ; nor can he dismiss, as altogether fictitious, the view recorded by more than one ancient Greek historian, that the retreat of Alexander was caused by the terror of the mighty power of the Nandas.

But if the invasion of Alexander was not crowned by military success like that of Nadir Shah or Tamerlane, it was nevertheless characterised by cruelties, which may differ in degree, but certainly not in kind, from those standing to the credit of these later heroes. The perfidious massacre of the garrison of Massaga, and the recorded instances of the blood-thirsty Greek troops slaughtering the inhabitants of captured cities, sparing neither man, woman nor child, tell their own tale. The Greek historians have recorded that during the campaign of the lower Sindhu valley alone, 80,000 of the natives were killed, and multitudes sold as slaves ; and howsoever the modern European historians may try to palliate or justify these crimes, an Indian historian can hardly be blamed for regarding Alexander only as a precursor of Nadir Shah and Tamerlane.

The death of Alexander was a signal for the disruption of his vast empire. The Indian territories, which cost him a toilsome and cruel warfare for about three years, declared their independence, and in less than five years they did away with the last vestige of Greek domination in the Panjāb.

APPENDIX

The Chronological Problem.

We have no definite data for fixing the chronology of the period before Alexander's invasion. According to the unanimous tradition of the Buddhists, the Buddha died in the 8th year of the reign of Ajātaśatru, and the chronology of the whole period is usually fixed with the help of this synchronism. Unfortunately, the date of the death of Buddha is not known with certainty. According to the tradition current in Ceylon, the event took place in 544 B. C. But this date is incompatible with the statement in the Ceylonese Chronicles that Aśoka's coronation took place 218 years after the death of Buddha. For the evidence of the Greek writers, and the known dates of the Greek kings mentioned in Aśoka's inscriptions as his contemporaries, leave no doubt that Aśoka's consecration took place within a few years of 269 B. C. Accordingly some scholars place the date of the death of Buddha in *c.* 487 (269+218) B.C. This view is supported by what is known as the dotted "record." It is said that a dot was put in a record each year after the death of Buddha, and this practice was continued in Canton up to the year 489 A. D. As the total number of dots in that year was 975, we get 486 B.C. as the date of the death of Buddha. This date has been accepted in this work and the chronology arranged accordingly, though the date of the death of Buddha still remains a vexed problem.

Once the date of Ajātaśatru's accession is fixed with reference to the date of the death of Buddha, we can determine approximately the dates of the kings who preceded and succeeded him by counting backwards and forwards with the help of their reign-periods stated in the Purāṇas and Ceylonese Chronicles. In this way we can approximately fix the chronology of the period going as far back as the Great War.

The known date of Alexander's invasion gives us the first fixed point in Indian chronology, and enables us to determine the date of Chandragupta Maurya. The dates of most other kings that succeeded him, with the exception of the Kushāna king Kanishka, are now known with a tolerable degree of certainty.

CHAPTER II

The Maurya Empire

I. Chandragupta.

The credit of freeing the country from the yoke of the Greeks is unanimously assigned to Chandragupta. The early career of this hero is all but unknown, although the brilliant achievements of his later life have surrounded his memory with a host of legends. Later Brāhmaṇical texts represent him as the son of a Nanda king of Magadha, by a low-born woman named Murā, from whom the dynastic name Maurya is supposed to have been derived. According to Buddhist chronicles, which are earlier in date, Chandragupta was a Kshatriya. It is probable, that Chandragupta belonged to the Kshatriya clan which is referred to as Moriyas of Pipphalivana in the Mahāparinivvāna Sutta. According to this Buddhist Sutta, the Moriyas were a well-known republican clan as far back as the time of Gautama Buddha.

Chandragupta

There are good reasons to believe, that the splendid success of Chandragupta was due, as much to his own military genius, as to the statesmanship of his Prime Minister Kauṭilya. Chandragupta drove away the Greek garrison from the Panjāb and Sindh and made himself master of these provinces. He then ascended the throne of Magadha by uprooting the Nanda dynasty about 322 B. C., and by a series of brilliant military conquests, established a vast empire stretching from the bank of the Sindhu to the mouth of the Gaṅgā. It is extremely fortunate that he did so, for ere long he had to meet with a terrible foe. Seleucus, one of the ablest generals of Alexander, obtained possession of the Asiatic dominions of his master, and after organising his empire from Syria to Afghānistān, he proceeded to take possession of the Panjāb. The desire was neither unnatural, nor illegitimate, in view of the recent conquests of Alexander, but, unfortunately for Seleucus, he had to reckon with a foe of a quite different character. The Panjāb was no longer parcelled out among numerous petty chieftains unable or unwilling to

Invasion of Seleucus

make a common cause against a foreign invader. It was part of a well-organised empire, at the head of which stood a great military genius, and a far-sighted politician. Singularly enough, the classical writers do not give any details of the conflict between Seleucus and Chandragupta. Some have therefore expressed doubt about any contest having actually taken place between them.

The otherwise inexplicable silence of the classical writers, as well as the net result of the expedition, however, clearly indicate that Seleucus met with a miserable failure. For he had not only to finally abandon the idea of reconquering the Panjāb, but had to buy peace by ceding Paropanisadai, Arachosia, and Aria, three rich provinces with the cities now known as Kābul, Kandāhār and Herāt respectively as their capitals, and also Gedrosia (Baluchistān), or at least a part of it. The victorious Maurya king probably married the daughter of his Greek rival, and made a present of five hundred elephants to his royl father-in-law. Some Greek writers have represented this gift as the price of the rich provinces ceded by Seleucus, which is of course absurd. It is difficult to believe that Seleucus would have readily agreed to part with his rich provinces for such paltry gifts unless he were forced to do so. It is therefore legitimate to hold that Seleucus was worsted in his fight with Chandragupta

The conflict between Seleucus and Chandragupta Maurya, if any, must be looked upon as the nearest approxmation to a fair trial of strength between the Greek and Indian military forces which history has recorded. The princelings in the Panjab can hardly be regarded as a fair match to Alexandar, the greatest military genius the world has ever seen, backed by the resources of a mighty empire, extending over three continents, and stretching from the Adriatic to the Sindhu. But the empires of Seleucus and Chandragupta do not compare unfavourably in point of resources. Both of them had fought their way to the throne within recent years, and the generalship of both was as fair a specimen as their countries could normally show. If, then, according to Dr. V. Smith, "the triumphant progress of Alexander from the Himalaya to the sea demonstrated the inherent weakness of the greatest Asiatic armies when confronted with European skill and discipline,"[1] it may be said, with far greater logic, that the triumph of Chandragupta over Seleucus demonstrated the inherent weakness

1. *Early History of India*, 3rd edition, p. 112.

of the greatest Hellenic armies when confronted with Indian skill and discipline.

2. *The Maurya Empire.*

The defeat inflicted upon the Greek hosts of Seleucus enabled Chandragupta to consolidate his mighty empire. It is unfortunately not yet possible to write a detailed account of his brilliant career. Nor can we trace the gradual steps by which an all-India empire, the unrealised dream of ages to come, was gradually brought into being. The available evidence, however, leaves no doubt, that during the reigns of Chandragupta and his son and successor Bindusāra, not only the whole of the Deccan, excepting the eastern coastal region, formed part of their empire, but even a considerable part of South Indian Peninsula was either incoporated in their dominions or was brought within their sphere of influence. The Tamil poet Māmūlanār, who flourished about the second or third century A.D., refers to a military expedition sent by the Moriar to reduce some Tamil chiefs in the South. The epithet Vamba (newly-risen) applied to Moriar seems to indicate that the reference here is to the early Maurya Emperor Chandragupta or Bindhusāra. The arms of the Mauryas were thus carried almost to the southern extremity of the Indian Peninsula; and the Maurya banner wafted across the vast stretch of land, from Herāt in the north-west, to Mādurā in the south.

The Maurya Empire at its height

India was now a leading power in the world, and maintained diplomatic relations with outside countries. The House of Seleucus sent regular embassies to the Court of Pāṭaliputra. We know, in particular two of these ambassadors, viz. Megasthenes, who lived in the Court of Chandragupta, and Daimachus who replaced him at the time of Bindusāra. We also hear of the exchange of friendly letters between Bindhusāra and Antiochus, the son and successor of Seleucus. There are also reasons to believe that diplomatic relations existed about this time between India on the one side, and China and the Central Asiatic powers on the other. Ptolemy Philadelphus, the Greek ruler of Egypt, also sent an embassy to the Court of the Mauryas. The Maurya rulers, too, despatched messengers to far-off countries, as will be described in the next section.

Foreign relations

A good idea of the power and magnificence of the Magadha empire about this period may be formed from the account of

Megasthenes and other Greek writers. The vast empire maintained a highly organised and well-equipped army, consisting of elephants, chariots, cavalry and infantry. The regular military establishment consisted of '600,000 infantry, 30,000 horsemen, 36,000 men with 9,000 elephants, and 24,000 men with nearly 8,000 chariots, or 690,000 men in all, excluding followers and attendants.'

Military strength

There was a highly organised system of military administration. Six Boards, consisting of five members each, looked after the six Departments, viz. (1) Admiralty: (2) Transport, Commissariat *etc.*; (3) Cavalry; (4) Infantry; (5) Chariots and (6) Elephants. The thirty members were no doubt collectively responsible for the whole military organisation.

Military Boards

The capital, Pāṭaliputra (modern Pātnā), at the confluence of the Gangā and the Sone rivers, was the greatest city in India. It was about 9 miles in length and a mile and a half in breadth. The wooden wall of the city, probably built of massive Sāl tree, had sixty-four gates, and was crowned with 570 towers. Surrounding the wall was a ditch, 'six hundred feet in breadth, and thirty cubits in depth.' The royal palace within the city was one of the finest in the whole world, and its 'gilded pillars, adorned with golden vines and silver birds' extorted the admiration of the Greeks. The municipal arrangements, too, were highly satisfactory. A Commission of thirty members administered the city. They were divided into six Boards of five members each. The members of the first Board looked after everything relating to the industrial arts. Those of the second looked after the comforts of the foreigners, resident in the city. The third recorded the births and deaths, while the fourth superintended trade and commerce. The fifth Board supervised manufactured articles, and the sixth collected the tenths of the prices of the articles sold. But, apart from the functions which these bodies separately discharged, the whole Commission, in its collective capacity, looked after matters of general interest, such as the keeping of public buildings in proper repair, the regulation of prices, and the supervision of markets, harbours and temples. There can be scarcely any doubt that this system of municipal administration prevailed in a large number of cities in the empire

The Capital City

Municipal Boards

The Maurya emperor himself probably administered the

government of Magadha and surrounding territories only. The distant provinces were under Viceroys, who were very often selected from the royal family. The Central Government kept watch over their administration by means of a class of persons called news-writers. Both in the Central Government, as well as in the provinces, the administration was carried on by a number of departments, each under a Superintedent, aided by a host of ministerial officers. There was a highly organised bureaucracy which efficiently managed the affairs of the vast empire. The different parts of the empire were connected by high-roads, one of them traversing the whole breadth of India from the Sindhu to the mouth of the Gangā. Irrigation works were undertaken even in such distant parts of the empire as the Kāthiāwār Peninsula, and, on the whole, the efficiency of the government was combined with peace, prosperity and contentment of the people.

System of administration

3. *Aśoka the Great*

Chandragupta and Bindusāra ruled for nearly half a century, and in or about 273 B. C., the throne of Magadha passed on to Aśoka, one of the greatest names in the history of the world. No figure in ancient Indian history is more familiar to us, and none leaves a more abiding impression of a towering personality, than this immortal son of Bindusāra.

Aśoka, the greatest king in ancient India

This is mainly due to the fact that for the first time in Indian history we come across original personal records of a king, composed probably by himself, engraved on imperishable rocks and stone-pillars. The inscriptions of Aśoka furnish a wealth of details about his life and reign such as we do not possess about any other king in ancient India. The more important of these inscriptions may be classified as follows :—

Aśoka's Inscriptions

I. Fourteen Rock Edicts—A set of fourteen inscriptions incised on rocks at eight different places, viz. Shāhbāzgaṛhī (Peshāwar District), Mānsehrā (Hazara District), Kālsī (Dehra Dun District), Girnar (near Junāgaḍh in Kāthiāwāṛ), Sopārā Ṭhāṇā District, Bombay), Dhauli and Jaugaḍā (Orissa), and Yerraguḍi (Kurnool District, Andhra Pradesh, eight miles from Gooty Railway Station). A copy of the Seventh Rock Edict of Aśoka in Shahbazgarhī is engraved on a bowl, originally found in the Gandhara region but now deposited in the Prince of Wales Museum in Bombay. This distribution is to be particularly noted as it is a valuable direct evidence of the great extent of the Maurya Empire.

noted as it is a valuable direct evidence of the great extent of the Maurya Empire.

II. Minor Rock Edicts—An edict incised on rocks at thirteen different places, viz. Rūpnāth (Jubbulpur District), Bairāt (Jaipur State, Rājpūtānā), Sasarām (Shāhābād District, Bihār), Maski (Raichur District), Gavimaṭh and Pālkīguṇḍu (Kopbal Tāluk in Mysore), Gujarrā (Datia District, Madhya Pradesh), Ahraura (Mirzapur Dt., U.P.) Now, Delhi Rājula-Maṇḍagiri (2 miles NNW. of Paṭṭikoṇḍa in Kurnool District, Andhra Pradesh), Yerraguḍi, and three neighbouring places in Chitaldrug district in Mysore. The last five also contain a Supplementary edict (No. II).

III. Seven Pillar Edicts—These were engraved on six fine monolith pillars, to be described in Chapter VIII. The complete set of seven edicts is found only on a single pillar now at Delhi (removed from a place called Toprā). The other pillars, found mostly in North Bihār, contain only six of the edicts. One of these, now at Delhi, was brought from Mirat.

IV. The remaining inscriptions engraved on rock, pillars and walls of caves, are of miscellaneous character. The most important of these, engraved on a pillar at Rumindei (Nepal Terai), records the visit of Aśoka to the place (Lumvinīvana) where Gautama Buddha was born, and marks that very site. Two short inscriptions, written in Aramaic script, have been found, one in Taxilā, and the other in Jalalābād District, Afghānistān. A bilingual inscription, written in Greek and Aramaic, has been found on a rock at Shar-i-Kuna near Kandahār in Afghānistān. Another similar record has also been found in the same locality. Four Aśokan edicts have been found at a site between the villages of Shalatak and Qargha in the province of Laghman in Afghānistān in 1969. One of these texts is in Aramaic, and the other hree are in "an old Indic language" (perhaps Prakrit) written in the Kharoshṭhī script.

These inscriptions supply the most valuable data for reconstructing the history of Aśoka. Unfortunately they tell us nothing about the early years of his reign, for which we have to depend solely on Buddhist traditions recorded in chronicles of a much later age.

Early Life

According to these, Aśoka was cruel and bloodthirsty, and seized the throne by killing his ninety-eight brothers. Many other stories are told of his ferocious nature which earned him the title Chaṇḍāśoka (ferocious Aśoka). These are hardly credible, and were undoubtedly intended to bring out in greater contrast his subsequent career influenced by Buddhism when he came to be known as Dharmāśoka (religious Aśoka). As to the story of killing all his brothers, it is interesting to note that in the records engraved long after his accession to the throne, Aśoka expressed great solicitude for the families of his brothers and referred to them in endearing terms. In any case the stories of Chaṇḍāśoka cannot be regarded as sober facts of history.

The same sources inform us that Aśoka was not formally consecrated till four years after his accession to the throne. This has been generally accepted by modern scholars, but its truth may be doubted, particularly as the long delay is alleged to have been caused mainly by the fratricidal war for succession to the throne.

The earliest event of Aśoka's reign, of which we possess reliable information, is his conquest of Kaliṅga, in the ninth year after his consecration to the throne. Kaliṅga usually denoted the long stretch of territory on the eastern coast of India between the rivers Suvarṇarekhā and Godāvarī, but its exact limits in the days of Aśoka cannot be determined. There is no doubt, however, that it was a populous and powerful State. The thirteenth Rock Edict of Aśoka gives a vivid account of the conquest of Kaliṅga after a terrible war in course of which 150,000 persons were captured, 100,000 were slain, and many times that number perished. Aśoka, who probably led the campaign in person, was struck by the horrors of the war and the amount of misery and bloodshed it involved. The feelings which they evoked in him are thus described in his inscription, probably in his own words :

Conquest of Kaliṅga

"Thus arose His Sacred Majesty's remorse for having conquered the Kaliṅgas, because the conquest of a country, previously unconquered, involves the slaughter, death, and carrying away captive of the people. That is a matter of profound sorrow and regret to His Sacred Majesty.

"There is, however, another reason for His Sacred Majesty feeling still more regret, inasmuch as in such a country dwell Brāhmans or ascetics, or men of various denominations, or householders...To such people in such a country befalls violence, or slaughter, or separation from their loved ones. Or misfortune befalls the friends, acquaintances, comrades, and relatives of those who are themselves well protected, while their affection is undiminished. Thus for them also that is a mode of violence."[1]

The feeling of remorse and misery led Aśoka to embrace the Buddhist religion, one of whose cardinal doctrines was non-injury to living beings. For about two years and a half

1. Rock Edict XIII. V.A Smith—*Aśoka*, pp. 172-173.

Aśoka remained a lay disciple; then he formally joined the Buddhist Order and became a Bhikkhu.

Propagation of Buddhism

From that time he exerted himself strenuously to propagate the religion in which he found the solace and comfort of his life. The means by which he sought to achieve this end were varied in character and have been graphically described in his own records. As early as the 11th year the emperor commenced a series of pious tours all over the country, spreading the gospels of his religion by his personal effort. He visited the holy places of Buddhism and wherever he went he arranged discussions on religious subjects. He instructed his high officials to proceed on circuit every five years and, in addition to their proper business, to spread the *dharma* (religious doctrines) among the people at large. Besides, he instituted a special class of officers called Dharma-mahāmātras whose sole business was to propagate *dharma* among the people. He also convoked a general Council of the Buddhists to settle internal differences. This was the Third General Council.

The Emperor organised a network of missions to preach the gospels in countries far-off and near. His missionaries visited not only the different parts of India and Ceylon, but also Western Asia, Egypt and Eastern Europe. Of the foreign kings, whose dominions thus received the message of the Buddha, five are mentioned in the inscriptions of Aśoka by name, viz. Antiochus Theos, king of Syria and Western Asia, Ptolemy Philadelphus of Egypt, Antigonus Gonatas of Macedonia, Magas of Cyrene and Alexander of Epirus. The names of the missionaries, whose sphere of work lay in India proper, are preserved in the Ceylonese literature. The relic caskets[1], unearthed about seventy years ago at Bhilsa, bear the names of some of them and vividly bring home to us the wonderful missionary activity of Aśoka. The great emperor even sent his own children, his son Mahendra and daughter Saṅghamitrā, to preach the religion in Ceylon.

But by far the most novel means adopted by the emperor to make the people realise the blessed doctrines of the Buddha, was to engrave them on rocks, pillars, and caves, throughout his vast dominions. Many of them have been lost, but we still possess about thirty-five separate records, which, in some respects, are the most wonderful that antiquity has bequeathed to us.

1. Those of Moggallāna and Sāriputta, recently exhibited in many towns of India, evoked unparalleled interest.

They contain a glowing personal narrative of the emperor, and give a detailed account of what he believed to be the *dharma*, and of what he did to bring it home to the millions of his subjects. The emperor was urged on by an anxious desire to uplift the morality of the people, by bringing home to them the essential features of his *dharma*. So he engraved these on imperishable stones, which even to-day, after the lapse of more than two thousand years, stand as an undying monument to his purity of life and sublimity of thoughts.

Aśoka's Dharma

The aspect of *dharma* which he emphasised was a code of morality, rather than a system of religion. He never discussed metaphysical doctrines, nor referred to God or soul, but simply asked the people to have control over their passions, to cultivate purity of life and character in inmost thoughts, to be tolerant to other's religion, to abstain from killing or injuring animals and to have regard for them, to be charitable to all, to behave with decorum to parents, teachers, relatives, friends, and ascetics, to treat slaves and servants kindly, and, above all, to tell the truth

Achievements of Aśoka

The emperor not only preached these truths but also practised them. He forswore hunting and gave up meat diet. He established hospitals for men and beasts, not only throughout his vast empire, but also in the dominions of his neighbouring kings. He made liberal donations to the Brāhmaṇas and followers of other religions. We read in his records, how, on the roads, he had rest-houses erected, and also caused wells to be dug and trees to be planted, for the use of men and beasts. He also issued various regulations to prevent the slaughter of animals.

Buddhism becomes a world religion

As a result of Aśoka's wonderful zeal and activities Buddhism, which was till then confined to an insignificant sect, was transformed into a world religion. He forswore the aggressive imperial policy of hisfore fathers and pursued instead the ideal of conquering the world by means of *dharma* (Law of Piety). In this object he succeeded to an extent beyond his wildest dreams. For it must be set largely to his credit that even to-day, more than two thousand years after his death, one-third of the people of the world follow the teachings of Buddha.

The most remarkable thing about Aśoka is that his ardour for Buddhism, great as it was, never made him neglect his duties

Aśoka as a king

as a king. As a matter of fact he may be justly regarded as one of the greatest monarchs in the whole world, ancient or modern. His conception of duties and responsibilities of a king, the zeal with which he pursued his ideals, and the extent to which he succeeded in giving effect to them—all alike are worthy of the highest praise. Probably no ruler ever expressed the relation between the king and his subjects in a simpler and nobler language. "All men are my children", said he, "and just as I desire for my children that they may enjoy every kind of prosperity and happiness, in both this world and the next, so also I desire the same for all men." Again he wrote in the same strain : "Just as a man, having made over his child to a skilful nurse, feels confident and says to himself, 'The skilful nurse is zealous to take care of my child's happiness,' even so my officials have been created for the welfare and happiness of the country."

Aśoka's zeal for public business, and his sense of responsibility for the sacred trust imposed on him as king, are well exemplified by another record. "For a long time past," runs the royal edict, "it has not happened that business has been dispatched and that reports have been received at all hours. Now by me this arrangement has been made that at all hours and in all places—whether I am dining, or in the ladies' apartments, in my bedroom, or in my closet, in my carriage, or in the palace gardens—the official Reporters should report to me on the people's business, and I am ready to do the people's business in all places. . . . I have commanded that immediate report must be made to me at any hour and in any place, because I never feel full satisfaction in my efforts and dispatch of business. For the welfare of all folk is what I must work for—and the root of that, again, is in effort and the dispatch of business. And whatsoever exertions I make are for the end that I may discharge my debt to animate beings, and that while I make some happy here, they may in the next world gain heaven."

Aśoka's conception of kingly duties was thus very noble. He did not take any credit for his great exertions to secure the welfare of the people, for in his views he merely discharged his debt thereby. And the welfare of the people he understood in the broadest sense—not only the security of life and property together with material prosperity here below, but also moral elevation leading to perpetual happiness hereafter. This conception of his duty was the logical outcome of his famous doctrine that all men are the children of the king. Just as a father ought not to rest satisfied by merely advancing the material prosperity of his children, but should also see to their moral development, in very much the same way the king should concern himself with both the material and the moral well-being of his subjects. This led Aśoka to adopt those extensive measures for the propagation of moral doctrines among his people to which reference has been made above. The same idea, again, is at least partly responsible for his assumption of the headship of the Buddhist Church. But Aśoka was not merely a great theorist; he was also an able administrator. In spite of his religious proclivities and avowed policy of non-aggression, he maintained peace and prosperity over his vast empire. As noted above, he annexed Kaliṅga after a hard-fought battle. It appears that the Tamil lands in the extreme south were lost to the Maurya Empire, but whether they broke off during Aśoka's reign or before his accession, it is difficult to say. It is certain, however, that in the 13th year of the reign of Aśoka, the Tamil kingdoms of Chera, Chola, Pāṇḍya, and Satyaputra were independent States, and the southern boundary of the Maurya empire was formed approximately by a line drawn from Nellore to the mouth of Kalyāṇapurī river on the western coast. But it comprised the rest of India proper (excluding probably Assam), in addition to modern Afghānistān and Baluchistān. Certain territories within this vast area enjoyed autonomy in internal administration, like the Native States in British India, while the rest of the empire was governed by a number of Viceroys, who had their seats of government at provincial capitals such as Suvarṇagiri, Tosālī, Takshaśilā and Ujjayinī. The vast organisation seems to have worked fairly well, and the magnificent works of art that Aśoka has left behind, and to which a detailed reference will be made in a later chapter, prove beyond all doubt, that the empire reached the high watermark of greatness and glory under him.

Extent of Empire

The Empire of Aśoka was not only vast in extent but was closely knit together as an administrative unit. One imperial writ ran from Peshāwar to Bengal, and from Kāshmir to Mysore. This never happened again in ancient India, and was but rarely witnessed before the middle of the 19th century A. D. Aśoka's inscriptions further prove that there was one common language for the whole empire, and the same script was

Political Unity of India

current except in a small region in the extreme north-west. Aśokan Empire thus brought about that political and cultural unity which is the dream of modern India, symbolised by her emblem of the capital of an Aśokan Pillar.

Art of Writing

Several other circumstances make the reign of Aśoka a memorable one. The earliest written record in India dates from his reign. His inscriptions, excluding the three written in Greek or Aramaic script, are engraved in two types of alphabets. The first, called Kharoshṭhī, derived from Aramaic, was confined to those at Shāhbāzgaṛhī and Mānsehrā, and soon went out of use. But the second, known as Brāhmī, used in all the other inscriptions, is the earliest Indian alphabet known to us, and all the Indian alphabetic systems known to-day are ultimately derived from it.

Art

Similarly the history of Indian art practically begins from Aśoka's reign. For, excluding the prehistoric examples found in the Sindhu Valley (p. 24), no other specimen of fine art has come down to us which may be definitely dated before the time of Aśoka. Aśoka seems to have introduced the art of building in stone, and although only a few specimens of his numerous works have survived, they form the first, though a brilliant, chapter in the continuous history of Indian art. Indeed his monolithic stone pillars, with their remarkable polish and still more wonderful animal sculptures on the top, still remain not only unsurpassed, but even unapproached anywhere in the world. But these will be more conveniently dealt with in the chapter on art.

4. *Downfall of the Empire.*

Downfall of the Empire

Aśoka died about 232 B. C., and seven kings followed him in regular succession, during a period of about fifty years. No detailed account of these kings is known to us, but the disruption of the empire began within almost a decade after the death of Aśoka. The Andhras, a powerful tribe in the Deccan, enjoying internal autonomy during Aśoka's rule, raised the banner of revolt, and freed the country south of the Vindhyas from the yoke of the Mauryas. The Mauryas ruled over the empire in Northern India till about 185 B. C., when they succumbed to internal dissensions and invasions from abroad.

It is necessary to go back a little, in order to understand aright the foreign invasions which brought about the downfall of the Mauryas. As has already been related, Seleucus and his descendants ruled from Syria over the whole of Western Asia up to the Hindu Kush mountains. About 250 B.C., Bactria and Parthia, two provinces of this vast empire, revolted against the Seleucid dynasty, and declared their independence. The Greek governor of Bactria and his successors formed a line of independent Greek rulers to the north of the Hindu Kush, while a national government was established in Parthia, the eastern part of modern Persia, by a native chief named Arsaces. The Seleucid emperors tried in vain to assert their supremacy over the revolted States, and Antiochus III led a campaign to Bactria with this object. But he failed and at last virtually acknowledged the independence of both Bactria and Parthia about 208 B. C. Shortly after this, the Graeco-Bactrian kings turned their eyes towards India. Demetrius, the son of the ruling king, and son-in-law of Antiochus III, invaded India about 190 B. C. and wrested from the Maurya Emperor Bṛihadratha, seventh in descent from Aśoka, a considerable portion of his empire in the north-west.

The successful revolt of the Andhras, the victorious raid of the Greek king, probably far into the interior of the Magadha empire, and the loss of the north-western dominions gave a terrible blow to the power and prestige of the Maurya empire. Apparently taking advantage of this state of confusion, Pushyamitra, the commander-in-chief of Bṛihadratha, made a plot against his royal master, and killed him, while engaged in reviewing the army. Thus ended the dynasty of Chandragupta and Aśoka after a rule of about 137 years (322-185 B.C.).

Pushyamitra was a traitor and regicide, but some modern historians have condoned his crime by holding it up as a necessity for saving the country. Too little is, however, known of the actual circumstances to justify such a lenient view. Though Pushyamitra ascended the throne, curiously enough, he retained the old title *Senāpati*. He made some amends for his foul crime by the energy he displayed in restoring order in the empire. There are reasons to believe that he successfully carried the arms of the Magadha empire up to the bank of the Sindhu and consummated his victories by the celebration of two *Aśvamedha* sacrifices. The great grammarian Patanjali refers to one of

Pushyamitra

these, and probably officiated as a priest on the occasion. We are told in the Sanskrit drama *Mālavikāgnimitram*, that Pushyamitra's valiant grandson Vasumitra, son of Agnimitra, the ruler of Vidiśā (Bhilsā), guarded the sacrificial horse, and rescued it from the Yavanas or Greeks after a terrible fight on the banks of the Sindhu. It has been held by many that this Sindhu river denotes a small stream like the Kālī Sindhu in Madhya Pradesh. But there is no valid reason why we should not identify the Sindhu of the drama with the famous river of that name. Intermittent fights with the Greeks continued throughout the reign of Pushyamitra and that of his descendants. Ultimately the Panjāb and Sindh were lost to the Magadha empire, and became the scene of contest for supremacy among the hosts of foreign invaders that began to pour into India. The emperor of Pātaliputra probably still claimed allegiance, however nominal, from the rest of Northern India. But it was quite evident that his actual power was dwindling day by day, for hosts of independent States, monarchical and republican, gradually sprang up in different directions all over the country.

The power of the Śuṅga dynasty—such is the name by which that founded by Pushyamitra is known in history—originated in foul treachery, and it met its end in the same way.

The Śuṅgas

Devabhūmi, the tenth king of the dynasty, was of dissolute character and was killed at the instance of his minister Vasudeva. The ten kings of the Śuṅga dynasty ruled for a period of 112 years (185-73 B.C.).

The Kāṇva dynasty, founded by Vasudeva, comprised only four kings and ruled over the Magadha empire for a period of

The Kāṇvas

45 years. The fourth king Suaśrman was overthrown by the Andhras to whom reference will be made later.

In the opinion of some modern scholars Aśoka must be held primarily responsible for the downfall of the great empire. The

Responsibility of Aśoka

empire was founded by a policy of blood and iron and could only be maintained by following the same policy. But by eschewing all wars and abandoning the aggressive imperial policy, Aśoka weakened the very foundations of the empire. There is no doubt that he could easily have completed the political unity of India by conquering the Tamil lands in the extreme south, if the only cared to send a powerful army instead of Buddhist missionaries to that region. It is also urged that the lack of all military activities after the Kaliṅga war and the constant preaching of the great virtue of *ahiṁsā* (non-injury) by the Emperor in person had a permanent effect, not only on the military organisation of the State, but also on the martial qualities of the people in general. The soldiers lost their skill and discipline and Indians generally became averse to war. This is the main reason why the army which successfully resisted the onslaught of Seleucus failed against the less powerful Bactrian Greeks.

There may be some truth in these accusations. But it must be remembered that the end of the Maurya Empire did not differ materially from that of many other powerful empires in India, though there was nothing like the pacifist policy of Aśoka to account for it. There were other factors at work, notably the weakness of the successors of Aśoka and the well-known centrifugal force in Indian politics. It may be easily surmised that the mighty Maurya Empire must have in any case come to an end, sooner or later, even without the policy of Aśoka. But this alone gave it the redeeming grace of having established a mighty moral force over an extensive portion of the world, and making an experiment of ending all wars, the necessity and wisdom of which did not again dawn upon the statesmen of the world till the second decade of the twentieth century A. D. Even if all the accusations against Aśoka prove to be true, he may well take comfort in the idea that he anticipated, by 2175 years, the policy of universal peace which the world is now slowly realising to be the only means of salvation for mankind. A modern historian may well remember the great saying of Thucydides that all mortal glory is doomed to destruction, but the memory of greatness lives for ever. The Maurya Empire has followed the way of all mundane glories, but the memory of Aśoka will last for ever.

CHAPTER III

From the end of the First to the beginning of the Second Magadha Empire (2nd century B.C. to 4th century A.D.)

1. *Foreign Invasions.*

It has been already recorded that the north-western Provinces of the Magadha empire had been wrested by Demetrius, the Greek king of Bactria, about the beginning of the second century B.C. Demetrius was so successful in his Indian expedition that the Greek writers gave him the appellation of "King of the Indians". But while he was busy in India, the Bactrian throne was usurped by one Eucratides, and Demetrius tried in vain to dislodge him. Eucratides, though successful against Demetrius, was not destined to enjoy his ill-gotten power for long. He was cruelly murdered by his own son, who drove his chariot over the dead body of his father.

The Greeks

These internal dissensions among the Greeks probably gave Pushyamitra a good opportunity to recover some of the lost territories and restore order in the empire. But they were followed by other terrible consequences for the Greeks. While they were quarrelling among themselves, Bactria was invaded by the Scythian hordes, and the Greek sovereignty in the fair valley of the Oxus was extinguished for ever (*c.* 120 B.C.). The Greeks, driven from Bactria, were forced to take shelter in their Indian dominions in Afghānistān and the Western Panjāb, where they ruled for two hundred years more. There were rival dynasties ruling in different localities, and it is at present impossible to deal with them in a consecutive narrative. But the interesting fact remains that within this narrow enclave, cut off from the mainland of Greece, and all but unknown to the Greek historians, there flourished two or more principalities ruled over by about thirty Greek kings. These, rather than Alexander and his host, were instrumental in introducing some elements of Greek culture in India to which reference will be made later.

The names of these Greek rulers are known to us from their coins, but we hardly know anything about most of them. Of the few kings, who are known to us from other sources also, Menander, King Milinda of the Buddhist literature, is the most prominent. His capital was Śākala, the present Sialkot, and he seems to have led several victorious expeditions into the interior of Northern India. Another king, Apollodotus, is also said to have conquered Kāthiāwāṛ Peninsula. In general, however, the sovereignty of the Greek kings was confined to Afghānistān and the Panjāb, and it is only at rare intervals that they temporarily carried their arms into the interior.

The Parthians

But the Greeks were not the only nation that harassed the Indian frontier. Several others followed in their wake, the most notable of them being the Parthians, the Sakas and the Kushāṇas. It has been already related how an independent national kingdom was established in Parthia, about the middle of the third century B.C., by a successful revolt against the Seleucid monarch of Syria. As early as the middle of the second century B.C., the Parthian king Mithradates I had carried his arms up to the Sindhu. At a later period, a powerful chief named Maues established a principality in the Western Panjāb. About the same time a line of Parthian princes ruled in the Kandāhār region, the most notable of them being Vonones and Azes. Towards the close of the first century A.D., Parthian chiefs were squabbling for power in lower Sindh. Some Parthian kings also ruled in the Peshāwar valley. Great interest centres round one of these Indo-Parthian chiefs, named Gondophares, whose record has been found at Takht-i-Bahi (in N. W. F. P.). A very early Christian tradition affirms that the Apostle St. Thomas visited his court, and converted him and his family to Christianity.

The Śakas

The Śakas were at first a nomadic tribe, and lived on the northern bank of the river Jaxartes or Syr Daria. Being dispossessed of their homelands by another nomadic tribe, the Yueh-chi, they fell upon Bactria, and destroyed the Hellenistic monarchy in that province, as has already been related. Later on, they proceeded south and east, and entered India in various bands, through different ways. They must have formed a strong settlement on the bank of the Helmund river, as the region was called Śakasthāna (now corrupted into Seistān) after them. In India, we can clearly trace three important Śaka principalities. Two of them were in Northern India, and had Mathurā and Takshaśilā as their respective capitals. The third comprised Mālwā and Kāthiāwār Peninsula in Western India. The rulers of all these countries called themselves Satraps or Viceroys. Though it is impossible to say anything about the overlord whose Viceroys they were, and although there is scarcely any doubt that they were practically independent monarchs, the nomenclature has been accepted by modern historians, who style the Śaka rulers of Mathurā and Takshaśilā as Northern Satraps, and those of Mālwā and Kāthiāwār Peninsula as the Western Satraps. Altogether four Northern Satraps are known to us, though we hardly possess any detailed information about them. The Western Satraps were more than twenty in number, and ruled for three centuries. Their history will be dealt with in the next section.

The Kushāṇas, the last but by no means of the least importance among these foreign invaders, belonged to a nomadic Turkish tribe, called the Yueh-chi, which originally settled in the Kan-su province in north-western China. Being driven by another nomadic tribe, called the Hiung-nu (Huns), about 65 B.C., they were forced to march westward, and fell upon the Śakas who occupied the territory to the north of the Jaxartes rivers. Hardly had they occupied the land of the Śakas, than they were once more defeated by their old enemy, the Huns, and forced to move towards the south. The migration of the Śakas in consequence of this event and their ultimate settlement in India have just been related. As mentioned above, the Yueh-chi drove away the Śakas, and occupied and settled in Bactria to the south of the Oxus. Here two important changes came over them. In the first place, they gave up their nomadic habit, and adopted a settled life. Secondly, the solidarity of the great Yueh-chi tribe was destroyed and five of its clans established five independent principalities in the conquered region.

The Kushāṇas

More than a century passed away, and then the chief of the Kushāṇas, one of the five clans of the Yueh-chi, found means to bring the other four clans under his sway. Kozola Kadphises or Kadphises I, who accomplished this great task, and laid the foundation of the greatness of his clan, did not rest content by merely establishing a united Yueh-chi principality. He cast longing eyes towards India, and made preparations for conquering that land. As a preliminary measure, he had to fight with the Greeks and the Parthians, who were now in possession of the territories immediately south of the Hindu Kush. Throughout his long career he was engaged in this task, and ultimately succeeded in finally extinguishing the Parthian and the Greek domination in the North-western frontier of India. A series of coins beautifully illustrate how the authority gradually passed from Hermaeus, the last Greek ruler of Kābul, to Kadphises I.

But although Kadphises I disposed of his enemies, viz. the Greeks and the Parthians, and occupied Kābul, he was not destined to enjoy the fruits of his labour. With the Indian empire almost within his grasp, he died, full of years and honours, at the age of eighty. But the task which he left unfinished was more than accomplished by his son and successor, Wema Kadphises or Kadphises II, who conquered India, probably as far as Banaras, if not further towards the east. He did not, however, rule his Indian dominions in person, but appointed military chiefs to govern them on his behalf. Thus was established a vast Kushāṇa empire which included large tracts on both sides of the Hindu Kush mountains.

Kadphises II

The next Kushāṇa emperor, the famous Kanishka, is probably the most familiar figure in ancient India after Aśoka. His memory has been fondly cherished by the Buddhists who looked upon him as one of their greatest patrons, and a number of traditions have gathered round his name. According to these he conquered the whole of Northern India including Kāshmir and Magadha, and his power extended up to the borders of the desert of Gobi in Central Asia. He is further credited with success in wars against the Parthians and the Chinese, and also with the conquest of three rich provinces belonging to the latter, viz. Kashgar, Yarkand and Khotan. It is even alleged that hostages from a Chinese principality lived in his court. How far these traditions may be accepted as historical it is difficult to say, but there is scarcely any doubt that Kanishka's Indian dominions included Kāshmir and Upper Sindh, and extended to Banaras in the east and the Vindhyas to the south.

Kanishka

Unlike Wema Kadphises, whose relationship with Kanishka is not yet known, Kanishka ruled his Indian territorries in person and selected Purushapura as his capital. The great relic-tower which he erected there excited the wonder and admiration of all for hundreds of years, and its ruins have been discovered near Peshāwar which represents that ancient capital city. This, along with the statue of Kanishka discovered in Mathurā, have rendered this famous emperor of old quite familiar to us. Traditions affirm that two learned men lived in the court of Kanishka, viz. Aśvaghosha, the famous Buddhist scholar and poet, and Charaka, who is supposed to be the same as the great medical authority whose treatises still occupy the highest place of honour in the indigenous system of medical treatment.

Kanishka's successors

Kanishka was followed by three kings Vāsishka, Huvishka, and Vāsudeva. Very little is known about them beyond the fact that they were probably successful in keeping the empire intact. Kanishka founded an era which is believed by many to be the Śaka era current to-day. This would place the accession of Kanishka in 78 A. D. But opinions widely differ on this point[1]. Certain it is that the four kings ruled for about one hundred years after which the great empire of Kanishka passed away.

Sassanian invasion

It is now generally recognised that the downfall of the Kushāṇa Empire was mainly due to the invasion of the Sassanians who had overthrown the Arsacid dynasty (pp. 116, 120) and founded a powerful kingdom in Persia early in the third century A. D. The Sassanian king Shāpur I (241-272 A. D.) is known to have made extensive conquests in Bactria and Afghānistān and subjugated the Kushāṇas. According to the latest theory on the subject, Shāpur's invasion, some time between 241 and 250 A. D., coincides more or less with the end of the reign of Vāsudeva; and consequently the accession of Kanishka, one hundred years before this, falls about 142 A. D.

1. The date of Kanishka has proved the most vexed problem of Indian chronology. Much has been written on this subject, but no final solution is possible without fresh evidence. Some place his accession in 78 A.D. and regard him as the founder of the Śaka era. The late Dr. Fleet, and some scholars following him, placed the same event in 58 B. C., thus regarding him as the founder of the Vikrama-Samvat. Others put his reign in the scond century A. D., while some even push it as late as third century A. D.

Cf. *J. R. A. S.* 1903 (1-65), 1913 (627 ff., 911 ff.) ; *Indian Antiquary*, 1908 (25 ff.) ; and a number of articles on this and cognate subjects in *J. R. A. S.* 1903-1915 ; Also Sten Konow's Introduction to CII, II. and articles in *J. I. H.*, XII, pp. 1-46. The latest view on the subject is given in *Journal Asiatique* Vol. CC XXXIV, p. 59.

But the overthrow of the Kushāṇa empire did not mean an end of the Kushāna power in India. Kushāṇa kings, known in history as the Later Kushāṇas, and bearing names of Kanishka and Vāsudeva, ruled in Kābul and a part of the Panjāb valley for a long time. They were ousted by another branch of the same clan, known as the Kidāra Kushāṇas, who ruled in the same region till the 4th century A. D.

Other Kushāṇa ruling families

2. *The Western Satraps.*

Reference has been made above (p. 121) to the Śaka Satraps or Governors ruling over Mālwā and Kāthiāwār Peninsula. Very little is known of Bhumaka, the earliest of them known to us, except that he belonged to the Kshaharāta dynasty, and ruled over extensive territories including Mālwā, Gujarāt, Kāthiāwār Peninsula, and probably also a part of Rājputāna and Sindh. The next Satrap Nahapāna, who assumed the title *rājan*, is a more distinguished figure. His known dates range between 119 and 125 A. D. and his coins and inscriptions leave no doubt that he ruled as an independent king over a vast dominion which extended as far as Ajmer in the north and the Nāsik and Poonā Districts in the south. But his power was crushed by the Sātavāhana king Gautamīputra Sātakarṇi, and the Satrapy passed into the hands of a new dynasty known as Kārdamaka.

Nahapāna

Chashṭana, the founder of this dynasty, is undoubtedly to be identified with Tiastenes who is mentioned in Ptolemy's Geography (written about 140 A. D.) as having ruled with Oozene (Ujjayinī) as his capital. Evidently he recovered from the Sātavāhanas at least some of the dominions of Nahapāna north of the Narmadā. But the struggle continued, and Chashṭana's successor, his grandson Rudradāman, is represented as the lord of all the countries conquered by Gautamīputra Śātakarṇi. He further claims to have twice defeated Śatakarṇi, lord of Dakshiṇāpatha, though he did not destroy the latter on account of close relationship between the two. A somewhat damaged record refers to the daughter of a Mahākshatrapa, the first letter of whose name, *ru*, alone has been preserved, as the wife of Vāsishṭhīputra Śātakarṇi. It has been plausibly suggested that the Mahākshatrapa was no other than Rudradāman and his son-in-law was Pulumāyi (or his

Rudradāman

brother according to some). The lord of Dakshiṇāpatha, defeated by Rudradāman, is generally taken to be Pulumāyi himself, though some identify him with his father Gautamīputra.

In any case, there is no doubt that the Sātavāhanas were finally driven from Mālwā, Gujarāt and Kāthiāwār, and Rudradāman not only ruled over these but also over Kachchha (Cutch), Svabhra (Sabarmati valley), Maru (Marwar), Sindhu, and Sauvīra (eastern part of Sindh), and inflicted a crushing defeat upon the Yaudheyas before 150 A. D., the date of the Junāgaḍh inscription, which supplies us the above account. This very important record also extols the manifold virtues of Rudradāman. He was, we are told, versed in grammar, polity, music, and logic, and was famous for his Sanskrit compositions in prose and poetry. Whatever we might think of these, the fact remains, that the long Sanskrit inscription, which was engraved by his order in A. D. 150, is the first official record in that language with the probable exception of one or two short epigraphs, out of hundreds that have so far come to light. According to this record Rudradāman won the hands of several princesses in *Svayaṁvara* ceremonies. Inter-marriage with Indian royal families seems to have been a deliberate policy pursued by the Kārdamakas in order to be merged into Hindu society.

Rudradāman was succeeded by his son Dāmajadaśrī who was associated with the administration during his father's reign.

Successors of Rudradāman

It seems to have been a regular practice for the king, who assumed the title Mahākshatrapa, to appoint his son or brother as joint ruler under the title Kshatrapa, with the right even to issue coins. As a matter of fact it is from the numerous dated coins issued by the Mahākshatrapas and Kshatrapas that we can trace, in an unbroken line, the genealogy of the Western Kshatrapas for more than 300 years with only occasional gaps here and there.

The death of Dāmajadaśrī was followed by a disastrous civil war between his son and brother in the last quarter of the second century A. D. which considerably weakened the power and prestige of the family.

Dissensions and decline

The Śātavāhana king conquered part of their dominions and a new ruler, Iśvaradatta by name, generally regarded as an Ābhīra, issued coins in his own name with the title Mahākshatrapa. Although order was soon restored and the family ruled peacefully for some time, troubles again arose about the second quarter of the third century A. D. Internal dissensions broke out once more and the Mālavas in the north and the Ābhīras in the south challenged the power of the Western Satraps. The Mālavas conquered a part of their northern dominions and the Ābhīras established a powerful kingdom in Northern Mahārāshṭra on the ruins of the Śātavāhana kingdom. It is generally believed that the era, starting in 248-9 A. D., and known later as the Kalachuri era, was founded by the Ābhīras, probably to commemorate this event. Mālwā was also probably lost as we find a Śaka chief Śrīdhara-varman ruling there as an independent king.

Change of dynasty

Mahākshatrapa Bhartṛidāman, whose known dates range between 289 and 296 A. D., is the last known member of Chashṭana's family to use this title. His son Viśvasena ruled as Kshatrapa till 305 A. D. but did not assume the higher title, which seems to have been in abeyance till 348-9 A. D. Viśvasena was ousted by Rudrasiṁha II whose relationship with his predecessor is not known. The change in the royal succession and the absence of the title Mahākshatrapa indicate a troublesome period, and it has been suggested that the kingdom was conquered by the Sassanians who placed a new chief on the throne as their vassal. But there is no positive evidence that the political influence of the Sassanians spread so far. The later history of the kingdom will be related in Book III, in connection with the Gupta Empire.

3. *The indigenous States in North India.*

There is no doubt that in spite of the successive foreign invasions, and the establishment of the Kushāṇa Empire, a large number of indigenous States flourished in North India during the long period of more than four centuries (c. 100 B.C. to 300 A.D.) that elapsed between the decline of the first and the rise of the second Magadha Empire. But although we can trace their existence from a large number of coins and a few inscriptions, it is not possible to deal with their history in detail. There were both kingdoms and non-monarchical States, and many of them had to submit, for a time, to the foreign invaders, notably the Kushāṇas. But many of them rose to power again with the decline of the foreign powers, and were not finally extinguished till the rise of the Gupta Empire in the fourth century A. D.

The coins of a large number of kings, many of whose names ended in Mitra, have been found principally at or near Ahichchhatra, in Rohilkhand, and also, in small quantities, over a wide region in Northern India. Some of them were probably identical with kings of the Śuṅga and Kāṇva dynasties (p. 117) mentioned in the Purāṇas, and others probably ruled after the end of the Kāṇvas. It would then appear that there was at least some semblance of an empire, not only up to the end of the Kāṇva dynasty, but probably even for some time after that.

Ahichchhatra

The large finds of these coins amid the ruins of Ahichchhatra (modern Rāmnagar in Bareilly District) indicate that this far-famed capital of North Pañchāla in early times was also an important seat of royal power during the period under review. In case the theory of some of these kings belonging to the Śuṅga and Kāṇva dynasty be not upheld, we may regard them all —twenty in number—as rulers of Ahichchhatra, who occasionally extended their power to distant lands. They probably ruled during the period 50 B. C. to 250 A. D.

Inscriptions prove that sometimes there was a matrimonial alliance between the rulers of Ahichchhatra and those of Kauśāmbī. The names of a number of kings ruling at Kauśāmbī are known from both coins and inscriptions. The earlier royal dynasty was probably overthrown by the Kushāṇas. But a new dynasty arose somewhat later whose kings generally had names ending with the word Magha. It has been suggested that they belong to the Megha Dynasty mentioned in the Purāṇas. They are known from coins and seals (mostly found at Bhitā near Allāhābād) as well as a large number of inscriptions found both at Kosam (Kauśāmbī) and Bandhogarh in Rewa State. Many of these contain dates, which are usually referred to the Śaka Era. Thus interpreted, the dates of these kings fall in the second and third centuries A. D.

Kauśāmbī

There was a third kingdom, with capital at Ayodhyā, the names of whose kings have come down to us. One of them, Dhanadeva, is represented in an inscription as sixth in descent from Senāpati Pushyamitra, the performer of two *Aśvamedhas*. There is no doubt that this Pushyamitra was the founder of the Śuṅga Dynasty (p. 116), and Dhanadeva probably traced his descent through a collateral or female line. Dhanadeva flourished

Ayodhyā

towards the end of the first century B. C., and the other kings, probably his successors, during the next two centuries. Another dynasty, issuing a different type of coins, probably flourished in the third century A. D.

Thus three important kingdoms, corresponding to Pañchāla, Kosala, and Vatsa of old days, flourished during the period under review, but we hardly know anything of them beyond the names of kings.

No less than three or four kingdoms, ruled by kings of Nāga families, flourished during the early centuries of the Christian era. The Purāṇas refer to Vidiśā (Bhilsa), Kāntipurī, Mathurā, and Padmāvatī (Padam Pawaya, near Nārwār in Gwalior State) as seats of their power. The Nāgas are usually regarded as non-Aryan tribes who either worshipped serpents (*nāga*) or used them as totem. But whether these royal Nāga dynasties possessed any distinctive ethnical or social peculiarities may be doubted. Many kings with names ending in *nāga* are known from coins, inscriptions, and literary traditions, and it is probable that they belonged to one or other of these Nāga families. It is also likely that some of the kings with names ending in *datta* or *mitra*, known from coins found at Mathurā, belonged to the Nāga family, as according to the Purāṇas seven Nāgas ruled at Mathurā. We learn from the same authority that nine Nāga kings ruled at Padmāvatī. One of these, Bhavanāga, is known from coins found in that locality.

Nagas

It is probable that he is identical with the Mahārāja Bhavanāga of the Bhāraśiva family who is represented as the maternal grandfather of the Vākāṭaka king Rudrasena I in the official records of that family. We learn from these records that the Bhāraśivas were so called because they carried a Śiva-liṅga on their shoulders. We are further told that they "were besprinkled on the forehead with the pure water of the Bhāgīrathī (Gangā) that had been obtained by their valour", and performed ten *Aśvamedha* sacrifices. Some modern writers have expressed the view that the *ghāṭ* at Banaras known as *Daśāśvamedha* (ten *Aśvamedhas*) owes its name to that fact, and they even go so far as to say that it was the Bhārasivas who overthrew the Kushāṇa power in India. But although none of these theories is very likely or has gained any support, there is no doubt that the Bhāraśivas were a very powerful ruling family in the third and fourth centuries A. D. But, as suggested above, they probably belonged to the Nāga

Bhāraśivas

royal family of Padmāvatī and extended their power far and wide, as far at least as the bank of the Gangā.

In addition to these kingdoms, a number of powerful republican or oligarchical tribal States flourished in North India, specially in East Panjāb and Rājputāna. They are mostly known from the coins which were issued in the name of the tribal republic (*gaṇa*) and not by any individual ruler. Many of them are also known from inscriptions. The chief among them were the Mālavas and the Yaudheyas.

The Mālavas are a very ancient people and are referred to in Pāṇini's grammar, along with the Kshudrakas, as *āyudhajīvins* i. e., 'those who live by the profession of arms. As noted above (p. 100), these two tribes formed a confederacy against Alexander. The Mālavas then lived in the Panjāb, to the north of the confluence of the Rāvi and the Chenab, and the Kshudrakas in the neighbouring Montgomery District. Their joint forces numbered 90,000 foot soldiers, 10,000 cavalry and 900 war chariots.

Mālavas

For more than three centuries after this we do not hear any thing about the Mālavas. But early in the Christian era we find a Mālava republic issuing coins, thousands of which have been discovered at Nagar or Karkoṭanagar in Uniyara in the Jaipur State. There is no doubt that it represents the ancient Mālava-nagara, the capital of this Republican State. The Mālavas fought successfully against the Śakas and other foreigners, as early as the beginning of the second century A. D., and we learn from an epigraphic record, dated 226 A. D., that the splendid victories of a Mālava chief (whose name is not unfortunately mentioned) brought back peace and prosperity to the country. This probably refers to a successful fight against the Śaka satraps with whom they had long been at war. It is also very likely that in course of this long-drawn struggle with the Śaka satraps the Mālavas gradually advanced further south and east and settled in the region (Mālwa) which is still called after them, and was known as such before, probably long before, the 6th century A. D.

The era beginning in 58 B. C., and later known as Vikrama Saṁvat, was long associated with the Mālava Republic and known as the reckoning of the Mālavas in the 5th century A. D. Before that it was known as the Kṛita era. No satisfactory explanation of this name has yet been forthcoming. But if, as some scholars believe, the era was founded by the Mālavas, we may take Kṛita as the name of an illustrious leader who probably freed them from foreign yoke and the era, started to commemorate this event, was at first named after him. Some are, however, of opinion that the era was founded by the Indo-Parthian chief Azes (p. 120) and later adopted and made popular by the Mālavas. The name Vikramāditya was associated with it at a later date. Whether this was the name or title of a historical person who flourished in 58 B. C., or of a Gupta Emperor (like Chandragupta) who ruled five centuries later, and was for some unknown reason associated with the era, it is difficult to say. But although the origin of the era of 58 B. C. is involved in obscurity, there is no doubt of its long and intimate association with the Mālavas.

Yaudheyas

The Yaudheyas were also an ancient people and included by Pāṇini amongst the peoples living by profession of arms (*āyudha-jīvi-saṅgha*). The clay seals and coins of the Yaudheyas indicate that though their main settlements were in the Eastern Panjāb they often exercised political authority over extensive territories in the adjacent districts of U. P. and Rājputāna. An inscription referring to the election of a general by this republican tribe has been found at Bijayagaḍh in the Bharatpur State. It is also very likely that the ancient Yaudheyas are now represented by the Johiyā Rājputs of Johiyabar on the border of the Bahāwālpur State.

Like the Mālavas and other republican tribes the Yaudheyas had to submit to the foreign invaders, but challenged their authority whenever any suitable opportunity offered itself. They fought with the Śaka satrap Rudradāman (c. 150 A. D.), and probably grew very powerful after the decline of the Kushāṇa power.

4 *Kaliṅga.*

Another powerful kingdom that arose out of the ruins of the Magadha empire was Kaliṅga. A large inscription in the Hāthigumphā cave in the Udayagiri hill near Bhuvanesvar (Orissa) gives us a detailed biography of king Khāravela—something unique in Indian history. Although the damaged condition of the rock does not enable us to understand the full import of the record, still enough remains to show that Khāravela made Kalinga an almost imperial power which played an important role in the history of North India.

Khāravela belonged to the third generation of the royal Chedi family of Kaliṅga. He was well instructed, as a young prince, in writing, accountancy, administration, and legal procedure. At the age of sixteen he was installed as *yuvarāja* (crown-prince) and was associated with the administration of the kingdom. Eight years later he was crowned king and began a career of conquest (*digvijaya*). In the second year of his reign his army advanced as far as the Kṛishṇabenā i. e. the Krishnā river in the south, and in the fourth year he subdued the Rāshṭrikas and the Bhojakas., who probably lived in Berar. Seven years later he conquered the region round Masulipatam. Although he made these extensive conquests in the Deccan he seems to have maintained friendly relations with the Andhras who established a powerful kingdom in that region. Without trying his strength with them, Khāravela turned his attention towards the north. In the eighth year he destroyed Gorathagiri (a fort in the Barabara Hills near Gayā) and attacked the city of Rājagṛiha (p. 96). Next year he defeated Bahasatimitra, king of Magadha, who was probably one of the Mitra rulers mentioned above (p. 127), and also conquered Aṅga. He threatened other rulers of Uttarāpatha, and caused so much terror in the heart of a Yavana (Greek) king that he fled away to Mathurā. The name of this king has been doubtfully read as Dimita and he has been identified with the Indo-Greek king Demetrius (p. 119). But this is very doubtful. After the conquest of Magadha, Khāravela proceeded to the far south and defeated the Pāṇḍya king.

But Khāravela was not merely a great conqueror. He was a good administrator and excelled in the arts of peace. Himself a great musician, he entertained the people by arranging all kinds of festive gatherings (*samāja*) including dance and music. He spent large amounts for irrigation and other works of public utility. He was also a great builder and decorated the capital city with gardens, gates, and houses including his own magnificent palace Mahāvijaya-prāsāda. He was a devout Jaina, and brought back from Magadha and Aṅga, as part of the booty, certain Jaina images which were taken away from Kaliṅga by a Nanda king. Khāravela excavated a number of caves in the Kumārī-parvata (Khaṇḍagirī hill) and probably also a monastery in the neighbourhood.

Even making due allowance for the exaggerations natural in a court record, we must regard Khāravela as a remarkable figure in the history of India. His conquering expeditions indicate a state of political chaos and confusion such as would have naturally followed the downfall of the Magadha Empire. Unfortunately we do not know what became of his conquests after his death. The history of Kaliṅga once more becomes obscure, and the brilliant figure of Khāravela appears and vanishes like a meteor without leaving any trace behind.

The date of Khāravela is not definitely known. His record refers to his repairing or enlarging a canal which was originally excavated by a Nanda king three centuries ago. This Nanda king was most probably Mahāpadma Nanda who established a mighty empire about 350 B. C. (p. 97) and presumably conquered Kaliṅga. The date of Khāravela would then fall in the first century B. C. Some scholars, however, place him in the first half of the second century B. C.

5. *The Andhras.*

While the Greeks, the Parthians, the Śakas and the Kushāṇas were harrying the north-western frontier of India, a powerful kingdom was established in the Deccan by the Andhras. The Andhras are an ancient people, and are referred to in a legend in the *Aitareya Brāhmaṇa* which shows that they lived on the border of Aryan settlements, and had a mixture of Aryan and non-Aryan blood in them. This notice may be dated about 800 B. C. Five hundred years later, we hear of them as a very powerful people, who possessed numerous villages and thirty towns, defended by walls and towers, and an army of 100,000 infantry, 2,000 cavalry, and 1,000 elephants[1]. Not long after this they had to acknowledge suzerainty of the Mauryas, although they seem to have preserved a great measure of autonomy in their internal administration. Their history is not definitely known, but it appears very probable that shortly after the death of Aśoka they threw off the yoke of the Maurya dynasty, and thereby brought about its downfall, as has been related above. King Simuka, who achieved this task, belonged to the Sātavāhana, family. The word Sātavāhana, in its corrupt form Sālivāhana, is almost a household word all over India, although the popular fancy has made the strange mistake of taking it for the name of an

Origin and early history

1. The statement is made by Pliny who probably got his information from Megasthenes.

individual king. In point of fact, Śālivāhana or Śātavāhana was the name of the royal family founded by Simuka. Simuka and his two successors extended their dominions from the mouth of the Krishnā to the whole of Deccan plateau. Pratishṭhāṇa, modern Paiṭhān or Pytoon on the Godāvari, was their western capital, while Dhānyakaṭaka, near Bezwada on the Krishnā, was the eastern capital. For nearly two hundred years the powers of the family were confined to the territories south of the Vindhyas, but according to the Purāṇas, the Śātavāhanas killed the last Kāṇva ruler, and became master of Magadha in the last century B. C.

Śālivāhana

The Purāṇas credit Simuka with this achievement, and accordingly some scholars refer him and the foundation of the Śātavāhana power to 27 B. C. or shortly before it. But this is incompatible with another statement of the same Purāṇas that the Śātavāhanas ruled for 456 years. For the Śātavāhana rule would in that case end in the 5th century A. D. when the Vākāṭakas were ruling in the Deccan. As a matter of fact we know definitely that the Śātavāhana rule came to an end about the middle of the third century A. D. If, therefore, we accept the Puranic statement that Simuka, the founder of the Śātavāhana family, destroyed the Kāṇvas, we must assign to them a total reign-period of 300 years for which there is some authority in the Vāyu Purāṇa. The scholars are thus divided in their views about the date of Simuka ; some place him about 220 B. C. and hold that the Andhras declared their independence shortly after the death of Aśoka. Others, however, place Simuka towards the end of the last century B. C. and regard him as having ended the supremacy of the Kāṇvas. Both, however, agree that the rule of his family ended about the middle of the third century A.D[1].

Date of Simuka, the first king.

However that may be, it is certain that in the first century B. C. there was a great Andhra empire which extended its sphere

1. For further study on this subject cf.

Sir R. G. Bhandarkar--Early History of the Deccan (2nd Edition.)

Dr. D. R. Bhandarkar—Dekkan of the Satavahana Period (*Ind. Ant.* 1918-1920).

Rapson--Catalogue of the Coins of the Andhra Dynasty (Introduction.)

V. A. Smith—Andhra History (*Z. D. M. G.* 1904)

Sir Asutosh Memorial Volume, published by J. N. Samaddar (1926-1928) Part II, p. 107.

of influence not only over the whole of the Deccan and South Indian peninsula, but also over Magadha and Central India (including Mālwa). More than hundred years passed in peace and prosperity, when the empire had to feel the terrible shock of the foreign invasions that convulsed North-western India. The Andhra emperors had to fight with the Greeks, the Śakas, and the Parthians, but the details of the struggle are unknown. Towards the end of the first century A. D., the Śaka chiefs, called the Western Satraps, of Mālwa and Kāthiāwār Peninsula, whose early history has been recorded above, dispossessed the Andhras of their dominions in Mālwa, conquered the North-western portion of the Deccan, and occupied the important city of Nāsik. It was a critical moment, not only for the Andhra kingdom, but also for the whole of Southern India, for the chances were that the whole country would be submerged under the barbarian invasions. Fortunately, a great hero arose in the Śātavāhana family in the person of Gautamīputra Sātakarṇi. He ascended the throne about 106 A. D., and inflicted a crushing defeat upon the Śaka chiefs of Mālwa and Kāthiāwār Peninsula. Thereby he not only recovered his paternal dominions in the Deccan, but also conquered large territories in Gujarāt and Rājputāna.

Fight with the foreign invaders.

Gautamīputra Satakarṇi.

His great exploits are described in detail in a record of his mother, queen Gautamī Balaśrī. She describes her son as a unique Brāhmaṇa, who totally uprooted the Kshanārāta dynasty and extirpated the Śakas, Yavanas (Greeks), and Pahlavas (Parthians). He is also said to have been lord of many countries including Aparānta (N. Konkan), Surāshṭra (Kāthiāwār), Ākara-Avanti (E. and W. Mālwa), Anupa, and Kukura, which together denoted regions in the neighbourhood of the preceding two. He totally defeated the Kshahārāta ruler Nahapāna, and having driven him out of Mahārashṭra restruck his coins in his own name for immediately putting them into circulation again.

Gautamīputra died after a glorious reign of about 25 years, and was succeeded by his son Pulumāyi. About that time the two Śaka principalities of Mālwa, and Kāthiāwār Peninsula were united under Rudradāman (p.124) and there ensued a long and protracted struggle between the two rulers. Rudradāman seems to have been successful in pushing back the Andhras to the Deccan proper, and enjoyed undisturbed his vast kingdom extending over Mālwā, Gujarāt and Rājputāna. A matrimonial alliance was established between the rival dynasties, by the marriage of Pulumāyi (or his brother) with the daughter of Rudradāman, but intermittent struggles continued.

A later Śātavāhana named Yajña Sātakarṇi seems to have conquered the southern dominions of the Western Satraps. His coins contain figures of ships, probably indicating the naval power of the Andhras. He not only ruled over Aparānta and the whole of the Deccan, but probably also over the eastern part of Central Provinces. He was the last great ruler of the Śātavāhana family. Soon after his death the vast kingdom was split up into several principalities, probably ruled by members of the ruling family. There were four or five successors of Yajña Sātakarṇi in the main line who continued to rule till about the middle of the third century A. D.

According to one Purānic account the dynasty comprised about thirty kings, who ruled for over 450 years, an unusually long period in Indian history. But according to another Puranic account there were 19 kings in the family who ruled for 300 years.

The different branches of the Śātavāhana family, which ruled in different parts of the kingdom after the decline of the central authority, were soon ousted by new powers some of which were probably feudatory states at the outset. As noted above, the Ābhīras established a kingdom in the north-western Deccan which probably included northern Konkan and southern Gujarāt. The Ikshvākus occupied the Andhra country proper between the mouths of the Krishnā and the Godāvari while the Bodhis and the Chuṭus ruled respectively in the north-western and south-western Deccan, the Bṛihatphalāyanas in the Masulipatam region, and the Pallavas in the South Indian Peninsula, iu the region round Kāñchī (modern Conjeeveram in Madras). But more powerful than these and several other powers that came into prominence on the ruins of the Andhra kingdom were the Vākāṭakas, who were the dominant power in the Deccan from the end of the third to the middle of the sixth century A. D.

6. *South India.*

South India specifically denotes that part of India which lies to the south of the Krishnā and the Tungabhadrā. From the earliest times of which we possess any record, three important kingdoms flourished in this land. The Pāṇḍya kingdom, probably named after the Epic Pāṇḍu, covered the southernmost region extending from coast to coast. Its northern boundary was formed by the river Vallaru in the Pudukkotai District. To the north-east and north-west of it lay respectively the Chola and Chera kingdoms. The former occupied the delta of the Kāveri and the adjoining region, and occasionally also included Toṇḍai (the region round Kānchi) though it is generally represented as an independent State. The Chera kingdom stretched along the west coast, probably as far north as Koṅkaṇ. The location of its capital Vañji is a matter of keen dispute among scholars. According to many it is represented by Tiru Vañjaikkalam in Cochin. Some modern scholars, however, identify it with Karuvūr. The Mysore plateau and the adjoining parts which lay beyond these three kingdoms contained a number of smallar States which owed allegiance to one or other of them. This entire region was known as the Tamil land proper and its northern boundary was formed by the hill of Tirupati.

The three kingdoms

The Aryans must have come into contact with South India long before the 4th century B. C. According to Tamil tradition Ṛishi Agastya came from the north and civilised the land. Megasthenes refers to the Pāṇḍya country being efficiently ruled by a queen. According to tradition recorded in classical Tamil-literature the Bomba (upstart) Moriyas conquered the whole land and advanced as far as Podiyil hill in the Madura-Tinnevelly border. The three kingdoms, together with Satyaputra, are mentioned in the Aśokan inscriptions as independent kingdoms. Satyaputra is evidently a tribal name, but as it is otherwise unknown, its identification is a matter of controversy, Some scholars have suggested that the Satyaputras (meaning members of the fraternity of truth) probably refer to the Kosar a people well known in Tamil literature for strict adherence to the plighted word. They inhabited the Koṅgu country (Salem and Coimbatore Districts).

It is impossible to write a connected history of these states, as scattered references in classical Tamil literature constitute at present our sole source of information for the early period with which we are dealing. It appears, however, that there was a constant struggle for supremacy among the three States, and the main

General condition

feature of South Indian History was the periodical ascendancy of one over the other two. To begin with, the Cholas seem to have exercised supremacy over the Cheras and the Pāṇḍyas from the beginning of the first century B. C. to the end of the first century A. D., or perhaps even a little later. Then followed the ascendancy of the Pāṇḍyas and of the Cheras. But the course of history did not flow in strict regularity with the above scheme. For much depended upon the personality of the ruler, and an able and strong monarch made his State the most powerful for the time being.

Chola

The figures of some such kings shine brilliantly in the classical Tamil texts whose composition is usually referred to the first five centuries of the Christian era, though recently some scholars have suggested a somewhat earlier date, *viz.* A. D. 100 to 250. The most distinguished among them was the Chola king Karikāla. Leaving aside the many romantic legends that have gathered round him, his two great achievements seem to be the crushing defeat he inflicted upon the joint forces of Chera and Pāṇḍya and the successful invasion of Ceylon.

Is appears that he defeated, in a great battle at Veṇṇi, 15 miles to the east of Tanjore, a confederacy of about a dozen rulers headed by those of Chera and Pāṇḍya, and thus established his supremacy over nearly the whole of the Tamil land. He is also credited with the construction of big irrigation channels by means of controlling the water of the Kāveri and the fortification of the famous sea-port Puhār, at the mouth of the Kāveri, chiefly with the labour of the Ceylonese prisoners of war. This led to the growth of trade and industry and all-round economic prosperity during his reign. He was a great patron of Tamil literature and many stories are told of his keen sense of justice. He was a follower of the Vedic religion and performed many Vedic sacrifices. At the same time he is represented as enjoying life to the full, eating heartily and indulging in wine and women without restraint. On the whole Karikāla offers a remarkable picture, full of human touches, of a great personality. His capital was Uraiyūr.

Pāṇḍya

Another distinguished figure is that of Neḍuñjeliyan, the Pāṇḍya king. The rulers of Chera, Chola and five other minor States combined against him and advanced to his capital Madurā. Neḍuñjeliyan drove them away and obtained a decisive victory at Talaiyālanganam.

This great victory was long remembered and is even mentioned in an inscription of the tenth century A. D. Neḍuñjeliyan also conquered Koṅgu and other minor States and increased the extent of his kingdom. He is eulogised by many poets whom he patronised, and was himself a poet of no mean order. He is also said to have performed many Vedic sacrifices.

Chera

Although not as distinguished as either Karikāla or Neḍuñjeliyan, the Chera ruler Neḍuñjeral Ādan also occupies a high position in the annals of the country. He conquered Kadambu near the sea, and perhaps this is the region which was later known as Kadamba, with its capital at Vanavāsi (near Goa). By a series of military campaigns, extending over many years, he is said to have defeated seven kings and thus claimed the rank of *adhirājar* or suzerain. At last he fought a battle with the Chola king. Both the kings were killed and their queens performed the *Sati* rite. Neḍuñjeral Ādan is also said to have defeated the Yavanas and brought some of them as prisoners, "their hands being tied behind and oil being poured on their heads." The reference is probably to the Greek or Roman traders who came in large numbers and set up colonies in south India, as we learn from both old Tamil poets and the classical writers of the West. There was an extensive maritime trade between South Indian ports and the Roman Empire in the early centuries of the Christian era, and possibly even before that. This sea-borne trade greatly enriched all the three kingdoms, some of whose rulers are known to have maintained diplomatic relations with Rome.

The younger brother of Neḍuñjeral Ādan, 'Kuṭṭuvan of many elephants,' was also a very powerful monarch and extended the Chera kingdom from sea to sea. Ādan's son Śenguṭṭuvan also figures very prominently in Tamil literature of a later age.

An interesting fact in connection with the history of the three kingdoms is the claim, made in Tamil literature, on behalf of several Pāṇḍya and Chera rulers, that they led victorious expeditions to the north as far as the Himālayas. As a matter of fact the Chera king Neḍuñjeral Ādan, mentioned above, is called *Imayavaramban*, i.e. 'he who had the Himālaya mountain as the boundary of his kingdom. Similar claim has been advanced also in respect of the Śātavāhana rulers of the Deccan. It is difficult to believe that any of these rulers had enough strength and resources for such military feats, but the stories probably indicate an intimate knowledge of North Indian politics on the part of the rulers of South India.

Before concluding this sketch reference must be made to some tribal movements in the Tamil land, towards the close of the period under review, which had important consequences for the future. A people, called Kalvār, who occupied the northern border of the Tamil land, seems to have been forced to migrate southwards by the advance of the Andhras. The Kalvārs, passing throug the Chola and Pāṇḍya countries, upset for a time the political equilibrium of these regions, though it was ultimately restored. But the effect on Toṇḍai or the region round Kānchi seems to have been of a more permanent character. For when the obscurity lifts again we see a new people, the Pallavas, settled in this region before the end of the third century A. D. These foreign immigrants (?) of unknown origin were destined to dominate over the Tamils for many centuries to come, but that history really falls into the next period.

Kalvārs

CHAPTER IV

Political Theory and Administrative Organisation

A. POLITICAL THEORY

1. *Arthaśāstra*

The period under review witnessed a remarkable development both in political theory and in administrative system. A large number of texts bearing on this subject were written, and though many are lost, a few have been happily preserved. The most remarkable among these is the Arthaśāstra attributed to Kauṭilya, the Prime Minister of Chandragupta Maurya. This is the most comprehensive treatise on the subject and was rightly regarded as the standard work on politics throughout the Hindu period and probably even long after it. Strangely enough the book was somehow completely lost, and it was not till the beginning of the present century that a copy was discovered by Pandit R. Shamasastry in a remote corner of South India. The newly discovered text fully sustains the reputation of the work, and its contents agree fairly well with the view that was formed about its scope and nature from the numerous references to, and quotations from, it in subsequent literature. What is more important, many passages in this text expressly describe it as the composition of Kauṭilya who uprooted the Nandas, thus clearly establishing his identity with the Prime Minister of Chandragupta. Nevertheless a critical examination of the contents has convinced some scholars that the text, as it is, was not the work of a single individual, but of a school of politics, and that it could not be composed in the third century B.C. but probably received its present form three or four centuries later. Although this view is now generally accepted, some distinguished scholars still regard the text as the genuine and long lost work of Kauṭilya. Whatever view we might take, it would be convenient and in accordance with general usage to designate it as Kauṭilīya Arthaśāstra or simply Arthaśāstra, without any qualification.

Kauṭilya's Arthaśāstra

In addition to the *Arthaśāstra* there are several other works on polity, among which the Rājadharma section of the Śāntiparva in *Mahābhārata*, and the *Manu-smriti* may be specially mentioned.

We learn from these books that the Hindus from a very early period studied politics with an ardour and enthusiasm which has probably no parallel in the ancient world. The science of politics was looked upon as the most important of all sciences, and some old writers even have gone so far as to declare, that there is only one science and that is the science of government, for it is in that science that all other sciences have their origin and end. The *Arthaśāstra* of Kauṭilya mentions no less than five schools and thirteen individual authors, who had contributed to the development of this science before him. All these strikingly indicate the progress and development of this science in ancient India.

2. *Origin of Kingship.*

The origin of kingship, one of the fundamental problems of politics, which already engaged the attention of political thinkers during the Vedic period (above, p. 74), is discussed in much greater detail, and though there is no striking originality in the views propounded, they are elaborated with greater thoroughness.

Divine Origin.

The theory of divine origin attains its most developed form in the *Manu-smṛiti* (VII. 3, 4, 8). "The Lord", it says, "created a king for the protection of this whole creation, taking (for that purpose) eternal particles of Indra, of the Wind, of Yama, of the Sun of Fire, of Varuṇa, of the Moon and of the Lord of Wealth (Kuvera)." From this follows the logical corollary: "Even an infant king must not be despised (from an idea) that he is merely mortal, for he is a great deity in human form."

Election.

The other view about the origin of king, viz. election by common consent, was modified in such a way as to offer a striking resemblance to the theory of Social Contract advanced by Locke in Europe nearly two thousand years later. This is full propounded in the *Mahābhārata* and summarised as follows in the *Arthaśāstra*. "People suffering from anarchy first elected Manu to be their king and allotted one-sixth of the grains grown and one-tenth of merchandise as sovereign dues. Fed by this payment kings took upon themselves the responsibility of maintaining the safety and security of their subjects." A further modification of this theory is found in the Buddhist canonical texts according to which the people elected, not the mythical Manu, but "the most handsome, gracious and powerful individual from among them on condition of giving him a portion of their rice." The democratic constitution of the Buddhist church evidently made its followers more inclined to this view even in a somewhat extreme form, for a Buddhist monk is represented as addressing a haughty king in the following words : "What is your pride worth, O King, who is a mere servant of the *gaṇa* (i.e. people) and receive the sixth part as wages." It is also legitimate to assume that the theory of Social Contract influenced practical administration in various ways. As an instance, reference may be made to the rule, occurring in most law-books, that "if the king cannot find out the stolen property he must compensate the owner."

3. *The State.*

The different theories of the origin of kingship were based on the assumption that there was a state of chaos and confusion which called for a protector. In some cases it is held that originally men lived happily and enjoyed peace and prosperity, till their wickendness brought about a state of anarchy and misery in which the might alone was right. Such a society was likened to a pond in which the bigger fish swallowed the smaller ones, and the proverbial state of anarchy was, from this analogy, technically termed *mātsya-nyāya* (like fish). This view may be compared to the theory of the 'state of nature' propounded by Hobbes and Rousseau.

The ancient political thinkers of India clearly distinguished the king from the State. The State was conceived as an organic whole, like a human body, and its constituent parts are actually called *angas* (limbs). On an ultimate analysis of the conception of State, seven such limbs were recognised, viz. the king, the minister, the country, the fort, the treasury, the army, and the friend. Kauṭilya has elaborately discussed each of these, and in the light of his remarks one can easily construe the essential pre-requisites of a State to be a fixed piece of territory, an organized government with adequate means, both financial and military, of maintaining internal peace and resisting foreign aggression, and recognition by other States. This is a surprisingly modern conception though, like many other political theories, it was never developed in later times.

Seven limbs

In one respect, however, the conception of State in ancient India strikingly differs from our own. Its scope of activities was all-embracing, and no distinction was made between personal and civic rights and duties, or between moral principles and positive law. Everything that had any bearing upon the moral and spiritual nature or material condition of a man came within the scope of State activities. This is best illustrated by an examination of the contents of the *Arthaśāstra*. It includes within the functions of the State not merely the security of life and property, administration of justice, and such economic control, including nationalisation of trade and industry, as is now being practised or advocated by the most advanced socialistic State, but also maintenance of proper relation between members of a family, the strict observance of rules prescribed by religion or social custom and etiquette.

Wide scope of activities

Thus the *Arthaśāstra* not only provides for State management of large scale trade and industry, and exercise of effective control over every profession, occupation (including that of physician and prostitutes), and even public amusements and entertainments (including gambling), and prescribes it to be the duty of the State to protect the helpless, the aged, and the orphan, and save the people from effect of natural calamities, but it also lays down what should be the proper relations between husband and wife, father and son, brother and sister etc., at what age and under what conditions one might renounce the world and adopt the life of a recluse or ascetic, when it was legitimate to use witchcraft for gaining the affection of wives or sweethearts, how to teach manners to refractory women etc. In short the State played an effective part over a man's social, economic, cultural, moral, and even spiritual life, and there was hardly any limit to its sphere of activity.

The wide outlook is no doubt the direct result of the philosophic conception of life as an integral whole in which man's activities were not divided into so many water-tight compartments under different labels, such as social, economic, religious etc. It was based on the conception of *Dharma*, which sustained life, as embracing all the activities of an individual which were interrelated to one another and subserved the sole purpose of human existence viz. spiritual salvation. This totalitarian view of life explains the totalitarian character of the State.

But although the State was totalitarian in its scope of activities, it did not adopt the totalitarian method in carrying out its function. A great deal of initiative and executive power was left to local assemblies as well as religious and social corporations, and on the whole there was a far greater degree of decentralisation of powers and authority than we see at the present day.

4. *Inter-State Relations.*

The relation between different States also received a great deal of attention, and Kauṭilya has given a most elaborate account of it. The normal relation between two neighbouring States is conceived to be one of hostility, and a State intervening between two others being common enemy of both, there was a natural alliance between them. This is the basis on which the entire convention of inter-state relations was built up.

According to Kauṭilya, material interests alone should guide the relation of one State towards another. A ruler should adopt the policy which is calculated to increase the power and wealth of his State, irrespective of any legal justice or moral consideration. The four traditional expedients for achieving this purpose are the *sāma*, (conciliation, treaty, alliance), *dāna* (gift, subsidy), *bheda* (sowing dissensions in a hostile State or among different enemy-States), and *daṇḍa* (aggressive action, chastisement). The condition or circumstances in which a State should follow one or other of these instruments of policy is minutely laid down in the *Arthaśāstra*. The governing idea of Kauṭilya seems to be that ethical considerations have no place in statecraft, but some writers insist that morality should be the watchword in private as well as public life. It would perhaps be wrong to judge Kauṭilya harshly on this ground, for he has merely frankly stated what every State in the world has actually done before and since his days, under false pretensions, and in spite of the most generous professions of high-sounding moral maxims. It should be remembered that Kauṭilya wrote a practical handbook for the guidance of statesmen and not a general text-book on political science.

B. ADMINITRATIVE ORGANISATION

1. *Kingdoms.*

The assiduous cultivation of political science, the evolution of the theory of State discussed above, and the growth of big kingdoms, culminating in the mighty Magadha empire must have exercised considerable influence upon the practical system of administration. It is impossible, however, to dwell upon the subject at great length in the present book, and we must therefore be content with a brief sketch of the salient features of public administration in ancient India.

The machinery of government was highly organised. At the head stood the king, assisted by a number of ministers, and a council. The detailed work of administration was divided among a number of departments, and managed by an efficient and highly organised bureaucracy. In order to have a rough idea of the system of government we must have some knowledge of each of these four elements, viz. the king, the ministers, the council, and the bureaucracy.

The King

The king was the supreme head of the executive, judicial, and military branches of administration. Sometimes the kings were elected by the people, though hereditary kingship became gradually the established practice. Females were not absolutely excluded from succession, though we hear very rarely of reigning queens. The prestige attached to the position of the sovereign varied in different times, and in different localities. He enjoyed special honours and privileges, and the theory of divine origin made his person almost sacrosanct. But in practice, the theory was never carried to the absurd or extreme length of investing the king with unfettered right over the life and property of the people. Even *Manu-smriti*, the great upholder of the divine origin of kings, expressly lays down that "a king who is voluptuous, partial, and deceitful will be destroyed," and the very *daṇḍa*, the symbol of royal authority, "strikes down the king who swerves from his duty." Actual instances are not wanting to prove that tyrannical kings were deposed and sometimes even killed. Even the Smṛitis quote such examples from ancient history or tradition to admonish the king and thereby indirectly support the punishment meted out to the kings.

Special care was taken to impart sound education and moral training to the future king. The text-books on polity lay great stress on this point, and provide that if the prince fail to reach a requisite standard, prove unruly, or show signs of wickedness or perverse character, he forfeits his right to the throne, and another shall be installed in his place. Kauṭilya goes so far as to say that if the only legitimate heir is lacking in knowledge and moral character, the king should even "try to beget a son on his wife by the system of levirate, but never shall a wicked and only son be installed on the royal throne."

The ancient writers on polity prescribe a daily round of duties, to which a king was expected to conform as closely as possible. The day and the night were each divided into eight parts, measured by water-clock or the shadow of the sun, and the following scheme lays down the duties to be performed during each of these parts.

Day :

(1) Receiving reports about the accounts and the defensive measures of the kingdom.
(2) Considering the prayers and petitions of the subjects.
(3) Bath, meal, and study.
(4) Attending to revenue and departmental heads.
(5) Attending to the business of the council and confidential reports from spies.
(6) Recreation or deliberation on State affairs.
(7) Inspection of royal forces.
(8) Consultation with the commander-in-chief about military affairs.

Night :

(1) Receiving the spies.
(2) Bath, meal, and study.
(3-5) Sleep.
(6) Reflection on sacred literature and his own duties.
(7) Consultation with the ministers and sending out spies.
(8) Attending to domestic duties, religious rites, ceremonies, etc.

Slightly varying details are given in different books, and it is not to be supposed that any of these time-tables was strictly followed by any king. But they certainly indicate methodical and business-like habits of ancient kings, and give us a general picture of their lives and duties.

The king was easily accessible to the people at large. Kauṭilya says that "when a king makes himself inaccessible to his people, and entrusts his work to his immediate officers, he may be sure to engender confusion in business, and to cause thereby public disaffection, and himself a prey to his enemies."

The paramount duty of the king was to protect the people and seek their welfare. Kauṭilya sums up the position very beautifully in the following verse : "In the happiness of his subjects lies his happiness ; in their welfare his welfare ; whatever pleases himself he shall not consider as good, but whatever pleases his subjects he shall consider as good."

The ancient writers on polity also emphasised the heavy responsibility of the king's position. By accepting taxes from the people, the king incurs definite obligations to them, and these he must fulfil by the due discharge of his duties. These ideal virtues of an ancient Indian king are embodied, to a considerable extent, in the character of the great emperor Aśoka to which reference has been made before (p. 113).

We must, however, bear in mind that kings in ancient India did not always approximate to this high standard, and that there were good and bad kings, as well as kings of average merit. But this is true not only of India but also of every other country under the sun. India's greatness lies in the fact that she produced at least one Aśoka, who still remains without a parallel in the history of the world.

Minister

Next in importance to the king were the ministers. Kauṭilya says: "Sovereignty is possible only with assistance. A single wheel can never move. Hence the king shall employ ministers and hear their opinion." Similarly other writers on polity, too, looked upon the ministers as an organic part of the government.

In view of the great importance of the position of the ministers, the ancient writers discussed in detail the proper modes of selecting them. Kauṭilya held the view that the "ministerial appointments shall depend solely on qualifications, and not on the considerations of family, or backstair influence." Before employing ministers on responsible duties, their characters were tested by secret agents, and the king employed those alone as ministers, who proved themselves superior to the allurements that usually lead a man astray from his duties. Those who failed in one or more tests, but were otherwise qualified, were appointed, in accordance with the ascertained degree of purity, to the various appointments in the civil service inferior in rank to that of the minister.

All kinds of administrative measures were preceded by deliberations in a council of ministers. The number of ministers varied according to circumstances, from three or four to twelve. Sometimes one of them was appointed Prime Minister. Individual ministers were in charge of separate departments. There were for instance finance minister, and the minister for war and peace. But they, in a body, advised the king on all important affairs of State. The following remarks of Kauṭilya indicate the nature of ministerial power and responsibility. "A single minister proceeds wilfully and without restraint. In deliberating with two ministers, the king may be overpowered by their combined action, or imperilled by their mutual dissension. But with three or four ministers he will not come to any serious grief, but will arrive at satisfactory results. In accordance with the requirements of place, time, and nature of the work in view, he may, as he deems it proper, deliberate with one or two ministers or by himself. The king may ask his ministers for their opinion, either individually or collectively, and ascertain their ability by judging over the reasons they assign for their opinions."

We read also in *Śukranīti* (a much later work, but probably embodying old traditions), that the king should receive in written form the opinions of each minister separately with all his arguments, compare them with his own opinion, and then do what is accepted by the many.

In addition to the body of ministers, there was a council to assist the king in the administrative work. King Bimbisāra, who had the sovereignty of 80,000 villages, is said to have once called an assembly of their 80,000 chiefs. Such big councils could, however, be summoned only on rare occasions. There was a smaller council, too, which formed a regular part of the machinery of government. Kauṭilya calls it *Mantri-Parishad*, but clearly distinguishes it from the council of ministers. We may designate them respectively as the State Council and Executive Council.

The Council

The State Council seems to have occupied the place of the *Samiti* or the Assembly of the Vedic period. It sometimes consisted of large numbers. Kauṭilya maintains, against the schools of politicians who would limit the number to 12, 16, or 20, that it shall consist of as many members as the needs of the dominion require. As regards the powers of this council, Kauṭilya expressly lays down that they had 'to consider all that concerns the parties of both the king and his enemy, and that in important cases the king shall hold a joint session of both the Executive and the State Councils, and ordinarily do whatever the majority of members suggest'. The constitutional importance of this body also appears quite clearly from the injunction of Kauṭilya, that the king should consult the absent members, if any, by means of letters.

A further constitutional development is indicated by a passage in the *Mahābhārata*, according to which 4 Brāhmaṇas, 8 Kshatriyas, 21 Vaiśyas, 3 Śūdras, and 1 Sūta formed the State

Council, and out of this body of 37, 'the king selected eight as ministers.' This seems to be the last stage of constitutional development in India, and it is interesting to note how, to a certain extent, it ran on parallel lines with that of England. As the great National Council of the English gave rise to the Parliament, from which the king selected his confidential ministers and formed the cabinet, so the *Samiti* of the Vedic period gave place to the *Mantri-Parishad* out of which the king selected a few to form a close Cabinet.

The Bureaucracy.

While the policy was formulated by the council and the ministers, the detailed work of administration was carried on by a bureaucracy. At the head of the bureaucracy were a few high officials whose number and status must have varied in different ages and different States. The following list includes the more important ones :—

1. The High Priest.
2. The Commander-in-Chief.
3. The Chief Judge.
4. The Door-keeper (*Pratīhārī*).
5. The High Treasurer (*Sannidhātā*).
6. The Collector-General (*Samāharttā*).

The general nature of heir duties is indicated by their names. There were also ceremonial officers, such as "The bearer of the Sunshade of the State," and "the State Sword-bearers." There were other officers like Viceroys and Ambassadors, whose sphere of work lay in distant parts of the country. All these formed the members of the higher branch of administration. Next came the lower branch, consisting mainly of the Superintendents of the various departments into which the administration was divided, and their staff. The number of these Superintendents must have varied in different kingdoms. In Kauṭilya's *Arthaśāstra* we read of the Superintendents of the following :—

1. Ocean-mines. 2. Treasury. 3. Mines. 4. Metals. 5. Mint. 6. Accounts. 7. Gold. 8. Store-house. 9. Commerce. 10. Forest produce. 11. Passports. 12. Weights and Measures. 13. Lineal measures. 14. Tolls. 15. Weaving. 16. Agriculture. 17. Liquor. 18. Slaughter-house. 19. Prostitutes. 20. Ships. 21. Cows. 22. Horses. 23. Elephants. 24. Chariots. 25. Infantry 26. Armour. 27. Pasture. 28. Harem.

Each Superintendent was the head of a department, and carried on his work with the help of a number of assistants and subordinates. His work was regularly checked by Commissioners appointed by the Collector-General, and punishments were inflicted upon him for dereliction of duty. The Superintendents were sometimes transferred from one department to another. As will be seen from the above list of departments, the Government directly carried on manufacture and commerce on their own account, and also worked the various mines of the kingdom.

Besides the officers named above, belonging to the central Government, there were local officers of various descriptions. The kingdom was divided into several districts, and each district into a number of villages. There was a District officer, called Sthānika, and a village accountant, named Gopa. There was, besides, a headman in every village, either nominated by the king or elected by the people of the village. The headman, assisted by an assembly of villagers, transacted the affairs of the village, and maintained peace and order. Each village formed a close corporation, invested with large powers and responsibilities. It had a very large control over persons and property belonging to the village, and was held responsible for the regular payment of royal dues. These were not necessarily paid in cash. Some villages supplied soldiers, some paid their taxes in the form of grains, cattle, gold or raw materials, and some supplied free labour and dairy produce in lieu of taxes. Some villages were altogether free from taxation. The general appearance of a village was very much like what it is to-day, but ancient villages were almost always surrounded by boundary walls or fencings.

Local administration.

The Gopa looked into the accounts and kept the statistics of a group of villages. He recorded and numbered plots of grounds, both cultivated and uncultivated, plains, marshy ands, gardens, vegetable gardens, forests, altars, temples of gods, irrigation works, cremation grounds, feeding houses, places where water was freely supplied to travellers, places of pilgrimage, pasture grounds, and roads within his jurisdiction. He fixed the boundaries of villages, of fields, of forests, and of roads, and registered gifts, sales, charities and remission of taxes regarding fields. He recorded the total number of cultivators, cowherds, merchants, artisans, labourers, slaves and animals. He also kept an account of the number of young and old men that resided in each house, and recorded their history, occupation, income and expenditure.

The Sthānika or the District officer supervised the work of the Gopas within his jurisdiction. The Collector-General, who was the highest officer in charge of these works, deputed special commissioners to inspect the work done, and the means employed by the village- and district-officers. He also employed secret agents to ascertain the validity of the accounts of these officers.

The administration of the city corresponded, on a small scale, with that of the country. It was divided into several wards, and each ward into several groups of households, like the corresponding divisions of the country into districts and villages. Similarly, a Gopa and a Sthānika were placed respectively in charge of a group of households and a ward. The superior officer in charge of the city, corresponding to the Collector-General, was called Nāgaraka or City-Superintendent. Corresponding to the village assembly there was municipal corporation in the city. A typical instance is furnished by the municipal body of the capital city Pāṭaliputra at the time of Chandragupta, to which reference has already been made (p. 107).

Elaborate regulations were laid down for the proper sanitary arrangements of the city and to prevent such calamities as the outbreak of fire. Most of the important cities had forts, walls, and other defensive works. Reference is also made to hidden passages for going out of the city.

Town-planning was regularly studied on scientific principles, and many ancient books give elaborate description of the proper arrangements for a city.

Cities were provided with temples, roads, foot-paths, reservoirs, wells for drinking water, travellers' sheds, hospitals, brilliant shops, pleasure gardens, big tanks, and various places of amusement. The Gopas kept a statistical record of cities like the corresponding officers of the village.

Spies.

In addition to the various officials described above, there was another class which played a prominent part in ancient Indian administration. These were spies or secret agents, maintained not only by the king, but by almost all the important officials as a check against their subordinates. The spies were divided into several classes, and employed for various purposes in various spheres of life. It is worthy of note that persons, who had necessarily to be fed by the State, were trained up for this purpose from their boyhood. Even women, including widows of the

Brāhmaṇa caste, adopted the profession of spy for earning their livelihood. The spies were distinguished by cleverness and an intimate knowledge of men and manners. They were also trained in various languages as well as in the art of putting on disguises appropriate to different countries and trades. Disguised as householders, cultivators, merchants, hermits, ascetics practising austerities, mendicant women and disciples or students, they mixed with all ranks of society, and collected information. The king employed them to watch the movements not only of his high officials, including the priests, ministers, and the commander-in-chief, but even of his own son and heir-apparent to the throne. The officials of the kingdom also followed the example set by their master. There were counter-spies for the detection of spies, and very often different bands of spies, unknown to one another, were employed on the same errand, so that the truth might be ascertained by comparing the different accounts given by them. The spies evolved systems of signs, symbols, and cipher-writing for communicating with one another.

Tribunals were organised throughout the kingdom for administering justice. There were local as well as central courts.

Judicial administration.

The local courts were three in number. The first consisted of the kindred of the accused; the second, the guild to which he belonged; and the village assembly formed the third. A great deal of importance was attached to these local courts, and this was based on the rational idea laid down in the *Śukranīti*, that "they are the best judges of the merits of a case who live in the place where the accused person resides, and where the subject-matter of the dispute has arisen." Proceeding on the same idea, Bṛihaspati recommends, that 'for persons roaming the forest, a court should be held in the forest; for warriors, in the camp; and for merchants, in the caravan.'

The central court was held in the capital. It was presided over by the king or the Chief Justice (*Prāḍvivāka*), and included four or five judges who were chosen for their character and erudition in law. This was the highest court of justice, and exercised a sort of general supervision over the administration of justice throughout the country.

Between the king's court and the local courts, there were other courts in important cities, where royal officers, assisted by judges, administered justice. Thus there was a regular gradation of courts,—court of kindreds, guild, village assembly, city court, and king's court. Each of these was more important than the preceding one, and heard appeals from its decision. But although they were courts of appeal, each of them was also an original court in respect of cases occurring within its jurisdiction. The first three could not decide cases involving serious crimes which were referred to the city courts. Both civil and criminal cases were tried by the same court.

It is difficult to conceive a more striking difference between ancient and modern societies than their standpoint with regard to law and its enactment. Accustomed as we are to a set of positive laws sanctioned by a definite authority, it requires a great effort on our part to adjust ourselves to a situation in which the difference between positive and moral laws was not clearly recognised, and the right of authorities to enact new laws positively denied.

Legislation.

Thus in ancient India there was no sharp distinction between religious ordinances, moral practices, and positive injunctions of secular law. All were jumbled together in law books, and an individual was expected to adjust himself to them as best he could.

Regarding the source of law, there was a great deal of difference between different authorities. They all, however, refer, as two primary sources, to the sacred literature, and the local usages. The sacred literature consisted of the Vedas, the Smṛitis, and the Purāṇas, and it was not always an easy affair to extract legal rules from them. The defect was removed by drawing up manuals of law based on sacred literature, and, in course of time, there grew up a body of practices and authoritative decisions which had the force of law.

The local usages were accorded a far greater importance than we can possibly imagine. Not only the usages and customs generally prevalent in the country, but also those of a village, of a profession, of a religious order, and even of a single family had the force of law. The king was bound to respect them and to keep a permanent record of "the history of customs, professions, and transactions of countries, villages, families, and corporations."

The source of law being limited to these two, there was theoretically no scope for new legislation. In practice, however, that was far from being the case. There were at least two distinct ways in which laws were either modified or enlarged. In the first place, commentaries were written to explain the sacred law, and these not infrequently altered the interpretation of original texts by straining the meaning of words, in order to suit them to the needs or tastes of the changed society. As a result, the same passage in sacred literature has given rise to diametrically opposite laws in different parts of the country.

Secondly, there was gradually evolved the custom of referring doubtful points in sacred law to a duly authorised body of Brāhmaṇas, called the Parishad. Although the Parishads were formed only to declare the true law as embodied in the sacred literature, in practice they altered the laws to a considerable degree by additions and alterations. The Parishad is thus the nearest approximation to a definite legislative body. Its constitution was not a stereotyped one, but differed in different localities. Accroding to a very ancient authority, it consisted of "four men who each know one of the four Vedas, one versed in Mīmāṁsā, one who knows the Aṅgas, one who recites (the works on) the sacred law, and three Brāhmaṇas belonging to three different orders."

Originally, the king had no power to enact laws, but with the development of political ideas, the royal edicts came to possess the force of law. The earliest notable instance in this direction is furnished by the case of the great Maurya Emperor Aśoka. He promulgated a number of ordinances, such as those prohibiting the slaughter of certain animals on certain days, and giving a brief respite of three days to condemned men lying in prison under sentence of death. He went even much further. His empire included a great many countries having different legal systems and practices, and he tried to introduce uniformity in judicial procedure and award of penalties all over his vast empire.

Before concluding the discussion on the monarchical form of government, it is necessary to say a few words about its general character. It has often been discussed whether ancient Indian monarchy was an absolute despotism, or there were some limitations upon its authority. Saturated as we are with the idea of modern constitutional development, we naturally look for constitutional checks upon the authority of kings, such as are to be found in most countries of modern Europe where monarchy prevails. The only check of this nature in ancient India seems to have been the *Mantris*

Character of ancient monarchy.

and *Mantri-Parishad*, roughly corresponding to the modern Executive and Legislative Councils. It will appear from what has been said above that the Ministers controlled the authority of the king to a great extent. We have also seen 'that the decisions arrived at the joint session of the two bodies were generally binding upon the king.' But our knowledge in this respect is very limited, for although the Legislative Council seems to have been of a representative character, we do not know for certain whether its members were nominated or elected.

There were, besides, many indirect restraints upon the authority of the king. In the first place, the law of the land had a sacred character and was binding equally upon him and his subjects. Secondly, the learned Brāhmaṇas of the land were guardians and expositors of this law, and in view of the position they held in society, he would be a bold king indeed who would dare to disobey them. Thirdly, the duty of the king was clearly defined in the Śāstras. In those days a man's status in society was looked at not so much from the point of view of his rights, as from that of his duty, which had moral and religious sanction behind it ; and it would have created as much sensation in those days, if the king had failed in his duties, as would follow the violation of people's right in modern days.

It is true that in spite of all these, a king might, and probably not unoften did, establish an arbitrary rule. But it must be remembered that even the most efficient constitutional checks that were devised in later ages in the western countries equally failed to curb the despotic authority of kings, until and unless the people demonstrated their will and power to force them to a reasonable frame of mind. The history of England amply illustrates this point, and further shows, that it is not the letter of the constitution, but the extent to which the people are willing and capable of exercising their undoubted rights, that really determines the character of the monarchy. The same is also true in ancient history. Octavius, for example, maintained the old constitution, but it would be a mockery to describe the Imperial Rome of his days as the old Republic or even a limited monarchy.

In judging of any constitution, therefore, the thing of primary importance is to determine the status and the political consciousness of the people. A close study of the *Arthaśāstra* reveals the fact that the people were reecognised as one of the most important factors of the State in ancient India. The theoretical recognition of this principle may be traced in various passages throughout the book. Some of these have been quoted above (pp. 146-7), and two more may be added. Addressing the army the king says: "I am a paid servant like yourselves." Again, we read: "It is unrighteous to do an act which excites popular fury." In practical politics, too, Kauṭilya attaches due importance to the power of the people. He refers again and again to the political organisation of the people, and to the causes and consequences of their disaffecion. He recommends that the king should bring round the disaffected by conciliation, and should show due deference to popular sentiment. To the king who has conquered a new territory, Kauṭilya suggests the following line of action: "He should follow the friends and leaders of the people. Whoever acts against the will of the people will also become unreliable. He should adopt the same mode of life, the same dress, language, and customs as those of the people. He should follow the people in their faith with which they celebrate their national, religious, and congregational festivals or amusements. Whoever has caused excitement to the people or incurred their displeasure should be removed and placed in a dangerous locality." But the surest testimony to Kauṭilya's regard for popular sentiment is furnished by the injunction that 'a prince, though put to troubles and employed in an unequal task, shall yet faithfully follow his father, unless that task costs his life, *enrages the people*, or leads him to commit any heinous sin (*pātaka*).' The author of *Śukranīti* says in the same strain that "the king should dismiss the officer who is accused by one hundred men." All ancient writers agree that the people have the undoubted right of dethroning a king, or even killing him, if he proves a tyrant.

All these things indicate a high political status enjoyed by the people at large. When everything is taken into consideration, it may be safely laid down that the ideal form of government in ancient India was one in which the three elements, the king, the bureaucracy, and the poeple, were equally balanced, and served as checks against one another. If we are to look for a modern prototype, the German government before the First Great War would approximate, in spirit, if not in form, to the ideal constitution of India in her best days.

2. *Non-monarchical States.*

It has already been mentioned above that monarchy was not the only form of government known in ancient India. From very early times both oligarchic and republican governments flourished in this country. They are not only referred to in ancient literature, coins, and inscriptions, but have also been noticed by the Greeks, who had far greater knowledge of the working of these constitutions than any other ancient people known to history.

We can trace the existence of these forms of government, as early as the sixth century B. C., among the Lichchhavis, the Śākyas, the Mallas, and many other tribes. Some of these, like the Lichchhavis, were very powerful and won great name and fame in ancient India.

Unfortunately, very few details with regard to the constitution of these States are known with certainty, and we can make only a tentative suggestion. It appears that the whole State was divided into a number of small administrative units, each of which was a State in miniature by itself, and possessed a complete machinery for carrying on the local administration. The business of the State as a whole was entrusted to an assembly consisting of the heads of those administrative units, under the guidance of a Chief or President elected for a definite period. In case the assembly was a large one, an Executive Council was chosen from amongst its members. The resemblance of this form of Government with the Cleisthenian constitution of Athens is obvious and need not be dilated upon.

The assembly consisted of both old and young men, and met in a hall called Santhāgāra. The Lord Buddha professed great admiration for the Lichchhavi assembly, and is said to have once remarked to his disciples : "Oh brethren, let those of the brethren who have never seen the Tāvatiṁsa gods, gaze upon this assembly of the Lichchhavis, behold this assembly of the Lichchhavis, compare this assembly of the Lichchhavis, even as an assembly of the Tāvatiṁsa gods." Buddha was also impressed with the inherent strength of the Lichchhavi constitution. For when Ajātaśatru, bent upon conquering the Lichchhavis, sent his ministers to him for advice, he replied that the Lichchhavis were invincible so long as their constitution remained unimpaired. There are grounds for believing that the Buddha modelled the democratic organisation of his Church on the constitution of the Lichchhavis.

We possess some information regarding the method in which justice was administered among the Lichchhavis. The system is chiefly remarkable for the ultra-democratic spirit which characterises it, and is calculated to give us some insight into the principles of administration followed in these non-monarchical States. We learn from an old text that a criminal was at first sent for trial to a class of officers called *Vinichchaya Mahāmātta*. If they found the accused innocent they acquitted him, but if he was guilty in their opinion, they could not punish him, but had to send him on to the next higher tribunal. The man had thus to pass through six judges, each of whom could acquit him, if he found him innocent, but had to send him on to the next higher tribunal if he appeared guilty in his eyes. The last tribunal, that of the President, alone had the right to convict the accused, and in awarding punishment he was guided by the *Paveni Pustaka* i.e. the book containing law and previous legal decisions. The position of the individual was thus safeguarded in a manner that has probably few parallels in the world. He could be punished only if seven successive tribunals had unanimously found him guilty, and he was quite safe if but one of them regarded him as innocent. And it is but fitting that the right of the people should thus be safeguarded in a State where the people governed themselves.

Republican and Oligarchical States.

Quite a large number of democratic States flourished in the fourth century B.C. Megasthenes says that most of the cities in his time adopted the democratic form of government, and other writers corroborate him. One of the most important democratic States in the 4th century B.C. was that of the Sabarcae, who, like many others, fought with the army of Alexander the Great. Their territory extended along the bank of the Sindhu, and they had 60,000 foot, 6,000 cavalry, and 500 chariots. Some other republican tribes have been mentioned above (p. 100) in connection with the invasion of Alexander the Great.

The Greek writers also refer to a number of oligarchical States. The city-state of Nysa, for example, had an oligarchical form of government and its governing body consisted of a President and 300 members of the aristocracy. In some cases the governing body consisted of as many as five thousand councillors. Reference is also made to another State in which the command in war was vested in two hereditary kings of two different houses, while a Council of Elders ruled the whole State with paramount authority. The Greek writer could not help emphasising its obvious similarity with the Spartan constitution.

The establishment of the Maurya empire proved ruinous to these non-monarchical States. The existence of independent democratic States is incompatible with the conception of a centralised empire, and Kauṭilya, in his *Arthaśāstra*, steadily advocates the policy of putting them down by all means, fair or foul. By his diabolical intrigues he seems to have been fairly successful in his task, and the oligarchies and democracies in the neighbourhood of Magadha vanished for ever. But after the downfall of the Maurya empire others arose in their place. The Yaudheyas, the Mālavas and the Arjunāyanas, among others, had democratic constitution and played important parts in Indian history. Like their predecessors they fought stubbornly against the foreign invaders, but like them, too, they had to succumb to an imperial power. For, as we shall see, Samudragupta conquered most of them in the 4th century A.D. Thus, a prey to imperialism within, and foreign invasion from without, these non-monarchical States finally vanished from India about the fifth century A.D.

There were two schools of thought in ancient India which held diametrically opposite views about the non-monarchical States. One, represented by the *Arthaśāstra*, being in favour of strong monarchy and imperialism, regarded these States as chief obstacles to this ideal, and strongly advocated their destruction by all possible means. The other, anxious to preserve the non-monarchical States, pointed out their inherent defects and dangers and suggested remedies for the same. A long passage in Śānti-parva (Ch. 107), for example, shows an intimate knowledge of these States and makes an eloquent appeal for their preservation. This passage is the only surviving relic of a school of political thought which favoured the democratic form of government that existed in India for more than a thousand years.

CHAPTER V

New Religious Movements

The sixth century B.C. may be regarded as an important landmark in the history of Indian culture. The old Vedic religion had gradually ceased to be a strong living force since the Upanishads had initiated freedom of speculation into the fundamental problems of life. Discontent with the existing state of things, brooding over the ills and sorrows of life, a passionate desire to remove them by finding out a new mode of salvation, and an earnest endeavour to discover the ultimate reality became the order of the day. It created a ferment of new ideas and philosophical principles, leading to the establishment of numerous religious sects, such as never occurred in India before or since.

Of these religious sects, which may be regarded as direct or indirect products of the thought-currents of this period, four alone deserve special mention as having permanently influenced the religious history of India. Two of these, Buddhism and Jainism, were heterodox and revolutionary in character, while the other two, Vaishṇavism and Śaivism, may be regarded as Reformist movements.

1. *Buddhism*.

Gautama Buddha.

Gautama, the founder of Buddhism, was a Kshatriya and belonged to the Śākya clan, whose territory is now represented by that part of the Nepal Terai which lies immediately to the norh of the Basti District in the Uttar Pradesh. Popular legends of a later date represented him as the son of a mighty king, born and brought up amidst the luxuries of a palace. The fact. however, is, that the Śākyas had a republican constitution, and the father of Gautama was probably elected to the chief position in the State for the time being. The date of his birth is a matter of dispute, but we may reasonably place it about 566 B.C. (p. 103). As he grew into manhood, he was caught by the prevailing spirit of the time, which was a sort of pessimism leading to spiritual aspirations. Popular tradition has dramatically represented, how Gautama was horrified at the sight of an old man, a diseased person, and a dead body, and then, being attracted by the saintly appearance of an ascetic, left his home, wife, and child in a sudden fit of renunciation. The fact seems to be, that the problem of getting rid of the evils of the world, among which old age, disease, and death are the most prominent, had been agitating the better minds of the Aryans, who realised the worthlessness of the material luxury that surrounded them. Gautama shared the growing pessimism of the day, and left his home in quest of higher truth. He studied for some time in the philosophical schools of two renowned teachers of Rājagṛiha, and then proceeded to Uruvilva near Gayā. Six years of concentration and profound meditation led to the discovery of truths which, he claimed, would cure the ills of the world, and thus Gautama became the Buddha or the enlightened.

Fundamental principles of Buddhism.

The fundamental principles of Buddha's teachings are represented by the four Noble Truths (Ārya-Satyāni), viz. (a) that the world is full of suffering ; (b) that thirst, desire, attachment etc. are the causes of the worldly existence (c) which can be stopped by the destruction of thirst etc.; and (d) that in order to do this one must know the right way. The chain of causes that lead to suffering is described in detail, and the means of deliverance from these sufferings are fully explained. This is the celebrated Eightfold Path (*Ashṭāṅgika-mārga*) *viz.* right speech, right action and right means of livelihood ; then right exertion, right mindfulness, right meditation ; and lastly right resolution and right view. The ultimate end of life is to attain *nirvāṇa*, the eternal state of peace and bliss, which is free from sorrow and desire, decay or disease, and, of course, from further birth and death.

Moral doctrines of Buddhism.

The moral doctrines preached by the Buddha were quite simple. Man is the arbiter of his own destiny, not any god or gods. If he does good deeds in this life, he will be reborn in a higher life, and so on, till he attains salvation or the final emancipation from the evils of birth. On the other hand, evil deeds are sure to be punished, and not only will salvation be retarded thereby, but man will be reborn into lower and lower life. Man should avoid both the extremes, *viz.* a life of ease and luxury, and a life of severe asceticism,—the middle path was the best. In addition to the ordinary moral code such as truthfulness, charity, purity and control over passions, Buddhism laid great stress on love, compassion, equanimity and non-injury to living creatures in thought, word, or deed.

In its negative aspect, Buddhism denied the efficacy of Vedic rites and practices for the purpose of salvation, and challenged the superiority assumed by the Brāhmaṇas.

Gautama Buddha adopted the life of a religious teacher at the age of thirty-five, and wandered in different places in Magadha, Kośala, and the adjoining territories, preaching his new gospel. The disciples, whom he thus recruited, fell into two categories, the *Upāsaka* or lay disciple, who lived with family, and the *Bhikshu* or monk, who renounced the world and led the life of an ascetic. The Buddha was endowed with a great organising capacity, and the community of Buddhist monks called *Saṁgha*, founded by him, became one of the greatest religious corporations the world has ever seen

A few striking characteristics of Buddhism may be noticed here. One was the admission of the female members into his church, as *Bhikshuṇī* or nun. Buddha was at first opposed to this, but was at last persuaded by his favourite disciple Ānanda to give his consent, though not without much misgivings about the future of his church. Secondly, the members enjoyed equal rights in his church, irrespective of the classes or castes to which they belonged. Thirdly, Buddha introduced the practice of holding religious discourses in the language of the common people, in preference to the highly elaborate Sanskrit tongue, unintelligible to the people at large.

All these factors contributed to make the religion of Buddha a highly popular one, and when he died at Kuśinagara at the advanced age of eighty (c. 486 B.C.), his loss was mourned by a wide circle of monks and lay disciples.

First General Council

Shortly after the death of Gautama Buddha, his disciples met together in a general council at Rājagṛiha, and made as complete and authentic a collection of the teachings of the master, as was possible. This was all the more important, inasmuch as Buddha did not nominate anybody to succeed him in the headship of the church, but expressly said to his disciples : "The truths and the rules of the Order which I have set forth and laid down for you, let them, after I am gone, be the Teacher to you."

The sacred literature of the Buddhists, which probably did not take final shape till one or two centuries later, is known as the *Tripiṭaka* or the three baskets. The first is the Vinaya-piṭaka, which laid down a body of rules and regulations for the guidance of the Buddhist monks, and the general management of the Church. The second, the Sutta- (Sūtra) piṭaka, was a collection of the religious discourses of the Buddha; and the third, the Abhidhamma-piṭaka, contained an exposition of the philosophical principles underlying the religion. [1]

Besides Buddha and his doctrines as embodied in the Tripiṭaka, there was yet a third factor which was of equal importance. This was the Saṁgha or the Buddhist Church. Even to-day, millions of Buddhists daily express their faith in the holy Trinity by uttering the sacred formula,—"I take refuge in the Buddha, I take refuge in the Dharma, I take refuge in the Saṁgha." The idea of a church, or a corporate body of men following a particular religious faith, was not certainly a new one, and there were many organisations of this type at and before the time of Gautama Buddha. His credit, however, lies in the thorough and systematic character which he gave to these organisations.

The Buddhist Church.

The membership of the Buddhist church was open to all persons, male or female, above fifteen years of age, irrespective of any class or caste distinctions, except certain specified categories, such as those affected with leprosy and other diseases, criminals, slaves etc. The new convert had to choose a preceptor who led him before an assembly of monks, and made a formal proposal for admitting him to the church. The consent having been obtained, the convert was formally ordained, and the life of destitution and stern morality, which he was expected to lead, was fully explained to him. A special training was necessary to accustom him to the new ideas and habits, and he had therefore to live for the first ten years in absolute dependence upon his preceptor. After this disciplinary period was over, he became a part and parcel of the great religious corporation. Henceforth his conduct, down to the minutest details, was regulated by specific ordinances, even the slightest violation of which was sure to bring down upon him the appropriate punishment. It was the cardinal principle of the Buddhist church that none but the founder of the sect could make laws for the fraternity. Others might explain and expound them, but could not formulate any new laws.

Its Membership.

1. For detailed account of the Buddhist Literature, see infra Chap. VI.

The Buddhist church consisted of the various local Saṅghas or communities of monks. There was no central organisation, co-ordinating the various local communities, and this defect was sought to be remedied by the convocation of general Councils, whenever any occasion arose. In theory, of course, all these local bodies were merely parts of one Universal Church, and thus any member of any local body was *ipso facto* a member of any other local community which he might choose to visit. These local bodies were governed on strictly democratic principles. The general assembly of all the monks resident in a locality constituted the supreme authority, and matters were decided by votes. No meeting of the assembly was legal, unless all the members were either present, or, being absent, formally declared their consent. The assembly, whose constitution and procedure would have probably satisfied the ultra-democrats of the present day, had complete authority over the individual monks and could visit their offences with various degrees of punishment. They carried on the necessary secular business of the monastery through the agency of a number of officers, appointed by them in due form. The nuns formed a distinct community which was practically subordinate to the community of monks. The general tendency of the Buddhist canon law was to assign a distinctly inferior position to the nuns (*Bhikshuṇīs*), as the great Buddha was of opinion, that their admission into the Buddhist chruch was calculated to destroy its purity. Many safeguards were devised to avert this evil, but the essential principles guiding the corporation of monks were equally applicable in the case of the nuns.

Its democratic character.

Special reference may be made to two important practices of the Buddhist Saṅgha. The first was the regular assembly of the local *Bhikshus* on the eighth, fourteenth, and fifteenth days of each fortnight, to recite the Dharma. On one of the last two days, a learned monk recited Pātimokkha, a short treatise containing a list of the crimes and offences which were to be avoided by the Buddhist monks. As the recitation proceeded, and at the end of the description of each class of offences, the question was put to the assembled monks and nuns, whether they were pure with regard to it. Any one, guilty of any of these offences, had to confess his guilt, and his case was treated according to rules and regulations.

The Confession.

The *Vassa* or the *Retreat* during the rainy season was another characteristic institution. It was ordained that for three months during the rainy season every year, the monks should live in a settled residence, and must not leave it except in case of emergency. The rest of the year the monks used to wander all over the country.

The Vassa.

The organisation of the church, sketched above, must have taken centuries to develop, but its groundwork was laid by Buddha himself. Its cheif defect was the absence of any co-ordinating central authority, which resulted in repeated schisms within the chruch. About 100 years after the death of Buddha, the monks of Vaiśālī observed certain practices, which were held by some monks to be unlawful. A general Council of the Buddhists was held, which was attended by monks from different parts of Northern India. The account of this Council is confusing and complicated, but it is certain that a great schism followed, and a new sect was established.

Second General Council.

We know very little of importance about the history of Buddhism, till we come to the reign of the Maurya emperor Aśoka who, as mentioned above (pp. 111 ff.), transformed the comparatively insignificant sect into a world religion. It was during his reign that the third General Council of the Buddhists was held at Pāṭaliputra.

Aśoka.

The grand personality of Aśoka, and the steadfastness of his purpose, backed by the resources of a mighty empire, gave an unparalleled impetus to the religion he patronised. Men were athirst for the knowledge that would relieve them from the woes and miseries of the world. That knowledge was vouchsafed to the noble son of the Śākyas, and the torch that would dispel the gloom of misery and ignorance was lighted at Gayā under the Holy Tree. Then appeared the torch-bearer, more than two hundred years later, who led the holy light from village to village, from city to city, from province to province, from country to country, and from continent to continent. Three continents now drank the nectar of bliss, thanks to the superhuman energy and undying zeal of the Maurya Emperor, and the time was not far distant, when the name of Buddha would be daily uttered in nearly one-third of the households of the entire world. It is not every age, it is not every nation, that can produce a king of this type, and the emperor Asoka still remains without a parallel in the history of the world.

Buddhism which was thus raised to the status of a world religion became, of course, the leading religion in India. The bands of foreign invaders that appeared on Indian soil were attracted by its catholicity, and must have been converted in large numbers. One of these, the Greek king Menander, still lives in the Buddhist tradition, as Rājā Milinda, and an interesting wor on Buddhist doctrines is associated with his name. But, by far the greatest name among the foreign patrons of Buddhism is that of Kanishka. His fame in the Buddhist world is only second to that of Aśoka. Like the Maurya Emperor Aśoka, he convoked a Buddhist Council—the fourth of its kind —to settle the text of the holy scriptures, and his political relation with the Central Asiatic states probably helped the propagation of Buddhism in Central and Northern Asia. Buddhism had already reached China on the one hand, and Burma, Siam, the Malaya Peninsula and islands in the Indian Archipelago on the other. Thus towards the end of the Kushāṇa dynasty, it was the leading religion in the whole of Asia.

Kanishka

Fourth General Council

But the period which saw the greatest expansion of Buddhism also witnessed the most serious dissensions within the Church. In describing the constitution of the Buddhist Church, we have already emphasised the absence of a central co-ordinating authority, which must have favoured the growth of split and dissensions. We have also seen how, about 100 years after the death of Buddha, a great schism followed the council of Vaiśālī. These schisms became more frequent in subsequent periods, and no less than eighteen different sects had grown up by the time of Kanishka. But the greatest split was yet to come. This was the growth of Mahāyānism which permanently divided the Buddhist Church into two hostile camps, as it were.

Growth of Mahāyānism

A detailed treatment of this new development cannot be attempted here, but some of its essential features may be briefly referred to. In the first place, the Mahāyānists introduced a belief in the *Bodhisattvas*, beings "who were in the process of obtaining, but had not yet obtained, Buddha-hood." A number of such Bodhisattvas soon claimed the faith and allegiance of the devotees, while the deification of the Buddha and image-worship with its usual accompaniments, such as elaborate rituals, formulae and charms, took the place of the simple faith in Buddha of the primitive times. Secondly, whereas the old school regarded the salvation of the individual as the goal, the new school had as its objective the salvation of all beings. Thirdly, whereas the Hīnayānists,—as the old sect was now called by way of contrast to the Mahāyānists,—practised self-culture and good deeds as the only way to salvation, the latter began to place more and more reliance on faith in, and devotion to, the various Buddhas and Bodhisattvas as leading to the goal. Fourthly, Sanskrit was adopted as the language of the religious literature, and a new canon was developed, differing from the old in many essential respects. Besides the points noticed above, there were fundamental differences between the two sects as regards metaphysical conceptions, the final goal of religious life, the true nature of Buddha, and sundry other matters.

The development of this sect is ascribed to Nāgārjuna, a contemporary of Kanishka, although it seems to be quite clear that it was already in an incipient state before the Kushāṇa period. In any case, from this time onward, the growing rivalry between the Mahāyāna and the Hīnayāna sects was the leading feature in the history of the Buddhist Church. The Buddha is said to have prophesied that his religion would remain pure for only five hundred years. Within that time limit, Buddhism had attained to the greatest glory, and reached the highest pinnacle of power. But now the tide was turned, and it was visibly going down. The story of its decline and fall is, however, reserved for another chapter.

2. *Jainism.*

The jaina religion is usually regarded as being founded by Vardhamāna Mahāvīra. Accoridng to the orthodox Jaina faith, however, Mahāvīra is only the last of a long series of illustrious teachers, to whom the religious sect owes its origin and development. These teachers, called *Tīrthaṅkaras*, are twenty-four in number. The first twenty-two of them, are, however unknown to history, and reasonable doubts may be entertained regarding the existence of most of them. But the twenty-third *Tīrthaṅkara*, Pārśva, seems to have had a real existence. The outline of his life and activity, so far as it is known to us, has a striking coincidence with that of Gautama Buddha and Mahāvīra. He was brought up amid luxury, left home at the age of thirty, attained the perfect knowledge after nearly three months of

Pārśva.

intense meditation, and spent the remaining life as a religious teacher, till death carried him away at the age of a hundred. This event may be placed in the eighth century B.C.

About 250 years after the death of Pārśva flourished Vardhamāna. He was born in Kuṇḍagrāma, a suburb of Vaiśālī, about the year 540 B.C. His father Siddhārtha was a rich Kshatriya belonging to the Jñātṛika clan, and his mother Triśalā was a sister of Cheṭaka, an eminent Lichchhavi noble of Vaiśālī. He married and had a daughter who was married to Jamāli. On the death of his parents, Vardhamāna left his home, and became an ascetic at the age of thirty. During the next twelve years he wandered about as a naked monk, practising the most rigorous asceticism. At the age of 42, he attained supreme knowledge and final deliverance from the bonds of pleasure and pain. Henceforth he was styled Mahāvīra or the great hero, and Jina or the conqueror. From this latter term his sect came to be known as the *Jainas*,—it being originally designated as the '*Nirgranthas*,' i.e. free from fetters. Mahāvīra spent the remaining thirty years of his life as a religious preacher, and died at Pāwā at the age of 72 (c. 468 B.C.).

Mahāvīra.

It appears that Vardhamāna Mahāvīra accepted, in the main, the religious doctrines of Pārśva, but reformed them by some additions and alterations. Pārśva laid stress on self-control and penance as well as on the four great commandments, viz. (1) Thou shalt tell the truth, (2) Thou shalt possess no property, (3) Thou shalt not injure any living being, and (4) Thou shalt not receive anything which is not freely given. To this Vardhamāna Mahāvīra added another, *viz.* (5) Thou shalt observe chastity. Mahāvīra introduced a further innovation by asking his followers to discard the use of clothes, and move about completely naked.

Mahāvīra was a junior contemporary of Gautama Buddha, and there are striking resemblances in the doctrines of these two teachers. Both started with a frank recognition of the fact that the world is full of sorrows and the salvation of a man means his deliverance from the eternal chain of birth and death; both derived their basic principles from the Upanishads, although they denied the authenticity of the Vedas as an infallible authority, and the efficacy of the rites prescribed in them for the purpose of salvation ; both ignored the idea of God; both laid great

Resemblance and contrast between Buddhism and Jainism.

stress upon a pure and moral life, specially non-injury to animate beings, rather than worship of, and devotion to, God as the means of salvation ; both emphasised the effects of good and bad deeds upon a man's future births and ultimate salvation ; both decried caste ; both preached their religion in the common language of the people, and lastly, both encouraged the idea of giving up the world, and organised a church of monks and nuns. Indeed the resemblance was so great that many scholars believed that Jainism was merely a branch of Buddhism. This notion is, however, erroneous, for apart from the fact that we can trace distinct historic origins of the two, they differ in fundamental conceptions about salvation and certain other matters which cannot be explained away as later additions. The Jaina conception of soul, for example, is radically different from the Buddhist. Again, Jainism laid great stress upon asceticism and practised it in a very rigorous manner, whereas Buddha decried it, and asked his disciples to follow the middle path between a life of ease and luxury on the one hand, and rigorous asceticism on the other. Besides, Buddha denounced the practice of going out naked, and the Jaina attitude of non-injury to animals was carried to far greater excesses than was ever contemplated by Buddhism. Further, Jainism did not oppose the caste system and was more accommodating to Hinduism than Buddhism.

There can thus be no doubt that Gautama and Mahāvīra were founders of independent religious sects. Both of them were products of the prevailing spirit of the time, and no wonder that both travelled the same way, up to a certain distance, in their search after truth. There was, however, a great deal of rivalry between the two sects, even during the lifetime of their founders, and Buddha condemned in no uncertain terms certain aspects of the rival religion. The two religious teachers lived and preached their religion in the same region, and recruited their disciples from the same class of people. So far as can be judged at present, both the religious sects had equal footing in the country at the time when their founders died, within a few years of each other. But it is in their later developments that the two sects differ widely ; for while, within five hundred years, Buddhism became a world religion, and was destined ere long to count nearly a third of the entire human race as its votaries. Jainism had never spread beyond the boundaries of India. On the other hand, while Buddhism practically vainshed from the land of its birth more than five hundred years ago, Jainism is still a living force in India, and has got a strong hold upon a large and influential section of the people.

At first Jainism seems to have made greater progress than Buddhism, and before the end of the fourth century B.C. it had spread to Southern India. The growing importance of the sect is probably due to a large extent to the patronage of Chandragupta Maurya. According to Jaina tradition, Chandragupta was not only a convert to Jaina religion, but had actually abdicated the throne and died as a Jaina *Bhikshu* in Southern India.

History of Jainism.

The genuineness of this story has been doubted, but the details that gathered round it are full of interest for the Jaina history. It is said that about two hundred years after the death of Mahāvīra, a terrible famine broke out in Magadha. At that time Chandragupta Maurya was the king, and the *Thera* Bhadrabāhu was the chief of the Jaina community. These two, with a crowd of followers, went to Karṇāṭa, leaving Sthūlabhadra in charge of the Jainas that remained in Magadha. Now Sthūlabhadra was the last man who knew all the 14 *Pūrvas* (*i.e.* old texts) in which the teachings of Mahāvīra were collected. He had learnt them all from Bhadrabāhu, but was forbidden to teach the last four to his successors. In view of the danger that threatened the loss of sacred scriptures, he convoked a council at Pāṭaliputra, in which the first 10 *Pūrvas* were re-arranged in 12 *Aṅgas*. The present scripture of the Jainas is merely a re-arrangement of the first 11 *Aṅgas* made in Valabhī in the 5th century A.D., the 12th *Aṅga* having already been lost by that time.

The Great Schism.

When the followers of Bhadrabāhu returned to Magadha, there arose a great dissension. The Jainas as a rule went naked, but the Jainas of Magadha had begun to put on white robes. This was objected to by the Jainas who returned from South India, as they held complete nudity to be an essential part of the teachings of Mahāvīra. Reconciliation was found to be impossible, and thus arose the two sects, the Śvetāmbaras (*i.e.* those who put on white robes) and the Digambaras (*i.e.* those who were stark naked), into which the Jaina Community is still divided. The unfortunate split was followed by other consequences. The Digambaras refused to accept the 12 Aṅgas as authentic. According to the tradition of the Digambara sect, the last man who knew all the *Aṅgas* died about 436 years after the death of Mahāvīra, and the knowledge of the *Aṅgas* was completely lost about 250 years later.

In spite of this internal dissension, the Jaina religion rapidly spread all over the country. It made headway also in South India, and ere long it became one of the important all-India religions.

Besides Buddhism and Jainism, there were other heterodox religious sects, like the Ājīvikas, which exercised considerable influence for the time being, but ultimately disappeared without leaving behind any trace whatsoever.

3. *Bhāgavatism*[1]

Between the heterodox religions like Buddhism and Jainism in the one extreme, and the orthodox Vedic religion in the other, there grew up certain religious systems which were destined to attain to considerable power at no distant date. These religious sects had no faith in the machanical system of worship prescribed in the Vedas. But while they agreed with Buddhism and Jainism to a large extent in this respect, the differences between them were very great. Buddhism and Jainism "discarded, or passed over in silence, the doctrine of the existence even of God, and laid down self-abnegation and a course of strict moral conduct as the way to salvation." The new theistic religions, however, centred round the idea of a supreme God conceived as Vishṇu, Śiva, Śakti or some other form. Salvation was possible through His Grace (*prasāda*) alone, and this could be attained only by *bhakti* i.e. intense love and devotion leading to complete surrender of self to the personal God.

The chief representatives of this new system were Bhāgavatism (known in later times as Vaishṇavism) and Śaivism. Bhāgavatism 'owed its orgin to the stream of thought which began with the Upanishads, and culminated, in the east, in Buddhism and Jainism.' It arose about the same time in the west among the Śātvatas, a branch of the Yādavas, who settled in the Mathurā region. Originally, it merely laid stress upon the idea of a supreme God, God of gods, called Hari, and emphasised the necessity of worshipping Him with devotion, in preference to older methods of sacrifices and austerities. It did not, of course,

1. This and the following section are mainly based on Dr. Bhardarkar's '*Vaishnavism, Saivism* etc'. and the quotations in the text, unless otherwise stated, are from this book.

altogether do away with either sacrifice or the Vedic literature which prescribed the same, but regarded them as of minor importance, and omitted the salughter of animals, which formed the principal feature of the Brāhmaṇical religion. The Sātvatas thus made "an attempt to introduce a religious reform on more conservative principles than Buddhism and Jainism did. The repudiation of the slaughter of animals, and the inefficacy of sacrificial worship and austerities are common to this religious reform with Buddhism. But that the supreme Lord Hari is to be worshipped with devotion, and that the words of the Āraṇyakas are not to be rejected are doctrines which are peculiar to it."

The religious reform received a strong impetus from Vāsudeva Kṛishṇa, son of Devakī, of the Vṛishṇi race, which was probably another name of the Śātvatas. He gave a definite shape to the reformed doctrine by promulgating its philosophical teachings in the *Bhagavadgītā*. This led to the regular growth of an independent sect, and ere long Vāsudeva was looked upon as the supreme deity, 'the supreme soul, the internal soul of all souls.'

Kṛishṇa

A passage in the *Chhāndogya Upanishad* refers to sage Kṛishṇa, son of Devakī, as a disciple of Ṛishi (ascetic) Ghora, and gives us some insight into the doctrines taught by the latter. He preaches such moral virtues as *dāna* (charity), *ārjava* (piety), *ahiṁsā* (non-injury), and *satya-vachana* (truthfulness), lays stress on *tapas* (meditation or asceticism), and deprecates *yojña* (sacrifice). As all these are also emphasised by Kṛishṇa in the *Gītā*,[1] he has been identified with the disciple of Ghora, and the beginnings of Bhāgavatism have been traced to the teachings of the latter.

Reference should be made to the doctrine according to which the four Vyūhas (phases of conditioned spirit) ultimately emanated from Vāsudeva, viz. Saṅkarshaṇa, Pradyumna, Aniruddha, and the Mahābhūtas (Elements). The first three of these are well-known members of the Vrishṇi family and there can be hardly any doubt that at first they, along with another, Sāmba, shared the divine honours with Vāsudeva, who was undoubtedly the chief figure and ultimately superseded the rest

In its ultimate form, as developed in the *Bhagavadgītā*, Bhāgavatism stood out prominently for two things. It counter-

1. The shorter form of *Bhagavadgītā*.

acted tendencies 'to look upon ascetic life as a *sine qua non* of religious elevation' by emphasising the supreme importance of doing one's worldly duties according to one's status in society. Secondly, it sought to turn men's minds away from 'dry, moral discourses, and thoughts of moral exaltation, unassociated with a theistic faith. Theistic ideas were, no doubt, scattered in the Upanishads, but it was the *Bhagavadgītā* which worked it up into a system of redemption, capable of being easily grasped.'

Gītā.

The new religious ideas seem at first to have been confined to the Mathurā District. The Greek ambassador Megasthenes notices that 'Herakles is held in special honour by the Sourasenoi, an Indian tribe, who possess two large cities, Methora and Cleisobora.' Thus even in the fourth, or the beginning of the third century B.C., Herakles, who is undoubtedly the same as Vāsudeva-Kṛishṇa, was sepcially worshipped by the Śūrasenas of Mathurā, through whose territory flowed the river Yamunā.

Original home.

Megasthenes also tells us a somewhat confused story associating Herakles and the Pāṇḍavas with the Pāṇḍya country in the far south (p. 136). This, as well as the name of its capital city Madurā, undoubtedly derived from Mathurā, has led some scholars to believe that Bhāgavatism penetrated into the southern extremity of India as early as the fourth century B.C.

But by the second century B.C., the new religion had certainly spread far beyond the confines of Mathurā. Inscriptions, recording the worship of Vāsudeva, are found in Mahārāshṭra, Rājputāna, and Central India. We learn from one of these, that a Greek ambassador of king Antialcidas, called Heliodora (Heliodorus), an inhabitant of Takshaśilā, styled himself a Bhāgavata, and erected a Garuḍadhavja (a pillar with an image of Garuḍa at the top), in honour of Vāsudeva, the God of gods, at Besnagar, the site of ancient Vidiśā, in the Gwalior State. It is thus apparent that Vaishṇavism, like Buddhism, made converts of the foreigners, and was distinguished enough in the second century B.C. to attract the most civilised nation among them. A Syrian leged further informs us that the cult of Kṛishṇa worship was prevalent in Armenia as early as the second century B.C. The popularity of the new cult about the same time is sufficiently demonstrated by the fact, that already the chief legendary exploits of Vāsudeva-Kṛishṇa formed the subject

Extension of influence.

of dramatic representations. From the second century B.C. the progress of the religion continued unabated, and epigraphic evidence proves that by the end of the period under review, it had gained a strong footing in South India, beyond the Kṛishṇā river.

The development of the local sect of Mathurā into what promised to be an all-India religion, in the second century B.C., seems to be due, at least partially, to an event of far-reaching importance. This was the adoption of the new sect into the fold of orthodox Brāhmaṇism. The reconciliation between the two is clearly demonstrated by the fact, that Vāsudeva-Kṛishṇa was successively indentified with two prominent Vedic gods, viz. (1) Vishṇu, originally a satellite of the Sun, but recognised to be a great god in the later Vedic period, and (2) Nārāyaṇa, probably a deified sage, who however appears later as Hari and the deity eternal, supreme, and lord. That this identification was completed before the second century B.C. is evidenced by the dedication of Garuḍadhvaja by Heliodorus, in honour of Vāsudeva, the God of gods, for Garuḍa was the recognised vehicle of Nārāyaṇa-Vishṇu, these two deities being ultimately regarded as one.

Reconciliation with Brāhmaṇical religion.

Why or how this amalgamation was brought about, it is difficult to say. The advance might have been made by the Brāhmaṇas themselves, as a protection against Buddhism, which grew predominant under the patronage of Aśoka and threatened utter ruin to them. The Bhāgavatas, on the other hand, probably thought it politic to attach to themselves the honour and prestige due to an old and time-honoured name. Whatever might be the reason, it must have cost the Brāhmaṇas a bitter pang. The memorable scene in the *Mahābhārata*, in which Śiśupāla poured forth the venom of his heart against Bhīshma for honouring Kṛishṇa as the most 'worshipful,' seems to be a reminiscence of the spirit of the die-hards, who refused to acknowledge the divine character of one who was not Brāhmaṇa by birth.

The reconciliation of Bhāgavatism with orthodox Brāhmaṇism not only assured a permanent position to the former, but gave an altogether new turn to the latter. Henceforth Bhāgavatism, or as it may now be called by its more popular name, Vaishṇavism, formed, with Śaivism, the main plank of the orthodox religion in its contest with Buddhism. It was mainly due to its influence that the worship of images, unknown in the Vedic period, gradually dominated the Brahmanical religion. The sacrificial ceremonies prescribed in the Vedas no doubt survived, but gradually receded into the background.

4. *Śaivism.*

The origin of Śaivism may be traced to the conception of Rudra in the Ṛigveda. Rudra represented the malignant and destructive phenomena in nature, which destroyed the cattle and caused diseases to the people. His wrath was sought to be appeased by offerings and prayers, a specimen of which is given below.

Rudra in Vedic literature.

"O Rudra, harm not either great or small of us, harm not the growing boy, harm not the full-grown man.

"Slay not a sire among us, slay no mother here, and to our own dear bodies, Rudra, do no harm.

"Harm us not, Rudra, in our seed and progeny, harm us not in the living, nor in cows or steeds.

"Slay not our heroes in the fury of thy wrath. Bringing oblations evermore we call to thee." (Ṛigveda I, 114).

'Rudra, however, occupies a minor position in the Ṛigveda,' though, like many other gods, he is occasionally described as possessing supreme power. It has been suggested that he represents the storm, 'not the storm pure and simple, but rather its baleful side, in the destructive agency of lightning.'

The conception of Rudra is further developed in the Yajurveda, in the famous Śatarudriya, where his benevolent characteristics are emphasised in addition to the malevolent ones. 'When his wrathful nature is thoroughly appeased he becomes Śambhu or benignant, Śaṅkara or beneficent, and Śiva or auspicious.' These three names, which occur at the end of the Śātarudriya, were destined to become famous at no distant date.

In the Atharvaveda, Rudra is looked upon as a supreme God, and the furthest point is reached when *Śvetāśvatara* Upanishad substitutes this active personal God in the place of the impersonal Brahman of the Upanishads. It asserts that "there is only Rudra—and they do not recognise another —who rules these worlds by his ruling powers, who is the inmost soul of all men, and creating all beings, protects them." "When there was simple darkness and no day or light, no entity or nonentity, Śiva alone existed. He was the one unchangeable thing, and he was the bright light of the sun, and from him sprang all intelligence. His form is invisible. Nobody sees him with the eye. Those who see him, dwelling in the heart, by the heart and the internal consciousness, become immortal." Lastly "Śiva, the God, the creator and destroyer, is said to be knowable by *Bhāva* (faith, love, or the pure heart)." It may be added that Umā Haimavatī, the spouse of Śiva, is also eulogised as a supreme deity in the *Kena* Upanishad. Saivism, as a distinct cult, therefore goes back to a very early period.

The supreme God Rudra-Śiva was at first the object of worship, not of a particular sect, but of the Aryans in general all over India, and this character it has retained down to the present day, in spite of the rise of innumerable Śaiva sects.

The existence of the Śaiva sects may be traced as early as the second century B.C. It is probable that a definite Śaiva system or school was established, in imitation of the Bhāgavata sect, by a person, called variously Lakulin, Lakuṭin, Lakulīsa and Nakulīśa. The Śaiva sects were at first generally known as Lākula, Pāśupata, or Māheśvara after the name of their God or historical founder. Before the end of the period under review, however, four important schools arose, viz. Pāśupata, Śaiva, Kāpālika and Kālāmukha. The main activity of these sects falls into the next period, and will be dealt with in another chapter.

The Śaiva sects.

The Śaivas, like the Buddhists and the Bhāgavatas, attracted foreigners to their creed. Wema Kadphises, the Kushāṇa conqueror of India, adopted the new religion, and the 'reverse' of his coins depicts the figure of Śiva, with a long trident, leaning on Nandī or bull behind him.

It must be noted here, that the image of Śiva, as an object of worship, was soon replaced by Liṅga or Phallus. Many eminent scholars think that this element of phallic worship and probably also the whole idea of Śiva as a God, were borrowed by the Aryans from the Sindhu Valley civilization (p. 25). But the Liṅga cult obtained a wide currency, and almost completely ousted the likness of Śiva as an object of veneration.

In addition to Vaishṇavism and Śaivism, other minor religious sects, of more or less the same general character flourished during the period under review. These were the followers of Śakti, Gaṇapati, Skanda or Kārttikeya, Brahmā, and Sūrya. Śakti was the wife of Śiva, while Gaṇapati and Kārttikeya, at first leaders of Gaṇas or hosts of Rudra-Śiva,

Minor religious Systems.

came to be regarded as his sons. Sūrya or the Sun was one of the principal deities in the Vedic age.

Brahmā, who later formed with Vishṇu and Śiva the famous Trinity, is not a Vedic God. He was derived from Prajāpati who occupied a very high position as the creator of gods in the Brāhmaṇas, and was identified with Brahman, the impersonal absolute of the Upanishads. From this the theists derived the name Brahmā.

As to the Vedic gods other than those mentioned above, some were still remembered, though occupying a distinctly inferior position, while others almost completely disappeared.

In order to complete the picture of religious condition, it is necessary to add that primitive belief in the spirits of the earth and mountains, in Yakshas, Gandharvas, and Nāgas, and worship of all these, as well as of animals like elephant, horse, cow, dog and crow, still retained a hold on the popular mind.

CHAPTER VI

Literature

1. *The Buddhist Literature.*

The Buddhist sacred literature was composed in several languages, viz. Pāli, a literary language based upon a provincial dialect of India, Sanskrit, and several other dialects. Of these we possess a complete text of the Pāli version alone, and only small fragments of the other versions have survived in original or Tibetan and Chinese translation.

As already mentioned, the Pāli canon of the Buddhists is divided into three classes, viz. (1) the Vinaya-piṭaka, (2) the Sutta-piṭaka, and (3) the Abhidhamma-piṭaka, dealing respectively with the disciplinary rules and regulations, religious doctrines, and philosophical principles.

The Pāli canon.

1. The Vinaya-piṭaka comprises the following texts :

   (1) The Suttavibhaṅga.

   (2) The Khandhakās.

   (3) The Parivāra, or Parivārapāṭha.

The Suttavibhaṅga, as the name implies, is the explanation (*vibhaṅga*) of the Sutta. The Suttas which it explains consist of what is known as Pātimokkha rules, *i.e.* a list of 227 different kinds of offences and the means of atoning for them. This list, which may be regarded as the nucleus of the Vinaya, was recited every new and full moon day before a gathering of monks and nuns, every individual member of which had to confess if he or she was guilty of one or more of them, and expiate the sin by appropriate punishment.

The Khandhakās are divided into two sections, the Mahāvagga and the Chullavagga, and lay down minute rules and regulations regarding such matters as admission into the Order, the mode of spending monsoon in a fixed retreat, the various ceremonies to be performed at fixed periods, probations and penances, as well as rules for foot-wear, seats, vehicles, dress, medicaments, houses, beddings, furniture etc., to be used by monks and nuns. These rules, which may be said, without much exaggeration, to have covered even the most insignificant details in the daily life of a monk or a nun, are generally prefaced by a short account of the occasion on which they were laid down by the Buddha. Incidentally, therefore, they contain many stories and legends about the life of Buddha, and throw a flood of light on the life and manners of the day.

The Parivāra, the last book of the Vinaya, is a sort of resume and index of the preceding books.

II. The Sutta-piṭaka forms the most important part of the Buddhist literature, and is divided into five Nikāyas or compilations, *viz.* (1) Dīgha-nikāya, (2) Majjhima-nikāya, (3) Saṁyutta-nikāya, (4) Aṅguttara-nikāya, and (5) Khuddaka-nikāya.

(1). The Dīgha-nikāya, or the compilation of the long (*dīgha*=Skt. *dīrgha*) *Suttas*, consists of 34 long *Suttas*, each dealing with one or more aspects of the Buddhist creed. The different *Suttas* have no connection with one another, and each of them is complete in itself. Each *Sutta* contains a short preface, describing the occasion on which Gautama Buddha delivered it, and some of the *Suttas* are put in the form of a Socratic dialogue between Gautama Buddha and an unbeliever. Thus in the Tevijja Sutta, the Brāhmaṇa Vāsishṭha (Vāseṭṭha) is forced to admit, after a severe cross-examination, that not the knowledge of the Vedas, but the Buddhist moral principles alone can lead to a realisation of the absolute Brahman.

Among other important topics, dealt with in this *Nikāya*, may be mentioned the origin of the universe, the artificiality of the caste system, the way to union with God, rebirths, *nirvāṇa*, self-mastery, self-concentration, asceticism, miracles, soul-theory, heretical doctrines, the previous Buddhas, the causes of things, and the true nature of a Brāhmaṇa. One of the most important *Suttas* in this series, the Mahāparinibbāna-Sutta, contains a very detailed and interesting account of the last days of Buddha, and his death and funeral ceremonies.

(2). The Majjhima-nikāya, or the compilation of the medium (*majjhima*—Skt. *madhyama*) *Suttas*, consists of 152 *Suttas*. These are shorter than the *Suttas* in the Dīgha-nikāya, but deal mostly with the same kind of topics. They contain discourses and dialogues, but a good many of them are *ākhyānas* or stories, narrated in prose and verse, and ending with a moral lesson.

(3-4) The Saṁyutta-nikāya, or the compilation of the joined or connected (*Saṁyutta*=Skt. *saṁyukta*) *Suttas*, consists of fifty-six groups of *Suttas*, divided in five great sections. The Aṅguttara-nikāya, or the compilation of *Suttas* arranged in an ascending numerical series (*aṅguttara*=Skt. *Aṅgottara*), consists of more than 2300 *Suttas* arranged in eleven sections in such a way, that "all the classes containing only one thing are treated of in the first book, all the dyads in the second, all the triads in the third, and so on." For example, the third section deals with the 'threefold way to the suppression of selfishness,' the 'three causes for the rise of *Kamma* and their extinction,' the 'threefold restraint' etc.; the fourth section deals with the 'four happy states, the four elements of popularity, four modes of producing a superabundance of merit, etc.'

The third and the fourth *Nikāyas* primarily deal with the same topics as the first two. But whereas owing to the conversational form in the latter, the doctrinal matters are necessarily treated in a discursive way, the same or allied topics being dealt with in many different passages, these are arranged in the third and the fourth *Nikāyas* with reference to their mutual relations. Thus in order to ascertain what Buddhism teaches on a particular subject, one has to ransack the whole of the first two *Nikāyas*, but the different points of view are actually brought together in the third and the fourth.

(5). The name of the last part of the Suttapiṭaka, Khuddaka nikāya or compilation of the small (*Khuddaka*=Skt. *Kshudraka*) *Suttas*, is misleading. It really consists of a large number of miscellaneous works, and some of them are very long indeed. Besides, it is quite apparent, that the different books comprised in this *Nikāya* were composed at different times, and did not originally form part of a single collection. These books are:—

1. The Khuddaka-pāṭha—A collection of nine short texts (*mantras*) to be first learnt during the noviciate.

2. The Dhammapada—One of the best and most well-known works in the Buddhist literature. It contains a fine exposition of the ethical teachings of Buddhism in 423 verses.

3. The Udāna—*lit.* an enthusiastic and joyous utterance. It is divided into eight sections of ten *suttas* each. Each *sutta* briefly narrates an event in Buddha's life, and ends with a maxim which Buddha delivered on the occasion.

4. The Itivuttaka ('Thus said the Buddha'). It consists of 112 short *suttas* in prose and verse, and expounds the teachings of Buddha without any narrative. As the title indicates, it purports to be actual reproductions of the sayings of Buddha.

5. The Suttanipāta. It is a collection of poetical *suttas* in five sections. Many of these are as old as the time of Buddha, and occur in other canonical texts. It is therefore of great importance for a knowledge of primitive Buddhism.

6—7. The Vimāna-vatthu and the Petavatthu. These describe the joys or sorrows which a man, doing good or bad deeds here below, respectively enjoy or suffer after death in heaven or hell. These two books belong to the latest strata of the Pāli canon.

8—9. The Thera-gāthā and the Therī-gāthā. These are collections of poems (*gāthā*) ascribed to various monks (*thera*) and nuns (*therī*). They are fine lyrics and, in the opinion of some critics, worthy of being ranked with those of Kālidāsa and Amaru.

10. The Jātakas. According to the Buddhist Mahāyāna doctrine, one can attain the status of a Buddha only by means of the accumulated merits of good deeds performed in countless births. Even the great Gautama Buddha had to pass through 84,000 previous existences before he could become a Buddha. The Jātakas contain more than 500 stories of such previous births of Gautama Buddha. Many of these stories are fairly old, some even possibly existing before the time of Gautama Buddha, and the Buddhists adopted them with slight alterations for the purpose of inculcating moral lessons in the shape of a previous-birth-story of Gautama Buddha. As these stories deal with different aspects of common life, they furnish very valuable materials for the study of economic conditions and social manners and customs in ancient India.

These stories are narrated in prose and verse. But it is only the verse which forms part of the canon, the prose portion merely supplying, by way of commentary, the details of the story briefly alluded to in the verses. As a matter of fact, however, some of the verses are quite unintelligible without the accompanying story in prose. The prose commentary was translated into the Siṁhalese language, and again re-translated in Pāli in the 5th century A.D. This Pāli text, with the original verses (*gātthās*), forms the present Jātaka-texts.

11. The Niddesa or Mahāniddesa. It is the title of a commentary to two sections of the Sutta-nipāta (No. 5). The fact that this commentary was included in the canon shows the relative antiquity of its composition.

12. The Paṭisambhidāmagga. It is really a philosophical work, and, properly speaking, belongs to Abhidhamma-piṭaka

13. The Apadāna. It is a collection of stories of good and virtuous deeds performed by the eminent Arhats (Buddhist Saints), both male and female, in their previous births. It is thus a counterpart of the Jātakas.

14. The Buddhavaṁsa. It consists of poetic legends of the 24 Buddhas who preceded Gautama Buddha during the last 12 *Kalpas*.

15. Chariyā-piṭaka, a collection of 35 Jātakas in verse, showing how Gautama Buddha possessed the ten *pāramitās* (perfections) in his previous births.

III. The Abhidhamma-piṭaka.

The term Abhidhamma is usually rendered as 'higher religion' or 'metaphysics,' but, as Rhys Davids pointed out long ago, there is very little of metaphysics in the Abhidhamma-piṭaka. As regards its philosophy, it is of the same character as that dealt with in the Sutta-piṭaka, so much so, that even the learned Mrs. Rhys Davids once remarked, that our knowledge of Buddhist philosophy would remain undiminished, even if the entire Abhidhamma-piṭaka were non-existent. Indeed the subjects dealt with in the Sutta-piṭaka and Abhidhamma are the same, only the latter deals with them in a more scholastic fashion, adding definition, classification, categories etc. The Abhidhamma is written mostly in the form of questions and answers, and its subject-matter is mainly derived from the Sutta- and the Vinaya-piṭaka. The Abhidhamma-piṭaka consists of seven books, of which the Kathāvattu, attributed to Tissa Moggaliputta, is the most important. It deals with such questions as follow: "Is there a soul? Can an Arhat lose his Arhatship ? Are there two kinds of Nirvāṇa? Can the father of a family become an Arhat?" All these questions are answered in the negative.

A few words must be said about the origin and antiquity of the Piṭakas. No one believes that these texts, attributed to Buddha, really contain only words uttered by him. Some, probably many, of Buddha's words and doctrines were, no doubt, current among his disciples, and incorporated into the Piṭakas, but the different texts, as we have them now, and their existing arrangement and classification, must have been the work of a long period of time, and separated, in some cases at least, by an interval of one or two centuries from the time when Gautama Buddha lived and preached.

Origin of the Pāli canon.

The great bulk of the Vinaya-piṭaka must have been composed before 350 B.C., and the same thing may probably be said of the first four Nikāyas of the Sutta-piṭaka. The miscellaneous works included in the Khuddaka-nikāya must have been composed at different periods. The loose character of this

Nikāya and its late origin are further demonstrated by the fact, that the Burmese version includes four texts which are not regarded as canonical in Ceylon, while seven texts are wanting in the Siamese edition of the Piṭaka. The bulk of the Khuddaka-nikāya, however, certainly existed in the third century B.C. As regards the Abhidhamma-piṭaka, its latest book, the Kathāvatthu, was composed during the reign of Aśoka, in the third century B. C.

Non-canonical Buddhist Literature.

In addition to the canonical works, there are other Buddhist books written in Pāli. One of the most famous is the *Milinda-Pañha*, which explains the Buddhist doctrines in the form of a dialogue between King Milinda and a Buddhist priest Nāgasena. King Milinda is no other than the Graeco-Bactrain king Menander, referred to above (p. 120), and the book was probably composed in North-Western India, about the first or second century A.D.

Commentaries.

The necessity of explaining the canonical texts gave rise to a vast literature by way of commentaries . These commentaries not merely explained the text by adding critical notes, but also systematically arranged the subject matter, and added legends and other extraneous matters. The commentators also attempted to reconstruct the life of Buddha from the scattered notices in the Piṭakas, and the result was the Nidānakathā. It relates the story of Buddha, from the day when he was born as Sumedha in the time of Dīpaṅkara Buddha, up to the grant of Jetavana to the Buddhist Order by the merchant Anāthapiṇḍika.

The greatest commentator of the Pāli canon was Buddhaghosha, who probably flourished in Ceylon during the reign of Mahānāma (c. 413 A.D.). He lived in the Mahāvihāra of Anurādhapura, and studied the Siṁhalese 'Aṭṭhakathā' or commentary. He is the author of Visuddhimagga, the first systematic and philosophic treatise on Buddhist doctrines, and wrote learned commentaries on almost all the books of the Pāli Tripiṭaka. It is, however, doubtful whether Buddhaghosha was the author of the famous commentaries on the Dhammapada and the Jātakas.

To complete the sketch of the non-canonical Buddhist literature, reference must be made to the two famous historical works of Ceylon, *viz.*, Dīpavaṁsa and Mahāvaṁsa. The

Dīpavaṁsa (the history of the island of Ceylon) was composed in the fourth or the beginning of the fifth century A.D., and was mainly based on the Siṁhalese Aṭṭhakathā or commentary. A far more successful effort to write .an historical epic of Ceylon is, however, to be found in the Mahāvaṁsa, probably the work of a poet Mahānāma, who flourished in the last quarter of the fifth century A.D. Many other Pāli works were composed in Ceylon, but they need not be referred to in detail.

Dīpavaṁsa and Mahāvaṁsa.

The Pāli literature, of which a short account has been given above, forms, however, the canon of only one class of Buddhists, called the Theravādins. Other sects had one or more different canons, written partly in Sanskrit, and partly in a Middle-Indian dialect, which is allied to Sanskrit, and may be called 'Mixed-Sanskrit.' This Sanskrit canon belongs mainly, though not exclusively, to the Mahāyāna school. The Sarvāstivādins of the Hīnayāna school, also, had a Sanskrit canon. This canon contained many voluminous works, but some of them have been recovered only in parts—a good many fragments being obtained in course of recent excavations in East Turkestan,—while others exist only in Tibetan and Chinese translations. It is thus impossible to give a detailed description of this canon, but it seems that both the Pāli and the Sanskrit canon originated from a common source, probably the lost Māgadhi canon. The canonical texts of the Mūlasarvāstivādins were so long known only from the Chinese and Tibetan translations, but the recent discovery of manuscripts at Gilgit has brought to light a large part of the original Sanskrit Vinaya texts. They show considerable agreement with, as sell as difference from the Pāli canon. The Vinaya of this canon corresponds in arrangement and substance to the Pāli Vinaya, and the Āgamas correspond to the Nikāyas; the Dīrghāgama, the Madhyamāgama, the Ekottarāgama, and the Saṁyuktāgama corresponding respectively to the Dīgha-, Majjhima-, Aṅguttara-, and Saṁyutta-nikāyas. There is also a Kshudrakāgama, but we do not know whether it contained all the works belonging to the Khuddaka-nikāya. The Sanskrit canon, however, contains Sūtranipāta, Udāna, Dharmapada, Sthaviragāthā, Vimānavastu and Buddhavaṁśa, corresponding, respectively, to Suttanipāta, Udāna, Dhammapada, Theragāthā, Vimānavatthu and Buddhavaṁsa. There are also seven Abhi-

The Sanskrit canon.

dharma books translated into Chinese, but it is doubtful whether they originated from the old canon.

All the Buddhist sects, however, did not possess a more or less complete canon like the Pāli Piṭaka of the Theravādins, or the Sanskrit canon of the Sarvāstivādins. But every sect had one or more treatises, which it looked upon as specially scared, and, for the rest, it appropriated select texts from an existing canon. One of the most famous of those special treatises is Mahāvastu, a book belonging to the Vinaya-piṭaka of the Lokottaravādins, a subdivision of the Mahāsāṁghikas, the sect which first broke off from the orthodox church after the council of Vaiśālī. But although classed as Vinaya, Mahāvastu contains hardly anything about the disciplinary rules of the monks. It merely contains legends about Bodhisattva and Buddha, which substantially agree with those found in the Pāli Piṭaka. It is thus a source of many Jātaka stories and other narratives found in the Buddhist literature. But although Mahāvastu belongs to the Hīnayāna school, some of its doctrines make a very near approach to the Mahāyāna system, and some of its hymns to Buddha are akin to the Purāṇic *stotras* addressed to Śiva or Vishṇu.

Mahāvastu.

We now come to the rich Sanskrit literature of the Mahāyāna school. One of the earliest texts of this school, which has obtained wide celebrity in the Buddhist world, is Lalitavistara, an embellished story of the life of Buddha. The work originally belonged to the Hīnayāna school, but was later definitely classed as Vaipulyasūtra or the Mahāyānasūtra.

These Vaipulyasūtras may be looked upon as the canonical books of the Mahāyānists. The latter, however, can hardly be said to possess a canon in the strict sense of the word, for these books originated at different times, and among different sects, though at present they are all looked upon with great reverence in Nepal. The Vaipulyasūtras consist of the following:—

The Vaipulya-sūtra.

1. Ashṭasāhasrikā Prajñāpāramitā, 2. Saddharmapuṇḍarīka, 3. Lalitavistara, 4. Laṅkāvatāra or Saddharmalaṅkāvatāra, 5. Suvarṇaprabhāsa, 6. Gaṇḍavyūha, 7. Tathāgataguhyaka or Tathāgataguṇajñāna, 8. Samādhirāja, and 9. Daśabhūmīśvāra.

The most important of these works is Saddharmapuṇḍarīka 'Lotus of good religion", a typical Mahāyāna work containing all the characteristic features of that school. The conception of a human Śākyamuni is here replaced by that of Buddha, God of gods, the self-created, and the creator of the whole world. This work was translated in Chinese between 265 and 316 A.D. and must therefore have been composed at least as early as the second century A.D.

The most important of the philosophical works of the Mahāyāna school is the Prajñāpāramitā. The word 'pāramitā' means the highest (*parama*) acquisition of certain virtues necessary to attain the state of Buddha. There were originally six of them (to which four more were added later) viz. charity (*dāna*), good conduct (*śīla*), forbearance (*kshānti*), strength (*vīrya*), meditation (*dhyāna*) and the true knowledge (*prajñā*). The Prajñāpāramitā texts deal with all these virtues, but more particularly with the last, the *prajñā,* which however, consists mainly in the realisation of 'Śūnyavāda' or 'nothingness of the world.' The book exists in four redactions of 100,000, 25,000, 10,000 and 8,000 ślokas, these being called respectively Śata-, Pañchaviṁśati-Daśa-, and Ashṭa-sāhasrikā Prajñāpāramitā.

The Mahāyāna literature also possesses a rich store of legends. The best known collections of these legends, called *avadānas*, are Avadānaśataka and Divyāvadāna, which were translated in Chinese in the third century A.D., and the Avadānakalpalatā of Kshemendra, a poet of Kāshmir, who flourished in the eleventh century A.D.

Reference may now be made to some of the greatest writers associated with the Buddhist Sanskrit Literature. The most famous of these is Aśvaghosha. He was a contemporary of Kanishka, and probably an inhabitant of Ayodhyā. A French savant has referred to him in the following enthusiastic strain. "He stands at the starting point of all the great currents that renewed and transformed India towards the beginning of the Christian era. Poet, musician, preacher, moralist, philosopher, playwright, tale-teller, he is an inventor in all these arts, and excels in all; in his richness and variety he recalls Milton, Goethe, Kant and Voltaire."[1]

Aśvaghosha.

The most important of Aśvaghosha's works is '*Buddhacharita*', a complete life of Buddha written in the form of Mahā-Kāvya. This great 'Buddha-epic' has been ranked along with the works of Vālmīki and Kālidāsa. Another work *Saundarā-*

[1] S. Lévi, in *Calcutta Review*, September, 1923. p. 377.

nanda-Kāvya is an excellent specimen of the *Kāvya* style. It, too, deals with Buddha's life, but dwells more particularly on those episodes which are either briefly related or altogether omitted in the *Buddha-charita*. The third great work of Aśvaghosha is the *Sūtrālaṁkāra*, a collection of legends written in prose and verse. Another work attributed to Aśvaghosha is *Vajrasūchī'* in which the Brāhmaṇical caste-system is decried, mainly by reference to or quotations from Brāhmaṇical works. Aśvaghosha's fame as a teacher of Mahāyānism is based upon a philosophical work called '*Mahāyānaśraddhotpāda*' which is used even to-day as the principal treatise in the schools and monasteries of Japan. A unique manuscript of a dramatic poem of Aśvaghosha, called '*Śāriputraprakaraṇa*', has been discovered in Central Asia. Other works are also attributed to Aśvaghosha but there are doubts about their true authorship.

Nāgārjuna.

Next to Aśvaghosha stands Nāgārjuna. He is said to be the author of the '*Śatasāhasrikā Prajñā-pāramitā*,' one of the earliest Mahāyāna-sūtras. He is also the author of *Mādhyamikasūtras*, and founder of the Mādhyamika school which teaches that the whole of the phenomenal world is a mere illusion. Other books are also attributed to him, but it is difficult to decide whether he was really the author of all of them. According to the biography of Nāgārjuna, which was translated into Chinese at the beginning of the fifth century A.D., he was born in a Brāhmaṇa family in South India. He studied the Vedas and other Brāhmanical scriptures, but was converted to Buddhism, and became one of the most important teachers of Mahāyāna Buddhism. He probably flourished towards the close of the second century A.D.

Āryadeva.

Āryadeva was probably a younger contemporary of Nāgārjuna. One of his books, *Chatuḥśatikā*, has recently been discovered. Another, of which only fragments are known, seeks to demonstrate the hollowness of Brāhmanical ceremonies.

Other writers.

A large number of Buddhist authors flourished after Āryadeva, and a brief reference to the most famous of them may be made to complete this sketch, although it would carry us beyond the period under review.

Asaṅga or Āryasaṅga was the founder of the Yogāchāra school of Mahāyāna Buddhism, and the author of *Mahāyāna-*

Sūtrālaṁkāra. The Yogāchāras deny the real existence of all except *vijñāna* or consciousness, and are therefore also called Vijñānavādins. Vasubandhu, younger brother of Asaṅga, was the author of *Abhidharmakośa*, a learned treatise on ethics, psychology, and metaphysics, held in great reverence by the Mahāyānists of China and Japan. He also wrote many other learned philosophical works and commentaries to Mahāyānasūtras. The two brothers Asaṅga and Vasubandhu probably flourished towards the end of the fourth, or the beginning of the fifth century A.D.

Asaṅga and Vasubandhu

Dignāga, the author of *Pramāṇa-Samuchchayā*, a famous treatise on logic, was a pupil of Asaṅga or Vasubandhu.

Chandragomin, a famous student of the school of Asaṅga, enjoys great celebrity all over the Buddhist world as a grammarian, philosopher, and a poet. Of his poetical works only the *Śishyalekhadharmakāvya*, an elegant religious poem written in the form of a letter to a student, is known to us. He flourished in the seventh century A.D.

About the same time flourished Śāntideva, the reputed author of three learned works, *Śikshāsamuchchaya*, *Sūtrasamuchchaya*, and *Bodhicharyāvatāra*. The last, 'a poem breathing a truly pious spirit, ranks foremost among the religious poetry of the Buddhists.'

In conclusion it may be pointed out that with the development of Buddhism as a world-religion, Buddhist literature also rose to the rank of a world-literature. It was studied all over Asia, and many of its legends, fables, and anecdotes found their way into Europe. Nay, it is even surmised by many, that the Christian Gospels, and particularly the story of Christ's life, were profoundly influenced by the Buddhist canon. Rudolf Seydel, who has gone more deeply into this branch of study than any other scholar, has pointed out a close agreement between a larger number of Buddhist and Christian legends, parables and maxims. From this he has derived the very natural conclusion that the Bible is indebted to a large extent to the Buddhist literature. Later scholars have disputed this theory, but have not been able to demolish it altogether. There is, however, no doubt that the Apocrypha, which originated in the second and third century A.D., and is admitted by the Roman Catholics into the Old Testament, borrowed largely from the Buddhist literature.

Buddhist Literature, a world literature.

The influence of Buddhism and Buddhist literature in Europe

at a later date is most conspicuously illustrated by the 'Barlaam and Josaphat,' 'one of the most widely spread religious romances of the Middle Ages, relating the conversion of the Indian prince Josaphat by the hermit Barlaam, his subsequent resistance to all forms of temptation, and his becoming a hermit.' The whole story is 'nothing more or less than a Christianised version of the legendary history of Buddha[1] agreeing with it in all essentials and many details.' The Romance was originally composed in the Pehlevi language about the sixth or the seventh century A.D., and translated in Arabic and Syriac at a later date. The Syrian version was rendered into Greek, and the Greek version was translated into many European languages. The book exists in Latin, French, Hebrew, Ethiopian, Italian, Spanish, German, English, Swedish, Dutch, Armenian, Russian and Rumanian versions, and was even translated as early as 1204 A.D. into Icelandic. It is also interesting to note that by the fourteenth century A.D., Barlaam and Josaphat were recognised as saints by the Holy Pope. Prof. Max Müller has pointed out how Gautama, the Buddha, under the name of St. Josaphat, is at the present day officially recognised and honoured throughout Catholic Christendom as a Saint of the Church of Christ. He justly remarks that few saints have a better claim to the title than the Buddha.

Barlaam and Josaphat.

2. *The Brāhmaṇical Literature.*

In addition to the Buddhist literature, the period witnessed the growth and development of the Jaina and the Brāhmaṇical literature as well. Unfortunately, the authentic Jaina literature of this period is completely lost, except in so far as it has been preserved in later works, of which a detailed account will be given in Chapter XVII. Of the Brāhmaṇical literature, the most important are the works belonging to the Vedāṅga class. A general account of it has already been given above (p. 35). We shall now refer briefly to the more important works under each of the six divisions of the Vedāṅgas.

1. Śikshā—Śikshā may be defined as the science dealing with pronunciation of letters, accents, organs of pronunciation, delivery and euphonic laws. The oldest text-books belonging to this class are the Prātiśākhyas. These are collections of pho-

1. 'Josaphat' is written in Arabic as Yudasatf which is simply a corruption of Bodhisat, the Arabic letters *y* and *b* being often confused with each other. Barlaam is probably to be traced to 'Bhagavān.'

netic rules peculiar to the different branches of the four Vedas. Besides giving general rules for the proper pronunciation of the Vedic language in general, they were intended to record what was peculiar in the pronunciation of certain teachers and their schools. The following may be mentioned among the more important texts belonging to the different Vedas.

1. The Ṛigveda-Prātiśākhya, attributed to Saunaka.
2. The Taittirīya-Prātiśākhya-Sūtra.
3. The Vājasaneyi-Prātiśākhya-Sūtra, attributed to Kātyāyana.
4. The Atharvaveda-Prātiśākhya-Sūtra, belonging to the Śaunaka school.

There are many later books belonging to this class which are attributed to such famous sages of old as Bharadvāja, Vyāsa, Vasishṭha, Yājñavalkya, etc.

2. Chhandas or Metre—Metre is dealt with in the Ṛigveda-Prātiśākhya. the Śāṅkhāyana-Śrauta-sūtra, and the Nidāna-Sūtra belonging to the Sāmaveda. One of the most important treatises is the Chhanda-Sūtra of Piṅgala. Although two recensions of it are attached respectively to the Ṛigveda and the Yajurveda, it is a comparatively late work.

3. Vyākaraṇa or Grammar—The older works on this subject were superseded by the Grammar of Pāṇini, called Ashṭādhyāyī. It has been rightly said about this work, that it presents 'the scientific treatment of a single tongue in a perfection which arouses the wonder and admiration of all those who are more thoroughly acquainted with it; it even now stands not only unsurpassed, but not even attained, and in many respects it may be looked upon as the model for similar work.'

Pāṇini was born in a village called Śalātura, in the North-West Frontier Province, not far from Attock on the Sindhu. His date is not definitely known, but he probably flourished in the fifth century B.C., though some scholars place him even two centuries earlier. His book, as the name implies, was divided into eight sections comprising about 4,000 *sūtras* and dealt mainly with the *bhāshā* or current language of his time, as opposed to the obsolete language of Vedic Saṁhitās. But the *bhāshā*, of which he writes the grammar, resembles more the language of the Brāhmaṇa texts than the Classical Sanskrit Literature.

Two great grammarians who wrote commentaries on Pāṇini's work are Kātyāyana, the author of *Vārttikas*, and Patañjali, the author of *Mahābhāshya*. These works not only explained but also amended and supplemented Pāṇini's *sūtra* in the light of the changes that had come over the spoken language since his days. Patañjali was a contemporary of Pushyamitra, the Śuṅga king, and lived in the first half of the second century B.C. Kātyāyana flourished a century earlier.

4. Nirukta or Etymology—As Grammar took its final shape in Pāṇini's work, so the etymological lexicography of Vedic terms was embodied in the *Nirukta* of Yāska, who flourished earlier than Pāṇini. All the older works on the subject, like those on Grammar, were superseded, and consequently forgotten.

5. Jyotisha—The only separate treatise on this subject is the Jyotisha-Vedāṅga, a small treatise of about 40 verses. It deals with the sun, the moon, and the 27 Nakshatras. The fact that it is written in verse, and not in the *sūtra* style, shows that it is a later work.

6. Kalpa—The treatises on ritual fall into three classes. The first, the Śrauta-sūtra, contains prescriptions for the solemn ceremonies, described in the Brāhmaṇas, and performed with the assistance of the priests with exact observance of the ritual. They include the Śulva-sūtras which give directions for the building of sacrificial places and fire-altars, and thus constitute the oldest works on Indian Geometry. The second, the Gṛihya-sūtra, deals with the various domestic ceremonies to be performed by a householder in all special circumstances of life, from the cradle to the grave, such as those connected with birth, initiation, marriage, death etc. (cf. pp. 79 ff). The third, the Dharma-sūtra, prescribes the moral rules to be observed in daily life with a view to fix the proper attitude of an individual, both towards other individuals, as well as towards the civic community at large. It has therefore to deal with the State and society and the relations of individuals thereto.

We have a collection of these four kinds of Sūtra-texts (including Śulva) belonging to the Baudhāyana and Āpastamba schools of the Black-Yajurveda. Closely connected with the Kalpasūtra of the Āpastamba school is that of the Hiraṇyakeśins. All these are attached to the Taittirīya-Saṁhitā, while to the Matirāyaṇī-Saṁhitā belong the Śrauta-, Gṛihya- and Śulva-sūtras of the Mānava school, and to the Kāṭhaka-Saṁhitā the Kāṭhaka-Gṛihyasūtra. The following list represents the other important works of this class, arranged under the different Vedas to which they are attached.

White-Yajurveda. (1) Kātyāyana-Śrautasūtra.
(2) Pāraskara-Gṛihyasūtra.
(3) Kātyāyana-Śulvasūtra.
Ṛigveda. (1) Āśvalāyana-Śrautasūtra.
(2) Āśvalāyana-Gṛihyasūtra.
(3) Śāṅkhāyana-Śrautasūtra.
(4) Śāṅkhāyana-Gṛihyasūtra.
Sāmaveda. (1) Lāṭyāyana-Śrautasūtra.
(2) Gobhila-Gṛihyasūtra.
(3) Khādira-Gṛihyasūtra.
Atharvaveda. (1) Kauśikasūtra.
(2) Vaitāna-Śrautasūtra.

All these works are of very great importance from historical point of view. They not only hold out before us a detailed picture of the social and religious condition of the Aryans, but also acquaint us with the form of their government and their political ideas. In short, they are the most important source of information about the Hindu civilization of this period.

There are other works which, properly speaking, belong to the Vedāṅga class, as they deal with the Saṁhitās, but are not really regarded as such. These are the Anukramaṇīs i.e. 'Lists' or 'Indices' of the contents of the Saṁhitās.

Anukramaṇīs.

Thus Śaunaka made an Anukramaṇī or list of (1) the Ṛishis, (2) the metres, and (3) the gods of the Ṛigvedic hymns, and another, of the hymns themselves. The most perfect Anukramaṇī is that of Kātyāyana, called Sarvānukramaṇī i.e. the index of all things belonging to the Ṛigveda. It gives, in the form of *sūtras*, the first words of every hymn, the number of verses, the name and family of the Ṛishi to whom it is ascribed, the deities to whom each individual verse is consecrated, and the metres of every verse. Another important work of the same class is the Bṛihad-devatā attributed to Śaunaka. It gives a list of deities referred to in the Ṛigvedic hymns, and contains many myths and legends about them.

In addition to the religious literature described above, reference should also be made to the six definite schools of philosophy that were distinguished at an early date, viz. the Sāṁkhya system of Kapila, the Yoga system of Patañjali, the Nyāya system of Gautama, the Vaiśeshika system of Kaṇāda, the Pūrva-Mīmāṁsā of Jaimini, and the Uttara-Mīmāṁsā or the Vedānta of Vyāsa. Besides these we have not only secular literature, such as dramas and poems (Kāvyas), but also the Smṛitis, the Purāṇas, and other classes of religious literature, of which the beginnings may be traced during the period under review. All these will be more conveniently dealt with together in a later chapter. But the two great Epics, the Rāmāyaṇa and the Mahābhārata, which belong to this period, deserve a special treatment in a separate chapter (cf. Chap. VII).

3. *Tamil Literature*

Tamil is the oldest of the Dravidian group of languages which include, besides, Kannaḍa (Kanarese), Telugu, and Malayālam. The earliest literary works in these three may be dated respectively in the 9th, 11th and 14th centuries. But the history of Tamil literature goes back to a hoary antiquity. Its earliest works are associated with the three Śangamas, i.e. academies or societies of learned men, all of which flourished in the Pāṇḍya kingdoma. Each Śangama consisted of a number of distinguished poets and erudite scholars who set their seal of approval on works submitted to them. Most of these approved works are now lost, and much of the account, at least of the first two Śangamas, is undoubtedly legendary. Nevertheless a few works associated with these Śangamas have come down to us, and they form the Tamil classics. As to the date of the Śangamas, opinions differ widely, but its extreme limits may be fixed at 500 B.C. and 500 A.D.

None of the works traditionally associated with the first Śangama has been preserved, and of the second, only a single work, *Tolkāppiyam* has come down to us. It is a grammatical treatise written in the form of *sūtras*, though it contains a great deal of extraneous matters throwing light on the manners, customsa, thoughts, and beliefs of the people.

All the other Tamil classics known to us belong to the third Śangama, and may be broadly classified as anthologies and the epics. Of the first the three important are: (i) *Patthupāttu* (Ten Idylls), (ii) *Ettuthokai* (Eight Collections), and (iii) *Padinenkīlkanakku* (Eighteen Minor Didactic Poems).

Among the idylls *Nedunalvādai* by Nakkīrar is one of the best known. It draws a contrast between the Pāṇḍya king Neduñjeliyan in camp and his lonely queen pining for him at home. Another idyll *Pattinappālai* by Rudran Kannanār beautifully depicts the internal struggle of the hero suffering from two opposite emotions—one calling him to the battlefield and the other to his beloved at home.

Of the Eight Collections, the last called *Purananūru*, is the best known, and contains the poems of one hundred and fifty poets including Kapilar, Avvai, and Kovūr-Kilār. Apart from literary merits these poems contain valuable data for the reconstruction of the social history of the Tamils.

Tirukkural, or *Kural*, of Tiruvalluvar is the best of the minor didactic poems, and its teachings have been described as "an eternal inspiration and guide to the Tamilians." The text is divided in three parts dealing with the *Trivarga* or well-known three objects of life viz. *dharma*, *artha*, and *kāma*, devoting ten stanzas to each of the 133 topics bearing upon different aspects of human life.

Of the ten epics, seven alone are now available, and two of these, *Śilappadikāram* and *Maṇimekhalai* deservedly occupy a very high place in Tamil literature. These two have been compared to the *Rāmāyaṇa* and the *Mahābhārata*, and supply very valuable data for reconstructing the history of the Tamils in the early centuries of the Christian era.

Śilappadikāram literally means 'the story that centres round an anklet.' "The hero Kovalan, infatuated by a courtezan named Mādavi (Mādhavī), squanders his fortune, and then, being disillusioned, returns to his chaste and faithful wife Kaṇṇaki. The two set out for Madura, where Kovalan wants to pursue a trade, and proposes to raise the necessary capital by selling a pair of anklets, the only remaining jewels of his wife. The State goldsmith of Madura, whom he approaches with one anklet for this purpose, had stolen a similar anklet of the queen, and now accuses Kovalan of the theft. The king, without further inquiry, executes Kovalan. Thereupon the distracted wife proves the innocence of her husband by breaking open the other anklet. The Pāṇḍya king dies of grief for the great act of injustice done by him but nemesis overtakes the city of Madura. Kaṇṇaki curses the city which is accordingly consumed by flames. She shortly joins her husband in heaven and is proclaimed the goddess of chastity."

Maṇimekhalai, which is a contemporary work, is really a sequel to the other epic. The heroine Maṇimekhalai, the daughter of Kovalan by Mādhavī, gets her inspiration from Kaṇṇaki, and passing through vicissitudes of fortune adopts the life of a Buddhist nun.

CHAPTER VII.

The Epics and the Hindu Society

1. *The Epics*

While the Vedic Sūtra literature is unmistakably Brāhmaṇical, the Epics may be said to represent the view-point of the Kshatriyas. Indeed they may be regarded as the last remnant of a vast Kshatriya literature, which was distinct in its origin and development from the Brāhmaṇical literature.

Origin of the Epics.

The latter refers to 'Gāthās' or Nārāśaṁsīs, literary compositions of the nature of 'hero-lauds,' describing in rapturous terms the heroism and other virtues of Kshatriya princes. It is quite clear that many of these compositions were regularly sung on the occasion of important ceremonies. They are mostly lost, but there can be no doubt that the origin of the Rāmāyaṇa and the Mahābhārata is ultimately to be traced to these sources.

Although edited and re-touched by the Brāhmaṇas at a later age, the Epics still retain their original characteristics to a great extent. They clearly testify to the fact that the political power of the Kshatriyas had not yet been subordinated to the Brāhmaṇas, as in a later age. This is a valuable historical truth, the importance of which cannot be overestimated.

Age of the Epics.

Neither the Rāmāyaṇa nor the Mahābhārata may be regarded as a composition of a single poet or even the product of a single age. It is certain that both of them, specially the latter, underwent considerable additions and alterations in successive ages, and did not assume their present form till the third or the fourth century A.D. Their beginnings must, however, be dated six to eight centuries earlier. Both the Epics are the products of new Hinduism. While Rāma and Kṛishṇa, the two chief incarnations of Vishṇu, play the most prominent part in them, they represent Śaivism also as a popular cult prevalent all over the country.

The historical importance of these two books is indeed very great. If any one would seek to realise what Hindu life and society was like during the period under review, he can do no better than turn to the two grand Epics, the Rāmāyaṇa and the Mahābhārata. They hold out before us a mirror reflecting the Indian society as it was two thousand years ago, and paint in glowing colours the virtues and vices that characterised the people, and the high ideals which inspired them.

The story of the Rāmāyaṇa.

The story of the Rāmāyaṇa may be briefly told. King Daśaratha of Ayodhyā had three queens, and four sons were born of them. He wanted to install the eldest, Rāmachandra, as crown-prince, but his favourite queen Kaikeyī wanted the throne for her own son Bharata. On the eve of the installation ceremony, she reminded the king of the two boons he had promised her long ago, and extracted a promise that he would grant them now. Her demands were terrible,—Rāma must go to the forest for 14 years, and Bharata should be placed on the throne. The old king would not swerve an inch from the path of rectitude, and though his heart was rent in twain, he could not refuse the demands he had solemnly promised to grant. Rāma, like a true hero, calmly accepted the position into which father's pledge had placed him, and banished himself from Ayodhyā. His loving brother Lakshmaṇa and young and faithful wife Sītā could by no means be dissuaded from accompanying him to the forest. On his way, he was hospitably entertained by Guha, a Nishāda chief, on the bank of the Gangā, and settled in the Chitrakūṭa mountain, modern Chitrakot in Banda District, about 65 miles from modern Allahabad. In the meantime Daśaratha died of a broken heart, and Bharata, who was at his maternal uncle's house, was hurriedly sent for. But Kaikeyī's cruel wish was not fulfilled. Bharata was overwhelmed with shame and sorrow at the part that she had played in the late transactions, and expiated the sins of his mother by trying to persuade Rāma to take back his legitimate throne. But Rāma was the worthy son of a worthy father who suffered himself to be literally killed by inches with a poignant sorrow, rather than deviate a hair's breadth from the path of honour. He refused the offer and Bharata went back to Ayodhyā in a dejected mood. He resolved henceforth to lead an ascetic life like Rāma, and having placed the latter's sandal on the throne, ruled the kingdom as his deputy.

Rāma retired further south into the Daṇḍaka forest, and lived near modern Nāsik on the banks of the Godāvari, served and cared for by his faithful brother and loving wife. There he had to fight against the marauding tribes of the forest, in order to protect the Aryan sages, but ere long this brought troubles upon him, and Rāvaṇa, the most notable non-Aryan chief of the south, carried away Sītā to his residence at Laṅkā, in the island of Ceylon. Rāma sought for and obtained the aid of Sugrīva, a non-Aryan chief of Kishkindhyā, by killing his elder brother Vāli. Tārā, the widowed queen of Vāli, became the willing spouse of Sugrīva, and with his help, Rāma defeated Rāvaṇa and recovered Sītā. Sītā's purity was tested by the ordeal of fire, and as it was now full 14 years since they left their home, the loving couple returned to Ayodhyā. Bibhīshaṇa, the faithless brother of Rāvaṇa, who had gone over to Rāma's side, was crowned at Laṅkā.

Rāma now began to reign in Ayodhyā, but sorrow and misfortune did not leave him for long. Soon his chief spy brought in the report that his subjects suspected the purity of Sītā's character on account of her long residence in Rāvaṇa's house. Rāma knew full well that Sītā's chastity was above suspicion, but nevertheless he thought it to be his duty as a king to discard her in deference to the popular will. Sorely grieved at heart, he banished Sītā to the hermitage of Vālmīki, the famous sage and the reputed author of the Rāmāyaṇa. There Sītā gave birth to twin sons through whom the royal Ikshvāku family (p. 68) was continued.

Historical truth to be deduced from the Rāmāyaṇa.

In its historical setting, the Rāmāyaṇa represents the most notable fact during the period under review, viz. the expansion of Aryan culture over Deccan and South India. It plainly hints at the methods employed by the conquerors, viz. the missionary enterprises backed by military power, and the setting up of one non-Aryan tribe against another. It also pays an indirect tribute to the high state of material and moral culture of the non-Aryans. The unfair means by which Vāli was killed by Rāma, and Indrajit by his brother Lakshmaṇa, only prove once more that a conquering race cannot always be scrupulous in its methods of warfare. The strength and resources of Rāvaṇa were by no means negligible, and the material civilisation of his country was hardly inferior to that of his opponents. In morality, there is at least one point in which Rāvaṇa towered head and shoulders above his opponents. We need only compare the barbarous treatment that Lakshmaṇa meted out to Rāvaṇa's sister Śūrpaṇakhā, on the slightest provocation, with the conduct of the outraged non-Aryan chief to his captive lady.

But the strength and excellence of the Aryan culture lay in their domestic virtues. The affectionate faithfulness of the brothers of Rāma, and the undying love of his consort Sītā contrast strangely with the faithless conduct of Bibhīshaṇa, Sugrīva, and Tārā. The sternness of Aryan character, and its spirit of sacrifice, as reflected in the characters of Daśaratha and his three sons, have no parallel in the effiminate luxury of Rāvaṇa's household.

Among the other virtues of the Aryans must be counted a supreme regard for truth, a spirit of manly enterprise which nothing could daunt, and a perseverance and dogged obstinacy which carried everything before it. Every one of these features is emphasised in the successful expedition of Rāma against enormous odds. There can hardly be a nobler and more stimulating example than of the helpless Rāma, rising above the most terrible calamity that can befall an honourable man, and fighting his way to a successful issue by dint of his stubborn will, energy, and prowess. The high ideals of Aryan life were embodied in Rāma, the faithful and dutiful son, the affectionate brother, the loving husband, the stern relentless hero, and an ideal king who placed the welfare of his State above the most cherished personal feelings—a strange combination, as an ancient text puts it, of the grace of flowers and the fury of thunders.

But the weak spots of Aryan life are also hinted at in the Rāmāyaṇa. The system of polygamy, and the weakness of king Daśaratha for feminine grace, not to put it more bluntly, brought all the disasters upon himself and his kingdom. Out of these germs developed the palace intrigues and the license of the court, which undermined the virility of political life in ancient India. The fire-ordeal of Sītā also points to the growth of superstitious practices, with ominous consequences for the future. The friendship of Rāma with the Nishāda and other non-Aryan chiefs clearly indicates the absence of the degrading influences of caste. It is to be noted, however, that the last book of Rāmāyaṇa, which was probably added at a later date, depicts Rāma as having killed a Śūdra for daring to perform the Brāhmaṇical sacrifices, and thus betrays the lamentable progress of that institution in the interval.

The story of the Mahābhārata is complex in character, and a great deal of its importance lies in the subsidiary legends and long discourses on political, social, moral, and religious topics, loosely attached to the main story.

The historical basis of the central theme of this grand epic has already been discussed (p. 72). Like the Rāmāyaṇa, it faithfully reflects an important feature of the history of India during the period under review, *viz.* the evolution of empire out of a host of petty States fighting for supremacy with one another. It shows considerable advance over the Rāmāyaṇa-period in war and diplomacy, and in various phases of society. The different characters of the book represent different aspects of Indian life. In Bhīshma we meet with the stern regard for truth, combined with a sense of duty, heroism, and filial love. Duryodhana is an embodiment of unscrupulous and insatiate greed for political power. The Pāṇḍava brothers typify the sweet brotherly relations of old. Yudhishṭhira is a model of unflinching rigid moral virtues, and Subhadrā, of a selfless, devoted wife and matron. But the typical figures of the Mahābhārata are Arjuna, Kṛishṇa, and Draupadī, representing some of the best and noblest traits of Aryan character. The first soldier of his age, Arjuna was equally devoted to high philosophy and fine arts, such as music and dancing. Kṛishṇa was the first great statesman that grasped the vital political problem of India, viz., the unification of the small States of India into one great empire, and applied his truly remarkable genius to its solution. He rose above the narrow parochial patriotism which distinguished most men of his age, and steered the ship of State cleverly through troubled waters. In Draupadī we find a unique type of women,—not merely a fond and devoted wife, but the true helpmate and partner in life. She was the best illustration of Kālidāsa's famous epigram—a good house-wife, wise counsellor, merry companion, and a beloved pupil in the pursuit of fine arts. The prowess, liberalism, and all-round culture of Arjuna, the masterly personality, profonnd philosophic insight, and political sagacity of Kṛishṇa, and the lofty, high-souled, and spirited Draupadī, proud in her virtue and noble in her indignation, formed the ideals that shed lustre on the society of ancient India.

Historical truths to be deduced from the Mahābhārata.

Several objectionable practices and customs referred to in the Mahābhārata throw an interesting light on the growth of Hindu society. Thus the marriage of Draupadī with five husbands points to the existence of polyandry. For, it must be remembered that the epic was based upon an ancient story, and the marriage of Draupadī was too essential a part of

Objectionable customs depicted in the Epic.

it to be modified in later versions. The attempt of the author to explain it away by a mythological story proves that although the system was in vogue in early times (p. 89), it had fallen into disuse during the period under review. The same may be said of another objectionable custom, *viz.* procreating sons on a childless widow by a relation, which we find in the birth-story of Dhṛitarāshṭra and Pāṇḍu.

It is difficult, however, to explain away the barbarity of Kaurava princes, who dragged Draupadī by her hair to an open assembly, and there forcibly took away her clothes. This cannot be conceived to be an essential part of the old story which the epic writer could not have avoided. It is part and parcel of the epic, though probably a later embellishment of the story, and we are bound to conclude that the Aryan society had already developed that characteristic disregard for woman's honour, which ultimately degraded her position in society. Some incidents seem o show that the primitive savage instincts were not yet wholly subdued. Fancy, for instance, how the Pāṇḍava prince Bhīma literally quenched his thirst for vengeance by drinking the blood of his opponent Kuru prince.

The long discourses scattered throughout the epic are both edifying and instructive and throw interesting sidelight on the social ideas, manners, and customs. We may take for example the growth of the caste-system. The divisions of society into different classes, to which we have referred in a previous chapter, were growing more and more rigid, and the Brāhmaṇas had already developed those social theories which we find to-day as accomplished facts. But the rational mind of India was not slow to challenge their extravagant pretensions and superstitious theories. Thus there are various passages scattered in the epic in which Brāhmaṇical pretensions are recorded, and others in which a rational view is taken of the growth of society. The following, for instance, is hard to match for its insolent bravado.

The Caste System.

"Brāhmaṇas are like flaming fire. Whether ill or well-versed in the Veda, whether untrained or accomplished, Brāhmaṇas must never be despised. Whether learned or unlearned, a Brāhmaṇa is a great deity".

Again, "through the prowess of the Brāhmaṇās, the Asuras were prostrated on the waters: by the favour of the Brāhmaṇas the gods inhabit heaven. The ether cannot be created, the mountain Himavat cannot be shaken, the Gaṅgā cannot be stemmed by a dam; the Brāhmaṇas cannot be conquered by anyone on earth".

Against all this we may quote the following:—

"Mahādeva says, "A man, whether he be a Brāhmaṇa, Kshatriya, Vaiśya or Śūdra, is such by nature. By evil deeds a twice-born man falls from his position. The Kshatriya or Vaiśya, who lives in the condition of a Brāhmaṇa , by practising the duties of one, attains to Brāhmaṇhood. And the foolish Brāhmaṇa, who having attained the Brāhmaṇhood, which is so hard to get, follows the profession of a Vaiśya, under the influence of cupidity and delusion, falls into the condition of a Vaiśya. A Brāhmaṇa who falls from his own duty becomes afterwards a Śūdra. But by practising the following good works a Śūdra becomes a Brāhmaṇa".

The period thus witnessed a conflict of ideas. In practice, the old class distinctions had not yet been reduced to a rigid caste, and the supremacy of the Brāhmaṇas was far from being an established fact.

2. *Hindu Society.*

If we turn from the Epics to the Buddhist literature we find the same state of things. The great Buddha denounced the arbitrary distinctions of caste, and proclaimed the equality of all. The Brāhmaṇic pretensions, no doubt, reached very high, but they were scattered to the winds by the irresistible logic of the great master. The supremacy of the Brāhmaṇas is never recognised in the Buddhist and the Jaina literature, and the preference is always given to the Kshatriyas. Thus in enumerating the four castes, they begin with the Kshatriya and not with Brāhmaṇa.

Marriage among different castes was in vogue, but the Brāhmaṇical literature of the period seems to imply, that although a Brāhmaṇa could marry a girl belonging to other castes, a Brāhmaṇa girl could not be married to any one but a Brāhmaṇa. This is categorically denied in the Buddhist literature, which maintains just the contrary view, *viz.* that a Kshatriya girl could not be married to a Brāhmaṇa, though a Brāhmaṇa girl might be married to a Kshatriya.

A comparison of these texts leaves no doubt that the caste was in the making, and although marriage within one's own class was preferred, there was as yet no absolute restriction against inter-marriage between different castes. The Brāhmaṇas and the Kshatriyas occupied the chief position in society, but none of them conceded the supremacy to the other. There was no question of the prohibition of inter-dining, and men might pass from one caste to another, though it was growing difficult in course of time.

The lot of the low castes, however, became more and more miserable. The marriage with the Śūdras was looked upon as degrading, and even eating food cooked by them was going into disuse. Some of them, like the Chaṇḍālas, were treated as Pariahs of the present day. They lived outside the city, and not only touch, but even the sight of them was impure.

Two new developments of the caste system during this period deserve special mention. The first is the influence of caste even in the legal status of a citizen. The provisions of both civil and criminal law were regulated according to caste and adversely affected the lower castes. The legal rate of interest, for example, was graded according to the caste of the debtor, that for the Śūdras being the highest. Similar was the case with fines and other penalties for criminal acts. Even capital punishment was awarded to the Śūdras for offences for which lighter punishments were provided for the other castes.

The second new feature was the rise of quite a large number of new castes. They are known as the Mixed Castes and their origin will be discussed later. But whatever the origin, we find, the society divided into numerous mixed castes, instead of the original four, and their number has been steadily on the increase. As a matter of fact the Kshatriyas, Vaiśyas and Śūdras soon ceased to denote any homogeneous group and even the Brāhmaṇas were divided into numerous classes or subdivisions.

The caste system was thus creeping like a shadow on the fair face of India, and the shadow was gradually lengthened with the declining day. It was a speck of black cloud that cast its shade on the brilliant culture and civilization of the Aryans. The cloud was as yet no bigger than a man's hand, but it was destined ere long to assume threatening proportions, and envelop the atmosphere in an impenetrable gloom, ushering in the dark night long before it was due.

It is refreshing to pass from the discussion of caste to a topic which showed the great liberality of Hindu society. It will be remembered that, during the period under review, foreign invaders like the Greeks, the Parthians, the Śakas and the Kushāṇas settled in India. All these elements were finally absorbed by the Hindu society, and not a trace remained of their separate individual characteristics. A number of inscriptions record the gradual transformation of these barbarian hordes,—how they adopted the languages, religion, manners, and customs of the people, and were finally incorporated into the Hindu society by matrimonial ties. The case of the Western Satraps furnishes a very good illustration. The names of its early kings were uncouth, such as Ghsamotika, Chashṭana and Nahapāna, but their successors bore purely Indian names like Viśvasena, Rudrasiṇha, Vijayasena, Rudrasena, etc. Then they gave up their barbaric language and religion, became pious devotees of Hindu gods, and adopted Sanskrit as their language. They went even further, and entered into matrimonial relations with Brāhmaṇical royal dynasties of India. Thus in everything they became pure Hindus.

Foreign elements in Hindu Population

The same liberal spirit was shown abroad by the Buddhist and Brāhmaṇical missionaries. The former carried their propaganda all over Asia, and brought its nomadic hordes within the pale of Indian culture, while the latter raised the people in the Far East from their primitive barbarism to a high state of progress and refinement.

On the other hand, the Indians freely borrowed from other nations in order to improve their arts and science. Their coinage drew its main inspiration from the Graeco-Bractrians. As regards other arts and architecture, too, we can say of them what has been said of the Greeks. 'They had a remarkable capacity for seizing what was good in the art of other nations. But although they borrowed largely, both from the Greeks and the Persians, not only technical processess, but decorative patterns, animal types and such-like motives,—the spirit of their productions was always inherently their own'. Thus the Indo-Aryans displayed remarkable capacity for assimilation and absorption, and in this respect they compare favourably with other nations, both ancient and modern.

The debt of the Hindus to foreign culture.

Further changes occurred during this period in the position of woman. Like the development of caste, we find the continuance of the retrograde movement in this direction. The change of attitude towards women is apparent in the reluctance of Buddha to admit them into his religious Order. He ultimately gave consent at the eloquent persuasion of Ānanda, and rationalism triumphed for the time being. The choice of Buddha was fully justified by the rare intellectual attainments of the Buddhist nuns, some of whose literary compositions are still preserved in the famous *Therī-gāthā*.

Position of Woman

The spirit of the time is also correctly indicated by Megasthenes. He says that the 'Brāhmaṇas do not communicate a knowledge of philosophy to their wives'. What a strange contrast to the relation between Yājñavalkya and Maitreyī that has been described above (p. 91) ! But Megasthenes admits that some women did pursue philosophy.

The general education of women is frequently referred to in the literature of the period. On the whole we must conclude that even in this period women had a fair share of culture and education, and sometimes reached high eminence in various branches of arts and sciences. But an idea was gradually gaining ground that knowledge and learning were not the proper sphere of women.

Early marriage.

This was partly the cause and partly the effect of the gradual lowering of the marriageable age of girls. Thus *Manu-smṛiti* prescribes that a man of thirty shall marry a maiden of twelve, or a man of twenty-four, a girl of eight. This marks the beginning of that tendency which ultimately regarded the marriage of girls before puberty as almost an inviolable sacred law. Many Smṛitis even laid down that the girls should be married when they were still *nagnikās* (lit. naked). The effect of this upon the mental development, particularly the educational activities, of women must have been very deplorable.

Prohibition of remarriage and divorce.

The new custom was evidently due to an anxiety to maintain the physical purity of women. The same anxiety also seems to be responsible for the gradual discouragement of the remarriage of women which was formerly allowed under specific circumstances such as the death of husband, his adopting an ascetic life or being abroad beyond a certain period. Similarly divorce or repudiation of husbands, permitted on certain grounds, was gradually disfavoured. On the other hand, *Manu-smṛiti*, which typifies the new spirit, permits the husband to discard the wife even on very flimsy grounds. Indeed Manu's injunctions in respect to the wife, in spite of some honeyed phrases of a conventional nature, are very painful reading.[1]

The discouragement of the remarriage of widows was accompanied by the growth of the custom of *satī* i.e. the burning of the widow with her dead husband. References in the Mahābhārata and some actual instances recorded by the Greek writers leave no doubt that this practice was in vogue during this period. The detailed account left by a Greek writer about the death of an Indian's wife by the *satī* rite in Irān in 316 B.C. is very interesting reading and proves the voluntary nature of the sacrifice. Aristobulus, who made some inquiry on this point, says that in some cases the women willingly immolated themselves on the funeral pyre of their husbands, but those who failed to do so were looked down upon by the society. This implies a general public encouragement to this abominable practice, though it is not sanctioned in the early Dharmaśāstras.

Satī.

Side by side with the gradual deterioration in the position of woman we find the rise of a class of courtesans who enjoyed high honour and distinction in society. The case of Ambapāli, the daughter of a rich citizen of Vaiśālī, and a contemporary of Buddha, may be cited as a typical example. It is said that on account of the great charms and accomplishments of this lady the democratic assembly of the Lichchhavis decided, in accordance with a well-known practice, that she must not be married, and lead the life of a public woman for the enjoyment of all. The king Bimbisāra of Magadha visited her and installed a similar courtesan in his own capital. Even Gautama Buddha deigned to accept her invitation in preference to that of others, and received a park as a gift from her. We know from other sources also that a class of cultured hetairae formed a distinctive feature of society in this and the succeeding ages.

Courtesans.

To complete the picture of the society reference must be made to the slaves whose existence from the earliest Vedic period to the modern times is proved by definite evidence. The Smṛitis refer to various processes by which one could attain the status of a slave, viz. birth (i.e. from a slave), purchase, gift, inheritance, maintenance during famine, pledge, indebtedness, captivity in war,

Slaves.

1. Cf. Bk. III, Ch. X.

wager, voluntary surrender of freedom, apostacy from asceticism, attachment to a female slave, and judicial punishment for crimes. It is somewhat curious that Megasthenes categorically states that there was no slavery in India. He was probably misled by the humane treatment accorded to the slaves in India which offered such a striking contrast to their lot in Greece. The Smṛitis lay down rules for the liberal treatment of the slaves and for their emancipation.

Life and manners of the people.

In conclusion we may briefly sketch the life and manners of the people at large. The wealth and luxury displayed in dwelling houses, furniture, dress and ornaments, to which a detailed reference will be made in the next chapter, seems to have been a characteristic feature, not merely of a few but of the people at large, for we are told that even the monks used costly utensils and furniture till they were forbidden to do so. Rich and varied articles of food and drink included rice, wheat, vegetables, fish, meat, the different preparations of milk, and a large number of fruits and their juice. Strong liquors of various kinds were also in use, and the literary evidence leaves no doubt that in spite of *śāstric* injunctions to the contrary intoxicating drinks were in common use, specially among the aristocracy. Although a few ascetics entertained pessimistic views of life, and the general people were plain simple folks, there was a large body of men enjoying their lives to the full by means of music, dancing, dramatic show and various other entertainments.

We may get a general picture of the life of a middle class citizen from the detailed description in Vātsyāyana's *Kāmasūtra* (Bk. I, Ch. IV). It portrays a life of ease and luxury with healthy and refined taste for artistic and social activities, in which wine and women played no inconsiderable part. The ordinary household life included daily bath and toilette with soap, sandal, incense, and ointment, and regular shaving of the chin and trimming of moustaches. Every bedroom was supposed to contain books, musical instruments, requisites for painting and "boards for different kinds of sports such as card-playing, and one for gambling". Every house had an attached garden with flowers, cages of pet birds such as parrots, and a *dolā* or swinging board. But this represents only one side of the picture. As a corrective to it we may quote the following statement of Megasthenes:

"The Indians live happily enough, being simple in their manners and frugal. They never drink wine except at sacrifices.

Theft is of very rare occurrence. Their houses and property they generally leave unguarded. The simplicity of their laws and their contracts is proved by the fact that they seldom go to law.

"Truth and virtue they hold alike in esteem. Hence they accord no special privileges to the old unless they possess superior wisdom".[1] At the same time Megasthenes disapproves of a custom which is prevalent to a great extent even to the present day, viz. that the Indians eat alone and have no fixed hours for meals.

We may therefore conclude that the Hindu society always contained diverse elements, both rich, ease-loving, and luxurious, as well as simple plain folks. But on the whole piety and morality were highly valued by them, and they had a high degree of intellectual culture and refined artistic sensibilities.

The general picture of Hindu society, described above, is a normal development or evolution of the Aryan society, as depicted in the Vedic literature, to which reference has been made above. The gradual expansion of the Aryans all over India led to the introduction of their religious and social ideas and institutions among pre-Aryan peoples with whom they came into contact. But as always happens in such cases, the Aryans themselves also assimilated, or were influenced by, the laws, ideas, manners and customs of the more primitive peoples who were admitted into their society. It may thus be taken for granted that the social and religious condition, as it was developed by the end of the period under review, represents a homogeneous culture resulting from the synthesis of Aryan and pre-Aryan elements. There were no doubt local variations or regional peculiarities, but the general framework of an all-India society had come into being. This may be truly called the Hindu society, taking the word Hindu in its original significance, denoting the country as a whole extending from the Himālayas to Cape Comorin and the Sindhu to the Brahmaputra.

The best evidence of this blending of Aryan and pre-Aryan elements into an organic whole is furnished by the picture of society in the Classical Tamil literature of the Śangam Age. Although going back to the early centuries of the Christian era, it shows such a complete fusion of Aryan and Dravidian elements that it is difficult to distinguish the purely Dravidian substratum from the

1. Megasthenes, *Indica*, pp. 69-70.

superimposed Aryan layer. The Vedic literature, the stories of the two Epics, and the injunctions of the Dharmaśāstras made as deep an impress upon literature, thoughts and traditions, as well as social, religious, and moral ideas, in the south, as in the north. The primitive ideas of marriage as a simple and a voluntary union of a boy and a girl were adjusted with the stereotyped eight forms of marriage enunciated in the Dharmaśāstras[1]. It is explicity stated in the *Tolkāppiyam* "that marriage as a sacrament attended with ritual was established in the Tamil country by the Āryas".[2] The social and occupational groups; the pre-eminence of the Brāhmaṇas; the political ideas and institutions; love of poetry, music and dancing; various forms of amusements, sports and pastimes; mixed bathing and picnic parties; superstitious beliefs in omens and portents; the important position and high status of special classes of courtesans; the position of women in general and of wife in particular, the hard lot of the widows, and the *satī* rite;—all these, mentioned in the Tamil Classics, remind one of the well-known characteristics of the Hindu society reflected in Sanskrit literature.

The Tamil Classics throw interesting light on the life led by the common people. In contrast with the practices of a later age the Brāhmaṇas "ate meat and drank toddy without incurring reproach."[3] The poets frequently refer to feasts arranged by their patrons, in which wine and meat formed the chief items of pleasure. "The flesh of animals cooked whole, such as pork from a pig which has been kept away from its female mate for many days and fattened for the occasion, the flesh of tortoises, and particular kinds of fish are mentioned as delicacies served at such feasts."[4] Special reference is made to "foreign liquor in green bottles"—evidently Greek wine,—and "toddy well matured by being buried underground for a long time in bamboo barrels."[5]

The Tamil Classics make specific references to some interesting customs and practices. We learn, for example, that watchmen, carrying torches, patrolled streets of big cities at night, that

1. This as well as the sketch of the Dravidian society that follows is based upon *A History of South India* by K. A. N. Sastri, pp. 124 ff.

2. *Ibid*, 125.

3. *Ibid*, 126.

4. *Ibid*, 130.

5. *Ibid*.

a select body of king's body-guards killed themselves when the king died, and that hero-stones were erected and regular worship was offered to them. To what extent these and a few other rites and customs were of southern and pre-Aryan origin, it is difficult to say. But there is no doubt that they became, sooner or later, general customs, not confined to any particular region or class of people.

CHAPTER VIII

Colonisation and Economic Condition

The various religious movements described above must not lead any one to suppose that the activity of the ancient Indians was confined to this sphere alone. Their spiritual achievements were no doubt very great, but these were not accompanied by a neglect of, or indifference to secular affairs, as is commonly supposed. In point of fact, the Indians of old were keenly alive to the extension of dominions, acquisition of wealth, and the development of trade, industry, and commerce. The material prosperity they gained in these various ways was reflected in the luxury and elegance that characterised the society. A brief reference to each of these topics is essential for a proper understanding of the ancient Indian civilisation.

1. *Expansion of Aryan Culture.*

We have already described how the Aryans had gradually spread over tne whole of Northern India. During the period under review they extended their supremacy over the whole of the Deccan and South Indian Peninsula. The process of conquest cannot be traced in detail, but it appears that the Aryan missionaries paved the way for the military conquest of many of these provinces. The story of Agastya shows their adventurous spirit in the south, and we read in the Rāmāyaṇa how the Aryan sages were often disturbed by the wild tribes, called Rākshasas, in their southern homes, and sought the aid of the Kshatriya princes. Things were probably not very different from what took place in the 19th century, giving rise to the apt epigram—"where missionaries go to-day, the gun-boat follows tomorrow." The result was not merely a military, but also a cultural conquest of South India. The language, literature, religion, manners and customs of the Aryans were adopted by the Dravidian people, when their last strong-holds in the extreme south were conquered by their eternal foes. Indeed it appeared as if the South would be as completely Aryanised as North India, and even the last vestige of Dravidian civilisation would be extinguished altogether. Future events showed, however, that it

The Aryan conquest of Deccan and South India.

was not to be. After a few centuries, there was a national awakening, and a distinct reaction in favour of the old order of things. The old language and literature was again assiduously cultivated, and although the modern Tamil, Telugu and other Dravidian languages show clear traces of extensive Aryan influence, they are assuredly of non-Aryan stock. In religion, social customs and other aspects of civilisation, too, although Aryan influence is supreme, the Dravidian element is clearly perceptible. There are even some peoples who have successfully preserved the old social order of the Dravidians, although it is radically different from the Aryan. But, on the whole, the fusion of Aryan and non-Aryan culture was so great, that henceforth the historian finds it necessary to use the term Indian, rather than Aryan. It is difficult to assign any precise date to the southern extension of the Aryans, but as noted above (p. 65), the whole movement may be generally referred to the period between 1,000 and 400 B.C. Thus, in course of 1500 years, the-Aryans reached the utmost limits of India.

The South not completely Aryanised.

The five centuries that followed witnessed further extension of their power, beyond the seas and mountains that gird India all around. Ceylon, Burma, Indo-China, East Indies and Central Asia imbibed Indian culture and civilization to a considerable extent.

As to Western Asia the facts are not so well-known, but there are grounds for the belief that Buddhism at one time spread from Hindu Kush to the Mediterranean. Brāhmaṇism had also some hold on these countries. There was a colony of Indians on the upper Euphrates in Armenia as early as the second century B.C., and temples were raised there in honour of Brāhmaṇical gods like Kṛishṇa. Thus the cultural conquest of India was more or less complete in the whole of Asia.

2. *Foreign Trade*

India also came into contact with foreign nations by means of trade from very early period. Reference has already been made above (p. 24) to trade relations between the Sindhu Valley and Western Asia in the third millennium B.C. Some find allusion in the Old Testament to Indian trade with Syrian coast as far back as 1400 B.C. Archaeological evidence shows that as early as the eighth century B.C., there was a regular trade relation, both by

Trade with foreign country.

land and sea, between India on the one hand and Mesopotamia, Arabia, Phoenica and Egypt on the other. The Chinese literary texts refer to maritime and trade activity between India and China as far back as the seventh century B.C. Recent archaeological finds in the Philippines, Malay Penninsula, and Indonesia seem to confirm this and we may reasonably presume that there was a regular trade relation between India and the Far-Eastern countries during the first half of the first millennium B.C. which continued down to the historical period beginning with the early centuries of the Christian era. From the fourth century B.C., trade and maritime activities were highly developed, and the Board of Admiralty and the Naval Department were efficiently organised by the Mauryas. It was this naval supremacy that enabled the Indians to colonise the islands in the Indian Archipelago. Shortly after, there grew up a regular traffic between India and China, both by land and sea. As a result of the invasion of Alexander (327-325 B.C.) India came into close and intimate contact with the Hellenic world. As we have seen above, embassies were sent to the Maurya court by the Greek rulers of Egypt and Syria, and Aśoka sent his missionaries to five Hellenic kingdoms. We learn from an ancient authority that in the processions of Ptolemy Philadelphus (285—246 B.C.) were to be seen Indian women, Indian hunting dogs, Indian cows, and also Indian spices carried on camels, and that the yacht of this Greek ruler of Egypt had a saloon lined with Indian stones. We have abundant evidence that the Ptolemies of Egypt, and later, the Roman Emperors, encouraged by all means the development of direct sea-trade with India. Everything indicates that there was a large volume of sea-trade between India and the western countries as far as African coast before the beginning of the Christian era. From the coast the goods were carried by land to the Nile, and then down this river to Alexandria which was a great emporium in those days.

The direct sea-voyage was at first a long and tedious journey, as the ships had to keep close to the coast. But the great discovery of Hippalus in 45 A.D. that there was a monsoon wind blowing regularly across the Indian Ocean enabled the ships to sail right across the sea. This fact as well as the establishment of the Roman Empire increased the volume of Indian trade in the early centuries of the Christian era. There was also a large volume of trade by overland route through the famous city of Palmyra.

There was a mercantile colony of Indians in an island off

the African coast in the first century A.D. The adventurous spirit of the Indians carried them even as far as the North Sea, while their caravans travelled from one end of Asia to the other.

A book, called the *Periplus of the Erythraean Sea*, written by a Graeco-Egyptian sailor in the first century A.D., gives a very detailed and interesting account of Indian trade from the author's personal knowledge. He came to India and found the Indian coast studded with ports and harbours, carrying on a brisk trade with foreign countries. The chief articles of export from India were spices, perfumes, medicinal herbs, pigments, pearls, precious stones like diamond, sapphire, turquoise and lapis lazuli, animal skins, cotton cloth, silk yarn, muslin, indigo, ivory, porcelain and tortoise shell; the chief imports were cloth, linen, perfume, medicinal herbs, glass vessels, silver, gold, copper, tin, lead, pigment, precious stones and coral.

The value of Indian trade may be estimated from the well-known passage of Pliny, in which he recorded that India drained the Roman empire of fifty million *sesterces* every year. Pliny's statement is corroborated by the discovery, in India, of innumerable gold coins of the Roman emperors, which must have come here in course of trade.

Most of these coins have been found in South India, and their evidence is corroborated by many passages in classic Tamil literature. We read of 'Yavanas of harsh speech' with many wares; of foreign merchants thronging sea-port towns like Māmallapuram, Puhār, and Korkai; of busy customs officials, and those engaged in loading and unloading vessels in the harbour.

The brisk trade activity between India and the Roman Empire through Palmyra and Alexandria can be traced till the third century A.D. Naturally political relations were also established, and there are records of no less than nine embassies sent by Indian States to the Roman Emperors during the first three centuries of the Christian era.

As a result of the growing trade the Romans and Indians visited each other's country in large numbers. Alexandria was the great meeting ground between the East and the West. According to Dio Chrysostom (c. 117 A.D.) Indians formed a part of the settled population of Alexandria. Some Brāhmaṇas who visited the city in 470 A.D. were the guests of its Consul. We also possess a short memorial record of an Indian in Egypt.

3. *Industry and Inland Trade*

The large volume of external trade pre-supposes keen industrial activity all over the country. Indeed, the literature and inscriptions of the period contain frequent references to various arts, crafts, and professions followed by the people at large. The army supplied occupation to quite a large number of people who served as foot-soldiers, charioteers, cavalry, and elephant-riders. They must have also supported such trade and industries as dealing in horses and elephants, and working in wood and metals in order to get the requisite supply of chariots, sea-going vessels, and weapons of war. The supply of wood and metals necessitated the clearing of forests and working of mines, and Kauṭilya lays down elaborate regulations for both. There was a royal officer called '*Ākarādhyaksha*', 'Superintendent of mines', possessing necessary scientific knowledge. Aided by experts in mineralogy, and equipped with mining labourers and necessary instruments, he was to examine and work at all the mines in the kingdom, only those which involved larger outlay being leased out to private parties. Another royal officer, Superintendent of metals, looked to the manufacture of copper, lead, tin, mercury, brass, bronze, bell-metal, and sulphurate of arsenic, as well as of commodities made out of them. The Superintendent of Ocean-mines attended to the collection of conch-shells, diamonds, precious stones, pearls, corals, and salt, and also regulated the commerce in these commodities. The Superintendent of forest produce looked to the preservation and maintenance of forests, and the manufacture of all kinds of wooden articles which were necessary for life or for the defence of forts. A very important industry, connected with this, was that of ship-building on a very large scale.

Industrial activity.

It would thus appear that the State carried on many industries and had a monopoly over some of them. To use modern phraseology there was a nationalisation of mines, armaments, forests, salt and other industries. Besides, the State not only had its own factories for textiles, oils, sugar, etc. but exercised a fair degree of general control over private trade and industry. The Superintendent of Commerce fixed both wholesale and retail prices, and took effective steps against smuggling, adulteration, use of false weights, and speculation or 'cornering' to enhance prices. The strike of workmen in order to increase wages was illegal. On the whole regulations concerning trade and industry in the *Arthaśāstra* have a surprisingly modern look.

The growing luxury of the people led to the development of various industries. The jewellers' and lapidaries' arts as well as the art of glass-making "had reached a high pitch of excellence long before the 3rd century B.C.". Working of gold, silver, ivory, and a variety of gems and other precious substances figures prominently in Kauṭilya's book. Fragrant substances of various descriptions, fine fabrics made of cotton, wool, and silk, variety of garments, blankets, and skins and beverages of all kinds were manufactured by a large section of the population. The art of painting, masonry, and stone-cutting had also risen to great importance on account of the palaces, temples and other monuments built by the kings, the merchants, and the aristocracy.

Agriculture was naturally one of the main industries, but not, as now, practically the sole industry of the people. Various kinds of grains, vegetables, roots, fruits, flowers, and medicinal herbs were produced, and oils and sugar were manufactured. Cattle-breeding, poultry, and fishery were important industries, which not only supplied milk, butter, and clarified butter, but also fish and meats of various birds and animals, for which there was a large demand. A host of other minor industries may be mentioned, such as those of potters, dyers, leather-workers, confectioners, garland-makers, rush-workers, basket-makers, weavers, blacksmiths, and stone-cutters of ordinary type, all supplying the necessaries or luxuries of life.

Internal Trade.

A host of traders and merchants carried the products of these various industries from one end of the country to the other by means of boats and bullock carts. Sometimes hundreds of bullock carts, gathering together and forming what is called a caravan, traversed from one end of the country to the other, and occasionally we hear of bands of volunteer police being hired to protect the merchandise on the way from thieves and robbers. By means of rivers, canals, and highways, the commodities were despatched to the ports and harbours with a view to their export to foreign countries in sea-going vessels. Traders and merchants of various descriptions and their fabulous wealth are very frequently referred to in books and inscriptions.

The trade and industry of the period were characterised by a highly developed organisation. The institution called 'Śreṇī' was a corporation of men following the same trade, art, or craft, and resembled the guilds of Mediaeval Europe. Almost every important industry had its guild, which laid down rules and regulations for the conduct of members, with a view to safe-guarding their interests. These rules and regulations were recognised by the law of the land. Each guild had a definite constitution, with a President or a Headman and a small Executive Council. Some times the guilds attained to great power and prestige, and in all cases the head of the guild was an important personage in Court. The guilds sometimes maintained armies and helped the king in times of need, though, at times, there were quarrels and fights between different guilds which taxed the power of the authority to its utmost. One of the most important functions of these guilds was to serve as local banks. People kept deposits of money with them with a direction that the interest accruing therefrom was to be devoted to specific purposes, every year, so long as the Sun and the Moon endure. This is the best proof of the efficient organisation of these bodies, for people would hardly trust them with permanent endowments if they were not satisfied with their working. Sometimes the guilds proved to be centres of learning and culture, and, on the whole, they were remarkable institutions of ancient India.

Organisation of Trade and Industry.

There were also other forms of corporate organisations besides guilds. Trade was carried on on Joint Stock principles; there was Traders' League, and sometimes we hear even of 'Corner' or 'Trust', *viz*, 'the Union of traders with a view to cause rise and fall in the value of articles and make profits cent per cent'.

The above facts prove beyond doubt that a keen business instinct characterised the society, and trade, commerce, and industry flourished in ancient India to a very high degree.

4. *Coinage.*

The most inportant feature of the economic development during this period was the use of coins as common currency. The system of barter, in vogue during the Vedic period, was gradually replaced by exchange in precious metals. Herodotus's statement that the Persian satrapy in India paid 360 talents of gold dust as annual tribute shows that even in the 6th century B.C. dust or ingots of gold and silver served as currency. But about the same time, or at least not long afterwards, we find the use of actual coins i.e. a piece of metal of regular shape, whose weight and fineness were guaranteed by a recognised

Introduction of Coins.

authority. They were regularly issued by rulers, individual merchants, or corporations, and the State had no monopoly in this respect. As one or more figures were marked on these coins by a punch, as symbols of the issuing authority, these coins are generally known as punch-marked coins. They however bore no names and, with rare exceptions, no legends at all, and some coins with similar devices were also cast. Thousands of these coins found in different parts of India show that they formed regular currency for a long period.

Indo-Greek Coins.

It is the Bactrian Greeks (p. 119) who first introduced coins with names and portraits of the rulers who issued them. The figure of the king on the obverse and of a deity or other symbols on the reverse are executed with a high degree of artistic skill. Not only the other foreign hordes who invaded India, but even the Indian rulers adopted the system and issued coins of similar type, though the execution is much inferior. The Imperial Guptas issued a series of fine gold coins which, though inferior to those of the Greeks, are yet of high artistic standard.

Standard.

The weight of the earliest coins was based on the system laid down in Manu-Saṁhitā. Its unit was the *rati* or *guñja berry* weighing approximately 1.83 grains or .118 grammes. Although no actual specimen of the *suvarṇa* or standard gold coin of 80 *ratis* is known, the silver *purāṇa* or *dharaṇa* of 32 *ratis*, and of the copper *kārshāpaṇa* of 80 *ratis*, as well as their various multiples and sub-divisions have been discovered all over India.

Metal.

When coins first came into use, only those of a single metal, preferably copper or silver, were generally current in a particular locality, but the example of two metals circulating side by side is also not unknown. It is definitely laid down in Kauṭilya's *Arthaśāstra* that coins of both silver and copper were in circulation and were linked in a certain definite ratio. The variation in the value of the two metals must have caused variation in weight from the standard, and it depended upon the predilection of the particular State, whether silver or copper would occupy the privileged position, leading to the change in the weight of the other in case of change in the relative value of metals.

The introduction of gold coinage on a large scale by the Kushāṇas led to a greater complexity which was partially obviated by linking up gold to copper and dropping silver altogether, and the Kushāṇa kings issued no silver coins. But the state of things was reversed by the Guptas who issued at first only gold, and then gold and silver, copper being retained only as a token currency.

Relative Value of Metals.

We have no definite knowledge of the relative value of gold and silver in India before the time of the Persian Emperor Darius (518 B.C.), when it was 1:8 in his Indian Satrapy while in Persia it was 1:13. This is due to the fact that while India had gold in abundance her supply of silver form indigenous sources was very restricted, and it had to be largely imported from outside. But gradually the ratio in India came to be the same as in the Western countries. The ratio between gold and copper did not exhibit the same fluctuation as that between gold and silver, as both gold and copper were procurable in this country. The fluctuation in the ratio between silver and copper was, however, great and, as noted above, led to the variation in weight of the two coins. The approximate ratio of the two metals was 1 : 5·7.

In the earliest period the copper Kārhsāpaṇa of 80 *ratis* (140 grains) was the standard coin. Kauṭilya refers to the silver Kārshāpaṇas of 32 *ratis*. The earliest Gupta gold coins follow the Kushāṇa standard of about 121 grains and were known as *dīnāra* (from Latin *denarius*). Skandagupta's coins are struck on two standards, one following a local standard of 132 grains, and the other, probably the *Suvarṇa* standard of 146.4 grains.

South Indian Coins.

The imperial Gupta coins show undoubted influence of the coinage introduced by the foreign invaders. But in South India, this foreign influence is hardly noticeable. Here gold and copper were almost exclusively used, though silver was not altogether unknown. Roman coins—gold, silver and probably also copper—have been found in the south in such a large number that it is probable that they were actually used as currency in South India in the second and third centuries A.D.

After the fall of the Gupta empire the various principalities issued their own coins, though the execution is rude and the number of coins of even important dynasties like the Pālas and the Pratīhāras is surprisingly small. There was no uniformity of design or standard of weight.

5. *Wealth and Luxury.*

The enormous trade activity, joined to the natural resources of the country, made India very wealthy. Indeed India was reputed to be the richest country, and the 'Wealth of India' became a proverbial expression from very early times. Many stories of the fabulous wealth of Indian merchants are recorded in ancient Indian literature. Anāthapiṇḍika, a celebrated merchant of Kośala, desired to present a fine park in Śrāvastī, called Jetavana, to Buddha, but the owner would not part with it save on the unreasonable condition that he must have as many gold coins as could be spread over the grounds in the park. Anāthapiṇḍika closed with the offer, and a carving on the railings of the Bhārhut *stūpa*, dating probably about the second century B.C., still depicts the whole scene, showing particularly how cartloads of coins were being spread over the ground.

The Wealth of India.

In a Jaina Canonical book, the householder Ānanda, who was ultimately converted to Jainism, is said to have 'possessed a treasure of four crore measures of gold deposited in a safe place, a capital of four crore measures of gold put out on interest, a well stocked estate of the value of four crore measures of gold, and four herds, each herd consisting of ten thousand heads of cattle.' Such stories are, no doubt, partly due to popular exaggeration and conventional way of describing things, but they indicate, in a general way, the economic condition of the country. An idea of the wealth of Indian merchant princes may also be obtained from the number of pious donations and endowments made by them. For example, the large Karle Cave, the finest in India and probably in the whole world, was the gift of a single merchant.

Wealth inevitably brings luxury in its train. Megasthenes observes that the Indians "love finery and ornament. Their robes are worked in gold and ornamented with precious stones, and they wear also flowered garments made of the finest muslin." The literature of the period contains abundant evidence of the luxury of the people. We read of fine buildings several stories high, of brick, stone or wood, with fine carved railings of the same material, rooms with coloured walls and painted frescoes, covered terraces, and over-hanging eaves; bath-rooms of stone and brick, with antechamber, fire-places, chimneys, and cells to be used as cooling rooms after steam bath; rectangular chairs, arm chairs, sofas, state chairs, cushioned chairs, chairs raised on pedestal, chairs with many legs, cane-bottomed chairs, straw-bottomed chairs; bedsteads of equally varied character,

The luxury of the people.

with carved legs, representing feet of various animals ; slippers of blue, yellow, red, brown, black, orange or yellowish colour; shoes with edges of the same variety of colours, having double, treble or manifold linings and adorned with lion-skins, tiger-skins, panther-skins, antelope-skins, cat-skins, squirrel-skins, and owl-skins; laced boots lined with cotton, boots of various hues like the wings of partridges, boots pointed with rams' horns and with goats' horns, boots ornamented with scorpions' tails and sewn round with peacocks' feathers; shoes made of wool, and ornamented with gold, silver, pearl, beryl, crystal, copper, glass, tin, lead or bronze; jewels and precious stones like diamond, ruby etc., used as ornaments by men and women; and costly utensils made of beryl, crystal, gold, silver, copper and glass, some of them being painted and set with jewels.

Other articles may be named, but the above list[1] is enough to give a fair idea of the ease and luxury of Indian life, and the height to which materialistic civilisation had reached in olden days.

But the wealth and luxury of ancient India was not counterbalanced, as in most modern countries, by a host of paupers. Fortunately there was no factory system to turn out generations of deformed humanity. Home industries organised on an elaborate plan brought subsistence and competence to every door, and although famine and other calamities were not absolutely unknown—for human ingenuity has not yet been able to provide permanently against them,—they were few and far between. On the whole, the following picture of Indian life drawn by Megathenes cannot be said to be very far from truth.

Economic condition of the masses.

"The inhabitants, in like manner, having abundant means of subsistence, exceed in consequence the orindary stature, and are distinguished by their proud bearing. They are also found to be well skilled in the arts, as might be expected of men who inhale a pure air and drink the very finest water. And while the soil bears on its surface all kinds of fruits which are known to cultivation, it has also under ground numerous veins of all sorts of metals, for it contains much gold and silver, and copper and iron in no small quantity, and even tin and other metals, which are employed in making articles of use and ornament, as well as the implements and the accoutrements of war.

1. The list is given in *Vinaya Piṭaka*.

"In addition to cereals, there grows throughout India much mill et, which is kept well watered by the profusion of river-streams, and much pulse of different sorts, and rice also, and what is called *bosporum*, as well as many other plants useful for food, of which most grow spontaneously. The soil yields, moreover, not a few other edible products fit for the subsistence of animals, about which it would be tedious to write. It is accordingly affirmed that famine has never visited India and that there has never been a general scarcity in the supply of nourishing food."[1]

1. Megasthenes—*Indica*, pp. 31-32.

CHAPTER IX

Art.

A life of ease and luxury is favourable for the growth of art and literature, and the period under review witnessed remarkable progress in both. In some respects India may even be said to have reached the high watermark of its artistic achievements during this age. It has been remarked by a high authority that the history of Indian art is written in decay, and that the period of Aśoka, the Maurya, may be said to be the culminating point in its progress. We know hardly anything of Indian art during the long interval between the end of the Sindhu Valley civilization and the time of Aśoka, and very little actual remains of this period have survived. It must not accordingly be supposed however, that the Indians had little or no knowledge of art before Aśoka. The literary testimony is sufficient to demolish this absurd hypothesis entertained too long by a group of European scholars, and no one can possibly doubt that the perfection of Aśokan art presupposes a long period of continuous and steady development of which no actual specimen has yet been found.

High development of art.

The artistic achievements of Aśoka may be classified under the following heads:

Aśokan Art.

1. Stūpas.
2. Pillars.
3. Caves.
4. Residential buildings.

1. The *stūpas* were solid domes of brick or stone masonry. The Buddlists and Jainas erected them, either to commemorate a noted event or a scared spot, or to deposit some relics of Buddha, Mahāvīra or other religious saints. The size and dimensions of the *stūpas* varied from small structures, known as votive *stūpas*, less than a foot in height and diameter, to those hundred times as big. Aśoka was a great builder of huge *stūpas*, and tradition ascribes to him 84,000 of them. Nine hundred years later, the Chinese pilgrim Hiuen Tsang found hundreds of them all over India and Afghānistān. Unfortunately, few of them have survived to our own day. The great *stūpa* at Sānchi is generally believed to

Stūpas.

have been built by Aśoka, and the following description of it may serve as a fair specimen of Aśoka's *stūpa*.

"The great *stūpa* consists of an almost hemispherical dome, truncated near the top, and surrounded at its base by a lofty terrace which served in ancient days as a procession path, access to which was provided by a double flight of steps built against it on the southern side. Encircling the monument on the ground level is a second procession path, enclosed by a massive balustrade of stone. This balustrade, which is of plain design unrelieved by carvings of any kind, is divided into four quadrants by entrances set approximately at the cardinal points, each one of which is adorned by a gateway lavishly enriched with relief on both the inner and outer sides."[1] It may be remarked here that the present gateways were later additions to the Aśokan *stūpa* which probably also underwent other additions or alterations in later ages.

Pillars.

2. Of the scanty remains of Aśokan art, the most beautiful and at the same time the most characteristic specimens are furnished by the stone pillars. It is not possible to determine the total number of stone pillars erected by Aśoka's command, but the number may be set down between thirty and forty, if not more. Each of these columns consists mainly of two parts,--the shaft and the capital. The shaft is monolithic i.e. made up of one piece of stone and so marvellously polished that even in modern age many mistook them to be of metal. The Lauriya Nandangarh Pillar represents one of the finest specimens and is thus described by V. Smith. "The shaft of polished sandstone, 32 feet 9½ inches in height, diminished from a base diameter of 35½ inches to a diameter of only 22½ inches at the top—proportions which render it the most graceful of all the Aśoka Columns."[2] The same scholar further observes with regard to the monolith shafts of Aśoka columns in general: "The fabrication, conveyance, and erection of monoliths of such enormous size—the heaviest weighing about fifty tons—are proofs that the engineers and stone-cutters of Aśoka's age were not inferior in skill and resource to those of any time or country."[3]

The capital which surmounted the pillars was also monolithic, and was chiefly remarkable for the animal figures in the

1. Marshall—*Guide to Sanchi*.
2. Smith—*Fine Art in India and Ceylon*, pp. 20-22.
3. Ibid., p. 22.

round which formed its topmost member. The lion and the elephant of the capitals respectively of Rāmpurwa and Sankisa pillars are fine examples. But by far the most magnificent capital is that of the Sārnāth column—"the finest piece of sculpture of its kind so far discovered in India." "The capital measures 7 feet in height. . . .It is surmounted by four magnificent lions standing back to back, and in their middle was a large stone wheel, the sacred Dharmachakra symbol. . . .It apparently had 32 spokes, while the four smaller wheels below the lions have only 24 spokes. The lions stand on a drum with four animal figures carved upon it, viz., a lion, an elephant, a bull, and a horse, placed between four wheels. The upper part of the capital is supported by an elegantly shaped Persepolitan bell-shaped member. The lion and other animal figures are wonderfully life-like and the carving of every detailing is perfect."[1]

As remarked before, the entire capital is made out of one block of stone. Its workmanship has evoked rapturous applause from all critics of art. V. A. Smith remarks that "it would be difficult to find in any country an example of ancient animal sculpture superior or even equal to this beautiful work of art, which successfully combines realistic modelling with ideal dignity and is finished in every detail with perfect accuracy.[2]" Sir John Marshall considers them to be "masterpieces in point of both style and technique—the finest carvings, indeed, that India has yet produced, and unsurpassed by anything of their kind in the ancient world".[3]

The Caves.

3. Aśoka and his grandson Daśaratha excavated cave dwellings for the residence of monks (*vihāras*). A series of interesting caves are situated in the Barābar Hills, 16 miles north of Gayā. The Sudāma cave, dedicated by Aśoka to the mendicants of the Ājīvika sect in his 12th year, "consists of two apartments: an outer, 32 ft. 9 inches in length, and 19ft. 6 inches in breadth, and beyond this a nearly circular apartment 19 ft. 11 inches by 19 ft."[4] The Karṇa Chaupār cave, excavated in the 19th year, is simply a rectangular hall, measuring 33 ft. 6 inches by 14, with an arched roof rising 4 ft. 8 inches above walls 6 ft. 1 inch in height."[5] These

1. *Ann. Rep. Arch. Surv.*, 1904-5 p. 69.
2. Smith—op. cit., p. 60.
3. *Ann. Rep. Arch. Surv.*, 1904-5. p. 36.
4. Fergusson—*History of Indian and Eastern Architecture* Vol. I. pp. 130-31.
5. Ibid—p. 130.

chambers, hewn out of the hard and refractory gneiss, had their interior walls "burnished like mirrior," and are "wonderful monuments of patient skill and infinite labour."

4. Unfortunately there are no extant specimens of the residential buildings of the Maurya age. But that they were magnificent appears not only from Megasthenes's description of the buildings of Pāṭaliputra, quoted above, but also from the rapturous applauses of Fa-hien. Speaking of the palaces of Aśoka, the Chinese pilgrim remarks: "The royal palace and halls in the midst of the city, which exist now as of old, were all made by spirits which he (Aśoka) employed, and which piled up the stones, reared the walls and gates, and executed the elegant carving and inlaid sculpture-work,—in a way which no human hands of this world could accomplish."[1]

Residential Buildings.

The Indian art, which thus attained to a high standard of excellence during the period of the Mauryas, continued to flourish in the subsequent periods, and in some respects made further progress. This is most notably the case in the cosnstruction of cave-dwellings. During the four or five hundred years that followed the downfall of the Mauryan empire, hundreds of these were erected in different parts of India. They not only served as *vihāras* or residences for the wandering monks, but also as *chaitya-halls* or churches. The caves of Aśoka, although showing high technical skill, were neither very large nor richly carved. But many of the large caves of the next period, such as those at Bhājā, Bedsā, Kondane, Junnar, Nāsik, Ajantā and Ellorā in the west, and Udayagiri (near Bhuvaneshvar in Orissa) in the east, not only show considerable developments in style, but are also highly decorated with fine sculptures and ornaments, and rank very high in point of artistic achievement. The cave at Karle, between Bombay and Poona, is the finest example of this later series of caves. 'It resembles an early Christian church in its arrangements; consisting of a nave and side-aisles terminating in an apse or semidome, round which the aisle is carried. The general dimensions of the interior are 124 ft. 3 inches from the entrance to the back wall, by 45 ft. 6 inches in width, the height being 45 ft. from the floor to the apex. Fifteen pillars on each side separate the nave from the aisle; each pillar has a tall base, an octagonal shaft,

Post-Mauryan Art.

1. *Fa-hien*, by Legge, p. 77.

and richly ornamented capital, on the inner front of which kneel two elephants, each bearing two figures, generally a man and a woman, but sometimes two females, all very much better executed than such ornaments usually are; behind are horses and tigers, each bearing a single figure."[1]

Another instance of the progress of Indian art is to be seen in the highly ornamented gateways added to the *stūpas*, the most notable case being that of the four gateways of the Sānchi *stūpa*. Nothing but a special treatise on the subject will enable the reader to appreciate the wealth of ornaments lavished on the four monuments which are covered with masses of sculpture 'representing scenes in the life of Buddha, domestic and sylvan scenes, processions, sieges, and groups of ordinary and extraordinary animals.'[2] The gateways and the railing of the Bhārhut *stūpa*, and the railing and the *stūpa* itself at Amarāvati were also decorated with a multitude of fine sculptures. In variety and phonetic value these sculptures have never been excelled in the whole history of art.

There were various schools of sculpture in the post-Aśokan period, the most notable being those of Gandhāra, Mathurā, Sārnāth and Amarāvatī. A number of good specimens with well-marked peculiarities of style and technique have been discovered in these and other places. These form subjects of special treatment in books dealing with Indian art which should be consulted for detailed knowledge of the subject. The Gandhāra school, as its name implies, flourished in the North-western frontier of India. As has already been related this region was ruled over by a number of Greek princes for about three hundred years. The influx of this new element produced a novel school of art in this meeting ground of East and West, in which the skill and technique of the Greek art was applied to Indian ideals and Indian subjects. The result was an Indo-Hellenic school, which produced some of the finest sculptures—notably images of Buddha and Bodhisatva—that ancient India can boast of. Its chief characteristic is the realistic representation of human figures, as opposed to conventional form lacking in physiological details generally found in India. It no doubt influenced to some extent, as it was itself influenced by, the other schools of Indian art, such as those of Mathurā and Amarāvatī,

The different Schools of Sculpture.

1. Fergusson, op. cit. pp. 143-5.
2. Smith, op. cit., p. 70.

but the nature and extent of this influence are matters of controversy. It failed however, to penetrate deeply into the interior, and had no share in the later development of Indian art. 'But outside India the Gandhāra school achieved a grand success by becoming the parent of the Buddhist art of Eastern or Chinese Turkestan, Mongolia, China, Korea and Japan'.

This brief sketch of the development of art may be concluded with a general observation. In India, art has always been a hand-maid of religion. The period under review saw the great preponderance of Buddhism, and hence the art was employed mostly in the service of that religion. The architects built Buddhist *stūpas*, monasteries, and churches, while the sculptors found their *motif* or subject-matter in the legends of Buddha and the stories associated with his life and religion.

General view of Indian Art.

But within this limitation, the artist showed a broad conception of life, and fine appreciation of the beauties of nature. Trees, plants, lakes, rivers, animals, human figures and other *motifs* drawn directly from nature are all depicted in lovely combinations, and 'every scene in the relief sculptures of Bhārhut or Sānchi is full of the joy of life'.

The Jainas and the followers of Brāhmaṇical religion also employed artists, but their extant products are far less in number. It has been customary to classify art as the Buddhist, Jaina or Brāhmaṇical. This is not, however, strictly accurate. True classification of art depends upon time and localities, and not upon the particular religion which the artist may be called upon to serve. It would be wrong therefore to think of Buddhist or Jaina style in the domain of art.

BOOK III.

From c. 300 A.D. to c. 1200 A.D.

CHAPTER I.

The Gupta Empire.

1. *The Foundation of the Empire.*

After the downfall of the Kushāṇas and the Andhras no great political power arose in India for some time. As we have seen above, for about a century India was divided into a large number of independent States whose varying fortunes and mutual struggles are the chief features of the history of this period. There were kingdoms as well as non-monarchial states, and on the whole the political situation was not unlike that at the beginning of the sixth century B.C.

The Rise of the Gupta Dynasty.

About the beginning of the fourth century A.D., a chief called Śrī Gupta, or Gupta, ruled over a petty kingdom in Magadha, which probably also comprised a portion of Bengal. He was succeeded by his son Ghaṭotkacha. Neither the father nor the son seems to have possessed any considerable power. But with Chandragupta, the son of Ghaṭotkacha, began a new epoch in the history of the family.

Chandragupta.

An era beginning in 320 A.D., and known as the Gupta era, is generally believed to have started from the accession of Chandragupta. Chandragupta is also styled *Mahārājādhirāja* in striking contrast to the title *Māhārāja* of his two predecessors. These facts indicate that he raised the small principality to the status of an important kingdom by extending its boundaries in all directions. The means by which he accomplished this are not definitely known. He married a princess of the Lichchhavi family named Kumāradevī and had her portrait engraved on his coins together with his own. His son and successor, the great emperor Samudragupta, took pride on his descent, on the mother's side, from the Lichchhavis. These facts give rise to a natural presumption that the matrimonial connection with the Lichchhavis materially contributed to the political greatness of the Guptas. This is, however, a mere conjecture for which definite proof is yet lacking. For it is just possible that the Guptas acquired great social prestige by matrimonial relation with an ancient Kshatriya clan like the Lichchhavis, and naturally proclaimed this fact in all possible ways.

The exact boundaries of Chandragupta's kingdom are unknown, but it probably extended to the west as far as Allāhābād. He died about 340 A.D. and was succeeded by his son Samudragupta.

Samudragupta is one of the greatest military genius that India ever produced. His whole reign was a vast military campaign. He was an embodiment of the political principles preached by Kauṭilya *viz.* "Whoever is superior in power shall wage a war", "Whoever is possessed of necessary means shall march against his enemy." He first of all waged a ruthless war of extermination against his neighbouring kings in Northern India. He seems to have advanced as far as the Chambal and within this area, all the kings were killed, and their kingdoms incorporated into the growing Gupta empire. It was unnecessary for the valiant emperor to proceed further, either towards the east or towards the west, for the eastern kingdoms like Bengal, Assam, and Nepāl, the western non-monarchical tribal states like those of the Mālavas, Yaudheyas, Arjunāyanas, Madras, and Ābhīras in the Panjāb and Rājputāna, and a host of minor ones in Mālwa and Madhya Pradesh proffered submission of their own accord, and agreed to pay homage and taxes to the Gupta Emperor. Indeed, the terror of the Gupta arms was such that even the distant Kushāṇa kings of Afghānistān and the Śaka Satraps of Gujarāt sought the favour of Samudragupta.

Samudraguta

His conquest in Northern India.

But the most difficult undertaking of the Gupta Emperor was unquestionably the great military expedition to the south along the coast of the Bay of Bengal. Passing through the forest tracts of Madhya Pradesh, he proceeded to the Orissan coast, and then marching through Ganjam, Vizagapatam, Godāvarī, Kṛishṇā and Nellore districts, his victorious army reached as far as the famous Pallava kingdom of Kāñchī, now represented by Conjeevaram, south-west of Madras. The march along the coast suggests a joint operation by the navy. Although there is no definite proof of this, we know that many islands in the Indian Ocean were either conquered by the great Gupta monarch, or submitted to him out of fear, thus clearly indicating his possession of a powerful navy.

His Southern Campaign.

The southern expedition of Samudragupta, though highly successful from a military point of view, did not lead to any permanent conquest. More than twelve kings were defeated in battle and taken prisoners, but as Samudragupta could not hope to rule over their dominions permanently, he took the prudent course of re-instating them, probably as tributary kings. It reflects great credit on the political sagacity of Samudragupta that he knew the limitation of his power and capacity. He was content with direct rule over a consolidated dominion in Northern India, and an acknowledgment of supremacy from the rest. Had he essayed the almost impossible task of ruling the whole of India, like Aśoka, the Gupta empire would probably have met with an early end like its predecessor. But it is chiefly due to the statesmanship of Samudragupta that the vast empire which he left behind was gradually extended and gloriously maintained by his successors for nearly a hundred years more.

The Empire.

The empire consisted of four categories of territory. The first, which formed its core, was directly administered by the Emperor with the help of viceroys and other officials. It was roughly bounded by the Himālayas on the north, the Yamunā and the Chambal on the west, the Brahmaputra on the east, and an irregular line running through Bhilsā and Jubbulpore on the south. To the east and the west of this lay the tributary States, monarchical and republican mentioned above, which formed the second category. Further beyond lay the dominions of the Śakas and the Kushāṇas who were independent in name, but thought it politic to be submissive to the great Gupta emperor. This, the third category, might be classed as States in subordinate alliance. The fourth category consisted of the twelve States in the Deccan whose rulers were defeated and re-instated, and presumably paid homage, if not taxes. It was the policy of the subsequent Gupta emperors to extend gradually the territory of the first category at the expense of the second, and to convert the territory of the third category into the second or the first.

Personality of Samudragupta

Samudragupta was really a hero of hundred fights, as the court-poet describes him in a long laudatory inscription incised on the Aśokan pillar at Allāhābād from which we know all the facts about him recorded above. He was, however, not merely the first soldier of his age, but a statesman of no mean order. He was, besides, a man of culture. The court-poet describes him not only as brave and skilful in battle, but also as a patron of learning, a celebrated poet and a musician. That these attributes were not merely fanciful exaggerations of the poet, appears from some coins of the emperor in which he is represented as playing upon the lyre. We are further told that he possessed a noble bearing, and was the favourite of his royal father as well as of the people at large. It even seems probable that although not the eldest son he was selected as his successor by Chandragupta I. The Gupta kings were patrons of Brāhmaṇical religion, and Samudragupta restored the *Aśvamedha* sacrifice which had fallen into abeyance for a long time. But he was of tolerant spirit, and extended his favour to other religions. This is well illustrated by his gracious permission to the Buddhist king of Ceylon to build a monastery for his subjects at Bodh-Gayā. It appears that the Ceylonese pilgrims to Bodh-Gayā felt great inconvenience for want of a suitable residence, and represented their grievances to the king Meghavarṇa of Ceylon. The latter sent an envoy with rich presents to Samudragupta to obtain permission to build a monastery for his subjects, and the Gupta emperor graciously sanctioned the laudable project, which was duly carried into effect.

Chandragupta II.

Samudragupta died in or shortly before 380 A.D. and was succeeded by Chandragupta, II,[1] the worthy son of a worthy father. He not only successfully maintained the vast empire that his father had left, but also added to it by conquests of his own. Following in the footsteps of his father, he proceeded on a career of conquest. He first directed his arms against the Śaka rulers known as Western Satraps (p. 126) ruling in Gujarāt and Kāthiāwār Peninsula. Since the usurpation of the throne by Rudrasiṁha II, mentioned above, the Śaka kingdom was passing through troublesome times. Neither he nor his son assumed the higher title of Mahākshatrapa, and after their reigns were over, no coins of this dynasty seem to have been issued for a period of 16 years from 332 to 348 A.D. A Śaka official, Śrīdharavarman, had already set up as an independent king in Mālwa, and there were probably similar revolts in other parts of the kingdom. The family of Rudrasiṁha II was ousted by Rudrasena III who restored the authority and prestige of the kingdom to some extent. He ruled from 360 to 380 A.D. in comparative peace,

1. See Appendix I.

but soon troubles broke out again. More than one rival king appeared on the scene after 380 A.D., and the Śaka kingdom was torn asunder by internal dissensions ending in the accession of Rudrasiṁha III, some time between 380 and 398 A.D. Chandragupta had inherited an empire which almost touched on the borders of the Śaka kingdom, and he evidently took advantage of its internal dissensions, even if he did not actually foment them, to reduce these foreign chiefs. He accordingly invaded their territory with a powerful army. The details of the struggle are unknown, but Rudrasiṁha III, the last of the long line of Śaka Satraps who had been ruling since 78 A.D. , was killed, and his dominions were annexed by Chandragupta II. This conquest destroyed the last vestige of foreign rule in India, and extended the Gupta empire up to the Arabian Sea, its natural frontier on the west. The new acquisitions were, however, also important from another point of view. The Gujarāt coast contained the important ports and harbours for vessels plying between India and the Western world. Masters of these stations, the Gupta kings came into possession of a vast source of wealth. Besides, their empire was now opened up, as it were, to the Western World, and the free intercourse between the two was probably of far-reaching consequence.

The end of Śaka rule.

Chandragupta II was probably engaged in other wars and conquests also. An inscription, engraved on the famous iron pillar near Qutb Minar at Delhi states that a king Chandra "defeated a confederacy of hostile chiefs in Vaṅga, and having crossed in warfare the seven mouths of the river Sindhu, conquered the Vāhlikas." This king Chandra is probably Chandragupta II, for we know of no other king of this name who could possibly carry on victorious military campaigns as far as Bengal in the east and beyond the Sindhu on the west.

Other wars.

If we accept the proposed identity, we must hold that Chandragupta II rounded off the Gupta empire and extended it to its natural frontier, not only in the west, as mentioned above, but also in the east and the north-west. The eastern campaign was probably necessitated by the rising of the petty chiefs of Bengal in a vain attempt to throw off the yoke of the Gupta empire which Samudragupta had already imposed on them. But they were defeated, and probably the whole of Bengal was now brought within the direct administration of the emperor.

The north-western campaign was undoubtedly directed against the Kushāṇa rulers of Afghānistān. If the Vāhlika territory conquered by Chandragupta really represents Balkh (Bactria), its normal connotation, we must credit him with an achievement to which no other Hindu king can lay any claim, not even his namesake of the Maurya family. But although it might have been a great success from a military point of view, its permanent results are uncertain. We do not know whether the tributary tribal States in the Panjāb, through which he must have passed, were incorporated into the empire like Bengal, or whether the Kushāṇa dominions, further beyond, were brought definitely within its fold. As a matter of fact, we have no further evidence that these territories were associated in any way with the Gupta empire after Chandragupta II. Chandragupta's chief queen was Dhruvadevī or Dhruvasvāminī whose name figures in the strange legend of Rāmagupta and gives it a semblance of reality.[1] But he also married a princess of the Nāga family named Kuveranāgā. The issue of this marriage was a daughter named Prabhāvatīguptā who was married to the Vākāṭaka king Rudrasena II. These two marriages were probably dictated by political considerations. For both the Nāgas and the Vākāṭakas held strategic positions on the frontier of the Gupta empire, and might have rendered great help or proved highly dangerous in respect of the expansion of the Gupta empire to the west and north-west. The daughters of the Kadamba ruler Kākusthavarman of Kuntala (N. Kanara in Bombay) were married in the Gupta family, and we have already seen that Chandragupta I married the Lichchhavi princess Kumāradevī. All these indicate that matrimonial relations with powerful royal families formed a part of the imperial policy of the Guptas.

Conquest of the Vāhlika country

The reigns of Samudragupta and Chandragupta, covering nearly three-quarters of a century, once more brought about the political unity of Northern India. In spite of numerous wars people enjoyed prosperity and security of life and property. The administration was highly organised and was far more liberal than in the Maurya times. Fa-hien, a Chinese pilgrim, travelled through the Gupta Empire during the reign of Chandragupta II,

Gupta Empire.

1. See Appendix 1.

and has left a very pleasing picture of the country. The taxes were light and the administration was very liberal. Cruel punishments, so much in vogue in Maurya times, were abolished, and harassing rules and regulations like Registration and Passports were unknown. Fa-hien everywhere witnessed the wealth and luxury of the people, and the economic condition was very satisfactory. Trade and commerce flourished, and the people followed various arts and crafts. The period also ushered in a tremendous intellectual and religious revival, accompanied by wonderful achievements in art and architecture, which will be described in detail in later chapters.

Vikramāditya.

The chief credit for all this undoubtedly belongs to Samudragupta and Chandragupta II. Both of them assumed the title Vikramāditya and none had probably a juster claim to the position occupied in popular mind by that legendary hero. It is possible that the exploits of that hero were recalled to the people by those of the two Gupta emperors (and their successors some of whom assumed the same title) and the whole thing was jumbled up in the developed form of Vikramāditya-saga of later times. Most of the scholars, however, do not believe in the existence of a real or legendary king Vikramāditya before Chandragupta II. They regard him as the king Vikramāditya whom Indian legends credit with having defeated the Śakas and established the famous *Vikrama Saṁvat* in 58 B.C., and whose court is said to have been graced by *Navaratna* (nine gems) including the famous Kālidāsa. Chandragupta II no doubt defeated the Śakas, and it is just possible that the poet Kālidāsa lived in his court. But it is difficult to explain his connection with the *Vikrama Saṁvat* which was current for about five centuries before his time. It has been suggested that the era was not originally founded by any Vikramāditya, but later on associated with a king of that name. Convincing proofs, are, however, lacking on this point, and the origin of the *Vikrama Saṁvat* and the identity of king Vikramāditya must still be reckoned among the unsolved problems of Indian history.

2. *Kumāragupta and Skandagupta.*

Kumārgupta.

Chandragupta II died about 413 A.D., and was succeeded by his son Kumāragupta, who enjoyed a long reign of more than forty years. He performed an *Aśvamedha* sacrifice, which usually implies some notable military conquest. But none is recorded, and we do not know of any of his achievements. The epigraphic records, however, show that he organised the administration of the vast empire. The very fact that he could consolidate the empire, and maintain intact its peace, prosperity and security for the long period of forty years, reflects no small credit upon his tact and ability. But towards the close of his reign hordes of the Pushyamitras, probably a tribe allied to the Hūṇas, that terrible scourge of mankind, invaded India and threatened the mighty fabric of the Gupta empire. For a long time, the fortune of the Guptas, nay of India, was tottering, but the heroic energy and the military genius of the crown-prince Skandagupta at last saved the situation. The barbaric hordes were defeated and the empire was saved. So terrific was the conflict that the heir to the mighty empire had to pass a night on the bare ground. India, which was thus delivered from the fury of these fierce barbarians, did not fail to show its gratitude to its saviour. We are told that songs of praise in honour of Skandagupta were sung in all directions by men, women and even children. In the midst of this great triumph, the old and aged emperor Kumāragupta breathed his last, and Skandagupta, the hero of the nation, succeeded him (455 A.D.).

Skandagupta

There are good grounds to believe that Skandagupta's succession to the throne was not a peaceful one, and there was a struggle between him and his half-brother Pūru-gupta, son of the chief queen of Kumāragupta. Probably Skandagupta's mother was a queen of an inferior rank and this gave an advantage to his rival. But Skandagupta triumphed at the end. It is stated in his own official record that "the goddess of sovereignty, of her own accord, selected him as her husband, having in succession discarded all other princes." The same idea is probably also visibly portrayed on a type of Skandagupta's coins in which a female figure stands before the king and offers him something like a fillet. This rivalry between Skandagupta and Pūrugupta did not end with the accession of Skandagupta, and probably had repercussion on the question of succession after his death. Certain it is that Skandagupta was succeeded by Pūrugupta or his sons, who in their official records traced the genealogy direct from Kumāragupta omitting altogether the name of Skandagupta.

Skandagupta's reign seems to have been full of wars. His greatest enemies were the Hūṇas, a ferocious barbarian horde who lived in Central Asia and were at this very moment threatening the mighty Roman Empire. One branch of them, known as the Ephthalites or White Huns, occupied the Oxus valley and advanced against both Persia and India. They crossed the Hindu Kush, occupied Gandhāra and hurled defiance at the mighty Gupta empire. It was a grave peril to the whole of India, and the magnitude of the danger must have been heightened by the tales of terrible atrocities and wholesale destruction which marked the advance of this cruel and vindictive race. The danger was perhaps far greater than the one which Skandagupta faced towards the close of his father's reign. Once more he rose equal to the occasion and inflicted such a terrible defeat upon the Hūṇas that for half a century they dared not disturb the Gupta empire though they wrought havoc on Persia during this period. In the light of subsequent events in India, and the history of the Hūṇa raids in other countries, the successful and effective resistance to them by Skandagupta must rank as one of the greatest achievements of the age. His grateful countrymen hailed him as the saviour of India and modern historians must endorse this popular verdict. This heroic feat fully entitled Skandagupta to assume the title Vikramāditya which Samudragupta and Chandragupta II did before him.

The Hūṇa war, and possibly other battles which are only vaguely mentioned in official records, must have proved a great strain on the financial resources of the empire, for this alone can satisfactorily account for the fact that the gold coins issued by Skandagupta were not only comparatively small in number and belonged to a single type, as opposed to a large variety of his predecessors, but also show depreciation in the purity of gold. Nevertheless, we have evidence of large works of public utility undertaken at a distant corner of his empire. Two interesting inscriptions, engraved on the Girnar Hill near Junāgaḍh, record the history of a big irrigation lake or reservoir, named Sudarśana, originally constructed in the regin of Chandragupta Maurya by building an embankment across a small gap in a natural depression on the hill. The rain water collected there was carried by irrigation channels to distant lands and fertilised them. Once in 150 A.D. the embankment burst and was repaired by the Śaka Satrap Rudradāman I, who left a record of his achievement in an inscription from which we know most of the details of his reign mentioned above (p. 124). The second inscription in this

Sudarśana Lake

locality tells us that owing to excessive rain, the Sudarśana lake once again burst its embankment in the year 136 of the Gupta era (455-6 A.D.) in the reign of Skandagupta, but his governor Parṇadatta, who was in charge of the province of Surāshṭra, repaired the damages and saved the people from a great calamity. These two inscriptions on the same hill testify to the great care bestowed on irrigation in ancient India ; they are also silent witnesses of the great change by which the Śaka kingdom became an integral part of the Gupta empire.

The inscription of Parṇadatta enables us to visualise the real nature of the mighty Gupta empire as it developed in the time of Skandagupta. It shows us that the process of empire-building initiated by Samudragupta was nearly completed so far at least as North India was concerned. The command of Skandagupta was obeyed by his governors of Bengal and Kāthiāwār Peninsula, and one imperial writ ran from the Bay of Bengal to the Arabian Sea.

3. *The Successors of Skandagupta.*

According to a contemporary record, peace and prosperity prevailed over this vast empire at the time of Skandagupta's death, which probably took place about 467 A.D. The history of the Gupta empire, immediately after this, is very obscure. We know the names of a number of kings, but their dates and relation to each other cannot always be determined. Scholars naturally put forward different views about the reconstruction of the history of this period, none of which is free from objections. The following sketch should, therefore, be regarded as nothing more than a reasonable hypothesis on the basis of facts known at present.

As mentioned above, the official genealogy traces the succession in the Imperial Gupta family from Kumāragupta to his son Pūrugupta by his chief queen Anantadevī, and omits all reference to Skandagupta. We do not know for certain whether Pūrugupta ascended the throne immediately after his father's death and was ousted by Skandagupta after his return from his campaign against the Pushyamitras or whether Pūrugupta succeeded Skandagupta immediately or shortly after his death, either by natural right or by removing the legitimate heir. There is, however, no doubt that Pūrugupta did rule for some time, though in either case his

Pūrugupta

reign was probably a very short one. He was succeeded by his son Budhagupta whose earliest known date is 477 A.D. But we have an inscription of a king called Kumāragupta (II) dated 474 A.D. His relation to Pūrugupta is not known, and his history is very obscure. It may be that he was Skandagupta's son or legitimate successor, who revolted against the usurpation of the throne by Pūrugupta, or by removing whom Pūrugupta ascended the throne. In any case Pūrugupta's son Budhagupta ruled from A.D. 477 to at least A.D. 495, and probably up to 500 A.D., without any rival, and there is no reason to suppose that the peace and prosperity of the empire suffered to any considerable extent during this period.

Kumāragupta II

Budhagupta

There were, however, ominous signs portending the break-up of the empire at no distant date. General Bhaṭārka of the Maitraka family, who was appointed governor of the distant province of Surāshṭra (Kāthiāwār Peninsula) with his head-quarters at Valabhī, made his position hereditary. Both he and his eldest son, who succeeded him, called themselves merely *Senāpati* (General), but the latter's younger brother and successor, Droṇasiṁha, assumed the title *Mahārāja* and claimed that the paramount ruler in person installed him in royalty by a regular ceremony. The paramount ruler is not named, but was almost certainly no other than Budhagupta. This shows that the Maitrakas were well on the way to found the independent kingdom of Valabhī, but it also proves that they formally acknowledged the suzerainty of the Gupta empire, certainly up to the end of the 5th century A.D., and possibly for many years more, as we shall see later.

Things were not so bad in the opposite corner of the empire, but it was not perhaps without significance that whereas the governors of North Bengal had the title *Uparika* in the days of Kumāragupta I, they now called themselves *Uparika Mahārāja*. The governors in Mālwa also assumed the title *Mahārāja*, and land-grants issued by several chiefs either do not contain reference to the reigning Gupta emperor, as was the custom, or simply refer to the Gupta sovereignty in general terms without mentioning the name of the emperor. These indicate that though theoretically the Gupta Empire did not suffer any substantial diminution and still extended from the Bay of Bengal to the Arabian Sea, its power and prestige were visibly on the decline. The war of succession, if any, after the death of Kumāragupta I, and again after the death of Skandagupta or shortly before it, is probably chiefly responsible for this, and the severe strain of the Hūṇa invasion might have been a contributing factor. There were probably other causes which we do not yet know, but there is no doubt that decline had already set in.

The death of Budhagupta was followed by a period of troubles caused by dissensions in the royal family, revolt of feudal chiefs, and foreign invasions,—all the three acting and reacting upon each other. It is not possible to give a chronological narrative, or even to indicate broadly the sequence of events during the first half of the 6th century A.D. All that we can do is to bring out clearly the main facts under the three heads mentioned above.

Successors of Budhagupta.

It appears from the official genealogy that Budhagupta was succeeded by his brother Narasiṁhagupta and the latter by his son and grandson, named respectively Kumāragupta (III) and Vishṇugupta. There are good grounds to believe that the last of these ended his reign about 550 A.D. and it is, therefore, reasonable to presume that the reigns of the three successors of Budhagupta covered the first half of the 6th century A.D. But epigraphic records show that at least two other Gupta kings ruled during the period. One of them, Vainyagupta, issued a land-grant in Eastern Bengal in 507 A.D., and his gold coins and seals leave no doubt that he belonged to the Imperial Gupta family. The other, Bhānugupta, is also known from a single inscription dated 510 A.D. on a memorial pillar found at Eran (Saugor Dist. M. P.). It tells us that "the mightly king, the glorious Bhānugupta, the bravest man on the earth," fought a battle in which his feudatory chief Goparāja was killed, and the latter's wife died with him in the same funeral pyre,—the earliest epigraphic record of the *Satī* rite in India.

No coin or seal of Bhānugupta has as yet come to light. But his name and the qualifying epithets leave no reasonable doubt that he belonged to the Gupta family. We can also surmise, without difficulty, the enemies against whom he fought the famous battle at Eran. We know from two other epigraphic records found in this locality that some time after the year 485 A.D., but within one generation, the region round Eran passed from the hands of the Guptas to a chief named Toramāṇa who was most probably a Hūṇa. It is almost certain, therefore, that Bhānugupta fought the great battle in 510 A.D. against this Hūṇa invader. Unfortunately, the result of the battle is not known, and we cannot say whether Bhānugupta opposed the invader and failed, or drove him out after a short occupation of the country.

The rule of two Gupta kings who cannot be made to fit in with the official genealogy, and the penetration of the Hūṇas as far as Eran, leave no doubt that within a decade or two of Budhagupta's death, the Empire was faced with internal dissensions and foreign invasions. There might have been other disturbing factors too. For the Vākāṭaka king Narendrasena is also said to have established his supremacy in Mālwa and other parts of the Gupta empire. The invasion by that ruler of the Deccan probably also falls in this period.

4 *The Huns and Yaśodharman.*

The Hūṇas who reappeared after half a century had grown very powerful in the meantime. Checked in India by Skandagupta, they had turned towards Persia. The Persian king Firuz, who opposed them, was defeated and killed. Emboldened by this success they spread far and wide and by the end of the 5th century ruled over a vast empire with their headquarters at Balkh; Gandhāra and probably also a part of the Panjāb were included in their dominion.

So far we are more or less on sure grounds. But no details of the further progress of the Huns into India, and the opposition, if any, offered by the Gupta empire at the frontier, are known to us. When the curtain lifts, we find Toramāṇa established in Eran, in the heart of the Gupta empire. Although there is no conclusive evidence that he was a Hūṇa, all the circumstantial evidence points in this direction. But even then we cannot say whether he represented the central authority of the Hūṇas in Balkh or Gandhāra, or was a freebooter who undertook the invasion on his own account, like Bakhtyār Khilji of a later period. In any case, the coins of Toramāṇa show that he was a foreigner, closely associated with the Hūṇas, and ruled over a vast dominion in India comprising Kāshmir, Panjāb, Rājputāna, Mālwa and parts of the U. P. He was succeeded by his son Mihirakula, whose record has been found at Gwālior and whose great power and incredible cruelties are echoed in the popular legends recorded by Hiuen Tsang and in the *Rājataraṅgiṇī*. According to the former his capital was at Sākala (Sialkot in the Panjāb). A book, called *Christian Topo-*

Toramāṇa.

Mihirakula.

graphy, composed by an Alexandrine Greek some time between 525 and 535 A.D., refers to the great power of the White Huns in India. Their country, he says, is on the other side of the Indus, but their chief Gollas "is the lord of India, and oppressing the people, forces them to pay tribute." Gollas is most probably to be identified with Mihirakula, and we may well believe that he became a regular terror to the whole of North India.

But Mihirakula was not destined to enjoy his power for long. Two different sources refer to his defeat and discomfiture in the hands of two different persons which not only put an end to his power but also to the Hūṇa menace in India.

Yaśodharman.

The first to oppose Mihirakula was Yaśodharman, whose brilliant career is known from a single record, engraved in duplicate on two pillars at Mandasor, in Mālwa. He probably belonged to an old family known as Aulikara, whose members ruled in Mālwa since the 4th century A.D., first as independent rulers, and then as feudatories of the Guptas. Yośodharman not only threw off the yoke of the Gupta emperor but carried his victorious arms far and wide. According to the official eulogy his suzerainty was acknowledged over the vast area bounded by the Himālayas in the north, the Mahendra mountains (Ganjam District) in the south, the Brahmaputra river in the east, and the ocean in the west. It is also claimed that he was lord of the countries which were not possessed by the Guptas or the Hūṇas. Finally we are told that "obeisance was made to his feet by even the famous king Mihirakula."

Even making due allowance for the obvious exaggerations of the court-poet, we may well believe that Yaśodharman made himself master of a large part of the Gupta empire and inflicted a defeat upon Mihirakula. All this probably took place before 530 A.D. as a record dated in that year refers to Yaśodharman as a great suzerain.

The victorious campaigns of Yaśodharman and the extent of his dominions, as described by his court-poet, would seem to imply that the Gupta empire had ceased to exist. But this was far from being the case. For we have good grounds to believe that the Gupta emperor Narasiṁhagupta not only survived the shock but transmitted his kingdom and the imperial tradition to his son and grandson. What is more important, he probably dealt the final blow which crushed Mihirakula. This we learn from Hiuen Tsang who describes in great detail how Mihirakula invaded Magadha, was defeated and captured by king Bālāditya; and how his life was saved at the intercession of the queen-mother of Magadha. Mihirakula returned to his dominions only to find that his brother had usurped the throne. He took shelter in Kāshmir, seized its throne by treachery, and conquered Gandhāra, but died within a year.

It is difficult to accept as true all the details recorded by Hiuen Tsang, but the general outline of his story, as given above, may be regarded as historical. There is also no doubt that Bālādityarāja of Magadha, as Hiuen Tsang puts it, refers to the Gupta emperor Narasiṁhagupta, whose gold coins show that he assumed the title Bālāditya. In an inscription at Nālandā, of the 8th century A.D., the king Bālāditya is described as "the great king of irresistible valour who after having vanquished all the foes enjoyed the entire earth". The fact that even two hundred years later Narasiṁhagupta Bālāditya lived in popular memory as a great king and conqueror lends some support to the story of Hiuen Tsang about him. It is interesting to note that both Hiuen Tsang and the 8th century inscription credit Bālāditya with having founded a great temple at Nālandā.

The question naturally arises, what had Narasiṁhagupta been doing during the first 30 years of the 6th century A.D. after the death of Budhagupta? We do not positively know, but may suggest that his power was kept in check, and possibly rendered nugatory, first by the rise of rival kings like Vainyagupta and Bhānugupta, and then by the successful revolt of Yaśodharman. It is also not unlikely that he ascended his ancestral throne only after the death of these rivals, hiding himself or leading an obscure life during this long period of thirty to forty years. For all we know, it is not unlikely that Vainyagupta or Bhānugupta, if not both, had a more legitimate claim to the throne, and that Narasiṁhagupta, by virtue of his descent, occupied the throne at a comparatively advanced age after the empire had been convulsed by the Hūṇas and the military campaigns of Yaśodharman.

5. *The Fall of the Gupta Empire.*

Whatever we may think of these possible alternatives, we may regard it as tolerably certain that Narasiṁhagupta and his two successors carried on the imperial tradition till about the middle of the 6th century A.D. This is proved, among others, by the fact that following the old tradition, all the land-grants of the Maitrakas of Valabhī, 14 in number, ranging in date between

526 and 545 A.D., express allegiance to *paramabhaṭṭāraka* or the paramount lord. The allegiance is no doubt nominal and formal, but this very fact shows that the paramount lord refers to the Gupta emperor. For such formal honour is usally paid to old royal families out of long-standing custom. A new authority either exacts real submission or is simply ignored.

Hiuen Tsang refers to Narasiṁhagupta as king of Magadha. Possibly his effective authority did not extend much beyond Magadha and North Bengal. A land-grant in North Bengal, dated 543 A.D., mentions as suzerain, one whose name is lost except the last two letters 'Gupta'. Possibly he was Vishṇugupta, son of Kumāragupta III and grandson of Narasiṁhagupta. All these three kings issued gold coins of the same type, but their continued debasement proves the rapid decline of the Gupta power.

Last three emperors

This decline was precipitated by the assumption of independence by the provincial governors and feudal chiefs. Yaśodharman set the fatal example which was perhaps nore disastrous to the Gupta empire than even the Hūṇa invasion. How Yassodharman's power came to an end, and what became of him or his successors, we do not know. He rose and vanished like a meteor without leaving any trace behind. This gave the Gupta empire some respite, but it was of short duration. Yaśodharman's example was followed by others. Among them the most powerful were the Later Guptas and the Maukharis who were at first feudatories to the Guptas but later established independent kingdoms in Magadha and the U.P. Independent kingdoms were also established in Bengal and other parts of India, and the Gupta empire now offered the same spectacle as was presented by the Mughul empire after the invasion of Nādir Shāh. But while the phantom Mughul emperors sat on the throne of Delhi for a century more, we do not hear of any Gupta emperor after Vishṇugupta, though it is possible that he might have one or more successors whose names are yet unknown to us.

Rebellion of Feudatory Chiefs.

A land-grant was issued in the Gayā district, in the very heart of Magadha, in 551-2 A D. by a person who calls himself *Kumārāmātya Mahārāja*. As no reference is made to the Gupta king, we must presume that by 550 A.D. the Guptas had ceased to exercise any effective authority even in Magadha. But the official name *Kumārāmātya* shows that like the *Viziers* of Āvadh, he dared not throw off the last vestige of homage to the Imperial House. But of that House itself we have no further evidence.

It would appear from what has been said above that the Hūṇa invasion was not the sole, or perhaps even the principal, cause of the downfall of the Gupta empire, as is generally supposed. The more important causes were the internal dissensions in the royal family and the revolt of the provincial governors or feudal chiefs. These were the immediate causes, though the Hūṇa, invasion might have been a remote cause and contributory factor of no mean importance.

The period of Gupta supremacy which covers more than two centuries is regarded by common consent as the most glorious epoch in Indian history. This view is fully justified by the wonderful outburst of intellectual activity in art, science and literature such as we witness not only during this period but also for a century more, which together constitute the Gupta Age, properly so called. It has been styled variously as the Golden, Classical, and the Periclean Age of India, and some account of its cultural achievements will be described in Chapters XVII and XX.

APPENDIX I

Rāmagupta

According to a popular story which forms the subject-matter of a dramatic work, *Devī-Chandraguptam*, Samudragupta was succeeded by his elder son Rāmagupta. This king, we are told, was so cowardly and devoid of a sense of honour, that once while he was closely besieged by a Śaka king and found no means to escape, he readily agreed to purchase his safety by surrendering his queen Dhruvadevī to his adversary. His younger brother Chandragupta, however, rejected this proposal with scorn. He disguised himself as the queen and, with a few brave followers similarly disguised as female attendants, visited the camp of the Śaka king in compliance with the terms of the treaty, killed the Śaka king, and returned in safety. Naturally he won high favour of the queen and the people who were thoroughly disgusted at the conduct of the king. Taking advantage of the unpopularity of king Rāmagupta, Chandragupta killed him, seized the throne, and married the widowed queen Dhruvadevī.

That this story had wide currency in later times is proved by both epigraphic and literary records. The earliest reference to it is to be found in a passage in *Harsha-charita* (7th century A.D.) which simply mentions the fact that Chandragupta, disguised in female attire, killed the Śaka king who coveted another's wife. The more important parts of the story viz. that Chandragupta deprived his elder brother of his life, wife, and throne, appears in a Rāshṭrakūṭa inscription of the 9th century A.D. Further references occur in literary works of later date.

In spite of this corroborative evidence it is difficult to accept the story as historically true. Apart from the inherent improbability of the story, the fact remains that the name of Rāmagupta never occurs either in the genealogical lists of the Gupta emperors supplied by numerous seals and inscriptions, or in a single coin out of the hundreds belonging to the dynasty that have been discovered so far. Epigraphia Indica, xix, pp. 139-51.

CHAPTER II

North India from C. 500 A.D. to C. 650 A.D.

1. *Up to the accession of Harsha-vardhana*

The break-up of the Gupta empire was followed by inevitable results. The provinces and feudatory States declared their independence and the whole of North India was divided into a number of independent States. In the home provinces of the Guptas we find a long line of rulers, all of whom except one had their names ending in Gupta. Hence the family is known in History as the 'Later Guptas of Magadha.' It is not possible to determine whether they were connected in any way with the imperial Guptas. Nor are we quite sure whether they occupied Magadha from the very beginning, as they certainly did in later times. It is held by some that they ruled in Mālwa till the time of Harsha-Vardhana. Some of the kings of this family were very powerful and carried their victorious arms as far as the Brahmaputra. More than one of them had to fight hard with their neighbour, the Maukharis, whose territory corresponded to the United Provinces or Uttara Pradesh, and who were rapidly rising to power. The Maukharis conquered part of Magadha and some branches of the family ruled even in the Gayā District. Two of their kings, Iśānavarman and his son Śarvavarman, styled themselves *Mahārājādhirāja*, and this pretension to supreme power was backed by conquest of extensive territories including the Andhra country. But the principal event in the history of the Maukharis, and the one which entitles them to be commemorated in Indian History, is the stubborn opposition they offered to the Hūṇas, who once more moved towards the heart of India. It has been already related how these black marauders, the scourge of the civilised world, more than once poured like a deluge upon the fair valleys and cities of India. It is painful to describe the scenes that followed. Rapine, massacre, and incendiarism marked the route of the barbarians. Cities were blotted out of existence, finest buildings were reduced to

Later Guptas.

The Maukharis

Hūṇas.

a heap of ruins, and temples and monastries, even where they were not violently pulled down, stood empty and desolate. The valley of the Kābul and Swat rivers, one of the most flourishing centres of Indian civilisation, was so completely devastated that the greater part of it has ever since remained outside the pale of civilisation, fit only for the habitation of wild tribes like those who live there today.

The terror which the advancing Hūṇas inspired in the millions of Indian hearts can better be imagined than described. It was at this critical moment that the Maukharis stood as bulwark of Indian civilisation. Under the leadership of Īśāna-varman the Indians fought stubbornly to protect their hearth and home. After a long and arduous struggle the Maukhari chief succeeded in checking the Hūṇas and thus saved Eastern India from their aggression.

Of the various other powers that arose out of the ruins of the Gupta empire, two only need specific mention. As related above, the Maitraka clan, under its leader Bhaṭārka, established a kingdom in Saurāshṭra with Valabhī as capital. The earlier chiefs of the dynasty were feudatory to the Guptas, but soon after the destruction of that power they declared their independence. From this time the boundaries of the kingdom were rapidly extended and Valabhī became not only a seat of learning and culture, but also a centre of trade and commerce. The Maitraka clan continued as an important power for well nigh three hundred years when they were probably overthrown by the Arab invaders from Sindh.

The Maitrakas of Valabhī.

Another State which was founded about the same time as Valabhī, but was destined to play a far more distinguished part in Indian history, was that of Thāneswar. The first three kings of this dynasty are mere names and do not seem to have exercised considerable powers. The fourth king Prabhākara-vadharna extended his kingdom at the expense of his neighbours, and assumed the imperial title of *Paramabhaṭṭāraka Mahārājādhirāja*. His sovereignty probably extended to the whole of the Panjāb in the north-west and part of Mālwa in the south. He was busy in his aggressive expeditions when he died in 604 A. D., leaving two sons, Rājya-vardhana and Harsha-vardhana, and a daughter Rājyaśrī married to the Maukhari king Grahavarman. Rājya-vardhana. being the elder of the two sons, succeeded his father.

Thāneshwar.

While Prabhākara-vardhana was rapidly extending the boundaries of his kingdom towards the west and south, two powerful kingdoms were established in Bengal and Assam. The people of Bengal are not known to have played any important political part in Indian history till after the downfall of the Imperial Guptas. About 525 A.D. an independent kingdom was established in Vaṅga i.e. East and South Bengal, but North Bengal still remained under the Guptas. When the Gupta empire fell, Gauḍa, comprising West and probably also North Bengal asserted independence, but was defeated by the Maukharis. Half a century later, the throne of Gauḍa was occupied by Śaśāṅka. He fixed his capital at Karṇasuvarṇa (near Murshidābād) and probably soon made himself master of the whole of Bengal. He belongs to the same type of military adventurers as Yaśodharman, and we know equally little of his predecessors and successors. Like Yaśodharman he rose and vanished like a meteor, leaving behind only the record of a splendid military career. Under him Bengal commenced that career of aggrandisement which was destined to raise her to the position of imperial supremacy. He cinquered Orissa and annexed it to his dominions. He also established his supremacy over the kingdom of Koṅgoda in the Ganjam district. He then advanced against Kanauj in the west. This region was then occupied by the Maukharis, whose enmity with Bengal commenced half a century ago, as mentioned above. But the Maukhari king Grahavarman, as already related, had married the daughter of Prabhākara-vardhana and this alliance no doubt strengthened his position. As a counter-move against this, Śaśāṅka contracted an alliance with the king of Mālava, who was glad to obtain the aid of such a powerful ally against the king of Thāneswar who was invading his territories.

Śaśāṅka of Gauḍa.

Thus, at the time when Rājya-vardhana ascended the throne, there were two political leagues in Northern India under the leadership of the two most powerful kingdoms of Bengal and Thāneswar. It appears that the Bengal group took the initiative and completely surprised the Maukhari capital. The king Grahavarman was killed and the queen Rājyaśrī thrown into prison.

So complete was the surprise that the first news of the battle and its tragic end reached Rājya-vardhana at the same time. He at once proceeded with a force of 10,000 cavalry to avenge the wrongs done to his sister. His promptness of action had its reward. He met with an advance-guard of the enemy under the king of Mālava and defeated him. Then with the small force at his command, he proceeded towards Kānyakubja. On the way, he was killed by Śaśāṅka, and his discomfited host returned to Thāneswar (606 A.D.).

An impenetrable mystery hangs round this tragic episode. The partisans of Rājya-vardhana have ascribed his murder to foul treachery on the part of Śaśāṅka, but there are reasons to believe that this is a perversion of truth for party purposes. Our sole authorities, Bāṇabhaṭṭa and Hiuen Tsang, were both hostile to Śaśāṅka, and cannot be looked upon as impartial. But while they agree as to the treachery of Śaśāṅka, they widely differ as to the circumstances under which it was played. On the other hand, the almost contemporary inscription of Harsha says that Rājya-vardhana "gave up his life in the mansion of his foe owing to his adherence to a promise." Between these widely divergent accounts, it is impossible to arrive at any definite conclusion. Certain it is, that Rājya-vardhana failed in his enterprise and lost his life.

2. *Harshavardhana*

Harsha-vardhana.

On the death of Rājya-vardhana the councillors of State offered the throne to his younger brother Harsha-vardhana, also known as Śīlāditya. At first the nobles of the court hesitated to offer, and the young Hasrha-vardhana was reluctant to accept the terrible responsibilities of kingship at such a critical time, but all doubts and fears were set at rest by the indomitable energy and military genius which the young king displayed on his accession (606 A.D.). He swore vengeance at Śaśāṅka and equipped a large expedition against him. He also entered into an alliance with Bhāskara-varman, king of Kāmarūpa, who was afraid of the growing power of Śaśāṅka. But Harsha's first care was for his sister. News arrived that she had been set free from the prison of Kanauj by the magnanimity of her foe, but felt so distracted at the news of her brother's death, that she retired to the Vindhya forest. There Harsha traced her, just at the very moment when, out of sheer desperation, she was going to throw herself into fire with all her attendants.

Having rescued his sister, Harsha joined his army on the bank of the Gaṅgā and then proceeded on a career of conquest to the east with a view to avenge the death of his brother by defeating Śaśāṅka. He was successful in his military enterprise, and conquered a great part of Northern India. Hiuen Tsang tells us that "he waged incessant warfare, until in six years, he had fought the five Indias. Then, having enlarged his territory, he increased his army, bringing the elephant corps upto 60,000, and the cavalry to 100,000, and reigned in peace for thirty years without raising a weapon." This sweeping statement about the success of Harsha's arms requires some correction. In the first place, the chief object of his military campaign was not fulfilled. For Śaśāṅka seems to have reigned in glory till at least 619 A.D., as in an inscription, dated in that year, he is invoked as the suzerain power by a feudatory chief in the Ganjam District. Secondly, Harsha's attempts to carry his arms beyond the Narmadā completely failed, and he sustained a decisive defeat in the hands of Pulakeśin, the Chālukya king of the south.

His conquest.

Towards the close of his reign Harsha undertook another military campaign to the east. Śaśāṅka was now dead and he had left no able heir to maintain his empire. Harsha had consequently no difficulty in overrunning it. He conquered Magadha and carried his victorious arms through West Bengal as far as Koṅgoda (Ganjam District), the southern limit of Śaśāṅka's empire. The rest of Śaśāṅka's dominions i.e. North, South, and East Bengal, passed into the hands of Bhāskaravarman, king of Kāmarūpa. The old alliance thus bore fruit in the disruption of Śaśāṅka's empire.

Much exaggerated notion is prevalent about the wide extent of Harsha's empire. But though his great power was recognised throughout North India, and many potentates, including the Maitraka king of Valabhī, his son-in-law, and Bhāskara-varman, his old friend, thought it politic to be submissive even to the extent of attending his court, it does not appear that Harsha exercised suzerain power over any considerable stretch of territorry outside the limit of the present provinces of Eastern Panjāb, Uttara Pradesh, Bihār, West Bengal, and Orissa. The idea that his empire included the whole of Northern India would not bear a moment's scrutiny. For Kāshmir, Western Panjāb, Sindh, Gujarāt, Rājputāna, Nepāl and Kāmarūpa were certainly independent States in his days. But even then we must regard him as a great conqueror and a powerful emperor.

His empire.

It is not, however, as a great conqueror alone that Harsha-vardhana figures in Indian history. He has earned an undying reputation for his peaceful activities, so vividly described by the Chinese pilgrim Hiuen Tsang who travelled all over India during his fourteen years' stay in this country (630-644 A.D.), and came into intimate personal contact with the great emperor.

Harsha-vardhana was unwearied in his efforts towards maintaining an efficient government in the country. He personally looked into the affairs of State, and constantly travelled over different parts of his empire to see things with his own eyes. The result was that his civil administration was carried on benign principles, though it is obvious that degeneration had set in since the days of the Imperial Guptas. The roads were evidently less safe, for the Chinese pilgrim himself was robbed by brigands more than once, and the criminal code was more sanguinary. Mutilation of the nose, ears, hands or feet was penalty for serious offences, and ordeals by fire, water, weighment, and poison seem to have been much in vogue.

His administration.

The great emperor was not only a patron of learning but himself an author of no small merit. Three of his Sanskrit plays, Nāgānanda, Ratnāvalī and Priyadarśikā have survived the trials of time, and deservedly achieved high reputation among lovers of Indian literature. He gathered around him a circle of learned men, of whom Bāṇabhaṭṭa, the author of Harshacharita (Biography of Harsha) and Kādambarī, is the most well-known.

His literary activities.

Harsha-vardhana was probably Śaiva in faith, but he was not only tolerant of, but actually devoted to, other religious sects as well. His charitable institutions were numerous. Like Aśoka, he built rest-houses and hospitals, and endowed numerous religious establishments both Brāhmaṇical and Buddhist. Later in his life, he seems to have shown a distinct partiality towards Buddhism, and forbade the slaughter of animals. He is said to have erected thousands of Buddhist *stūpas* on the banks of the Gaṅgā, and a number of monasteries at the sacred places of the Buddhists. Besides, he annually summoned a convocation of the Buddhists, where discussions and disputations were held among the Brethren, and rewarded those who were most successful in debate. Moral excellence was the only passport to his favour. He befriended

His religion.

princes and statesmen who were virtuous, and would not even deign to converse with those who were of opposite character.

Harsha-vardhana became the patron of Hiuen Tsang who is lavish in his praises of the great emperor. Most of the facts we have stated about Harsha-vardhana are known from the wonderful records left by the pilgrim, which, besides, give us a detailed picture of the condition of India such as we do not find anywhere else. Harsha-vardhana met the Chinese pilgrim in West Bengal, and being delighted in his company, held a special assembly at Kanauj in his honour. It was attended by twenty tributary kings, four thousand Buddhist monks, and about three thousand Jainas and orthodox Brāhmaṇas. On the west bank of the Gaṅgā, the king built a spacious monastery, and a tower 100 ft. high, and put a golden image of Buddha of his own height within the latter. A little to the west of this was built the temporary palace of the king and pavilions for other guests. Every morning a small golden image of Buddha, 3 ft. in height, was carried in splendid procession from the royal palace to the tower. The king himself, dressed as Śakra (Indra), and escorted by 500 war-elephants, held the canopy and scattered pearls, gold, silver flowers, and various other precious substances on the way. A long train of caparisoned elephants carried the tributary kings, their escorts, and other guests, and 100 great elephants carried musicians who sounded their drums and raised their music. After the procession was over, the king offered to the image of Buddha tens, hundreds, and thousands of silken garments, decorated with precious gems. Then, after the feast, the men of learning assembled in the hall to discuss the most abstruse subjects, the Chinese pilgrim being of course accorded the place of honour. In the evening the guests retired to their dwellings. This solemn programme was repeated every day, for about a month, when the monastery suddenly took fire, and was partially destroyed. Harsha-vardhana was surveying the scene from the top of a *stūpa* when a fanatic, knife in hand, rushed towards him. The attempt on his life failed, and the assassin confessed that he was engaged by the Brāhmaṇas who were infuriated at the excessive favour shown by the king towards the Buddhists. These men had deliberately set the monastery on fire in order to kill the king in the confusion which would follow. The chief culprits were punished and the rest were pardoned.

Hiuen Tsang.

Harsha's assembly at Kanauj.

After the ceremony at Kanuaj had closed amid these tragic incidents, the emperor, accompanied by the Chinese pilgrim, proceeded to Prayāga (Allāhābād), where he used to celebrate another solemn festival at the end of every five years, at the confluence of the Gaṅgā and the Yamunā. All the vassal kings attended, and the king had already summoned there the followers of different religious sects, the poor, the orphan, and the needy for receiving gifts.

Religious assembly at Prayāga.

Towards the west of the junction of the two rivers there was a great plain, called "the Arena of charitable offerings," as from very ancient times kings from different parts of India frequented this spot for the purpose of practising charity Here the emperor amassed his treasure and performed the ceremony, which lasted for about 3 months, and has been vividly described by the biographer of Hiuen Tsang.

"On the first day they installed the image of Buddha and distributed precious articles of the first quality and clothing of the same character.

The second day they installed the image of Āditya-deva (Sun-god) and distributed in charity precious things and clothing to half the amount of the previous day.

The third day they installed the image of Iśvara-deva and distributed gifts as on the day before.

The fourth day they gave gifts to 10,000 Buddhist Bhikkhus, each receiving 100 pieces of gold, one pearl, one cotton garment, various drinks and meats, flowers and perfumes.

For the next twenty days gifts were bestowed upon the Brāhmaṇas.

For the next ten days alms were bestowed upon those who came from a distance to ask for charity.

For the next month gifts were made to the poor, the orphans and the destitute.

By this time the accumulation of five years was exhausted. Except the horses, elephants, and military accoutrements, which were necessary for maintainng order and protecting the royal estate, nothing remained. The king even freely gave away his gems and goods, his clothing and necklaces, ear-rings, bracelets, chaplets, neck-jewel, and bright head-jewels.

All being given away, he begged from his sister an ordinary second-hand garment, and having put it on, he paid worship to the Buddhas of the ten regions, and exulted with joy with his hands closed in adoration.

This ceremony being over the assembled kings severally distributed among the people their money and treasure for the purpose of redeeming the royal necklaces, head-jewels, court vestments, etc., and restored them to the king; and then after a few days these same things were again given away in charity, as before."

Thus finished the remarkable ceremony which emperor Harsha-vardhana performed after the example of his ancestors, at the end of every five years. As he informed the Chinese pilgrim, this was the sixth of its kind during his reign. Shortly after this ceremony Hiuen Tsang returned home and the emperor took all possible steps to facilitate the journey.

Embassies to China.

Harsha-vardhana evidently knew a great deal of China even before he met Hiuen Tsang, and in 641 A.D. sent an envoy to the Chinese emperor, who also sent an envoy in return. Soon after his meeting with Hiuen Tsang Harsha sent a Brāhmaṇa envoy to the Chinese emperor who sent a second mission in 643 A.D. Shortly after Hiuen Tsang's return to China, and probably as a result of the detailed report submitted by him, the Chinese emperor sent a third mission under Wang-hiuen-tse. This mission left China in 646, but when it arrived in India, Harsha-vardhana was no more. The great emperor died at the end of 646 or at the beginning of 647 A.D.

Harsha's successors.

Harsha-vardhana does not appear to have left any heir to his throne which was usurped after his death by his minister Arjuna or Aruṇāśva. A curious story is related in Chinese books of a fight between Arjuna and Wang-hiuen-tse. Arjuna is said to have plundered the property of the mission led by the latter, and killed some of its escorts, upon which Wang-hiuen-tse fled to Tibet. The king of Tibet, who was married to a Chinese as well as a Nepālese princess, helped him with troops, and so did Nepāl. With these he came back, defeated Arjuna, and by dint of several victories conquered a considerable territory in Indian plains. It is difficult to estimate the historical value of this somewhat strange episode, and in any case the truth of the details may be doubted.

CHAPTER III

North India from c. 650 A. D. to c. 800 A. D.

Amid the confusion which followed the death of Harsha-vardhana his great empire passed away without leaving any trace behind. The futile attempts of his minister to govern the kingdom, and the strange Chinese expedition which his own folly had invited, have been referred to above. The victorious Chinese army which dealt the death-blow to the empire is said to have received substantial aid from Bhāskara-varman king of Kāmrūpa or Assam valley, and there is good evidence that he played an important part in Indian politics about that time.

1. *Kāmarūpa*

The ancient kingdom of Kāmarūpa generally remained outside the currents of Indian history. It does not appear to have been included in the Maurya empire, nor, so far as we know, had it any political relations with other early kingdoms. While the rest of India was convulsed by the upheaval of new religious sects, Kāmarūpa retained the Brāhmaṇical religion to the last.

Kāmarūpa

The kings of Kāmarūpa traced their descent from Naraka, the son of Vishṇu, and Naraka's son was the great epic hero Bhagadatta. But the earliest historical dynasty is undoubtedly that founded by Pushya-varman early in the fourth cenurty A.D. The first six kings of this dynasty acknowledged the supremacy of the Guptas, but perhaps the seventh king, who claims to have performed two horse-sacrifices, threw off the yoke. Under the next king Bhūti-varman, who flourished about the middle of the 6th century A.D., Kāmarūpa became a powerful kingdom. It included the whole of the Brahmaputra valley and Sylhet, and extended to the west as far as the Karatoyā river which continued to be the traditional boundary of Kāmarūpa for a long time. The successors of Bhūti-varman came into conflict with the later Guptas who once advanced up to the Brahmaputra, but both sides claimed victory.

Bhāskara-varman, fourth in descent from Bhūti-varman, ascended the throne towards the end of the sixth or the beginning of the seventh century A.D. He sent an ambassador to Harsha-vardhana, immediately after the latter's accession, with a view to establish friendly relations between the two kingdoms. It is not difficult to divine the real object of this embassy, if we remember the height of power to which the kingdom of Bengal was raised about this time by Śaśāṅka. The king of Kāmarūpa dreaded the power of this neighbour, and tried to secure his position by availing himself of the enmity which had sprung up between Śaśāṅka and the Lord of Thāneswar. There was thus the combination of Thāneswar, Kanauj, and Kāmarūpa against that of Bengal and Mālwa—with what results we have already seen. Bhāskara-varman must have realised, when it was too late, the consequences of alliance between unequal powers. For, though after the removal of the dreaded rival by the death of Śaśāṅka the latter's kingdom was divided between the two allies, Bhāskara-varman soon came to be looked upon by Harsha more as a feudatory vassal than an equal ally. He was not only forced to send the Chinese pilgrim Hiuen Tsang to Harsha-vardahana at the point of bayonet, but had also to attend the pompous ceremonies at Kanauj and Allāhābād along with other vassal States of the Kanauj empire. No wonder that he fed fat his grudge by aiding the Chinese expedition against the successor of Harsha-vardhana on the throne of Kanauj. He was, however, too shrewd to lend this aid for nothing, and when that strange episode was over, he made himself master of Eastern India. He pitched his victorious camp in the capital of his late rival Śaśāṅka, and thus increased the power and prestige of the kingdom of Kāmarūpa to an extent never dreamt of before.

But the greatness of the family did not last long. Bhāskara-varman's kingdom was shortly after overthrown by a barbarian, Sālastambha by name, and Kāmarūpa passed under the Mlechchha rule.

2. *Later Guptas*

The next power to rise into importance were the Later Guptas. It has been already related how this dynasty was founded at the break-up of the Gupta empire. Mahāsenagupta, the fifth king of this line, defeated Susthita-varman, the father of Bhāskara-varman, on the bank of the Lauhitya (Brahmaputra) But later in life he was visited by a great calamity, the exact nature of which is not known. He seems to have lost his life

The Later Gupta.

and his kingdom, and his two sons Kumāra-gupta and Mādhava-gupta took refuge in Thāneswar whose king Prabhākara-vardhana was his near relation. The two young princes became great friends of Rājya-vardhana and Harsha-vardhana. Evidently with the help of the latter Mādhava-gupta became king of Magadha. About 675 A.D. Ādityasena, son of Mādhava-gupta, gained sufficient power and prestige to justify the asssumption of imperial titles. Under him and his three successors, Deva-gupta, Vishṇu-gupta and Jīvita-gupta, who all assumed imperial titles, the kingdom of Magadha occupied the position of supremacy in Eastern India. Two other kings of this family bearing imperial titles, namely Rāma-gupta and his son Jīva-gupta are known to have ruled in Bihar from inscriptions. They probably succeeded Jivita-gupta.

3. *Yaśovarman*

But once more Kanauj came to be the dominant power in North India. The history of this kingdom, since the abortive attempt of the minister of Harsha to maintain his master's empire, is obscure in the extreme. In the beginning of the eighth century A.D., however, we find a very powerful monarch on the throne of Kānyakubja. This was Yaśovarman, another military adventurer of the type of Yaśodharman and Śaśāṅka. He was not only a great conqueror but also a patron of poets. Bhababhūti, the sweet neightingale of Sanskrit literature, lived in his court, and as long as Sanskrit language survives, Yaśovarman's name will remain bound up with one of its greatest poets. Other poets of lesser renown also graced his court, among whom the name of Vākpati stands pre-eminent. This poet sought to immortalise his patron king by describing his exploits in a Prākṛit poem of unusual merit, called *Gauḍa-vaho* or the 'Slaying of the king of Gauḍa.' We learn from this poem that the king of Gauḍa, probably Jīvita-gupta II, the great-grandson of Ādityasena, ruled over extensive territories, including Magadha, but his capacity was not equal to the task of governing such a vast kingdom. On the approach of Yaśovarman he took fright and fled, apparently leaving Magadha in possession of the victor. The nobility of Bengal, were, however better than their master, and next year they forced their cowardly king to face the invader. Vākpati describes with eloquence the brave fight put up by the Bengali heroes. But all the same the battle ended in their defeat and the death of their king, and Yaśovarman overran the whole of Bengal up to the sea-shore.

Patron of poets

Yaśovarman is next said to have proceeded in his career of conquest towards the south, and then, marching along the Narmadā towards the west, reached the Western Ghāts. Thence he moved northwards and conquered Marudeśa (Rājputāna) and Śrīkaṇṭha (Thāneswar), and after visiting the Himālaya mountains returned to his capital at Kanauj.

How far this conventional description of conquest may be regarded as historically true it is difficult to say, but Yaśovarman was unquestionably the most powerful king about this time. He maintained diplomatic relations with the great Chinese emperor. In the year 731 A.D. he sent his minister to the Chinese court, but neither the object nor the result of the mission is known to us. We know, however, that in alliance with Lalitāditya, king of Kāshmir, he led a campaign against the Tibetans, defeated them and blocked the passes leading to that mountainous territory. As the Chinese emperor was then engaged in hostilities with the Tibetans, Yaśovarman probably sought to make a common cause against his northern foe. The enmity between Yaśovarman and the Tibetans is easily explained when we remember how they had taken part in Indian politics and already conquered Nepāl. Moreover, the Tibetan king had helped Wang-hiuen-tse to successfully defy the power of Kanauj and plunder the rich cities of India shortly after the death of Harsha-vardhana. It is, however, not also unlikely that Yaśovarman wanted to make a common cause with China against the growing power of the Arabs.

Yaśovarman ruled with glory and splendour till about 740 A.D., when his ambitious ally Lalitāditya, king of Kāshmir, grew jealous of him, and sought to play the imperial role at his expense. Hostilities broke out on the most flimsy pretext, and a protracted struggle followed, ending in the defeat and perhaps also death of Yaśovarman, and the absorption of his kingdom in the growing empire of Kāshmir.

4. *Kāshmir.*

Kārkoṭa Dynasty.

The early history of the kingdom of Kāshmir is full of legendary traditions, but not long before the middle of seventh century A.D., Durlabha-vardhana, a chief of obscure origin, obtained the throne by marrying the daughter of the late king and founded the famous royal dynasty known as the Kārkoṭa. It was during his reign that Hiuen Tsang visited Kāshmir. As the pilgrim informs us, Durlabha-vardhana ruled not only over

Kāshmir proper, but a part of the north-western Panjāb as well. He was followed by his son Pratāpāditya II who ruled with moderation and justice, and built the town of Pratāpapura. He was succeeded by his three sons. The eldest Chandrāpīḍa, who was powerful enough to be recognised as king by the emperor of China in 720 A.D., was renowned for his piety and justice. It is recorded in Kalhaṇa's *Rājataraṅgiṇī*, which henceforth forms a valuable source for the detailed history of Kāshmir, that when the king began to build a temple, a leather-tanner refused to give up his hut which lay on the site. When the matter was reported to the king, he considered his own officers to be at fault, not the tanner. "Stop the building," he cried out, or "have it erected elsewhere." The tanner himself came to the king and represented: "Since my birth this hut has been to me like a mother, witness of good and evil days. I cannot bear to see it pulled down to-day." Still he agreed to give up his hut "if His Majesty would come to his dwelling and ask for it in accordance with propriety." As soon as the king heard this, he went to his home and bought up the hut with money. The reign of this king was full of just acts like this, and he may almost be said to have fallen a martyr to them. Once he punished a Brāhmaṇa who had secretly murdered another Brāhmaṇa by means of witchcraft. The former felt deep wrath over his punishment and was instigated by the king's younger brother Tārāpīḍa to use his witchcraft against the king. Thus died the noble king Chandrāpīḍa after a reign of eight years and a half. The fratricide Tārāpīḍa then ascended the throne. His inglorious rule of four years was full of cruel and bloody deeds. He was followed by his younger brother Lalitāditya Muktāpīḍa, the greatest king of the dynasty.

Lalitāditya ascended the throne about 724 A.D. He was 'eager for conquests and passed his life chiefly on expeditions.'

Lalitāditya.

As already related, he entered into an alliance with Yaśovarman and defeated the Tibetans. Like Yaśovarman, and probably for similar reasons, he sent a diplomatic mission to the Chinese emperor in order to induce him to make a common cause against the Tibetans. The mission was received with honour by the emperor who recognised the king of Kāshmir as his royal ally, but no military assistance was sent from China. But even unaided, Lalitāditya succeeded in defeating not only the Tibetans but also the mountanious tribes on the north and north-western frontier of his kingdom, such as the Dards, Kāmbojas and Turks.

But the most important of the expeditions of Lalitāditya was that against Yaśovarman to which reference has already been made. By that victory Lalitāditya not only made himself master of Kanauj, but also acquired the theoretical right of suzerainty over the vast conquests of his late rivals. In order to effectively assert these rights, Lalitāditya marched towards the east and overran Magadha, Gauḍa, Kāmarūpa, and Kaliṅga. He then marched against the Chālukyas of the south, but it is difficult to ascertain how far he had penetrated into the Deccan and the amount of success he achieved in this direction. He next seems to have conquered Mālwa and Gujarāt, and defeated the Arabs of Sindh, somewhere near the border of his country. These extensive conquests made the kingdom of Kāshmir, for the time being, the most powerful empire that India had seen since the days of the Guptas. No wonder that for centuries the Kāshmirians celebrated the victories of the great emperor whom, with pardonable exaggeration, they chose to call the universal monarch.

Lalitāditya lavished the great resources of this mighty empire in adorning his kingdom with beautiful towns, and decorating the towns with fine buildings, monasteries, temples, and images of gods. The most famous of his works is the Mārtaṇḍa temple, ruins of which still form "the most striking remains which have survived of the ancient architecture of Kāshmir."

Kalhaṇa, the author of *Rājataraṅgiṇi*, has drawn a magnicent picture of this celebrated king. But two incidents have left an indelible stain on the character of this great emperor. Once in a fit of drunkenness he ordered the town of Pravarapura to be burnt down, though afterwards he repented of it and was glad to find that the ministers had disobeyed his orders. The second case was more serious. He summoned the king of Gauḍa (Bengal) to Kāshmir and promised him safe-conduct, making the image of Vishṇu Parihāsakeśava the surety for his promise. All the same he had the king killed by assassins. It is as difficult to find any motive for this foul treachery as to condone it in any way. The sequel of this story is interesting in the extreme. A few devoted followers of the murdered king undertook the long journey from Bengal to Kāshmir, and invested the temple of the god who had been made the surety. The priests closed the gates, but they were forced open. The Bengali heroes reached the statue of Vishṇu Rāmasvāmin, and mistaking it for that of Parihāsakeśava, overturned it and broke it into pieces, while they were all being cut up by the Kāshmirian soldiers who had just arrived from the capital. Kalhaṇa pays a just tribute to the heroism of the small but devoted band of Gauḍa. "What of the long journey which had to be accomplished, and what of the devotion for the dead lord? Even the creator cannot achieve what the Gauḍas did on that occasion. Even to this day the temple of Rāmasvāmin is seen empty whereas the world is filled with the fame of the Gauḍa heroes."

Lalitāditya died about 760 A.D. after a reign of thrity-six years. He was followed by a succession of weak kings who were unable to maintain the power and prestige of the family. One among them, Jayāpīḍa, fifth in descent from Lalitāditya, seems to have made a serious attempt to regain the lost supremacy but no conspicuous success attended his efforts.

Successors of Lalitāditya

While the Kāshmirians were gradually receding into the background two new powers arose in Northern India that were destined to play the imperial role with far greater success. These were the Pālas and the Gurjaras the story of whose rise, growth and decay carries us almost to the end of the period of Hindu supremacy. Indeed, from the close of Lalitāditya's reign to the invasions of Mahmūd of Ghazni the history of Northern India is chiefly the history of these two mighty powers.

5. *The Gurjaras*

The early history of the Gurjaras, the ancestors of the modern Gujars, is shrouded in mystery. It is generally held that they entered India at a comparatively late period, probably along with the Hūṇas, towards the close of the fifth century A.D. Cities and districts named after the Gurjaras mark the successive stages of their advance through the Panjāb to Jodhpur in the heart of Rājputāna. There, to the west of the Aravalli hills, they formed their main settlements for which the region was long known as Gurjaratrā, the earlier form of Gujarāt, before it came to be called Rājputāna, early in the Muslim period. Prabhākaravardhana, the king of Thāneswar, waged wars against them, but apparently without success, for they ruled over an independent kingdom even when Harsha-vardhana founded his empire in Northern India. The ruling family belonged to the Pratīhāra clan, and hence the royal dynasty is known in history as the Gurjara-Pratīhāra. It appears that the Gurjaras proceeded from their main settlements at Rājputāna further towards the east and south, and one branch dynasty was ruling at Broach, and another at Mālwa.

6. *The Arab Conquest of Sindh*

The Gurjara-Pratīhāras had been settled in Rājputāna for a century and a half when a formidable rival appeared in the west. These were the Arabs who had imbibed along with their new religion a national consciousness and a warlike spirit from the Prophet Muhammad Their energetic and enthusiastic nature bordering on fanaticism was thoroughly roused, and they rushed forth to spread the new religion and carry on military conquests all over the world. Verily they wrought wonders. Syria and Egypt were conquered within six years of the death of the Prophet; Northern coast of Africa, Spain, and Persia fell in quick succession; and before a century had elapsed, the empire of the Caliphs, as the successors of the Prophet were called, extended from the Loire in the heart of France to the Oxus and Kābul rivers.

The Arabs

Such was the formidable people who had reached the frontiers of India, and cast longing eyes on her fair plains and cities. They made several plundering raids into India both by land and sea, but could not gain any important success till 712 A.D. About this time the king of Ceylon sent to Hajjāj, the governor of Irāq, some women who were born in his country as Muslims, their fathers, who were merchants, having died. But the ship in which they were sailing was captured by the pirates of Debal, a seaport of Sindh. Hajjāj thereupon wrote to Dāhar, king of Sindh, to set the women free, but Dāhar pleaded inability, saying 'I have no control over the pirates who captured them.' Hajjāj regarded this as the *casus belli* against Sindh, and determined to make renewed effort on a large scale for conquering a country which had so long defied the arms of Islam. The Caliph was at first unwilling to sanction the risky expedition, but ultimately gave his consent at the importunities of Hajjāj. Hajjāj thereupon sent 'Ubaidallāh to raid Debal, but he was defeated and killed. Then a second expedition was sent by way of sea from Oman under Budail. Budail got reinforcements from Muhammad ibn-Hārūn and marched towards Debal. Dāhar, on hearing the news, sent a force under his son Jaisiṁha to protect Debal. A pitched battle ensued, which lasted the whole day. At the end the Muslim army was routed and Budail was killed.

Early invasions of Sindh.

Hajjāj then made elaborate preparations for the invasion of Sindh, after obtaining necessary permission from the Caliph

Wālid. He appointed his nephew and son-in-law Muhammad Ibn Qāsim as commander of the expedition, and provided him with soldiers, arms and ammunitions on a most lavish scale. He asked for and obtained from the Caliph the services of 6000 Syrian soldiers fully armed. The petty kingdom of Sindh was hardly in a position to offer any effective resistance to this vast and well-organised army. But still Dāhar opposed a brave resistance. Muhammad first conquered Debal, Nerun, Siwistān and a few other strongholds and, according to *Chach-nāma*, treachery, specially of the Buddhists, played no small part in these campaigns. Muhammad then met Dāhar and his main army before the fort of Raor. Dāhar fought bravely for two days but an unfortunate incident practically decided the fate of this battle. The Muslim army was routed and victory inclined to the side of Dāhar when his elephant, being wounded, rushed away from the battle-field, and the disappearance of the king led to so great a panic and confusion, that although the king, himself wounded, returned to the field shortly after, order could by no means be restored. Dāhar fought with desperate courage and gallantly fell fighting in the midst of his enemies.

The widowed queen collected the remains of the army and defended the fort with stubborn courage till provisions failed. Then followed a strange scene, a precursor of many others in India but without any parallel in the history of the world, both ancient and modern. Faced with the alternatives of death or dishonour the men and women of the capital chose the former. A big fire was kindled in the courtyard. The women gaily decorated themselves, took leave of their husbands and other relations, and then with joyous face threw themselves and their children into the blazing flame. The men silently watched the terrible scene till the fire had devoured all that was dear and near unto them in this world; then they threw the gates wide open, and, sword in hand, rushed into the midst of the enemy. The Muhammadan soldiers long remembered the day when the handful of Indians perished to a man, after having fought with the desperate courage which certain death never fails to inspire When the victorious Muhammadan general made his triumphal entry into the capital, the dying embers of the flame told him the awful tale of heroic sacrifice, known as Jauhar.

Jaisiṁha, the son of Dāhar, now strongly fortified Bāhmanābād and the capital city of Alor, and himself moved with an army to harass the enemy and cut off its supplies. Muhammad besieged Bāhmanābād. 'Every day the besieged came out and offered battle and fierce fight continued from morning till evening.' But though the besieged fought valiantly foi six months, some leading citizens betrayed the fort to the Muslim general, who then laid siege to Alor. The capital city was defended for some time by Fofi, another son of Dāhar, and when the residents wanted to make peace with Muhammad, he withdrew with his forces. After the submission of Alor and the conquest of a few more forts, Muhammad proceeded to Multān. The people offered a brave resistance for two months, when a traitor pointed out to Muhammad the source of water-supply for the town. Muhammad cut it off and Multān was forced to surrender.

Shortly after this the death of Hajjāj in 714 A.D. and that of Caliph Wālid in 715 A.D. brought in evil days for Muhammad. The new Caliph Sulaiman and his governor of Irāq were both great enemies of Hajjāj. Muhammad Ibn Qāsim was recalled from India and put to death, along with several other adherents of Hajjāj.

According to *Chach-nāma* Muhammad had proceeded from Multān to the frontiers of Kāshmir and at the same time sent an expedition to Kanauj. It then relates the story how two virgin daughters of Dāhar, who were sent as prisoners to the Caliph Wālid, brought about the death of Muhammad Ibn Qāsim by falsely accusing him of having outraged them before sending them to the Caliph. But this story is hardly credible

Such was the beginning of the Arab domination in India. Surpirse has often been felt why the victorious forces were satisfied with Sindh alone, and failed to carry their arms into the interior of India. Various theories have been put forth to explain why the 'conquerors' of the world stopped merely at the gates of India, and even failed to retain what they had conquered. The real explanation is not, however, far to seek. It has been already related that Lalitāditya, the king of Kāshmir, gained success against the Arab forces, and it is legitimate to suppose that the imperial forces of Kāshmir checked their onward progress for the time being. Further, there is incontestable evidence that from the very beginning the Gurjaras stood as bulwarks of Indian defence against the vanguards of Islam. That there was no lack of desire on the part of the Arab government to extend their dominions into the interior of India is proved by the military expeditions they sent for the purpose from time to time. The most formidable o

The Arab advance checked by the Gurjaras.

these was despatched about 725 A.D., when the Muhammadans overran Cutch, Kathiāwār Peninsula, northern Gujarāt and sothern Rājputāna, and probably even advanced as far as Mālwa. It appeared as if the whole of Northern and Southern India would fall within their grasp. But Northern India was saved by a chief of the Gurjara-Pratīhāra clan, and the gates of the Deccan were successfully defended by the forces of the Chālukya king of Bādāmi led by his viceroy named Avanijanāśraya Pulakeśirāja who received from his grateful sovereign the proud titles of "Solid pillar of Dakshiṇāpatha" and "repeller of the unrepellable."

The Pratīhāra chief who had thus saved Northern India was Nāgabhaṭa, the ruler of Avanti, the present Mālwa, in the first half of the eighth century. His power and prestige must have been considerably increased by his great victory over the Arabs, and he extended his kingdom by incorporating many of the smaller principalities overrun by them. He was succeeded by his two nephews Kakkuka and Devarāja, and then came Vatsarāja, the son of the last named king. Vatsarāja, who is known to have been ruling in 783 A.D., was a very powerful ruler, and consolidated the Pratīhāra dominion by extensive conquests in Northern India. He even claims to have easily defeated the king of Gauḍa or Bengal. He had thus well-nigh established unquestioned supremacy over the greater part of Northern India when an unforeseen event deprived him of the great prize almost within his grasp. Before, however, proceeding to describe this incident it will be well to take note of the condition of Bengal which thus fell an easy prey to the Pratīhāra king.

The early successes of the Gurjaras.

7. *The Rise of the Pālas*

After the death of Śaśāṅkā, Bengal had lost all political solidarity. As we have seen above, it was conquered by Harsha-vardhana as well as Bhāskara-varman of Kāmarūpa. At the beginning of the eighth century, a king of the Śaila dynasty made himself master of Pauṇḍra or Northern Bengal, and this was followed by the invasions of Yaśovarman and Lalitāditya as has been recorded above. About the middle of the eighth century, a king named Harsha, probably of Kāmarūpa, conquered the country.

Pitiable condition of Bengal.

These successive foreign invasions brought about complete anarchy and confusion throughout the kingdom. There was no central authority and each landlord established an independent principality like the feudal barons of Middle Ages. Might was right, and the sword was the only arbiter. In short, all the miseries of an anarchical state were harassing the people of Bengal. But the evil brought its own remedy. The chiefs, unable to endure this state of things any longer, agreed to elect Gopāla as the ruler of the whole kingdom. Unfortunately, no details of this remarkable act of personal sacrifice and political sagacity have been preserved to us. It reminds us of a similar event in Japan, not very long ago, when the semi-independent feudal barons surrendered their powers to the Mikado, and thereby made their country great and respected in the world as a First Class Power for three-quarters of a century. Whether the events in Bengal were parallel to those of Japan we cannot say, but the results were equally remarkable. Gopāla consolidated his dominions in Bengal from the Himālayas to the sea, and brought peace and prosperity after the anarchy and misrule of a century and a half, during which the country had sunk to the lowest pitch of misery and degradation. As the name of Gopāla and his successors ends in Pāla, the dynasty founded by him is known in history as the Pāla dynasty. The date of his accession is not definitely known, but may be placed in the last half of the eighth century A.D. He died about 780 A.D. and left a flourishing kingdom to his son Dharmapāla, who was destined to raise it to a height of greatness and splendour not dreamt of before.

Election of Gopāla.

Dharmapāla was undoubtedly the greatest king that ever ruled in Bengal, and made his position supreme in North India. He had to spend almost his whole life in military campaigns which carried him as far as Kedāra in the Himālayas. His career was a chequered one, and he suffered defeat in the hands of the Gurjara and Rāshṭrakūṭa kings as will be related later. But he survived all this and ultimately established an empire that embraced a considerable part of Northern India. Most of the details of his reign are found in an inscription engraved on a copperplate found at Khālimpur. Fortunately his supremacy in North India is also known from a literary work, composed in the 11th century, which refers to him as lord of North India.

Dharmapāla

Dharmapāla assumed imperial titles and ruled for more than 32 years. The Pālas were Buddhist and Dharmapāla was a great patron of Buddhism. He founded many Buddhist monasteries, but his greatest achievement was the foundation of the famous Vikramaśīla University which soon almost rivalled Nālandā.

CHAPTER IV

The Deccan up to the rise of the Rāshṭrakūṭas

In South India, as in the North, the downfall of an Imperial dynasty almost inevitably gave a fresh lease of life to the independent provincial powers. So, after the Śatavāhana family had passed away in the first half of the third century A.D., the Deccan plateau as well as the Southern Peninsula witnessed the rise of a number of independent kingdoms. For about three centuries, the whole country south of the Narmadā was partitioned among various powers, too numerous to be mentioned in detail.

Various kingdoms in Deccan and South India.

The most important among these were the Pallavas who rose to political greatness in the Toṇḍai-maṇḍalam (region round Kāñchī) in the 3rd or 4th century A.D., and soon became the dominant power in South Indian Peninsula, a position which they maintained till the 10th century A.D. along with another great power, the Pāṇḍyas of Madura. The history of these as well as some other minor powers like the Gaṅgas and Kadambas, which arose respectively in Mysore and the region to its west and north-west during the period, will be related in detail in a later chapter. For the present we confine our attention to the Deccan, i.e. the region to the north of the Krishnā.

1. *The Vākāṭakas*

(a) *Early History*

The Vākāṭakas were the most powerful among the ruling dynasties that arose in the Deccan after the fall of the Śātavāhanas. Not much is known about its founder Vindhyaśakti, not even the locality to which he belonged. This, the early home of the family, has been placed by some in Mālwa and by others in the southern part of the Deccan, but the most reasonable view seems to be that it was situated in the Madhya Pradesh (C. P.), the region where most of their epigraphic records have come to light.

Vindhyaśakti.

Vindhyaśakti was a Brāhmaṇa, and according to the Purāṇas ruled for 96 years. This figure is evidently a mistake, and may denote the length of his life rather than that of his reign. He probably flourished in the third quarter of the third century A.D.

Pravarasena

The real founder of the greatness of the family was Vindhyaśakti's son and successor Pravarasena whose glorious achievements are recounted in the records of his successors. He was a great conqueror and extended his kingdom in all directions. He is the only Vākāṭaka ruler to whom the title *Samrāṭ* is given, and there is no doubt that he fully deserved it. Although we may dismiss, as ridiculous, the view propounded by some scholars that the Vākaṭaka empire embraced a large portion of North India as well as the whole of the Deccan, the dominions of Pravarasena certainly extended from Bundelkhand in the north to Hyderābād State in the south. Pravarasena is said to have preformed quite a large number of Vedic sacrifices including four *Aśvamedhas*. He married his son Gautamīputra to a daughter of king Bhavanāga of the powerful Bhāraśive family, and it is not unlikely that this alliance was of great help to him in increasing his political power. The Purāṇas assign him a reign of 60 years, and he probably died about 330 A.D.

The empire of Pravarasena was divided, at least into two parts, after his death His eldest son, Gautamīputra, probably died before him, and in any case did not rule. Gautamīputra's son Rudrasena I succeeded his grandfather and was the founder of what may be called the main branch of the family ruling with Nandivardhana, near Rāmtek hill, 22 miles from Nāgpur, as its capital. Sarvasena, another son of Pravaraśena, ruled over the western part of the empire with his headquarters at Vatsagulma, modern Basim, in the Akola District of Berār.

(b) *The Main Branch.*

Not much is known about Rudrasena I or his son Pṛithivīsheṇa I, except that the latter's dominion probably extended up to Bundelkhand. But even if it were so, this region was shortly conquered by Samudragupta. Curiously enough, the long inscription on Allāhābād Pillar enumerating the conquests of that Gupta emperor does not refer to the Vākāṭakas; rather it seems that he studiously avoided the Vākātaka dominion though he must have passed along its border in his famous campaign to the south. There is no doubt that tne Vākāṭakas were much more powerful than the Guptas when Chandragupta I laid the foundations of their power, and it is natural that the two such aggressive empire-builders would come into conflict. But there is no evidence of any struggle between the two, except on the very improbable suggestion that Rudradeva, one of the nine rulers of North India exterminated by Samudragupta, was identical with the Vākāṭaka king Rudrasena I. Apart from the fact that Rudrasena I could hardly, with much propriety, be classed among the rulers of Āryāvarta (North India), his kingdom, with the possible exception of a small outlying district, was certainly not extinguished and inscorporated with the Gupta empire, as the Allāhābād incription would have us believe. Besides, if Samudragupta had defeated the powerful Vākāṭaka ruler, it is natural to expect that the fact would have been more prominently mentioned. But the most important argument against the proposed identification is the undisputed fact that Rdudrasena's grandson Rudrasena II married Prabhāvatīguptā, daughter of Chandragupta II. It stands to reason that Pṛithivishena I would never have married his son to the grand-daughter of one who killed his father. It is therefore more reasonable to suppose that the two great political powers of the fourth century A.D. entered into an amicable arrangement regarding their spheres of activity and cemented it by a matrimonial alliance.

Rudrasena

There are good grounds to suppose that ere long, with the growing power of the Guptas, the Vākāṭakas gradually sank into the position of subsidiary allies and were strongly under the influence of the Gupta emperor. This perhaps explains why Rudrasena II, whose forefathers were Śaivas, became a devotee of Vishṇu, like his father-in-law. The influence of the Gupta court increased still further, when Rudrasena II died, and the administration was carried on by Prabhāvatīguptā, as regent for her minor son Divākarasena.

Divākarasena died before ascending the throne which was successively occupied by his two brothers Dāmodarasena and Pravarasena II.[1] The widowed queen-mother Prabhāvatīguptā lived for more than one hundred years, and had the great misfourtune to survive her first two sons, if not the third also. Pravarasena II changed his

Pravarasena II

1. These two are generally regarded as identical, but cf. *JRASBL.* XII, p. 3.

capital to Pravarapura, a city named after, and probably founded by him. He is usually, though not unanimously, identified with the royal poet Pravarasena, the author of *Setubandhakāvya*, written in Māhārāshṭri Prākṛit, and some even suggest that Kālidāsa, the famous poet, was deputed to supervise his education by his grandfather Chandragupta. The vicinity of the Vākāṭaka capital to the Rāmtek hills, undoubtedly identical with the Rāmagiri mountain, immortalised in Kālidāsa's famous poem *Meghadūta*, no doubt lends some colour to this story; but this, as well as many other anecdotes associated with Kālidāsa in this connection, can hardly be regarded as authentic.

Narendrasena

Pravarasena II was succeeded by his son Narendrasena. According to official records his command was 'honoured by the kings of Kosala, Mekala, and Mālava.' The first denotes the present Chhattisgarh Division and the second, the country near the Amarkantak hills. It would appear then that Narendrasena, probably taking advantage of the decline of the Gupta power, made a bold bid for extending his power to Central India and Mālwa. Whatever the extent of his success, it was shortlived, and soon some great calamity overtook the Vākāṭaka kingdom. For Narendrasena's son and successor Pṛithivīsheṇa II claims to have twice recovered the fallen fortunes of his family. The calamity was probably caused by the invasion of the Vākāṭaka king of the Vatsagulma family, which had now grown very powerful. In any case Pṛithivīsheṇa II is the last known king of the main branch of the Vākāṭaka family. His reign-period is not known with certainty, but may be placed in the first part of the 6th century A.D.

(c) *The Vatsagulma Branch.*

Dharmamahārāja Vindhyaśakti II, son of Sarvasena, had a long reign of 37 years or more, and his kingdom comprised the southern part of Berār, northern part of Hyderābād State, and probably also some adjoining territories. He, if not his brother, claims to have defeated the ruler of Kuntala, which designates the country round Banavāsi, then under the Kadambas.

Harishena.

The most notable king of this family was Harisheṇa, fourth in descent from Vindhyaśakti. II. The official records give a long list of countries over which Harisheṇa exercised his influence or authority. The list comprises eastern part of the Madhya Pradesh, the entire eastern coast of the Deccan, Central India, Mālwa, Southern 'Gujarāt, Koṅkan, and even North Kanara. It is difficult to believe that Harisheṇa conquered or maintained effective control over this vast region. But he seems to have been a powerful ruler, and conquered neighbouring regions, including perhaps the dominions of the main branch.

Nothing is known of either of the two Vākāṭaka families after the reign of Harisheṇa, which probably ended some time before 550 A.D. How the Vākāṭaka power came to an end is not definitely known, but it is significant that the Vākāṭakas are not mentioned among the various States which had to be subdued by the Chālukyas before they could establish their supremacy in the Deccan in the third quarter of the sixth century A.D.

2. *The Chālukyas.*

Their origin.

The Chālukyas are regarded by some as an indigenous Kanarese family, but it is not unlikely that they had immigrated into South India from the north at some unknown period in history. They claimed to have originally ruled over Ayodhyā for a pretty long time, but this can hardly be accepted as an historical fact. Certain it is that about 540 A.D. one of their chiefs, called Pulakeśi[1], carved a small principality around Vātāpipura (Bādāmi in the Bijāpur District) which henceforth became its capital. Pulakeśi performed *Aśvamedha* and other sacrifices. His sons, who succeeded him, were also great conquerors. The elder, Kīrtivarman (566-597 A.D.) defeated the Kadambas and annexed part of their territory. Later on, he defeated also the Mauryas and the Nalas who ruled respectively over Koṅkaṇ in the north, and Bellāry and Kurnool districts in the south. He is also credited with conquests of distant countries like Bengal and Bihār in the north, and the Chola and Pāṇḍya kingdom in the south; but it is difficult to say how far these exaggerated claims are based on fact. The younger, Maṅgaleśa, defeated the Kalachuris and extended the boundaries of the kingdom to the river Mahi. The kingdom thus embraced nearly the whole of the old State of Bombay south of that river.

1. The name is also written as 'Pulakesin'. Similarly the dynastic name is variously written as Chalikya, Chalukya, or Chālukya.

Maṅgaleśa wanted to leave the throne to one of his sons. Pulakeśi II, the son of Kīrtivarman, however, put forth his legitimate claim and there ensued a civil war which ended in the defeat and death of Maṅgaleśa. Pulakeśi secured the throne (610-11 A.D.), but internal discord and confusion proved to be the signal for the revolt of the newly conquered provinces, and what was worse still, the Chālukyas were themselves attacked by other powers. It reflects no little credit upon the valour and generalship of Pulakeśi II that he not only overcame the difficulties and reasserted his supremacy over the revolted territories, but also made extensive conquests in the north and south.

Pulakeśi II

A detailed account of these victories, as well as the early history of the Chālukyas, recorded above, is given in a long inscription engraved on the walls of a Jaina temple at Aihole in 634-35 A.D.[1] This *praśasti* or royal eulogy was composed by a Jaina poet named Ravikīrti who claimed an equal rank with poets Bhāravi and Kālidāsa. This is, for the present, the earliest document of a known date which mentions the great poet Kālidāsa.

We learn from this record that in the south Pulakeśi II captured Vanavāsi, the capital of the Kadambas, and defeated the Gaṅgas of Mysore. In the north he defeated the Mauryas of Koṅkaṇ and reduced by a naval attack the island city of Puri (Elephanta island near Bombay) which was probably their capital. Further north he subdued the Lāṭas, Mālavas, and Gurjaras i.e. parts of Mālawa and Gujarāt.

While Pulakeśi had thus established his supremacy in the Deccan and was making aggressive raids in Western India, Harsha-vardhana was busy consolidating his empire in Northern India. As both of them were fired by imperial ambitions, a clash between the two was inevitable. We learn from both the Aihole inscription and Hiuen Tsang's account that Harsha-vardhana was defeated by Pulakeśi. It was a decisive battle and prevented Harsha from ever extending his power to the Deccan. The time or the place of this great battle is not known. Some place it before 612 or 613 A.D. i.e. only two or three years after Pulakeśi's accession. But this seems very improbable. Most likely the battle was fought between 630 and 634 A.D.

Immediately after describing the victory over Harsha the Aihole inscriptiom refers to Pulakeśi's presence in the region of

1. *EI*. VI. 1ff.

the Vindhyas and the Revā (Narmadā). From this it has been inferred that the battle took place on the bank of the Narmadā while Harsha attempted to cross it. This cannot, however, be regarded as anything more than a mere hypothesis. But although we do not know definitely either the time or the place of the battle, or the immediate cause of it, there is no doubt that Pulakeśi had every reason to feel proud of the great achievement which saved the Deccan from the domination of the North. It was long remembered by a grateful posterity, and not only the successors of Pulakeśi, but even his enemies, centuries later, referred to his great exploit of defeating the glorious Harsha-vardhana, the warlike lord of all the region of the North.

Pulakeśi apparently turned towards the east from the Vindhya region. For we are told that he defeated the South Kosalas and the Kaliṅgas (probably the Gaṅgas of the Ganjam and Vizagapatam districts). He then turned south, and proceeding along the coast reduced the fort of Pishṭapura (Pithāpuram) and overthrew the royal family. He next conquered Veṅgi (between the Krishṇā and Godāvari), inflicted a crushing defeat upon the Pallavas, and advanced within a few miles of their capital, Kāñchī. He then crossed the Kāverī and made friends with the Cholas, Keralas, and the Pāṇḍyas. These accepted the alliance of the Chālukya king who again dispersed the Pallava army.

These great victories made Pulakeśi II the undisputed master of not only the whole of India south of the Vindhyas, but also of considerable territories to the north of that natural frontier. His reputation seems to have travelled beyond the confines of India, and it is believed that letters and presents were interchanged between him and king Khusrū II of Persia.

The Chinese traveller Hiuen Tsang pays a just tribute to the power and virtues of Pulakeśi and the valour and heroism of his subjects. We read in his memorable account the following interesting sketch of the people of Mahārāshṭra and their king Pulakeśi II.

Hiuen Tsang's account.

"The disposition of the people is honest and simple; they are tall of stature, and of a stern, vindictive character. To their benefactors they are grateful ; to their enemies relentless. If they are insulted, they will risk their life to avenge themselves. If they are asked to help one in distress, they will forget themselves in their haste to render assistance. . . . If a general loses a battle they do not inflict punishment, but present him with woman's clothes, and so he is driven to seek death for himself. The country provides for a band of champions to the number of several hundred. Each time they are about to engage in conflict, they intoxicate themselves with wine, and then one man with lance in hand will meet ten thousand and challenge them in fight. . . . . .Moreover, they inebriate many hundred heads of elephants, and, taking them out to fight, they themselves first drink their wine, and then rushing forward in mass, they trample everything down, so that no enemy can stand before them. (But in spite of these military habits) the men are fond of learning."

So far about the people, but the Chinese pilgrim continues: "The king, in consequence of his possessing these men and elephants, treats his neighbours with contempt. His plans and undertakings are wide-spread, and his beneficent actions are felt over a great distance. His subjects obey him with perfect submission."[1]

Hiuen Tsang then records how Harsha-vardhana, although master of the whole of Northern India, failed to conquer these stubborn people. We read how "Harsha-vardhana has gathered troops from the five Indies, and summoned the best leaders from all countries, and himself gone at the head of his army to punish and subdue these people, but he has not yet conquered these troops."

This account was written about 641 A.D., when Pulakeśi II was evidently at the zenith of his power. But hardly a year rolled by before his name and fame were a thing of the past.

The death of Pulakeśi II.

The Pallavas, who were so disastrously defeated by Pulakeśi in the earlier part of his reign, had now grown in power under their capable ruler Narasiṁha-varman I. But Pulakeśi undertook a campaign against him. After defeating the Bāṇas, who were feudatories of the Pallavas, he overran the Pallava dominions and once more threatened their capital Kāñchī. But he was defeated by Narasiṁha in several battles and had to retire in disgrace. Narasiṁha now invaded the Chālukya dominions. The great emperor Pulakeśī was defeated and killed, and his empire lay prostrate before the victorious hosts of the enemy. The Pallavas plundered and devastated Bādāmi, the Chālukya capital, and the Chālukya sovereignty, at least in the heart of the kingdom, practically remained in abeyance for about thirteen years. Thus

1. Beal's Tr. II. 256.

ended the career of the great emperor Pulakeśi II, adding one morc illustration of the proverbial instability of the goddess of royal fortune.

The Eastern Chālukyas.

While the Chālukyas were thus shorn of power and dignity, a branch of them was rapidly consolidating its power over the territories between the Krishnā and the Godāvari. These were conquered by Pulakeśi II and left in charge of Yuvarāja Vishṇu-vardhana, "dear younger brother" of the king. But, sometime before 632 A.D. , the Yuvarāja established himself there as an independent king, and founded what was known as the Eastern Chālukya Branch. He at first fixed his capital at Pishtapurī and then removed it to Veṅgi. His dominions extended as far north as Vizagapatam District and he probably ruled from 624 to 642 A.D. The family remained independent of the main or Western Branch, and exercised uninterrupted sway over kingdom down to the 12th century A.D.

Restoration of Chālukyan Power

But the main Chālukya dynasty was not long in recovering its fortune. Vikramāditya I, a younger son of Pulakeśi II, but one who claims to have been specially selected by the emperor for the succession, was ruling in some part of the Chālukya kingdom. He had, however, to contend not only with the feudatories who had declared independence, but also with his own brothers who refused to acknowledge his authority. But Vikramāditya I was a very capable ruler and made unceasing efforts to retrieve the fortunes of his family. His efforts were crowned with success after thriteen years, when, at the end of a long and protracted struggle, the Pallavas were defeated and driven away, and Vikramāditya I had the supreme satisfaction of finding his authority re-established in the whole of his paternal dominions.

Vikramāditya.

But Vikramāditya was not satisfied with this. In order to take full vengeance he now carried the fight into the Pallava territory. He claims to have defeated no less than three successive Pallava kings, viz. Narasiṁha-varman, Mahendra-varman II and Parameśvara-varman I. He then captured the capital Kāñchī and received obeisance from the Pallava rulers who had humbled his family and destroyed his ancestral kingdom. We are further told that he defeated the kings of the Cholas, Pāṇḍyas, and Keralas, and thus became the lord of the whole earth bounded by the three oceans (i.e. Bay of Bengal, Arabian Sea, and the Indian Ocean). But the Pallavas soon retaliated, and king Parameśvara-varman I is said to have not only defeated Vikramāditya I but also destroyed his capital city Bādāmi. It is difficult to follow chronologically the alternate victory and defeat of the two parties. But it seems that Vikramāditya, though helped by the Pāṇḍya army, was finally defeated by the Pallava king and forced to give up his southern conquests.

Vikramāditya appointed his younger brother Jayasiṁha-varman, viceroy of the Gujarāt region. He is said to have annihilated the army of one Vajjaḍa (Vajrāṭa) between the Mahi and Narmadā rivers. Vajrāṭa was evidently a powerful ruler, for even in later ages this victory, along with the defeat inflicted upon Harsha-vardhana, was mentioned as the two great achievements of the Chālukya army even by their enemies, the Rāshṭrakūṭas. Vajjaḍa has been identifed with the Maitraka king Śīlāditya III of Valabhī. This is probable, but by no means certain.

Vikramāditya I died in 681 A.D. and may be regarded as the worthy son of a worthy father. He found the Chālukya empire in ruins and restored it almost to its former glory and prestige.

Vinayāditya

Vinayāditya (681-96 A.D.), the son and successor of Vikramāditya, who had already distinguished himself by his military exploits during his father's reign, is credited with victory over a large number of peoples such as Pallavas, Kalabhras, Keralas, Cholas, and Pāṇḍyas in the south, and Mālavas and Haihayas in the north. It is further claimed that Vinayāditya defeated the lord of entire Uttarāpatha and acquired from him the banner called *Pālidhvaja*. The name of this emperor of North India is not mentioned. But the reference is most probably to Yaśovarman of Kanauj, who is also said to have carried on military campaigns in the Deccan.

It was probably in course of this campaign of Vinayāditya to the north that *Yuvarāja* Vijayāditya distinguished himself by deafeating the hostile forces in front of his father and acquired the Gaṅgā and Yamunā symbols and the *Pālidhvaja* banner as wall as a rich booty. Unfortunately he was captured by the retreating enemy forces, though he somehow managed to escape.

Inscriptions of a later period credit Vinayāditya with levying tribute from Pārasīka (Persia)[1] and Siṁhala (Ceylon). This appears, on the face of it, highly improbable. We should remember, however, that both these countries were passing through troublesome times at this period, and some kind of help asked by and rendered to their dethroned or fugitive rulers might have been exaggerated by the court poet.

Vinayāditya was succeeded by his son Vijayāditya (696-733 A.D.). His reign was on the whole a peaceful one. But towards the close of his reign he sent an expedition against the Pallavas under the crown-prince Vikramāditya. Whether it was a purely aggressive action on the part of the Chālukya king, or the Pallavas gave any provocation, we do not know. But the result was highly gratifying. Vikramāditya conquered Kāñchī and levied tribute from the Pallava king Parameśvara-varman II. This took place in or shorty before 731 A.D.

Vijayāditya

Vikramāditya II ascended the throne after the death of his father and ruled from 733 to 746-7 A.D. The hostilities with the Pallavas continued or were resumed, and the new king made a sudden attack on the Pallava kingdom in order to uproot this 'natural enemy'. Evidence from both sides indicates that he obtained phenomenal success. He defeated and put to flight the Pallava king Nandivarman II and then entered the capital city Kāñchī. But far from destroying the city he made rich donations to its temples. Vikramāditya II then defeated the Chola, Pāṇḍya, Kerala, and Kalabhra kings and planted his pillar of victory on the shores of the southern ocean.

Vikramāditya II

The most memorable event in the reign of Vikramāditya II was the invasion of the Arabs who had, as already related, obtained a footing in Sindh as early as 712 A.D., and then, after overrunning Northern Gujarāt, proceeded towards the Deccan with the desire of conquering all the southern kings. They entered Lāṭa, the northernmost province of the Chālukyas, but were defeated, as noted above (p. 267), by the local Viceroy and forced to retreat. Southern India was thus saved, but this was the last great act of the dynasty whose record is full of brilliant achievements. For,

1. According to Sir R. G. Bhandarkar this may refer to the Syrians on the Malabār coast (*EHD* 3rd *Ed*. p. 98).

under the next king Kīrtivarman II, the sovereignty was wrested by the Rāshṭrakūṭas and the Chālukya supremacy came to an end. This event may be placed at about 753 A. D., although Kīrtivarman nominally ruled over some parts of his kingdom for a few years more.

The fall of the Chālukyas

3. *The Rāshṭrakūṭas.*

The Rāshṭrakūṭas, who thus secured the mastery of the Deccan, seem to have been an indigenous people of the country. The word Rāshṭrakūṭa is used as the name of an official in early records of the Deccan, and probably indicates 'the head of a *rāshṭra* or province.' It seems likely that the founder of the Rāshṭrakūṭa family was an official of this class, and so it continued to be designated by that name, like the Peshwās of later days. Several Rāshṭrakūṭa families are known to have been ruling in different parts of the Deccan since the 5th century A.D. Two of these ruled in Satara region. Another ruled over a small principality with its capital at Achalapura (Ellichpur) in Berar, as a feudatory of the Chālukyas, in the first half of the seventh century A.D. Either this family or another in the Aurangābād District ultimately established a powerful kingdom. The first ruler of note in this family was Indra who married a Chālukya princess. He was succeeded about 710 A.D.[1] by his son Dantidurga who founded the greatness of the family.

Origin

Dantidurga, like his ancestors, began his career as a feudatory and probably took part as such in the two famous campaigns of his overlord Vikramāditya II, viz., against the Pallavas of Kāñchi and the Arab invaders of the north. Gradually his ambition grew, and as soon as Vikramāditya II died, he launched upon a career of conquest on his own account. He conquered the Gurjara kingdom of Nandipurī (near Broach) and the Gurjara-Pratīhāra kingdom of Mālwa, and also extended his authority over the eastern part of Madhya Pradesh. He carefully avoided any aggressive action against his Chālukya overlord, but Kīrtivarman II being apprehensive of the growing power of his feudatory, decided to

Dantidurga

1. This is the view of Mirashi who takes the date of his Ellora grant to be 463 and refers it to Kalachuri Era (*POC.* XV.). Others take the date to be 663 Śaka=741 A.D.

curb it. In the battle that ensued Dantidurga was completely successful and, by 753 A.D., he was master of a large part of the Deccan.

Shortly after this Dantidurga died without leaving any son, and his uncle Kṛishṇa ascended the throne some time before 758 A.D. The Chālukya emperor, who had retired to the south after his defeat, made a final attempt to reassert his supremacy, but was again defeated by Kṛishṇa, and the Chālukya power practically came to an end in 760 A.D. Kṛishṇa next defeated the Gaṅgas of Mysore and the Eastern Chālukyas of Veṅgi. The latter entered into an alliance with him and the Rāshṭrakūṭas now became the ruler of practically the whole of the Chālukya empire. Kṛishṇa died about 773 A.D. He consolidated the Rāshṭrakūṭa power by his conquests, but his greatest achievement was the building of the famous rock-cut temple of Kailāsa at Ellora. The next king Govinda II was hopelessly addicted to sensual pleasures, and hence his younger brother Dhruva took the reins of government in his own hands. Govinda II attempted to recover his power with the help of friendly chiefs, but Dhruva defeated him in a pitched battle and formally deposed him.

With the accession of Dhruva a new era began in the history of the Rāshṭrakūṭas. They were no longer content with their dominions in the south, but looked wistfully towards the rich plains of Northern India. Their history, at this stage, forms a part of the general history of India and will be described in the next chapter.

CHAPTER V.

Struggle for supremacy—the Rāshṭrakūṭas, the Pālas, and the Gurjara Pratihāras

1. *The Tripartite Struggle.*

The detailed account given in the last two chapters will make it quite clear that towards the close of the 8th century A.D. there were three great powers in India, viz. the Pālas, the Gurjara-Pratīhāras, and the Rāshṭrakūṭas. The Pratīhāra king Vatsarāja, one of whose known dates is 783 A. D., seems to have ruled over considerable territories in Rājputāna and Central India. It appears that while Vatsarāja was laying the foundations of the future greatness of his family in the west, the Pālas had established a strong monarchy in Bengal in the east. The former gradually expanded his kingdom towards the east while the latter did the same in the opposite direction. Under the circumstances it was inevitable that there would be a trial of strength between the two. As a matter of fact there was an encounter between Vatsarāja and the king of Gauḍa, but we do not know definitely when and where it took place. The Chāhamāna ruler Durlabharāja of Śākambharī (near Ajmer), who was a feudatory of Vatsarāja and probably accompanied him, is said, in a very late work, to have overrun the whole of Bengal up to the confluence of the Gaṅgā and the sea. This seems highly incredible, and most likely the fight took place somewhere between the Gaṅgā and the Yamunā. The king of Gauḍa, who must have thus extended his power at least as far as Allāhābād in the west, was defeated by Vatsarāja. The vanquished king was either Gopāla or more probably his son Dharmapāla, and this struggle may be said to have originated the eternal hostility between the Pālas and the Gurjaras. But while the Pratīhāras and the Pālas were fighting for an empire in Northern India, a new claimant appeared on the scene. These were the Rāshṭrakūṭas, who had already established undisputed supremacy in the Deccan, and were now trying to assert their supremacy in the north. King Dhruva crossed the Vindhyas and inflicted a crushing defeat upon Vatsarāja who fled across the desert of Rājputāna. Dhruva next

The three great Powers.

advanced against Dharmapāla and defeated him. In this case we know definitely that the encounter took place somewhere in the Gaṅgā-Yamunā *doab*, and it is therefore likely that the fight between Vatsarāja and the Gauḍa king also took place in the same region.

Thus commenced that tripartite struggle for empire between the Pālas, the Gurjaras, and the Rāshṭrakūṭas which was the most important factor in the political history of India during the next century. The keynote of the struggle seems to have been the possession of the imperial city of Kanauj for which each of these tried and succeeded in turn. In order that the account of this struggle might be intelligently followed we arrange below, in a tabular form, the list of kings of the three rival dynasties so far as we are concerned with them here.

Gurjara—Pratīhāra	Rāshṭrakūṭa	Pāla
Vatsarāja (783 A.D.)	Dhruva (C. 779-793 A. D.)	Dharmapāla (c. 780-815 A.D.)
Nāgabhaṭa (815 A. D.)	Govinda III (794-813 A.D.)	Devapāla c. 815-855 A.D.)
Rāmabhadra.	Amoghavarsha (814-877 A.D.)	
Bhoja (836-885 A. D.)		Vigrahapāla (c 855-860 A.D.
Mahendrapāla (885-910 A. D.)	Kirshṇa II (878-914 A.D.)	Nārāyaṇapāla (c. 860-915 A. D.)

As will be seen from the above table, the first encounter took place between the Rāshṭrakūṭa king Dhruva, the Pratīhāra Vatsarāja, and the Pāla king Dharmapāla. The Rāshṭrakūṭas achieved a complete triumph, but the death of Dhruva, some time before 793 A.D., ushered in a period of confusion in their kingdom. Twelve kings in the south formed a confederacy against Govinda III, the son and successor of Dhruva, and the new king had also to cope with the treacherous hostilities of the Gaṅga chief. While his own hands were thus busy in the south, he seems to have left his northern possessions in charge of his younger brother Indrarāja. To the northern kings this was a good respite and they were not slow to take advantage of it.

Short-lived triumph of Dhruva

2. *The Pāla Empire.*

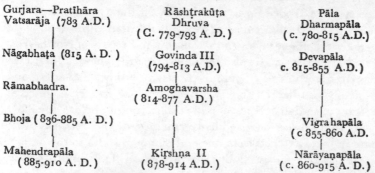

Dharmapāla, who was probably less affected by the Rāshṭrakūṭa blow, seems to have first entered the field and made his suzerainty acknowledged by almost all the important States of Northern India. In particular he defeated Indrāyudha, king of Pañchāla, and placed his own nominee Chakrāyudha on the throne of Kanauj. The great imperial assembly which he held at that famous city was attended by the vassal kings of Bhoja, Matsya, Madra, Kuru, Yadu, Yavana, Avanti, Gandhāra and Kīra. In the presence of this assembly he consecrated himself, both literally and figuratively, as the suzerain of North India. We are told that the assembled chiefs, with bowed heads, acknowledged the new political status of Dharmapāla, while the sacred water of consecration was being poured over his head from a golden pitcher by the elders of Pañchāla. The list of chiefs who attended this Imperial *Durbar* gives us a rough idea of the extent of Dharmapāla's empire. It included Central Panjāb (Madra) and probably extended up to the Sindhu, for the Yavanas can only refer to the Muslim rulers of Sindh or Multan while Gandhāra denotes the upper valley of the Sindhu and a part of North-West Frontier Province. It also included Kangra valley (Kīra), East Panjāb (Kuru, Yadu), Jaipur (Matsya), Mālwa (Avanti) and probably also Berār (Bhoja). Bengal, which hardly counted as a factor in Indian politics for more than a century before the Pālas came into power, now suddenly emerged as the mistress of an empire that stretched from one end of North India to the other.

Empire of Dharmapāla

The ever-shifting political combination of the time, however, made it difficult, if not impossible, for any king to enjoy undisturbed a long and prosperous reign. The Gurjara power was merely stunned by the Rāshṭrakūṭa blow, but not destroyed, and Nāgabhaṭa, the son and successor of Vatsarāja, set himself to the task of retrieving the fortunes of his family. He first made himself master of Sindhu, Andhra, Vidarbha and Kaliṅga, and then felt strong enough to try his strength with his two great rivals. He attacked and defeated Chakrāyudha, the nominee of Dharmapāla on the throne of Kanauj, and this necessarily precipitated a conflict with Dharmapāla himself. The battle probably took place at Monghyr, and Nāgabhaṭa scored a great victory over his rival. Urged on by his triumph, Nāgabhaṭa conquered in quick succession the Ānartta, Mālava, Kirāta, Turushka, Vatsa, and Matsya countries.

Nāgabhaṭa

While Nāgabhaṭa was thus wresting the empire from the hands of Dharmapāla, the latter probably sought the aid of the

Rāshṭrakūṭa king Govinda III who had settled the affairs of his kingdom by this time. Either in response to such an appeal or on his own initiative, Govinda III undertook a military expedition to the north like his father. Dharmapāla, with his protege Chakrāyudha, waited upon him. Nothing could resist the onslaught of the Rāshṭrakūṭa forces, and Nāgabhaṭa fled away in fear, nobody knew whither. Govinda III overran his territory and proceeded up to the Himālaya mountains. Well might he exclaim like the later Peshwās, that his horse could run from the Himālayas tc Cape Comorin without treading upon others' territory.

Govinda III.

Thus the imperial dreams of Nāgabhaṭa, like those of his father, were rudely shattered by the lancers of the south. But the Rāshṭrakūṭa king was not left free to enjoy his conquests. His dominions were torn asunder by internal dissensions. The governor of Lāṭa was expelled by his younger brother in 812 A.D., and the revolutionary movement, thus set on foot, afterwards developed into an attempt to prevent the accession of Amoghavarsha, the son of Govinda III.

This unexpected imbroglio in the Rāshṭrakūṭa affairs once more left the Pālas and Gurjaras free to fight among themselves. It is difficult to follow the details of the struggle, but the Pālas seem to have got the upper hand. Dharmapāla seems to have recovered his empire, at least to a large extent, and when he died, at an advanced age, about 815 A. D., his son and successor Devapāla ruled as the undisputed master of a large part of Northern India. On the other hand, Rāmabhadra, the son of Nāgabhaṭa, possessed very little power. Devapāla is said to have defeated the Draviḍas, Gurjaras, and the Hūṇas, and conquered Utkala and Kāmarūpa. It is therefore not without justification that the court poets described his empire as extending from the Himālayas to the Vindhyas and from the Bay of Bengal to the Arabian sea.

Devapāla

Devapāla ruled for about 40 years, and the fame of his prowess reached the distant isles in the Indian Archipelago, where centuries ago adventurous Indians had established a colonial empire. Mahārāja Bālaputradeva, the Śailendra king of Suvarṇadvīpa[1], erected a monastery at Nālandā, and at his request Devapāla granted five villages for its maintenance.

Weak successors of Devapāla

1. For the Śailendras cf. Ch. XXII, §1.

With Devapāla ends the most glorious period of the Pāla history. His successor Vigrahapāla ruled for a short period and preferred an ascetic life to an aggressive military career. He was followed by Nārāyaṇapāla whose long reign of more than half a century saw the decline of the great imperial fabric raised by Dharmapāla and Devapāla.

3. *The Pratīhāra Empire.*

While the fortunes of the Pāla empire were in the hands of weaklings who preferred ascetic life to an aggressive military career, a youth of remarkable energy and military skill had ascended the throne of the Pratīhāras. This was Bhoja who had succeeded his father Rāmabhadra in or about 836 A.D. Almost immediately after his accession he tried to re-establish the glory of his family. He had some initial success and was master of both Kanauja and Kālañjara. He was, however, defeated by Devapāla and fared no better against the Rāshṭrakūṭas. He was probably also defeated by the Chedis of Tripurī who were gradually rising into prominence. But although his early attempts proved a failure, Bhoja did not give up all hope. The death of Devapāla and the pacific policy of his successors, followed by the Rāshṭrakūṭa invasion of Bengal, must have furnished a golden opportunity to the Pratīhāra king. He secured the aid of the powerful Chedi rulers of Gorakhpur and probably also of the Guhilot king. Assisted by these powerful chiefs, Bhoja had probably no great difficulty in inflicting a crushing defeat upon the unwarlike king that sat upon the throne of Dharmapāla and Devapāla. Fortune also favoured Bhoja in another direction. The Rāshṭrakūṭa king Kṛishṇa II was involved in a life and death struggle with the Eastern Chālukyas who occupied and burnt his capital. Bhoja seized this opportunity to take the offensive. He defeated Kṛishṇa II, probably on the bank of the Narmadā, and occupied Mālwa. He then advanced towards Gujarāt and occupied the territory round Kheṭaka (Kaira District). But although this was recovered by Kṛishṇa II, Bhoja maintained his supremacy over the whole of the Kāthiāwār Peninsula. A sanguinary battle was fought between Bhoja and Kṛishṇa II at Ujjayinī which was long remembered by posterity. But it led to no decisive result, and Mālwa remained in the hands of the Pratīhāras.

Bhoja

Having thus triumphed over the two great rival powers,

Bhoja had no difficulty in establishing his suzerainty over the Panjāb, Oudh and other territories. Thus with the exception of Kāshmir, Sindh, the Pāla dominions in Bihār and Bengal, and the Kalachuri kingdom in Jubbulpore region, the rest of Northern India was conquered by Bhoja. Having fixed his capital at the imperial city of Kanauj, the great emperor seems to have enjoyed the undisturbed possession of these extensive territories. He died about 885 A.D., leaving a consolidated empire, for which Vatsarāja and Nāgabhaṭa had fought in vain, to his son and successor Mahendrapāla, whose known dates are 893 and 907 A.D.

Mahendrapāla.

Under Mahendrapāla Magadha and at least a considerable portion of North Bengal were added to the Pratīhāra empire. Thus the victory over the eastern rival was complete after a struggle of more than a century, and the Pratīhāra empire reached its high watermark of success and glory.

At the beginning of the tenth century, the Pratīhāra king Mahendrapāla ruled over an empire that, to quote the phraseology of the court poet of Devapāla, stretched from the source of the Gaṅgā to that of the Revā (i.e. from the Himālayas to the Vindhyas) and almost from the eastern to the western ocean. The struggle for empire between the three great rival powers of the ninth century A.D. had thus had its logical end. Dhruva and Govinda III, Dharmapāla and Devapāla, Bhojadeva and Mahendrapāla,—each pair played in turn the imperial role. But their empires, like the waves of the ocean, rose to the highest point only to break down. So it had proved with the Pālas and Rāshṭrakūṭas, and so it was destined to be in the case of the Pratīhāras. For the later history of this dynasty is but the history of the decline and downfall of the mighty empire.

CHAPTER VI.

Downfall of the Pratīhāra empire.

1. *The decline of the Pratīhāra empire.*

The emperor Mahendrapāla was succeeded by his two sons, Bhoja II and Mahīpāla. Of the first we know very little, but the reign of the second was a prosperous one in its earlier part.

Mahīpāla

The empire remained intact and the poet Rājaśekhara, who lived in the court of Mahīpāla, describes him as the *Mahārājādhirāja* of Āryāvarta, and refers to his victories over the Muralas, the Mekalas, the Kaliṅgas, the Keralas, the Kuntalas, and the Ramaṭhas.

The great extent and prosperity of the Pratīhāra empire is also attested to by the Muhammadan traveller Al Masūdī, a native of Baghdad, who visited India in the year 915-16 A.D. It appears from his statements that the Pratīhāra empire reached the Rāshṭrakūṭa territory in the south and included a part of Sindh and the Panjāb. Masūdī says that the king is rich in horses and camels, and maintains four armies in the four quarters of N. India, each 700,000 or 900,000 strong. Regarding the political relations of the king of Kanauj, we are told by Masūdī that of the four armies maintained by him, that of the north wars against the Muslim ruler of Multān, and that of the south fights against Balharā i.e. the Rāshṭrakūṭa king.

The hostility with the Rāshṭrakūṭas, which Mahīpāla had inherited from his predecessors, proved, however, as fatal to his flourishing empire as it was to those of Vatsarāja and Nāgabhaṭa.

Sack of Kanauj

Within a year or two of Masūdī's visit, the Rāshṭrakūṭa king Indra III invaded North India, defeated Mahīpāla and pursued him up to the junction of the Gaṅgā and the Yamunā, while the imperial city of Kanauj was devastated by his soldiery. Thus the Rāshṭrakūṭas had a complete victory over the Pratīhāras, and the empire of Bhoja and Mahendrapāla lay prostrate at the feet of their southern rival. But Indra III did not stay long in North India. He returned to the Deccan in 916 A.D. and the internal circumstances of the Rāshṭrakūṭas proved extremely unfavourable for the maintenance of their possessions in the north. Mahīpāla seized this opportunity, and was loyally supported by his feudatory chiefs in his endeavour to restore the fallen fortunes of his family. Whether he was able to recover all the territories he had lost, it is difficult to determine. At the time of his death, in 913 A.D., his kingdom stretched as far as Banaras in the east. The Yamunā, the Betwā and the Dasan rivers seem to have formed its boundaries on the south-east while to the south it probably reached the Vindhyas.

But although Mahīpāla may be credited with retrieving his fortunes to a large extent, there can be no question that the prestige of the Pratīhāras sustained a serious blow. As is usual in these circumstances, subordinate chiefs began to assert independence and new powers arose within the empire. The Rāshṭrakūṭas also renewed their invasion shortly before 940 A.D., and probably seized the two famous fortresses of Kālanjara and Chitrakūṭa (Chitor). Thus began the decline and downfall of the great Pratīhāra empire, and the process of disintegration presents a historic parallel to that which overtook the Mughal empire in the eighteenth century. The history of the Pratīhāra kings after Mahīpāla is somewhat obscure and even the succession of kings cannot be settled with certainty. But it seems that he was succeeded by his three sons, Mahendrapāla II (945 A.D.), Devapāla (948 A.D.), and Vijayapāla, one of whose known dates is 960 A. D. During the reigns of these three kings the disintegration of the Pratīhāra empire was all but complete.

The successors of Mahīpāla

The new political situation is best illustrated by the history of the several new powers that arose on the ruins of the Pratīhāra empire. A brief reference to each of them is, therefore, necessary before resuming the history of the Pratīhāras.

2. *The Chandellas.*

The Chandellas, who were later included among the 36 Rājput clans, claimed to be descended from the sage Chandrātreya, who was born of the moon. They rose into prominence in the 9th century A.D., and established a kingdom, later known as Jejākabhukti, in the Bundelkhand region. The capital of this kingdom was Kharjuravāhaka, represented by the modern village of Khajrāho in the Chhatarpur State, whose beautiful temples still testify to the glory of the Chandellas.

They were feudatories of the Pratīhāra emperors, and their chief, Harshadeva (c. 900-925 A.D.), had loyally assisted Mahīpāla in regaining his kingdom. Yaśovarman, son of Harshadeva, however, practically threw off the allegiance, and was described as a scorching fire to the Gurjaras. The decline of the Pratīhāra empire left the field free for his ambitious enterprises. He conquered the famous fortress of Kālanjara and extended his kingdom as far as the Yamunā in the north. He then launched upon a career of conquest and, according to official records, carried on successful wars against the Gauḍas, Kosalas, Kāśmīras, Mithilas, Mālavas, Chedis, Kurus, and Gurjaras. In spite of obvious exaggerations there is no doubt that he made extensive conquests in North India and made the Chandellas a formidable power. The fort of Kālanjara henceforth became the stronghold of this kingdom. The Pratīhāra ruler was indeed still invoked as the suzerain power in official documents, probably very much in the same way as the rulers of Oudh and Hyderābād found it convenient to pay a nominal allegiance to the emperors at Delhi, but Yaśovarman carved out a principality which was independent for all practical purposes.

Yaśovarman.

The Chandella power rapidly advanced under Dhaṅga, the son and successor of Yaśovarman. He is said to have obtained the empire after defeating the Kānyakubja king, which means that he gave up even the formal acknowledgment of the Pratīhāra suzerainty. By the year 954 A.D. his kingdom extended up to the Yamunā in the north, Gwalior in the north-west, and Bhilsā in the south-west. The occupation of Gwalior must have been a severe blow to the power and prestige of the Pratīhāras, as their powerful rival thereby obtained a secure footing in the very heart of the kingdom. In course of his long reign, extending over the latter half of the tenth century A.D., Dhaṅga made further encroachments upon the territory of the Pratīhāras, and seems to have extended his kingdom far to the north of the Yamunā and as far as Banaras in the east.

Dhaṅga.

Dhaṅga also directed his arms against the Pālas and invaded Aṅga (Bhāgalpur). He then proceeded to Rāḍha (west Bengal) and South Kosala, and also came into conflict with the kings of Andhra and Kuntala. He also claims to have defeated the kings of Kratha, Siṁhala and Kāñchi—which is possibly a mere hyperbole.

Dhaṅga's known dates are 954 and 1002 A.D. He was the first independent Chandella king and assumed the title *Mahārājādhirāja.* According to Firishta the Raja of Kālinjar joined the confederacy of Indian chiefs organised by Jayapāla against Sabuktigīn. He must be identified with Dhaṅga who and his successors called themselves 'lords of Kālanjara'. This is confirmed by an inscription which states that Dhaṅga, "by the strength of his arms equalled even the powerful Haṁvīra" i.e. the Yamīnī king who used the title Amīr. Dhaṅga died at Allāhābād at the ripe old age of 100.

3. *The Kalachuris.*

The Kalachuris, also known as the Haihayas, were an ancient people. Their legendary history, known from the Epics and the Purāṇas, has been referred to above, (p. 69).

Early history

An era starting from 249 or 250 A.D was later used by the Kalachuris and known as the Kalachuri era. But the Kalachuris are not known to have been a political power in the third century A.D. and probably had nothing to do with the foundation of this era. In historical times we first come across them in the latter half of the sixth century A.D. when they ruled over a powerful kingdom comprising Gujarāt, northern Mahārāshṭra, and later, even parts of Mālwa. Three kings of this family are known viz. Kṛishṇarāja, his son Śaṁkaragaṇa, and the latter's son Buddharāja. They had to fight with the two powerful neighbours; the Maitrakas of Valabhi and the Chālukyas of Bādāmi. As noted above, the Chālukya king Maṅgaleśa put to flight Buddharāja and conquered his dominions. Evidently the Kalachuris were not exterminated. For the Chālukya king Vinayāditya defeated the Haihayas, and his grandson Vikramāditya II married two Haihaya princesses. These Haihayas undoubtedly refer to the Kalachuris who were till then (i.e. middle of the 8th century A.D.) probably ruling over Eastern Mālwa and the neighbouring regions.

About this time, or shortly after, several branches of the Kalachuris were settled in different parts of Northern India. One of them founded a principality in Sarayūpāra in the modern Gorakhpur District. The other, which soon became very powerful, ruled in Chedi country in Bundelkhand.

The Kalachuris of Chedi, also known as kings of Ḍāhala, had their capital at Tripurī, represented by the modern village of Tewār, six miles to the west of Jubbulpore. The royal dynasty was founded about 845 A.D. by Kokalla[1] who was one of the greatest military leaders of the age. The Kalachuri inscriptions credit him with victories over many powerful kings, and it is difficult to say how far we can regard them as historical facts. But there is no doubt that Kokalla carried his victorious arms far and wide and established a powerful kingdom.

Kokalla I

As noted above (p. 286) he probably came into conflict with the Pratīhāra king Bhoja I, for he is said to have granted Bhoja 'assurance of safety or protection' (literally, freedom from fear). He also looted the treasuries of Śaṅkaragaṇa, probably the Kalachuri ruler of Sarayūpāra, Harsharāja, probably the Guhila chief, and Guvāka, the Chāhamāna king of Śākambharī. As the last three were vassals of Bhoja I, it may be presumed that Kokalla gained a great victory against the Pratīhāra king, helped by his feudal chiefs, but afterwards came to amicable terms with him.

Next, he defeated the Turushkas, who were undoubtedly some Turkish forces of the ruler of Sindh. Unfortunately no details are known and we cannot say whether Kokalla took the aggressive or merely checked one of the periodical raids of the Arabs. He is also said to have plundered Vaṅga i.e. East and South Bengal, which probably was no longer under the Pālas and formed an independent kingdom.

Towards the close of his long reign Kokalla invaded Northern Koṅkaṇ and helped the Rāshṭrakūṭa king Kṛishṇa II (878-914 A. D.), who had married his daughter, probably against the Eastern Chālukyas and the Pratīhāras.

These extensive conquests made the Kalachuris for the time being almost an imperial power, but this position was not maintained for long, and the actual dominions of the Kalachuris even under Kokalla never extended much beyond Madhya Pradesh. A more stable empire was founded by his early rival, the Pratīhāra king Bhoja I, as noted above.

Kokalla married a Chandella princess and had eighteen sons. The eldest succeeded him on the throne while the others were appointed rulers of different *maṇḍalas* or Divisions. This led to the disintegration of the kingdom, for we know that the descendants of one of these founded a separate kingdom in South Kosala with its capital at Tuṁmāṇa.

[1] Also written Kokkalla, Kokkala etc.

Kokalla was succeeded by his son Śaṁkaragaṇa some time between A.D. 878 and 888. He defeated a Somavaṁśi ruler of South Kosala and conquered some territories from him near Ratanpur in Bilāspur district. He came to the rescue of the Rāshṭrakūṭa king Kṛishṇa II when the latter was attacked by the Eastern Chālukya king Vijayāditya III, but was defeated. There were several matrimonial alliances between the Kalachuris and the Rāshṭrakūṭas.

Śaṁkaragaṇa.

Śaṁkaragaṇa was succeeded by his two sons Bālaharsha and Yuvarāja. The latter ascended the throne about the middle of the 10th century A.D. and defeated the Pāla king of Gauḍa and the Gaṅga ruler of Kaliṅga. He was, however, defeated by the Chandella king Yaśovarman and also by his near relative, the Rāshṭrakūṭa king Kṛishṇa III, who probably occupied a part of the Kalachuri kingdom for some time. But Yuvarāja soon defeated and drove out the Rāshṭrakūṭa forces. In order to celebrate this great victory the famous poet Rājaśekhara, who now lived in the Kalachuri court, staged his drama *Viddhaśālabhañjikā*. The Kalachuri inscriptions credit Yuvarāja also with successful raids against Kāshmir and the Himālayan region.

His successors.

Yuvarāja's son Lakshmaṇarāja, who ruled in the third quarter of the 10th century A.D., was also a great conqueror. He invaded Vaṅgāla, south Bengal, which was then probably under the Chandra dynasty. The king of Orissa conciliated him by offering him a jewelled image of the serpent Kāliya. The Somavaṁśi king of South Kosala was also defeated by him. In the west he invaded Lāṭa, ruled by a feudatory of the Rāshṭrakūṭas, and defeated the king of Gurjara, probably Mūlarāja I, the founder of the Chalukya Dynasty. After further conquests he advanced as far as Somanātha and worshipped at the temple of Someśvara. He is further credited with the conquest of Kāshmir and Pāṇḍya, in the extreme north and south—which is probably a mere conventional boast.

Lakshmaṇarāja's two sons, Śaṁkaragaṇa II and Yuvarāja II, who successively sat on the throne, were unworthy sons of a worthy father. The kingdom suffered serious reverses during the reign of the latter which covered the last quarter of the 10th century A.D. His maternal uncle Taila II, who had re-established the Chālukya supremacy in the Deccan by defeating the Rāshṭrakūṭas, carried on raids into his dominions. Far more disastrous was the invasion of the Paramāra king Muñja of Mālava. Yuvarāja II was defeated and fled, and his capital city fell into the hands of the enemy. Though the enemy forces soon withdrew, the ministers did not allow the cowardly king to return, and placed his son Kokalla II on the throne. He restored the power and prestige of the dynasty by his brilliant military career. He invaded the Deccan and by his victories took revenge for the defeat inflicted upon his father by Taila II. He also led successful expedition against the Gurjaras in the west, Kuntala in the south, and Gauḍa in the east. Thus by the end of the 10th century A.D. the Kalachuris had again become a great power.

4. *The Paramāras.*

Immediately to the west of the Kalachuris were the Paramāras ruling in Mālava. The Paramāras came to be known as Pavar Rājputs in later days and a story was told of their origin from a fire-pit in Mount Abu. But according to the earlier records the Paramāra rulers were born in the family of the Rāshṭrakūṭas. This is more probable and it seems that Upendra *alias* Kṛishṇarāja, the founder of the Paramāra dynasty, was originally the governor of Mālwa, appointed by the Rāshṭrakūṭa emperor Govinda III after he had conquered the province from Nāgabhaṭṭa II. The family remained loyal to the Rāshṭrakūṭas and lost possession of Mālwa when it was conquered by the Pratīhāras, who were in possession of it till at least 946 A.D. Shortly after this Vairisiṁha, a descendant of Upendra, recovered his ancestral dominions, evidently with the help of the Rāshṭrakūṭas. An inscription tells us that "Vairisiṁha proved by the strength of his sword that Dhārā belonged to him". Dhārā, the capital of the Paramāras, is now represented by Dhar, in Central India.

Origin.

Vairisiṁha's son and successor Sīyaka II was a brave general and defeated several neighbouring chiefs. Like his father he acknowledged the suzerainty of the Rāshṭrakūṭa emperor Kṛishṇa III, but as soon as the latter died he declared himself independent. The new Rāshṭrakūṭa king advanced against the rebel, and a sanguinary fight took place on the bank of the Narmadā in A.D. 972. Sīyaka completely defeated Khoṭṭiga and pursued him up to his capital city Mānyakheṭa which he mercilessly sacked.

Sīyaka II thus founded the independent kingdom of Mālava which was bounded by the Tāpti on the south, Jhālawar on the north, Bhilsā on the east and the Sābarmati on the west. He died shortly after, and was succeeded by Muñja, who was probably his son, though some old authorities represent him to be an adopted son.

Muñja.

Muñja, also known as Utpala and Vākpatirāja II, was the most powerful ruler of the family and one of the greatest generals of his age. His whole reign was full of wars and conquests. He defeated the Kalachuri king Yuvarāja II and the Guhilas of Medapāṭa, and plundered their capital cities. He also defeated the Hūṇas who ruled over a small principality known as Hūṇa-maṇḍala, to the north-west of Mālava, evidently the last remnant of the vast empire of Toramāṇa and Mihirakula. He attacked the Chāhamānas of Naḍḍula, and wrested from them Mt. Abu and considerable territories in the south of modern Jodhpur State. Muñja next defeated Mūlarāja, founder of the Chaulukya kingdom of Aṇahilapāṭaka, who fled to the desert of Mārwar.

But the greatest enemy of Muñja was Taila II, who had conquered the Deccan from the Rāshṭrakūṭas and naturally wanted to assert his authority over Mālava which once belonged to them. Taila led no less than six campaigns against Mālava in each of which he was defeated by Muñja. In order to put an end to this trouble Muñja decided to take the offensive. Success at first attended his arms and he defeated Taila on the bank of the Godāvari. He then pursued the enemy beyond the river, but was unfortunately defeated and taken prisoner. His officers made a secret attempt to rescue him, but the plan miscarried, and he was put to death by Taila II who annexed all the territories up to the bank of the Narmadā.

The tragic end of Muñja was brought about by his own folly in advancing too far from his base into the interior of the enemy's country. A story is told that his wise minister Rudrāditya counselled him strongly never to cross Godāvari river, and as soon as he heard that his master had gone to the other side in pursuit of the enemy, he committed suicide so that he might not live to see the great calamity which, he instinctively felt, would befall his master. In spite of his sad end Muñja must be remembered as a mighty warrior, a beneficent ruler, and a great patron of art and literature. A large number of poets including such famous names as Dhanañjaya, Halāyudha, Dhanika, and Padmagupta graced his court and enjoyed his munificence. He is also credited with the excavation of a number of big tanks and construction of temples.

Muñja's defeat and death took place shortly after A.D. 993. He was succeeded by his younger brother Sindhurāja who avenged his disgrace by defeating the Chālukya king and recovering the lost territories. The great poet Padmagupta took the life of the king, also known as Navasāhasāṅka, as the theme of his famous work *Navasāhasāṅka-charita*. The allegorical and mythical way in which some of the events of his life are narrated makes it difficult to find out sober historical truth about him. It is, however, suggested, on the basis of this work, that Sindhurāja, helped the Nāga king of Bastar against some non-Aryan ruling chief of Wairagarh (Chanda District, M. P.). Sindhurāja was in any case a great conqueror. He defeated the Somavaṁśīs of South Kosala, the Śīlāhāras of Koṅkaṇ, and the ruler of Hūṇa-maṇḍala. He also conquered Lāṭa (South Gujarāt) and tried without success to subjugate the Chaulukya kingdom of North Gujarāt. He died about A.D. 1000 and was succeeded by his son Bhoja.

5. *The Chaulukyas.*

Some time about 940 A.D. Mūlarāja of the Chaulukya dynasty conquered Sārasvata-maṇḍala (country on the bank of the Saraswati) and established an independent kingdom with its capital at Aṇahilapāṭaka or Aṇahilapattana now represented by Pātan. The Chaulukya is regarded by some as only a variant form of the Chālukya, but this is not probably a correct view, as the two families have different traditions about their origin. The Chaulukyas were later known as the Solaṅki Rājputs.

Mūlarāja.

Mūlarāja soon extended his kingdom by conquering the eastern part of Saurāshṭra and Kachchhadeśa (Cutch). But he had soon to face the hostility of his powerful neighbours. The Chāhamāna king Vigraharāja from the north and Barappa, the feudatory chief of Lāṭa and a general of Taila II, from the south, simultaneously invaded the newly founded kingdom. Mūlarāja retired to Cutch, while Vigraharāja overran his kingdom as well as Lāṭa and reached the Narmadā. Mūlarāja concluded a treaty with Vigraharāja, and as soon as the latter withdrew, defeated and killed Barappa. But he had no respite. The Paramāra king Muñja overran his kingdom and Mūlarāja fled to Mārwār. Although he recovered his kingdom some time later, he was again defeated by the Kalachuri king Lakshmaṇarāja. It reflects no little credit upon Mūlarāja that he survived all these disasters and saved his kingdom. It is even claimed in Gujarāt chronicles that Mūlarāja defeated Sindhurāja and the ruler of North Kosala Mūlarāja's known dates are A.D. 942 and 994 and he probably died in 995 A.D. At the time of his death the Chaulukya kingdom extended upto the Sābarmati river on the east and south. In the north it included Sanchor in the Jodhpur State.

Mūlarāja's son and successor Chāmuṇḍarāja had also to fight against the Paramāras and Kalachuris. He died in 1008 A.D.

6. *The Chāhamānas.*

The Chāhamānas, later known as the Chauhān Rājputs, are known to have been ruling in different parts of Gujarāt and Rājputāna as early as the 7th and 8th centuries A.D. The most important branch ruled over Sapādalaksha country with its capital at Śākambharī, now represented by Sambhar in Jaipur. The Chāhamāna rulers of this kingdom acknowledged the suzerainty of the Pratīhāras. As already mentioned above (p. 282), Durlabharāja of this dynasty accompanied Vatsarāja in his expedition against Gauḍa. His son and successor Govindarāja *alias* Guvāka, a feudatory of Nāgabhaṭa II, is mentioned in a literary work as having repulsed an attack of Sultan Vega Varisa. This Sultan has been identified with Bashar, the governor of Sindh under Caliph Al-Māmūn (A.D. 817-833). According to another literary work the Guhila king Khommāṇa II and other chiefs are said to have resisted an Arab invasion during the Caliphate of Al-Māmūn. Nāgabhaṭa II, the Pratīhāra emperor, is also said to have defeated the Turushkas. Probably all these relate to the same event, and we may presume that Nāgabhaṭa II, with the help of his feudatory chiefs, including the Chāhamāna and Guhila rulers, successfully resisted an Arab invasion led by Bashar, the Arab governor of Sindh.

The Chāhamānas were loyal to the Pratīhāras till the beginning of the 10th century A.D. But after the disastrous defeat of Mahīpāla in the hands of the Rāshṭrakūṭas they gradually asserted independence. Vākpatirāja I, who ruled in the first quarter of the 10th century A.D., is said to have harassed Tantrapāla who was coming with a message of his overlord. If this overlord is Mahīpāla I, we must presume that Vākpatirāja had already begun to defy the authority of his suzerain. His son and successor Siṁharāja, whose known date is 956 A.D., openly declared independence and assumed the title *Mahārājādhirāja.* It is even said that he imprisoned a number of Pratīhāra feudatories, and his overlord had to come in person to his house in order to secure their release. This overlord must have been one of the successors of Mahīpāla I, and the incident shows the depths of degradation to which the Pratīhāra empire had fallen. Siṁharāja's son and successor Vigraharāja II, whose known date is 973 A.D., overran the Chaulukya kingdom and Lāṭa, and carried his victorious arms up to the bank of the Narmadā as mentioned above (p. 296). Though he had to withdraw from these parts he left a powerful State with Śākambharī as its capital.

Assertion of independence.

Lakshmaṇa, the youngest son of Vākpatirāja I, founded a kingdom at Naḍḍula, modern Nadol in Jodhpur, which flourished for several centuries.

Branch Families.

Two other Chāhamāna families are known to have been ruling in Dholpur and Partābgarh in Rājputāna. Both of them were feudatories to the Pratīhāras. Chaṇḍamahāsena, lord of Dhavalapurī (Dholpur) in 842 A.D., claims to have been served by the Mlechcha lords settled on the bank of the Charmaṇvatī (Chambal). These Mlechcha lords were probably Arab chiefs taken prisoner in course of the fight between Nāgabhaṭa II and Bashar, the governor of Sindh, noted above. In that case we should presume that Chaṇḍamahāsena or his predecessor also joined his overlord along with other feudatory chiefs.

7. *The Guhilas.*

The Guhila-putras or Guhilots of Medapāṭa (Mewar), later known as Śiśodīya Rājputs, occupied a unique place in the mediaeval history of India, and naturally many romantic tales and bardic sagas have clustered round their names, and obscured their true history. The earliest epigraphic record containing a full genealogy of the family is an inscription, dated A. D. 977, found at Atpur. It gives the names of 20 kings in an

Origin.

unbroken line of succession, beginning from Guhadatta and ending in Śaktikumāra. Allowing five reigns to a century we may place Guhadatta in the second half of the 6th century A.D. This view is corroborated by other epigraphic evidences, but goes against the bardic tradition that Guha, the founder of the family, was the son of Śīlāditya, the last ruler of Valabhī, as the latter was on the throne till at least 766 A.D.

The most surprising thing in the genealogical account of Atpur Ins. is the omission of the name of Bappa Rāwal, who figures so prominently as the founder of the dynasty in bardic chronicles and later records dating from 13th century A.D. Different versions are current of his early history, according to some of which he obtained royalty through the grace of a sage and captured Chitrakūṭa (Chitor) by defeating the Mlechchhas (or the Mori kings, according to some version).

Bappa.

The story of Bappa Rāwal cannot be dismissed as a pure myth. It seems that Bappa was not the proper name but the designation of one of the Guhilot kings mentioned above. In view of the fact that all the chronicles place him in the first half of the 8th century A.D., he cannot of course be regarded as the founder of the family, and he has been identified by some with Kālabhoja, and by others with Khommāṇa or Khummāṇa, the eighth and ninth king respectively, in the genealogical list of the Atpur Ins.

The Guhilots were ruling in Mewar for at least two centuries before Bappa. Their earliest capital was Nāgahrada[1] and it was replaced by Āghaṭa (Ahar) in the 10th century. The tradition about the conquest of Chitor by Bappa may however have some basis in fact. It is likely that the Mauryas (Moris), who were ruling at Chitor, fell before the great onslaught of the Arabs which, as noted above (p. 267), overwhelmed nearly the whole of Western India about 725 A.D., and that Bappa, like Nāgabhaṭa I (p. 267), was one of those Indian rulers who distinguished themselves by brave resistance against the Arabs and secured some important cities and strongholds which they were able to wrest from the foreign invaders. The heroic part which Bappa played at this critical moment of India's history probably raised his power and fame to such an extent that posterity regarded him as the real founder of the family, particularly as the capital of

1. Modern Nagda, 14 miles north of Udaipur.

the kingdom was later removed to Chitor, the famous fortress which he had seized by his own prowess.

In addition to the main branch of the Guhilots ruling in Mewar, there was another ruling in Jaipur. Both these branches acknowledged the suzerainty of the Pratīhāras, and reference has been made above (p. 286) to the loyal Guhila chiefs fighting on behalf of their Pratīhārā overlords.

But some time in the second quarter of the tenth century A.D. the Guhila ruler Bhartṛipaṭṭa threw off the yoke of the Pratīhāras. In an inscription, dated A.D. 943, he assumes the title *Mahārājādhirāja*. His son and successor Allaṭa, whose known dates are A.D. 951 and 953, killed in battle Devapāla, probably the Pratīhāra king of that name who is known to have been ruling in Kanauj in 948 A.D. and had the ignominy to come in person to the house of his Chāhamāna feudatory in order to secure the release of other feudatory chiefs whom the latter had imprisoned (p. 298).

The Guhila kingdom flourished till, in the reign of Śakti-kumāra, the great-grandson of Allaṭa, the Paramāra king Muñja invaded the dominion and destroyed Āghāṭa, the capital city and 'the pride of Medapāṭa'. But Śaktikumāra survived this disaster and ruled up to the close of the 10th century A.D.

8. *The Shāhis (Shāhiyas)*.[1]

A family of Indianised foreigners ruled in Kābul valley and North-West Frontier Province up to the 9th century A.D. Alberūnī calls them descendants of Kanishka, and they are known as Turkish Shāhiyas. About the middle of the 9th century king Lagatūrmān of this dynasty was dethroned by his Brāhmaṇa minister named Kallār who founded a new royal dynasty known as Hindu or Brāhman Shāhiyas. When Kābul was seized by the Saffarid Yāqūb ibn Layth in 870 A.D. the capital of this kingdom was fixed at Udabhāṇḍapura, or Ohind, modern Und, a small village on the right bank of the Sindhu, about 15 miles above Attock.

Kallār, the founder of this new kingdom, is generally identified with Lalliya Shāhi who is highly praised in the *Rāja-taraṅgiṇī* and whose glory is said to have outshone that of all the

1. The name of the dynasty is written variously as 'Śāhi' 'Shāhi' and 'Shāhiya'. The form 'Sāhi' is used in an epigraph of the dynasty (Ep. Ind. XXI: 298).

rulers in the north, many of whom found safety in his capital city. The new Shāhi kingdom had intimate political association with Kāshmir. Lalliya's son Toramāṇa was expelled by a usurper, but with the help of Kāshmir he recovered the kingdom. After the death of Toramāṇa, also known as Kamaluka and Kala (Kamala?)-varman, his son ascended the throne under the title *Mahārājādhirāja Parameśvara* Sāhi Śri-Bhīmadeva. The famous queen Diddā of Kāshmir was the daughter's daughter of Bhīmadeva and consequently he exercised great influence on that kingdom during the reign of her husband Kshemagupta (A.D. 950-958).

The next important king is Jayapāla, but we do not know whether he was related to Bhīma or belonged to a different family. A fragmentary inscription engraved on a hill in Upper Swat mentions *Paramabhaṭṭāraka Mahārājādhirāja Śrī* Jayapāla-deva, and some pious foundations at Vajirasthāna, obviously the same as modern Wāziristān. Some Muslim chronicles describe in detail how Jayapāla annexed the kingdom of Lohur or Lahore in 999 A.D. It is clear from all this evidence that Jayapāla ruled over an extensive kingdom which comprised the Western Panjāb as far as Sirhind on the east and Multān in the south, North-West Frontier Province, and Eastern Afghānistān as far as Lamghān (or Laghmān) on the west. Jayapāla was thus guarding the gates of India when a powerful Turkish State was founded in his immediate neighbourhood with Ghazni as capital. The Principal event in the reigns of Jayapāla and his successor is the prolonged fight with the rulers of this kingdom which will be described later.

9. *The Minor States.*

In addition to the powerful kingdoms mentioned above, most of which arose out of the ruins of the Pratīhāra empire, there were a few other States, less powerful, that freed themselves from the yoke of the Pratīhāras, but did not play any important part in contemporary politics outside their local sphere.

Four of these were in Kāthiāwār Peninsula which formed an integral part of the Pratīhāra empire. Beginning from the west there were the Saindhavas, also known as the Jayadratha dynasty, ruling from its capital Bhūmilikā, now represented by Bhumili or Ghumli, 25 miles to the north-east of Porbandar, in a gorge of the Bardā Hills. Pushyadeva, the earliest known king of this dynasty,

Saindhavas.

was probably ruling when, some time about 739 A.D., the Arabs of Sindh invaded this kingdom. Seventeen years later Hishām, the governor of Sindh, sent a fleet against it. This naval attack was repulsed by the Saindhavas who called themselves "masters of the Western sea" (*apara-samudr-ādhipati*). The naval expedition was repeated in 776 A.D. According to Arab chronicles the outbreak of an epidemic forced the Arab fleet to withdraw after the death of a number of soldiers. It is more likely, however, that the Saindhava navy repulsed the Arab fleet, for according to a Saindhava inscription, one of their kings, Agguka I, "rescued his country which was being drowned in an ocean of naval force sent by powerful enemies." In any case the Arabs henceforth ceased to send any naval expedition against Indian coast land. The credit of saving India from Arab invasion by sea justly belongs to the Saindhavas, who are chiefly remarkable as being one of the few powers in ancient India with a distinguished record of naval exploits.

Success against the Arabs.

During the reign of Agguka's son and successor Rāṇaka, the Saindhavas were conquered by Nāgabhaṭa II and accepted his suzerainty. This, however, did not prevent them from fighting with the Chāpas, another feudatory of the Pratīhāras. *Mahāsāmantādhipati* Jāika II, whose known dates are 904 and 915 A.D., is the last known king of the family after whom the kingdom was conquered by the Ābhīra chief Grahaṛipu. It has been suggested that the Saindhava ruling family is now represented by the Jeṭhwā Rājputs.

The Chāpas, also known as Chāvaḍās and Chāvotkaṭas, ruled in a part of the Kāthiāwār Peninsula in the 9th century A. D. with their capital at Vardhamāna, modern Wadhwan. They were vassals of the Pratīhāras till about the middle of the 10th century A.D., when Mūlarāja Chaulukya defeated them and annexed their kingdom.

Chāpas.

A Chālukya dynasty ruled in Junāgaḍh region since the latter part of the 8th century A.D. They became feudatories of the Pratīhāras, and their ruler Vāhukadhavala claims to have defeated Dharma (i.e. Dharmapāla), a Karṇāṭa army (i.e. the Rāshṭrakūṭas), and many other kings. Evidently he joined the forces of his suzerain Nāgabhaṭa II against those enemies. Avanivarman II, the great-grandson of Vāhukadhavala, was ruling

Chālukyas.

in 889 A.D. as a vassal of Mahendrapāla. He fought with the Chāpas, and was defeated by the Paramāra king Sīyaka II. About the middle of the 10th century A.D. the Ābhīras conquered this kingdom.

Abhīras.

The Ābhīras grew very powerful during the reign of Graharipu in the middle of the 10th century A.D. He had his capital at Vāmanasthali, now represented by the village Vanthali, 9 miles west of Junāgaḍh. As noted above, he defeated the Saindhavas and the Chālukyas and brought nearly the whole of Southern and Western Saurāshṭra under his sway. Graharipu is described as a *mlechchha* chief who ate beef and plundered the pilgrims to Prabhāsa-*tīrtha* (Somnāth) which was within his territory. These anti-Brāhmanical activities brought upon him the wrath of the Chaulukya Mūlarāja who invaded his dominion and took him prisoner.

Chāpas.

To the north of the Kāthiāwār Peninsula ruled another branch of the Chāpa dynasty, probably since the 8th century A.D., with its capital at Aṇahilapāṭaka. The dynasty was supplanted by the Chaulukyas whose founder Mūlarāja (p. 296) is said to have been descended on his mother's side from these Chāpas.

Tomaras.

To the north-west of the Chāhamānas lived the Tomaras, who were reckoned later as one of the thirty-six Rājput clans. The Tomaras ruled over the Hariyāṇa country and their capital was Dhillikā which became famous in later days as Delhi. According to tradition Delhi was founded by the Tuars, evidently an abbreviated form of Tomaras, in A. D. 736. But the earliest epigraphic reference to the Tomaras does not go beyond the 9th century A. D. when they were vassals of the Pratīhāras. They probably shook off the yoke of the Pratīhāras by the middle of the 10th century A.D. when they were constantly engaged in hostilities with the Chāhamānas. The Tomaras continued to rule over the region round Delhi until they were overthrown by the Chāhamāna king Vigraharāja III Vīsaladeva in the 12th century.

Kachchhapaghatas.

To the east of the Chāhamānas, the Kachchhapaghātas, known in later days as Kachchwā Rājputs, established a powerful kingdom in the latter of the 10th century A.D. Vajradāman of this dynasty defeated the king of Gādhinagara i.e. the Pratīhāra king of Kanauj and conquered Gopagiri, i.e. the famous fort of

Gwalior, some time before 977 A.D. As Gopagiri was in possession of the Chandellas about this time, it appears that Vajradāman had defeated both the Chandella king Dhaṅga and his Pratīhāra overlord who also joined him in defending this stronghold. Probably after this ignominious defeat Dhaṅga shook off even the nominal suzerainty of the Pratīhāras.

CHAPTER VII.

Invasions of Sultān Mahmūd

The review of the political condition of India in the last chapter will make it clear that when Pratīhāra Rājyapāla, son of Vijayapāla (p. 289), ascended the throne of Kanauj in the last quarter of the tenth century, A. D., India presented the same political features as inevitably followed the disruption of a mighty empire. The Pratīhāra rule was practically confined to Kanauj and its neighbourhood, while the rest of North India was divided among rival independent kingdoms fighting with one another. As so often happened in the past, a political re-adjustment would probably have taken place sooner or later, if the Indian States were left to themselves. But this was not to be. Just when the military strength of North India had been exhausted by the age-long struggle for supremacy among the great powers, and before as yet the country had time to take its breath, an Islamic power appeared in the west, and changed the whole situation. The States that were fighting for supremacy were all involved in a common ruin.

About 933 A.D. Alptigīn, a Turkish slave of the Sāmāni kings, had carved an independent principality in the Soleiman Hills round Ghaznī. The kingdom passed on, some time after his death, to one of his Turkish slaves named Sabuktigīn about 977 A.D. He claimed to be descended from the last ruler of Persia, but his family came to be regarded as Turk on account of long residence in Turkistān. In his early life Sabuktigīn was taken prisoner and sold as a slave to Alptigīn. But by dint of his ability he rose high in office and married the daughter of Alptigīn. After the death of the latter chaos and confusion followed, and Sabuktigīn took advantage of it so seize the throne. His accession was approved b y the Sāmāni king to whom he still paid nominal allegiance.

Sabuktigīn.

Immediately after his accession Sabuktigīn extended his kingdom on all sides by conquering the neighbouring States. Jayapāla, the Shāhi king who, as already related, ruled over extensive territories from the Hakrā river in the east to the mountains of Kābul in the west, did not like the rise of a strong Muhammadan power so near his borders. But when Sabuktigīn led several expeditions into his kingdom he could not tolerate it any longer and invaded the new kingdom. The two armies met near Jelalabād, but before there was any engagement, a furious thunderstorm broke out, and induced Jayapāla to retreat, after concluding a treaty with Sabuktigīn. Once safely back in his kingdom Jayapāla refused to observe the treaty. This brought about exactly what Jayapāla had hitherto sought to prevent, and Sabuktigīn assembled an army with a view to invade India. Jayapāla, who foresaw the danger of a Muhammadan invasion long ago, did not underrate its gravity, and asked for the assistance of other Indian chiefs to save the honour of their motherland. The appeal was immediately responded to by the king of Kanauj, as well as the Chāhamāna and Chandella kings.

As has already been related, the Islamic forces had obtained a footing in India as early as the eighth century A.D. They, however, failed to make any lasting impression beyond the territory of Sindh. This was mainly due to the Pratīhāras, who had stood as a bulwark against the aggression of the Muslims ever since their first raids into India proper. Nāgabhaṭa, the founder of the dynasty, owed his greatness to a successful campaign against them early in the 8th century A.D., when they seemed to carry everything before them (p. 267). During the following period, when the power of the Pratīhāras was at its highest, they were looked upon as the greatest enemies of the Muhammadan faith. Masūdī says that while the Rāshṭrakūṭas were friends of the Muhammadans, the Gurjara king of Kanauj was constantly at war with them. As a matter of fact, the Muslim rulers of Multān could save themselves only by holding out the threat that if they were attacked they would destroy the famous image of the Sun-god of that place revered all over India. With the decline of the Pratīhāras no power was left strong enough to oppose a successful resistance to the aggressions of Islām, and when the Ghaznavid kings seized this favourable opportunity to push forward the outpost of Islām into the heart of India, Jayapāla, the king immediately affected, could only send a piteous appeal to the powerful chiefs of India. The Pratīhāra king of Kanauj, though shorn of power and dignity, remembered the proud role his family had played, and when the call of duty came about 991 A.D., he joined the confederacy that Jayapāla had formed against his Muhammadan foe, along with his whilom vassal chiefs of the Chāhamānas and the Chandellas. The imperial banner of the Pratīhāras was unfurled in the valley of the Kurram river in far distant Afghānistān in defence of faith and country. But although the river was dyed red with the blood of hundreds and thousands of Indian patriots, Sabuktigīn gained the day and made himself master of all the territories up to the Sindhu.

Defeat of the Hindu confederacy.

Sabuktigīn died in 997 A.D. His son Mahmūd had been appointed governor of Khurāsān, a rich province in eastern Persia, by the Sāmāni kings who had at last been reconciled to the new dynasty. Sabuktigīn nominated his younger son Ismāīl for the throne of Ghaznī, and the latter caused himself to be proclaimed as king immediately after his father's death. But he was defeated by Mahmūd, who conquered Ghaznī and declared himself king. About this time anarchy and confusion in the Sāmāni State enabled Mahmūd to throw off his allegiance to that power. He received investiture from the Caliph and assumed the title of Sultān, indicating his independent sovereignty. The Caliph also conferred upon him the title Yamīn-ud-Daullah from which his family is known as the Yamīnī dynasty.

Sultān Mahmūd.

Mahmūd was undoubtedly the first soldier of his age. Master of extensive territories from the Sindhu to the heart of Persia, he determined to pursue the aggressive policy of his father on a much bigger scale, and marched towards India with 10,000 chosen horse. The old king Jayapāla met his adversary near Peshāwar, but was defeated and taken prisoner, and Mahmūd pursued his march beyond the Sutlej. Although Jayapāla was released on promise of paying tribute, he did not choose to survive the disgrace, and burnt himself to death in a pyre which he set on fire with his own hands.

What followed took the breath of India away. Year after year Mahmūd repeated his incursions into India. He directed his march against a notable place, plundered everything that fell on his way, destroyed the temples within his reach, and returned home, laden with booty, with the supreme satisfaction of advancing his own religion by the destruction of the image of Hindu gods. He was out for ruthless devastation of territories and the desecration of temples. He did not care so much for establishing an empire in India, but his ambition was satisfied by plundering her rich treasures and breaking the images of her numerous temples.

But the Indians were not insensible to the danger which threatened their country and religion. Ānandapāla, the son and successor of Jayapāla, had organised a confederacy in which the kings of the principal States of western and central India took part. The old king Rājyapāla of Kanauj, true to the traditions of his family, joined the holy war, and the Chandellas also took prominent part in it. The immense host, the largest Indian army that had yet taken the field in defence of their faith and country, boldly advanced into enemy's territories. It was the last desperate struggle for Indian's freedom and so well was this understood, and so profoundly did the sacred cause impress the heart of India, that not only contingents daily came from far and near to augment the immense host, but even, "Hindu women sold their jewels, melted down their golden ornaments, and sent their contributions from a distance to furnish resources for this holy war." The only notable power in Northern India that did not join this great national movement was the Pāla king Mahīpāla of Bengal who was too much involved in troubles at home to think of sending an army abroad.

Second Hindu confederacy.

But with this one notable exception, the sons of Āryāvarta nobly responded to the call of their motherland, and for once falsified the charge that modern historians have brought against them, *viz.* lack of union and patriotism at the time of a national crisis.

Sultān Mahmūd did not underrate the strength of his enemy; but he was a hero of hundred fights, and the courage and military genius that enabled him to rout the innumerable host of Ilak Khān, king of the whole of Tartary up to the walls of China, did not fail him at this critical moment. With the true instincts of a general, he did not risk everything by a general assault, but took up a defensive position near Peshāwar and fortified it by means of trenches. His plan was to provoke the Indians to attack his entrenched camp so that his deficiency in numbers might be made up by the strength of his position. For once in his life he made a miscalculation. The Indians attacked the camp with "astonishing fury", and cut down horse and rider till three to four thousand men of Mahmūd were killed in the first charge.

Napoleon once said that it is not *the men* but *a man* that decides the fate of a battle. Never was the truth of this dictum more fully demonstrated. Mahmūd, undaunted by these reverses, kept discipline in his army and calmly surveyed the situation, while the Indian army, flushed with success, did not maintain either order or discipline. The Indian general himself took part in the melee, while one of those unfortunate incidents, that have again and again decided the fate of Indian battles, snatched away this victory from his grasp. The elephant on which he was mounted took fright and fled from the battlefield. The Indians lost heart at what they took to be the desertion of their general, and the fury of their charge abated. The keen eye of Sultān Mahmūd at once detected the true situation, and he charged home with 10,000 select horse. The Indians dispersed in all directions but the Sultān would give them no quarter. It was then a pure butchery, and twenty thousand Indians lay dead on the field. In spite of the stubborn bravery of the Indian soldiers, the day was lost on account of bad generalship.

Victory of Mahmūd.

The Sultān followed up his victory by the plunder of Nagarkot. There was no garrison to protect it as they had joined the late wars, and "700,000 golden *dinārs*, 700 *mans* of gold and silver plate, 200 *mans* of pure gold in ingots, 2000 *mans* of unwrought silver, and twenty *mans* of various jewels, including pearls, corals, diamonds, and rubies," fell into his hands.

Henceforth the Sultān hardly met with any opposition worth the name in his periodical excursions into India. Altogether seventeen expeditions are set to his credit, all characterised by massacre, plunder, devastation, and desecration of temples. Two of these were directed against the imperial city of Kanauj which exceeded all others in splendour and magnificence. Rājyapāla tried in vain to check Mahmūd in the frontier of his kingdom, and, unable to defend his capital with his small following, crossed over to Bāri on the other side of the Gaṅgā, about 30 miles to the east of Kanauj. The Sultān captured the seven forts that guarded Kanauj and then massacre and plunder were let loose on the fair city (1019 A.D.). Next year he captured Bāri and then proceeded against the Chandella king, but could not gain much success. Jayapāla II, the successor of Ānandapāla, opposed him and the Sultān annexed the whole of the Panjāb to his kingdom.

Sack of Kanauj.

The last important expedition of Mahmūd was directed against the celebrated temple of Somnāth. It was included within the dominions of the Chaulukyas whose early history has been mentioned above. It is a sad reflection on the Indian kings in general, and the Chaulukya king Durlabharāja, son of Chāmuṇḍarāja, in particular, that at the very moment when North India was crumbling before the hard knocks of Sultān Mahmūd, they should have quarrel among themselves over a bride in a *Svayaṁbara* ceremony. For when Durlabharāja won the hands of a Chāhamāna princess in such a ceremony, he had to fight with a number of Indian rulers who were disappointed suitors. He also dissipated his energy in conquering Lāṭa. He abdicated the throne in 1022 A.D. in favour of his nephew Bhīmadeva I. At the news of Sultān Mahmūd's approach Bhīma fled to Cutch. The Sutlān occupied the capital city Aṇahilapāṭaka and then proceeded towards Somnāth where he arrived early in 1025 A.D. The guards of the temple, though deserted by their cowardly leader who fled, offered a brave resistance, and for three days repulsed the Muslim hordes from the walls of the city. In the battle that ensued, the Muhammadan army was almost beaten back, but the stubborn courage and superior skill of Mahmūd reversed the fortunes of the day. When the Sultān entered the temple over the dead bodies of its fifty thousand defenders he was struck with awe at the grandeur and magnificence of the structure. The priests of the temple implored him to protect the image and even wanted to pay a handsome ransom. The reply of the Sultān was characteristic of the man. He said that he would rather be remembered as the breaker than the seller of idols, and with his own hand broke the image, probably a Śivaliṅga, to pieces. The treasures which the Sultān secured at this place were incalculable and are said to have exceeded all his former captures. On its way back to Ghaznī, the Sultān's army suffered great miseries in the desert of Rājputāna. It is said that a priest of Somnāth, in order to avenge its destruction, assumed the role of a guide to Mahmūd's army and lured it to what he thought would be a sure destruction. The Sultān, however, extricated his army and reached Ghaznī in safety. His attention was now drawn to the western territories and he conquered the greater part of Persia. Soon after this brilliant achievement the Sultān died at Ghaznī in A.D. 1030.

Sack of Somnāth.

Sultān Mahmūd was undoubtedly one of the greatest military genius that the world has ever seen. His cool courage, prudence, resourcefulness and many other good qualities of head and heart command universal respect and admiration. But in spite of all these, the historian of India cannot regard Mahmūd save as a freebooter of the worst type. He drained the country of its enormous wealth and brought incalculable misery upon its inhabitants. His ferocity and avarice knew no bounds and his religious zeal, bordering on fanaticism, led him to violate wantonly the most sacred sentiments of a great people. We miss in him that dignified idealism which seldom fails to impart a grace and charm even to the most ruthless conqueror. His imagination was not fired even by the ambition of founding an empire to which the common consent of all ages and nations has attached something of a noble and generous impulse. From first to last his Indian policy was inspired merely by the primitive instincts of plunder, devastation, massacre, and desecration.

Character of Sultān Mahmūd

It is too often assumed that the invasions of Sultān Mahmūd had no permanent results, so far as India was concerned. Nothing can be a greater mistake. He terribly drained the military and economic resources of the country, and the Muslim occupation of the Panjāb served as the key to unlock the gate of Indian empire. Big cracks had already been made therein and it was no longer a question of whether but when that mighty structure would fall.

CHAPTER VIII

Northern India in the 11th and 12th centuries A. D.

1. *General Review.*

A century and three-quarters elapsed between the last invasion of Sultān Mahmūd and the conquest of the greater part of North India by the Muslims. The history of India during this period is a melancholy but an interesting study. The view, commonly held, that India enjoyed a respite from Muslim invasion during this long period is not correct. For, as we shall see, the successors of Sultān Mahmūd never disguised or concealed their policy to carry their victorious arms into the heart of India whenever they could, and actually sent several military expeditions into the interior. The Indian ruling chiefs could, therefore, hardly fail to recognize that the establishment of an aggressive Islamic State in the Panjāb was a grave danger to the whole of India. At least they had no reasonable pretext to ignore or minimise it. We would naturally like to know what steps they took to ensure the safety of their motherland, and whether their ultimate failure was due to their want of foresight, lack of unity, inferiority in military skill and organisation, or any other cause over which they had no control. Posterity naturally holds them responsible for the great betrayal which subjected this country to foreign domination and imposition of an alien culture, from the effects of which it has never been, nor will ever be, able to recover. It is the duty of the historian to find out, as far as possible, the true facts on the basis of which alone we can pass a just verdict on the people and rulers of India who stand condemned before the bar of public opinion. Unfortunately, the historian is not in a position to discharge this duty. For no contemporary Indian ever thought fit to chronicle the events of that critical period, nor anyone in centuries immediately following cared to inquire into the circumstances which led to such a momentous change in the fortunes of his country. Our knowledge of the history of this period is mainly confined to isolated facts such as fights and victories by individual rulers, rise and fall of royal dynasties, perpetual shifting of boundaries of kingdoms etc., derived from contemporary epigraphic records. Although these are by no means few in number, we are not always able to connect the different events and find out their mutual relations and consequences in order to fit them into an integrated picture of the country as a whole. We get brilliant flashes, but not an unbroken outline; important and interesting episodes, but not a continued narrative. These are offered in the following pages, arranged under different States and dynasties. But in order to enable the reader to appreciate as far as possible the true bearing of the facts upon one another, and their relation to the general history of India, a few conclusions of a general nature may be added by way of preface.

In the first place it is significant that many great military leaders arose during this period such as Kalachuri Gāṅgeyadeva and Karṇa, Paramāra Bhoja, Gāhaḍavāla Govindachandra, Chaulukya Jayasiṁha-Siddharāja and Kumārapāla, Chāhamāna Vigraharāja, Chālukya Vikramāditya, and the Chola king Rājendra the Great. Even excluding the last, whose seat of authority was too far away, all the rest are credited with victories and conquests in North India to such an extent that it passes our comprehension why they failed to overthrow the domination of the Ghaznavids in the Panjāb, particularly when these were almost perpetually suffering from internal dissensions and foreign invasion. That the Indians were not altogether insensible to the great danger of India is proved by the recorded invasion of the Panjāb by some Indian rulers, and there is at least one instance of a concerted action against the Ghaznavids in 1043 A.D. The boastful expression of an Indian ruler that Āryāvarta was again made by him true to its meaning (i.e. the land of the Āryas) by the destruction of the *Mlechchhas*, implies that the Indians were also fully alive to the peril with which Muslim invasion threatened their religion and culture. We have also contemporary records of defeats inflicted upon Muslim army by the Hindus, proving thereby that the former could not claim any inherent superiority in military skill and discipline. One may then well wonder how or why, in spite of all these, the Mulsim rule was allowed to continue in the Panjāb as a great potential danger to the security of India.

For a true explanation we must look to the other side of the shield, too. Rulers like Karṇa and Bhoja no doubt defeated the Muslims; it has even been suggested, perhaps quite correctly, that they effectively prevented the Muslim aggression which was resumed after their death. But it is a fact that they also carried their victorious arms far and wide against other Indian rulers. One might well ask why these rulers did not concentrate their energy and resources to extinguish finally the great national enemy. Indeed the most striking thing in Indian history during this period is the constant warfare going on between Indian rulers at the very moment when the Muslim armies were carrying fire and sword into the heart of India; even one Indian ruler attacking another who was actually engaged in fighting with the Muslims, or was in a position to do so, if left unhampered by his Indian enemy. Nor are instances altogether lacking of an Indian chief actively helping the Muslim invaders for the sake of personal gain, though, fortunately, these are very rare and there is not one single case which is proved beyond all doubt. Nevertheless, it becomes painfully evident that the pecple lacked a true conception of Indian or Hindu nationality, as we understand the term; that the policy of Indian rulers was not guided by the common concern of India as a whole, nor even by the enlightened self-interest and true statesmanship which would correctly visualise the remote, as opposed to the immediate, gain or loss.

Perhaps further reflections and other conclusions would present themselves to a thoughtful mind as it considers the known facts of the period, and subjects them to a careful review; but illustration and confirmation of what has been said above meet us at almost every step as we go through the brief outline of the history of the different powers which is offered below.

In order to complete the history of Hindu India and to give a full picture of Hindu resistance against Muslim invasion, the history of certain dynasties or States has been brought down to their final conquest by the Muslims, though it has carried us sometimes more than a century beyond A.D. 1200, which is usually regarded as closing the ancient period and has been adopted as the general limit of this chapter.

2. *Kanauj and the Gāhadavālas.*

The sack of Kanauj and Bari by Sultān Mahmūd dealt the death-blow to the Pratīhāras. The empire passed away, but its carcase remained, and then followed the feast of vultures. The Chandellas and the Kachchhapaghātas fell upon the old unfortunate Rājyapāla, and he met a heroic death on the battlefield. He was succeeded by Trilochanapāla, one of whose known dates is 1027 A.D. With him ended the line of the Imperial

Pratīhāras, who had fully justified their designation by defending the gates of India for more than two hundred years.

For half a century Kanuaj was ruled by petty chiefs of a Rāshṭrakūṭa family. During the third quarter of the 11th century A.D. the Chālukya king Someśvara I and the Chola king Vīrarājendra invaded Kanauj. Some time after A.D. 1085, Mahmūd, the son of the Ghaznavid Sultān, conquered Kanauj. Thereupon the Rāshṭrakūṭa chiefs left that city and settled in Vodamāyuta, modern Budaun, where it continued to rule till 1202 A.D. when it was conquered by Qutbuddīn.

Mahmūd is said to have an ally in Kanauj named Chānd Rāi, whom he appointed to look after his elephant forces there.

Chandradeva

It is generally believed that this Chānd Rāi is no other than Chandradeva of the Gāhaḍavāla clan who carved out a kingdom with Kanauj as capital, and assumed the proud title of *Mahārājādhirāja*, some time before 1090 A.D. The inscriptions of this dynasty refer to a tax called Turushka-daṇḍa, the exact significance of which is unknown. It was undoubtedly a special imposition upon the people either to defray the expenses of war against the Turkish invaders from the Panjāb, or to make up the heavy annual tribute payable to them. If Chandradeva really owed his throne to the Muslim ruler of the Panjāb, the latter view is the most probable one. On the other hand it is noteworthy that Chandradeva claims in his records to have protected the holy places of Upper India, presumably against the Muslim invaders. Chandradeva defeated the ruler of Pañchāla, evidently belonging to the Rāshṭrakūṭa family mentioned above, and probably extended his dominions as far as Allāhābād and Banaras, at the expense of the Kalachuris. He was, however, defeated by the ruler of Magadha. Banaras, which was thus near the eastern boundary of his kingdom, was almost like a second capital of the Gāhaḍavālas, for they are often referred to as the rulers of Kāsi.

Chandradeva's known dates are 1090 and 1100 A.D. He was succeeded by his son Madanachandra. Evidently the Gāhaḍavālas defied the authority of the Yamīnī rulers, for we know from Muslim chronicles that Mas'ūd III (1099-1115 A.D.) invaded, 'Hindusthān of which the capital was Kanauj and took its king prisoner'. According to these chronicles the king Malhi (possibly a corruption of Madanachandra) released himself by paying a heavy ranson. Fortunately we have also the Indian version of this incident. According to a contemporary epigraphic record, Govindachandra, son of Madanachandra, gained a great victory against the Muslims while he was yet a *yuvarāja* (heir-apparent) i.e. during the lifetime of his father. The one sided version of the conflict, as given by the Muslim chroniclers, cannot therefore be regarded as the whole truth.

Govindachandra, who succeeded his father some time before 1114 A.D. was undoubtedly the greatest king of the dynasty.

Govindachandra

More than forty inscriptions, ranging in date between A.D. 1114 and 1154, testify to the length and glory of his reign. He achieved many victories and his dominions included not only the greater part of the Uttar Pradesh but also a considerable part of Magadha. This latter was the bone of contention between him and the Pāla king of Bengal. Some time after 1143 A.D. he carried his victorious arms as far as Monghyr, but within ten years the Pāla king recovered this city. It seems that Govindachandra had also to fight with the Senas. He defeated the Chandellas and wrested Eastern Mālava from them. Govindachandra came into conflict with the Kalachuris of South Kosala and probably also with other great powers of the time, and maintained diplomatic relations with the Chaulukya ruler of Aṇahilapāṭaka and the king of Kāshmir. An intimate association of Govindachandra with the Cholas is indicated by an incomplete record, engraved on a stone in the Chola capital some time after 1111 A.D., which gives the genealogy of the Gāhaḍavāla kings. It would thus appear that Govindachandra was an all-India figure and once more raised the city of Kanauj almost to the status of an imperial city.

Govindachandra's son and successor, Vijayachandra, whose known dates are 1168 and 1169 A.D., repulsed an attack of the Yamīnī ruler, probably Khusrav Malik. He was succeeded in 1176 A.D. by his son Jayachandra[1] who is described by some

Jayachandra

Muslim historians as the greatest sovereign in India. In any case Jayachandra enjoys a high degree of fame or notoriety in Indian traditions on account of his romantic relations with Pṛithvīrāja and disastrous defeat by Shihabuddīn Muhammad to which reference will be made later His inscriptions, ranging in date between 1170 and 1189 A.D., show that he maintained intact the vast dominions inherited by him. But he was involved in a

1. Also called Jayachchandra

prolonged war with the Senas of Bengal. He conquered the Gayā District after the downfall of the Pālas, but Lakshmaṇa Sena not only recovered it, but even carried his victorious arms as far as Banaras and Allāhābād. It is an irony of fate that these two powerful rulers of North India should have exhausted their strength and resources by fighting with each other at the very moment of Muhammad's invasion which involved both of them in a common ruin. There is, however, nothing to support the current story that Jayachandra invited the Muslim king to invade India to weak his vengeance against Pṛithvīrāja.

3. *Bengal under the Pālas and Senas*

To the east of the Gāhaḍavālas ruled the Pālas. We have already described the brief spell of imperialism enjoyed by the early kings of this dynasty, and the gradual decline of their power on the rise of the Pratīhāras. From that time the Pālas ruled as a local power in eastern India, although continually troubled by foreign invasions. The Kalachuris, Chandellas, and the Rāshṭrakūṭas made occasional raids into their territory and sometimes conquered portions of their dominions. Towards the latter part of the tenth century A.D., the Kāmbojas occupied North and West Bengal during the reign of the Pāla king Vigrahapāla; but his son Mahīpāla I (c. 980-1030 A.D.) recovered the paternal territories. Taking advantage of the weakness of the Pālas the Kalachuris probably advanced as far as Mithilā before 1019 A.D., and about the same time the Chola king Rājendra Chola and a Chālukya king invaded the Pāla dominions. To the credit of Mahīpāla it must be said that he not only recovered the paternal dominions from the Kāmboja usurper, and successfully defended his country against the Kalachuris, Cholas, and Chālukyas, but also extended his dominions up to Banaras before 1025 A.D. But Mahīpāla had probably no hold over South and West Bengal which was ruled by several dependent chiefs. It is only fair to emphasise the fact that the domestic and foreign troubles through which his country was passing must have made it impossible for Mahīpāla to take part in the confederacy of Hindu States against Sultān Mahmūd.

Mahīpāla I

Nayapāla, the son and successor of Mahīpāla, was involved in a prolonged war with the Kalachuris of Tripurī. As mentioned above, there are some grounds to believe that the Kalachuri king Gāṅgeyadeva seized Mithilā sometime before 1019 A.D., but

Nayapāla

Mahīpāla must have reconquered it and was in possession of Banaras, in 1026 A.D. But Gāṅgeyadeva renewed his struggle against the Pālas either towards the end of Mahīpāla's reign or at the beginning of that of Nayapāla. The Pāla king was defeated, and Gāṅgeyadeva seized Banaras which was in his possession in 1034 A.D.

We learn from the Tibetan accounts that there was a protracted war between Nayapāla and Karṇa, the son of Gāṅgeyadeva. Karṇa had some initial success and advanced into the heart of Magadha, but was ultimately defeated by Nayapāla. The famous Buddhist scholar Dīpaṅkara Śrījñāna, also known as Atīśa, who was then residing in Bodh-Gayā, gave shelter to Karṇa and, at his mediation, a treaty was concluded between Karṇa and Nayapāla. But soon after the accession of Vigrahapāla III, the son and successor of Nayapāla, Karṇa renewed hostilities and invaded Gauḍa. But he was again defeated by the Pāla king and concluded a treaty of alliance which was cemented by a marriage between his daughter Yauvanaśrī and the Pāla king.

Vigrahapāla III had three sons,—Mahīpāla II, Śūrapāla II, and Rāmapāla. Mahīpāla II succeeded his father about A.D. 1070, but was soon involved in great troubles. An almost contemporary poetical work, the *Rāmacharita*, gives us a detailed account of the history of this period. It appears that some of the vassal chiefs rose against Mahīpāla and there was a general upheaval in the country. To make matters worse, it was reported to Mahīpāla that his two brothers were conspiring against him. Mahīpāla was of a hasty temper. Without making any proper inquiry into the truth of the allegations against his brothers he threw them into prison, and then, against the advice of his ministers, he marched against the rebel vassals though he had no adequate force for the purpose. He was defeated and killed, and an official named Divya (or Divvoka), Kaivarta by caste, made himself master of Varendrī or N. Bengal. This is the famous Kaivarta revolt of which we find a detailed account in the *Rāmacharita*.

Kaivarta revolt

In the midst of these turmoils Śūrapāla and Rāmapāla escaped from the prison and took shelter in Magadha. Śūrapāla died after a short reign and was succeeded by Rāmapāla. The whole of Bengal had now practically passed out of the hands of the Pālas. East Bengal was ruled by a dynasty of kings whose names ended in Varman and who claimed to belong to the Yādava dynasty of Siṁhapura, a place which cannot be identified with certainty. Divya, the rebel Kaivarta chief, consolidated his dominions in N. Bengal, even though king Jātavarman of East Bengal claims victory over him. Divya left a peaceful and prosperous kingdom to his brother Rūdoka, who was succeeded by his son Bhīma. The rest of Bengal was divided among more than a dozen independent chiefs, though some of them might still nominally acknowledge the suzerainty of the Pālas.

Rāmapāla

For many years Rāmapāla could do nothing to retrieve the situation. At last, by literally begging from door to door, he could enlist the sympathy and support of a large number of chiefs with whose help he defeated and killed Bhīma and recovered his ancestral kingdom Varendrī or North Bengal.

Rāmapāla was an able ruler and soon conquered Kāmarūpa and forced the Varman ruler of East Bengal to submit to his authority. He also sent an expedition against the Gāhaḍavālas, and though it was repulsed by Govindachandra, the further progress of the latter towards the east was checked. In the south he interfered in the politics of Orissa where two rival kings were fighting for power. One of them seized the throne with the help of Anantavarman Choḍagaṅga, the powerful ruler of Kaliṅga. Rāmapāla supported the other and succeeded in placing him on the throne, presumably after defeating the forces of Anantavarman. But his success was shortlived as we find Anantavarman's nominee on the throne of Orissa in 1112 A.D.

After a long and eventful reign Rāmapāla died about 1120 A.D. He had a remarkable personality and his achievements were undoubtedly very great. He found the Pāla kingdom in a state of complete disintegration, but by his energetic efforts restored its strength and prestige to a considerable degree.

But the recovery was of short duration. During the reign of his two sons Kumārapāla and Madanapāla, the disintegration of the Pāla kingdom proceeded apace, thanks to internal dissensions, successful rising of feudal chiefs, and foreign invasions. Two feudal chiefs of Magadha and the governor of Kāmarūpa declared independence. The minister Vaidyadeva put down the revolt in Kāmarūpa, but ultimately made himself an independent ruler of this kingdom. The Gāhaḍavālas conquered western Magadha and even proceeded upto Monghyr, while Anantavarman Chodagaṅga carried his victorious arms up to modern Hooghly on the bank of the Bhāgīrathī (or Gaṅgā).

It must be said to the credit of Madanapāla that he made a heroic effort to save his kingdom and attained some successes.

End cf the Pālas

He recovered Monghyr from the Gāhaḍavālas, but was soon to reckon with a new royal family, originally hailing from Karṇāṭa, which carved a kingdom in Mithilā or N. Bihār. The invasion of these Karṇāṭa rulers kept him busy in the north, while a new power, the Senas, rose in Rāḍha or W. Bengal, and finally extinguished the Pāla power in Bengal. Madanapāla continued to rule over a part of Bihār till his death about 1160 A.D. He is the last ruler of the family of Dharmapāla. Another king, Govindapāla, is known to have been ruling in the Gayā District till 1162 A. D. when his kingdom was destroyed, either by the Gāhaḍavālas or by the Senas. But we do not know whether Govindapāla belonged to the Pāla family.

The Senas belonged to a Kshatriya clan of Karṇāṭa and probably came to Bengal along with Vikramāditya VI when

Senas.

that Chālukya prince undertook an expedition against Bengal, Assam, and other northern countries. The Senas at first settled in Rāḍha (W. Bengal). The first notable king of the new dynasty wat Vijaya Sena who defeated the Pāla king Madanapāla and conquered Bengal.

Vijaya Sena

He pushed his conquests to Assam and Mithilā, and probably also to part of Magadha, although the Pāla king still ruled over a portion of the last named province. Vijaya Sena was succeeded by his son Ballāla Sena

Ballāla Sena

who was a powerful ruler and finally subdued Mithilā. He was a learned scholar and author of several works, and his reign is associated with important social changes the effect of which is still to be seen to-day.

Lakshmaṇa Sena

Ballāla Sena was succeeded by his son Lakshmaṇa Sena who ascended the throne in 1178 A.D. He received his military training by joining the campaigns of his father and grandfather against Gauḍa, Kāmarūpa, and Kaliṅga. The victories against these kingdoms, with which he is credited, probably refer to those campaigns rather than any new ones during his reign. But even as a king he had to carry on arduous military campaigns. In the south he gained some successes in Orissa and planted a pillar of victory in Purī. But his greatest fight was against the Gāhaḍavālas. He achieved conspicuous success and carried his victorious arms to Banaras and Allāhābād, where he is said to have planted two more pillars of victory. There is no doubt that Lakshmaṇa Sena was in possession of a considerable part of Bihār. For even now there is an era known as Lakshmaṇa *Saṁvat* (*La Saṁ*) current in North Bihār, and we have epigraphic evidence that such an era was used in the Gayā District long after the reign of Lakshmaṇa Sena was over.

Lakshmaṇa Sena was a patron of poets, and a number of them including Jayadeva lived in his court. He himself composed poems and completed a learned treatise left unfinished by his father. An almost contemporary Muslim chronicle bestows high praise on him for his charity and other qualities of head and heart, describes him as the chief among the Indian rulers like the Caliph in the Muslim world and prays for his salvation after death, an unusual thing for a Muslim writing of a non-Muslim. But in spite of his bravery, military skill, and manifold virtues Lakshmaṇa Sena's reign had a tragic end. There is, of course, no basis for the popular belief that he was such a worthless and cowardly ruler that eighteen horsemen under Bakhtyār Khilji captured his capital and he took to flight. But it is a fact that Bakhtyār, by a sudden raid, seized the city of Nadiyā where the old king was staying, and made himself master of a considerable part of Bengal.

4. *Kāmarūpa.*

After the death of Bhāskara-varman, Kāmarūpa was occupied by a *Mlechchha* ruler named Sālastambha. But we do not know anything of him or his successors beyond the names of some of them. One of them, Harisha, is generally identified with king Harsha of the Bhagadatta dynasty who was lord of Gauḍa, Oḍra, Kaliṅga, and Kosala, according to a Nepāl inscription, but this is very doubtful. About the beginning of the 9th century A.D. this dynasty was overthrown by Prālambha who claimed descent from Bhagadatta and, therefore, might have been connected in some way with the dynasty which ended with Bhāskara-varman. This change of dynasty nearly coincides with the conquest of the country by the Pāla king Devapāla and might not be

Harjara

altogether unconnected with it. But Prālambha's son Harjara-varmadeva, who assumed imperial titles some time before 829 A.D., seems to have freed his country from the yoke of the Pālas. During his son's reign the kingdom extended at least up to the Trisrotā (Tistā) river in the west, and we may therefore accept the traditional account that Karatoyā formed the western boundary of Kāmarūpa or Prāgjyotisha. The dynasty of Prālambha ruled from their capital at Hārūppeśvara on the Brahmaputra till about 1000 A.D.

On the death of Tyāgasiṁha, the last ruler of this dynasty, the people elected Brahmapāla as the king. He fixed his capital at Durjayā, which has been identified by some with Gauhāti. His son Ratnapāla is said to have defeated the kings of Gurjara, Gauḍa, Kerala, and Dākshiṇātya. This appears to be highly improbable. But we know that the Chālukya prince Vikramāditya, son of Someśvara, led an expedition against Kāmarūpa some time before 1068, and it is not unlikely that the forces of the above countries formed part of his army. The dynasty of Brahmapāla was overthrown by Rāmapāla of Bengal, and Tiṅgyadeva ruled the province as his feudatory. Shortly afterwards Tiṅgyadeva revolted, and the Pāla king Kumārapāla sent his minister Vaidyadeva against him. Vaidyadeva quelled the rebellion, but some time later, probably after the death of the Pāla king, assumed independent powers.

5. *The Kalachuris.*

The Kalachuris of Ḍāhala rose to be the greatest political power in India during the 11th century A.D. This was mainly due to the military genius of Gāṅgeyadeva, son of Kokalla II mentioned above (p. 294). Perhaps an important factor contributing to his success was the fact that his kingdom escaped the devastating raids of Sultān Mahmūd which affected most of the other great powers to its north and north-west.

The epigraphic records of the period refer to the numerous conquests and alliances of Gāṅgeyadeva, but it is difficult to arrange them in proper sequence. We may therefore describe them according to geographical order. Gāṅgeyadeva joined his western neighbour, Paramāra Bhoja, and the great king of the South, Rājendra Chola, in an expedition to the Deccan. But the Chālukya king Jayasiṁha defeated the confederate troops. Somewhat later, Gāṅgeyadeva quarrelled with his ally the Paramāra king Bhoja, but sustained reverses in his hand. His effort to subdue the Chandellas of Bundelkhand also met with failure.

Gāṅgeyadeva

Being frustrated in the north, south, and west, he turned towards the east, and here he achieved conspicuous. success. He had an old score to pay against Mahāśivagupta Yayāti, the Somavaṁśi king of South Kosala, who had defeated the Kalachuris and devastated their dominions. Gāṅgeyadeva invaded his kingdom and so completely defeated him, that he could easily march further and conquer Orissa as far as the sea-coast. In token of his great victory he assumed the proud title of Trikaliṅgādhipati, 'Lord of Trikaliṅga'.

Gāṅgeyadeva was equally successful in the north-east. Passing through Baghelkhand he advanced as far as Banaras and annexed all these territories to his kingdom. He also led a successful expedition against Aṅga (Bhagalpur) which was under the Pālas. As noted above (P.337) it is probable that Mithilā or N. Bihār was in his possession for some time.

Shortly after Gāṅgeyadeva had conquered Banaras, the city was raided by the Muslim troops under Ahmad Niyāltigīn, the governor of the Panjāb. They plundered the *bazar* and carried immense riches, but left it without delay. It was evidently nothing more than a plundering raid, and the city being taken by surprise, there was no regular fight. But Gāṅgeyadeva's boast that he carried his arms to the Kīra country (Kāngra Valley), which was part of the Ghaznavid province of the Panjāb, may refer to a sort of retaliatory expedition against the Muslim power. In any case, it proves the ability and willingness of Gāṅgeyadeva to fight the Muslims in their dominions. It also shows that for this purpose he could count on something like a free passage through the territories of other independent rulers.

Gāṅgeyadeva assumed the title Vikramāditya. He died at the sacred city of Prayāg (Allāhābād), and no less than one hundred of his wives accompanied him on the funeral pyre, perhaps the most terrible case of *Satī* on record. The reign-period of Gāṅgeyadeva is not definitely known. Probably he ascended the throne before 1019 A.D. and died about 1040 A. D.

Karṇa

Gāṅgeyadeva was succeeded by his son Lakshmī-karṇa, better known simply as Karṇa. He was also a veteran general like his father, and a hero of hundred fights. He is credited with an expedition against the Kīras, but it is probable that it refers to the campaign undertaken during the reign of his father. He was in possession of the city of Allāhābād which was also probably conquered by his father. His fights with the Pāla kings Nayapāla and Vigrahapāla in Magadha have been referred to above (p. 318). It appears that after concluding the treaty with the latter he proceeded further east, conquered Rāḍha or West Bengal and Vaṅga or South and East Bengal. Jātavarman, king of Vaṅga, is known to have married Vīraśrī, a daughter of Karṇa, and it is probable that as in the case of Vigrahapāla, the marriage cemented the treaty of alliance between Karṇa and Jātavarman.

Karṇa next carried his victorious arms along the eastern coast as far as the country round Kañchī, which was then ruled by the Cholas. Karṇa is said to have defeated a number of peoples in the south such as the Pallavas, Kuṅgas, Muralas, and even the Pāṇḍyas who lived in the extreme south. It is more likely that these peoples helped the Cholas, and Karṇa defeated them all in a single fight, than that he separately raided their several countries. He also claims to have defeated the ruler of Kuntala, probably the Chālukya king, Someśvara I, who, on the other hand, claims to have utterly destroyed the power of Karṇa. These victorious expeditions to the south took place before A.D. 1048. They no doubt reflect great credit upon his military genius but do not seem to have led to any permanent results.

Karṇa was more successful than his father not only in the south but also in the north and west. He defeated the Chandella king Kīrttivarman and, for a time, occupied a large part of his dominions. He made an alliance with the Chaulukya king Bhīma, and the two simultaneously attacked Mālava from the east and the west. The Paramāra king Bhoja died about this time (1055 A.D.) and the two allies got possession of Mālava. But Bhoja's son made an alliance with the Chālukyas and with their help recovered his kingdom. Then a quarrel broke out between the two allies, Karṇa and Bhīma, over the spoils of the Mālava war. Bhīma invaded Ḍāhala and forced Karṇa to give up some of the rich booties conquered from Mālava.

In spite of his numerous wars and conquests the permanent results achieved by Karṇa, by way of addition to his territories, were insignificant. The reconquest of Mālava by the Paramāras and his ignominious defeat in the hands of Chaulukya Bhīma obscured his earlier glory, and the Kalachuris had suffered a great deal in power and prestige when, in 1072 A.D., Karṇa abdicated the throne in favour of his son Yaśaḥkaraṇa.

Oblivious of this great change the new king began his reign like his father and grandfather, by leading two military expeditions, one against North Bihār and the other against the Eastern Chālukyas. But soon his own kingdom became the target of attack of all the great powers who had suffered from the aggressive imperialism of his two predecessors. The Chālukyas of the Deccan successfully raided his kingdom, the Paramāras plundered his capital and encamped for some time on the Narmadā, and he was also defeated by the Chandellas. All these defeats weakened his power and he had the mortification to see Allāhābād and Banaras conquered by the Gāhaḍavālas.

Yaśaḥkarṇa

Gayakarṇa, the son and successor of Yaśaḥkarṇa, was defeated by the Chandella king Madanavarman. His second son Jayasiṁha, who ascended the throne between A.D. 1159 and 1167, seems to have partly recovered the fortunes and prestige of the family. He achieved some success against the Chaulukya king Kumārapāla and the king of Kuntala, probably Bijjala, who had wrested the Deccan from the Chālukyas. But Bijjala, who belonged to a minor branch of the Kalachuri clan, also claims to have defeated Jayasiṁha. During his reign the Turushkas invaded his dominions, but were repulsed. This probably refers to the invasion of Khusrav Malik. But the revival was short-lived. During the reign of Jayasiṁha's son Vijayasiṁha, who succeeded him between 1177 and 1180 A.D., the Chandella king Trailokyavarman conquered nearly the whole of the Kalachuri kingdom, including Baghelkhand and Ḍāhala-maṇḍala. This took place about 1212 A.D. and we hear nothing more of the Kalachuris. The Hayobansi Rājputs of the Balia District in U. P. claim descent from them.

Jayasiṁha

Early in the 11th century A.D. a scion of the royal Kalachuri family of Ḍāhala founded a kingdom in South Kosala, with its capital first at Tuṁmāṇa, modern Tumāna in the Bilāspur District in C. P., and later at Ratanpur, 16 miles north of Bilāspur. The family remained feudatory to the Kalachuris of Ḍāhala for about a century till Jājalladeva declared his independence during the latter part of Yaśaḥkarṇa's reign, early in the 12th century A.D. He extended his power by imposing tribute upon a large number of petty principalities in

Minor Kalachuri dynasties

Orissa and eastern part of C. P. His family continued to rule with power and prestige in this locality for another century.

Other branches of Kalachuris are also known. One of them ruled in the neighbourhood of Kasia in the Gorakhpur District. Another conquered the Deccan by defeating the Chālukyas and ruled as a powerful dynasty though for a short period.

6. *The Paramāras*

Reference has already been made, more than once, to the Paramāra king Bhoja, son and successor of Sindhurāja (p. 296). He ascended the throne about 1000 A.D. and ruled for more than half a century. His military career during this period resembles that of his great contemporary Karṇa. It brought him glory and credit, but little by way of accession of dominions and increase in power, and his reign ended in a veritable tragedy.

Bhoja fought with all his powerful neighbours. He made an alliance with Gāṅgeyadeva and Rājendra Chola against his hereditary enemies, the Chālukyas of the Deccan, but in spite of preliminary success the allies were forced to retire. Later, the Chālukya king Someśvara took revenge on Bhoja by invading his dominions. The strong fortress of Māṇḍu, the famous city of Ujjain, and even Dhārā, the capital of the Paramāras, fell into the hands of Someśvara, and were plundered by him.

Bhoja failed in his fight against the Chandellas, the Kachchhapaghātas of Gwalior, and the Rāshṭrakūṭas of Kanauj. He had some success against the Chāhamānas of Śākambharī, but met with serious reverses in the hands of the Chāhamānas of Naḍḍula.

Bhoja at first gained some successes against the Chaulukyas, his western neighbours. The Chaulukya king Bhīma, following true Kauṭilyan policy, formed an alliance with Bhoja's eastern neighbours, the Kalachuris, whose king Gāṅgeyadeva, though at first an ally of Bhoja, was later defeated by him. Kalachuri Karṇa now joined Bhīma, and the two simultaneously attacked Mālava from the east and the west. While engaged in this unequal war, the old king Bhoja fell ill and died about 1055 A.D. His kingdom lay prostrate before his enemies.

In spite of this tragic end Bhoja must be regarded as a ruler of remarkable ability. He was undoubtedly a military leader of consummate ability, though, like his great contemporaries, he wasted his energy and resources in fruitless aggressive wars all through his life. But what distinguished him from them was his profound scholarship, patronage of learning, and great care for the spread of education among his people. He is credited with having composed more than twenty books on a variety of topics including such diverse subjects as architecture, astronomy, and poetry. Men of letters like Dhanapāla and Uvaṭa lived in his court, and he established a Sanskrit college within the precincts of the temple of Sarasvatī, remains of which still exist. He built a large number of temples, and also a city named after him Bhojapura. Popular tradition has invested him with all the qualities of an ideal king, and even today the name of Bhoja stands for all that was good and great in an Indian king.

Jayasiṁha

Bhoja's successor Jayasiṁha ascended the throne at a time when the greater part of his kingdom was overrun by the Kalachuris and the Chaulukyas. In this grave crisis he turned for aid towards his southern neighbours, the Chālukyas of the Deccan. Nothing illustrates more forcibly the shifting nature of political combinations of the time than that the Paramāras should seek for, and receive, help from their hereditary enemies. The fact, however, seems to be that almost all he great powers being engaged in hostilities with one another, expediency, rather than sentiment or a fixed policy, determined their mutual relations at any particular moment. The Chālukyas responded to the appeal of Jayasiṁha, and prince Vikramāditya cleared Mālava of its enemies. The Chaulukyas and the Kalachuris were forced to retire and Jayasiṁha recovered his kingdom. The grateful king naturally became a staunch ally of Vikramāditya and helped him in his wars against the Eastern Chālukyas. But this generous attitude proved his ruin. Someśvara II, the Chālukya king, regarded his younger brother Vikramāditya as a rival for the throne. He either suspected Jayasiṁha of actually conspiring with his brother, or generally disliked the idea of an alliance between the two as it would inevitably strengthen the latter in the impending contest for the throne. Whatever may be the ground, Someśvara made an alliance with the Chaulukya king Karṇa, son of Bhīma, and invaded Mālava. Jayasiṁha fell in the battle, and Mālava was occupied by the two allies.

Udayāditya, a brother of Bhoja, now sought for aid from

the Chāhamānas of Śākambharī, and with their help defeated the invaders and recovered his kingdom. His known dates are A.D. 1080 and 1086. His son Lakshmadeva had a distinguished military career. He defeated the Kalachuri king Yaśaḥkarṇa and raided Aṅga Gauḍa, and Kaliṅga. He successfully defended his kingdom against the invasion of Mahmūd, the Ghaznavid governor of the Panjāb, and, probably in retaliation, invaded the Kīra country (Kangra valley) which was part of the latter's dominions. Lakshmadeva is probably to be identified with Jagadeva, a son of Udayāditya, the stories of whose great victories figure so prominently in the folk-tales of Western India. Among other military feats he is said to have defeated the Chaulukya king Karṇa and, in alliance with Vikramāditya VI, invaded the dominion of the Hoysalas.

Lakshmadeva

The next king Naravarman (1094 A.D.) began his career well and became master of a large part of Madhya Pradesh, as far as Nāgpur. But he was defeated by the Chandella king and was soon involved in a prolonged war with the Chaulukya king Jayasiṁha Siddharāja. It dragged on for twelve years and ended in a disastrous defeat for Naravarman. He fell a prisoner into the hands of his enemy, and though he secured his release, the power and prestige of his family suffered a great loss. Its full effect was seen in the reign of the next king Yaśovarman (1133 A.D.). Dewas, a principality in the very heart of Mālava, became an independent State, and the Chandellas occupied the Bhilsa region. Ujjain itself was attacked by the Chāhamāna king. To crown all, the Chaulukya king Jayasiṁha Siddharāja, helped by the Chāhamānas of Naḍḍula, defeated Yaśovarman, took him prisoner, and annexed the whole of Mālava about 1135 A.D. Though Yaśovarman's son Jayavarman recovered Mālava, it was soon conquered by the joint forces of the Chālukya king Jagadekamalla and Hoysala king Narasiṁha, who placed one Ballāla on the throne. But Ballāla was dethroned by the Chaulukya king Kumārapāla, who again annexed the whole of Mālava, as far as Bhilsā.

Naravarman

Yaśovarman

The Chaulukyas maintained their hold over Mālava for nearly 20 years after which Vindhyavarman, son of Jayavarman, recovered his ancestral kingdom by defeating Chaulukya Mūlarāja II. He had to fight with the Hoysalas and the Yādavas who had supplanted the Chālukyas in the Deccan. Although

Vindhyavarman

he fared badly in these wars, he once more made Mālava a strong and prosperous kingdom before his death which took place shortly after 1193 A.D.

His son and successor Subhaṭavarman now turned the table against the Chaulukyas and successfully invaded Gujarāt. He made himself master of Lāṭa, stormed the capital city Aṇahilapāṭaka, and even advanced as far as Somnāth before he was forced to retreat. He was however defeated by the Yādavas.

Subhaṭavarman

Arjunavarman, who succeeded him before 1210 A.D., also successfully fought with the Chaulukyas, but was badly defeated by the Yādava king Siṅghaṇa. He was an author of some repute and patronised various scholars the most distinguished of whom, Madana, wrote the drama *Pārijāta-mañjarī*, whose theme was furnished by the king's marriage with the daughter of his Chaulukya adversary Jayasiṁha.

Arjunavarman

Devapāla, the next king (1218-1232 A.D.)[1], was again attacked by Siṅghaṇa who took prisoner his vassal chief of Lāṭa named Śaṅkha, but soon a treaty was concluded between the two. About this time the Muslims, who had already conquered a large part of Northern India, invaded Gujarāt. While the Chaulukyas were engaged in a life and death struggle with the Muslims, the Yādavas and the Paramāras made an unholy alliance and attacked the southern part of Gujarāt. Fortunately, the shrewd diplomacy of the Chaulukya Governor saved the situation by bringing about dissensions between the two allies. But the Mālava king soon reaped the fruit of his unwise policy. He lost the southern Lāṭa to the Chaulukyas, and his dominions were invaded by Sultān Iltutmish who captured Bhilsa and plundered Ujjain in 1233 A.D.

Devapāla

But though Mālava survived the first shock of Muslim invasion, bad days were in store for it. During the reign of the next king Jaitugi, it was raided by the Yādavas and the Vāghelās of Gujarāt sacked the capital city Dhārā, about the same time when Sultān Balban also invaded it in 1250 A.D.

Decline and fall

From this time Mālava showed signs of rapid distintegration. The Chāhamānas of Ranthambhor inflicted a crushing defeat

1 The dates, within bracket, refer to known dates, not necessarily the first and last years of a reign.

upon king Jayasiṁha who shut himself up in the famous hill-fort of Maṇḍapa (Māṇḍu). His death in 1270 A.D. was followed by a disastrous civil war between king Arjunavarman II and his minister which led to the division of Mālava into two parts. Arjunavarman II had also to suffer invasions from the Chāhamānas, Yādavas, and the Vāghelās. During the reign of Bhoja II, who came to the throne after 1283 A.D., Mālava was again raided by the Chāhamānas and Sultān Jalāluddīn Khiljī. In 1305 Alāuddīn Khiljī invaded the country. The last Paramāra king Mahlak Deo, being defeated, took shelter in Māṇḍu. He was killed there by Alāuddīn's general and Mālava passed into the hands of the Muslims. There were several branches of the Paramāras ruling in the region near Mt. Abu, at Vāgaḍa (modern Banswara and Dungarpur), Jāvālipura (Jalor), and Bhinmal (in Southern Mārwar) who were all ultimately conquered by the neighbouring States such as the Guhilas and the Chāhamānas.

Branch dynasties

7. *The Chandellas*

When king Dhaṅga died, some time after A.D. 1002, his son Gaṇḍa inherited a kingdom which, in power and prestige, exceeded all others in North India. After a short reign he was succeeded by his son Vidyādhara, whose reign is memorable for the successful resistance to Sultān Mahmūd's invasion. Dhaṅga and Gaṇḍa had joined the confederacy against the Sultān, but their kingdom had hitherto escaped his invasion. After his conquest of Kanauj, the Kachchhapaghāta chief Arjuna, who was a feudatory of the Chandella king, killed Rājyapāla for having tamely submitted to the Sultān. This brought upon the Chandellas the wrath of the Sultān who twice invaded their kingdom, in 1019 and 1022 A.D. The Chandellas appear to have adopted a 'scorched earth policy' and retreated before the Muslim army without offering any battle. The Sultān, afraid of penetrating too far into the interior, had each time to retreat without much gain, and ultimately established a friendly relation with Vidyādhara, who had thus the unique distinction of being the only Indian ruler who effectively checked the triumphal career of Sultān Mahmūd and saved his kingdom from wanton destruction by that ruthless conqueror.

Successful resistance to Mahmūd

After the departure of Sultān Mahmūd the Chandella kings were engaged in the usual pastime of fighting with their neighbours. Vidyādhara and his successor Vijayapāla defeated respectively Paramāra Bhoja and Kalachuri Gāṅgeyadeva. But Vijayapāla's son Kīrtivarman (1070 A.D.) was defeated by Kalachuri Karṇa, who occupied his kingdom for some time. Gopāla, one of the powerful feudatories of the Chandellas, however, recovered the kingdom of his suzerain by defeating Karṇa. Krītivarman was also defeated by Mahmūd, the Ghaznavid governor of the Panjāb, who plundered Kālanjara, a feat which even his great namesake could not accomplish.

The next great king of the family was Madanavarman whose known dates are 1129 and 1163 A.D. He conquered Bhilsa from the Paramāras but had to surrender it to Chaulukya Siddharāja, who invaded his kingdom and advanced as far as Mahobā, the capital city. He also fought with the Gāhaḍavāla Govindachandra and defeated the Kalachuris.

Madanavarman was succeeded by his grandson Paramardideva, whose known dates range between A.D. 1165 and 1201.

Paramardideva

His early career was very successful and he recovered the Bhilsa region from the Chaulukyas some time after 1173 A.D. But in or before 1182A.D. his power was shattered by a disastrous defeat inflicted upon him by the Chāhamāna Pṛithvīrāja who overran his whole kingdom. The date of this sanguinary battle between the two premier States of North India is of melancholy interest, for in 1181 A.D. Shihābuddīn Muhammad had already reached the gate of Lahore.The victor Pṛthvīrāja succumbed to the onslaught of this Muslim chief in 1192 A.D., and ten years later came the turn of the vanquished. In 1202 A.D. Muhammad's general Qutbuddīn besieged Kālanjara, the strong citadel of the Chandellas. Paramardi resisted for some time and then proposed to conclude peace on condition of payment of tribute.

Then followed a scene, the like of which is seldom met with in Indian history. Ajayadeva, the proud minister of Paramardi, remembering the old glories of Dhaṅga and Vidyādhara,

Muslim conquest

refused to bow to the Muslims. He killed his royal master and bravely continued the fight. But the failure of water supply forced him to surrender. The fort of Kālanjara and, later , the capital city of Mahobā fell into the hands of Qutbuddīn who appointed his own governor to administer the conquered territories.

But the resistance of Ajayadeva, though unsuccessful, was not in vain. He inspired a new kind of patriotic fervour which bore fruit. The son of Paramardi, known as Trailokyavarman or Trailokyamalla (1205-1241 A.D.), organised a strong force and, in A.D. 1205, fought a pitched battle with the Muslim army at a place now known as Kakarādaha, south-east of Bedwara. He won a complete victory and recovered all his dominions including Kālanjara. It was a great achievement and Trailokyavarman lived long to enjoy the fruit of his hard-earned victory. He also conquered Rewā and the Kalachuri kingdom of Dāhalamaṇḍala. The Muslims again invaded Kālanjara during the reign of Iltutmish, but though they plundered some of the surrounding townships, they could not conquer any territory.

Recovery of the kingdom

When Trailokyavarman died, he had the supreme satisfaction of leaving an extensive and powerful kingdom to his son Vīravarman. He ascended the throne some time before A.D. 1254 and maintained intact this precious heritage. He was succeeded by Bhojavarman and Hammīravarman, probably his sons, who ruled at least till 1303 A.D. Next year Alāuddīn Khiljī conquered the greater part of the kingdom. A king named Vīravarman II ruled in Bundelkhand as late as 1315 A.D., but nothing is known of him or of his kingdom after that year.

Final conquest

8. *The Chaulukyas*

The pusillanimous king Bhīma, who had fled to Cutch at the approach of Sultān Mahmūd, returned to his capital after the departure of the enemy. But although too cowardly to resist the Muslim invader, he turned his arms against the petty principalities in the neighbourhood. He conquered Mt. Abu and Bhinmal, which were ruled by two branches of the Paramāras. His conquest of Mālava in alliance with Kalachuri Karṇa, and subsequent fight with him have been related above. The stories told in a literary work of his victorious expeditions to Sindh, Kāsi, Ayodhyā etc. do not deserve credence. He abdicated the throne in favour of his son Karṇa in 1064 A.D.

Karṇa's conquest of Mālava and subsequent defeat by Udayāditya and Jagaddeva have been mentioned above. He invaded southern Mārwar but was defeated by the Chāhamānas of Naḍḍula. When he died about 1094 A.D., his son Jayasiṁha being too young, the queen-mother, a daughter of the Kadamba king of Goa, acted as regent during his minority.

Jayasiṁha, who assumed the title Siddharāja, was one of the greatest kings of the dynasty. He carried his victorious arms on all sides and defeated almost all his neighbouring powers. He defeated and took prisoner the Ābhīra chief of Saurāshtra and annexed it to his kingdom. He annexed Bhinmal by defeating its Paramāra rulers. The Chāhamāna rulers of both Naḍḍula and Śākambharī submitted to him and ruled their States as his vassals. His brilliant campaigns against the Paramāra rulers Naravarman and Yaśovarman, ending in the annexation of Mālava, have been related above. He also invaded the Chandella kingdom and proceeded as far as Kālanjara and Mahobā. The Chandella king Madanavarman was forced to buy peace by returning Bhilsa which he had conquered from the Paramāras. He also gained a victory over the Chālukya king Vikramāditya VI. Although the Paramāras of Mālava and Chāhamānas of Naḍḍula recovered their dominions before the close of Jayasiṁha's reign, he ruled over an extensive kingdom and raised the power and prestige of the Chaulukyas to a height unknown before.

Jayasiṁha Siddharāja

In spite of his military activities Jayasiṁha, like Paramāra Bhoja, was a great patron of learning, and established institutions for the study of *Jyotisha*, *Nyāya*, and Purāṇa. His court was graced by the great Jaina scholar Hemachandra whose prolific literary activities have been described elsewhere.

Jayasiṁha Siddharāja died in or shortly after 1143 A.D. He had no son and nominated his minister's son Bāhaḍa as his successor. But after the death of the king, Kumārapāla, a remote descendant of Bhīma I, seized the throne some time between 1143 and 1145 A.D. Bāhaḍa's cause was taken up by the Chāhamāna ruler Arṇorāja of Śākambharī who, in alliance with the Paramāras of Mālava and Mt. Abu, simultaneously invaded the Chaulukya dominions from the north and east. But Kumārapāla defeated all his adversaries. Arṇorāja was defeated and concluded a treaty which was cemented by the marriage of his daughter to Kumārapāla. The Paramāra ruler of Mt. Abu was dethroned and his nephew was made the king. The ruler of Mālava was killed in the battle and the whole country up to Bhilsa was again annexed to the Chaulukya kingdom.

Kumārapāla

In 1150 Kumārapāla again invaded and devastated the dominions of his father-in-law Arṇorāja as the latter had insulted his own queen, a daughter of the Chaulukya king Jayasiṁha

Siddharāja. But though Arṇorāja was defeated, he was allowed to rule his kingdom. Kumārapāla also established his sway over the Chāhamānas of Naḍḍula and Paramāras of Bhinmal and conquered Koṅkaṇa between 1160 and 1162 A.D.

Kumārapāla had a remarkable personality, and looms large in the Jaina chronicles of Gujarāt. He adopted Jainism before 1164 A.D., probably under the influence of Hemachandra, to whom he was extremely devoted. Although he still showed his reverence to the family deity Śiva, there is no doubt that with the proverbial zeal of a new convert he forbade the slaughter of animals, and this regulation was enforced not only in his own kingdom but also in some of his feudatory States. Even the Brāhmaṇas had to substitute grains for animals in their customary religious sacrifices. By another remarkable ordinance he stopped gambling in the State.

Kumārapāla's death in A.D. 1171-72 was followed by a struggle for the throne between his sister's son and brother's son, backed respectively by the Jainas and the Brāhmaṇas. The latter, Ajayapāla, succeeded to the throne and is represented by the Jaina chroniclers as a persecutor of their religion. He defeated the Guhila chief Sāmantasiṁha who had invaded his dominions, and fought successfully against the Chāhamānas of Śākambharī. But he was killed by a Pratīhāra[1] about 1176 A.D.

Mūlarāja II, the son of Ajayapāla, being too young, his mother, queen Nāiki, daughter of Paramardin, the Kadmba chief of Goa, acted as regent. Soon she was confronted by a grave danger. In 1178 A.D. Shihābuddīn Muhammad attacked Gujarāt, but the brave queen, with the boy king on her lap, herself led the army and inflicted a defeat upon the Muslim hosts near Mt. Abu. It was a highly creditable achievement, though, taking advantage of this crisis, Mālava successfully asserted her independence.

Mūlarāja II

Mūlarāja II died in 1178 A.D. and was succeeded by his younger brother Bhīma II, who had a long reign of 60 years. It is a sad commentary on the political wisdom even of the upper classes of the country, that almost immediately after they had actually passed through the grave crisis of a Muslim invasion, they should have utilized the opportunity to further their own personal interests at the cost of the State, instead of concerting measures to

Bhīma II

1. This may denote a high royal official or a chief of the Pratīhāra clan.

strengthen it against future dangers. Apparently taking advantage of the situation caused by the Muslim invasion and the succession of one minor king by another, many of the provincial governors declared independence, and some of the ministers set up as ruling chiefs in different parts of the kingdom. Indeed, the kingdom was threatened with complete disintegration when the able and energetic Vāghelā chief Arṇorāja saved the situation. He belonged to the Chaulukya clan and was related to Kumārapāla who granted him, in recognition of his loyal and faithful service, the village of Vyāghrapalli, 10 miles south-west of the Chaulukya capital. From the name of this village, where the family settled, it came to be known as the Vāghelās.

Vāghelās

Arṇorāja loyally stood by the young king and subdued the rebellious elements. He lost his life in course of this struggle, but his son Lavaṇaprasāda continued the task left unfinished by his father. He virtually carried on the administration of the State in the name of the king, from his headquarters at Dholka (Kaira Dist.), and with the help of two brothers, Tejaḥpāla and Vastupāla who served as his ministers, saved the State from internal dissensions and heroically struggled against foreign invasion. The Yādavas led repeated invasions against Gujarāt, and the Paramāras overran the country, but both were ultimately repulsed by Lavaṇaprasāda. But the greatest enemies were the Muslims who had become the dominant power in Northern India by defeating Pṛithvīrāja in 1192 A.D. and occupying Ajmer in the following year. When the Muslims attacked the Mhers the Chaulukyas sent an army to their help which pursued the Muslims almost up to the city of Ajmer. To punish this, Qutbuddīn, with a fresh contingent from Ghaznī, invaded Gujarāt and plundered its capital city, but retired shortly afterwards.

Lavaṇaprasāda

Even this dire threat to the very existence of the kingdom could not stop the internal dissensions. Some time before 1210 A.D. the throne of Gujarāt was forcibly occupied by one Jayantasiṁha or Jayasiṁha, and the usurpation continued for nearly fifteen years till Lavaṇaprasāda and his able son Vīradhavala drove him out between 1223 and 1226 A.D.

The Yādava Siṅghaṇa continued the aggressive policy against Gujarāt and formed an alliance with the neighbouring powers for the purpose. It is shameful to record that when Iltutmish, the Muslim Sultān of Delhi, invaded Northern Gujarāt, Siṅghaṇa attacked its southern part in alliance with the Paramāra king and chief of Lāṭa. To the credit of Vīradhavala and Vastupāla it must be said that they heroically faced this great danger and repulsed respectively the two great enemy forces.

Lavaṇaprasāda concluded a treaty with Siṅghaṇa and retired from public affairs in 1231 A.D. Henceforth his son Vīradhavala became the real ruler of Gujarāt, though he acknowledged Bhīma II as the nominal ruler. Bhīma II died in 1238 A.D. and was succeeded by Tribhuvanapāla. During his reign the Yādava king Siṅghaṇa again invaded Gujarāt in alliance with the Parāmāra and Guhila rulers, but Viśvamalla or Vīsala, son of Vīradhavala, routed the enemies. Shortly after this Vīrama, another son of Vīradhavala, seized the throne by driving away Tribhuvanapāla. Vīrama was deposed by his brother Vīsala, who ascended the throne before 1251 A.D. but abdicated it in favour of Arjuna, the son of his other brother, between 1261 and 1264 A. D. Arjuna was succeeded in 1274 A.D. by his son Sāraṅgadeva who repulsed an invasion of Balban, the Sultān of Delhi. He also defeated Arjunavarman II, the Paramāra king of Mālava, and successfully defended his kingdom against the Yādava king Rāmachandra. Even then Kāthiawār and Cutch were included in his dominions. He died in 1296 and was succeeded by his nephew Karṇa. In the very first year of his reign the whole of Gujarāt was conquered by Alāuddīn Khiljī. He fled to Devagiri but his queen and daughter fell into the hands of Alāuddīn Khiljī.

9. *The Chāhamānas.*

(a) *The main Branch of Śākambharī*

The Chāhamānas of Śākambharī did not suffer much from the invasions of Sultān Mahmūd. Throughout the 11th century A.D. they maintained their position as a rising local power and as usual, had to fight with the neighbouring States. One record refers to their battle with the Mātaṅgas, which mean *Mlechchhas,* and probably refer to the Muslims.

Ajayarāja, who ruled early in the 12th century A.D., was the first to begin an aggressive imperial policy. He invaded Ujjain and captured the commander of the Paramāra forces. He is also said to have killed in battle three kings. But we do not know whether

Ajayarāja.

the boundaries of his kingdom were extended by these victories. He founded a city called after him Ajayameru, better known in later days in its abbreviated form Ajmer. It is interesting to note that some of his coins bear the name of his queen Somaladevī, a rare thing in Indian history.

Arṇorāja.

Arṇorāja, the son and successor of Ajayarāja, ascended the throne before 1139 A.D. Reference has been made above to his hostilities and marriage alliances with the Chaulukya kings Jayasiṁha Siddharāja and Kumārapāla. But though defeated by them Arṇorāja claims to have defeated and killed a large number of Turushkas (i.e. Muslims of the Panjāb) who invaded his dominion. He was killed by his own son who, however, had a short rule and yielded to his younger brother Vigraharāja IV, also called Vīsaladeva.

Vigraharāja IV.

Vigraharāja, whose known dates range between A.D. 1150 and 1163, was a great conqueror and raised the Chāhamānas to the status of an imperial power. He conquered Jābālipura, Naḍḍula and other smaller States in Southern Rājputāna which acknowledged the suzerainty of Kumārapāla, and thus took revenge for the defeat inflicted upon his father by the Chaulukyas. But he earned undying fame by his victories in the north. He conquered Ḍhillikā (Delhi) by defeating the Tomaras and then advanced to the Eastern Panjāb. He overran the Hissar District and obtained several victories over the forces of the Ghaznavid ruler of the Panjāb. His proud boast that he made Āryāvarta once more true to its designation by exterminating the *Mlechchhas* (i.e. Muslims) had undoubtedly some justification, though, unfortunately, we do not possess any details of his fight with the Muslims. The epigraphic records of his reign prove that his kingdom extended in the north as far as Siwālik hills, and in the south, at least up to Jaipur District in Udaipur. Vigraharāja was an author of repute and a few fragments of his drama *Harakeli-nāṭaka*, engraved on stone, still exist in Ajmer. Similar stones containing fragments of *Lalita-Vigraharājanāṭaka*, composed in honour of the king by the great poet Somadeva, have been discovered in a mosque at Ajmer.

Vigraharāja's son having died after a short rule, the throne was occupied by Pṛithvirāja II, a grandson of Arṇorāja. His governor in Eastern Panjāb fought successfully with the Muslims and even claims to have burnt one of their cities and taken its ruler prisoner.

Pṛithvīrāja was succeeded by his uncle Someśvara, son of Arṇorāja by the Chaulukya princess (daughter of Jayasiṁha Siddharāja). Someśvara had spent his boyhood and youth in the Chaulukya court and helped Kumārapāla in his wars. While he was still there he had married a Kalachuri princess named Karpūradevī, and two sons were born of her named Pṛithvīrāja and Harirāja. When the Chāhamāna ruler Pṛithvīrāja II died young, after a short reign, his ministers invited Someśvara to occupy the throne of Śākambharī. Someśvara accordingly came from Gujarāt and ascended the throne in A.D. 1169. His reign was uneventful and, on his death about A.D. 1177, his minor son Pṛithvīrāja III became king, and the queen-mother acted as regent.

The name of Pṛithvīrāja occupies a unique place in Indian history. As the last great Hindu emperor of Northern India, his memory has been embellished by popular legends and formed the theme of many a popular ballad. The celebrated poet Chand Bardāi has immortalised him in his famous epic *Pṛithvīrāja Rāso*, but the book in its extant form can hardly be regarded as a contemporary and authentic account of his life. Another biographical work called *Pṛithvīrāja-vijaya* is earlier and more reliable, but only a fragment of it has so far come to light. On the basis of these and almost contemporary Muslim accounts, supplemented by epigraphic records, we may draw up a brief sketch of the life and career of Pṛithvīrāja bereft of romantic and incredible details.

Pṛithvīrāja III

Pṛithvīrāja probably assumed the reins of government in his own hands in A.D. 1178. He had soon to face a rebellion by his cousin Nāgārjuna, son of Vigraharāja, but suppressed it without difficulty. According to a literary text he set out for a *digvijaya* (world-conquest), but apart from some minor conquests, the only important expedition which he is known to have led with success was that against the Chandellas. He defeated Paramardi, the Chandella king, and ravaged his kingdom in A.D. 1182, but could not retain it long.

In 1187 A.D. he invaded Gujarāt, but could not gain much success and concluded a treaty with Chaulukya Bhīma II. It does not appear that Pṛithvīrāja enlarged the boundary of his kingdom or achieved conspicuous military victories such as distinguished many Indian kings during the preceding two centuries. There is no ground to suppose that he was either the most powerful of Indian kings or the greatest general of his age. The almost contemporary Muslim historians also do not convey any such impression. It is really the romantic tale of Chand Bardāi that has cast a spell around him. But there is no historical basis for the central theme of this work, which has gained a great deal of currency, viz. that the Gāhaḍavāla king Jaychandra of Kanauj was his sworn enemy, and that the hostility between the two paved the way for the destruction of Indian independence. As to the origin of this hostility, two circumstances have usually been accepted as historical facts. It is said that both Pṛithvīrāja and Jayachandra were grandsons of the Tomara king through their mothers, and as the latter, having no male issue, adopted Pṛithvīrāja as his heir, Jayachandra was jealous of his cousin. This story is, however, discredited by *Pṛithvīrāja-vijaya* according to which Pṛithvīrāja's mother did not belong to the Tomara clan at all. The second circumstance explaining the enmity between the two chiefs savours more of romance than history. We are told that Jayachandra celebrated a *Rājasūya Yajña* at Kanauj, followed by a *Svayaṁvara* ceremony for the marriage of his daughter Saṁyuktā.[1] The latter served as a bait and almost all the notable chiefs attended. Pṛithvīrāja, however, disdained to join the assembly and thereby tacitly admit Jayachandra as his superior. He was thereupon represented by a stone statue. Saṁyuktā, however, placed the nuptial wreath round the neck of the statue, and during the night Pṛithvīrāja, who was present in the city in disguise, carried her off in the cover of darkness, but not without a severe fighting.

But the true fame of Pṛithvīrāja rests upon his fight with the Muhammadan invaders from Ghūr which will be related later.

b. The Minor Branches.

Occasional references have been made in the preceding chapters to the Chāhamānas of Naḍḍula who ruled over their petty principality throughout the period, though occasionally defeated and subjugated by neighbouring powers. Naḍḍula became an independent State under Kelhaṇa some time after 1178 A.D. He and his brother Kīrtipāla, with the help of the Chaulukyas, defeated the forces of Shihābuddīn Muhammad who plundered Naḍḍula in 1178 A.D. Kīrtipāla overran

Naḍḍula

1. Also called Saṁyogitā.

Mewar, and wrested from the Paramāras the principality of Jābālipura (Jalor) where his successors ruled for more than a century. The kingdom of Naḍḍula was invaded by Qutbuddīn in 1197 A.D. during the reign of Kalhaṇa's son Jaitrasiṁha, but seems to have soon passed into the hands of the Chaulukya king Bhīma II from whom it was reconquered by Udayasiṁha of the Jābālipur branch some time after 1226 A.D. Udayasiṁha capitulated to Iltutmish when he invaded Jalor, but later helped the Vāghelā chief Vīradhavala against the Sultān. Udaya's successors ruled in Jalor till its final conquest by Alāuddīn Khiljī in 1310-11 A.D.

The Satyapura (Sanchor in Jodhpur) branch of the Chāhamānas was founded by a member of the Naḍḍula family. One of the rulers claims to have recovered Bhinmal from the Muslims, probably after 1310 A.D.

The Devḍā branch founded by a member of the Jalor family, conquered Mt. Abu, and ruled till 1337 A.D.

But by far the most important, though the latest, branch of the Chāhamānas was that which ruled at Raṇastambhapura, modern Ranthambhor in Jaipur. It was founded towards the close of the 12th century by a member of the main branch who is said to have been banished by Pṛithvīrāja III. After the extinction of the main branch Ranthambhor seems to have grown into importance. The history of this small principality possesses a singular interest on two grounds. In the first place we have an Indian text, *Hammīra-Mahākāvya*, which gives a continuous narrative of its struggle with the Muslims and enables us to judge the value of Muslim chronicles which form our only source of information for the history of the rest of India during this period. Secondly, the heroic resistance of a small State, continually exposed to the attacks of the Sultāns of Delhi, throughout the 13th century A.D., throws a new light on India's struggle for independence against the Muslims. The tenacious fight for freedom against heavy odds by the small band of Chāhamānas gives lie to the general belief, partly engendered by Muslim chroniclers and partly due to ignorance, that after the battle of Tarain, the Muslims had an easy walk-over so far as the rest of India was concerned. Unfortunately we have before us only the picture painted by the victors, and that certainly does not convey the whole truth. The history of Ranthambhor thus possesses a special degree of importance.

Ranthambhor.

After the overthrow of Pṛithvīrāja and his brother Harirāja and the capture of Ajmer by the Muslims, the members and followers of the royal family found shelter in Ranthambhor. But it was soon conquered by the Muslims and its ruler Bālhaṇadeva was a tributary to Iltutmish in 1215 A.D. Shortly after, Bālhaṇa threw off the yoke, but Ranthambhor was reconquered in 1226 A.D. Shortly after the death of Iltutmish in 1236 A.D., the Chāhamāna ruler Vāgbhaṭa again got possession of Ranthambhor. Balban led two invasions against him in 1248 and 1253 A.D., but without success. The contemporary Muslim chronicle refers to Bāhar-deo (i.e. Vāgbhaṭa) as the greatest of the Rais of Hindusthān, and well did he deserve the title for his organised resistance against the Muslims. For, according to *Hammīra-Mahākāvya*, he took elaborate precautions to guard the frontier by always stationing adequate forces at strategic points.

Fight against the Muslims.

Vāgbhaṭa.

Jaitrasiṁha, son and successor of Vāgbhaṭa, carried on successful wars against the neighbouring Hindu chiefs, but was defeated by Sultān Nāsiruddīn Mahmūd in 1259 A.D. and forced to pay tribute. But Ranthambhor soon became independent again.

Hammīra, who succeeded his father Jaitrasiṁha in 1283 A.D., was the greatest king of this dynasty. Śākambharī formed a part of his kingdom, though it is not known with certainty whether he or his predecessors conquered it from the Muslims. He ruled over an extensive kingdom which included Seopur district in Gwalior and Balvan in Kotah. The *Hammīra-Mahākāvya* gives an elaborate account of his *digvijaya* or career of conquest. He ravaged Medapāṭa (Mewar), defeated the Paramāra kings of Mālava and Mt. Abu, and proceeded as far as Kāthiāwār Peninsula.

Hammīra.

The decline of the Sultānate of Delhi probably gave Hammīra the requisite opportunity to carry on this victorious expedition against his Hindu neighbours. He had soon to repent bitterly that the opportunity was not taken advantage of to strengthen his defence against the Muslims by organising a confederacy of Hindu rulers. The decadent Slave dynasty of Delhi was overthrown by Jalāluddīn Khiljī, and the new ruler lost no time in invading Ranthambhor. But this expedition of 1290 as well as several others led by Alāuddīn Khiljī's general Ulugh Khān proved unsuccessful. Then Alāuddīn himself led a well-equipped army against Ranthambhor. Hammīra fought bravely and offered a heroic resistance, but he was ultimately defeated and killed, and Ranthambhor fell in Muslim hands in 1301 A.D.

10. *The Guhilas of Mewar.*

The history of the Guhilas during the 11th century was uneventful. During the next century the Guhilas had to submit for some time to Chaulukya Kumārapāla who was in possession of Chitrakūṭa, the famous fort of Chitor, in 1151 A.D. Shortly after the Guhila chief Sāmantasiṁha had recovered his kingdom (1171 A.D.) it was conquered by Kīrtipāla of Naḍḍula. Sāmantasiṁha thereupon settled in Vāgaḍa (Dungarpur), but his younger brother Kumārasiṁha drove out Kīrtipāla before 1182 A.D. with the help of the Chaulukya king, and established himself at Āghāṭa, modern Ahar, in Udaipur, which had already risen to the position of a second capital of the kingdom early in the 11th century A.D.

The first powerful king of this dynasty was Jaitrasiṁha whose known dates range between 1213 and 1252 A.D. Early in his reign his kingdom was invaded by Sultān Iltutmish who overran the country and destroyed the capital Nāgahrada, but on receipt of the news that the Vāghelā chief Vīradhavala of Gujarāt was coming to help Jaitrasiṁha, the Muslim forces left Mewar.

Jaitrasiṁha

In spite of this early reverse Jaitrasiṁha frittered his energy and resources in carrying on campaigns against his Hindu neighbours. He fought with the Chāhamāna king of Ranthambhor, the only bulwark against the Muslim encroachment in that region, and invaded Gujarāt whose ruler had saved him from the Muslims earlier in his reign. This lapse was, however, more than made up by his grandson Samarasiṁha (1273-1301) A.D.) who helped the Vāghelā chief Sāraṅgadeva in overthrowing the Muslim forces which invaded Gujarāt some time before 1285 A.D. But later when Ulugh Khān, the general of Alāuddīn Khiljī, advanced against Gujarāt, Samarasiṁha meekly submitted to him. But this pusillanimity did not save his kingdom. During the reign of his son and successor Ratnasiṁha, who ascended the throne in 1301 or 1302 A.D., Alāuddīn Khiljī invaded Mewar in 1303 A.D. and pitched his camp near the famous citadel of Chitor. Ratnasiṁha bravely resisted for two months, but then lost heart, and stealing out from the city surrendered himself to Alāuddīn.

A branch of the Guhilas ruled as vassals of the main family at Sisoda, and thus came to be known as Sisodiyā Rājputs.

Sisodiyās

Their chief Lakshmaṇasiṁha, who had married Padminī, the daughter of Ratnasiṁha, bravely defended Chitor, even after the desertion of its cowardly king. The heroic resistance of Lakshmaṇasiṁha, in course of which he died with his sons, has been immortalised by the bards of Rājputāna. But it was all in vain, and Alāuddīn occupied Chitor in 1303 A.D. The well-known story of Alāuddīn's infatuation for Padminī, and the release of Ratnasiṁha by a stratagem, belongs more to romance than to history. It is certain, however, that the Guhilas maintained their independence and continued the fight even after the fall of Chitor. Alāuddīn soon recalled his son whom he had left in charge of that fort, and handed it over to Chāhamāna Māladeva, sister's son of Ratnasiṁha, who ruled in Chitor as a vassal of Alāuddīn Khiljī.

CHAPTER IX.

The Muslim conquest of Northern India.

1. *The Panjāb under the Yamīnī Dynasty*

The death of Sultān Mahmūd in A.D. 1030 was followed by a struggle for succession between his two sons, Muhammad and Mas'ūd. The former was dethroned after a reign of 7 months and Mas'ūd ascended the throne of Ghaznī in A.D. 1031. He appointed Ahmad Niyāltigīn governor of the Panjāb. Niyāltigīn continued the policy of Sultān Mahmūd and led military expeditions into the interior of the country. In 1034 he is said to have suddenly appeared in Banaras, plundered its markets from morning till midday, and then left the city and returned to the Panjāb with his spoils. How these plundering raids were conducted without any serious engagement with the powers that ruled over the intervening region it is difficult to say.

Expedition of Niyāltigīn

Three years later Mas'ūd personally led a big army to India and conquered Hānsi, Sonpat, and neighbouring territories in East Panjāb. But shortly afterwards the Saljūq Turks repeatedly invaded his dominions and he was forced to leave Ghazni. On his way to India his Turkish and Hindu slaves revolted and killed him.

Mas'ūd

After the usual struggle for succession Maudūd, son of Mas'-ūd, made himself master of both Ghaznī and the Panjāb. But the Saljūq attacks continued and, taking advantage of this, the Indian rulers seem to have made a combined effort under the leadership of the Tomara king of Delhi to wrest the Panjāb from him. The confederacy of Indian rulers, probably comprising, among others, the Paramāra king Bhoja, the Kala-churi Karṇa, and the Chāhamāna Aṇahilla (of Naḍḍula) conquered Hānsi, Thāneswar, Nagarkot, and other places, and at last besieged Lahore itself, in 1043 A.D. The garrison in Lahore were reduced to great straits, and being in utter despair made a sally. The Indian army, taken unawares, took to flight.

Indian Confederacy

In the light of later events, this failure, entirely due to lack of generalship, may be said to have paved the way for the final conquest of India by the Muslims.

The death of Maudūd in A.D. 1049 was followed by the usual palace intrigues, and no less than six Sultāns gained and lost the throne during the next ten years. Nevertheless, even during this period of turmoil, the governor of the Panjāb reconquered Nagarkot, and Sultān Ibrāhīm, who ascended the throne in 1059 A.D., led an expedition and conquered a number of places in East Panjāb. His son Maḥmūd, who was appointed governor of the Panjāb in 1085 A.D., advanced further into the interior and captured Kanauj and Agra; but he failed to take Ujjain and Kālañjar which were successfully defended by the Paramāra and Chandella rulers. During the reign of Ibrāhīm's successor Mas'ūd III (1099-1115 A.D.), the Muslims made another plundering raid beyond the Gaṅgā in course of which they took prisoner Malhi, the king of Kanauj. As noted above (p. 316), he is probably to be identified with Gāhaḍavāla Madanachandra, and his son Govindachandra defeated the Muslims and secured his release.

Maḥmūd

On the death of Mas'ūd III his two sons successively occupied the throne, but the latter was defeated and killed by another son Bahrām with the help of his maternal uncle, the Saljūq Sultān. Bahrām ruled from 1118 to c. 1152 A.D. Towards the close of his reign he came into conflict with the Shansabānī princes of Ghūr, a small principality to the west of Ghaznī and east of Herāt. It was a dependency of Ghaznī, and a member of its ruling family took shelter with Bahrām. The latter, however, killed him on suspicion, and this led to a sort of blood-feud between the rulers of Ghaznī and Ghūr which was accompanied by unusual acts of cruelty and treachery. At last Bahrām was defeated and his kingdom fell into the hands of his rival. The city of Ghaznī, embellished by the Indian spoils of Sultān Mahmūd, was at that time one of the most splendid in the whole world. But Alāuddīn, king of Ghūr, treated the capital of Sultān Mahmūd in exactly the same way as the latter had done in his Indian expeditions. Ghaznī was given up to flames, ravage, and massacre for three (according to some accounts seven) days. Almost all its magnificent buildings were destroyed and the finest city of Asia was all but blotted

Ghūr

Destruction of Ghaznī

from the face of the earth. Thus did terrible Nemesis do her work and the grave injury done to India was cruelly avenged, though by foreign hands.

Bahrām recovered Ghaznī before he died, and was succeeded by his son Khusrav Shāh. The larger part of his dominion was conquered by the rulers of Ghūr, and at last he was driven out of Ghaznī by the Ghuzz Turks shortly after A.D. 1157. He fled to Lahore where he ruled till 1160 A.D. and was succeeded by his son Khusrav Malik. Even the Indian dominion of the Ghaznavids showed clear signs of disintegration, and the governors and vassal chiefs practically behaved like independent rulers. All the while hostility continued with the rulers of Ghūr. That kingdom shortly passed into the hands of Ghiyāsuddīn who wrested Ghaznī from the Ghuzz Turks in 1174 A.D. and appointed as its ruler his brother Shihābuddīn Muhammad, also known as Mu'azzuddīn Muhammad. The epithet Ghūrī is usually attached to both of them in Indian history. Shihābuddīn, who was entrusted with eastern affairs, naturally turned his attention to India. He advanced into the Panjāb and took Uch, but, as noted above, was disastrously defeated in an expedition to Gujarāt by the Chaulukya king Mūlarāja II. Shihābuddīn was, however, more successful in Sindh and twice invaded Lahore in 1181 and 1184 A.D. In 1186 A.D. he led a third expedition and wrested the Panjāb from Khusrav Malik, the last king of the Yamīnī Dynasty of Ghaznī.

Khusrav Malik

2. *Shihābuddīn Muhammad Ghūrī*

The conquest of the Panjāb brought the dominions of the Ghūrī kings to the confines of the kingdom of Pṛithvīrāja, and a struggle between the two was inevitable. Already in 1178 A.D., while Shihābuddīn was marching against Gujarāt, he had sent an agent to Pṛithvīrāja, apparently with a view to making a common cause against that country. To the credit of Pṛithvīrāja it must be said that he did not agree, and even decided to march against the Muslim invader, when the latter conquered Naḍḍula. It is interesting to note that this zeal of the young king to crush the Muslims was not shared by his aged minister Kadambavāsa who thought it more expedient to allow the two enemies, the Muslims and the Chaulukyas, to exhaust themselves by fighting with each other. As a matter of

Pṛithvīrāja

tact, Pṛithvīrāja desisted from his military preparations as soon as he heard that Mūlarāja had routed Shihābuddīn's army; and, as noted above, even after Shihābuddīn had conquered the Panjāb, he was engaged in fighting with Chaulukya Bhīma, rather than making a common cause with him against the Muslim invader. It was not till Shihābuddīn actually carried on depredations into the kingdom of Pṛithvīrāja and conquered the strong fort of Tabarhindah, that the latter awoke to the gravity of the danger. Indeed it was impossible to ignore it any longer. The Governor of Delhi and other chiefs reported to him how the Muslims ravaged the land and dishonoured the women, with the result that refugees from the Panjāb filled the hills and dales on this side of the border. On hearing this Pṛithvīrāja decided to fight Shihābuddīn and set out with a vast army. The battle took place in 1191 A.D. near the village of Tarāin, or Torawana, 27 miles from Bhatinda. Shihābuddīn vigorously charged the centre of the Indian army, but his wings gave way and he was completely surrounded. He was severely wounded, but with great difficulty, and by dint of stubborn courage, he extricated himself with a few followers. Pṛithvīrāja gained a complete victory and routed the army of his opponents. It was the last great military achievement of the Hindus like the last bright glimmer of the lamp before it is finally extinguished. But, curiously enough, the retreating and scattered Muslim forces were not pursued and allowed to retire in safety.

First Battle of Tarāin

Shihābuddīn never forgot this great insult, and is reported to have said that "he never slumbered in ease, or waked but in sorrow and anxiety." Burning for revenge he collected a vast army of the hardy mountaineers of Central Asia, and next year again marched towards India.

After his success in the first battle Pṛithvīrāja besieged the fort of Tabarhindah which capitulated after 13 months. Besides recovering this strong fort Pṛithvīrāja did not take any advantage of the respite of more than a year to organise proper defence against the future aggression of the enemy. He could easily have conquered the Panjāb during the absence of Shihābuddīn and held the mountain passes, for the Panjāb, newly conquered, was seething with discontent, and there was no strong Ghurī garrison left in India. What is worse, he even did not make any adequate arrangement for defending Tabarhindah which guarded his kingdom on the west. Shihābuddīn easily reconquered in a few days the fort which defied Pṛithvīrāja for 13 months even after the departure of the army of Shihābuddīn. As a matter of fact, Shihābuddīn hardly met with any opposition till he reached Tarāin, the scene of the first battle, where Pṛithvīrāja was waiting with his army. Strangely enough, Pṛithvīrāja's veteran general Skanda, who won the last battle, was engaged in a war elsewhere even at this critical moment. Pṛithvīrāja was joined by contingents of a number of other Indian kings who displayed once more their sense of unity in face of a common danger. He sent a message to Shihābuddīn asking him to retire, and the latter complacently replied that he was referring the matter to his brother, the king. Having thus allayed the suspicions of the Indians who were encamped quite close by, Shihābuddīn suddenly attacked them about day-break and threw them into confusion. But order was at last restored in the Indian camp and the Indian army advanced to the attack. Baffled in his attempts to overwhelm the Indian army by a surprise attack, Shihābuddīn now adopted a new strategy. He kept with him a strong reserve, and having divided the rest of his army into small groups instructed them to attack vehemently and then pretend to retreat. As he foresaw, the Indian army pursued them in hot haste. Once more the lack of generalship and discipline among the Indian soldiers snatched away the victory which their bravery had won. Eager for pursuit they advanced pell-mell in scattered and disorderly groups, while the army of Shihābuddīn, even in course of flight, maintained excellent order and discipline. As soon as Shihābuddīn saw the rank of his enemy broken and disorderly, he charged home with 12,000 chosen horse which he had kept in reserve, and completely routed the Indian hosts. A number of Indian chiefs vainly endeavoured to rally and lay dead on the field. Pṛithvīrāja himself was taken prisoner and killed in cold blood. Thus ended the terrible day and the sun of Hindu glory set for ever on the fatal plain of Tarāin (1192 A.D.).

Second Battle of Tarāin

The rest may be briefly told. Shihābuddīn followed up his victory by the conquest of Ajmer which became a tributary State under the young son of Pṛithvīrāja. Shihābuddīn conquered a number of fortresses and returned to Ghaznī, leaving his general Qutbuddīn in charge of Indian affairs. Qutbuddīn took

Muslim conquest of North India

possession of Delhi and conquered other places. Next year Shihābuddīn himself defeated Jayachandra of Kanauj and thereby carried the banner of Islam to Banaras. Shortly afterwards Harirāja, younger brother of Pṛithvīrāja, overthrew his nephew and became independent king of Ajmer. But, it is sad to relate, his licentious habits made him very unpopular, and when Qutbuddīn invaded Ajmer, there was hardly any opposition at all. But in the last hour of his life Harirāja proved himself worthy of his great ancestry. Instead of surrendering to the enemy and leading an ignoble life of a slave, he burnt himself with his family on a funeral pile. His followers took shelter in Ranthambhor, and Ajmer fell into the hands of Qutbuddīn.

The eastern conquests were completed by Muhammad Bakhtyār Khaljī,[1] an adventurer and a soldier of fortune. He wrested Southern Bihār, defeated Lakshmaṇa Sena of Bengal by a sudden raid upon the city of Nadiyā, and conquered Western and Northern Bengal. The only effective check which Qutbuddīn received was from the Chaulukya king of Gujarāt who was supported by other chiefs. Qutbuddīn was defeated and forced to shut himself up at Ajmer till reinforcements from Ghaznī enabled him to take the field. He occupied the capital, Anhilwāra, but could not subdue the province. He, however, defeated the Chandellas, and the only power in Central India that remained unsubdued was the Paramāras of Mālwa. Thus in less than ten years after the second battle of Tarāin, the whole of Northern India, with the exception of Eastern Bengal, Northern Bihār (Tirhut), Mālwa, and Gujarāt, passed into the hands of the Ghurī king. But the Chandellas, as noted above, recovered their kingdom and even annexed the dominions ruled by the Kalachuris. Reference has also been made above to the brave resistance offered by some minor powers to the Muslim invaders.

Shihābuddīn Ghurī ascended the throne after his brother's death, but was himself killed in 1206, probably by a party of hill tribes called Khokars, on the bank of the Sindhu, in course of his return journey to Ghaznī from India. After his death the Ghurī dominions in Northern India passed to Qutbuddīn.

1. His full name is Ikhtiyāruddīn Muhammad Bakhtyār Khaljī. Some take him to be a son of Bakhtyār. He belonged to the Turkish tribe of Khalj which afterwards gave a line of Sultāns to the Muslim empire of Delhi, commonly known as Khiljī.

It is needless to add that the Muhammadan conquest of India was attended with horrors and cruelties beyond description. When Ajmer was captured, thousands of its inhabitants were put to the sword and the rest sold as slaves; and this was by no means an exceptional incident. Even religious establishments suffered the same fate. So completely did they massacre the monks in a Buddhist monastery in Bihār, that when they looked for somebody to explain the books in the library, not a living soul was to be found. Temples, monasteries, and other splendid monuments were wilfully destroyed and their materials used for buildings mosques.

CHAPTER X

Nepāl and Kāshmir

In order to complete the historical sketch of Northern India we must give some account of the two outlying kingdoms of Nepāl and Kāshmir, of which alone we possess some indigenous historical chronicles.

1. *Nepāl*

Nepāl is the only kingdom of ancient India that has maintained its independence without interruption up to the present time. The early history of the country is purely traditional. It is said to have been ruled at first by a dynasty of cowherds (*gopālas*) consisting of eight kings. They were overthrown by a dynasty of Āhirs or Ābhīras, who, as we have seen above, played an important part in the history of Western India in the early centuries of the Christian era. During the reign of the third king of this dynasty Nepāl was conquered by the Kirātas. The Kirāta is a well-known tribal name in ancient India. It is referred to in Vedic, Epic, and subsequent literature, and was probably a general designation of the Tibeto-Burman families living between the Himālaya and the Gangetic delta. Twenty-nine Kirāta kings ruled in Nepāl when the country was conquered by a Kshatriya prince from India named Nimisha. The dynasty of Nimisha consisted of five kings, the last of whom was overthrown by the Lichchhavis.

Early history.

With the Lichchhavi conquest begins the authentic history of Nepāl. The Lichchhavis were a well-known clan living in Videha at the time of Gautama Buddha. They were conquered by Ajātaśatru (p. 96) at the beginning of the fifth century B.C., and we do not hear of them again till they reappear under a monarchical constitution in Nepāl in the second or third century A.D. It is probable that when North India was invaded by the barbarous hordes from Central Asia, the Lichchhavis left the plains and sought the protection of the fastnesses of the Himālayas. About twenty-eight kings of this dynasty ruled for four or five hundred years, and their names are preserved in the genealogical lists and epigrphic records.

The Lichchhavis.

As has been said above, a Lichchhavi princess was married to Chandragupta I at the beginning of the fourth century A.D., and under Samudragupta Nepāl had to acknowledge the suzerainty of the Gupta empire. But with the decline of the Gupta empire the Lichchhavis became very powerful, and under Mānadeva, who reigned towards the end of the fifth or the beginning of the sixth century A.D., their sway extended beyond the valley of Nepāl both towards the east as well as towards the west. About the beginning of the seventh century A.D. there were some internal troubles, due perhaps to the resuscitation of the power of the Ābhīras. Aṁśuvarman, a powerful minister at the court, took advantage of this to establish his own supremacy, and ultimately usurped the throne. He probably married the daughter of the last Lichchhavi king, and founded a new royal dynasty which is known as Vaiśya-Thākuri, Vaiśya being the name of a Rājput clan to which Aṁśuvarman belonged.

Aṁśuvarman,

Shortly before this time the nomads of Central Asia, who lived to the west of the Chinese empire, were organised by a powerful leader who founded a kingdom in Tibet. Under the second king of this dynasty, Srong-btsan-Gam-po, the Charlemagne of Tibet, the kingdom was extended in all directions. The king of Nepāl, with some other potentates of India, had to acknowledge the supremacy of this new power, and was practically forced to give his daughter in marriage to its barbaric chief.

The death of Aṁśuvarman was followed by some troubles, and the Lichchhavi line was restored by Narendradeva who ascended the throne before 643 A.D. Śivadeva, son of Narendradeva, married a Maukhari princess, a grand-daughter of Ādityasena, the emperor of Magadha, while his son Jayadeva married the daughter of Harsha, the lord of Gauḍa, Oḍra, Kaliṅga, Kośala and other places. As this Harsha is said to have belonged to the race of Bhagadatta, he was probably a king of Kāmarūpa. We thus find that the kings of Nepāl had matrimonial relations with all the neighbouring chiefs.

For about 150 years after the death of Jayadeva Nepāl was a dependency of Tibet, which was then one of the most powerful States in Asia. In 838 the kingdom of Tibet passed on to one Dharma, or Glaṇ Darma. His brutality and cruelty led to revolutionary outbreaks, and the consequent dismemberment of the Tibetan empire. Nepāl took this opportunity to free itself from the

Tibetan Supremacy.

yoke, and the event was apparently celebrated by the foundation of a new era, known as Nepāla *Saṁvat*, in the year 879 A.D. In any case the new era marks a new chapter not only in the political history of Nepāl, but also in its economic prosperity. Flourishing towns grew up on all sides and Kātmāndu, the present capital city, was either established or raised to an important position about this time.

Nepāla Era.

From about the beginning of the eleventh century A.D. the feudal princes became very powerful in Nepāl. The kingdom was divided among two or three kings ruling in different parts, with Pātan, Kātmāndu, and Bhatgaon as their capitals, and the feudal barons often elected new members to the kingship. Towards the close of the 11th century A.D. Nepāl was conquered by the Karṇāṭaka king of Tirhut, called Nānyadeva, who made himself master of the entire territory, and reigned in all the three capitals (1098-1118 A.D.). After his death, the old dynasty was re-established in Nepāl, although it probably acknowledged the nominal suzerainty of the successor of Nānyadeva who ruled at Tirhut.

Nānyadeva.

Then a new line of kings, with names ending in Malla, appear in Nepāl. They probably belonged to the old Malla clan which, with the Lichchhavis, played such a prominent part in ancient India at the time of Gautama Buddha. Arimalladeva, the founder of this Malla dynasty, flourished at the beginning of the 13th century A.D. In 1287 the Khāsias invaded Nepāl from the east and devastated the country. Although their conquest was short-lived, the political solidarity of Nepāl was lost, and it was destined to be subjugated by another enemy at no distant date.

Malla Dynasty.

The descendants of Nānyadeva continued to rule at Tirhut long after the greater part of Northern India had passed into the hands of the Muhammadans. In the cold season of 1324-1325 A.D. Ghiyāsuddīn Tughlak came to Tirhut on his way from Bengal to Delhi. The reigning king Harisiṁha, unable to resist, fled to Nepāl and established his suzerainty over it without much difficulty. The kings of the Malla dynasty were suffered to exist as local chiefs, and the successors of Harisiṁha remained the real suzerains of the land for about 100 years, till Yaksha Malla, who ascended the throne about 1425 A.D., became undisputed master of the Nepalese territory. He was a great conqueror,

Harisiṁha.

and is reckoned to be the greatest king of the Malla dynasty. But an unwise move on his part brought ruin to his family.

He divided his vast possessions into four kingdoms, and gave them to his four children, a daughter and three sons. The inevitable struggle between these States, and the anarchy and confusion that set in, exhausted the resources of Nepāl till in 1768 it fell an easy prey to Pṛithi Nārāyan (Pṛithvī-Nārāyaṇa), the Rājput king of Gurkhā, a small principality in the basin of the seven Gaṇḍakis. The present rulers of Nepāl are descendants of this chief.

Gurkhā conquest

2. *Kāshmir*

The history of Kāshmir possesses a unique interest inasmuch as we are in a position to follow its course in a far more detailed manner than is possible with any other kingdom in India. This is due to the remarkable historical work by Kalhaṇa called *Rājataraṅgiṇī* to which reference has already been made.

a. *The end of the Kārkoṭa Dynasty*

We have already traced the history of Kāshmir up to the reign of Jayāpīḍa. He was followed by his son Lalitāpīḍa, one of the most infamous kings that disgraced the throne of Kāshmir. He ascended the throne towards the close of the eighth or the beginning of the ninth century A.D., and ruled or misruled for 12 years. He was a slave to his passions and neglected his royal duties. No wonder that the kingdom became the prey of courtesans and was defiled by immorality'. He had a concubine, the daughter of a spirit-distiller, named Jayādevī. Lalitāpīḍa was succeeded by his brother and the latter by the son of Jayādevī, called Bṛihaspati. During Bṛihaspati's reign the royal power was usurped by the five brothers of Jayādevī, who ultimately killed him. The brothers squandered the resources of the country, and at last fell out among themselves. Bloody battles ensued, and the fabric of government almost completely collapsed. A few puppets of the family of Lalitāditya were placed on the throne by the contending parties, till at last Avantivarman, grandson of Utpala, the eldest of the five brothers, was raised to the throne by the minister Śūra. Thus ended the Kārkoṭa dynasty which produced brilliant kings like Chandrāpīḍa and Muktāpīḍa

Lalitāpīḍa.

b. The Utpala Dynasty.

Avantivarman

The new king Avantivarman (855-883 A.D.) restored peace and put the government on a firm basis. He founded the town of Avantipur and built a large number of temples which, "though not equal in size to Lalitāditya's structures, yet rank among the most imposing monuments of ancient Kāshmir architecture." The minister Śūra wielded exceptional authority owing to the part he had played in the elevation of his master to the throne. But he was a type of the just and able statesmen who have played such prominent part in Indian history as royal ministers. He was a great patron of learned men and honoured them with a seat in the king's court. We are told that "the scholars, who were granted great fortunes and high honours, proceeded to the court in vehicles worthy of kings." He built a town, erected temples, and endowed monasteries. The king and the minister felt mutual regard for each other and Kalhaṇa tells an interesting story in this connection. One of the feudal barons of Kāshmir was attached to the minister and, emboldened by this connection, took away the villages belonging to a temple where the king had gone to worship Śiva. The king noticed the poverty of the priests and, on enquiry, learnt the truth. He did not say anything, but 'left the worship under pretence of indisposition.' On being apprised of the situation, Śūra sent for the feudal baron, and as soon as the latter arrived, cut off his head. He then inquired after the health of the king, and made him rise from his couch and complete the worship. The historian truly remarks that "such a king and such a minister, whose relations were never disfigured by the blemish of mutual hatred, have not otherwise been seen or heard of." One of the most important events in the glorious and peaceful reign of Avantivarman was the great engineering operations which were carried out by the skilful Suyya for the drainage of the valley and its irrigation. These not only protected the country from disastrous floods, but also extended the area of cultivation. The immense material benefits thus conferred upon the country stirred the popular imagination, and the memory of the great engineer is still preserved by the town of Sūryapura called after him. The manner of Avantivarman's death was characteristic of his life. He was a Vaishṇava at heart, but, out of regard for the minister, bore himself outwardly as a worshipper of Śiva. When his end was drawing near, he disclosed the secret to

Śūra with folded hands, and "listening to the end to the recital of the *Bhagavadgītā* and thinking of *Vaikuṇṭha* or the residence of Vishṇu, he cast off his earthly life with a cheerful mind."

The death of Avantivarman was followed by a struggle for succession among the numerous descendants of Utpala, but his son Śaṁkaravarman secured the throne, mainly owing to the exertions of the Chamberlain Ratnavardhana. Śaṁkaravarman's reign (885-902 A.D.) is memorable for his foreign expeditions. He first of all conquered Dārvābhisāra and Trigarta, and thus recovered the hill tracts immediately to the south of Kāshmir which were lost during the last days of the Kārkoṭa dynasty. But the greatest victory of Śaṁkaravarman was against the king of Gūrjara (between the Jhelum and Chenāb) in the Panjāb, which extended the territories of Kāshmir in that direction. The king of Gūrjara was supported by the illustrious Lalliya Shāhi, mentioned above (p. 300). King Śaṁkaravarman desired to remove Lalliya Shāhi from his sovereign position, but did not meet with much success. The result of his encounter with the Pratīhāra king Bhoja seems to have been equally indecisive.

Śaṁkarvarman.

At home Śaṁkaravarman digraced his reign by "skilfully designed exactions" and all kinds of oppression. Specially oppressive for the cultivators were the excessive demands made for forced labour. Kalhaṇa describes with much bitterness the baneful effects of this regime, 'which favoured only the rapacious tribe of officials, and left men of learning unprovided with emoluments.' Śaṁkaravarman's reign had a tragic end. After conquering numerous territories on the banks of the Sindhu he was returning through Urasa,[1] when, in course of a conflict with the inhabitants on account of the quartering of his troops, a man of a low caste struck him with an arrow. It is interesting to note how his death was concealed by his ministers till they reached a place of safety. We are told that by means of cords, which made his head bend down and rise like that of a puppet, they caused him to return the greetings of feudatories who had come to do homage. Gopālavarman, the son of Śaṁkaravarman, then ascended the throne, and ruled the kingdom (902-904 A.D.) under the guardianship of his mother Sugandhā. The widowed queen-mother was a woman of dissolute character, and bestowed her favours on the minister Prabhākaradeva. The

1. Hazara District.

latter plundered the riches of the kingdom, and when the king remonstrated, had his royal master murdered by sorcery (904 A.D.). Gopālavarman's brother was then raised to the throne, but he died after 10 days. Then Sugandhā herself assumed the royal power, but after two years the Tantrin soldiers, the Praetorian guard of Kāshmir, placed on the throne a child of ten years called Pārtha (906-921 A.D.). Eight years later Sugandhā returned at the head of an army, but was defeated, imprisoned, and killed. The Tantrins now became all-powerful in the State. The fabric of civil government almost completely collapsed, and the whole kingdom was a scene of oppressions, miseries, and calamities. A terrible famine broke out in 917-18 A.D. and while the people died in thousands, the king's ministers and the Tantrins became wealthy by selling stores of rice at high prices. The wretched king had to contest his position with his father, Paṅgu, and sometimes the one and sometimes the other gained the power through intrigues with the Tantrins. The court was dissolute and licentious in the extreme, and the two queens of Paṅgu vied with each other in offering to their ministers, as fees, the pleasures of love along with rich presents, in order to secure the throne for their respective sons. At last in 921 A.D. the Tantrins dethroned Pārtha and began to make and unmake kings at their pleasure. The throne was usually offered to the highest bidder. Thus Chakravarman and Śūravarman were successively placed on the throne and set aside. Then Pārtha was restored, only to be driven away, and Chakravarman, who offered great riches, was once more made king. As he could not pay the Tantrins, he fled in fear, and Śambhuvardhana was installed as king. Chakravarman now gathered a number of feudal chiefs, and with their countless hosts set forth to regain the kingdom. The Tantrins were signally defeated in a great battle and Chakravarman became king for the third time. Once firmly seated on the throne, Chakravarman abandoned himself to vile cruelties and excesses. He raised a low caste Ḍomba girl to the rank of chief queen, and subservience to her low-caste relatives became the only passport to high office and royal favour. The licentious practices of the court are too revolting to be described. At last Chakravarman was assassinated in the chamber of the Ḍomba girl, and such was the degradation of the court morality, that the murderers were freely urged

Sugandhā.

The Tantrins

Chakravarman

on by the king's own wives to crush his knees with a large stone, as he lay dying in the embrace of the Ḍomba girl (937 A.D.).

The next king Unmattāvanti, or mad Avanti was one of the worst despots that have ever disgraced a royal throne. The first acts of this depraved king were to starve his half-brothers to death and then to murder his father Pārtha. The horrible brutality that accompanied this act has no parallel in either history or fiction. The old man was dragged aways from his crying wife and children, and pulled along the street by his hair, and "then they killed him, unarmed as he was, emaciated by hunger and parched up, crying and naked." The king looked at the dead body with supreme pleasure, while his officers extolled before him their own prowess by pointing out the limbs where they had severally dealt their blows. One of them now struck his dagger into the dead body of Pārtha and, amused thereby, the king struck up a long continued laugh.

Mad Avanti

This mad and miscreant parricide had the womb of pregnant women cut open in order to see the child, and also used to cut off limbs of labourers in order to test their power of endurance. At last death carried away the vile king in 939 A.D. and a supposititious son Śūravarman (II) succeeded him. Before a week was over Kamalavardhana, the Commander-in-Chief, rose in revolt and occupied the capital. Strangely enough, he did not ascend the throne, but left the choice of the king to an assembly of Brāhmaṇas. The late king had destroyed all his relatives, and in the absence of a member of the royal family, the assembly elected a learned but poor commoner, Yaśaskara by name, to the throne of Kāshmir (939 A.D.).

Election of a king

The choice of the electors was fully justified by the benevolent rule of Yaśaskara. He restored order and discipline in the country, and Kāshmir obtained a much needed respite after the late troubles. Kalhaṇa praises the manifold virtues of this king and the beneficent nature of his rule. The unruly officials who plundered the royal treasury, were brought under control. and the land became so free from robbery that at night the shops were left open in the *bazzars*, and the roads were secure for travellers. Trade and agriculture flourished, and the moral tone of the people rapidly improved. The king's reputation

Yaśaskara

for justice and fairness spread in all directions, and some interesting anecdotes about it have been preserved by Kalhaṇa.

On the death of Yaśaskara his child-son became king in 948 A.D., but he was killed by the minister Parvagupta who usurped the throne (949 A.D.). Parvagupta died next year and was succeeded by his son Kshemagupta. Bad by nature, be became still more terrifying through the society of wicked persons, and was given to dissipation with dice, wine, and women. This licentious king married Diddā, daughter of the chief of Lohara and grand-daughter (daughter's daughter) of the Shāhi king Bhīma (p. 301). He died of a foul disease (958 A.D.) and his child-son Abhimanyu became king under the guardianship of Diddā. The queen-mother was a remarkable figure. Cruel, suspicious, unscrupulous, and licentious in the extreme, she combined in her character an inordinate lust for power with statesmanlike sagacity, political wisdom, and administrative ability. She drove away powerful officials from the court, and put down repeated revolts and popular risings by force or cunning. As Kalhaṇa relates, those treacherous ministers who, during sixty years (901-960 A. D.), had robbed sixteen kings, from Gopālavarman to Abhimanyu, of their dignity, lives, and riches, were all, together with their descendants and followers, quickly exterminated by the angry queen, whose rule was firmly established over the whole land. On the death of Abhimanyu, his young son Nandigupta became king in 972 A.D. But Diddā destroyed both Nandigupta and two other grandsons who succeeded him, and herself ascended the throne in 980 A.D. Her debauchery and licentiousness now knew no bounds, and one of her paramours, Tuṅga by name, and originally a *Khaśa* herdsman, was made Prime Minister. During her rule of 23 years, rebellions constantly broke out against Tuṅga, and the Brāhmaṇas held solemn fasts against him. But Diddā ruled over the whole kingdom till her death in 1003 A.D. when her nephew Saṁgrāmarāja of the Lohara dynasty obtained peaceful possession of the throne.

Ḍiddā.

c. Lohara Dynasty

The notable event in the reign of the new king was the expedition under Tuṅga sent to help the Shāhi king Trilochanapāla, son of Ānandapāla, against Sultān Mahmūd. Tuṅga obtained some successes, but was ultimately defeated and on his return to Kāshmir he was treacherously murdered with his son.

The next king Harirāja died after a reign of 22 days (1028 A.D.). The licentious queen-mother, who is credited with the murder of her royal son, tried to secure the crown, but her young son Ananta was raised to the throne.

Ananta

The early years of Ananta were full of troubles, but his courage was equal to the task. A revolt of the feudal chiefs was put down, and an invasion of the Dards and Muhammadans successfully repelled. Ananta's pious queen Sūryamatī played a leading part in this reign. She checked the extravagance and vagaries of the king, and gradually assumed full charge of the royal affairs. Her administration proved strong and efficient, and the authority of Kāshmir was established over neighbouring hill tracts. But one feminine weakness destroyed all the good she had done. Blinded by filial affection, she made the king abdicate the throne in favour of her son Kalaśa (1063 A.D.). Kalaśa was a licentious youth, and his dissolute character soon disgusted his parents. Open hostilities broke out, and after a prolonged struggle, Ananta committed suicide. Sūraymatī atoned for her faults by following her husband on the funeral pyre.

Kalaśa

Kalaśa 's character changed for the better after his parent's death, and he extended and consolidated the kingdom of Kāshmir. His son Harsha, however, revolted against him. The king put him in prison and designated his second son Utkarsha as his successor. He was, however, exasperated by his son's rebellion, and again took to the licentious life of his youthful days. On his death in 1089, due to these excesses, Utkarsha succeeded to the throne. He kept Harsha in confinement but soon a rebellion broke out, and Harsha took advantage of it not only to regain his freedom, but to secure the throne which belonged to him by right.

Harsha.

King Harsha was a remarkable person in many ways. Possessed of exceptional prowess, he obtained renown by merits rarely to be found in other kings. Versed in many languages, a good poet in all tongues, and a repository of different branches of learning, be hecame famous even in other kingdoms. But there were strange contrasts in his character. "Cruelty and kindheartedness, liberality and greed, violent selfwilledness and reckless supineness, cunning and want of thought,—these and other apparently irreconcileable features in turn display themselves in Harsha's chequered life."

The first acts of the king bore marks of sagacity and prudence. He retained the officials of the late regime, although some of them had acted against him. His confidence was well deserved, for when his brother raised a rebellion it was crushed without difficulty. Harsha introduced many elegant fashions in his court and encouraged learning by munificent gifts. He passed his nights in the assembly-hall, which was illuminated by a thousand lamps, attending meetings of learned men, musical performances and dances. But Harsha fell a prey to the licentiousness which proved a veritable ruin to many of his predecessors. He placed three hundred and sixty women in his seraglio and squandered his riches right and left.

Harsha sent an expedition against Rājapurī (Rajaori) and compelled its king to pay tribute. A dangerous conspiracy against him by his half-brother was sternly put down, and Harsha not only killed its authors but also other near relatives who took no part in it.

The reckless extravagance of the king involved him in grave financial difficulties. New and oppressive taxes were imposed, and the king not only seized the treasures of the temples, but even melted their images for the valuable metal of which they were made.

Harsha then abandoned himself to sensuality and excesses of all kinds, and spent the ill-gotten money in wicked follies of revolting character. It is probable that the king had a streak of insanity. That alone satisfactorily explains his incredible infatuations and horrible cruelties.

But the evil brought its own remedy. The king ruthlessly persecuted the feudal chiefs all over the kingdom and had arches and garlands made of their heads. The remaining chiefs combined under two brothers, Uchchala and Sussala of the Lohara family, and raised the standard of rebellion. Troops and officials deserted the doomed monarch, who fought till the last and, when the palace was burnt down, fled at night amid heavy downpour, accompanied by only two attendants. He was, however, soon overtaken and beheaded (1101 A.D.).

Uchchala, who now ascended the throne, was an able ruler and a cunning diplomat. He managed to put down the turbulent nobles and officials and consolidated the kingdom. But he fell a victim to a treacherous plot in 1111 A.D. A period of confusion followed, but ultimately Sussala occupied the throne in 1112 A.D. His cruelties and exactions provoked constant rebellions headed by the feudal chiefs. Bhikshāchara, the grandson of Harsha, put himself at the head of the rebels and drove away Sussala (1120 A.D.). The reign of Bhikshāchara was full of confusion and troubles, and at the end of a year Sussala recovered the throne. Bhikshāchara, however, continued the war with the help of some feudal lords, and at last had Sussala murdered in 1128 A.D. The latter's son Jayasiṁha, however, gained the throne, and within four months forced Bhikshāchara to leave the kingdom.

Jayasiṁha.

Although nominal peace was thus restored, the kingdom was utterly exhausted by the recent struggles. The power of the feudal lords had risen very high, and secure in their fortified residences like the feudal lords of Europe in Middle Age, they defied the power of the king. Sussala's whole reign was an unceasing but unsuccessful struggle to break their power by force of arms. Jayasiṁha wanted to achieve the same object by cunning diplomacy and unscrupulous intrigues which sometimes led him to commit acts of striking ingratitude and treachery.

Before two years were over, Jayasiṁha was faced with open rebellions of the feudal chiefs, and Bhikshāchara returned to try his luck once more. After a hard fight Bhikshāchara was defeated and killed, but almost immediately a new rival arose in Loṭhana, a half-brother of Uchchala, who crowned himself at Lohara. The royal troops sent against him were forced to retreat, and the retreat soon developed into a complete rout. But Jayasiṁha's intrigue succeeded where his forces had failed, and Lohara was retaken. By similar ignoble means the king got rid of a number of powerful feudal barons, and although these broke into rebellion again and again, his cunning diplomacy was always successful. Jayasiṁha ruled for twenty-seven years (1128-1155) and he enjoyed comparative peace during the last ten years of his reign. We even hear of a successful expedition undertaken by the king against the Yavanas during this period. Kalhaṇa brings his memorable history to a close with the reign of Jayasiṁha. But Hindu rule was continued in Kāshmir for two centuries more, and the old story of a succession of rebellions and internal disturbances repeated itself till 1339 A.D. when Shāh Mīr deposed queen Koṭā, the widow of the last Hindu ruler, and founded a Muhammadan dynasty.

Muslim conquest.

d. Lessons of the History of Kāshmir.

Although the history of Kāshmir possesses in the main only a local interest, the somewhat prolonged narrative of events given above is not without importance even from the point of view of Indian history as a whole. As may be easily gathered from a perusal of the preceding pages of this book, by far the greater part of Indian history merely resolves itself into a history of the provincial States. Unfortunately, very few details of any provincial history are known to us, and we are therefore not in a position to form any concrete idea of these provincial governments. Kalhaṇa's history furnishes a detailed account of one of these States, and this may serve as a type of the rest.

Kalhaṇa's history teaches us several striking lessons. It shows us to what great extent the fate of a kingdom was dependent upon the character of its sovereign, and how little there was of that political consciousness of the community at large, which in every healthy State shapes its destiny. People patiently endured acts of wanton cruelty and despotic whim, and although there were rebellions, they were prompted by the class interests of the feudal barons, and not by the interests of the people at large.

The second great lesson of the history of Kāshmir is the evil influence of harem upon the king and the kingdom. The incredible sensuality of the kings and queens of Kāshmir, which brought untold sufferings upon the State, throws a lurid light on the manners and customs of the age, and gives a rude shock to the fond illusion of benevolent despotism of our ancient rulers.

Thirdly, the history of Kāshmir portrays a sad lack of character among officials, both high and low. Among the large crowd which Kalhaṇa has drawn on his canvas, including persons of all ranks from the king to the meanest official, the number of those who showed steadfast loyalty, stern morality, a deep sense of duty, or even an appreciation of ordinary moral rules is meagre in the extreme.

Fourthly, Kāshmir holds out before us a ghastly picture of court life, where debauchery reigns supreme, and intrigues and rebellions follow one another in quick succession.

Fifthly, patriotism or statesmanship in a broad sense is conspicuous by its absence. We do not find anything like a national rising against the Muhammadans. Nay, the kings of Kāshmir even employed them to subserve their own ends.

There is hardly any consciousness of India as motherland, characterising the actions of any of the Kāshmir kings.

Some of these characteristics, notably the last, may be due to the isolated position of Kāshmir, but it will not be unfair to assume that the rest, or most of them, are applicable to other mediaeval Indian States as well.

On the other hand, there are many relieving features to this dismal picture, equally typical of Indian States as a whole. Although in political development and barbarous cruelty the people of Kāshmir might very well be likened to the Europeans in Middle Age still in refinement, culture, and all that go to make up civilization, they were in a far more advanced stage. Learning flourished and was very much appreciated in the country. Fine arts like music and dance were cultivated by the king and people alike. Art and architecture greatly prospered, and even the worst kings and their officials continued the pious practice of building temples and monasteries. In religion and philosophy Kāshmir showed remarkable progress, and evolved a new school of Śaivism, whose humanity and rationality are in strange contrast to the horrible and ghastly picture of many Śaiva sects that preceded it.

Although administration was sadly disgraced by wicked kings and their parasites, noble examples like those of Chandrāpīḍa, Avantivarman, and Yaśaskara show that the ideals of justice and good administration were both high and noble. A very interesting feature was the administrative ability displayed by the queens. Although , unfortunately, it was in most cases accompanied by a dissolute character, still the careers of Diddā, Sugandhā and Sūryamatī, apart from a host of minor ones, throw interesting light on the opportunities afforded to women in public life, and their capacity for utilising them.

But the best period of Kāshmir history is the one in which she enjoyed a brief spell of imperialism under Lalitāditya. All that was good and bright in a nation brilliantly shone forth, and the petty provincial State was raised to the pinnacle of glory by a succession of eminent rulers. The history of Kāshmir since that date is written in decay.

CHAPTER XI

Rise and Fall of Empires in the Deccan

1. *The Rāshṭrakūṭas.*

We have already recounted how the Rāshṭrakūṭa dynasty wrested the supreme power from the Chālukyas and then entered into a struggle for Indian empire with the two northern powers, the Pālas and the Gurjaras. We shall now deal with the history of the dynasty from the accession of Dhruva I where we left it (above, p. 281). After defeating and dethroning his elder brother Govinda II, about 780 A.D., Dhruva proceeded to punish the kings of Gaṅgavāḍi (Mysore) and Kāñchī who had espoused the cause of the latter. He defeated the Gaṅga king Śrī Purusha Muttarasa, took his son Śivamāra prisoner and annexed the whole of Gaṅgavāḍi, thus extending the Rāshṭrakūṭa kingdom as far as Kāveri to the south. The Pallava ruler was also forced to come to terms.

Dhruva

After thus settling the affairs in the south, Dhruva planned an elaborate campaign to North India. The struggle between Vatsarāja and Dharmapāla, the two premier rulers of North India, gave him the requisite opportunity and, as we have seen above, he defeated them both and carried his victorious arms to the Gaṅgā-Yamunā *doab*. To commemorate his great victory, the symbols of these two rivers were included in the Rāshṭrakūṭa banner. Dhruva perhaps never intended his northern campaign to be anything more than a victorious march or a plundering raid. In any case, he did not make any effort to consolidate his conquests and returned to his kingdom in 790 A.D. When he died, three years later, the power and prestige of the Rāshṭrakūṭas rose very high indeed. He had humbled all the great rulers of India and there was none between the Himālaya and Cape Comorin to challenge his authority.

Dhruva nominated a younger son Govinda III as his successor, and appointed the elder son Stambha as viceroy of Gaṅgavāḍi. As could be expected, Stambha rebelled against his brother, and was helped by the Pallava king and the Gaṅga crown-prince Śivamāra whom Govinda III had magnanimously released from prison. What is unusual, however, is that after defeating and imprisoning Stambha, Govinda III again made him viceroy of Gaṅgavāḍi and he remained loyal throughout his life—a rare instance in history. Śivamāra was again put into prison and the Pallava king came to terms.

Govinda III

Like his father Govinda III also led a military expedition to North India and his success was equally brilliant. As noted above, he defeated Nāgabhaṭa, and both Dharmapāla and Chakrāyudha submitted to him. Govinda III is even said to have proceeded up to Himālaya and visited Prayāga (Allāhābād), Banaras, and Gayā. Whether Govinda III intended to make a prolonged stay in North India and consolidate his dominions there, we do not know. But events in the south forced him to return, about 800 A.D., and the whole North Indian campaign probably did not last for more than two years.

Taking advantage of Govinda's absence in the north, the Eastern Chālukya ruler of Veṅgi, Vijayāditya II, rose against the Rāshṭrakūṭas, but Govinda III defeated him and put his younger brother Bhīma on the throne (c. 802 A.D.). More formidable was the hostile confederacy of the Gaṅga, Pallava, Pāṇḍya, and Kerala rulers, but Govinda defeated them all and even occupied Kāñchī, the capital of the Pallavas (802 A.D.). Once more all the powers between Himālaya and Cape Comorin were defeated, and practically the whole of India had to acknowledge the Rāshṭrakūṭa supremacy.

The Rāshṭrakūṭas had reached the high watermark of power and glory, but decline set in soon after the death of Govinda III in 814 A.D. His son and successor Amoghavarsha was a boy of 13 or 14, and Karka, the nephew of Govinda III and viceroy of Gujarāt and Mālava, was appointed regent. But soon rebellion broke out on all sides and it assumed so serious proportions that the boy king had to flee from his capital in 818 A.D. But Karka restored order and Amoghavarsha recovered his throne within three years.

Amoghavarsha

Vijayāditya, who was dethroned by Govinda III, had recovered the throne of Veṅgi and headed the rebellion. Amoghavarsha defeated him in 830 A.D. and occupied Veṅgi for more than ten years till it was recaptured by a general of Vijayāditya some time before 845 A.D.

Amoghavarsha, however, lost Gaṅgavāḍi. After almost continuous war for twenty years the Rāshṭrakūṭa forces had to evacuate the kingdom, and an alliance between the two rulers was established by the marriage of Amoghavarsha's daughter with the Gaṅga prince Būtuga.

Karka, the regent in the minortiy administration, had saved the Rāshṭrakūṭa kingdom in a great crisis, and retired to his own viceroyalty of Gujarāt and Mālava after Amoghavarsha attained majority and took up the reins of administration in his own hands. Cordial relation subsisted between the two, but soon after Karka died (c. 830 A.D.) and was succeeded in his office by his son Dhruva I, a disastrous war broke out between the king and the new viceroy. It continued for 25 years and was only concluded when Pratīhāra Bhoja threatened the northern provinces of the Rāshṭrakūṭa dominions. Dhruva II, the grandson of Dhruva I, came to an understanding with Amoghavarsha and the unity of the Rāshṭrakūṭas frustrated the efforts of Bhoja I, as mentioned above.

Amoghavarsha died about 878 A.D. after a long reign of more than sixty years. He did not inherit the military genius of his father or grandfather, and though he maintained peace and order, the Rāshṭrakūṭa power suffered a visible decline during his reign. But he had a remarkable personality and is an admirable illustration of the famous dictum that peace hath her victories as well as war. He was himself an author of repute, and composed a work on poetics named *Kavirājamārga*, one of the earliest texts in Kanarese literature that have come down to us. A number of famous Jaina and Hindu authors lived in his court, and his catholicity extended even to the religious creeds. He revered both Jaina and Brāhmaṇa gods, and in later life spent much time on religious devotion and practices. His ideal of royal duties was such that on the outbreak of a severe epidemic he actually cut off his own finger and offered it to a goddess in the belief that it would be an effective remedy. He died as he lived, and drowned himself in the sacred river Tuṅgabhadrā in right Jaina fashion.

Kṛishṇa II

The reign of Kṛishṇa II, the son and successor of Amoghavarsha, was a disastrous one. The Eastern Chālukya king Vijayāditya III invaded his dominions, inflicted serious defeats upon him, though he was helped by the Kalachuris, and even advanced as far as the Rāshṭrakūṭa capital and burnt it. Kṛishṇa II ultimately succeeded in defeating the Chālukyas, and even captured king Bhīma, the successor of Vijayāditya III. Bhīma obtained his release by agreeing to rule as a feudatory to the Rāshṭrakūṭa king; then he rebelled and was again defeated. As mentioned above, Kṛishṇa II was also unsuccessful in his wars with the Pratīhāra Bhoja I who conquered Mālwa and Kāthiāwār Peninsula. The Gujarāt Branch of the Rāshṭrakūṭa viceroys also came to an end shortly after 888 A.D.

Kṛishṇa II died about 914 A.D., and was succeeded by his grandson Indra III, whose father Jagattuṅga had already died.

Indra III

Soon after his accession Indra III led a brilliant military campaign to North India in course of which he defeated Pratīhāra Mahīpāla and devastated his capital city Kanauj. It was however a plunderig raid and led to no permanent conquest. Indra was also successful in his war with the Eastern Chālukyas. He defeated and killed their king Vijayāditya V, but did not annex his kingdom.

Indra III died in 922 A.D. and was succeeded by his son Amoghavarsha II. But soon Govinda IV seized the throne by murdering his elder brother. His vicious life, tyranny, and oppression alienated the people and the officials, who invited his uncle Amoghavarsha to occupy the throne. Govinda was easily defeated and Amoghavarsha III became king in 936 A.D.

Amoghavarsha III had a short reign of three years during which the administration was really carried on by his son

Kṛishṇa III

Kṛishṇa. The latter defeated the Gaṅga king and put on the throne his younger brother Būtuga who had married a daughter of the Rāshṭrakūṭa king. Kṛishṇa also led a successful expedition to North India and captured the two important fortresses of Kālañjar and Chitrakūṭa.

Soon after his accession in 939 A.D. Kṛishṇa III, in alliance with his brother-in-law Būtuga, the ruler of Gaṅgavāḍi, led a campaign to South India. They captured Kāñchī and Tanjore in 943 A.D., and six years later inflicted a crushing defeat upon the Cholas at the famous battle of Takkolam in which the Chola crown-prince Rājāditya was killed by Būtuga. Following this great victory Kṛishṇa marched triumphantly up to Rāmesvaram and planted his pillar of victory on the shore of the southern sea. The Cholas recovered their kingdom, but Kṛishṇa annexed Toṇḍaimaṇḍalam (Arcot, Chingleput, and Vellore Districts).

Kṛishṇa also interfered in the affairs of Veṅgi and put on its throne Bāḍapa (956 A.D.) who remained a loyal feudatory to him. Kṛishṇa also led another expedition to North India in 963 A.D. He proceeded to Mālwa and captured Ujjayinī, and advanced as far as Bundelkhand. By his brilliant victories Kṛishṇa III once more raised the power and prestige of the Rāshṭrakūṭas to a high degree. But it was the last flicker of the lamp before it finally went out.

Khoṭṭiga

Khoṭṭiga,[1] who succeeded his elder brother Kṛishṇa in 967 A.D., was old and a weak ruler. The Paramāra king Sīyaka, in revenge for the occupation of Ujjayinī by Kṛishṇa III, invaded the Rāshṭrakūṭa dominions. He marched triumphantly up to the capital city Mālkheḍ, and sacked it in 972 A.D. Shortly afterwards Khoṭṭiga died of a broken heart.

Karka II, the nephew and successor of Khoṭṭiga, far from restoring the shattered prestige of the kingdom, made the situation worse by his vicious maladministration. Taking advantage of the resulting chaos and confusion, Chālukya Taila (or Tailapa), a feudatory chief of Tardavāḍi (Bijāpur District), rebelled against the king and defeated him in a pitched battle in 973 A.D. Although Karka II fled to Mysore and continued to rule over a small principality there till 991 A.D., the Rāshṭrakūṭa kingdom was seized by Taila. The Gaṅga king Mārasiṁha made an effort to regain it for his nephew Indra, a grandson of Kṛishṇa III, but was defeated in 974 A.D. Both Mārasiṁha and Indra became Jaina monks, and Taila became the undisputed ruler of the Deccan.

2. *The Later Chālukyas.*

Taila II

The second Chālukya dynasty, known in history as the Chālukyas of Kalyāṇa from the name of their capital city (Kalyāṇa or Kalyāṇapura, modern Kalyāṇi in the Nizam's dominions), was probably allied to, but not a continuation of the first, though Taila, who founded the new dynasty, claimed direct descent from the Chālukyas of Bādāmi. Immediately after his accession he was involved in a war with Pañchaladeva who had made himself master of the northern part of the Gaṅga kingdom. Though at first reduced to great straits Taila II (counting Taila

1. Also spelt 'Khoṭika' and 'Koṭṭiga'.

of Bādāmi as the first ruler of that name) ultimately defeated him and seized his kingdom. He also gained a victory over the Chola king Uttama some time before 980 A.D. In the north he defeated the Śilāhāras of Southern Koṅkaṇ as well as the Yādavas of Seuṇa-*deśa* (region round Daulatābād), and both, hitherto feudatories of the Rāshṭrakūṭas, now acknowledged his supremacy. He also conquered Lāṭa and placed it in charge of his general Bārappa. Having thus consolidated his dominions in the Deccan, Taila, as already mentioned above, carried his victorious arms against the Chālukyas of Gujarāt, the Paramāras of Mālwa, and the Kalachuris of Chedi. His fight with Muñja, the Paramāra king, and the defeat and death of the latter, have already been referred to above.

Satyāśraya

Satyāśraya, who succeeded his father Taila II in 997 A.D., was defeated by the Paramāra Sindhurāja who recovered the dominions wrested from Muñja. The Kalachuri Kokalla II also claims to have defeated him. Satyāśraya, however, defeated the Śilāhāras of Northern Koṅkaṇ who acknowledged his supremacy.

The most memorable event in Satyāśraya's reign was his fight with the Cholas. Rājarāja the Great invaded his kingdom with 900,000 soldiers and at first carried everything before him. He advanced far into the Deccan and ravaged the country, but was ultimately defeated and forced to retreat. Satyāśraya then took the offensive and conquered all the enemy territories up to Kurnool and Guntur districts.

Jayasiṁha II.

Satyāśraya was succeeded by his three sons who ruled one after another. The youngest of them, Jayasiṁha II, whose known dates range between A.D. 1015 and 1043, was faced by a hostile confederacy of three such powerful kings as Kalachuri Gāṅgeya-deva, Paramāra Bhoja, and Rājendra Chola. They simultaneously attacked him from the north and south, but in spite of some initial successes they ultimately gained nothing. It reflects great credit upon Jayasiṁha II, that single-handed he defended his kingdom against three such powerful adversaries and drove out all of them. It is interesting to note that the confederacy was organised by the Paramāra and Kalachuri kings some time before 1019 A.D., i.e. at the very moment when Sultān Mahmūd was harrying North India. How one would wish that such a powerful confederacy were organised against him rather than against an Indian ruler. Jayasiṁha II showed equal ability in suppressing the rebellion of his feudal chiefs and officials. He ruled from Kalyāṇa, in Bidar District, where the capital was removed from Mānyakheṭa. either during his reign or shortly before it.

Someśvara I Āhavamalla, the son and successor of Jayasiṁha II, had a long and eventful reign whose known dates range between A.D. 1043 and 1068. Immediately after his accession he was involved in a war with the Cholas which dragged on, with short intervals, almost throughout his reign, and even beyond it. The Chola king Rājādhirāja invaded his dominions, defeated successively three armies that opposed him, and marched triumphantly to Kalyāṇa which was sacked and burnt. Someśvara fled and Rājādhirāja returned home, richly laden with booty, after overrunning the whole of the Deccan. Rājādhirāja led two more expeditions, one before 1047 A.D. and another in 1051-52 A.D. The last is famous for the great battle that was fought at Koppam, a place not yet satisfactorily identified. Rājādhirāja was killed and the Chola army broke into confusion, when his brother Rājendradeva rallied it and obtained a decisive victory. Someśvara, who lost his brother and many generals, fled and the Chola Rājendradeva crowned himself king in the battlefield.

Someśvara

But Someśvara also retaliated by invading the Chola dominions. Some time before the battle of Koppam he had captured Kāñchī. He led two more expeditions between 1058 and 1061 A.D., but was defeated in the last.

Vīrarājendra, who succeeded Rājendra, claims to have defeated Someśvara no less than five times. Some of these battles took place in connection with the Eastern Chālukya kingdom and will be related elsewhere. The most famous battle between the two rival kings was fought in 1062 A.D. at Kūḍalsangam, a place not yet definitely identified. After a fierce battle, which was fought with great fury on both sides, the Chālukyas were completely beaten. Someśvara fled with his sons, but his wife and treasures fell into the hands of Vīrarājendra. The Cholas long remembered with justifiable pride this great victory over the Chālukyas. Someśvara sought to avenge this defeat, but was defeated again and again between 1063 and 1067 A.D. His son Vikramāditya, however, led a successful expedition in 1067-68 A.D. and plundered the Chola capital. On the whole this long-drawn war led to no permanent gain of territories on either side.

In spite of almost continual war with the Cholas Someśvara found time to engage in hostilities with other powers. He not only conquered North Koṅkaṇ but also invaded Gujarāt and Mālava and fought with Kalachuri Karṇa as mentioned above (p. 324). He raided South Kosala in the east and Kerala on the west, and subdued the revolt of the Yādavas of Seuṇa-*deśa*. Someśvara wanted to install his second son Vikramāditya as *yuvarāja* on account of his remarkable abilities, but he declined the honour in favour of his elder brother. Instead, he set out on a campaign of 'world conquest' and conquered a large number of countries including Bengal, Assam, Veṅgi, Chola, Pāṇḍya, Kerala, and Ceylon.

Someśvara was succeeded by his eldest son Someśvara II in A.D. 1068. But the Chola king Vīrarājendra, who had married his daughter to Vikramāditya, led an expedition against him to secure the crown for his son-in-law. He gained some successes at first, but was ultimately defeated by Someśvara II, and Vikramāditya also submitted to his brother. Someśvara II then led an expedition to the north and occupied Mālava for some time as related above (p. 327).

Vikramāditya was acting as the governor of southern territories under his elder brother when his father-in-law Vīrarājendra died. As there was some trouble, Vikramāditya marched to the Chola country, put down the revolt, and placed Vīrarājendra's son Adhirājendra on the throne. But Adhirājendra lost his life in a popular outbreak, and Kulottuṅga occupied the Chola throne. Vikramāditya tried, but failed, to dislodge him. While engaged in hostility with the Cholas, Vikramāditya rose against his brother Someśvara II, defeated and imprisoned him, and ascended the throne in 1076 A.D. Bilhaṇa's *Vikramāṅka-charita* or Life of Vikramāditya justifies his patron's action on the ground that Someśvara II was a vicious and cruel king who neglected his duties. But it is difficult to say how far the court-poet gives us the whole truth.

Vikramāditya VI

Vikramāditya VI had a glorious reign of 50 years (1076-1126 A.D.) and is chiefly known for his victorious military expeditions both in the north and south. He had fought in the numerous wars of his father's reign, and undertook a world-conquest even while he was a prince. According to the *Vikramāṅka-charita* and the numerous inscriptions of his reign Vikramāditya VI conquered Gurjara, Ḍāhala, Maru, Sindhu, Turushka,

Kāshmir, Vidarbha, Nepāl and Vaṅga in North India. This is undoubtedly a great exaggeration, but there is no doubt that Vikramāditya crossed the Narmadā some time before 1088 A.D. and came into conflict with the Chaulukyas and Kalachuris of Ratanpur.

But we possess more detailed and definite information about his conquests in Deccan and South India. His younger brother, who had revolted against him after A.D. 1082, was defeated and imprisoned. He also successfully put down the revolts of the Hoysalas of Dorasamudra (Mysore), Kadambas of Goa, the Śilāhāras of Koṅkaṇ and the Yādavas of Seuṇa. The Hoysala king Vishṇuvardhana fought valiantly and gained some victories, but had to acknowledge the supremacy of Vikramāditya.

The war with the Cholas was continued during his reign. Some time before 1085 A.D. he captured Kāñchī. There was a prolonged fight with Kulottuṅga Chola over the possession of the Eastern Chālukya kingdom, which frequently changed hands.

Vikramāditya assumed the title Tribhuvanamalla, and started an era from the year of his accession. The new *Vikrama-Saṁvat*, however, did not long survive his death. His empire extended as far as the Narmadā in the north and Cuddapa district and Mysore in the south. In the east, it sometimes extended up to the sea, as it certainly did in the west. Besides the great Kāshmirian poet Bilhaṇa, mentioned above, the celebrated jurist Vijñāneśvara, the author of *Mitāksharā*, lived in his court.

Someśvara III

Someśvara III, the son and successor of Vikramāditya VI, had to fight hard with the Hoysala king Vishṇuvardhana who invaded his dominions, but ultimately defeated this powerful feudal chief. He is credited with conquest of Andhra, Tamil country, Magadha and Nepāl. The first two no doubt refer to his fight with the Cholas, but though he might have attained some success at first, he lost the Eastern Chālukya kingdom some time before 1134 A.D. It is difficult to believe that he led expeditions to Magadha and Nepāl. But it is true that some dynasties of Karṇāṭa origin ruled in Nepāl, Bengal, and Bihār about this time. They were porbably founded in the wake of the invasion of Vikramāditya VI, and the Chālukya officials regarded them as subordinate to Someśvara III. He was a very learned scholar and composed the work *Mānasollāsa* or *Abhilasitārtha-chintāmaṇi*.

Jagadekamalla, who succeeded Someśvara III in A.D. 1138, had to face the rebellions of a number of feudatories including the Hoysalas and Kadambas, but put them down. His invasion of Mālava and fight with Chaulukya Kumārapāla have been mentioned above (p. 328). He also fought successfully with Kulottuṅga Chola II and Anantavarman Choḍagaṅga of Kaliṅga. He was succeeded by his younger brother Taila III in or shortly after 1151 A.D.

Taila III was attacked by the Chaulukya Kumārapāla and Kulottuṅga Chola II. Shortly after he had repulsed them the feudatory Kākatīya chief Prola of Telingana revolted, and Taila marched against him. Taila was, however, defeated and taken prisoner. Though Prola released him, this incident gave a severe blow to the prestige of the Chālukyas. Some time before 1162 Rudra, successor of Prola, again severely defeated Taila III and crushed the power of the Chālukyas. Feudatory chiefs revolted on all sides and one of them, Bijjala of the Kalachuri clan, seized the sovereignty of the Deccan in 1156 A.D. He occupied the capital city some time before 1160 A.D., but paid nominal allegiance to Taila III so long as he lived.

Taila III

Bijjala restored order in the kingdom by defeating the numerous feudatory chiefs who had revolted, and also fought successfully with the Cholas, Gaṅgas of Kaliṅga, the Chaulukyas, and the Kalachuris of Tripurī. The statement in some later records that he conquered Aṅga, Vaṅga, Magadha, Nepāla, Turushka, and Siṁhala seems to be merely a conventional praise.

Usurpation by Bijjala

According to a tradition, recorded in many literary works of a late period, Bijjala, who was a patron of the Jainas, quarrelled with his minister, Basava, the founder of the Liṅgāyat sect, and was killed by him. But the truth of this story may be doubted, as according to earlier and more reliable epigraphic evidence, Bijjala abdicated the throne in 1168 A.D. in favour of his son Someśvara.

Someśvara is credited with many victories, including those against the Cholas, Gaṅgas, and Chaulukyas, and died in 1177 A.D. His younger brother Saṅkama, who ruled from 1177 to 1180 A.D., is also said to have conquered many countries from Bengal to Ceylon.

Successors of Bijjala

Āhavamalla, the younger brother and successor or Saṅkama, also makes similar boastful claims. But during his reign, Someśvara IV, son of the Chālukya king Taila III, wrested a considerable portion of the Deccan and restored the Chālukya kingdom in 1181 A.D. Though Āhavamalla still continued to rule over a small principality, and was succeeded by his younger brother Siṅghaṇa in 1183 A.D., the latter submitted to Someśvara IV within a year.

But Someśvara IV was not destined to enjoy his ancestral kingdom for a long time. The Yādavas drove him out of the Deccan before 1189 A.D., and he took refuge with his feudatory chief of Goa who acknowledged his supremacy till 1198 A.D. Nothing is known of him or of his family after this date.

3. *The Yādavas.*

The Yādavas claimed to belong to the family of Yadu to which the epic hero Kṛishṇa belonged, and literature and inscriptions contain elaborate account of their genealogy. Within histroical times we find two of their ruling families, one in Seuṇa-*deśa*, i.e. the country round Devagiri or Daulatābād, and the other, better known as Hoysalas, at Dorasamudra (modern Halebid) in Mysore. Both these families were feudatories to the Rāshṭrakūṭas and Western Chālukyas, and first came into prominence about the tenth century A.D. The southern family became very powerful at the beginning of the twelfth century A.D. and Vishṇuvardhana even invaded the Chālukya territory with a view to establish his suzerainty in the Deccan. His attempts were, however, foiled by the Chālukya kings as noted above. The northern family was equally ambitious and more successful.

Bhillama

Bhillama (1185-1193) defeated both the Kalachuris and the Western Chālukyas, and made himself master of the greater part of the Chālukya empire in the Deccan. He established his capital at Devagiri (modern Daulatābād) and henceforth the family was known as the Yādavas of Devagiri.

The Hoysalas were not slow to take advantage of the situation and renewed their efforts for establishing a preponderant position in southern politics. They easily defeated the nominal Chālukya king, and then ensued a contest for supremacy between the two Yādava families.

Bhillama was at first more successful and overran the dominions of Hoysala Vīra-Ballāla II as far as Seringapatam on the Kāveri. He even defeated the Chola king Kulottuṅga III. But later, Ballāla II defeated Bhillama

c. 1188 A. D. and forced him to leave the Hoysala country. Four years later Ballāla II took the aggressive and conquered the Yādava dominions in the south as far as the Krishnā.

Bhillama, though checked in the south, carried his victorious arms in the north and defeated Vindhyavarman of Mālava and Bhīma II of Gujarāt. He is also credited with victories over many other States, but was defeated by the Chāhamānas of Naḍḍula.

Bhillama's son and successor Jaitrapāla or Jaitugi (1193-1200 A.D.) was also a great conqueror. He successfully fought with the Kākatīyas, the Gaṅgas, and the Cholas in the south and the Paramāras and Chaulukyas in the north.

Siṅghaṇa.

Jaitugi's son and successor Siṅghaṇa was the greatest ruler of the family. He defeated the Hoysalas, wrested back the territories acquired by them from his grandfather, and established the undisputed supremacy of the family in the Deccan. He made extensive conquests in the north. He successfully invaded Gujarāt several times and conquered Lāṭa. He also defeated the king of Mālava, a Muhammadan ruler of the north, and the Kalachuris, or Chedis of Chattisgarh and Jubbulpore. The Śilāhāras of Kolhāpura, the Kadambas of Goa, and various other petty principalities in the Deccan submitted to him. In commemoration of his victorious expedition against the Hoysalas he erected a column of victory on the bank of the Kāveri. Thus during the long reign of Siṅghaṇa (1200-1247), who assumed the full titles of a paramount sovereign, the Yādavas of Devagiri ruled over an extensive empire which not only embraced nearly the whole of the Deccan, but also a part of southern India beyond the Kṛishnā.

Siṅghaṇa was succeeded by his two grandsons Kṛishṇa (1247-1260 A.D.) and Mahādeva (1260-1271 A.D.). They maintained the empire intact and fought successfully with the powerful neighbouring kings in the south and the north, as well as with the petty chiefs in the Deccan. Some territories beyond the Tuṅgabhadrā were wrested from the Hoysalas, and Northern Koṅkaṇ was annexed by Mahādeva. His minister was the famous Hemādri who credits his master with decisive victory against the Vāghelās of Gujarāt, the Paramāras of Mālava and the Kākatīyas of Telingana (Warangal).

The next king Rāmachandra, son of Kṛishṇa, made a final attempt to annex the Hoysala country. He sent a well-equipped force which advanced up to the capital city Dvārasamudra, but was driven away from its gates. He also met with failure in his invasion of Gujarāt. but won some successes against a number of petty chiefs. He was the last independent king of the dynasty. Alāuddīn Khiljī, the nephew of the Muhammadan ruler of Delhi, invaded his dominions in 1296 (or 1295). Being defeated in the open field, the king shut himself in his fort, and concluded a peace on condition of an annual tribute, cession of certain territories, and an immediate payment of "600 maunds of pearls, two of jewels, 1000 of silver, 4000 pieces of silk and other precious things." This shattered the power and prestige of the Yādavas, and the Hoysalas in the south and the Kākatīyas in the east, far from making a common cause against the Muslims, aggrandised themselves at the expense of the Yādavas. Some years later Rāmachandra refused to pay tribute, but was defeated by the Muhammadan general Kāfūr[1] in 1307 A.D. He was taken prisoner to Delhi, but was released and ruled his state as a vassal chief. Five years later his son Śaṅkara (or Siṅghaṇa II)[2] again asserted independence, but was again defeated and killed by Kāfūr in 1313 A.D. After the death of Alāuddīn Khiljī, Harapāla, the son-in-law of Rāmachandra, raised a revolt, but was taken prisoner and flayed alive. Then the Deccan became a Muhammadan province.

Rāmachandra

4. *The Kākatīyas.*

The Kākatīyas traced their descent from one Karikala-Chola, Śūdra by caste and belonging to Durjaya family, who settled in Kākatipura. The earliest known king of this family was Beta I who took advantage of the confusion caused by the invasion of Rājendra Chola and carved a small kingdom in the Nalgonda district (Hyderābād). His son and successor, Prola I, rendered distinguished services to his suzerain the Chālukya Someśvara I, and received as reward Anmakoṇḍa-vishaya (Hanamkonda in Warangal, Hyderābād). The next king Beta II (1079-1090 A.D.) received further territories from Vikramāditya and established his capital at Anmakoṇḍa.

1. Kāfūr got the title Malik Nāib or Lieutenant of the kingdom, and is commonly referred to as Malik Kāfūr.

2. There is difference of opinion among scholars about the correct form of this name.

His son and successor, Prola II (1115), took advantage of the disintegration of the Chālukya dominion to aggrandise himself by conquering the feudal chiefs in Telingana and Andhra countries. The Chālukya king Tailapa III attacked him, but was defeated and made a prisoner, as noted above. Prola II released him, but henceforth ruled as an independent king.

Rudra I, the son and successor of Prola II, again defeated Tailapa III, some time before 1162 A.D., and conquered the Kurnool District before 1185 A.D.

The next king Mahādeva was defeated and killed by the Yādava Siṅghaṇa. Mahādeva's son Gaṇapati, who ascended the throne in 1198 A.D., was the most powerful ruler of this family. The disintegration of the Chola empire led to a triangular fight between the Pāṇḍyas, Hoysalas, and the Kākatīyas. Ganapati conquered nearly the whole of Andhra, Nellore, Kāñchī, Kurnool and Cuddapah districts and thus ruled over a vast empire, though some time after 1250 A.D. Jaṭāvarman Sundara Pāṇḍya defeated him and wrested Nellore and Kāñchī. Gaṇapati transferred his capital to Oruṅgallu (Warangal).

Gaṇapati was succeeded by his daughter Rudrāmbā some time after 1261 A.D. She was defeated by the Yādava king Mahādeva. Ambadeva, the feudal chief of Cuddapah and Kurnool districts, declared independence. But Marco Polo, who visited Moṭupalli, the important seaport of the Kākatīyas, in 1293 A.D., has highly praised the administrative qualities of the queen.

Rudrāmbā was succeeded by her daughter's son Pratāparudra who succeeded in restoring the power and prestige of the family. He defeated Ambadeva and reconquered Cuddapah and Kurnool districts, and also attacked Nellore. But his southern campaign was interrupted by the invasion of Kāfūr in 1309-10 A.D. He fought bravely, but had to buy peace by paying a vast amount of treasure. Yet, instead of husbanding his resources against Muslim invasion in future, he resumed his southern campaign, conquered both Nellore and Kānchī, and even carried his victorious arms as far as Trichinopoly. In spite of these brilliant achievements he was ruined by his own folly. As could be easily foreseen, his kingdom was invaded by the Muslims in 1323 A.D. Ulugh Khān (afterwards Muhammad Tughluq) defeated Pratāparudra and took him prisoner, and the Kākatīya kingdom formed part of the Delhi Sultānate.

CHAPTER XII

Eastern and Western Deccan.

A. Western Deccan

A number of minor dynasties ruled in the Western Deccan. Beginning from the south we have the Gomins who had their capital at Chandrapur (Chandor in Goa). Two kings of this family are known viz. Devarāja and Chandravarman who probably belonged respectively to the fourth and fifth century A.D. Another royal family, called Bhoja, ruled in the same region in the 6th-7th centuries A.D. Three kings of this family are so far known, *viz.*, Śrī Kāpālivarman Dharmamahārāja, Pṛithvīmalla-varman, and Anirjitavarman.[1]

Gomins

Bhojas

To the north of these were the Rāshṭrakūṭas ruling from their capital Mānapura (probably Mān in Sātarā district). Mānāṅka, the founder of the dynasty, probably ruled in the fifth century A.D. and was succeeded by his son, two grandsons, and one great-grandson named Abhimanyu.

Rāshṭrakūṭas

Further north were the Traikūṭakas who derived their name undoubtedly from the Trikūṭa hill, probably situated in Northern Koṅkaṇ. The first important king of the family was *Mahārāja*, Dahrasena, son of Indradatta. He reigned in 465 A.D. and performed an *Aśvamedha* sacrifice. His son Vyāghrasena (490 A.D.) is said to have been the lord of Aparānta (Northern Koṅkaṇ) and other countries. Inscriptions of this family have been found at Kanheri, Sorat and Pardi, 50 miles south of Surat; but their coins have also been found in southern Gujarāt and the region beyond the Western Ghāts.

Traikūṭakas

The Traikūṭakas are the earliest rulers who are definitely known to have used the era beginning in 248-9 (or 249-50) A.D. This era, later known as the Kalachuri era, is generally

1. *POC* xv. (Summary of Papers, p. 99).

believed to have been founded by the Ābhīras who are known to have been ruling in Northern Mahārāshṭra about this time. It is held by some scholars that the Traikūṭakas were originally feudatories of, or held offices under, the Ābhīras, and later supplanted them. Some even regard the Ābhīras as a great, almost an imperial, power in Western Deccan in the third century A.D., but our direct knowledge of the Ābhīras as a political power is very scanty.

Kalachuri era

Ābhīras

The Traikūṭakas were probably supplanted by the Kalachuris who are known to have ruled in the same region in the sixth century A.D. and used the same era. Their history has been described above (p. 291).

Kalachuris

The Śilāhāras appear to have been an independent power in the Deccan before the rise of the Chālukyas, but there is no certain evidence of this. Three of their families come to our notice as dependent chiefs of the Rāshṭraktūas in northern and southern Koṅkaṇ and Kolhapur. The Śilāhāras of northern Koṅkaṇ ruled for a period of 450 years from about 810 A.D. to 1260 A.D. They ruled over the present districts of Thana and Kolaba under the Rāshṭrakūṭa sovereignty, and when that power was overthrown by the Chālukyas, they declared their independence. But it was of short duration, for the Chālukyas of Gujarāt established their supremacy over the State and later on it was conquered by the Yādavas of Devagiri. There were altogether 20 kings in the dynasty. The Śilāhāras of southern Koṅkaṇ ruled from about 808 to about 1100 A.D., at first under the Rāshṭrakūṭas, and then under the Chālukyas, till their territories were conquered by the Kolhāpur branch. This family comes into notice about the time of the downfall of the Rāshṭrakūṭas, and seems to have been the most powerful of the three. They enjoyed semi-independence during the last days of the Later Chālukyas, and one of their chiefs helped Vijjala to overthrow the last Chālukya king. After that event they ruled as an independent power till their country was annexed by the Yādava king Siṅghaṇa.

Śilāhāras

B. *Eastern Deccan*

1. *The Nalas.*

A dynasty of kings, who called themselves 'descended from king Nala' (presumably the king of Nishadha whose pathetic story is told in the *Mahābhārata*,) ruled in the Jeypore State (Vizagapatam District) with their capital probably at a city called Pushkari. About the middle of the 6th century A.D. this dynasty was in occupation of Nandivardhana, the old capital city of the main branch of the Vākāṭakas, near the Rāmtek Hill. This shows that the Nalas had conquered a large part of the Vākāṭaka dominion. But they were soon defeated and their capital city was sacked by an enemy, whose identity is unknown. Skanda-varman, son of Bhavadatta-varman, recovered the fortunes of the family and repeopled the deserted capital city. Bhavadatta and Arthapati Bhaṭṭāraka, another king of this dynasty, issued gold coins which have been discovered in the Bastar State. The inscriptions of the Chālukya king Vikramāditya I refer to the Nalavāḍi-*vishaya* which comprised parts of Bellary and Kurnool districts. Some rulers in the Raipur District in C.P., belonging to about the same period, also claimed descent from Nala. All these indicate that the Nalas, in one or more branches, had at one time or another ruled over extensive territories from Southern Kosala as far as the Kurnool District in the south. But it is not possible to give a detailed or consecutive history of this family.

2. *South Kosala.*

Dynasty of Śūra

South Kosala, so designated to distinguish it from Kosala in the north (Awadh), comprised roughly the present districts or Rāipur, Bilāspur and Sambalpur. It was included in the Śātavāhana empire and probably formed an independent kingdom after its downfall. But its king Mahendra was defeated by Samudragupta, and it remained a part of the Gupta empire till the latter part of the 5th century A.D., when a new dynasty was founded by Śūra in the Rāipur District. He was followed by his five successors, the last of whom Bhīmasena II ruled about the beginning of the 7th century A.D. (though some push back this date by a century). About the same time another dynasty was founded in the Rāipur district by a king named Śarabha with his capital at a city, named after him as Śarabhapura, the exact location of which is not known. The capital was later removed to Śrīpura, present Sirpur in Rāipur District. Six kings of this dynasty are known, the last of whom, Pravararāja, probably ruled about 550 A.D.

Śarabhapura dynasty

This dynasty was overthrown by another known as Pāṇḍuvaṁśīs or rulers of the Pāṇḍava family who originally ruled in the region round Kālanjar (Banda District U. P.). King Nanna and his son Tīvara conquered the whole of South Kosala and ruled there, but it is not known whether they also ruled over Kālanjara region. Tīvara probably ruled in the last part of the 6th century A.D. (though some refer him to the 8th century A.D) and one of his successors, Bālārjuna, who assumed the title Śivagupta (or Mahāśīvagupta), was probably the king defeated by Chālukya Pulakeśi. The dynasty was probably overthrown by the Nalas.

Pāṇḍuvaṁśīs

A branch of the Pāṇḍuvaṁśīs ruled in the country known in ancient times as Mekala—a name still preserved in the Maikal range near the source of the Narmadā river. Four kings of this family are known who probably ruled in the 5th century A.D.

Pāṇḍuvaṁsīs of Mekala.

The Pāṇḍuvaṁśa is also called Somavaṁśa i.e. the family of the moon. But this title is specially reserved for another royal family that ruled in this region about the 10th century A.D. The first known king of this family is Śivagupta, but his son Janamejaya Mahābhavagupta I was the founder of the greatness of the family. He conquered Orissa and assumed the title 'Lord of Trikaliṅga'. He ruled for more than 34 years, and was followed by four more kings, after which there were great troubles as there was no legitimate heir. The ministers (*amātyas*) thereupon raised to the throne Mahāśivagupta III, a grandson of Mahābhavagupta I, who restored order both in Kosala and Utkala. The troubles were probably brought about by the conquest of both Kosala and Orissa by Rājendra Chola, as mentioned above. Mahāśivagupta not only freed his country from foreign domination and unruly elements, but is also said to have defeated the kings of Karṇāṭa, Gurjara, Lāṭa, Rāḍha, and Gauḍa. His son Udyotakeśarī Mahābhavagupta IV, who ascended the throne about the middle of the 11th century, is also said to have defeated the kings of Ḍāhala, Oḍra, and Gauda. But after the reign of Udyotakeśarī the family was shorn of its power and prestige, being attacked by the Later Gaṅgas of Kaliṅga on one side and the Kalachuris on the other. Orissa was conquered by Anantavarman Choḍagaṅga some time before 1118 A.D., though it is likely that for some time the Somavaṁśī ruler there was made a pawn in the diplomatic game and political warfare between

Somavaṁśīs

Rāmapāla and Anantavarman. About the same time the Kalachuris of Tuṁmāṇa gradually conquered the whole of South Kosala and the Somavaṁśī power came to an end in the first quarter of the 12th century A.D. It appears likely that during Udyotakeśarī's reign the chief seat of authority of the Somavaṁśīs was in Orissa, with their capital at Yayātinagara (modern Jajpur), founded by, and named after, Yayāti Mahāśivagupta I, son of Janamejaya Mahābhavagupta.

3. *Orissa.*

The history of Orissa after the reign of Khāravela is very obscure. It acknowledged the suzerainty of the Guptas till at least 570 A.D. Shortly after this Śambhuyaśas, who was either himself a member of the Māna dynasty or a feudatory of this family, ruled over Northern and Southern Tosalī which comprised the greater part of Orissa extending from Balasore to Puri District. His known dates, 260 and 283, referred to the Gupta era, would give us A.D. 580 and 603, as his regnal years. The use of the Gupta era also indirectly proves the suzerainty of the Guptas, after whose downfall the Mānas and the Śailodbhavas established two independent kingdoms in Orissa.

Śailodbhavas.

The Śailodbhavas ruled over Koṅgoda, a region extending from Chilka lake to Mahendragiri mountain in the Ganjam District. The kings of this dynasty had somewhat peculiar names or titles such as Raṇabhīta who founded the dynasty, Sainyabhīta, and Ayaśobhīta. At the beginning of the 7th century A.D. Śaśāṅka of Bengal conquered both Orissa and Koṅgoda. The Māna rule came to an end and Orissa was ruled by the governors of Śaśāṅka. But the Śailodbhavas continued as feudatories of Śaśāṅka. After the death of Śaśāṅka Orissa was overrun by Harsha. But about the middle of the 7th century A.D. the Śailodbhava king Sainyabhīta Mādhavavarman, also called Śrīnivāsa, declared independence. He was a powerful ruler and performed an *Aśvamedha* sacrifice. His son also did the same and probably extended the boundary of his kingdom up to the Mahānadi in the north. The Śailodbhavas were shortly after weakened by a civil war, but continued to rule till the middle of the 8th century A.D., and possibly somewhat later.

During the next two centuries and a half several dynasties ruled in different parts of Orissa, but we hardly know anything definite about their chronology or exact location. The most important among them were the Karas and several branches of the Bhañjas.

The Kara kingdom comprised the coastal districts of Balasore, Cuttack, and Puri, and the hinterland corresponding to them.

Karas

We know the names of sixteen rulers of this dynasty, of whom no less than five were females. The names of all the kings ended in Kara. One of them, Śivakara, *alias* Unmaṭṭasiṁha, claims to have defeated the king of Rāḍha (W. Bengal) and carried his daughter. He is probably to be identified with the king of Orissa who sent an autograph Buddhist manuscript to the Chinese Emperor Te-tsong in 795 A.D., for the Chinese rendering of the name, "the fortunate monarch, who does what is pure, the lion," exactly applies to Śivakara and Siṁha. His son, Śudhākara, is credited with the conquest of Kaliṅga.

The Karas were defeated by Devapāla, and for some time their kingdom formed a part of the Pāla empire. The Kara inscriptions probably allude to this when they refer to a great calamity that seized the kingdom after which the queen-mother Tribhuvanamahādevī took the administration in her own hands and restored the fortunes of the family. The dynasty continued to rule till the middle of the tenth century A.D. Their capital was Guhadevapāṭaka which has not yet been identified.

Bhañjas

Although we possess no less than thirty inscriptions of kings with names ending in Bhañja, we do not know the detailed history of the family. There were undoubtedly several dynasties, the more important being those that ruled at Khijiṅga and Khiñjali.

Khijiṅga

Khijiṅga is now represented by the ruins at Khiching in Mayurbhanj and there can be hardly any doubt that the recent ruling chiefs of this State continued the tradition of the old Bhañjas. There are good grounds to believe that the late ruler, whose name also ended in Bhañja, was the last of a continuous royal line which had ruled over this region for more than a thousand years, a thing almost unique in Indian history. Though we do not know the detailed history of Khijiṅga, the images and ruins of temples found there testify to a very high development of art and architecture, and indirectly to the great power and culture of the rulers and the people.

Khiñjali, which cannot be identified, lay to the south of Khijiṅga, and this kingdom originally comprised the present

States of Baud and Sonpur. Later, its boundaries were extended to the Ganjam District, and it was divided into two parts, one to the north and the other to the south of the Mahānadi. Śatrubhañja and his son Raṇabhañja were two early kings who established the greatness of this family. Curiously enough, the same two names occur as those of two powerful kings in Khijiṅga, but they were obviously different persons. The kingdom of Khiñjali continued from 750 till 1000 A.D., and probably even somewhat later. Bhañja kings are known to have ruled in Baud even in the 15th century A.D., and there are still Bhañja families living in a place called Kinjili between Aska and Berhampore (Ganjam District). This Kinjili thus naturally reminds us of old Khinjali.

Khiñjali

4. *Andhra.*

(a) *Minor Powers*

The Andhra country, properly so called, lay between the lower courses of the Godāvari and the Krishnā, but probably as a result of the Śātavāhana conquest, its boundary was extended to the south of the Krishnā.

The earliest dynasty known to be ruling in this region after the Śātavāhanas is the Ikshvāku. Whether it was connected in any way with the famous Ikshvākus of Ayodhyā (Awadh) is not known, but reappearance of well-known names like Kosala and Ikshvāku in the Deccan may be taken to indicate a migration of the tribe from the north.

Ikshvākus

The founder of the royal Ikshhvāku family of the Andhra country was Chāṁtamūla I (Śāntamūla I) who probably flourished about the middle of the 3rd century A.D. He performed *Aśvamedha* and other Vedic sacrifices and ruled in the lower Krishnā valley. The records of his son Virapurisadata (Vīrapurushadatta) have been found in the three famous Buddhist sites, Amarāvati, Jagayyapeta, and Nāgārjunikoṇḍa. The family was overthrown by the Pallavas towards the end of the third century A.D. To the north of the Ikshvākus, in the region round Masulipatam, ruled a dynasty known as Bṛihatphalāyana. But this was also ousted by the Pallavas at the end of the third century A.D.

Bṛihatphalāyana

The Pallava domination of Andhra was, however, of short

duration. For we find an independent dynasty ruling in the Guntur District about the middle of the fourth century A.D. This family was founded by Kandara (Kṛishṇa) of the Ānanda *gotra*, and only two kings are known to have ruled after him, viz. Attivarman and Dāmodaravarman.

Ānandas

To the north of the Ānandas ruled the Śālaṅkāyanas, with their capital at Veṅgi, modern Peddavegi near Ellore in Godāvari District. To this dynasty belonged Hastivarman defeated by Samudragupta. Hastivarman's successors ruled the Andhra country proper till they were subdued by the Vishṇukuṇḍins about the beginning of the 6th century A.D.

Śālaṅkāyanas

The name Vishṇukuṇḍin is probably derived from the original home-land of the dynasty which may be identified with modern Vinukoṇḍa, about 60 miles east of Śrīparvata (modern Nallamalais range). For the kings of this dynasty were worshippers of the God Śrīparvata-svāmī. The Vishṇukuṇḍins thus belonged to the same locality as the Ikshvākus mentioned above.

Vishṇukuṇḍins.

A king of this dynasty named Mādhavavarman I claims to have performed eleven *Aśvamedha* sacrifices, one thousand *Agnishṭomas*, and the *Hiraṇyagarbha Mahādāna*. The Vishṇukuṇḍins were powerful rulers and fought successfully with the Gaṅgas of Kaliṅga. Their kingdom, at its greatest extent, comprised Guntur, Krishnā, Godāvari and Vizagapatam Districts.

There is sharp difference of opinion among the scholars regarding the genealogy and chronology of the seven or eight kings of the dynasty so far known to us. The kingdom was probably founded in the second half of the fifth century A.D. and continued till it was conquered by Chālukya Pulakeśi II about 624 A.D.

(b) *The Eastern Chālukyas.*

After the conquest of the eastern coastland including the kingdom of Pishṭapura and Veṅgi, about 624 A.D., the Chālukya king Pulakeśi II appointed his younger brother named Kubja-Vishṇuvardhana viceroy over this region, extending from the Vizagapatam to Nellore District. Soon Vishṇuvardhana assumed independent powers, and founded a royal dynasty which is known as the Eastern Chālukya dynasty. He at first ruled

Foundation of the Kingdom

from Pishṭapura and then fixed his capital at Veṅgi. His son and successor Jayasiṁha I did not render any help to either Pulakeśi II or his sons when their kingdom was overrun by the Pallavas from 642 to 655 A.D.

The Rāshṭrakūṭas, who had seized the dominions of the Chālukyas of Bādāmī, naturally wanted to complete the conquest by annexing the Eastern Chālukya kingdom. Some time before 769-70 A.D. the Rāshṭrakūṭa king Kṛishṇa I sent an expedition under his son Govinda II against the Eastern Chālukya king who was defeated and forced to submit. This was the beginning of that prolonged struggle which continued with alternate success and failure on both sides till the end of the Rāshṭrakūṭa dynasty.

Struggle with the Rāshṭrakūṭas

Like some other unfortunate rulers Vishṇuvardhana IV, the king of Veṅgi, wanted to improve his position by supporting Govinda II against his brother Dhruva in the struggle for the throne, but was severely chastised by the latter.

Vijayāditya II (799-c 847 A.D.), son of Vishṇuvardhana IV, was opposed by his brother Bhīma-Sālukki who gained the throne with the help of the Rāshṭrakūṭa king Govinda III. But during the period of troubles that followed the accession of Amoghavarsha, Vijayāditya not only recovered the kingdom by defeating his brother and the latter's Rāshṭrakūṭa allies, but even overran a large part of the Rāshṭrakūṭa kingdom. He is said to have fought 108 battles in course of his prolonged struggle with the Rāshṭrakūṭas and Gaṅgas extending over twelve years. Ultimately the Rāshṭrakūṭa king defeated the Eastern Chālukya army and reasserted his supremacy over Veṅgi.

Vijayāditya I

Vijayāditya III (848-92 A.D.), the grandson of Vijayāditya II, was the most powerful ruler of the dynasty. He defeated the Pallavas, Pāṇḍyas, and Western Gaṅgas in the south, and the kings of South Kosala, Kaliṅga, and various other minor chiefs in the north. He obtained a great victory over the combined forces of Rāshṭrakūṭa king Kṛishṇa II and Kalachuri Śaṅkaragaṇa at the battle of Kiraṇapura (Bālāghat, C.P.), burnt Achalapura (Ellichpur), and overran the Rāshṭrakūṭa kingdom.

Vijayāditya III

But the Rāshṭrakūṭas avenged the defeat by pillaging and occupying a part of the Eastern Chālukya kingdom during the reign of the next king Chālukya-Bhīma I (892-922 A.D.) who was repeatedly defeated. But towards the close of his reign Bhīma seems to have defeated and driven away the Rāshṭrakūṭa forces. The death of his grandson Amma I (922-29) was followed by a prolonged struggle for succession among various claimants. One of them, Yuddhamalla II (930-36), gained the throne with the help of the Rāshṭrakūṭas who practically ruled the country in his name. But he was expelled by Chālukya-Bhīma II (936-46). His son Amma II Rājamahendra transferred the capital to a city founded and named after him Rājamahendrapura (Rajahmundry). After a rule of 11 years he was driven out by Bāḍapa, son of Yuddhamalla, who became king with the help of the Rāshṭrakūṭa Kṛishṇa III. But Amma II, who took shelter in Kaliṅga, soon regained the throne. He was, however, killed in A.D. 970 by his elder brother Dānārṇava who, in his turn, was killed in A.D. 973 by Jaṭāchoḍa Bhīma, brother-in-law of Amma. Bhīma became king of Veṅgi, but Śaktivarman I, son of Dānārṇava, who had fled to the Chola court, regained the throne in 999 A.D. after defeating and killing Bhīma with the help of Rājarāja the Great. Henceforth the Eastern Chālukyas ruled as proteges of the Cholas. Vimalāditya, the younger brother and successor of Śaktivarman, married Kundavvai, the daughter of Rājarāja the Great, and also another Chola princess, who respectively bore him two sons, Rājarāja and Vijayāditya.

Civil War

Chola influence

Rājarāja , who ascended the throne in 1018 A.D., married Ammaṅgayāmbā, the daughter of Rājendra Chola, and had a son named Rājendra Chola II, better known by his later name Kulottuṅga. Vijayāditya revolted against his brother in A.D. 1030 and ruled over a small principality in Vizagapatam District. Later, in 1060 A.D., Vijayāditya usurped the throne of Veṅgi.

As noted above, a prolonged struggle was going on about this time between the Cholas and the Later Chālukyas, and each wanted to establish political influence in the Andhra country as a point of vantage against the enemy. The Chālukya Vikramāditya took advantage of the internal troubles and, with the help of Paramāra Jayasiṁha, defeated Vijayāditya. The Chola king Vīrarājendra, however, reinstated him on the throne by defeating his enemies. But shortly after the death of Vīrarājendra the Chola throne was occupied by Kulottuṅga I (A.D. 1070-1118),

Kulottuṅga

as described above. He naturally asked his uncle to return the Andhra kingdom which rightly belonged to him. Vijayāditya's position was worsened by the invasion of the Kalachuri Yaśaḥkarṇa who overran his kingdom shortly before 1073 A.D. He surrendered the Andhra country which henceforth formed an integral part of the Chola empire. In reality the Eastern Chālukya king Kulottuṅga now ruled over the vast Chola empire, and the history of the Eastern Chālukyas was merged into that of the Cholas which will be described later. Vijayāditya took shelter with the Gaṅga king who allowed him to rule over a small principality.

5. *Kaliṅga.*

(*a*) *Minor Powers*

We do not know much of the history of Kaliṅga after the reign of Khāravela. It probably formed a part of the Sātavāhana empire and, after its downfall, was divided into a number of petty States, such as we find in the time of Samudragupta's victorious march over this region (p. 231). Two of the kingdoms which submitted to the Gupta emperor, viz. Pishṭapura (Pithāpuram, in East Godāvari district) and Devarāshṭra (Vizagapatam District) continued in later times, but nothing is known of the rest.

Pitṛibhaktas

Several dynasties ruling in this region in the fifth and sixth centuries A.D. are known from epigraphic records. One of them used the designation Pitṛibhakta (devoted to father) and ruled in Central Kaliṅga with its capital at Siṁhapura (Singupuram, near Chicacole). This dynasty was probably overthrown by the Māṭharas of South Kaliṅga who had their capital at Pishṭapura but also issued grants from Siṁhapura. The Māṭharas were, in their turn, ousted by the Vasishṭhas. The Vasishṭhas were originally rulers of Devarāshṭra in Central Kaliṅga, but king Anantavarman, who probably ruled at the beginning of the sixth century A.D., had his capital (*adhishṭhāna*) at Pishṭapura. The kings of all these dynasties assumed the title 'lord of Kaliṅga', but most of them were rulers of either Central or Southern Kaliṅga, with occasional supremacy over both. Ultimately, the kingdom of Pishṭapura or Southern Kaliṅga, of which a few more rulers are known, was conquered by the Chālukyas of Bādāmi. Central Kaliṅga was absorbed by the Gaṅgas who rose to power in North Kaliṅga

Māṭharas

Vasishṭhas

about the time when the rulers of Central and Southern Kaliṅga, mentioned above, were struggling for supremacy.

(b) *The Early Eastern Gaṅgas.*

The Gaṅgas have left quite a large number of records dated in their own era which was probably started about 550 A.D. This date evidently commemorates the foundation of the Gaṅga kingdom in this region. As we shall see later, there was a Gaṅga dynasty ruling in the Mysore region from an earlier period, and it is very probable that the Gaṅgas of Kaliṅga were an offshoot of the Gaṅgas of Mysore. The epithets 'Eastern' and 'Western' are respectively added to the two to distinguish them from each other.

The Eastern Gaṅgas had their chief capital at Kaliṅga-nagara (Mukhaliṅgam in the Ganjam District) and a secondary capital at Dantapura (Palur). The charters of this family begin with an obeisance to Gokarṇeśvara Śiva on mount Mahendra i.e. Mahendragiri hill in the Ganjam District.

Indravarman

The earliest Gaṅga king known to us is Indravarman who ruled in the year 39 of the Gaṅga Era. It is not unlikely that he was the founder of the family whose regnal year was continued by his successors and thus gave rise to an era. We know the names of a large number of kings of this dynasty, all ending in 'Varman', from their charters, but hardly anything is known about them. Some of them assumed the title 'Lord of the whole of Kaliṅga' or 'Lord of Trikaliṅga'. The exact meaning of Trikaliṅga is not known, but it perhaps originally designated the forest region between South Kosala and Kaliṅga, though occasionally it might have been used to denote the three (north, central and south) parts of Kaliṅga. It appears from their charters that their kingdom normally comprised both Ganjam and Vizagapatam Districts, though occasionally some kings extended their power further towards the north, south or west. The family ruled for more than 400 years, the last known ruler, Devendravarman IV, having issued a grant in the year 397 of the era (c. 893 A.D.)

During the next century we do not hear much of the Gaṅgas, but Kaliṅga was conquered, first by the Eastern Chālukyas, and later by the two Chola rulers, Rājarāja the Great and Rājendra.

(c) *Later Eastern Gaṅgas.*

In the eleventh century A. D. we find another Gaṅga family ruling in this region. These rulers are called Later Eastern Gaṅgas to distinguish them from the earlier ones. The early history of this family is obscure, and we do not know whether it was connected with the earlier one. The first king of this family of whom we know something is Vajrahasta-Anantavarman who ascended the throne in 1038 A.D. He assumed the title Trikaliṅgādhipati and issued a number of inscriptions from his capital at Kaliṅganagara. But it was his grandson Anantavarman-Choḍagaṅga who was the founder of the greatness of the family. He was associated in the government by his father Rājarāja before formally ascending the throne in A.D. 1078.

Vajrahasta

Anantavarman Choḍagaṅga

The shelter given to the Eastern Chālukya king Vijayāditya (p. 389) provoked the wrath of Kuloṭuṅga Chola who twice invaded the Gaṅga dominions and conquered the whole of Kaliṅga shortly after 1083 A.D. But Anantavarman not only recovered his kingdom, but also wrested Vizagapatam District before 1090 A.D. He even conquered the Godāvari District, but it was recovered by Kulottuṅga Chola.

The decline of the Somavaṁśī power in Orissa and a contest for the throne between two rival claimants tempted both Rāmapāla of Bengal and the Gaṅga rulers to seize it by interfering in its internal affairs. Karṇakeśarī, placed on the throne by Rājarāja, was dethroned by Rāmapāla, but he or his successor was again re-instated by Anantavarman. As could be easily foreseen, this was the first step to the annexation of Orissa, which actually took place before 1118 A.D. Henceforward the Gaṅga kings called themselves 'the Lord of Utkala' as well as 'the lord of Trikaliṅga.'

Conquest of Orissa

But Anantavarman was not content with Orissa alone. Taking advantage of the decline of the Pālas he invaded Bengal and pushed his conquests up to the Gaṅgā in the Hooghly District. Anantavarman had a long reign and ruled at least up to 1150 A.D. Although he was not very successful in his fights with the Kalachuris and Paramāras, he left a vast empire which extended from the Gaṅgā to the Godāvari. He constructed the famous temple of Jagannātha at Puri.

Other Conquests

The successors of Anantavarman could not retain South-West Bengal which passed into the hands of the Senas, and, as noted above, the Sena king Lakshmaṇasena even claims to have planted a pillar of victory at Puri. But the Senas were soon overwhelmed by the invasion of Muhammad Bakhtyār who occupied North and West Bengal and thus advanced up to the border of Orissa about 1200 A.D. In 1205 A.D. Bakhtyār sent an army against Orissa which failed to achieve any success against Rājarāja III, grandson of Anantavarman Choḍagaṅga, who then occupied the throne. His son and successor Anaṅgabhīma III, whose known dates are 1216-1235 A.D., also repulsed the invasion of Khiljī Ghiyāsuddīn 'Iwaz, the Muslim ruler of Bengal. He also fought successfully with the Kalachuris of Tuṁmāṇa, but was disastrously defeated by the Kākatīya Gaṇapati.

Struggle with the Muslims.

Narasiṁha I, son and successor of Anaṅgabhīma III, distinguished himself by boldly invading the Muslim dominions in Bengal in 1243 A.D. His general defeated the Muslim governor at Katasin, captured Lakhnor by defeating and killing its commander and even advanced up to the very gate of the capital, Lakhanawati (Gauḍa); but he returned on hearing that a large Muslim contingent from Awadh was coming to help the ruler of Bengal. He fought four more battles, but was defeated in the last, whereupon the Muslims occupied some territories of the Gaṅgas. Narasiṁha I, who thus offered a heroic resistance to the Muslims, was the builder of the famous temple of Konārak, near Puri.

Narasiṁha I.

Narasiṁha II, the grandson of Narasiṁha I, not only recovered the territories conquered by the Muslims, but drove them from South-West Bengal and advanced as far as the Gaṅgā, from the banks of which he issued some land-grants in A.D. 1296. The Muslims of Bengal now remained quiet, but Ulugh Khān, after conquering Warangal in 1323, invaded the Gaṅga kingdom from the west. He was, however, repulsed by Bhānudeva II, son and successor of Narasiṁha II.

Narasiṁha II.

Throughout the 14th century the Muslim attacks continued. To make matters worse, the Gaṅgas had also to defend themselves from the aggressions of Vijayanagara. Bhānudeva III (1353-1376 A.D.), grandson of Bhānudeva II, suffered greatly from the invasions of Shamsuddīn Illyās Shah of Bengal, Bukka of Vijayanagara, and lastly of Firoz Tughluq, Sultān of Delhi. Bhānudeva

III submitted to the Sultān, but declared independence after his departure. During the reign of his son Narasiṁha IV (1379-1424 A.D.) Muslim rulers of the Deccan, Jaunpur, and Mālwa led expeditions against Orissa. But be it said to the credit of Narasiṁha IV that he survived these shocks and maintained his hold on Orissa and Kaliṅga. But soon after his death the minister Kapilendra usurped the throne and founded a new dynasty called Sūryavaṁśa in A.D. 1434.

The Gaṅgas thus achieved the unique distinction of being the only Indian royal dynasty that successfully resisted the Muslim onslaught for more than two centuries and maintained their independence to the very end after the Muslims had conquered the rest of India, literally from Himālaya to Cape Comorin.

CHAPTER XIII

South India

From the close of the 3rd cent. A.D. (p. 139) the history of South India remains very obscure until about the sixth century. From that period onwards we can trace it in detail, practically without any break. During the next three hundred years, i.e. from 6th to 9th century A.D., we find the Pallavas and the Pāṇḍyas on two sides of the Kāveri as the dominant powers in the south, the triangular fight between these two and the Chālukyas or the Rāshṭrakūṭas constituting the chief feature in the politcal history of the period. The Cholas, destined to be the greatest imperial power in the south, hardly counted as a political power till they emerged from obscurity in the 9th century A.D. The Cheras of old and some new powers like Gaṅgas and Kadambas played only a minor part and, like many petty principalities, transferred their allegiance from one suzerain power to another as best suited their convenience and opportunity.

1. *The Pallavas*

After the fall of the Śātavāhanas the south-western part of their empire, i.e. the region round Banavāsi or Vaijayantī (Kanara Districts), was occupied by the Chuṭu family whose kings bore the title Śātakarṇi and were probably allied to them. They, however, never grew very powerful and their rule was of short duration. The eastern region, to the south of the Krishṇā, passed into the hands of the Pallavas who ruled over Toṇḍaimaṇḍalam, the region round the city of Kāñchīpuram (Conjeeveram) which was their capital.

The Pallavas are not referred to in the classical Tamil literature of the Śangam age, and are generally regarded as foreigners who immigrated into the Tamil land during the rule of the Śātavāhanas, probably as their governors or military officials. Some have even identified Pallava with Pahlava or Parthian. Others, however, take them to be an indigenous tribe, either identical with, or allied to the Kurumbas.

Origin

The names of some early Pallava rulers like Siṁhavarman and Śivaskandavarman are known from a few copper-plate charters, written in Prākrit and probably belonging to the third century A.D. All that we can definitely say about them is that they performed Brāhmanical sacrifices and ruled over a well organised kingdom that covered the northern part of the peninsula, extending from sea to sea. Later than these were the kings, about eight in number, whose names are known from charters written in Sanskrit. Attempts have been made to arrange them in chronological and genealogical order, though no theory has met with general acceptance. In general they may be placed between the fourth and sixth centuries A.D. Vishṇugopa of Kāñchī, defeated by Samudragupta, was certainly a Pallava ruler of this period.

Early kings.

With the reign of Siṁhavishṇu during the last quarter of the sixth century A.D., we tread upon firm ground. It is interesting to note that the Pāṇḍyas also emerge from obscurity about the same time and their ruler Kaḍungon, like his contemporary Siṁhavishṇu, is said to have begun his rule by putting down the Kalvārs (p. 139). It has been suggested that these semi-barbarous and anti-Brāhmanical people were an important factor in South India till Siṁhavishṇu and his contemporary Pāṇḍyan king Kaḍungon inaugurated a new era, both political and cultural, in this region.

Siṁhavishṇu.

Siṁhavishṇu (c. 575-600 A.D.) is said to have seized the Chola country, and his dominions extended from the Krishṇā to the Kāveri. His son and successor Mahendravarman. (c. 600-630) was a versatile genius. He wrote some Sanskrit farces, introduced the practice of scooping entire temples out of solid rock, and was highly versed in music. But unfortunately he was involved in a war with the Chālukya king Pulakeśi II who defeated him and wrested the northern provinces of his dominions.

Mahendra-varman.

The war, thus begun, continued so long as the Chālukyas ruled in the Deccan and, after them, with the Rāshṭrakūṭas who supplanted them. Narasiṁhavarman I (A.D. 630-68), the son and successor of Mahendravarman, not only resisted successfully the renewed invasion of Pulakeśi, but shortly took the

Narasiṁha-varman I.

aggressive. He advanced as far as Bādāmi and occupied it after a siege, in course of which Pulakeśi was defeated and lost his life (c. A.D. 642).

Struggle with the Chālukyas

Narasiṁhavarman is said to have defeated the Cholas, Cheras and Kalabhras. He gave shelter to a Ceylonese prince Mānavarman and sent two naval expeditions to Ceylon to help him to secure the throne of that country. He was the most powerful king in the South and raised the power and prestige of the Pallavas to a height unknown before. The complete collapse of the Chālukya power and its restoration by Vikramāditya about A.D. 655 have been described above (p. 277). Vikramāditya is said to have defeated not only Narasiṁhavarman, but also his two successors, his son Mahendravarman II, and the latter's son Parameśvaravarman I. The Chālukya king, helped by the Gaṅgas of Mysore and the Pāṇḍyas of the south, invaded the Pallava kingdom and Mahendravarman II (c. 668-70 A.D.) was probably defeated and killed, while resisting the invasion, somewhere in Mysore. But Parameśvaravarman I (c. 670-95 A.D.),[1] though defeated by the Pāṇḍyas in the south, made a successful raid on Bādāmi. Vikramāditya, in revenge, devastated the Pallava dominion and advanced as far as Urāiyur, near Trichinopoly, on the Kāveri. In a battle in this region, Parameśvara is said to have "made Vikramāditya, whose army consisted of several *lākhs*, take to flight, covered by a rag." Whatever we may think of this, it was a decisive victory which forced the Chālukyas to retire, and there was a lull in the conflict between the two powers.

Narasiṁha-varman II.

Narasiṁhavarman II (c. 695-722 A.D.), also known as Rājasiṁha, the son and successor of Parameśvaravarman, had thus a peaceful reign, and is chiefly known for his remarkable architectural activities which inaugurated the peculiar Dravidian style. Of the many temples built by him the most famous is the Rājasiṁheśvara or the Kailāsanātha at Kāñchī. The art of painting also flourished, and most probably the great Sanskrit author Daṇḍin lived in his court. He also sent ambassadors to China in A.D. 720 and was highly honoured by the Chinese emperor who,

1. There is no unanimity of opinion among scholars regarding the dates of king Parameśvaravarman and his successors. Prof. K. A. N. Sastri adopts a different system of chronology in his book *'A History of South India'*, Ch. VIII.

curiously enough, also gave a honorary title to the Pallava army "which was to be employed to chastise the Arabs and the Tibetans." The significance of this is not quite clear to us.

Parameśvaravarman II, the son and successor of Narasiṁha varman, had to face a Chālukya invasion, and even Kāñchī, the capital city, was conquered by the enemies, who, however, soon retired.

Nandivarman II

Parameśvaravarman II died about A.D. 731 without leaving any issue, and Nandivarman II, a boy of 12, belonging to a collateral branch of the royal family, was elected king by the chief citizens of the State. The young king, known as Pallavamalla, enjoyed a long reign of sixty-five years or more. At the very beginning he was engaged in prolonged hostilities with the Pāṇḍya king Rājasiṁha I who took up the cause of a pretender to the Pallava throne. Both sides claim victory in a number of engagements and evidently the Pāṇḍyas did not achieve any conspicuous success. Nandivarman owed his success mainly to the loyal devotion and great ability of his general Udayachandra who also conquered for his lord some territories in the north by defeating a Nishāda chief, tributary to the Eastern Chālukyas. In order to check the aggressive designs of the Pāṇḍyas, Nandivarman organized a confederacy against them with the rulers of Koṅgu and Kerala. But the Pāṇḍya king Jaṭila Parāntaka defeated them, annexed the whole of Koṅgu, and even advanced into the Pallava dominions as far as the Pennar river. Thus the efforts of Nandivarman miserably failed.

The Chālukya king Vikramāditya II, who had invaded the Pallava dominions and conquered Kāñchī even while he was a crown prince, about 730 A.D., again defeated Nandivarman and occupied the capital city, but far from damaging it, returned to the temples the wealth that belonged to them. Later in Nandivarman's reign, the Chālukyas made another raid and took a rich booty. Some time about 750 A.D. the Rāshṭrakūṭa Dantidurga, who had overthrown the Chālukya power, invaded Kāñchī. In spite of all these defeats Nandivarman maintained his kingdom intact. He seems to have even defeated the Gaṅga king Śrīpurusha and conquered some territories from him. But later his alliance with the Gaṅga king Śivamāra II and the Rāshṭrakūṭa Govinda II brought upon him the wrath of Dhruva who had succeeded the latter, and Nandivarman had to conciliate the Rāshṭrakūṭa king by rich presents.

During the rule of the next king Dantivarman (c. 796-840 A.D.) the Pallavas suffered severely from the attacks of the Pāṇḍyas in the south and the Rāshṭrakūṭas from the north. The next king Nandivarman III, however, defeated the Pāṇḍyas and recovered the territories conquered by them. He was a powerful ruler and is said to have built up a powerful fleet. A Tamil inscription at Takuapa, in the Malay Peninsula, refers to a temple of Vishṇu and a tank called Avaninārāṇam. This is regarded by some as referring to Nandivarman III who had this title.[1] But towards the close of his reign he was defeated by the Pāṇḍyas and died soon after, about A.D. 865. The defeat was avenged by the next king Nṛipatuṅga, who inflicted a crushing defeat upon the Pāṇḍya king Śrīmāra and once more recovered the power and prestige of the Pallavas. Later in his reign, about A.D. 880, the Pāṇḍyas were defeated again in a decisive battle at Śrī Purambiyam by the Pallava ruler Aparājita, who was greatly helped by the Cholas and other feudatories. The history of Aparājita is obscure but he was probably a relation of Nṛipatuṅga and associated by him with the government of the country. Nṛipatuṅga ruled for 41 years though Aparājita seems to have played the chief role in the kingdom during the last part of his reign.

Struggle with the Pāṇḍyas.

But even the brilliant success of Aparājita could not save the Pallavas. The Chola chief Āditya, hitherto a feudatory, now entertained the ambition of reviving the old glory of the Cholas by overthrowing the Pallavas whose weakness was manifest in the recent fights with the Pāṇḍyas. Some time before A. D. 891 he defeated Aparājita in a pitched battle and conquered Toṇḍaimaṇḍalam. Thus the Pallava power was destroyed, not by its hereditary enemies, the Pāṇḍyas and the Rāshṭrakūṭas, but by its own feudatory, the Cholas, who now took its place as the dominant power in the South.

End of the Pallava power.

2. *The First Pāṇḍya Empire.*

As noted above (p. 395), the Pāṇḍya power was revived by Kaḍungon in the last quarter of the 6th century A.D. But very little is known of its history till we come to the reign of the fourth king Arikesari Māravarman (or Parāṅkuśa) (c. 670-710 A.D.). He extended his kingdom by conquering Kerala and other

Arikesari Māravarman.

1. Cf. K. A. N. Sastri, *Op. Cit.* p. 153.

principalities, and made a common cause with the Chālukya king Vikramāditya I against the Pallavas. Though he defeated the Pallava king Parameśvaravarman, neither he nor his ally could gain any permanent success. Kochchaḍayan (710-35 A.D.), who succeeded Arikesari, followed his imperial policy and conquered the greater part, if not the whole of the Koṅgu country (Coimbatore and Salem Districts). The fight of his successor Māravarman Rājasiṁha I (735-65 A.D.) with Nandivarman, the Pallava king, has been mentioned above. But though Rājasiṁha could not gain any conspicuous success against the Pallavas, he won about A.D. 750 a brilliant victory at Veṇbai against the confederate forces of the Gaṅgas and their overlord the Chālukyas. His successor Jaṭila Parāntaka alias Varaguṇa (765-815 A.D.) also won many brilliant victories and extended the boundaries of his kingdom which now included Trichinopoly, Tanjore, Salem and Coimbatore districts. His success against the coalition organised by Nandivarman has been mentioned above.

Māravarman Rājasiṁha I

Jaṭila Parāntaka

Śrīmāra Śrīvallabha (815-862 A.D.), the son of Jaṭila, began his reign with brilliant victories. He is said to have defeated at Kumbakonam a hostile confederacy consisting, among others, of the Gangas, Pallavas, Cholas, Kaliṅgas and Magadhas. He also led an expedition to Ceylon and sacked its capital. But later in his reign he met with serious disasters. His son Varaguṇavarman rebelled against him and, at his invitation, the Ceylonese king invaded his dominion. In the meantime he was attacked by the Pallava king Nṛipatuṅga. He was badly defeated by the latter, and during his absence his capital city fell into the hands of the Ceylonese forces. Śrīmāra made an attempt to recover his capital, but was defeated and died soon after. It is probable that the Ceylonese and Pallava rulers acted in concert on this occasion, and found a good tool in Varaguṇavarman II who now occupied the throne as a feudatory of the Pallava king Nṛipatuṅga.

Śrīmāra Śrīvallabha.

Varaguṇa made an attempt, later in his reign, to free himself from the yoke of the Pallavas, but was disastrously defeated at Srī Purambiyam about A.D.880, as mentioned above. He died shortly after and was succeeded by his younger brother Śrī Parāntaka *alias* Vīranārāyaṇa Śaḍayan (880-900 A.D.). During the rule of

Chola conquest

this king and his successor Māravarman Rājasiṁha II (c. 900-920 A.D.) the Pāṇḍyas came into conflict with the Cholas who were rapidly rising as a great power on the ruins of the Pallavas. Parāntaka, son of Āditya Chola, captured the Pāṇḍya capital Madurā before 910 A.D. The Pāṇḍyas formed a coalition with Ceylon, but their combined forces were defeated at Velūr, near Madurā, about 920 A. D. Rājasiṁha fled first to Ceylon, and then to Kerala, and was heard of no more. With him ended the Pāṇḍya kingdom founded by Kaḍungon after a glorious existence of more than three hundred years.

3 *The Gaṅgas, Kadambas and other minor powers.*

(*a*) *The Western Gaṅgas.*

The Western Gaṅgas, so called to distinguish them from the Eastern Gaṅgas of Kaliṅga, ruled over a large part of modern Mysore, called after them Gaṅgavāḍī. The kingdom was founded by Koṅkaṇivarman Dharmamahādhirāja, who probably ruled in the second half of the 4th century A.D. and had his capital at Kolar. Harivarman, who ruled from c. 435 to 460 A.D. and was a feudatory of the Pallavas, removed his capital to Talakād (Talkād, near Sivasamudram) on the Kāveri.[1] Durvinīta (c. 540-600) threw off the yoke of the Pallavas and conquered Punnāḍ (Southern Mysore) and Koṅgudeśa. He kept friendly relations with the Chālukyas. Like some of his predecessors and successors Durvinīta was a great scholar in Sanskrit and is the reputed author of several works. The next important king is Śrīpurusha (728-788). Koṅgudeśa was lost to the Pāṇḍyas, and Śrīpurusha occupied the unenviable position of ruling over a buffer state between two sets of rivals, the Rāshṭrakūṭas and the Pallavas on the one hand, and the Pallavas and Pāṇḍyas on the other. He was an ally of the Pāṇḍyas and won a great victory over Nandivarman Pallavamalla, though that did not save him from the Rāshṭrakūṭa invasions. Śrīpurusha on the whole acquitted himself creditably and assumed the imperial title Konguṇi-Rājādhirāja-Parameśvara. He transferred his capital to Mānyapura (Manne, near Bangalore) and his kingdom

Koṅkaṇivarman.

Śrīpurusha.

1. It has been suggested by some that there was a division of the kingdom and a brother of the king ruled at Kolar.

was known as Śrīrājya, evidently on account of its prosperity. The Nolambas of Nolambavāḍi (Chitaldrug District) acknowledged his suzerainty.

Śivamāra II, the son and succesor of Śrīpurusha, was defeated and twice imprisoned by Rāshṭrakūṭa Dhruva and Govinda III, as mentioned above. The Gaṅgas successfully revolted during the troublesome period that followed the accession of Amoghavarsha on the Rāshṭrakūṭa throne, and maintained their independence till Kṛishna III placed on the throne his brother-in-law Būtuga II in 937 A.D. During this period, and even later, the Gaṅgas took part in the wars of the Pallavas against the Pāṇḍyas, and of the Rāshṭrakūṭas against the Cholas, and also fought against the Bāṇas and the Eastern Chālukyas. In 1004 A.D. the Cholas captured Talakād and the Gaṅga ruler had to accept their suzerainty. But gradually the Gaṅga rule, even as feudatory, came to an end.

Śivamāra II

(b) *The Kadambas.*

The Kadambas claim to have migrated from North India but seem to be an indigenous dynasty of Kuntala (North Kanara District). A very early inscription gives an interesting account of the origin of this royal dynasty. It is said that Mayūraśarman, a learned Brāhmaṇa, who had gone to Kāñchī for study, was insulted by a Pallava official. Burning for revenge he took to military profession, defeated the frontier-guards of the Pallavas, and conquered some territories. Ultimately he came to terms with the Pallavas and, in return for loyal services, obtained a feudal principality on the western coast. There may be some truth in this, and Mayūraśarman probably ruled in the third quarter of the fourth century A.D. It is not unlikely that the political confusion caused by Samudragupta's invasion enabled him to set up an independent kingdom with its capital at Banavāsi. His son and successor Kaṅgavarman changed the family title from Śarman to Varman and assumed the title *Dharmamahārājādhirāja*. He was probably the king of Kuntala who was defeated by the Vākāṭaka king Vindhyasena. His grandson Kākusthavarman (c. 430-450 A.D.) seems to have been a powerful king, and he claims to have made many marriage alliances with the Guptas and other kings.

Origin

Shortly after the death of Kākusthavarman the southern

part of the kingdom was formed into an independent principality under his younger son. Mṛigeśavarman (c. 475-490 A.D.) of the senior branch claims to have defeated the Western Gaṅgas and the Pallavas. The next important king was Ravivarman who defeated the Western Gaṅgas and made the junior branch of the Kadambas his feudatory. But the glory of the family was shortlived. During the rule of his son Harivarman (c. 537-547 A.D.) the feudatory Chālukya chief Pulakeśi established an independent kingdom at Bādāmi, as noted before. Harivarman himself was defeated by Kṛishṇavarman II, ruler of the junior branch.

Division of the kingdom.

Kṛishṇavarman's predecessors had to acknowledge the suzerainty, first of the Pallavas and then of the senior branch. Though he reunited the Kadamba kingdom and performed a horse-sacrifice like his namesake, the founder of the junior branch, his son Ajavarman had to submit to the Chālukyas. Ajavarman's son tried to recover his independence, but Pulakeśi II captured Banavāsi and put an end to the Kadamba kingdom.

End of the Kadamba kingdom

(c) *Minor Kingdoms.*

But though the Kadambas disappeared as an independent power, individual chiefs and feudatory families belonging to the clan are met with as late as the tenth century A.D., and even somewhat later. Several other dynasties flourished in South India about the same time as the Kadambas. The Ālupas ruled in South Kanara known as Tuluva country which, together with two other kingdoms, Koṅgu (Coimbatore and Salem Districts) and Kerala (Chera), existed from a very early period, long before the Kadambas rose to power. None of them ever attained any political importance and their history may be briefly told.

Ālupas

The Ālupas were conquered by the Chālukyas and other great powers, though occasionally we come across some rulers of importance who probably exercised independent powers. The Hoysalas conquered them and annexed their kingdom.

Koṅgudeśa, as noted above, passed successively into the hands of the W. Gaṅgas, Pāṇḍyas and Cholas.

Koṅgu

In Kerala the old dynasty of the Perumals ended with Chera-man Perumal. It is generally held that he was converted to Islam or Christianity, and the Kollam or Malayalam era, which started in 824-25 A.D., marks the beginning of the new dynasty. Sthānu Ravi of the new dynasty was an ally of Āditya I Chola. The Keralas supplied queens both to the Pāṇḍya and Chola courts and gave shelter to the Arabs in the 9th century A.D. whose descendants, born mostly of Indian mothers, are now known as Moplahs. It is also held that the Jews settled in this region in the first century A. D., but the earliest epigraphic evidence is a charter of Bhāskara Ravivarman (978-1036 A.D.) recording grant of lands to Joseph Rabban near Kranganur on the west coast.

Kerala

The Bāṇas, who traced their descent from *Asura* Bāṇa, ruled in Kolar and North Arcot districts as feudatories of the Pallavas. They gained independence in the ninth century and fought successfully against the Western Gaṅgas and Nolambas. Even though Parāntaka I claims to have extirpated them, we find them fighting on the side of the Rāshṭrakūṭas against the Cholas in the famous battle of Takkolam in 949 A.D. They were later defeated by the Cholas. But though the kingdom of the Bāṇas disappeares we hear of Bāṇa chiefs holding responsible posts even in Pāṇḍya country as late as the 16th century A.D.

Bāṇas

The Vaidumbas, who occupied the Ranaṇḍu country (Cuddapah District) in the 9th century were probably feudatories to the Ālupas and helped them in their wars against the Western Gaṅgas. They were conquered by the Cholas along with the Bāṇas.

Vaidumbas

4. *The Cholas*

After playing an important role in the history of South India during the Śaṅgam age, the Cholas ceased to exercise any effective political power for more than five hundred years, due, no doubt, mainly to the invasion, first of the Kalabhras and then of the Pallavas. The name and tradition of the Cholas were, however, continued by the Telugu Choḍas who ruled in Renaṇḍu (Cuddapah District) as feudatories of the Pallavas, Chālukyas, or Rāshṭrakūṭas. About the middle of the 9th century A.D. the obscurity lifts, and we find a powerful Chola chief ruling as a feudatory of the Pallavas in the region round Uraiyūr, the old capital of the early Cholas like Karikāla.

Vijayālaya

As the Pallavas were at constant feuds with the Pāṇḍyas, the Cholas, who lived in the borderland between the two, aggrandised themselves at the cost of the Pāṇḍyas or their feudatories. Thus Vijayālaya conquered Tanjore from the Muttarayar, feudatory of the Pāṇḍyas, and soon his principality extended from the north to the south Vellar along the lower course of the Kāveri and the Coleroon. Tanjore became the capital of this new kingdom.

Āditya

As noted above, Āditya I (871-907 A.D.), the son and successor of Vijayālaya, loyally helped his Pallava overlord Aparājita against the Pāṇḍyas in the decisive battle of Śrī Purambiyam. The grateful suzerain rewarded the services of his feudatory chief by granting him more territories, but the latter had seen the weakness of the Pallavas and was now fired by the ambition of establishing an independent kingdom and reviving the old glory of his family. The final clash between the two was not long in coming, and probably took place some time before 891 A.D. Āditya defeated and killed the Pallava king and added Toṇḍaimaṇḍalam to his dominions. He next conquered Koṅgu country and defeated the Western Gaṅgas who transferred their allegiance to him. The task so successfully begun by Āditya, was completed by his son and successor Parāntaka who ascended the throne in 907 A.D. As noted above, he defeated the Pāṇḍyas though the latter were aided by the Siṁhalese forces, and annexed their kingdom. The last remnants of the Pallava power were extinguished, the Bāṇas were uprooted, and the Vaidumbas were defeated. Thus by 930 A.D. the Cholas ruled over the whole of South India from the north Penner to Cape Comorin with the exception of the western coast ruled by the Keralas.

Parāntaka

But their glory proved to be of short duration. The old enmity between the Pallavas and the Chālukyas had now devolved upon their successors, the Cholas and the Rāshṭrakūṭas. The Rāshṭrakūṭa king Kṛishṇa III, evidently alarmed at the growing power of the Cholas, conquered the Gaṅga kingdom and invaded South India as mentioned above (p. 368). He inflicted a crushing defeat upon the Cholas at Takkolam in 949 A.D. and

Battle of Takkolam

annexed Toṇḍaimaṇḍalam. It was a severe blow to the power and prestige of the Cholas and they lost their empire, as the Pāṇḍyas and other smaller powers recovered independence.

Parāntaka I did not long survive this great disaster which undid his life's work, and probably died in 953 A.D. The history of the Cholas during the next 32 years is somewhat obscure. The Chola king Sundara Chola or Parāntaka II (957-973 A.D.) defeated Vīra Pāṇḍya and his Siṁhalese allies, but could not gain any decisive or permanent success. But he recovered Toṇḍaimaṇḍalam from the Rāshṭrakūṭas whose power was crumbling (p. 368).

The accession of Rājarāja I, the son of Sundara Chola, in 985 A.D. marks the beginning of the most brilliant period in the history of the Cholas. He set on foot a new fashion of adding a detailed list of conquests by the king at the beginning of his official records, and this enables us to trace the rapid growth of the Chola empire. Rājarāja once more began the aggressive imperial policy which received such a rude shock in the hands of the Rāshṭrakūṭas. The Western Chālukyas had replaced the Rāshṭrakūṭas but inherited the hostility to the Cholas. Rājarāja began by conquering the Western Gaṅga country and annexing it to his dominions. Then followed the prolonged but indecisive warfare with the Western Chālukyas to which reference has been made above.

Rājarāja the Great

But Rājarāja gained brilliant success in the south. He defeated the Kerala ruler, destroyed his ships at Kāndalūr-Śālai (Trivandrum), and attacked Kollam (Quilon); he defeated the Pāṇḍya king and seized Madura; and he took possession of the stronghold of Udagai in Kuḍamalai (Coorg) which gave him a position of vantage against both the Pāṇḍyas and Keralas. He also conquered the Maldive islands by means of his powerful navy. To crown all, he invaded Ceylon and annexed the northern part of the island.

Rājarāja also interfered in the affairs of the Eastern Chālukya kingdom to prevent the growth of an alliance between the Eastern and Western Chālukyas. He conquered Veṅgi, put on its throne his own nominee Śaktivarman, and cemented the alliance by marrying his daughter Kundavvai to Vimalāditya, the younger brother of Śaktivarman, a marriage which was big with future consequences. Rājarāja also came into conflict with the Gaṅgas of Kaliṅga, who had an eye on Veṅgi, and defeated them.

Rājarāja was one of the greatest rulers of South India, and fully deserved the title, "the Great", that is usually applied to him. He was a great conqueror and laid the foundation of the mighty Chola empire. He also made excellent arrangement for the administration of his vast dominions, to which reference will be made later. The great land-survey, which he commenced in A.D. 1000, and the growth of local self-government constitute great landmarks in the administrative history of India. Another practice followed, though perhaps not inaugurated, by him, was also calculated to improve the administrative system. In A.D. 1012 he associated his son Rājendra with him in the administration. It gave valuable practical experience to the future king and prevented struggle for succession.

Rājarāja was a great builder, and the famous temple at Tanjore, named after him as Rājarājeśvara, still testifies to the glory of Chola art. Rājarāja was himself a Śaiva but he also erected temples for Vishṇu and helped the Śailendra king of Java, Māravijayottuṅgavarman, to construct and endow a Buddhist *vihāra*.

Rājendra

Rājendra ascended the throne on his father's death in 1018 A.D., but his reign-period was held to commence from A.D. 1012 when he was crowned a *yuvarāja* and associated with the government of his father. Rājendra himself followed the practice adopted by his father and crowned his son Rājādhirāja as *yuvarāja* in A.D. 1018.

His conquests

Rājendra, usually known as Rājendra Chola, was the worthy son of a worthy father and raised the Chola power to the high watermark of greatness. His extensive conquests are referred to in his records, and may be briefly enumerated. In the south he not only conquered the Pāṇḍya and Chera countries, as well as Ceylon, but ruled all these as provinces of his empire. He severely defeated the Chālukyas in several engagements, and even sacked the capital city, but could not gain any permanent success.

Expedition to the north.

Two military expeditions of this reign deserve special notice. one, sent along the eastern coast, passed through Kaliṅga, Oḍra (Orissa) and south Kosala to Bengal, and defeated not only three petty rulers of West and South Bengal, but even the great Pāla king Mahīpāla. The avowed object of the expedition, which proceeded up to the bank of the Gaṅgā, was to bring the sacred water of that river, and it is said that the defeated kings were made to carry it on their shoulders. But in any case, it was of the nature of a raid, and did not lead to any addition to the empire. The other expedition may be regarded as unique in the history of India. It was a big naval expedition, equipped on a scale unknown before or since in ancient India, with the object of conquering the Śailendra empire which comprised the Malay Peninsula, Java, Sumatra, and many other neighbouring islands.

Expedition against the Śailendras

The Śailendras were on friendly terms with Rājarāja, and the reasons for the hostility of Rājendra are unknown. But he achieved brilliant success. His fleet crossed the Bay of Bengal and landed an army which conquered successively a number of feudal principalities in Sumatra, and possibly also in Java, and then crossing over to Malay Peninsula conquered Kaṭāha or Kaḍāram (Keddah), the chief stronghold of the Śailendras. The mighty Śailendra empire, the biggest naval power in the east, lay prostrate before the victorious Chola army, and Rājendra Chola had the proud satisfaction of seeing his banner floating from the bank of the Gaṅgā to the island of Ceylon, and across the Bay of Bengal over Java, Sumatra, and Malay Peninsula.[1]

Rājendra Chola was without doubt one of the greatest conquerors in Indian history and was fully justified in assuming the proud titles of Kaḍārangoṇḍa and Gaṅgaikoṇḍa in memory of his great victories. He also built a new capital called Gaṅgaikoṇḍaśolapuram and lavishly decorated it with temples and palaces. One of his greatest achievements was a magnificent irrigation tank sixteen miles in length. He also established a big college for teaching the various branches of Vedic study. Rājendra Chola was thus not only a great conqueror, but also excelled in arts of peace. Like his illustrious predecessors he improved the efficiency of administration to an extent unknown before.

Rājādhirāja, the son of Rājendra Chola, who had been associated with his father in the government as early as 1018, succeeded him in 1044 A.D. He spent his time mostly in quelling the rebellions that frequently occurred in the vast empire left by his predecessors. He was eminently successful in main-

1. The current view that Rājendra Chola conquered Pegu is wrong.

taining order in his kingdom by inflicting crushing defeats upon the revolted kings of Chola, Pāṇḍya, Ceylon and other minor States. He then invaded the Chālukya dominions and carried fire and sword wherever he went. The Chālukya king Someśvara met him at Koppam, and in the sanguinary battle which ensued the Chola king lost his life (1052 or 1053 A.D.). The victory was, however, gained by Rājendra, the brother of the deceased Chola king, who got himself crowned in the battlefield.

Rājādhirāja

The struggle between the Cholas and the Chālukyas continued and many a sanguinary battle took place, the most notable of them being fought at Kūdal-Śangamam, a place not yet definitely identified. Vīrarājendra, the Chola king, who ascended the throne in 1063 A.D., gained victory in many battles and successfully ruled over the vast empire. He was succeeded by his son in A.D. 1070, but the latter was driven away within a year and the Chola empire passed on to Kulottuṅga I.

Kulottuṅga I, the son of the Eastern Chālukya king, Rājarāja, had a great deal of Chola blood in him. His father's mother was the daughter of Rājarāja the Great, his own mother was the daughter of the great Rājendra Chola Gaṅgaikoṇḍa, and he had married the daughter of Rājendra, the victor at Koppam. He set aside Adhirājendra, the son of Vīrarājendra, put down the rebellions raised on his behalf, and firmly established himself on the Chola throne (1070 A.D.). He was a brave and vigorous king and many a martial exploit is set to his credit. During his long rule (1070-1118 A.D.) he repelled repeated invasions of the powerful Chālukya king Vikramāditya VI (who espoused the cause of Adhirājendra whose sister he had married), and subdued the rebellions in his kingdom. But Ceylon became independent.

Kulottuṅga

Kulottuṅga appointed his sons as viceroys of Veṅgi and defeated Anantavarman Choḍagaṅga of Kaliṅga. But about 1118 A.D. Vikramāditya VI took possession of Veṅgi, as mentioned above. The rise of the Hoysalas about this time was another ominous factor, and already they had driven the Cholas beyond the Kāveri, thus freeing the Mysore Plateau from their domination. Kulottuṅga made two land-surveys, one in 1081 and another in 1110 A.D.

The reigns of the successors of Kulottuṅga during the next hundred years (1118-1216) were uneventful from a political point of view, except for a prolonged war with the Ceylonese king on behalf of one of the rival claimants to the Pāṇḍya kingdom, and the rise in power of a number of feudatory States such as the Telugu-Choḍas (of Renaṇḍu), Bāṇas, and Kāḍavas. Other noticeable features were the rapid growth of the Hoysalas, Pāṇḍyas, the Eastern Gaṅgas of Kaliṅga, and the Kākatīyas.

The effect of all these factors was clearly seen in the reign of Rājarāja III (1216-1246). He was severely defeated by the Pāṇḍyas who even seized his capital. The Hoysalas had established a powerful kingdom, and more than once the Chola king had to invoke their aid in order to put down the rebellious chiefs. During most of the period the Chola rulers were, for all practical purposes, proteges of the Hoysalas.

On one occasion, the Chola king became a prisoner in the hands of Ko-Perunjinga, one of his feudal barons, and this was a signal for the disruption of the mighty empire. Rājendra III (1246-1279 A.D.) obtained some success against the Pāṇḍyas but suffered a severe blow when Gaṇapati Kākatīya occupied Kāñchī (1250 A.D.). Taking advantage of the state of confusion that followed, Jaṭāvarman Sundara Pāṇḍya marched north, defeated the Cholas, Hoysalas, and the Kākatīyas, advanced as far as Nellore, and occupied it. The Chola king Rājendra III henceforth ruled as the feudatory of the Pāṇḍya, and the last vestige of the Chola kingdom was swept away by the invasion of Malik Nāib Kāfūr in 1310 A.D.

The fall of the Chola Power

5. *The Hoysalas*.

Reference has just been made above to the rising power of the Hoysalas. They first came into prominence as chiefs of the borderland during the prolonged struggle between the Later Chālukyas and the Cholas. When the Chālukyas finally conquered the region which was formerly ruled by the Western Gaṅgas, the Hoysala chiefs were appointed governors of the frontier outposts, and thus gradually became powerful. Early in the 12th century, or somewhat earlier, the Hoysala chief Ballāla I ruled over a small principality as feudatory of the Chālukyas, with his capital at Belur; but it seems that Dvārasamudra (modern Halebīḍ) was also an alternative capital.

Origin.

Shortly after 1106 A.D. Ballāla was succeeded by his

younger brother Biṭṭideva, or Vishṇuvardhana, who laid the foundation of the greatness of the family. He conquered and annexed Gaṅgavāḍi and Nolambavāḍi (Bellary District), and by A.D. 1131 extended the boundary of his kingdom to the Krishṇā. It thus not only comprised the whole of Mysore but even some borderlands to the north. This brought him into conflict with the Western Chālukya emperors Vikramāditya and Someśvara III and other chieftains of petty principalities in the neighbourhood, but Vishṇuvardhana claims to have defeated them all. Though in A.D. 1137 he performed the Tulāpurusha ceremony, which is a symbol of assuming sovereign power, he nominally acknowledged the suzerainty of the Western Chālukyas till his death in 1141 A.D. or shortly after.

Vishṇuvardhana.

It was Vīra Ballāla II (1173-1220), the grandson of Vishṇuvardhan, who finally declared independence in A.D. 1193, evidently taking advantage of the decline of the Chālukya power. This brought the Hoysalas into conflict with the Yādavas as described above (p. 375). Ballāla's son and successor Narasiṁha II (1220-1234 A.D.) was also a powerful ruler and supported the declining Chola power against the Pāṇḍyas and other refractory vassals (p. 409). His son Someśvara (1234-1262 A.D.) took the Chola kingdom under his protecting wings, and settled himself with his younger son Rāmanātha in a new capital city which he built at Kannanur near Śrīraṅgam, leaving the Hoysala kingdom proper in charge of his elder son Narasiṁha III. Someśvara fought vigorously and frequently against the Pāṇḍyas, but was ultimately defeated and killed, while the latter drove the Hoysalas from the Kāveri region in the south and overran the Chola kingdom (p. 410). On the death of Someśvara his kingdom was divided between his two sons. Narasiṁha III (1262-1291 A.D.) fought successfully against the Yādavas, but his younger brother, being finally driven by the Pāṇḍyas from the south, rebelled against him and occupied part of his territory. The unity of the kingdom was restored by Vīra Ballāla III, the son and successor of Narasiṁha. Ballāla ably defended his kingdom against the Pāṇḍyas, and had to fight hard against the Yādavas and a number of refractory feudal chiefs who had risen to power in the south on the fall of the Chola empire.

Vīra Ballāla II

Someśvara

While he was thus engaged, the Muslim invasion broke in upon South India. He was defeated in 1310 A.D. by Kāfūr, but for more than 30 years maintained the struggle, first against Khiljīs and then against Muhammad Tughluq. Although Tughluq menace diminished on account of the rebellions by which that emperor was faced, Ballāla III had to fight against the Muslim dynasty established at Madurā which posted a strong garrison at Kannanur, the old southern capital of the Hoysalas. He fought bravely against them and died in a battle near Trichinopoly in 1342. He was succeeded by his son who ruled for a short while and then the Hoysalas disappear from history.

Muslim conquest

6. *The Second Pāṇḍya Empire*

After the overthrow of the Pāṇḍya kingdom by Chola Parāntaka I, early in the 10th century A.D., the Pāṇḍyas made several attempts to reassert their independence, but without success, being severely defeated by Rājendra Chola, Kulottuṅga I, and Kulottuṅga III. The last named, who ruled from 1178 to 1216 A.D., led three campaigns against the Pāṇḍyas in 1182, 1189 and 1205 A.D., and defeated Jaṭāvarman Kulaśekhara who had assumed royal power (1190-1216) and conquered Travancore.

Kuleśekhara's successor Māravarman Sundara Pāṇḍya (1216-1238), however, turned the table completely against the Cholas. He defeated Kulottuṅga III and burnt Uraiyūr and Tanjore. But Kulottuṅga got back his kingdom with the help of the Hoysalas, though he had probably to acknowledge the suzerainty of the Pāṇḍyas. The Chola Rājarāja III renewed the struggle and was again defeated, but was saved again by the intervention of the Hoysalas. Though twice foiled by the Hoysalas in his struggle against the Cholas, Māravarman ruled over an extensive territory including Trichinopoly and Pudukkottai. His successor Māravarman Sundara Pāṇḍya II (A.D. 1238-1251) was defeated by Rājendra III, and probably acknowledged the overlordship of the Cholas. But this was fully avenged by the next king Jaṭāvarman Sundara Pāṇḍya I (1251-1268 A.D.) who was the most powerful king of this period and established the Second Pāṇḍya empire. He defeated the Chera king, overthrew the Hoysala power in

Māravarman

Jaṭāvarman

the south, and completely destroyed the Chola power as mentioned above. He also conquered Northern Ceylon, and put down the turbulent chiefs that rose to power on the decline of the Cholas. He captured Kāñchī, defeated Gaṇapati Kākatīya, and advanced triumphantly as far as Nellore. He annexed both the Chola kingdom and Koṅgudesa, and ruled over a vast empire that included the whole of South India (excluding Mysore) as far as Nellore in the north, and also northern Ceylon. He lavished the enormous wealth he had plundered from the conquered countries in decorating and endowing the temples, particularly those of Śrīrangam and Chidambaram which were provided with golden roofs.

Kulaśekhara

The Pāṇḍya kings followed the Chola practice of associating the princes in the government, and these often issued imṣcriptions in their own names even before they had actually ascended the throne, taking credit for victories which they perhaps won during the preceding reign. Thus Jaṭāvarman Vīra Pāṇḍya I (1253-1275) was associated with both Jaṭāvarman Sundara Pāṇḍya I and his successor Māravarman Kulaśekhara Pāṇḍya (1268-1310 A.D.), who in his turn associated no less than four other princes, viz., Jāṭāvarman Sundara Pāṇḍya II (1276 A.D.), Māravarman Vikram Pāṇḍya (1283 A.D.), Jaṭāvarman Vīra Pāṇḍya II (1296 A.D.) and Jaṭāvarman Sundara Pāṇḍya III (1303 A. D.). This explains the wrong notion held by even contemporary foreign writers, that the Pāṇḍya kingdom was divided among a number of independent rulers.

Kulaśekhara maintained intact the vast empire he had inherited. He captured Kollam (Quilon) and sent a victorious expedition to Ceylon which returned with the famous Tooth relic of Buddha. Parākramabāhu, the king of Ceylon, however, offered submission and regained the relic.

The Venetian traveller, Marco Polo, who visited the Pāṇḍya country in 1293 A.D., has left a detailed account of the power, wealth and grandeur of the empire which he calls "India, the Greatest, best of all the Indias," and "the finest and noblest in the world". It contained a number of ports which were the great centres of world-trade, a detailed account of which we get also from Muslim historians specially Wassaf.

Māravarman had two sons, a legitimate one named Jaṭāvarman Sundara Pāṇḍya and an illegitimate one named Jaṭāvarman Vīra Pāṇḍya. As the latter was chosen the heir-apparent, the former killed his father and ascended the throne in A.D. 1310. But Vīra Pāṇḍya soon expelled the parricide who thereupon appealed for help to Malik Nāib Kāfūr who had invaded the Hoysala kingdom. Kāfūr was only too glad at this invitation, for Vīra Pāṇḍya had helped the Hoysala ruler against him, and the quarrel between the two brothers gave him an excellent opportunity to extinguish the last Hindu kingdom in the extreme south of India.

The invasion of Kāfūr in 1310 A.D. destroyed all the Hindu kingdoms in this region which once formed part of the Chola and the Pāṇḍya empires, but half a century later a new empire arose which fairly rivalled them. This was the empire of Vijayanagara, the story of which occupies a promiment place in the Muhammadan period of Indian History

CHAPTER XIV

Political Theory and Public Administration

No remarkable changes are noticed in political theories or in the system of public administration, at least during the earlier part of the period. The royal power and prestige was undoubtedly on the increase. This is testified to by the assumption of high-sounding titles such as *Mahārājādhirāja* and *Paramabhaṭṭāraka*. Even the official records emphasise the divinity of kings. Samudragupta, for example, is described not only as equal to the gods Indra, Varuṇa, Kuvera and Yama, but also as a 'god dwelling on the earth'. These ideas are crystallized in the title *Parameśvara* or *Paramadaivata*, assumed by the Gupta emperors and many other kings in subsequent periods. In the preceding period such titles were used by the rulers of foreign origin such as the Greeks or the Kushāṇas, but never by kings of Indian origin.

Royal Power.

But the old ideals of popular government are freely expressed in *Śukranīti*, one of the latest political treatises written in ancient times. It lays down in the right old spirit that "the ruler has been made by Brahmā a servant of the people, getting his revenue as remuneration." It emphasises the necessity of a Council "for the deliberation of proposals and consideration of problems." The king was to rule with the help of his ministers.[1] It is ordained that 'he should receive in written form the opinions of each separately with all his arguments, compare them with his own opinion, and then do what is accepted by the many.' It is further laid down that the 'king should take the side, not of his officers, but of his subjects', and 'should dismiss the officer who is accused by one hundred men.' Lastly, it is boldly decreed that "if the

Popular Ideals

1. "Even the king who is proficient in all the sciences and a past master in statecraft should never by himself study political interests without reference to ministers.

The wise ruler should ever abide by the well thought-out decision of councillors, office-bearers, subjects and members attending a meeting, never by his own opinions."

king be an enemy of virtue, morality "and strength, people should desert him as the ruiner of the state."

The Guptas continued the old bureaucratic type of administration, though it was more elaborately organised. The title *mahā* prefixed to many known official titles (e.g. *Mahā-balādhikṛita, Mahā-pratīhāra, Mahā-daṇḍanāyaka*) probably refer to Imperial officers of high rank. Two new classes of officers were introduced by the Guptas. These were *Sāndhi-Vigrahika* (Foreign Minister, *lit.* Minister of Peace and War) and *Kumārāmātyas* a large body of top-ranking officials attached not only to the king-emperor but also to the crown-prince, and sometimes placed in charge of districts. Another class of important officials, called *Āyuktas*, are probably the same as *Yuktas* mentioned in Aśokan Inscriptions and Kauṭilya's *Arthaśāstra*.

The administrative system seems to have been more elaborately organised. The kingdom was regularly divided into *Bhuktis, Vishayas, Maṇḍalas, Bhogas* and *Grāmas*,[1] roughly corresponding to the modern, Divisions, Districts, Subdivisions, *Thānās* and Villages. The governor of a *Bhukti*, generally called *Uparika*, was appointed by the Central Government, and he, in his turn, appointed the officer in charge of a *Vishaya*. Some epigraphic records of the Gupta period have thrown interesting light on the functions of these '*Vishayapatis*.' 'They had their headquarters

Local Board

in towns where they had their own officers, and were aided in their administrative work by a Board of Advisers consisting of four members representing the various important interests, viz. the *Nagara-Śreshṭhin* (Guild-President), the most wealthy man of the town representing, perhaps, the guilds in particular and the rich urban population in general; (2) the *Sārthavāha* (the chief merchant) representing, perhaps, the various trading communities; (3) the *Prathama-kulika* (the chief artisan) representing, perhaps, the various artisan classes, and (4) the *Prathama-Kāyastha* (the chief scribe) who might have represented the Kāyasthas as a class, or might have been a Government official of the type of a Chief Secretary of the present day. This body was known as *Adhishṭhān-ādhikaraṇa*, but two more bodies of this nature are referred to as Vi*shay-ādhikaraṇa* and *Ashṭakul-ādhikaraṇa*, whose compositions are not precisely known. But the latter included

1. The names of these units varied in different ages and different localities.

the village headman and the *Kuṭumbins* (householders), and probably served the same function in the rural areas as the first did in the towns.

List of officials.

The minute organisation of the government during the later period is indicated by the very large number of officials, referred to in contemporary epigraphic records, although the exact nature of these functionaries is not always easy to determine. Thus, in the Khālimpur copper-plate of Dharmapāla, the emperor's commands conveying a grant of land are issued to the following:—

1.	Rājan	... Feudal chiefs.
2.	Rājanaka	... Nobility.
3.	Rājaputra	... Royal princes.
4.	Rājāmātya	... Royal minister or Councillor.
5.	Senāpati	... Commander of army.
6.	Vishayapati	... Governor of a Vishaya.
7.	Bhogapati	... Governor of a Bhoga (territorial unit).
8.	Shashṭhādhikṛita	... (A Superintendent or Controller of the sixth part of the produce, due to the king);
9.	Daṇḍaśakti	... (See No. 46 below)
10.	Daṇḍapāśika	... Executioner or Police-officer.
11.	Chauroddharaṇika	... Police-officer who has to deal with thieves.
12.	Dauḥsādha-sādhanika	... (See No. 45 below)—porter or superintendent of villages.
13.	Dūta	... Ambassador.
14.	Khola	... Spy.
15.	Gamāgamika	... Messenger (?)
16.	Abhitvaramāna	...
17a-17e.	Hasty-aśva-go-mahish-ājāvik-ādhyaksha	... Inspectors of elephants, horses, cows, buffaloes, goats and sheep.
18.	Naukādhyaksha	... Inspector of fleet.
19.	Balādhyaksha	... Inspector of the forces.
20.	Tarika	... (Probably overseers of ferries, tolls and forests).
21.	Śaulkika	... Custom-officer.
22.	Gaulmika	... Military officer.
23.	Tadāyuktaka	...

24. Viniyuktaka ...
25. Jyeshṭhakāyastha ... The chief writer (clerk or record-keeper).
26. Mahāmahattara ...
27. Mahattara ... (Village elder ?)
28. Daśagrāmika ... Probably the officer in charge of a group of ten villages.
29. Karaṇa ... Accountant.

The copper-plates of the Pāla, Chandra, Varman and Sena kings of Bengal add a few more officials as follows:—

30. Rāṇaka ... (Feudatory rulers ?)
31. Purohita ... Priest
32. Pramātṛi ... (Survey or Judicial officer)
33. Mahā-dharmādhyaksha... Chief Justice.
34. Mahā-sāndhivigrahika ... Minister of peace and war.
35. Mahā-senāpati ... Commander-in-chief.
36. Mahā-mudrādhikṛita ... Keeper of royal seal.
37. Antaraṅga ... Royal physician.
38. Bṛihad-uparika ... Governor-General (?)
39. Mahākṣhapaṭalika ... Keeper of records.
40. Mahā-pratīhāra ... Chief Warden.
41. Mahā-bhogika ... Chief groom.
42. Mahā-vyūhapati ... Chief master of military arrays.
43. Mahā-pīlupati ... Chief elephant-keeper.
44. Mahā-gaṇastha ... Commander of a Gaṇa Squadron.
45. Ḍaussādhika ... (probably same as No. 12 above).
46. Daṇḍanāyaka ... (probably same as No. 9 above) Magistrate or Leader of army.
47. Mahā-sarvvādhikṛita ...
48. Koṭṭapāla ... The officer-in-charge of the fort.

We get similar lists of officials in the inscriptions and literary works of other parts of India. Among these mention may be made of the following additional designations.

49. Divirapati ... Head of the clerks (?)
50. Draṅgika ... A class of military officers.
51. Śāsayitā ... Executor of a royal charter.
52. Rājyādhikṛita ... Chief Minister.
53. Tairthika ... Officer in charge of fords.
54. Rahasyādhikṛita ... Head of the Secret Service (?)

55. Maryādādhurya ... Warden of the Marches.
56. Rājāsthānīya ... Viceroy (?)
57. Tantrapāla ... Representative of the Emperor in a feudatory or vassal State.
58. Nagarādhipa ... Superintendent of the City.
59. Dvārapati ... Guard of the Passes.
60. Kampaneśa ... Commander-in-chief.

This list is by no means exhaustive. For even the very inscriptions, which give long lists from which the above names are taken, conclude with the following phrase: "and all other dependents of the king who are mentioned in the list of *adhyakshas* (heads of departments) but not specially named here",—the reference being apparenly to a list of *adhyakshas* such as we meet with in Kauṭilya's *Arthaśāstra.* Thus we see the old spirit still intact, and the old framework of the constitution still in vogue, though modified and in some cases elaborated in course of time.

As a type of the prevalent system we may refer to the administration of the Cholas which is known to us in some details from contemporary records. It was highly systematised from a very early date. The unit of administration was the village community, composed often of a single village or oftener of a group of villages. Each of these Unions had an assembly of its own. This assembly , subject to supervision by the divisional officers, exercised an almost sovereign authority in all the departments of rural administration (for a detailed account of these bodies see the next Chapter).

The Chola administration.

A number of these village Unions (*kūṟṟam*) constituted a District (*nāḍu*) and a number of these again formed a Division (*koṭṭam* or *valanāḍu*). A number of these Divisions went to make a Province (*maṇḍalam*). Each Province was placed under a Viceroy who was generally selected from the royal family. The whole Chola empire was divided into six such Provinces.

The lands under cultivation were carefully surveyed, and holdings registered, at least a century before the famous Domesday record of William the Conqueror. The inscriptions show that the Survey was correct to $\frac{1}{50,000}$ of a square inch. The royal dues were fixed and taken either in kind or in gold or in both. The total demand upon land, including customary taxes, came up to nearly four-fifteenths of the gross out-turn.[1]

1. Aiyangar *Ancient India*, pp. 158 ff.

The emperors personally supervised the administration of State and issued orders which were committed to writing by the Royal Secretary. "Whatever was the order, it had to be approved of by the Chief Secretary (*Olaināyakam*) and another high dignitary. Finally it was transmitted to the party concerned by the dispatching clerk, which, again, meeting with the approval of the Viceroy or Governor and the Assemblies concerned was registered and sent into the record office."[1]

But the general tendency of the times, specially after the downfall of the Gupta empire, seems to be towards the weakening of the popular control, and the establishment of unchecked bureaucracy or autocracy. How or when this state of things was gradually brought about it is not easy to determine. Different causes must have operated at different times and in different localities. But we may notice several circumstances which must have contributed more or less to this state of decline.

Anti-democratic spirit.

In the first place, the final triumph of orthodox Brāhmaṇism against heterodox religious sects brought about a coalition between priestly and royal power. The priest looked to the king for patronage and maintenance of his creed, and not unoften purchased the royal support by placing his own spiritual power and prestige at the disposal of his royal master. Thus it was that the king protected the social and religious hierarchy of the neo-Brāhmaṇism, if necessary even by force, while a sense of gratitude as well as motives of self-interest induced the Brāhmaṇa writers and expositors of the sacred law to exaggerate the royal power and prestige in extravagant terms and decry all popular sentiment.

Secondly, the rapid growth of a rigid caste system which divided the Indian community into so many water-tight compartments, while helping the growth of local corporate feelings, operated against the development of national sentiments. With the ideas of superiority and inferiority as well as impurity and untouchability inherent in the later growth of castes, it was idle to expect a concerted action on the part of the people in political matters. And the dissensions among the people served as a golden opportunity for the king to play the autocrat.

Thirdly, the wide development of religious sects was detrimental to the growth of the nation. The best intellects of the

1. *Ibid*, p. 177.

country devoted their energies to religious and philosophical studies, and only the mediocrities played any part in politics. It is a significant fact that politics as a science ceased to grow during the period, and the few books that were written merely recapitulated old ideas without adding anything new.

All these and other causes combined to bring about a set-back in the growth of political ideas. But it is idle to lament over the result. We must remember that nations, like individuals, have to pass through boyhood, youth and old age. It is no more feasible for a nation than for an individual to keep up perpetually the brightness of boyhood or the vigour of youth, and retard for ever the decay of old age. We have traced the history of India from about 1500 B.C. and witnessed the growth of a vigorous civilisation from the primitive beginnings of Ṛig-vedic Age. Towards the close of the period under review unerring signs of old age and decay are visible in the body-politic. The creative energy and adaptability to environments which distinguished it of old now give way to idle superstitions and an orthodox conservatism in social and political matters. The result is at first a stagnation and then a process of decay. Curiously enough, as in the case of an individual in old age, it is only in philosophy and religion that a faint shadow of the old acuteness can still be perceived. But nothing could be of much avail when the whole civilisation was in the iron grip of death.

CHAPTER XV

Growth of Local Self-Government

Although the period under review did not witness any important development in the political theories or any radical changes in the system of public administration, it was characterised by a remarkable growth of the local self-governing institutions such as the Village Communities and District Unions. Their existence from a very early period has already been noticed before, but hundreds of inscriptions, mainly from South India, throw a flood of light on their nature and work, and testify to the most wonderful organisation that the political genius of India had evolved. The subject is too vast for adequate treatment here, and we shall briefly discuss it under the following heads:

Village community

1. The powers and functions of the Village Community.
2. The Constitution of the Village Community.
3. Larger Corporate Organisations.

1. *Powers and Functions.*

The village corporation practically exercised all the powers of a State within its narrow sphere of activity, and was looked upon as an integral part of the Constitution. It possessed corporate property which it could sell or mortgage for public purposes. It had extensive judicial powers and tried all cases, except serious crimes, arising within the boundary of the village. It was a trustee for public charities of all kinds, and received deposits of money, land, and paddy, on condition to provide, out of their interest, the things stipulated by the donors. The corporation could regulate the market, impose taxes, and even levy extra tolls for specific objects of public utility. It had also the power to exact forced labour from the inhabitants of the village. The provision of drinking water and proper maintenance of garden, irrigation, and means of communication demanded special care of the village corporations. During famine and scarcity the village corporations helped the poor people to tide over their difficulties. They borrowed money from the

Powers and functions

temple treasury and sometimes sold their property or the purpose. The Government recognised the heavy responsibility of the corporation and empowered them to regulate the payment of government dues with a view to the actual condition of the country. The village corporations fully realised their responsibility for maintaining temples and other local institutions. They also made provision for educational and charitable institutions, and in most cases these were associated with local temples. We learn from an interesting record of the time of Rājendra Chola, that in order to secure success to the arms of the king, a village corporation made detailed provision for 340 students and 10 Professors for various branches of study. The corporation adopted measures for the safety of the village from robbers and enemies, and entertained high sense of honour for the local patriots who distinguished themselves in its defence. One Viśālayadeva repelled the Muhammadan raiders from a local temple and reconsecrated it. As a mark of gratitude the corporation assigned to him a specified quantity of corn from the harvest reaped by each individual, and conferred on him certain privileges in the temple. There are records of rent-free lands being granted to several persons for having shed their blood in the cause of the country. In the 8th year of Rājarāja I a certain Kalipperumāṇ lost his life in the act of defending his village, and the corporation provided for a permanent lamp to burn in the local temple in order to secure merit for the martyr. An interesting record registers the decision of a village corporation that the residents of their village should not do anything against the interests of their village, nor against the local temples and other institutions; that if they did so, they must suffer as the *grāmadrohins* (traitors to the village) do and should not be allowed the privilege of touching Śiva.

The corporations possessed absolute authority over the village lands and were generally left undisturbed in the internal management of the villages. They were, however, responsible for the payment of taxes due from the village, and we have an instance on record where the members of a Village Assembly were arrested and imprisoned for the unpaid balance of the revenue. The royal officers supervised their accounts from time to time and they were liable to fine for dereliction of duty. In one case the corporation was actually fined by the king on the complaint brought by the temple authorities that it was misappropriating part of the revenues assigned to them. On the other hand, the corporation could bring to the notice of the king any misdoings of the servants of any temple within the area of the village. Some of the regulations passed by the corporation required the sanction of the king. On the other hand any royal charter affecting the status of a village had to be sent for approval to the Village Assembly before it was registered and sent to the Record Office. Sometimes the members of a village corporation had audience of the king on public business, and there are frequent references to cordial relations between the two.

2. *The Constitution.*

The Assembly (*Sabhā* or *Mahāsabhā*) was the supreme governing body of all these village corporations, and exercised full authority in all matters concerning the village. Its constitution differed in different localities and probably also at different times. In some cases it consisted of all the male adults of the village, in others it was a select body. In such cases regulations were prescribed for qualifying a villager for the membership of the Assembly. The number of men composing the Assembly varied. In one case it was 300, the total number of citizens being 400. In another case the strength of the Assembly was 512, but sometimes it reached the astoundingly high figure of 1000. In most cases, if not in all, there was a headman of the village. The status of the village assemblies, so far as it may be inferred from their meeting places, considerably varied, probably according to the importance of the villages which they represented. In some instances we hear of halls built by kings for their meetings. Generally, however, they met in local temples, while in some cases, the shade of a tamarind tree seems to have been considered as good enough for the purpose.

The Committees

Although the Assembly was the supreme authority in the village corporations, the detailed administrative work seemed to have been carried on in most cases by one or more committees. The following list of more important committees will indicate their nature and importance.

1. Great men elected for the year.
2. Great men elected for charities.
3. Great men elected for tank.
4. Great men elected for gardens.
5. Great men elected for supervision of justice.
6. Great men elected for gold supervision.

7. Great men elected for supervision of wards.
8. Great men elected for supervision of fields.
9. Great men elected for management of temples.
10. Great men elected for the supervision of ascetics.

The first committee, called also 'Annual Supervision Committee', probably looked over general and miscellaneous affairs not covered by the other Committees whose nature and duties are quite evident from their designation. Young and old men served in these committees, and in one instance we hear of a lady as a member of the Committee of Justice.

We are fortunate in possessing a very interesting and detailed account of the constitution of these Committees in a particular instance. The village in question was divided into thirty wards. The inhabitants of each ward assembled together and drew up a list of persons eligible for these committees. Honest villagers between 35 and 70 years of age, and possessing certain property and educational qualifications, were alone eligible for election. Out of these, again, those who had been on any of the committees but did not submit their accounts, and those guilty of any of the five great sins, together with their kinsmen and relations, were left out of consideration. Men guilty of various offences and malpractices, the nature of which is recorded in minute details, were similarly disqualified. Out of the persons thus selected in every ward as eligible for serving on the committees, one was elected by lottery, and all possible precautions were taken for ensuring fair play in the matter. The minute and lengthy regulations recorded for the purpose serve as a very interesting commentary on the political training of the people. The thirty persons thus chosen were then allotted to different committees on consideration of their specific knowledge and past experience. The elaborate rules laid down for the election of committees most strikingly illustrate the ultra-democratic character of these village corporations. It is evident that the functions of the corporations were mainly carried on by means of these committees, and that is undoubtedly the reason why so great precautions were taken to safeguard them against corruption. The natural evils of a popular and democratic constitution were sought to be eradicated without injuring its spirit and vitality, and the regulations which were drawn up for the purpose must be pronounced to be a remarkable piece of legislation, characterised alike by sagacity and foresight. There was a regulation that

Election of Committees

only those who have not been on any of these committees for the last three years would be chosen. It was certainly calculated to give every villager a fair chance of serving on them and thus gaining the political training requisite for the responsible membership of the corporation to which he belonged. The method of electing members, carefully eliminating as it did all chances of corruption and personal influence, may be fairly compared with all that we know about the republican States of ancient and modern world.

3. *Larger corporate organisations.*

In addition to village corporations, the communal spirit among the people of South India was manifested on various occasions by the corporate acitivity of the populace of wider areas. Reference is made to a great district assembly meeting in a royal abode, and consisting of, among others, 'the sixteen' of the eight districts. In another case the people living in a district made an agreement with two persons that they should levy brokerage on all the betel-leaves imported into the said district and annually supply a stipulated quantity of them to the local temple out of the proceeds. The people of the district and the 'blameless five hundred men of the district' were appointed to supervise this arrangement. A Pāṇḍya inscription records that the residents of the eighteen sub-divisions of the seventy-nine districts assembled together and set apart the income derived by them from certain articles of merchandise to meet the cost of repairs to the temple. A Chola inscription informs us that the residents of a district imposed a tax upon themselves for the conduct of worship in a particular temple. In another case the residents of a district imposed a certain contribution upon every village in order to construct an embankment on a river.

Many cases are on record where the people of a district assembled to try cases. We further hear of judicial assemblies consisting of the people from "the four quarters, eighteen districts, and the various countries", "the agriculturists from the districts and the one thousand and five hundred men of the four quarters." The last phrase, together with such expressions as "the sixteen of the eight districts" and "the blameless five hundred of the district" clearly shows that the principle of representation was fully understood, and in one case there is a pointed reference to 32,000 representatives of various localities. This fact, taken along with reference to the "district assembly" and "the headman of the district", leaves no doubt that in some cases at least there was a definite and permanent organisation of a district. Intermediate between the organisation of a village and a district we find that of a subdivision.

But there were corporate organisations of areas larger than a district. An inscription of Rājarāja Chola refers to the "Great Assembly of twelve districts", and an inscription of Travancore, of the 12th century A.D., mentions a corporate body of six hundred for the whole State.

We thus find a regular gradation of self-governing institutions with a village corporation at one end and the council of the whole State at the other. This was possible because of the principle, of "representation." No ancient nations, including the Greeks and the Romans, ever hit upon this political expedient which alone could reconcile the principles of democracy with big territorial expansion. The political genius of India alone evolved this new machinery in politics which was to work miracles in other lands in subsequent ages.

CHAPTER XVI

Religion

1. *Buddhism*

In a preceding chapter we have described the rise of Buddhism and its growth and expansion as a world-religion. We have now to trace its decline and downfall in India. It is always difficult to assign a particular date for important religious movements, and therefore, without attempting to be too precise, we may say in a general way, that the period of Gupta supremacy was the dividing line between Buddhist ascendancy and decadence.

The Gupta emperors were followers of Brāhmaṇical religion, and although they were not hostile to the Buddhists, the latter did not find in them such special patrons as the Maurya or Kushāṇa emperors. The change in religious outlook is indicated by the statement in the Gupta inscriptions that Samudragupta restored the Aśvamedha sacrifice which had long been in abeyance. With the restoration of sacrificial forms we find also a revival of the worship of Brāhmaṇical gods and goddesses. Indeed the fourth and fifth centuries A.D. during which the Guptas exercised political supremacy in Northern India, were definitely marked by a strong revival of Brāhmaṇism and the decline of Buddhism. Nothing more significantly points to this change than the fact that whereas the numerous inscriptions of the pre-Gupta period, with only a few exceptions, refer to non-Brāhmaṇical religious sects like Buddhists and Jainas, the great majority of the inscriptions of the Gupta period refer to Brāhmaṇical religion. Towards the close of the fifth century A.D. the Hūṇa invasion dealt a deathblow to Buddhism in North-Western India. The Hūṇas destroyed Buddhist temples and monasteries and massacred the Buddhist monks. Now Buddhism derived its spirit and vitality from the monastic system, and to destroy that was practically to destroy the religion. The monasteries were so to speak the garrisons which maintained the influence of Buddhism in surrounding countries, and as soon as they fell, Buddhism

Downfall of Buddhism

almost vanished from the neighbouring area. The monasteries, on account of their central situation, splendour and magnificence always served as a target of attack to the foreigners. Thus whereas the Hūṇa invasion, and later the Islamic invasions, spelt utter ruin to the Buddhists, other religious sects were not so hard hit

The effects of the Hūṇa invasion can be clearly perceived in the annals of Hiuen Tsang. Throughout North-Western India he scarcely came across any trace of living Buddhism, but the ruins of thousands of temples and monasteries, deserted and dilapidated, told the tale of its former splendour. When Hiuen Tsang visited this country (629-645 A. D.), Harshavardhana's patronage of Buddhism gave a temporary lease of life and vigour to the decaying religion in North India, but although the Chinese pilgrim did not plainly admit it, the facts recorded by him are sufficient to show that Buddhism had lost its strong hold except in Bengal and the Uttar Pradesh. In other parts of India Buddhism was carrying on a life and death struggle with Jainism and the newly revived Brahmaṇical religion or Hinduism.

In the Pāla emperors of Bengal and Bihar, Buddhism found its last strong pillars of support. During the four centuries that the dynasty was in power, Buddhism enjoyed their unstinted patronage. The monasteries at Bodh-Gayā, Nālandā, Odantapurī (Bihar), and Vikramaśīla, kept up the traditions of old, and the Buddhist missionaries of the Pāla kingdom renovated the religion in Tibet where it still flourishes with unabated vigour.

Before the close of the 12th century A.D. Buddhism was driven away even from this last stronghold. The Senas conquered Bengal about the middle of the century and firmly established Hinduism in the province. The Buddhists were now confined in the enclave of Bihar, and when this province was conquered by the Muhammadans about 1198 A.D. Buddhism had no refuge in the land of its birth. Individuals, or even small sects, directly or indirectly professing the religion, might be found in the country for centuries to come, and may be said to exist even now, but Buddhism as a force in society vanished from India since 1200 A.D. never to return.

The extinction of Buddhism in India was brought about by many circumstances. The loss of royal patronage, and the foreign invasions, to which reference has been made above, served as potent causes of its downfall. To these may be added the internal dissensions caused by the rise of numerous sects, the spiritual decay brought about by the spread of abhorrent, licentious practices in the Buddhist Church, and renovated vigour of its old rival, the Brāhmaṇical Hinduism. The latter asserted its power and violently attacked the shortcomings of Buddhism. Two names stand out prominently in this contest of Hinduism against its late powerful rival, viz. Kumārila Bhaṭṭa (*c.* 700 A.D.) and Śaṅkarāchārya (c. 788-820 A.D.). Tradition has preserved the memory of many a successful disputation which these heroes held with their opponents, on the express condition that the vanquished should either adopt the religion of his opponent, or forfeit his life and surrender the property of the religious establishments, if he had any. Whatever we might think of these traditional stories, there can be hardly any doubt that the downfall of Buddhism and the success of Hinduism was due in no inconsiderable degree to the intellectual superiority of the latter. Further, this victory was hastened and rendered easier by the degraded and sometimes depraved manners and customs of various sects of Buddhists.

Cause of the downfall of Buddhism.

But although we are accustomed to say that Buddhism has vanished from the land of its birth, that statement is hardly an accurate expression. As a matter of fact Buddhism was assimilated by the neo-Brāhmaṇical religion popularly known as Hinduism. Mahāyānism, by its adoption of Sanskrit language, the worship of images, and the stress it laid upon faith and devotion as a religious factor, made a very close approach to Brāhmaṇical theism, and the later Buddhist sects like Sammitiya made a still nearer approach. On the other hand the Hindus imbibed the essential teachings of Buddhism. The Buddhist and Jaina doctrine of *ahiṁsā* or abstention from the slaughter of animals made such a profound impression, that even to-day the high class Hindus of the greater part of India are strict vegetarians. To crown all, the Buddha was included in the Hindu Pantheon and is still regarded as one of the ten incarnations of Vishṇu by every orthodox and pious Hindu. This process of assimilation is visible even to-day in many temples all over India, where Buddhist images have been converted into Hindu gods and are being daily worshipped by pious Hindus.

Buddhism absorbed by Hinduism.

Thus while internal causes brought about the rapprochement between the two sects, external causes such as have been noticed above broke the spirit of Buddhist sectarianism. The result was a fusion between the two. The Buddhist monasteries were broken by foreign foes, the monks were dispersed, and the vast population of lay devotees silently entered the fold of Hinduism. A similar process of fusion is going on to-day before our very eyes in Nepāl.

2. *Jainism*

Jainism, unlike Buddhism, made considerable progress during the first part of the period under review. The Early Chālukyas and the Rāshṭrakūṭas, as well as the Gaṅgas and Kadambas, patronised the Jaina religion, and it made great progress in the South during their rule. But from the 7th century A.D. Jainism began to decline in South India on account of the influence of Śaiva and Vaishṇava saints. Under the Later Chālukyas, it ceased to be the conquering religion that it was, and, in the twelfth century A.D., Śaivism and Vaishṇavism superseded it to a considerable extent, even in the Deccan. Bijjala, the Kalachuri chief who usurped the throne of the Later Chālukyas, was a Jaina, but succumbed to a revolution of the Liṅgāyat sect (i.e. those who worshipped the phallic form of Śiva). The Hoysalas, too, were Jainas, and though converted to Vaishṇavism, protected the religion. But the Cholas and the Pāṇḍyas were bigoted Śaivas and are said to have persecuted the Jainas. The Pāṇḍya king Sundara is said to have impaled 8000 of them, and pictures on the walls of the great temple at Madurā represent their torture. Fortunately stories of such persecution are very rare, and are more than counterbalanced by numerous recorded instances of mutual toleration, sympathy, and reconciliation.

But Jainism, like Buddhism, suffered more from the assimilative power of Hinduism. The process of Hinduisation is still going on, but Jainas, unlike Buddhists, have not been extinct in the land of their birth. At present there are about 14 *lakhs* of Jainas in India. This difference is chiefly to be explained by the fact that Gujarāt and Rājputāna, their chief strongholds, had suffered less from the iconoclastic fury of the first Muhammadan invasion.

3. *Śaivism*

The Hinduism, which thus triumphed over the heterodox sects, was, however, essentially different from the Brāhmaṇical religion of the Pre-Buddhist period. The new religion was no doubt theoretically based on the old Vedic system and beliefs, but it had characteristic features of its own which were fundamentally distinct, and it imbibed not a little of the spirit of the heterodox sects like Buddhism which were so long dominant in the country.

Neo-Brāhmaṇical religion

The chief charcteristic of the new religion was the predominance it gave to theistic systems like Vaishṇavism and Śaivism. Of course Vedic texts were still recited, and Vedic sacrifices were not forgotten, but the new religion looked for inspiration to a new class of literature, mainly the Epics and the Purāṇas, and its rituals were quite different. The belief in Vishṇu, Śiva, or Śakti as the supreme deity was quite distinct from the Vedic conception of a host of gods none of whom could claim to be superior to the other. Again *śraddhā* (faith), the watch-word of the Vedic relgion, or *jñāna*, the knowledge of Reality, emphasised in the Upanishads, was replaced by *bhakti* or devotion. In ritual the differences were equally great. The elaborate sacrifices in the open ground or simple structures designed for the purpose, for propitiating gods and gaining favours of them, gave way to personal worship of the images of the supreme deity Vishṇu or Śiva in temples dedicated to Him, and there arose Hindu temples which in grandeur and magnificence far surpassed even the sacred structures associated with Jainism and Buddhism.

But the most significant change in the new Brāhmaṇical religion was the growth and development of sects, notably in Śaivism and Vaishṇavism, the rise of which has already been noticed in an earlier chapter.

The worship of Śiva, apart from any sectarian spirit, seems to have been a general practice in early days. Great kings like Śaśāṅka and Harsha-vardhana, great poets like Kālidāsa and Bhababhūti, and great masters of prose like Subandhu and Bāṇabhaṭṭa seem to have been ardent worshippers of Śiva without probably belonging to any particular sect. The same might be said of quite a large number of ordinary people. By the 6th century A.D. Śaivism had spread to the extreme south of India and also become the predominant religion in Annam and Cambodia.

But the Śaiva sects also developed very rapidly. In the 7th century A.D. the Chinese traveller Hiuen Tsang found 'very many professed Pāśupatas' as far west as Baluchistān. Even then Banaras was a stronghold of the Śaivas. It was adorned with many temples and there was a copper statue of god Maheśvara 'somewhat less than 100 ft. high.' The Chinese pilgrim describes the followers of Maheśvara as follows: "Some cut their hair off, others tie their hair in a knot and go naked, without clothes; they cover their bodies with ashes and by the practice of all sorts of austerities they seek to escape from birth and death."

Śaiva sects.

This description is confirmed by what we know of the different Śaiva sects from their literature.

Thus according to the "Pāśupata" system, the following, among others, were recommended for bringing about righteousness, and attaining the highest powers of knowledge and action.

The Pāśupatas.

(1) "Besmearing the body with ashes and lying down in ashes."

(2) "Making of the sound 'hā! hā' by the forcible stretch of the throat and the lips."

(3) "Huḍukkāra (a holy sound resembling that of an ox made by striking the tongue on the palate)."

(4) "Walking as if one's legs and other limbs were disabled."

(5) "Doing a thing condemned by all as if one were devoid of the sense of discrimination between what should be done and what should be avoided."

'These fantastic and wild processes' were, however, backed by philosophic, metaphysic, and psychological concepts of no mean order.

The "Śaiva" school professed more moderate and rational doctrines. It laid stress upon "twilight adorations, worship, muttering of formulas (*japa*), throwing oblations into the fire, occasional ceremonies for the attainment of eternal bliss, methods of the restraint of breath, abstraction, meditation, concentration, absorption in thought (*samādhi*), penances, purificatory ceremonies and the worship of the various phallic forms.'

The Śaiva school.

The theories and practices of two other Śaiva sects, the "Kāpālas" and "Kālāmukhas," are most revolting in character. Some of them cannot be mentioned in a modern book for the sake of decency. Among others may be noted "(1) eating food in a skull;

The Kāpālas and Kālāmukhas.

(2) besmearing the body with the ashes of a dead body; (3) eating the ashes; (4) holding a club; (5) keeping a pot of wine; and (6) worshipping the god as seated therein." These horrible practices may be a reflex of the original character of the terrible and outlandish god Rudra-Śiva, or of the mental and moral condition of the classes from which the disciples were recruited.

Sir R. G. Bhandarkar aptly remarks that "it is a relief to turn away from this ghastly picture of the wild aberrations of human intellect and spirit to the system of Kāshmir Śaivism which is more human and rational." The two branches of Kāshmir Śaivism flourished respectively in the 9th and 10th centuries A.D. The metaphysical conceptions of this school were characterised by bold originality, and the religious practices enjoined by it were healthy and conducive to the growth of spirituality. It kept clear of the wild and fantastic courses of discipline followed by the other schools mentioned above, and created an honourable place for Śaivism among the different systems of religion. This changed aspect of Śaivism seems to be due in no small measure to the influence of the great philosopher Śaṅkarāchārya (c. 788-820 A.D.).

Kāshmir Śaivism

Śaivism of a purely devotional character flourished in South India from about 500 A.D. A large number of saints, called Nāyanārs, poured forth, in devotional hymns, some of the highest spiritual sentiments that religion can offer, and set up Śaivism on a strong foundation. The number of these saints is usually given as 63 and their hymns are still widely read and held in great veneration. The highly sectarian character of Śaivism may be inferred from the statement of Tirumūlar that "to feed a Śiva-jñānin once is more meritorious than the gift of a thousand temples or the feeding of a crore of Brahmins versed in the Veda". But at the same time he holds that "the Āgama (i.e. Śaiva canon), as much as the Veda, is truly the word of God."

Śaivism in South India.

Among the important Śaiva sects of South India must be mentioned the Vīraśaivas or Liṅgāyats, whose philosophy was influenced both by Śaṅkara and Rāmānuja, and who gave great prominence to the Liṅga (Phallus) and the Nandin or Bull. This sect was raised into prominence, if not actually founded, by Basava, the Prime Minister of the Kalachuri king Bijjala (see *ante* p. 374). Basava fell out with the king and had him murdered by one of his

Liṅgāyats.

disciples. Under Basava and his nephew Chenna-Basava the position of the sect was firmly established. It laid great stress upo [illegible] i.e. love and self-surrender, truth, morality, and cleanliness. It was further characterised by an anti-Brāhmaṇical spirit, and according to some, it originated among non-Brāhmin Hindus out of a spirit of jealousy of the power exercised by the Brāhmaṇas. It is interesting to note how the Liṅgāyats deviate from some well-known Brāhmaṇical practices. Their widows are allowed to marry again. Instead of Yajnopavīta or sacred thread, they hang the *liṅga* by means of a silken cloth suspended round their neck, and a Śaivite formula is substituted for the usual *Gāyatrī mantra*. A similar anti-Brāhmaṇical spirit is noticeable in other Śaiva sects. The Kālāmukhas maintain, for example, that people of other castes may become Brāhmaṇas by a process of simple initiation.

The Śaiva religion became very popular in the south under the patronage of the Rāshṭrakūṭas and the Cholas, and magnificent temples and monastic establishments still testify to its former grandeur. Even the Buddhist Pāla kings of Bengal established Śaiva temples for the Pāśupata sects. The Sena kings were professed Śaivas and an inscription of Vijayasena refers to the erection of a magnificent temple in honour of Pradyumneśvara.

4. *Vaishṇavism*

Vaishṇavism, too, made rapid progress during the period under review. It was patronised by the Gupta, Chālukya and Hoysala kings, among others, and a large number of temples with Vishṇuite images indicate its wide extent all over India. It also spread to Indian colonies in the Far East.

The doctrine of Vaishṇavism, however, underwent some important changes. In the first place the theory of *Avatāra* or incarnation, i.e. the birth of the Divine Being in human form, assumed great preponderance. The origin of this conception may be traced to a fairly early period of its history, but it played a very important part only during the period under review.

Avatāras.

The number and nature of these *Avatāras* are variously given in different treatises. At first the total number was four or six, but later the number was raised to ten and even more (24 or 39). Ultimately even Ṛishabha, the first Tīrthaṅkara of the Jainas and Buddha came to be looked upon as *Avatāras* of Vishṇu. Naturally enough, Kṛishṇa was also regarded as an *Avatāra*, though for historical reasons mentioned above, he stands on a special footing. Of the other *Avatāras*, Rāma and Dattātreya alone still command a large number of followers.

Myths about Kṛishṇa

The next great change in the Vaishṇava religion was the addition of two new chapters in the life of Vāsudeva Kṛishṇa. The first is the story of the Child Kṛishṇa brought up among the cowherds, and the second is his amorous dalliance with the *gopīs* or cowherd girls. These phases of Kṛishṇa's life occupy such an important position in modern Vaishṇavism that it looks like heresy to assert that they did not form part of the original creed. Still that seems almost undoubtedly to have been the case. Some ideas of a pastoral Kṛishṇa might be of fairly early age, and there is no inherent improbability in a religious teacher beginning his life as a shepherd, but many episodes connected with Kaṁsa, Nanda and Yaśodā, the miraculous elements in the story, such as the holding up of Govardhana, killing of Putanā etc. are evidently of later origin, as they are not referred to in early literature. Some scholars hold that these elements were added to the Kṛishṇa legend by the Ābhīras (p. 125), a foreign tribe of nomadic character, who were settled in western India in the early centuries of Christian era or even before that. The romantic and amorous episodes of Kṛishṇa and the *gopīs* or cow-herd girls seem to be of still later origin. A further development of this latter phase was the introduction of Rādhā, the chief beloved, though not the consort, of Kṛishṇa.

Ālvārs.

The power and influence of Vaishṇavism was very much developed in South India by the Ālvārs or Vaishṇava devotees who held the same position as Nāyanārs among the Śaivas.[1] Their Tamil songs are so much marked by depth of feeling and true piety that they are looked upon as Vaishṇava Veda. These songs are still very popular in South India, and their authors are held in so great veneration that their images are worshipped side by side with those of Vishṇu and his *Avatāras*.

But the devotional cult of Vaishṇavism was faced with a great danger from two sides. On the one hand there was the vigorous growth of Mīmāṁsā school represented by Śabarasvāmin and Kumārila Bhaṭṭa, who maintained that the old

1. For an account of the Alvārs and Nāyanārs, cf. Ch. XVII, Sec. 5.

Vedic scarificial rites were the only way to salvation. On the other hand, there was an upheaval of philosophic teachings which laid stress upon spiritual knowledge, rather than faith, love, or devotion, as the chief means of salvation. The famous Śaṅkarāchārya preached his Advaitavāda theory, according to which nothing really existed excepting one Universal Spirit, and there was, therefore, no scope for love or devotion, as that obviously requires two distinct entities, 'the lover' and the 'beloved'. The truly remarkable genius of Śaṅkarāchārya, his profound learning, wonderful personality, and unrivalled polemic abilities seemed to carry everything before him from one end of India to the other. The Vaishṇavas, however, proved equal to the occasion. A class arose, known as *Āchāryas*, who devoted themselves to the task of defending their faith on philosophic grounds. The first three *Āchāryas* were Nāthamuni, Yāmunāchārya, and the famous Rāmānuja (11th century A.D.). Rāmānuja's name is only second to that of Śaṅkara, and he gave a new turn to Vaishṇavism by his Viśishṭādvaitavāda theory which was a reply to Śaṅkara's Advaitavāda.

Āchāryas.

The most important Vaishṇava *Āchārya* after Rāmānuja was Madhva or Ānandatīrtha who flourished in the 13th century A.D. He propounded new philosophical doctrines, but the most important change introduced by him was the elimination of the *Vyūhas*, Vāsudeva and others (p. 172). The supreme spirit is mostly referred to as Vishṇu, and the old Bhāgavata system was thus replaced by pure Vaishṇavism. It may be noted that both Rāmānuja and Madhva discarded the "Cowherd" and the "Gopī (cowherd girls)" elements of Vaishṇavism, but these again came into prominence in the system of Nimbārka who flourished after Rāmānuja. Though a Tailaṅga Brāhmaṇa by birth, he lived and preached in Northern India. Kṛishṇa, surrounded by thousands of Gopīs with Rādhā as his chief lover, forms the most essential element of his sect, and these features still continue to form the preponderating element in Vaishṇavism of Northern India, thanks to the impetus given to it at a later date by Chaitanya. Nimbārka lived at Bṛindāvana, near Mathurā, the reputed scene of the early-life of cowherd Kṛishṇa and his dalliance with the Gopīs.

There were many other important Vaishṇava *Āchāryas*, but their history falls beyond the scope of the present work.

CHAPTER XVII

Literature.

I. BRĀHMAṆICAL LITERATURE

It is impossible to form a correct appreciation of the culture and civilisation of the ancient Indians without some reference, however brief, to their wonderful literature, and the system of education of which it was the visible product. Unfortunately, it is not possible here to write the history of Indian literature either in detail or in strict chronological order, and a general account of the important and characteristic works must suffice.

The literary efforts before the Guptas were mainly inspired by religion, and we have already referred above to the Vedic, Buddhist and Jaina literature. Similarly, during the period under review, the new Brāhmaṇical religion produced a literature of its own. This may be classified as Epics, Smṛitis, Purāṇas, and philosophic works.

The two epics Rāmāyaṇa and Mahābhārata have already been discussed above (Book II, chapter VII). The Smṛitis are metrical texts containing the rules and regulations for the guidance of society. They are based on Dharma-Sūtras and Gṛihya-Sūtras of the Vedic literature, but additions and alterations have been freely made to make them suitable to the changed conditions of society. Manu-Smṛiti,[1] the most well-known work of the kind, was probably composed between 200 B.C. and 200 A.D., but other important Smṛitis like Vishṇu, Yājñavalkya, Nārada, and Bṛihaspati were composed during the first five centuries of the Christian era. The total number of such works is quite large and the commentaries on them larger still. The commentaries not only explain the Smṛitis, but in doing so considerably modify their doctrines in order to bring them in a line with the changed conditions of society. The present Hindu society is guided to a great extent by these commentaries, some of which were composed as early as 900 A.D., and others as late as the 16th century A.D.

Smṛitis

1. Also called Manu-Saṁhitā.

It is difficult to define the Purāṇas or give an exact idea of their contents. They are a store-house of traditions, legends, myths, dogmas, rituals, moral codes, and religious and philosophic principles. The origin of this class of literature has probably to be traced to an earlier period, but the extant Purāṇas are almost without exception associated with new Hinduism, and products of the period under review. According to well established tradition, the Purāṇas are eighteen in number, but we actually find a greater number of texts, and there are, besides, upa-Purāṇas, or supplementary works. The Purāṇas served as the canon of the new religion, and being composed in simple language were extremely popular. Some of them are sectarian in character, and both Vishṇuites and Sivaites have special Purāṇas eulogising their particular deities. The more well-known among the Purāṇas are, Vāyu-Purāṇa, Matsya-Purāṇa, Vishṇu-Purāṇa, Mārkaṇḍeya-Purāṇa, Bhāgavata-Purāṇa, and Skanda-Purāṇa, the first four of which were probably composed between A.D. 300 and 600.

Purānas.

The philosophical works of the period are many and varied in character. They are almost invariably associated with religion, and thus we have philosophic works of the Mahāyāna and other schools of the Buddhists, and those of the various schools of the Śaivas and Vaishṇavas. The best known name is that of Śaṅkara (c. 788-820 A.D.) who established the Vedānta system on a sound basis and has secured a world-wide reputation. Next to him may be mentioned Kumārila who flourished between 650 and 750 A.D. and Rāmānuja. The Buddhist and Jaina philosophers were many but need not be mentioned in detail.

Philosophy.

II SECULAR LITERATURE

The religious literature mentioned above was supplemented by secular literature such as Kāvya or poetical works, drama, lyric, prose romance, and fables.

The name of Kālidāsa stands foremost in the history of secular Indian literature, and he is credited with having written the best works in the first three classes. His Kāvyas such as *Raghuvaṁśa* and *Kumārasambhava*, dramas such as *Śakuntalā* and *Vikramorvaśī*, and lyric poems like *Meghadūta* are read all over the world, and will keep his name alive as long as man has any taste for literature.

Kālidāsa.

Yet, curiously enough, scarcely anything authentic is

known of this famous poet. Not to speak of any details of his life, we are ignorant even of the time when he flourished. According to tradition, he graced the court of Vikramāditya, the king of Ujjayinī, who is credited with the foundation of an era known as Vikrama *Saṁvat* in 58 B.C. There are, however, many difficulties in the way of accepting this tradition (p. 236) and scholars now generally agree in placing Kālidāsa in the fifth century A. D.; probably Chandragupta II or Kumāragupta I was his patron.

Although Kālidāsa was the central and the most prominent figure, the secular literature did neither begin nor end with him. Thus the Kāvyas flourished even long before the Christian era. The most famous work of the earlier period is the *Buddha-charita* of Aśvaghosha, the poet, philosopher, and religious teacher who flourished, according to the Buddhist tradition, at the time of Kanishka. Then some of the inscriptions of the Gupta emperors are written in good Kāvya style, and Harisheṇa, the author of the Allahabad Praśasti (p. 232), "shows a mastery of style rivalling that of Kālidāsa and Daṇḍin." Of the later Kāvyas the more important are *Kirātārjuniya* of Bhāravi (6th c. A.D.), *Rāvaṇa-vadha* (*Bhaṭṭikāvya*) of Bhaṭṭi (7th c. A.D.), *Śiśupāla-vadha* of Māgha (7th or 8th C. A.D), and *Naishadha-charita* of Śrīharsha (12th c. A.D.). A less known Prākṛita work is *Gauḍa-vaho* (slaughter of the king of Gauḍa) of Vākpatirāja who flourished in the court of Yaśovarman of Kanauj, and extolled his master's victory over the king of Gauḍa.

Kāvyas.

In the field of lyric poetry Kālidāsa had no notable predecessor that we know of, with the exception of Hāla, a Śātavāhana king, who probably flourished in the first century A.D. His work, known as '*Saptaśataka*' or *Gāthāsaptaśatī* (700 verses), written in Prākṛita, contains many beautiful poems.[1] Of the later poets Amaru (7th c. A.D. ?). Bhartṛihari (7th c. A.D. ?), Bilhaṇa (11th c. A.D.), and Jayadeva (12th c. A.D.) are well-known.

Like Kāvya, the origin of Indian drama can be traced to great antiquity, but very few works anterior to Kālidāsa's time have survived. The dramatic work of Aśvaghosha has been referred to above (p. 186). Thirteen Plays of Bhāsa, a poet mentioned with respect by Kālidāsa, were discovered in 1910 A.D.,[2] and some of them such

Drama.

1. Keith refers this work to the period from 200 to 450 A. D. (*His. Sans. Lit.*, p. 224.)

2. Some scholars, however, do not accept them as works of Bhāsa.

as *Svapna-Vāsavadattā* and *Pratijñā-Yaugandharāyaṇa* have won well-deserved praises. In this field, however, Kālidāsa was followed by a number of worthy successors, such as Śūdraka (c. 5th or 6th c. A.D.), the author of *Mṛichchhakaṭika* (Clay Cart), and the famous emperor Harsha-vardhana, the reputed author of *Ratnāvalī* and *Nāgānanda*. But by far the greatest name of this period is that of Bhavabhūti (8th c. A.D.), second, if at all, only to Kālidāsa. He lived in the court of Yaśovarman of Kanauj, and his best works are *Uttara-Rāma-Charita* and *Mālatī-Mādhava*. Next in point of time comes Viśākhadatta, the author of *Mudrā-Rākshasa* (c. 800 A.D.).[1] About hundred years later flourished Rājaśekhara. He lived in the court of the Pratīhāra emperors Mahendrapāla and Mahīpāla, and his best known works (written in Prākṛita) are *Karpūra-mañjarī* and *Bāla-Rāmāyaṇa*.

Prose Romances.

Of the Prose Romances, the earliest notable work is *Daśa-kumāra-charita* by Daṇḍin (6th c. A.D.), and *Vāsavadattā* of Subandhu is next in point of time (6th c. A.D.). Bāṇabhaṭṭa, the court-poet of emperor Harsha-vardhana (p. 251), was probably the greatest writer in this line. His works *Kādambarī* and *Harsha-charita* are masterpieces of diction and style.

Fables.

Sanskrit literature is particularly rich in fairy tales and fables. One of the most interesting works is *Pañchatantra* which was translated into Pehlevi, Arabic and Syriac at an early date, and thus found its way to the western countries and translated in almost all European languages. The celebrated and popular work *Hitopadeśa* is based upon *Pañchatantra*.

An early work, *Bṛihat-kathā* by Guṇāḍhya (1st or 2nd c. A.D.), is now lost, but its substance exists in two[2] later versions. These are Kshemendra's *Bṛihat-kathāmañjarī* and Somadeva's *Kathā-sarit-sāgara*, both belonging to the eleventh century A.D. The latter is a massive work of about one-fourth the size of *Mahābhārata*. Other well-known works of this class are *Vetāla-pañcha-viṁśati*, *Siṁhāsana-dvātriṁśikā* and *Śuka-saptati*.

Besides the general secular literature mentioned above

1. Some scholars place the author even as early as 4th or 5th century A. D.

2. Buddhasvāmin's *Ślokasaṅgraha*, of which only a fragment exists, is another version of *Bṛhat-katha*

there were others of a technical character. Lexicons, grammar, dramaturgy and books on metrics and poetics, too numerous to mention in detail, have deservedly received a high recognition.

Technical literature.

Historical literature was least developed in ancient India. Besides *Harsha-charita* and *Gauda-vaho* mentioned above, reference may be made to six other similar works viz. *Vikramāṅkadeva-charita*, or the life of the Later Chālukya king Vikramāditya VI, by the Kāshmirian court-poet Bilhaṇa, *Navasāhasāṅka-charita* or the life of the Mālwa king Sindhurāja by Padmagupta (1000 A.D.), *Bhoja-prabandha* or the life of the Paramāra king Bhoja by Ballāla, the *Pṛithvīrāja-raisa* and *Pṛithvīrājavijaya*, *Kumārapāla-charita*, or the life of the Chaulukya king Kumārapāla, by Hemachandra (12th c. A.D.), and *Rāmā-charita* or the life of Rāmapāla, one of the last Pāla kings of Bengal, by Sandhyākara Nandī (12th c. A.D.). These works, though dealing with historical subjects, cannot be strictly called history in the modern sense of the term. The only work which can claim this character is *Rājataraṅgiṇī*, a history of Kāshmir, written by Kalhaṇa in the 12th century A.D. There are, besides, many works containing royal genealogies which supply materials for history.

Historical literature.

But although history received but scant attention, the allied sciences of Politics and Economics reached a high degree of development. Many schools and individual writers flourished, but their works are mostly lost. Of the extant works the *Arthaśāstra* of Kauṭilya is the best known. It isg enerally attributed to Kauṭilya or Chāṇakya, the famous minister of Chandragupta Maurya, but some think that it is a production of a much later date. It deals not only with political philosophy and administrative system, but also with International Law, military science, trade, commerce, industry, mining, metallurgy, and sundry connected topics. The other well-known works are *Nītisāra* of *Kāmandaki* (c. 7th c. A.D.) and *Śukra-nīti*, a work of quite late date, which mentions the use of gun-powder.

Politics and Economics.

In Mathematics and Astronomy Indian intellect reached a high level of success. The earliest scientific works were the Siddhāntas (4th c. A.D.) of which only a portion has survived. Of the later scholars who developed the science, the more well-known are Āryabhaṭa (born in 476 A.D.), Varāhamihira (6th c. A.D.),

Scientific literature.

Brahmagupta (born in 598 A.D.) and Bhāskarāchārya (born in 1114 A.D.). Some progress was also made in Physics and Chemistry.

Medical literature,

In medical science the Indians had made considerable progress. According to early tradition, Charaka, the author of *Charaka-saṁhitā*, was a contemporary of Kanishka. The next important name is that of Suśruta, the author of the well-known Saṁhitā, who flourished earlier than fourth century A.D. Other well-known writers are Vāgbhaṭa (7th c. A.D.) and Chakrapāṇidatta (11th c. A.D.). Interesting medical treatises form part of the contents of a manuscripts found at Kashgar in Chinese Turkestan. The collection belongs probably to the fifth century A.D. and is known as the Bower Manuscript after its founder.

Miscellaneous.

Indian literature deals with sundry other subjects which cannot be noticed here in detail. The sexual science had a rich literature. There were treatises on horses, elephants, agriculture and horticulture, histrionic art (Bharata's *Nāṭyaśāstra*), dancing, music (*Saṅgītaratnākara*), fine art and architecture (*Mayamata* and *Mānasāra*). Even the arts of stealing and hawking had a literature. In short Sanskrit literature thoroughly represents the different phases of human thoughts and activities to which there is hardly any parallel except in quite modern times.

III. JAINA CANONICAL LITERATURE

Reference has already been made to the circumstances which divided the Jaina community into two rival sects, the Śvetāmbaras and the Digambaras, and led to the compilation of the twelve Aṅgas by the former. The existing sacred texts, including these Aṅgas, thus belong exclusively to the Śvetāmbara sect, and were finally arranged in a council at Valabhī in the middle of the 5th century A.D. The texts were, however, based on those compiled in the council at Pāṭaliputra at the biginning of the third century B.C., and are thus ultimately traceable to Mahāvīra and his immediate disciples.

The sacred literature of the Svetāmbaras is written in a form of Prākṛita called Ārsha or Ardha-Māgadhī, and may be classified as follows:—

I. The twelve Aṅgas.
II. The twelve Upāṅgas.
III. The ten Prakīrṇas.
IV. The six Chhedasūtras.

V. The four Mūlasūtras.
VI. Miscellaneous texts, four in number.

I. *The Twelve Aṅgas*

1. The first Aṅga, *Āyāraṁga-sutta* (*Āchārāṅgasūtra*), deals with the rules of conduct which a Jaina monk was to follow. Minute prescriptions are laid down to safeguard the lives of the least sentient beings, and great emphasis is laid upon the various forms of self-mortification. A monk should rather allow himself to be frozen to death than break his vow.

2. The second Aṅga, *Sūyagaḍaṁga* (*Sūtrakṛtāṅga*), is mainly devoted to a refutation of the heretic doctrines, with a view to enable the young Jaina monks to defend their faith against the arguments of the heretic teachers.

3-4. The third and fourth Aṅgas, *Thāṇaṁga* (*Sthānāṅga*) and *Samavāyaṁga*, like *Aṅguttaranikāya* of the Buddhists, present the Jaina doctrines in an ascending numerical series.

5. The fifth Aṅga, the *Bhagavatī*, is one of the most important of Jaina canonical texts. It contains a comprehensive exposition of the Jaina doctrine, and gives a vivid description of the joys of heaven and the tortures of hell as conceived by the Jainas. One of the most important sections of the book contains legends about Mahāvīra and his predecessors and contemporaries. The fifth book, for example, contains an interesting account of Gosāla Makkhaliputta, the founder of the Ājīvika sect.

6. The sixth Aṅga, called *Nāyādhammakahāo* (*Jñātādharmakaṭhāḥ*), teaches the main principles of the doctrine by means of parables, legends and stories.

7. The seventh Aṅga, *Uvāsagadasāo* (*Upāsakadaśāḥ*), narrated the story of ten rich merchants who were converted to Jaina faith, and having performed most rigorous ascetic practices, ultimately went to heaven.

8-9. The *Aṁtagaḍadasāo* (*Antakṛiddaśaḥ*) and *Aṇuttarovavāiyadasāo* (*Anuttaraupapātikadaśāḥ*), the eighth and ninth Aṅgas, contain stories of Jaina ascetics who 'saved their souls by following a course of rigorous self-torture', leading to death. From literary point of view the texts are rather poor, their style being 'alike frigid, mechanical and dreary in the extreme'.

10. *Paṇhāvāgaraṇāiṁ* (*Praśṇavyākaraṇāni*) is a dogmatic treatise dealing with the ten precepts, ten prohibitions etc.

11. The eleventh Aṅga, *Vivāgasuyaṁ* (*Vipākaśrutam*), con-

tains legends illustrating the consequences, after death, of good and bad deeds of a man done in this life.

12. The contents of the lost twelfth Aṅga *Diṭṭhivāya* (*Dṛishṭivāda*) are only imperfectly known from allusions in other texts. It seems to have contained miscellaneous doctrines of a varied character.

II. To every one of these Aṅgas belongs one Upāṅga. The twelve Upāṅgas, however, possess very little literary interest, as their contents are mostly dogmatic and mythological in character. The second *Rāyapaseṇaījja* is of some literary merit, and contains a dialogue between the Jaina monk Kesi and a king Paesi (probably Prasenajit of Kosala). The fifth, sixth, and seventh Upāṅgas deal with Astronomy, Geography, Cosmology etc. The eighth Upāṅga *Nirayāvalīsuttam* contains an interesting account of Ajātaśatru, but its historical authenticity is very doubtful.

III. The ten Prakīrṇas, as the name signifies (Prakīrṇṇa—scattered), deal with various doctrinal matters and are written in verse.

IV. The six Chhedasūtras, like the *Vinaya-piṭaka* of the Buddhists, deal with disciplinary rules for monks and nuns, and illustrate them by various legends. The best known work is *Kalpasūtra* attributed to Bhadrabāhu, who was the sixth thera (head of the church) after Mahāvīra, and flourished about 170 years after the latter's death. The *Kalpasūtra* forms a part of the fourth Chhedasūtra and consists of three sections. The first, Jina-charita, describes the lives of the Jinas, particularly of Mahāvīra, in a grandiloquent style. The second, Therāvalī, gives a list of the different Jaina schools, their branches and their founders. The third section deals with the rules to be observed by the monks. There is also another *Kalpasūtra* which forms the fifth Chhedasūtra and is looked upon as the principal treatise on the rules of conduct of the Jaina monks and nuns.

V. The four Mūlasūtras are very valuable Jaina texts. The first, the *Uttarajjhayaṇa* (*Uttarādhyayanasūtra*), forms, as a piece of religious poetry, one of the most important portions of the canon, and contains parables, maxims, ballads and dialogues.

VI. Among the separate canonical texts which do not belong to any group, mention may be made of *Nandisutta* (*Nāndīsūtra*) and *Aṇuyogadāra* (*Anuyogadvāra*) which are encyclopaedic texts, containing accounts of the different branches of knowledge pursued by the Jaina monks. This is not confined to religious matters but also includes poetics, Arthaśāstra, Kāmaśāstra etc.

IV. THE NON-CANONICAL JAINA LITERATURE

In the field of non-canonical literature, mention must first be made of commentaries to the canonical texts. The oldest of these, called Nijjuttis (Niryuktis), may be traced as far back as the time of Bhadrabāhu. These were later developed into elaborate Bhāshyas and Chūrṇis written in Prākṛita, and Ṭīkās and Vṛittis written in Sanskrit.

Commentaries.

One of the most famous commentators was Haribhadra who obtained great celebrity as a scholar and a poet. He flourished in the second half of the ninth century A.D. and is reputed to have composed 1444 works. Three other well-known commentators, Sāntisūri, Devendragaṇi and Abhayadeva flourished in the 11th century A.D. These commentaries, while preserving historical or semi-historical traditions of old, also contain quite a large number of legends and stories which are evidently of later origin. Indeed legends and fables form quite a prominent feature of the Jaina literature and there are many independent works containing single stories or collections of the same. Some of these are mentioned below :

Single Stories

(1) *Kālakāchārya-kathānaka*—It is looked upon as very old and gives a legendary account of the conquest of Ujjayinī by the Śakas.

(2) *Uttama-charitra-kathānaka*—A story containing episodes full of remarkable adventures.

(3-4) *Champaka-śreshṭhikathānaka*, and *Pāla-Gopāla-kathānaka*; written by Jinakīrtisūri in the middle of the 15th century.

Collections of Stories

(1) *Samyaktvakaumudī*—It describes how a merchant and his eight wives attained samyaktva (perfection) in religion.

(2) *Kathākosa*—A rich mine of stories some of which have travelled beyond the boundaries of India. It contains the Jaina version of the Nala-Damayantī episode of the Mahābhārata.

(3) *Antarakathā-saṁgraha* by Rājaśekhara (14th c. A D.).

(4) *Kathāmahodadhi* by Somachandra (15th c. A.D.)

(5) *Kathāratnākara* of Hemavijaya (16th c. A.D.).

(6-7) *Kāthākośa* and *Panchaśatī-prabodhasambandha* by Śubhaśilagaṇi (15th c. A.D.)

The Jainas further possess an extensive poetic literature of what are called Charitras and Prabandhas. The former narrate the stories of Tīrthaṅkaras and mythical sages, while the latter give the story of Jaina monks and laymen who flourished in historical times. As these books are didactic in character, they should be ragarded rather as collections of edifying stories grouped round an individual than a biography in the true sense of the term. The Charitras contain the story of individuals or the story of all the holy sages. One of the most famous works of this last type is *Trishashṭiśalākā-purusha-charita* (lives of 63 best men) of Hemachandra.

Hemachandra.

The name of Hemachandra stands foremost among the Jaina authors. He was a versatile genius, and excelled in grammar, lexicography, poetics, and metrics, in addition to Jaina religious teachings. He was born at Dhundhūka, a town in the neighbourhood of Ahmedabad, in the year 1089 A.D. and died at the advanced age of 84 (1172 A.D.). Most of his life he spent at the capital of Gujarāt under the patronage of the Chaulukya king Jayasiṁha Siddharāja (1094-1143 A.D.) and his successor Kumārapāla (1143-c. 1171 A. D.). Kumārapāla was converted to the Jaina faith by Hemachandra, and with the zeal of a new convert he tried his best to establish Jainism firmly in his kingdom. He prohibited slaughter of animals, erected Jaina temples and patronised the literary men of the Jaina sect. It was during his reign that Hemachandra wrote his famous biography of 63 good men, mentioned above, which ranks as a Mahākāvya among the Jainas. The book is divided into ten parvas and the last parva *Mahāvīra-charita*, dealing with the life of Mahāvīra, is naturally regarded as very important. But more valuable still, from the point of view of literary history, is the appendix to this book, '*Pariśishṭaparvan*' or '*Sthavirāvali-charita*,' the biography of the earliest teachers of Jainism, whose names and order of succession may be regarded as historical. The stories themselves have seldom any historical value, but they have preserved modified version of those known from other sources, sometimes beyond the boundaries of India.

Lists of Jaina teachers are also furnished in various Paṭṭāvalis and their history in the *Gurvāvalīsūtra* of Dharmasāgaragaṇi and the *Therāvalī* of Merutuṅga. The *Prabhāvaka-charitra* of Prabhāchandra and Pradyumnasūri (c. 1250 A.D.) gives the story of 22 Jaina teachers including Hemachandra himself.

There are also semi-historical works like *Prabandha-chintāmaṇi* of Merutuṅga (1306 A.D.) and the *Prabandha-kośa* of Rājeśekhara (1349 A.D.) in which groups of legends are centred round historical persons, including Jaina teachers and kings like Bhoja, Vikramāditya, Śīlāditya etc.

The Digambaras sometimes style the Charitras as Purāṇas, e.g. *Padma-charita* or *Padma-purāṇa* by Vimalasūri. There is also a Mahāpurāṇa, written partly by Jinasena and partly by his disciple Guṇabhadra, which contains, like Brāhmaṇical Purāṇas, an account of the various rites and ceremonies. Jinasena is also the author of *Harivaṁśa-purāṇa*, which was completed in 783 A.D. The Jainas possess many prose romances. Mention may be made of "*Samarāichchakahā*' of Haribhadra, and *Upamiti-bhavaprapañchā-kathā* of Siddharshi (906 A.D.).

The Jaina literature also contains a large number of romances in poems. Bāṇa's *Kādambarī* served as the model of Somadeva's *Yaśastilaka* (959 A.D.) and Dhanapāla's *Tilakamañjarī* (970 A.D.). The poet Harichandra wrote a Mahākāvya (Epic) called *Dharmaśarmābhyudaya* in imitation of Māgha's *Śiśupālavadha*. There is an interesting poem called *Nemidūta* by Vikrama in which the last line of every stanza is taken from Kālidāsa's *Meghadūta*. There are also other epic poems independently written, such as *Malayasundarī-kathā*, *Yaśodhara-charita* of Kanakesena Vādirāja (10th c. A.D.) and *Mṛigāvatī-charita* of Maladhāri-Devaprabha (13th c. A.D.).

Kāvyas.

The Jaina literature is rich in religious lyrics. Mention may be made of *Bhaktāmara-stotra* of Mānatuṅga, *Pavayanasāra* (*Pravachanasāra*) of Kundakunda (7th c. A.D.), *Uvaesamālā* of Dharmadāsa, *Śṛiṅgāravairāgya-taraṅgiṇī* of Somaprabha (1276 A.D.), and *Gāthākośa*, an anthology by Munichandrasūri (c. 1122 A.D.).

Lyrics.

This brief sketch of Jaina literature may be concluded by a reference to a few other writers who are held in high estimation by the Jainas.

Famous writers.

1. Umāsvāti or Umāsvāmin is reputed to have composed no less than 500 works. His *Tattvārthādhigamasūtra*, looked upon as authority both by the Digambaras as well as the Śvetāmbaras, deals with cosmology, metaphysics and the ethics of the Jainas. Another of his works, *Śrāvaka-prajñapti*, gives a systematic exposition of the Jaina religion mainly intended for the lay followers. He probably flourished in the 7th c. A.D.

2. Amitagati, the author of *Subhāshitaratna-saṁdoha* and *Dharmaparīkshā*, flourished during the latter part of the tenth and the beginning of the eleventh century A.D. His books contain a severe attack against the Brāhmaṇical religion, particularly the caste system. It is noteworthy that he reproduces many episodes from the *Rāmāyaṇa* and the *Mahābhārata* in a distorted version.

3. Chāmuṇḍa-Mahārāja composed in 978 A.D. his *Chāritrasāra*, which deals with ethical principles of the Digambaras.

4. Śāntisūri's *Jivaviyāra* is a remarkable work, dealing with Theology, Zoology, Botany, Anthprology, and Mythology at one and the same time.

V. DRAVIDIAN LITERATURE

1. *Tamil*

The Tamil literature of the period mainly consists of a large number of secular works, resembling those of the Śangam Age mentioned above (p. 193), and the devotional songs of the Śaiva and Vaishṇava saints which are characterised alike by the depth and sincerity of feeling and the beauty of literary expression. Among the Śaiva saints, known as Nāyanārs, Tirumūlar, Sambandar, Appar, Sundarar and Māṇikkavāchagar, who all lived in the 7th and early part of the 8th century A.D., occupy a very high position. The hymns composed by them are collected into eleven Tirmurais which are held in great veneration by the Tamil Śaivas. It has been said of Māṇikkavāchagar's *Tiruvāchakam*, that one who is not moved by it is verily a stone. It presents the spiritual excellence of Tamil Saivism at its best. Another important work, the *Periyapurāṇam*, contains the lives of 63 Śaiva saints. These include men and women of all classes and castes, and some of them are even 'untouchables'; but all of them are held in great veneration, showing the catholicity of the religion.

Śaiva Nāyanārs.

The Vaishṇava saints, known as Ālvārs, also belonged to both the sexes and different classes and castes, ranging from a king to a *vellāla* and *kalla*. They are traditionally twelve in number and may be placed between the 7th and 9th century A.D. The collection of their works, known as *Nālāyira-prabandham*, consists of 4,000 stanzas. Four poems by Nammālvār, the greatest of the Ālvārs, form the most important part in this collection, and the Śrī-Vaishṇavas

Vaishṇava Ālvārs.

regard them as the Tamil redaction of the four Vedas. Similarly the six poems of Tirumaṅgai, the last of the Ālvārs, are regarded as the six Vedāṅgas. Another Ālvār, Kulaśekhara, originally a king of Malabar, is the author of two exquisite poems *Perumāl-Tirumoli* and *Mukundamālā*, the last of which, on account of its lyric beauty, has been compared to *Gītagovinda* of Jayadeva.

The popularity of this extensive religious literature, the adoption of the *Nālāyira-prabandham* as a sacred text, and the celebration of it in special festivals in all the prominent temples of South India raised the status of Tamil and made it equal to that of Sanskrit. It also led to the growth of voluminous commentaries the object of which was to expound the *Prabandha* and discuss its obscure points, thus usherring in a new type of religious literature, half Sanskrit and half Tamil.

In the field of secular literature mention may be made of *Jīvakachintāmaṅi* of the Jaina ascetic and poet Tiruttakkadevar who flourished in the tenth century A.D. It is a romantic poem describing the many love-adventures of the hero Jīvaka ending in marriages. Another famous work is the *Kalingattupparaṇi*, a war-poem written by the Chola court-poet Jayangondār with the Kaliṅga war of Kulottuṅga I as its theme. A still more famous poet is Oṭṭakkūttan who graced the courts of the three immediate successors of Kulottuṅga I and wrote laudatory poems on each of them. But the greatest Tamil poet was Kamban who composed the Tamil *Rāmāyaṇa* during the reign of Kulottuṅga III. This is justly regarded as the greatest epic in Tamil literature. There were also several reputed works on grammar, prosody, poetics and lexicography.

2. *Kaṇṇaḍa*

Next to Tamil, Kaṇṇaḍa or Kanarese literature is the most ancient among the Dravidian group. The history of this literature really begins with *Kavirājamārga*, a work on poetics by the Rāshṭrakūṭa king Amoghavarsha (814-778 A.D.), though a few earlier texts are known to us. The next century saw the high watermark of this literature. It was the age of Pampa, Ponna, and Ranna, the three Gems, whose poetical works, based on the lives of Jaina Tīrthaṅkaras as well as the *Mahābhārata*, have attained great distinction.

Pampa, the greatest among them, was a court-poet of Arikesari II of Vemulavāḍa, a feudatory of Rāshṭrakūṭa

Kṛishṇa III, and is famous for his two works, the *Ādipurāṇa*, dealing with the life of the first Jaina *Tīrthaṁkara* and the *Pampa-Bhārata* with Arjuna as its hero.

Among later writers may be mentioned Durgasiṁha the author of a Champū work *Pañchatantra* based on the *Bṛihatkathā*, and Nāgachandra who wrote a Champū on the story of Rāma, giving it a completely Jaina garb.

The Kaṇṇaḍa literature is very rich in works based on the Sanskrit Epics and Purāṇas, the Jaina traditions, as well as romantic stories and poems based on Sanskrit models.

Like the Jainas the Vīraśaivas contributed a great deal to the development of Kaṇṇaḍa literature. The prose literature introduced by them and known as Vachana constitutes a landmark in Kaṇṇaḍa literature and enjoys great popularity among the masses even today. More than two hundred writers, including some women, are said to have contributed to the growth and development of this literary form, simple in style and easily understood by the common people.

Like the Śaiva and the Jaina there were also Vaishṇava works of repute. One of the earliest was Rudra Bhaṭṭa's *Jagannātha-vijaya*, a Champū based on the legends of Kṛishṇa.

3. *Telugu*

The Telugu literature proper may be said to have begun with the translation of the Ādi and Sabhā parvas of the *Mahābhārata* by Nannaya in the eleventh century A.D. Tikkana (c 1220-1300), the greatest among the Telugu poets, took up the translation from Virāṭa-parva to the end. The intervening Vana-parva was translated by Yerrāpragaḍa (1280-1350). These three poets (*kavitraya*) occupy a very high position in Telugu literature.

There were two Telugu translations of the *Rāmāyaṇa*, one by Kona Buddharāja in the thirteenth, and the other by Hullakki Bhāskara in the fourteenth century.

Many other works in Sanskrit were translated into Telugu, including *Daśakumāra-charita* of Daṇḍin, two treatises on Mathematics, and Vijñāneśvara's *Mitāksharā*. There were also books on grammar and politics as well as Purāṇas based on Sanskrit models.

CHAPTER XVIII

The System of Education

The extensive literature described above is the visible product of a rational system of education which had no parallel in the history of the ancient world. The importance of education was realised in India from very early times, and utmost emphasis was laid upon the acquisition of knowledge. The educational institutions were many and varied in character. In its simplest form it was the gathering of one or more students in the house of a teacher. The students were brought up as members of the household and they looked upon the teacher and his wife as their father and mother. As regards tuition fees, the practice varied. In some cases no fee was taken except something voluntarily given at the end. In other cases, the sons of rich men paid a lump sum to teachers as honorarium at the commencement of their study, while the poor students performed menial services in the teacher's house in lieu of paying fees.

Object of Education.

The object of this system of education was threefold: the acquisition of knowledge, the inculcation of social duties and religious rites, and, above all, the formation of character. All the three aims were kept distinctly in the forefront, but the greatest emphasis was laid upon the last. Even the greatest champion of Brāhmanism boldly laid down that "neither the study of the Vedas, nor liberality, nor sacrifices, nor any self-imposed restraint, nor austerities ever procure the attainment of rewards to a man whose heart is contaminated by sensuality." And the control of passions must be of a thorough-going character, for "when one among all the organs slips away (from control), thereby (man's) wisdom slips away from him, even as the water (flows) through the one (open) foot of a (water-carrier's) skin." In order to achieve this high ideal of perfect mastery over senses, a life of strict discipline was prescribed for the student. He had to shun sensual pleasures of all kinds, and lead a simple austere life. He was inspired by the high ideals of the teacher with whom he lived in close and intimate contact, and imbibed social and moral virtues by his precept and example. At the same time the tender side of his nature was nourished, and domestic virtues developed by the sweet and affectionate relationship with the wife and sons of the teacher.

Subjects of Instruction.

The subjects of instruction were fairly comprehensive, and included not only literature, both sacred and secular, with its accessories, Grammar, Metrics, Poetics, Logic and Philosophy, but also technical and Scientific literature such as Medicine, Military Science, Astronomy, Astrology Mathematics, Politics, Economics, as well as divination, magic and mechanical arts of all descriptions. The practical character of the teaching in science is well illustrated by the story of Jīvaka. After he had studied medical science at Takshaśilā for seven years, his teacher adopted the following device in order to put his knowledge to the test. "Take this spade," said he, "and seek round about Takshaśilā a *yojana* on every side, and whatever plant you see which is not medicinal, bring it to me." Jīvaka accordingly walked round the city with a spade in hand but did not see anything that was not medicinal. When he reported this to his teacher, the latter was satisfied about his pupil's learning and permitted him to go home.

Takshaśilā (Taxila) was the most famous seat of learning in ancient India till the rise of Nālandā in the fifth century A.D. It had many famous teachers, and attracted students not only from all parts of India but also from other parts of the world.

Origin of University.

There were other cities besides Takshaśilā which grew to be important seats of learning. Sometimes hundreds of students gathered round a teacher in these cities and were maintained at public expense. In some cases the teacher found the surroundings of the city life to be hindrances to proper education of his students, and retired to a solitary place. There the teacher lived in humble huts with his students, and maintained a precarious living with the assistance of their kinsfolk. As soon, however, as the reputation of the teacher spread abroad, the public help placed them above all wants. From these humble beginnings arose important institutions like the University of Nālandā, the crest-jewel of the educational institutions in the whole of Asia.

It is difficult for us to realise at this distance of time the position and achievements of this famous university of old. Advanced students from different parts of Asia flocked to it in order to complete their education, and nobody without a Degree of Nālandā was thought much of in the educated world.

The Chinese traveller Hiuen Tsang studied at Nālandā

for several years and has left a short but impressive accounts of its magnificence. 'There were thousands of similar institutions in India', says he, 'but none comparable to Nālandā in grandeur. There were 10,000 students who studied not only the Buddhist literature in all its branches, but even other works such as the Vedas (including Atharvaveda), Logic, Grammar, Medicine, Sāṅkhya Philosophy etc. and discourses were given from 100 pulpits every day. Piety of generations of kings not only adorned the place with magnificent buildings, both residential and lecture halls, but supplied all the material necessaries of this vast concourse of the teachers and the taught. The revenues of about 100 villages were remitted for this purpose, and two hundred householders in these villages supplied in turn the daily needs of the inmates.' The Chinese pilgrim aptly remarks: "Hence the students here, being so abundantly supplied, do not require to ask for the four requisites, clothes, food, bedding and medicine. This is the source of the perfection of their studies, to which they have arrived."

Nālandā.

Hiuen Tsang was impressed by the atmosphere of learning that prevailed at Nālandā. "The day is not sufficient for asking and answering profound questions. From morning till night they engage in discussion; the old and the young mutually help one another."

Nālandā was meant for advanced students only, and the candidates for admission had to pass a severe preliminary test. Hiuen Tsang says that the teachers and students were men of the highest ability and talent, and their fame rapidly spread through distant regions. Learned men from different cities came in large number to settle their doubts, and the students of Nālandā were sure of honour and renown, wherever they went. In a word, the University of Nālandā was the embodiment of the highest ideal of education, and it was the visible monument of the role which India played as the teacher of Asia.

Nālandā continued as an important centre of learning down to the latest days of Hindu independence. Throughout this period famous universities like Vikramaśīla and thousands of educational institutions, both great and small, flourished all over India and imparted education in all branches of study. These were maintained, sometimes by pious donations, and sometimes at public expense, for the Indians never hesitated to loosen their purse strings for purposes of education. The type of men turned out by these educational institutions may be best

Result of Education

described in the words of Hiuen Tsang. 'When they have finished their education and have attained thirty years of age, then their character is formed and their knowledge ripe. There are some deeply versed in antiquity, who devote themselves to elegant studies and live apart from the world, and retain the simplicity of their character. These rise above mundane presents and are as insensible to renown as to the contempt of the world. Their name having spread afar, the rulers appreciate them highly, but are unable to draw them to the court. The chief of the country honours them on account of their (mental) gifts, and the people exalt their fame and render them universal homage. Forgetting fatigue they expatiate in the arts and sciences; seeking for wisdom while "relying on perfect virtue" they count not 150 miles a long journey. Though their family be in affluent circumstances, such men make up their mind to be like the vagrants and get their food by begging as they go about. With them there is honour in knowing truth and there is no disgrace in being destitute."

It is not every age, it is not every nation, that can boast of the type of men described by Hiuen Tsang. But the effect of the wonderful system of education was also seen in the high level of average men in ancient India. The most unimpeachable testimony on this point is furnished by the foreign travellers who visited India from time to time. We have already quoted above (p. 206) the observations of Megasthenes, the Greek statesman who visited India in the 3rd century B.C. Let us now turn to the account of a Chinese scholar in the 7th century A.D. Hiuen Tsang tells us:—"The Kshatriyas and Brahmans are clean-handed and unostentatious, pure and simple in life and very frugal. They are pure of themselves and not from compulsion. With respect to the ordinary people, although they are naturally light-minded, yet they are upright and honourable. In money matters they are without craft, and in administering justice they are considerate. They are not deceitful or treacherous in their conduct, and are faithful to their oaths and promises. In their rules of government there is remarkable rectitude, whilst in their behaviour there is much gentleness and sweetness." Thus according to the standards both of the East as well as of the West, Indian character was high and honourable. This was undoubtedly the result of the grand system of education which they had evolved,—a system which produced the most comprehensive literature and the best type of men.

CHAPTER XIX

Economic Condition

1. *Trade and Commerce*

During the period under review trade and commerce was in a flourishing condition. Not only was there a coasting trade between different parts of India, but a regular mercantile traffic was carried on between India on the one hand and the Eastern and Western countries on the other. Ships plied between ports on the Bay of Bengal and those in Further India, islands in the Indian Archipelago, and China. Tāmralipti, represented by modern Tamluk in Bengal, was a famous port, and we read of many voyages to it from the Chinese ports. The people of Kaliṅga and the Tamil States had also a great share in this traffic, and there was regular commercial intercourse between the eastern coast of India and the Indian colonies beyond the sea. Similarly there was a brisk trade between the western coast of India and the western countries such as Western Asia, Africa and Europe. Fa-Hien, who came to this country in the 5th century A.D., sailed from Tāmralipti to Java *via* Ceylon, and again from Java to China in Indian merchantmen. Hiuen Tsang also refers to both inland and foreign trade of India. Referring to Surāshṭra he says, "the men all derived their livelihood from the sea and engage in commerce and exchange of commodities." Of the people of another kingdom in the west he says, "commerce is their principal occupation." From ninth century A.D. we get accounts of Indian trade from the Arab writers, for at this period the Arabs took a leading part in the trade of the Western world. Indian inscriptions also refer to the activities of merchants. Numerous clay-seals, discovered in the ruins of the ancient city of Vaiśālī, bear the names of a large number of traders, bankers and merchants, and refer to their corporate organisation. Dr. Bloch, who discovered them, concludes that "something like a modern Chamber of Commerce existed in Northern India, at some big trading centre, perhaps at Pāṭaliputra." Similarly the merchants of Southern India were also distinguished for their cor-

Maritime trade

Mercantile Organisations.

porate organisations. We read of "organisation of 505 merchants", and "an assembly of merchants from 18 sub-divisions of 79 districts meeting together in a conference." The Baṇañja community had a most powerful organisation embracing merchants of different classes from distant parts of India. They are frequently referred to, and sometimes highly praised, in contemporary records. We learn from one of them "that they were brave men born to wander over many countries, penetrating regions of the six continents by land and water routes, and dealing in various articles such as horses, elephants, precious stones, perfumes, and drugs, either wholesale or in retail." Some of these trade-corporations enjoyed large prerogatives and political rights.

2. *Wealth and Prosperity*

The highly flourishing trade and commerce made the country enormously wealthy, and the reputation of the riches of India spread far and wide. Hiuen Tsang says with regard to Valabhī that "there are some hundred houses (families) or so who possess a hundred *lakhs*. The rare and valuable products of distant regions are here stored in great quantities." Similar accounts of the enormous wealth of India are given by the Muhammadan writers. "The immense wealth," "plenty of gold" etc. of India are referred to in general terms by the Arab travellers of the ninth and following centuries. Again, the Arab historians refer to the enormous quantity of wealth plundered by the Muhammadan conquerors from India. Thus we are told that after the fall of Multān, Muhammad Ibn Qāsim obtained a treasure amounting to thirteen thousand and two hundred *maṇs* weight of gold in one temple alone. Again, when Sultān Mahmūd conquered Bhim-Nagar (Kangra), a contemporary writer records that the "treasures and precious jewels accumulated in it had attained such an amount that the backs of camels would not carry it, nor vessels contain it, nor writer's hands record it, nor the imagination of an arithmetician conceive it." Coming to details he says: "The treasures were laden on the backs of as many camels as they could procure and the officers carried away the rest. The stamped coins amounted to seventy thousand thousand royal *dirhams*, and the gold and silver ingots amounted to seven hundred thousand four hundred *maṇs* in weight". The Sultān on reaching Ghaznī spread his booty on a carpet in the courtyard of his palace, and the foreign ambassadors assembled to see the wealth which they had never yet even read of in books of the ancients, and which had never been accumulated by kings of Persia or of Rūm, or even by Karun who had only to express a wish and God granted it." Such is the description of the wealth of a single temple which was by no means the richest in India, for the same writer says with regard to the riches plundered at Thāneswar that "it is impossible to recount them." Similar stories of riches untold are narrated with regard to the sack of other cities. By the treaty between Alāuddin Khiljī and the Yādava king of Devagiri, the latter paid, among other things, "600 *maunds* of pearls, two of jewels and 1000 of silver." These accounts may be exaggerated to some extent, but they suffice to give a general idea of the immense riches of the country.

CHAPTER XX

Art and Architecture.

A. Gupta Age

The enormous wealth of the country led to the development of art and architecture. The Gupta period, remarkable for the religious and intellectual renaissance, also witnessed brilliant developments in respect of all the three branches of fine art, viz architecture, sculpture, and painting

Although the political supremacy of the Guptas ended about 550 A.D., the culture in general, and the type of art in particular, ushered in by them continued for a century or even a little more Hence the whole period between 300 to 600 or 650 A.D. may be said to constitute the Gupta Age.

1. *Architecture*

The Gupta architecture continues the tradition of the old and at the same time marks the beginning of a new age. The *stūpas* and the rock-cut caves (both *chaitya*-halls and *vihāras*) continue the old forms, but possess striking novelty. The Dhamekh *stūpa* at Sārnāth, probably of the sixth century A.D., consisting of a circular stone drum with a cylindrical mass of brickworks above it, and rising to a height of 128 ft., shows the final form of evolution of this type of structure. The caves, notably those at Ajantā[1] (Nos. XVI,XVII, XIX), while retaining the essential features of old, strike an altogether new line by the great beauty of their pillars of varied design and the fine paintings with which the inner walls and ceiling are decorated. Another notable groups of rock-cut monasteries and *chaitya*-halls are those of Ellora.

The structural *chaitya*-halls and the Hindu temples with apsidal ends follow the old traditions. Small flat-roofed temples, sometimes surrounded by pillared halls, are characteristic of the early Gupta period, and the small but elegant temple at Sānchī furnishes a good example. But a few shrines, with a *śikhara* on the roof, usher in a new style in North India which later came to be adopted all over the country. Though these

1. The name of this place is also written as Ajanta and Ajaṇtā.

temples of the Gupta period were neither imposing in dimensions nor very beautiful in design, they mark the beginning of the temple architecture, properly so called, in North India, which was destined to exercise profound influence even in far-off lands. Two best examples of this type are furnished by the brick temple at Bhitargaon and the Daśāvatāra temple at Deogarh.

2. *Sculpture*

But it is in the domain of sculpture that the Gupta period witnessed the highest development of art in India. The figures of Buddha, found in large number at Sārnāth and other places, show a fully evolved form which was regarded as the model for succeeding ages in and outside India. It was derived from the Mathurā type and owes nothing to Greek or any other foreign influence. Indeed the Gupta sculpture may be regarded as typically Indian and classic in every sense of the term. As a great art critic has observed the "Gupta art marks the zenith in a perfectly normal cycle of artistic evolution." The fine image of Buddha at Sārnāth exhibits at once the grace and refinement as well as delicacy and repose, and offers a unique combination of perfection in technique with the expression of the highest spiritual conception which makes it a masterpiece. This high quality generally marks also the figures of Brāhmaṇical gods as illustrated by the images of Śiva, Vishṇu and others in the sculptured panels of the Deogarh temple. On the whole the evolution of the perfect type of divinities may be said to be the chief glory of Gupta sculpture. These divine images not only possess beautiful figures, at once charming and dignified, but are also beaming with a radiant spiritual expression. These characteristics, to a more or less degree, are present in all the figure sculptures, both human and mythical.

The beauty and charm which distinguishes human figures is equally present in the terracottas and decorative sculptures which are at once vigorous and well-designed. The deeply carved scrolls, with rich foliage and diminutive human and animal figures, deserve the highest praise for their naturalism and beautiful execution.

Metal Work

The Gupta artists and craftsmen were no less capable in working metals. The famous iron pillar at Delhi, near the Qutb Minār, is a marvel of metallurgical skill. The art of casting copper statues on a large scale by the *cire perdue* process was practised with conspicuous success. A copper image of Buddha, about 80 feet high, was erected at Nālandā in Bihār at the close of the sixth century; and the fine Sultanganj Buddha, 7½ feet high, is still to be seen in the Museum at Birmingham.

In general, a sublime idealism, combined with a highly developed sense of rhythm and beauty, characterises the Gupta sculptures, and there are vigour and refinement in their design and execution. The intellectual element dominates Gupta art and keeps under control the highly developed emotional display and the exuberance of decorative elements which characterise the art of succeeding ages.

3. *Painting.*

Literary evidence leaves no doubt that the art of painting was cultivated in India from very remote times, for decorative paintings in walls of houses and lifelike portraits are referred to in the canonical Pāli texts as well as in the Epics. But the most ancient extant paintings in India do not go back more than a century or two before the Christian Era. These are painted frescoes in the Jogimārā cave of the Rāmgarh hill in the Surguja State, M. P. Traces of painting also exist in the Bedsa cave and probably belong to the 3rd century A.D.

But the best fresco painting in India is illustrated in the series of Ajantā caves constructed between the first and seventh century A.D. These caves are 29 in number, and even as late as 1879 A.D. traces of painting remained in sixteen caves. Much has disappeared since and what remains today is only a very small fragment of the pictures which originally adorned the walls and ceilings of the caves.

Ajantā.

The bulk of the painting undoubtedly belongs to the period 400-640 A.D., and was mainly executed under the patronage of the Vākāṭaka and the Chālukya kings. Although the pictures are termed frescoes, the process is somewhat different from that which is understood by that term in European painting. In Ajantā the rock-walls of the caves were first covered by a mixture of clay, cowdung, and pulverized traprock, and then a thin coating of fine white plaster was applied. The ground thus prepared was carefully smoothed and kept moistened, and this produced a surface on which the design was first sketched and then painted, the usual colours being white, red and brown in various shades, a dull green, and blue.

The pictures depict figures of Buddha and various episodes of his present and past lives i.e. Jātaka stories. Animal and vegetable world is drawn upon in profusion for ornamental decorations, and the designs are as varied and graceful as they are fanciful. As regards the technical skill and aesthetic value of these paintings the following observations of Griffiths, who spent 13 years in closely studying them, may be said to represent the general views.

'In spite,' he writes, 'of its obvious limitations, I find the work so accomplished in execution, so consistent in convention, so vivacious and varied in design, and full of such evident delight in beautiful form and colour, that I cannot help ranking it with some of the early art which the world has agreed to praise in Italy. . . .The Ajantā workmanship is admirable; long subtle curves are drawn with great precision in a line of unvarying thickness with one sweep of the brush; the touch is often bold and vigorous, the handling broad, and in some cases the *impasto* is as solid as in the best Pompeian work. . .The draperies, too, are thoroughly understood and though the folds may be somewhat conventionally drawn, they express most thoroughly the peculiarities of the Oriental treatment of unsewn cloth. . . .For the purposes of art education no better examples could be placed before an Indian art-student than those to be found in the caves of Ajantā. Here we have art with life in it, human faces full of expression, limbs drawn with grace and action, flowers which bloom, birds which soar, and beasts that spring, or fight, or patiently carry burdens; all are taken from Nature's book—growing after her pattern, and in this respect differing entirely from Muhammadan art, which is unreal, unnatural, and therefore incapable of development.'

A Danish artist, who has published a valuable professional criticism of Ajantā paintings, declares that 'they represent the climax to which genuine Indian art has attained'; and that 'everything in these pictures from the composition as a whole to the smallest pearl or flower testifies to depth of insight coupled with the greatest skill.'

Bāgh

Some fine specimens of Indian paintings adorned the caves at Bāgh, a village in the Gwalior State, even as late as 19th century. But very little of them now remains. These paintings possessed the same high quality as those at Ajantā and probably belonged to the 6th or first half of the 7th century A.D.

B. Post-Gupta Age

1. *Architecture*

(a) *Rock-cut caves*

During the period of six hundred years that followed the Gupta age we find a remarkable development in architecture. As before we have only specimens of religious structure. The rock-cut caves now enter the final phase of development and are gradually replaced by structural buildings. Nevertheless we have a few fine examples such as the Brāhmaṇical series (as distinguished from the earlier Buddhist ones) at Ellora, and the fine Brāhmaṇical temples at Elephanta and Salsette islands (near Bombay), all excavated between the 7th and 9th century A.D. Somewhat earlier than these are (1) a number of pillared halls, and (2) the seven monolithic temples popularly called *rathas* or *Pagodas* at Māmallapuram, 35 miles south of Madras, erected respectively by the Pallava kings Mahendravarman and Narasiṁhavarman (p. 395) in the 7th century A.D. The *rathas* culminated in a complete reproduction of massive structural temple cut out of rock, of which the unique example, unrivalled anywhere else in the world, is furnished by the Kailāsa temple at Ellora built by the Rāshṭrakūṭa king Kṛishṇa. An entire hill-side was cut off to the extent of 160 ft. by 280 ft., and was converted into a magnificent monolithic temple with spacious halls and finely carved pillars. Fergusson refers to it as "one of the most singular and interesting monuments of architectural art in India," and V. Smith calls it "the most extensive and sumptuous of the rock-cut shrines," and "the most marvellous architectural freak in India."

Kailāsa Temple.

The Jaina caves at Ellora (800-950 A.D.) bring to an end, for all practical purposes, the rock-cut architecture of India, whose gradual evolution we can trace from the days of Aśoka. They were gradually superseded by the structural examples i.e. temples built by means of dressed stone masonry, which is undoubtedly the more normal and rational mode of construction, once the technique had sufficiently developed.

(b) *Structural Temples*

These structural temples may be broadly divided into two classes, according to the shape of the *śikhara* i.e. the towering superstructure above the sanctum containing the image of the god. Those in North Indian temples look like a solid tower with curvilinear vertical ribs,

Two styles.

bulging in the middle and ending in a very narrow necking covered by a distinct ribbed piece of round stone known as *āmalaka*. The *śikharas* in Southern India have the appearance of straight-lined pyramidal towers, made up of a series of gradually receding stories divided by horizontal bands, and ending in a dome, or occasionally, a barrel-roofed ridge. Both the North and South Indian *śikharas* are decorated with sculptures, which often, specially in the former, take the form of miniature reproduction of the *śikhara* itself. According to geographical distribution these two styles of architecture are known respectively as North Indian or Indo-Aryan and South Indian or Dravidian.

(c) *North Indian Style*

The large number of temples at Bhuvanesvar in Orissa illustrate the evolution of the North Indian style. The temples consisted mainly of two parts, the cella or sanctum (*garbha-griha*) roofed by the *śikhara*, and a *maṇḍapa* or porch in front covered by a low pyramidal roof. Of the numerous temples at Bhuvanesvar, the Mukteśvara, Rājarāni, and the Liṅgarāja (the Great Temple) with its *śikhara*, 160 ft. in height, are the three best specimens. The famous but dilapidated temple at Konārak is remarkable for its marvellous sculptures and the beautifully designed pyramidal roof of the porch, happily intact, which has been praised as "the most perfectly proportioned structure." The temple of Jagannāth at Puri is also another fine specimen. From the Orissa coast on the east to Kāshmir on the west, the whole of North India was studded with temples of this style. An important group of them is found at Khajarāho, the capital of the Chandellas, and they were built by the rulers of this dynasty between 900 and 1150 A.D. A beautiful variation of this style, found in Rājputāna and Gujarāt, "is characterized by a free use of columns, carved with all imaginable richness, strut brackets, and exquisite marble ceilings with cusped pendants." The two best specimens of this style are those at Mt. Abu, built wholly of white marble in 1031 and 1230. A.D. "The beauty and delicacy of the carving and the richness of design" of these two temples surpass all description.

We get a vivid idea of the splendour and magnificence of these North Indian temples from the following account of the temples of Mathurā by Al Utbi, Secretary to Sultān Mahmūd of Ghaznī.

"In the middle of the city there was a temple larger and finer than the rest, which can neither be described nor painted. The Sultān thus wrote respecting it: "If any should wish to construct a building equal to this, he should not be able to do it without expending an hundred thousand thousand red *dinārs* and it would occupy two hundred years, even though the most experienced and able workmen were employed." Among the idols there were five made of red gold, each five yards high, fixed in the air without support. In the eyes of one of these idols there were two rubies of such value, that if any one were to sell such as are like them, he would obtain fifty thousand *dinārs*. On another, there was a sapphire purer than water and more sparkling than crystal; the weight was four hundred and fifty *miskāls*. The two feet of another idol weighed four thousand four hundred *miskāls*, and the entire quantity of gold yielded by the bodies of these idols was ninety-eight thousand three hundred *miskāls*. The idols of silver amounted to two hundred, but they could not be weighed wthout breaking them into pieces and putting them into scales. The Sultān gave orders that all temples should be burnt with naphtha and fire, and levelled with the ground."

(d) *South Indian Style*

The earliest examples of the Dravidian style are the rock-cut temple known as Dharmarāja-*ratha* at Māmallapuram and the structural temples at Kānchī, known as Kailāsanātha and the Vaikuṇṭha Perumal,—all built by the Pallava kings. The first is a monolithic structure which, along with six others on the same site, are known as the seven *rathas* or *Pagodas*, and show the ingenuity of the Pallava artists.

The Cholas, who succeeded the Pallavas as the dominant political power in the south, were mighty builders. They built, among others, two magnificent temples at Tanjore and Gangaikoṇḍacholapuram in the Trichinopoly District. The great Śiva temple at Tanjore is 'the largest, highest and the most ambitious' religious structure in India. The temple is 180 feet long; the base of the sanctum is 82 ft. square and two stories in height; above this rises, in 13 stories, the massive pyramidal tower 190 ft. high. While every inch of this vast exterior was richly carved with sculptures, the interior walls of the cella were decorated with fine paintings.

(e) *Temple in the Deccan*

The Deccan plateau had at first no independent style of its own, and we find temples both of North and South Indian style at Aihole, Bādāmi and Pattadakal. From after 1000 A.D., however, we find some notable changes gradually leading to the evolution of a distinct style, which some regard as intermediate in type between North and South Indian styles, and others, merely as a variation of the latter with hardly any influence of the former. The low pyramidal *śikhara* of these temples, however, undoubtedly has the appearance of a blending of the northern and southern types, and in height and composition may be regarded as intermediate between the two. The influence of the North Indian style is clearly emphasised by the introduction of miniature North Indian *śikhara* as a decorative element. There is, however, no doubt that the influence of the South Indian style is more marked.

Most of the temples of this type were built by or during the reigns of the Later Chālukya and Hoysala kings. Hence the new style is often called after these royal dynasties, Chālukya, Hoysala or Chālukya-Hoysala. Apart from the shape of the *śikhara*, these temples, which are mostly found in modern Mysore, 'are characterised by a richly carved base or plinth, supporting a polygonal or star-shaped temple.' The wealth and variety of sculptures on the base is unrivalled in any buildings, ancient or modern, and the Hoysala temples are appropriately referred to "as one of the most marvellous exhibitions of human labour to be found even in the patient east."

Hoysala style.

The Hoysaleśvara temple at Dorasamudra is the best example of this style. It really consists of two temples built side by side and connected by the adjacent transepts. Each of these is 112 ft. long and 100 ft. wide, and cruciform in plan, so that its exterior shows a large number of projections and angular surfaces. The two structures with their *nandi* pavilions rest on a platform having angles corresponding to those of the main buildings. Its entire external elevation of 25 ft. is covered by a continuous series of mouldings of animal figures and floral scrolls which are carried round the whole building covering a length of about 710 ft. The figures of elephants, which cover the lowest frieze and are minutely carved with rider and trappings, are about two thousand in number. More than ten such carved friezes decorate the lower part above which begin the big sculptured figures on the walls. It has been rightly remarked by a great art critic that "this temple, chiefly on account of the emphatic prodigality of its sculptural embellishment, is, without exaggeration, one of the most remarkable monuments ever produced by the hand of man."

2. *Sculpture.*

In striking contrast with architecture, the art of sculpture suffered a great decline during the post-Gupta age. The main reason seems to be the undue weight of religious conventions, for the artists had to follow scrupulously the descriptions of the deities in religious texts without any regard to aesthetic considerations The result was generally a grotesque, and at best a dull lifeless conventional, figure which hardly made any aesthetic appeal. Nevertheless, numerous specimens all over India show that the sculptors still possessed high technical skill and sometimes even produced works distinguished alike by charm and elegance. The sculptures of Eastern India during the Pāla period form a class by themselves and show a fair degree of excellence. The figures as well as decorative sculptures of Orissa often reached a high standard of excellence. The earlier Chola sculptures also maintain a very high level, and some of the bronze figures of Naṭarāja from South India have elicited high admiration of art critics. In the Deccan some of the sculptures of the Kailāsa temple, Ellora, and the reliefs of Elephanta cave (8th century A.D.) may be regarded as finest examples of sculpture of this age.

3. *Painting.*

The ceilings of the rock-cut temple at Kailāsa and the adjoining caves (Indrasabhā, Lankeśvara, and Gaṇeśa Lena) contain paintings of a type and style different from those of Ajantā and Bāgh. The walls were also probably painted, but only a few traces have been preserved. Most of these paintings are coeval with the temple itself and thus belong to the 8th century A.D.

The cave temple Sittannavasal in Pudukottai (Madras) contains some fine paintings of the time of the Pallava king Mahendravarman. They are elegant and beautiful, and show the degree of excellence which the art had attained during the Pallava rule.

Chola paintings of the 11th century A.D. have been found in the Great Temple at Tanjore. These were overlaid with later paintings and have only recently been exposed. Their high quality recalls those of Ajantā and offer a striking contrast to the later paintings which covered them so long.

The art of painting in later periods is mostly known from illuminations on palm-leaves of manuscripts found in Eastern India and Gujarāt. But although they are basically related to those of Ajantā, they are much inferior. Although some of the paintings in the manuscripts of the Pāla period are of good quality, they cannot be compared with the earlier paintings, specially those at Ajantā, Bāgh, and Sittannavasal in respect of colour, expression, or drawing of line. In these elements which constitute the essence of the art, the specimens of the earlier age up to the 7th century A.D. represent the high watermark of the art of painting in India.

CHAPTER XXI

Degradation of Hindu Society.

We have had occasion to notice in a previous chapter that one of the chief distinctions of Indo-Aryan culture was its great power of assimilation and absorption. We have seen, how, not only the aborigines with whom the Indo-Aryans first came into contact in this country, but also the foreign hordes like the Greeks, Parthians, Śakas, and Kushāṇas were gradually absorbed in the vast Indian society. To this list we may now add the Hūṇas and the Gurjaras. For, in spite of their pretended pedigrees reaching back to mythical heroes of the *Rāmāyaṇa* and the *Mahābhārata*, it has now been satisfactorily established that the Hūṇas and other allied tribes who invaded India in the 5th and 6th centuries A.D. form important elements among the Rājput clans. The Hūṇas are still reckoned as one of the thirty-six Rājput clans. The Gurjaras were also most probably of foreign origin, and the imperial Pratīhāras, admittedly of Gurjara stock, re-appear in mediaeval history as the Partīhāras, one of the four famous "Agnikulas" i.e. the Rājput clans who are alleged to have issued out of the fire-pit at Mount Abu.

The catholicity of the Hindus.

It is thus quite clear that at the beginning of the period under review the Indo-Aryan society had the same catholicity as of old. The last crowning act of this spirit was the absorption of Buddhism by the Hindu society to which reference has already been made.

The power of assimilation also remained unabated. The Indians drew inspiration from foreign art and numismatics and derived considerable help from the Romans in the development of astronomy.

In strange contrast, however, with this liberal catholicity of old times, we find the growth of a spirit of narrow exclusiveness which was destined to bring utter ruin to the Hindus. This aspect of their civilization is forcefully described by Alberuni in the following words:—

Growth of narrowness.

"All the fanaticism of the Hindus is directed against those who do not belong to them, against all foreigners. They call them Mlechchhas i.e. impure, and forbid having any connection with them, be it by intermarriage or any other kind of relationship, or by sitting, eating and drinking with them, because thereby they think they would be polluted. They consider as impure anything which touches the fire and the water of a foreigner; and no household can exist without these two elements. They are not allowed to receive anybody who does not belong to them, even if he wished it, or was inclined to their religion. This, too, renders any connection with them quite impossible and constitutes the widest gulf between us and them.

"The Hindus believe that there is no country but theirs, no nation like theirs, no king like theirs, no religion like theirs, no science like theirs.' They are haughty, foolishly vain, self-conceited and stolid. They are by nature niggardly in communicating that which they know, and they take the greatest possible care to withhold it from men of another caste, among their own people, still much more, of course, from any foreigner. According to their belief, there is no other country on earth but theirs, no other race of man but theirs, and no created beings besides them have any knowledge or science whatsoever. Their haughtiness is such that, if you tell them of any science or scholar in Khurāsān and Persis, they will think you to be both an ignoramus and a liar. If they travelled and mixed with other nations, they would soon change their mind, for their ancestors were not as narrow-minded as the present generation is."

The sad picture of narrowness and bigotry, so brilliantly sketched by the shrewd and critical Arab scholar, is an unerring sign of the degradation of the Hindu society in the 11th century A.D. It is all the more disheartening if we remember the previous history of the Indians in their relation with the outside world. Well might an historian exclaim "From what heighth fallen into what low pit thou seest."

Evil effects of the caste system.

In looking out for a cause for so great a change our attention is immediately drawn to the caste system which had assumed a rigid form since the revival of Brāhmaṇical religion. It has already been noted that in the Vedic period society was divided into distinct classes such as the Bhrāhmaṇas, Kshatriyas, Vaiśyas, and Śūdras. This was neither unusual nor productive of great evils. Similar distinctions are still observable in European society. Compare, for example the Lords, the Clergy, the Middle class, and the Labourers in Englnad. But these class distinctions are a long way off from the rigid system of caste, and there were many intermediate stages between the two. The essential features of the caste system, viz. the ascendancy of the Brāhmaṇas, the determination of caste by the accident of birth, and the prohibition of inter-dining and intermarriage between different castes, are all matters of slow growth. None of these was sanctioned by ancient scriptures and none of them was established without a hard struggle which continued almost up to the end of the Hindu period. In the end, however, the Brāhmaṇas succeeded in spite of stubborn resistance of the Kshatriyas, and the decline and fall of Buddhism set the final seal to their supremacy. Once assured of their supreme position, the Brāhmaṇas set to work with a vigour, consistency, and organisation which should have been reserved for a better cause. It is difficult to name any social change more miraculous than what the Brāhmaṇas had accomplished. Taking their stand on ancient *śāstras* or sacred scriptures, they introduced new elements into society which were utterly against the spirit and letter of those very *śāstras*. Thus in spite of practical instances to the contrary, recorded in ancient books, they enunciated the bold doctrine that none but an issue of Brāhmaṇa parents could become a Brāhmaṇa. In the face of the fact that even the late *Manu-saṁhitā* approves of certain forms of intermarriage between different castes, marriage was strictly confined within the caste. But the strangest phenomenon was reserved to the last. Though the sacred literature permits the cooking of food, even sacrificial food, by a Śūdra, and although no ancient books having the least pretension to a sacred character, prohibit inter-dining among different castes, elaborate regulations were laid down for controlling 'food' and 'touch', and the Brāhmaṇas were polluted if they even crossed the shadow of a low caste!

Slowly but steadily the Brāhmaṇas managed to degrade the rest of the society to a state of marked inferiority and subordination. The Kshatriyas wielded royal authority and hence enjoyed some amount of social prestige, but this was counterbalanced by gradually restricting the rank and title of Kshatriyas to a microscopic minority. The Vaiśyas were similarly dealt with. Ultimately the Kshatriyas and Vaiśyas practically vanished from Indian society, and their descendants, divided among the large number of professional castes we see around us to-day sank into the position of the Śūdras, to which the descendants of various aboriginal races, incorporated in Aryan society, had already been consigned, as so many different castes.

Thus we find that in *Manu-saṁhitā* the Ābhīras, Mallas, Khasas, Andhras, Vaidehas, and Māgadhas are described as castes, whereas they were really famous tribes. Similarly, the weavers, potters, carpenters, goldsmiths, blacksmiths etc. originally denoted groups of men following those professions, but they were later stereotyped as castes. This took place later than the age of *Manu-saṁhitā*, for they are there included in the list of professions and not of castes. But in *Manu-saṁhitā* we find a systematic attempt at explaining the origin of this motley group of castes by definite and comprehensive theory. These castes are divided into two categories. The castes of the first category are said to have been formed by those Brāhmaṇas, Kshatriyas, and Vaiśyas, who were at various times degraded to the rank of Śūdras for omitting their sacred duties or failure to consult the Brāhmaṇas. The origin of castes of the second category is explained by what is known as the theory of Mixed Caste.

According to this theory the issue of a marriage between different castes formed altogether a separate caste, and a large number of castes were derived by mixed marriages among the original four castes and the resultant sub-castes. The theory bears the stamp of absurdity on its very face and need only be stated to be rejected in scorn. Fancy, it seeks to explain the origin of the Chīnas, Yavanas, Śakas, Sātvatas and Ābhīras in one of these ways! Nor is the theory, when carefully scrutinised, always complimentary to the Brāhmaṇas. The Chaṇḍālas, for example, are said to have been the off spring of Śūdra father and Brāhmaṇa mother. As the number of Chaṇḍālas is considerably larger than that of the Brāhmaṇas, at least in certain localities, are we to believe that the Brāhmaṇa girls were more attached to the Śūdras than to men of their own caste, although there could be no legal marriage between the two? But whatever we might think of the theory, the resulting state of things was entirely satisfactory to the high pretensions of the Brāhmaṇas. The position of honour now incontestably belonged to them, and as law-makers of society they were the arbiters of the destiny of the rest of the population. They practically monopolised all learning and culture. The Kshatriyas and Vaiśyas of old shared it with them, but there were hardly any remnants of them left in society, and those that were, were at the tender mercies of the Brāhmaṇas who could degrade them into Śūdra castes. The political condition of the last three or four centuries also helped the Brāhmaṇas a great deal. The royal authority mainly rested in the hands of the descendants of the Hūṇas and Gurjaras like the Rājputs, or the aborigines of the soil recently incorporated in Aryan society like the Chandellas. These kings no doubt ranked as Kshatriyas, but they had no glorious traditions behind them, and their recent origin obliged them to look up to the Brāhmaṇas for the social prestige and status which was in the power of the Brāhmaṇas alone to give. These were, therefore, naturally subservient to the Brāhmaṇas who could always use them as lever against anybody who dared to contest their supremacy.

The Hindu society now resembled that unfortunate human being whose head and feet alone were active but whose intermediate limbs were maimed or paralysed. It is obvious that the one was as little capable of healthy growth and progress as the other. It is equally obvious that the Brāhmaṇas alone cannot be held responsible for this lamentable state of things. After all, people get what they deserve. The Brāhmaṇas could not have asserted their ascendancy if the people possessed a manly spirit and vigour, and could tear asunder the chains of superstition by which they were bound to the perpetual servitude. Anyone who, not unnaturally , wonders how a gifted people like the Hindus could readily submit to the yoke of these superstitions, need only look around him to-day. He will see how groups of men, not inferior in moral and mental qualities to any on earth, are still bound down to those very shackles of superstition. He will see how, in spite of the knowledge of the ancient Vedas, Brāhmaṇas, Sūtras, and Smṛitis, millions of men in Bengal unwittingly submit to the dictates of a Brāhmaṇa writer of the 15th century,—dictates which are in flagrant contrast with the injunctions of the ancient sacred literature. He will be confronted with the strange spectacle of a people adhering neither to common sense nor to traditions of her best days, but bowing down with reverent awe to an all-devouring Moloch—the superstitious customs of degenerate days.

The rigid system of caste, with its attendant evils such as untouchability and prohibition of inter-dining and inter-marriage, to an extent not contemplated even in the Smṛitis, produced disastrous effects on Hindu society. It arrested the development of intellect and education among the masses, degraded arts and crafts by relegating their votaries to a position of inferiority, and checked the growth of trade and commerce by emphasising ceremonials of purity and condemning the crossing of the seas and visiting *mlechchha* countries. The division of people into close compartments prevented the growth of a national feeling. A Brāhmaṇa of Bengal had more in common with a Brāhmaṇa of Kanauj, than either had with a mechanic or peasant of his own province. Like mediaeval Europe India was divided horizontally and not vertically. In Europe, however, the class interests were gradually subordinated to national interests, but the rigidity of the caste system in India kept the class interests perpetually alive, and true national sentiment was never awakened in the minds of the people. Above all, the caste system, with its superstitious outgrowths and purificatory ceremonials, brought about that narrowness of outlook and haughty exclusiveness which have been noticed by Alberuni. This exclusiveness, again, was in a way responsible for the political downfall of India. For it is the aloofness from the outer world which kept the Hindus ignorant of the development of science, particularly of military science, among other Asiatic nations, and neither high ideals nor brilliant courage could make up for that deficiency. A careful study of the series of Mumhammadan invasions which ultimately overwhelmed the Indian States leaves the impression upon every mind that the Indian soldiers were not a whit inferior to the Muhammadans in respect of courage, valour, and endurance, but they suffered defeat in spite of this, because the Hindus did not keep pace with the progress of military science abroad, and they were unaware of those military tactics in which their opponents excelled. It is true that the foreigners had conquered India even before, but their conquests seldom extended beyond the borderlands and were never of long duration. The Indians successfully contested their grounds and always succeeded in ultimately repelling the foreign foe. Their inability to do the same in the case of Muhammadan invasions, leading to the subjugation of the whole country by this foreign race, is a measure of their degradation which was brought about in no small degree by the system of caste. It may, of course, be argued that the caste is not the cause, but a phenomenon of the weakness and degradation of the people which made Muhammadan conquest possible. There is possibly a great deal of truth in this argument, but there can hardly be any doubt that the growth of caste and the degradation of people acted and reacted upon each other, and each stage in the development of the caste system was but a milestone in the downward march of the Hindus to sure destruction.

But the caste system was not the only untoward feature of the society that the neo-Brāhmaṇical religion had evolved. The lowering of woman as a class from the high position she had once enjoyed marked its degradation in no less conspicuous manner. This changed attitude is evident from the tone of *Manu-saṁhitā*, the Veda of the Brāhmaṇical revival. Manu has no doubt some honeyed phrases echoing the noble sentiments of old.

Degradation of woman as a class.

We read for example: "Women must be honoured and adorned by their fathers, brothers, husbands, and brothers-in-law who desire their own welfare. Where women are honoured, there the gods are pleased; but where they are not honoured, no sacred rite yields rewards". But these sweet phrases are cast into shade by the practical regulations recommended by the law-giver. The fundamental doctrine of women's perpetual subjection is boldly laid down: "In childhood, a female must be subject to her father, in youth to her husband, when her lord is dead, to her son: a woman must never be independent." The natural affectionate relation between husband and wife is completely marred by the studied inferiority in which women are placed. "Though destitute of virtue, or seeking pleasure (elsewhere), or devoid of good qualities, (yet) a husband must be constantly worshipped as a god by a faithful wife. She who shows disrespect to (a husband) who is addicted to (some evil) passion, is a drunkard, or diseased, shall be deserted for three months (and be) deprived of her ornaments and furniture." But the husband is not required to follow a similar line of conduct. For "she who drinks spirituous liquor, is of bad conduct, rebellious, diseased, mischievous or wasteful, may at any time be superseded (by another wife)"! Nay, more; the husband could supersede his wife on much less serious grounds. "A barren wife may be superseded in the eighth year, she whose children (all) die in the tenth, she who bears only daughters in the eleventh, but she who is quarrelsome, without delay." And the poor wife was to bear this degradation with stoic calmness; for "a wife who, being superseded, in anger departs from her husband's house, must either be instantly confined or cast off in the presence of the family." Sometimes she could even be beaten with a rope or a split bamboo. The poor wife was expected to follow her husband even in death by burning herself alive, but the husband, 'having given sacred fires to his wife who dies before him, may marry again, and again kindle the fires.' Strangest of all, women, who once even composed Vedic hymns, were not allowed to study the Vedas and perform sacrificial rites.[1]

Manu prohibited the remarriage of Hindu widows, but it is quite evident that such remarriage was prevalent in his time. Similarly, in other respects, too, the injunctions of *Manu-saṁhitā* were probably a foretaste of what was desired to happen in future, rather than an indication of the actual circumstances in his time. But the deliberate attempt to degrade the position of women, which is perceptible in the *Manu-saṁhitā*, was destined to bear fruit at no distant date.

The iniquitous barrier which the Hindus had raised between man and man, and man and woman, sapped the strength and vitality of national as well as domestic life. No wonder they fell an easy prey to the followers of a religion which not only preached but practised the universal brotherhood of its adherents.

1. Manu V. 154, 168 ; IX. 14-18, 78-83 ; VIII. 299

CHAPTER XXII

Indian Colonies in the Far East

The beginnings of Indian colonisation in Burma, Indo-China and Indonesia have been referred to above. During the period under review many of these colonies grew into powerful kingdoms and empires under kings with Indian name and most probably of Indian descent. It is not possible to deal with each of them in detail and a brief general account must suffice.

1. *Suvarṇadvīpa*

The Hindu colonists established several States in Malay Peninsula during the first five centuries of the Christian era. Although we know some interesting facts about them from Chinese chronicles and ruins of temples and images in various parts of the country, it is not possible to write a connected history of them. But there is no doubt that the Malay Peninsula

Malay Peninsula.

served as the main gate of the Indian colonial expansion in the Far East. Takkola, modern Takua Pa, was the first landing stage of the Indian traders and colonists. From this some followed an all-sea route along the coast, but many passed across the narrow Isthmus of Kra directly to the opposite coast round the Bay of Bandon, and then proceeded further east, by land or sea, to Siam, Cambodia, and Annam. The archaeological remains indicate the existence of flourishing Indian colonies along this trans-peninsular route, the most important of which were Nakhon Sri Dhammarat (Ligor), and Chaiya, a little to the north, both mainly agriculturist, on the eastern coast, and Takua Pa and a few others, which prospered by the exploitation of tin and gold mines, on the western coast. Even to-day persons of an Indian cast of features are common on the west coast near Takua Pa, while colonies of Brāhmaṇas of Indian descent survive at Nakhon Shri Dhammarat and Patalung and trace the arrival of their ancestors from India by an overland route across the Malay Peninsula.

Java.

We have four Sanskrit inscriptions of a king called Pūrṇavarman who ruled in Western Java about fifth century A.D. Two or three centuries later Sañjaya founded a powerful kingdom in Central Java, with its capital probably at Matarām.

Sumatra.

The kingdom of Śrīvijaya was founded in Sumatra in or before the fourth century A.D.

All these States—Malay Peninsula, Java and Sumatra—were conquered by the Śailendras who founded a powerful empire in the eighth century A. D. They established their sway over nearly the whole of Suvaraṇadvīpa, comprising Malay Peninsula, Sumatra, Java, Bali, Borneo, and the other islands of the East Indies. The Śailendra Empire is

Śailendras.

referred to by various Arab writers who designate it as Zābag, Zābaj, or the empire of *Mahārāja*, and describe its wealth and grandeur in glowing terms. The *Mahārāja* is said to have been overlord of a large "number of islands extending over a length of 1000 *parsangs* or more. Even the most rapid vessels could not complete in two years a tour round the isles which are under his possession." This is supported by contemporary epigraphic evidence which shows that the Śailendras also established political authority for some time over Kambuja, and probably raided the coast of Champā. The Śailendras were Buddhists and maintaineed diplomatic relations with China as well as with the Pāla and Chola emperors who helped them to build Buddhist sanctuaries at Nālandā and Negapatam. The Śailendras were also great builders and the famous Barabuḍur in Java is an undying monument to their power and glory.

The Śailendra empire declined after the 9th century A. D., but continued for two centuries more. The defeat of the Śailendras by the Cholas has been mentioned above. Not long after this the Śailendras gradually pass from our view. Java threw off the yoke of the Śailendras in the 9th century A.D. But gradually the central political authority was shifted to the eastern part of the island, and both Western

Eastern Java.

and Central Java lost their importance. A number of powerful kingdoms flourished in Eastern Java among which those of Kaḍiri and Singhasāri were the most important. By the 14th century A.D. the city of Majapahit became the seat of a great empire under Rājasanagara, who ascended the throne in A.D. 1350. A detailed list of the States subordinate to him is given in a contemporary literary work, *Nāgara-Kṛitāgama.* The long list shows the hegemony of nearly the whole of Malay Peninsula and Malay Archipelago under him, the only notable exception being the Philippines. Roughly

Majapahit empire.

speaking, the empire of Rājasanagara comprised the Dutch possessions in the East Indies with the addition of Malay Peninsula, but excluding perhaps

Northern Celebes. The *Nāgara-Kṛitāgama* refers to a number of countries which had trade relations with Majapahit, and from which Brāhmaṇas and Śramaṇas visited the Javanese capital. Thus we read: "There came unceasingly, in large numbers, people from all lands such as Jambudvīpa, Kāmboja, Chīna, Yavana, Champā, Karṇāṭaka, Gauḍa, and Siam. They came in ships with merchandise. Monks and distinguished Brāhmaṇas also came from these lands and were entertained." Jambudvīpa, of course, refers to India, while Karṇātaka and Gauḍa are specially mentioned, probably to indicate a closer intimacy with Bengal and Kanarese districts. The Javanese had indeed a high regard for India, for in one verse (83.2) the *Nāgara-Kṛitāgama* says that Jambudvīpa and Java are the good lands *par excellence.* The intimate relation between the two countries is also indicated by the fact that the laudatory poems in honour of the Javanese king were written by the monk Buddhāditya of Kāñchī (Conjeevaram) and the Brāhmaṇa named Mutali Sahṛidaya, probably a Tamil Brāhmaṇa.

The decline of the empire set in early in the 15h century. Among its succession States Malacca occupied the most important position both as a political power as well as a big centre of trade and commerce. Its Hindu king married the daughter of a Muslim ruling chief in Sumatra, and became a convert to the new faith. Some members of the royal family of Java also adopted the Muslim religion which was introduced in this region by Indian merchants, mostly from Gujarāt. The gradual and peaceful penetration of Islam forced the Hindu king with his followers to take refuge in the island of Bali, which had been colonised by the Hindus more than a thousand years before and was then subordinate to Java. The island of Bali henceforth became the seat of a highly flourishing Indo-Javanese culture, and it still retains the proud position of being the last refuge of Brāhmaṇical religion in the East Indies or Suvarṇadvīpa of old.

Bali

2. *Champā*

Along the eastern coast of Indo-China, now known as Annam, a Hindu kingdom was established as early as the second or third century A.D. The capital of this kingdom was the city of Champā, and this designation was also applied to the whole country. We have got an inscription of king Śrī Māra written in Sanskrit, which is usually referred to the second or third century A.D. though it may be

Śrī Māra.

somewhat later. The history of this kingdom is known in some details from a large number of inscriptions and references in Chinese chronicles. Bhadravarman, one of the early kings, ruled nearly over the whole of Modern Annam (excluding Tonkin and Cochin-China), divided into three provinces known as Amarāvatī Vijaya, and Pāṇḍuraṅga. Tonkin, the country immediately to the north, was peopled by the Annamites, and formed a part of the Chinese empire. The Hindu kings of Champā, anxious to extend their power northwards, often came into conflict with the Chinese and suffered invasion by the Imperial troops, sometimes with disastrous consequences. Later, when the Annamites threw off the yoke of China and established an independent kingdom, there were constant hostilities between them and Champā. We know the names of quite a large number of kings of Champā belonging to different dynasties such as Sambhuvarman, Satyavarman, Indravarman, Harivarman, Siṁhavarman etc. Champā was often invaded by its western neighbour, the kingdom of Kambuja, and on one occassion, Jayavarman VII, the king of Kambuja, defeated Jaya Indravarman VIII, the king of Champā, took him captive, and governed Champā as a conquered province (1190 A.D.). But though after a prolonged war of more than thirty years Champā regained independence, she suffered a great deal from the invasion of the great Mongol Chief, the famous Kublāi Khān, during 1282 to 1285 A.D. Shortly after this hostilities broke out with the Annamites who had now become very powerful. During the next two centuries the Annamite emperors led successive expeditions against Champā and gradually conquered nearly the whole country before the end of the 15th century A.D.

Fight with China.

Kambuja Invasions

Mongol invasion

Annamite conquest.

3. *Kambuja*

The earliest Hindu kingdom in Cambodia; the land of the Khmers, was called Fu-nan by the Chinese. According to a Chinese account, dating back to the third century A.D., this kingdom was founded by a Brāhmaṇa named Kauṇḍiṇya. He came from India and, having subdued the local queen, married her. The natives of the country were semi-savages, and both men and women went about naked. But gradually they were brought within

Fu-nan.

the pale of civilization by the Hindu rulers who established their authority over the whole of Cambodia and Cochin-China. Some of these Hindu rulers even conquered Siam and parts of Laos and Malay Peninsula, and thus established the first Hindu empire in Indo-China. They maintained diplomatic relations with both China and India. We possess Sanskrit inscriptions of Kulaprabhāvatī, the chief queen of Jayavarman, and of Rudravarman, the son of the latter, both of whom ruled in the 6th century A.D.

Early in the seventh century A.D. Kambuja, originally a vassal State of Fu-nan, became very powerful and conquered Fu-nan. Henceforth Kambuja became the leading power and gave the name to the whole country. For a time, in the eighth century A.D., Kambuja came under the influence of the Śailendras, but Jayavarman II re-established its independence early in the 9th century A.D. Popular tradition in Cambodia regards him as the greatest ruler and surrounds his memory with a divine halo. There is no doubt that with him began a new and glorious era in the history of the country, and we can follow the course of events without any break down to the present. day. Two of his achievements deserve special mention. He removed the capital of the kingdom to the Angkor region, which henceforth became the centre of culture and was decorated with architectural monuments which have made the name of Kambuja famous all over the world. He instituted the Tantric cult of Devarāja, which became the State religion of Kambuja, and ordained that the royal priest should be chosen exclusively from a single family. We possess an interesting record giving the history of these royal priests in an unbroken line of succession for 250 years. Jayavarman II ruled from 802 to 854 A.D. and was succeeded by his son who died in 877 A.D. According to a Chinese chronicle, written in 863 A.D., the kingdom of Kambuja at that time included the whole of central Indo-China and touched the frontiers of Yunnan in southern China.

Kambuja

Jayavarman II

The most powerful king after Jayavarman II was Yaśovarman who ruled from 889 to 908 A.D. He was one of the most remarkable kings that sat on the throne of Kambuja. A great conqueror and a versatile scholar, he was also a great builder. He is said to have mastered various *śāstras* and *kāvyas* and composed a commentary on Patañjali's *Mahābhāshya*. He built a large number of tem-

Yaśovarman.

ples and *asramas.* We possess a large number of Sanskrit inscriptions containing detailed regulations for the inmates of these monastic establishments which throw interesting light on the religious and social life of Kambuja, perfectly modelled on Hindu lines. He founded a new capital which was called, at first Kambupurī, and later Yaśodharapura, and included a large part of the later capital city now known as Angkor Thom. The region round this capital city remained the seat of Kambuja empire throughout its period of greatness and became the centre of the Angkor civilisation which forms the most brilliant chapter in the history of Kambuja.

The dynasty to which Yaśovarman belonged ruled for a century and a quarter (877-1001 A.D.). The political authority of Kambuja was established during this period over Siam and Laos, and probably also over Yunnan. Indravarman, father of Yaśovarman, even claims in his record that his commands were respectfully obeyed by the rulers of Chīna, Champā, and Yavadvīp.

Sūryavarman I, the founder of the next dynasty, established the authority of Kambuja over Northern Siam and probably even invaded Lower Burma. From this time, Khmer art and

Sūryavarman I

culture were firmly established in the Menam valley, and Khmer civilization spread in the north as far as Sukhothai and Savankalok in Siam. Th next powerful king was Sūryavarman II (1113-45 A D.) whose dominions, according to the Chinese, included Lower Burma and northern part of the Malay Peninsula He also reduced the northern part of Champā but could not retain it for long. He has earned undying fame by constructing the famous Angkor Vat, one of the veritable wonders of the world.

The war with Champā continued long after the death of Sūryavarman, and in 1177 Jaya Indravarman, king of Champā, sent a naval expedition which plundered the capital city. But

Jayavarman VII

the accession of Jayavarman VII, the grand monarch of Kambuja, in A.D. 1181, ushered in a new period of glory. As already noted, he made Champa, a vassal state of Kambuja. He also fought with the Annamites and conquered a considerable portion of Lower Burma. Thus the Kambuja empire reached its greatest extent during his reign and embraced the whole of Indo-China with the exception of Upper Burma, Tonkin, and the southern part of Malay Peninsula. But although fully engaged in wars and conquests it is mainly for his peaceful pursuits that he ranks as one of the greatest kings of Kambuja.

Angkor Thom.

Jayavarman VII planned a new capital city worthy of his great empire. This is the famous Angkor Thom (Nagaradhāma ?). The town was surrounded by a high stone wall with a ditch beyond it, 110 yds. wide. The ditch, like the wall, has a total length of nearly 8½ miles, and its sides are paved with enormous blocks of stone. The enclosing wall was pierced by five huge gates which gave access to the city by means of five grand avenues, each 100 ft. wide and running straight from one end of the town to the other. Each gateway consisted of a huge arched opening, more than 30 ft. high and 15ft. wide, surmounted by figures of four human heads placed back to back. The town was square in shape, each side measuring about two miles. The grand avenues converge to the Temple of Bayon which occupies almost the central position of the city, and is justly regarded as a masterpiece of Kambuja architecture. To the north of Bayon is a great public square, a sort of forum, about 765 yds. long and 165 yds. wide, surrounded by famous structures such as the Baphuon, the Phimenakas, the Terrace of Honour etc., each of which forms a splendid monument by itself.

Public works of Jayavarman VII

The religious foundations and works of public utility undertaken by Jayavarman VII were also on a scale befitting the mighty empire over which he ruled. The account of royal donations to a single temple makes interesting reading, and reveals the magnitude of his resources and depth of religious sentiments. It is not possible here to record all the details, but a few facts may be noted. Altogether 66, 625 persons were employed in the service of the deities of the temple, and, 3,400 villages were given for defraying its expenses. There were 439 Professors and 970 scholars studying under them, making a total of 1409, whose food and other daily necessaries of life were supplied. There were altogether 566 groups of stone houses and 288 groups of brick. Needless to say that the other articles, of which a minute list is given, were in the same proportion, and included huge quantities of gold and silver, 35 diamonds, 40,620 pearls, and 4,540 other precious stones. The inscription, from which the above is quoted, informs us that there were 798 temples and 102 hospitals in the whole kingdom, and these were given every year 117,200 *khārikās* of rice, each *khārikā* being equivalent to

3 mds. 8 srs. Jayavarman VII also established 121 *Vahni-gṛihas* which were travellers' rest-houses like the *dharmaśālās* of the present day. They were set up along the principal highways of the kingdom for the convenience of pilgrims.

Jayavarman VII was the last great king of Kambuja. We know very little of the history of Kambuja during the century following his death. There is, however, no doubt that from the 14th century A.D. its power and prestige rapidly declined. The chief cause of this lay in the rapid progress of the Thais who, proceeding from Yunnan, advanced towards Burma and Siam. Towards the close of the 13th century A.D. Rām Kamheng, the famous Thai king of Sukhodaya, carried his victorious arms to the heart of Kambuja. The Thai kingdom of Ayodhyā (Ayuthia), which replaced that of Sukhodaya about 1350 A.D., made itself the master of nearly the whole of Siam and Laos. On the east, the Annamites gradually conquered nearly the whole of the kingdom of Champā by the fifteenth century. Kambuja was now hard pressed by these two important Thai powers on two sides, who steadily encroached upon its territory.

Fall of Kambuja

This simultaneous pressure from the two flanks proved the ruin of Kambuja. Its weak and helpless rulers tried to save themselves by playing off their two powerful enemies against each other, but with disastrous consequences to themselves. For centuries Kambuja remained the victim of her two pitiless aggressive neighbours. At last, shorn of power and prestige, Ang Duong, the king of Kambuja, now reduced to a petty State, placed himself under the protection of the French in 1854, and thus the once mighty kingdom of Kambuja, became a petty French Protectorate.

4. *Brahmadeśa* (*Burma*).

The Indian colonists proceeded both by land and sea and set up various kingdoms in different parts of both Upper and Lower

Mons or Talaings

Burma. Of the various indigenous peoples among whom the Hindu colonists settled, three deserve special mention. Beginning from the south we first come across the Mons who were also known as Talaings. This name seems to have originally denoted the Indian colonists who came from Telingana, i e the Telugu speaking region on the east coast of India, and was ultimately applied to the whole people. The Hinduised Mon settlements in Lower Burma were known collectively as Ramañña-deśa. But the Mons spread their power further to the south, as far as the important king of Dvāravatī which comprised the lower valley of the Menam river in Siam. It was a powerful kingdom in the 7th century A.D., and from this centre the Hinduized Mons spread their power and influence to the more inaccessible regions in North Siam and West Laos. The Mons were Hīnayāna Buddhists, and a large number of Pāli chronicles give an account of the various local ruling families and their religious foundations.

Pyus and Śrīkshetra.

To the north of the Mons the Hinduized Pyus established a kingdom with Śrīkshetra (modern Ḥmawza, near Prome) as the capital. The Pyus occupied the Irāwadi valley as early as the third century A D. and continued as a great political power till 9th ventury A.D. A Sanskrit insciiption of about 7th century A. D. on the pedestal of a Buddha image records that it was set up by king Jayachandravarman. The Chinese accounts show that the Pyu kingdom was a powerful one in the 7th and 8th centuries A.D. It touched the frontiers of Eastern India, Yunnan, Kambuja, and Dvāravatī, and was 500 miles from east to west and 700 or 800 miles from north to south. It would appear that the Hinduized Pyu kingdom included a large part, if not the whole, of Upper and Central Burma in the 9th century A.D. Shortly after this the power of the Pyus steadily declined. The Thai king of Nan-chao (Yunnan) invaded the Pyu kingdom in 832 A.D. and sacked its capital. It is probable also that a new racial element, the Mrammas, came into prominence in Upper Burma. Pressed by the Mons from the south, and the Mrammas from the north, the Hinduized Pyus gradually lost all political power and were ultimately merged into their powerful neighbours without leaving any trace of their separate entity.

Mrammas.

Popular philology derives the tribal name Burman from the Sanskrit word Brahma, invested with a sacred character. It seems to be more probable, however, that Mramma (*var.* Myamma) was the original ethnic appellation of a branch of the Tibeto-Dravidian tribe who settled in Burma and ultimately gave its name to the whole country and its peoples of diverse origin. It has been suggested that the name of the tribe was derived from the Brahmaputra river, on whose banks it lived for a long time.

The Mrammas poured into Burma in large numbers in the 9th or 10th century A.D., but they had probably established their authority at a much earlier period. They must have come under the influence of the Hindu colonists who were settled in that region from remote times. Soon the Hinduized Mrammas founded an independent kingdom with Pagan as its capital. The classical name of this city is Arimardanapura and the kingdom was known as Tāmbradipa.

The first Hinduized Mramma king of importance was Aniruddha (Anawrath, according to Burmese pronunciation), who ascended the throne in A.D. 1044. About this time a debased form of Buddhist Tāntrism dominated the religious and social life of Upper Burma. But king Aniruddha was converted to the pure Theravāda by a Brāhmaṇa monk from the Mon kingdom of Thaton, named Arahan, known as Dharmadarśī, and the two together brought about a great religious reform. The king now sent envoys to the Mon king of Thaton for bringing complete copies of Buddhist Tripiṭakas. The latter, however, not only refused the sacred books, but also insulted the royal messengers. Aniruddha now decided to seize by force what he could not secure by peaceful means. He marched with an army and besieged Thaton. After 3 months' siege Thaton capitulated. Aniruddha returned in triumph to Pagan with the royal captive Manuha, bound in golden chains, and accompanied by all the monks and a large number of prisoners, including artisans and craftsmen. But the most priceless treasures, in the eyes of the king, were the Buddhist scriptures and sacred relics which were carried by thirty-two white elephants of the vanquished king. On his way king Aniruddha razed the walls of the ancient Pyu capital Śrīkshetra (near Prome) and carried away the relics enshrined in its pagodas for many centuries.

Aniruddha.

Introduction of Hīnayāna Buddhism.

The conquered Mons then made a complete cultural conquest of the Mrammas, and the Theravāda form of Buddhism, together with Pāli language and the Mon scripts, was adopted by the latter. Aniruddha, fired by the proverbial zeal of a new convert, built numerous *pagodas* or temples and monasteries, and his example was followed by his successors.

Aniruddha was also a great conqueror. He defeated the king of North Arakan and the Shan chiefs of the east. He is said to have visited "the Indian land of Bengal" and also led a victorious campaign against Burma's old enemy, the Thais of Yunnan. By these victories Aniruddha brought nearly the whole of Burma,

Conquests

excluding Tenasserim, under his authority, and a political union of the country was effected for the first time in its history.

Aniruddha gained a position of international importance. He married an Indian princess and the Burmese chronicles give a long account of her journey to Burma. When Ceylon was invaded by the Cholas its king sought for the aid of Aniruddha, and later asked him for Buddhist monks and scriptures. In return the Ceylonese king sent him a duplicate of the tooth relic of Buddha. As soon as the ship carrying the relic arrived, king Aniruddha himself waded through the river to the ship, placed the jewelled casket on his own head, and carried it in procession to the shrine he had built for it—the famous Shewzigon Pagoda which still attracts worshippers from all over Burma.

The reign of Aniruddha (1044-1077 A.D.) was thus a turning point in the history of Burma. He raised the small principality of Pagan into an extensive kingdom including the greater part of modern Burma, and introduced elements of higher culture and civilization among a rude people. Aniruddha was succeeded by his two sons. The latter, known as Kyanzittha, ascended the throne in 1084 A.D. and assumed the title Tribhuvanāditya-dharmarāja. He desired to marry his daugther to the prince of Paṭṭikera (E. Bengal), but his ministers objected to it. The prince's love for the daughter of Kyanzittha, ending in suicide, forms the theme of many Burmese poems and dramas, which are acted on the stage even now.

Kyanzittha.

During Kyanzittha's reign, Burma was in intimate touch with India. Many Buddhists and Vaishṇavas went from India and settled in his kingdom. It is said that the king fed eight Indian monks with his own hands for three months, and hearing from them the description of Indian temples, designed and built the famous temple of Ānanda, the masterpiece of Burman architecture. Whatever we might think of this story, there is no doubt that the Ānanda temple was designed on Indian models[1]. A modern European author writes:

Ānanda temple.

"Still in daily use as a house of prayer, the Ānanda, with its dazzling garb of white and its gilt spire glittering in the morn-

1. Cf. p. 497.

ing sun, is to-day one of the wonders of Pagan. Inside the temple, two life-size statues kneel at the feet of a gigantic Buddha; they have knelt there for more than eight centuries. One of these is the king and the other his teacher Arahan. The face of the king is not Burmese—his mother was an Indian lady."

Kyanzittha completed the Shewzigon Pagoda begun by his father, and built some 40 smaller *pagodas*. He even repaired the famous temple of Bodh-Gayā. We read in the chronicles:

"King Kyanzittha gathered together gems of divers kinds and sent them in a ship to build up the holy temple at Buddha-Gayā, and to offer lights which should burn for ever there. Thereafter king Kyanzittha builded anew, making them finer than before, the great buildings of king Aśoka, for they were old and in ruins."

Kyanzittha is also said to have persuaded a Chola king of India to adopt Buddhism. The latter offered his daughter with rich presents to the Burmese king.

Kyanzittha sent an expedition against South Arakan and compelled its chief to acknowledge his suzerainty. He also sent a mission to China in 1106 and insisted on precedence over the Chola ruler. The Board of Rites reported in favour of Pagan as it was a sovereign State.

Kyanzittha died in 1112 A.D. and was succeeded by his grandson (daughter's son) Alaungsithu, who had a long reign of fifty-five years. His reign was troubled with rebellions. The chief of South Arakan, who raided frontier villages, was beheaded, and the king himself suppressed a rising in Tenasserim. The king of North Arakan, dispossessed of his throne by a usurper, sought the protection of the court of Pagan. Alaungsithu sent an expedition both by land and sea and restored the rightful owner to his throne. When the grateful king of Arakan wanted to do something in return, he was asked by Alaungsithu to repair the Bodh-Gayā temple; he sent his agent with enough funds to do the same.

The family of Aniruddha continued to rule in Pagan till 1287 A.D. The last king of the dynasty, Narasiṁhapati, was murdered by his subjects on account of his cowardly flight from the capital for fear of the Mongols. A grandson of Kublāi Khān then marched to Pagan which perished 'amid the blood and flame of the Tartar terror.' Thus ended the great kingdom of Aniruddha after a glorious existence of two hundred and forty years, but the

Fall of Pagan.

great Indian culture which the people imbibed during his reign has lasted up to the present day.

5. *Hindu culture and civilization in the Far East*

The peoples of the Far East who came into contact with the Indian colonists belonged to all grades of civilization, from the semi-savages of Cambodia, who went about naked, to the people of Java who seem to have already advanced beyond the primitive state of culture. All of them, however, felt the impact of Indian civilization, and absorbed it to a very large extent. There is abundant evidence to show that the language, literature, religion, art, and political and social institutions of India made a thorough conquest of these peoples and largely eliminated the indigenous elements in these respects.

(a) *Language and Literature.*

Inscriptions written in Sanskrit have been found in Burma, Siam, Malay Peninsula, Cambodia, Annam, Sumatra, Java, and Borneo. The earliest of them goes back to the second or third century A.D. and they were in use for a period of more than thousand years. The Pāli, a derivative from Sanskrit, is still in daily use in a large part of Indo-China.

Sanskrit Inscriptions.

More than one hundred Sanskrit inscritpions have been discovered in Champā. Those in Kambuja are not only larger in number but are also of higher literary merit. They are composed in beautiful and almost flawless *Kāyva* style such as would do credit to any Indian *Paṇḍiṭ*. Some of these inscriptions run to great lengths. Four inscriptions of Yaśovarman contain respectively 50, 75, 93, and 108 verses each; one of Rājendravarman contains 218 and another 298 verses.

The authors of these inscriptions have very successfully used almost all the Sanskrit metres and exhibit a thorough acquaintance with the most developed rules and conventions of Sanskrit grammar. rhetoric and prosody. Besides, they show an intimate knowldge of the Indian Epics, *Kāvyas*, Purāṇas and other branches of literature, and a deep penetrating insight into Indian philosophical and spiritual ideas; they are also saturated with the religious and mythological conceptions of the different sects of India,—all this to an extent which may be justly regarded as marvellous in a community separated from India by thousands of miles.

The epigraphic records make specific references to the study of Veda, Vedānta, Smṛiti, the religious texts of the Brāhmaṇical sects as well as of the Buddhists and the Jainas, the Epics, *Kāvyas*, Purāṇas, grammar of Pāṇini with the *Mahābhāshya* of Patañjali, and the works of Manu, Vātsyāyana, Viśālāksha, Suśruta, Pravarasena, Mayūra and Guṇāḍhya. The influence of Kālidāsa seems to have been very great, and one inscription contains no less than four verses which are distinct echoes of four verses from *Raghuvaṁsa*, repeating sometimes the very words used by the great poet.

Branches of study

The kings and high officials took a leading part in literary activity. We have reference to three scholarly kings of Champā. One of them was versed in the four Vadas; another was proficient in the six systems of Indian philosophy, Buddhist philosophy, Pāṇini's grammar with Kāśikā, and the Ākhyāna and Uttarakalpa of the Śaivas; while the third studied grammar, astrology, the Mahāyāna philosophy and the Dharmaśāstras, notably the Nāradīya and the Bhārgavīya. King Yaśovarman of Kambuja is said to have been fond of *śāstras* and *kāvyas*, and composed a commentary on *Mahābhāshya*. One of his ministers was an expert in *Horāśāstra*. Sūryavarman I of Kambuja was versed in Bhāshyas, *Kāvya*, six philosophical systems, and Dharmaśāstras. Another king of Kambuja learnt from his priest, astronomy, mathematics, grammar, Dharmaśāstra, and all the other śāstras.

Scholarly kings.

In Java, the people not only studied Sanskrit literature, but evolved out of it an extensive literature of their own. For nearly five hundred years (1000-1500 A.D.) Indo-Javanese literature had an unbroken and flourishing career under the patronage of the kings of Kaḍiri, Siṅghasāri and Majapahit.

Indo-Javanese Literature

The language of this literature is Javanese with a large admixture of Sanskrit words. Its poetry follows rules of Sanskrit metre and its subject-matter is derived mainly from Indian literature. Among the important works may be mentioned the Old-Javanese *Rāmāyaṇa* and the prose translation of the great epic *Mahābhārata*. The latter also supplied themes for numerous *Kāvyas* which exhibit merit of a very high order. Among these may be mentioned *Arjuna-vivāha*, *Bhārata-yuddha*, *Smara-dahana*, and *Sumanasāntaka* (death caused by a flower). The last work is based on the story of Indumatī, the queen of Aja and mother of Daśaratha, immortalised by Kālidāsa in his *Raghuvaṁśa*.

There were also works of the nature of Smṛitis and Purāṇas, and also those dealing with history, linguistics, and medicine. Indeed whether we look at the variety, quality or the quantity, the Indo-Javanese literature forms one of the most remarkable features of ancient Indian colonisation in Java. Nowhere else, outside India, has Indian literature been studied with so much advantage and with such important consequences.

The same remark applies to Burma and Ceylon in respect of the Buddhist Pāli literature. The study of the Buddhist canons in these two colonies led to the adoption of the language of the sacred texts as a classic, which has evolved a new literature and continued its unbroken career down to the present time.

(b) *Religion*

In all the colonies mentioned above, the religious ideas and practices of India had a complete hold of the people. Buddhism was the dominant religion in Burma and Siam, but in the remaining colonies the Purāṇic form of Brāhmaṇical religion was firmly established, and Buddhism played, comparatively speaking, only a minor part. Images of all the known Hindu gods and goddesses have been found, and the following observation of Crawfurd, made more than a century ago, can hardly be regarded as an exaggeration: 'Genuine Hindu images, in brass and stone, exist throughout Java in such variety that I imagine there is hardly a personage of the Hindu mythology, of whom it is usual to make representations, that there is not a statue of."

Purāṇic religion

Although the worship of the Trinity i.e. Brahmā, Vishṇu, and Śiva, was widely prevalent, the place of honour seems to have been accorded to Śiva. Vishṇu occupied the second place, while the worship of Brahmā as a separate deity was rather rare, as in India. The invocations to Śiva and Vishṇu in the various inscriptions, and the extant images of these and their satellite gods and goddesses, clearly prove that the people were fully conversant with the philosophy and mythology of these two sects. Of course, we should not expect that the indigenous faiths and practices vanished altogether. As in India, these were partly eliminated by, and partly absorbed into, the higher and more developed system, but in some respects, the latter was also affected and moulded by the former.

Reference may be made in this connection to an image.

Bhaṭāra-Guru

usually styled Bhaṭāra-Guru, which is very popular in Java. It is a two-armed standing figure of an aged pot-bellied man with moustache and peaked beard, and holding in his hands trident, water-pot, rosary, and fly-whisk. This image is usually regarded as a representation of Śiva Mahāyogin (the great ascetic), and his universal popularity is explained by supposing that an originally Indonesian divinity was merged in him. Some are, however, of opinion, that the image represents the sage Agastya. The extreme veneration for, and the popularity of the worship of, Agastya in Java are reflected in the inscriptions, and this view seems eminently reasonable.

Buddhism

Both Hīnayāna and Mahāyāna forms of Buddhism, and even the most debased Tāntrik cults, found their way into these colonies. In short, if we exclude Jainism, we find in these far-off lands an almost exact replica of the religious system that prevailed in India during the first millennium. How close was the resemblance can be seen even today in Burma and the island of Bali, in cases, respectively, of Buddhism and Brāhmaṇical religion.

Renowned centres

It is interesting to note that some localities in this distant region became renowned centres of Buddhism. Thus Śrīvijaya was an important centre of Buddhism in the time of I-tsing who stayed there for seven years (688-695 A.D.), studying and translating the original texts, either Sanskrit or Pāli. Again we hear that Dharmapāla of Kāñchī, the great professor at Nālandā in the 7th century A.D., and Dīpaṅkara Śrījñāna, also known as Atīśa, who later became the High Priest of Vikramaśīla monastry, visited Suvarṇadvīpa. The latter went there, early in the 11th century A.D., with the express object of studying Buddhism under the guidance of Chandrakīrti, the High Priest of Suvarṇadvīpa.

We learn from inscriptions in Kambuja that many Brāhmaṇas of India visited that country and obtained high honours, one of them even marrying a princess. Learned Brāhmaṇas from Kambuja also visited India. The most important instance is that of Śivasoma, the *guru* of king Indravarman (877-889 A.D.), who learnt the *śāstras* from Bhagavat Śaṅkara who is undoubtedly the great Śaṅkarāchārya.

Āśramas

Another interesting feature was the large number of *āśramas* which were set up all over Kambuja by royal munificence and private efforts. King Yaśovarman claims to have founded no less than one hundred of them. The sites of twelve of them are marked by twelve inscriptions which describe in detail the rules and regulations of these *āśramas*. Although some of these were specially meant for Vaishṇavas, Śaivas, or Buddhists, they were generally open to all sects and classes of peoples. These *āśramas* supplied necessaries of life not only to the resident pupils, but also to the boys, old men, poor, and destitute. There can be hardly any doubt that these *āśramas* served as strongholds or citadels of the Hindu culture and civilization in its progress of conquests over the primitive culture of the land.

(c) *Society*

The caste system which forms the fundamental basis of the Hindu Society was introduced in most of these colonies. But although the four broad divisions into Brāhmaṇas, Kshatriyas, Vaiśyas, and Śūdras were known, the system had not attained the rigidity we find in India to-day. Thus intermarriage and inter-dining, permitted in *Manu-saṁhitā*, were also prevalent in these regions. On the whole, the caste system, as it prevails today among the Balinese of Bali and Lombok, may be regarded as typical of old times. The theory of untouchability did not degrade the society, and the different castes were not tied down to specific occupations.

Caste system

The ideals of marriage, details of the ceremony, and the conjugal relations generally resembled those of India. The *Satī* system was also in vogue. But in general the women occupied a much higher position and status than in India. Some of them ascended the throne in their own right, even when they had brothers, and others occupied high positions in administration. There was no *purdah* system and the women could choose their husbands.

Position of Women

Gambling, cock-fight, music, dancing, and theatrical performances were among the principal amusements. The most popular form of the last in Java was the shadow-play called *Wayang*, in which the actors are represented by shadows which the painted leather-puppets throw from behind on a white screen in front of the audience. The perfomer sits behind the screen under a lamp and manipulates the puppets so as to suit their actions to the speech which he himself recites from behind on behalf of all the actors. The themes of the *Wayang* were usually derived from the two Indian epics, the *Rāmāyaṇa* and the *Mahābhārata*, and this is

Amusements

also the case to-day though the people of Java are now all Muhammadans.

As in India, rice and wheat formed the staple food, and the people drank wine made from flowers, palm-tree, and honey.

Food and dress

The chewing of betels was also much in vogue. The dress and ornaments resembled those in ancient India. The upper part of the body, even in cases of females, was uncovered a practice which still persists in Bali. The ancient Indian sculpture also represents both men and women in the same way.

(d) *Art*

The art in the colonies, as in India, may be described as the handmaid of religion. All the monuments of this art so far discovered—and their number is legion—are religious structures. The earlier phase of this art was wholly Indian in character, and many early temples and images have even been supposed to be the handiworks of Indian artists and craftsmen who migrated from India. But gradually different local styles were evolved without losing the essentially Indian character. It is impossible to refer, even briefly, to the magnificent temples and fine images that abound in these colonies, and we shall only try to convey an idea of their massive grandeur and artistic excellence by describing a few typical specimens.

The most important monument in Java is Barabuḍur which was built during 750 to 850 A.D. under the patronage of the

Barabuḍur

Śailendras. This noble building consists of a series of nine successive terraces, each receding from the one beneath it, and the whole crowned by a bell-shaped *stūpa* at the centre of the topmost terrace. Of the nine terraces the six lower ones are square in plan, while the upper three are circular. The lowest terrace has an extreme length of 131 yds (including projections) and the topmost one a diameter of 30 yds. The five lower terraces are each enclosed on the inner side by a wall supporting a balustrade, so that four successive galleries are formed between the back of the balustrade of one terrace and the wall of the next higher one. The three uppermost terraces are encircled by a ring of *stūpas*, each containing an image of Buddha within a perforated framework. From the ninth terrace a series of circular steps lead on to the crowning *stūpa*. The balustrade in each terrace consists of a row of arched niches separated by sculptured panels. All the niches support a superstructure which resembles the terracedro of of a temple, with bell-shaped *stūpas* in the corners and the centre, and contain the image of a Dhyānī-Buddha within. There are no less than 432 of them in the whole building.

There is a staircase with a gateway in the middle of each side of the gallery leading to the next higher one. The doorway is crowned by a miniature temple-roof like the niches of the balustrade. The beautiful decorations of the doorways and the masterly plan in which they are set—commanding from a single point a fine view of all the doorways and staircases from the lowest to the highest—introduce an unspeakable charm and invest them with a high degree of importance in relation to the whole construction.

The series of sculptured panels in the galleries form the most striking feature of Barabuḍur. On the whole there are eleven series of sculptured panels, the total number of which is about fifteen hundred.

It may be safely presumed that the sculptures in the different galleries follow prescribed texts, and it is not possible to interpret tnem without the help of those texts. Fortunately, these have been traced in many cases, and thus the work of interpretation has been comparatively easier in these instances. They depict the life of Gautama Buddha, the Jātakas, i.e. previous births, and Avadānas or great deeds of the Buddha, and the story of Sudhanakumāra, who made sixty-four persons his *gurus*, passed through a hundred austerities, and ultimately obtained perfect knowledge and wisdom from Manjuśrī. The other reliefs have not been satisfactorily interpreted. All of them show a high artistic skill.

The detached images of Buddha in Barabuḍur and of Bodhisatvas in Mendut may be regarded as the finest products of Indo-Javanese sculpture. Fine modelling, as far as it is compatible with absence of muscular details, refined elegance of features, tasteful pose, close-fitting smooth robe, and a divine spiritual expression of face are the chief characteristics of these figures. The art must have, therefore, been ultimately derived from the classical art of the Gupta period in India.

Although no Brāhmaṇical temple in Java makes even a near approach to Barabuḍur, the Lara-Jongrang group in the Prambanan valley may be regarded as the next best. It consists of eight main temples, three in each row with two between them, enclosed by a wall, with three rows of minor temples round the wall on each side making

Lara-Jongrang

a total of 156. Of the three main temples in the western row, the central one is the biggest and the most renowned, and contains an image of Śiva. The one to the north has an image of Vishṇu, and that to the south an image of Brahmā.

The Śiva-temple in the centre is the most magnificent. Its basement, about 10 ft. high and 90 ft. long, supports a platform on which the temple stands, leaving a margin about 7 ft. wide on each side, which served as a path of circumambulation. The platform is enclosed by a balustrade decorated with reliefs on both sides. The inner side of the balustrade consists of a continuous series of relief-sculptures in forty-two panels depicting the story of *Rāmāyaṇa* from the beginning up to the expedition to Laṅkā. The story was persumably continued on the balustrade of the temple dedicated to Brahmā. These reliefs constitute the chief importance and grandeur of the Lara-Jongrang temples. They may justly be regarded as the Brāhmaṇical counterpart of the Buddhist reliefs on Barabuḍur and are hardly, if at all, inferior to them.

The sculptural art of Lara-Jongrang is more naturalistic than that of Barabuḍur, and is characterised by a greater feeling for movements and human passions. It is more informed by human life and activity, though not devoid of the graceful charm of idealism. It has brought the divinity of idealism to the earth below, but with less abstraction and more animation than is the case with Barabuḍur. It is dramatic and dynamic while the latter is passive and static. In short the sculptures of Barabuḍur and Lara-Jongrang represent respectively the Classic and Romantic phases of Indo-Javanse art.

Kambuja

In Kambuja the earlier series of monuments at Angkor consists of isolated temples which show great resemblance with Indian temples. But gradually a new style is evolved in the eleventh and twelfth centuries A.D., first by the introduction of gallery, and later still by pyramidal construction in several stages. The combination of these two features results in a series of concentric galleries, enclosing each successive stage of the pyramid, with a crowning tower at the centre of the top or the highest stage. Similar towers are added at the four corners of each stage of the pyramid, and finally we have the *gopurams* at one or all the four faces, each consisting of a gateway with a vestibule, surmounted by an ornamental tower in the form of a stepped pyramid as we see in South India. The central and corner towers are of the North-

Indian or *Śikhara* style. The best and the complete example of this type is Angkor Vat. An innovation is introduced in Bayon, where the towers are capped by four heads facing the four directions.

The gallery, referred to above, is, in its final shape, a long narrow running chamber with vaulted roof supported by a wall on one side and a series of pillars on the other. It has a *verandah* with a half-vaulted roof of lower height supported by columns of smaller dimensions. The walls of these galleries are generally covered with continuous friezes of bas-reliefs and other sculptures.

The wide ditcnes surrounding the temples and cities, with paved causeways over them, form an important feature of construction, and the figures of long rows of giants pulling the body of a serpent, which serve as the balustrades of the causeway on its two sides, are justly regarded as one of the most ingenious and interesting architectural devices to be seen anywhere in the world.

An idea of the massive character of these monuments may be had from the measurements of Angkor Vat. The moat or ditch, surrounding the temple and running close to its boundary walls, is more than 650 ft. wide,and is spanned on the western side by a stone causeway, 36 ft. broad. This ditch, like the wall of enclosure which completely surrounds the temple, has a total length of two miles and a half. The broad paved avenue which runs from the western gateway to the first gallery is 1560 ft. long and raised 7 ft. above the ground. The first gallery measures about 800 ft. from east to west and 675 ft. from north to south, with a total running length of nearly 3000 ft. The central tower, on the third or highest stage, rises to a height of more than 210 ft. above the ground level.

Angkor Vat.

These few details would serve to convey an idea of the massive character of Kamuja temples. But it is not by the massive form alone that they appeal to us. Their fine proportions, the general symmetry of the plan, and above all the decorative sculptures invest them with a peculiar grandeur.

In Burma the finest temple is the Ānanda at Pagan. It occupies the centre of a spacious courtyard which is 564 ft. square. The main temple, made of bricks, is square in plan, each side measuring 175 ft. A large gabled porch, 57 ft. long, projects from the centre of each face of this square, so that the total length of the temple, from end to

Ānanda temple

end, on every side, is nearly 290 ft. In the interior the centre is occupied by a cubical mass of brickworks, with deep niche on each side, containing a colossal standing Buddha image 31 ft. in height above the throne which itself is about 8 ft. high. The central mass is surrounded by two parallel corridors, with cross passages for communication between the porch and the Buddha image on each side.

Externally, the walls of the temple, 39 ft.high, are crowned with a battlemented parapet, having a ringed pagoda at each corner. Above the parapet rise in succession the two roofs over the two parallel corridors below, each having a curvilinear outline and an elongated *stūpa* at the corners, and a dormer-window in imitation of the porches at the centre. Above these two roofs are four receding narrow terraces which serve as the basement of a *śikhara* crowned by a *stūpa* with an elongated bell-shaped dome and a tapering iron *hti* as its finial. Each of the receding stages has the figure of a lion at the corners and small imitation porch openings in the centre. Apart from the graceful proportions and the symmetry of design, the beauty of the Ānanda temple is enhanced by the numerous stone sculptured reliefs and glazed terra-cotta plaques that adorn its walls. The stone-reliefs, eighty in number, and some of the plaques illustrate the principal episodes in the Buddha's life, and 926 plaques depict the Jātaka stories. The unique character of the plan of the temple has evoked much discussion about its origin. But, as noted above, there is no doubt of its derivation from Indian type. Temples of the same type existed in Bengal and most probably suggested the model of the Ānanda temple. This is the view of Duroiselle who has made a special study of the subject in recent times. He further observes as follows:

"There can be no doubt that the architects who planned and built the Ānanda were Indians. Everything in this temple from *Śikhara* to basement, as well as the numerous stone sculptures found in its corridors, and the terra-cotta plaques adorning its basement and terraces, bear the indubitable stamp of Indian genius and craftsmanship. . . .In this sense, we may take it, therefore, that the Ānanda, though built in the Burmese capital, is an Indian temple."

BIBLIOGRAPHY

A short and select bibliography is given below for the use of advanced students who want to study in greater detail the different topics that are necessarily dealt with very briefly in this work. The 'General Bibliography' given at the beginning includes recent standard works dealing with the ancient history of India as a whole or some particular periods of it. These will not be ordinarily repeated in the 'Bibliography' that follows, which contains list of books arranged in accordance with the topics dealt with in different chapters of this book. Neither list is exhaustive, the aim simply being to include only those books which would prove very helpful to advanced students. As the list is intended to be short and practical, the exclusion of any work does not mean any disparagement of its merit or usefulness. Books in language other than English are not included.

GENERAL BIBLIOGRAPHY

Aiyangar, S. K.—*Ancient India and South Indian History and Culture* (1941).

Basak, R. G.—*The History of North-Eastern India* (from about 320 to 750 A.D.) (1934).

Cambriage History of India, Vol. 1. Edited by E. J. Rapson. (It deals with the history from the earliest times to about the middle of the first century. A.D.). Though this volume appeared in 1922, the second volume has not yet been published.

Chattopadhyaya, Sudhakar—*Early History of North India* (Calcutta, 1958).

Chaudhuri, Sasi Bhusan—*Ethnic Settlements in Ancient India* (Calcutta, 1955).

Cunningham, A.—*Ancient Geography of India* (Reprint, edited by S. N. Majumdar).

Dutt, R. C.—*History of Civilization in Ancient India* (1893). (Though considerably out of date, it still contains much useful information and thoughtful observations).

Kane, P. V.—*History of Dharmaśāstra* (a learned treatise dealing with social institutions with reference to original sources).

Majumdar, R. C. and Altekar, A. S.—*The Vākāṭaks-Gupta Age* (1946), being Vol. VI. of *A New History of the Indian People.* (It deals with the period 200-500 A.D.;—the series is now amalgamated with the History of India in 12 volumes planned by the Indian History Congress).

Masson-Oursel, P—*Ancient India and Indian Civilisation* (London, 1934).

Ray, H. C.—*The Dynastic History of Northern India*, 2 vols. (1931, 1936). (It gives a detailed account of the mediaeval States that flourished after the downfall of Harsha's Empire).

Raychaudhuri, H. C.—*Political History of Ancient India*, 5th Edition (1950). (It deals with the political history from the accession of Parīkshit to the extinction of the Gupta Dynasty).

Sastri, K. A. N.—*A History of South India from Pre-historic Times to the Fall of Vijayanagar* (Oxford University Press, 1955).

———*Age of the Nandas and Mauryas* (1952).

———*Foreign Notices of South India* (Madras, 1939).

Smith, V. A.—*Early History of India*, 4th Edition (1924). (It deals with the political history from the 6th century B. C. to the end of the Hindu Period).

Vaidya, C. V.—*History of Mediaeval Hindu India.*

Bombay Gazetteer—Vol. 1. (It deals with the History of Gujarāt, the Deccan and the Kanarese Districts, different chapters being written by Bhagavan Lal Indraji, R. G. Bhandarkar and J. F. Fleet).

The History and Culture of the Indian People. (A comprehensive History of India, in 10 volumes, planned by Bhārātīya Itihāsa Samiti, Bombay, and Edited by Dr. R. C. Majumdar.—The first five volumes, deal with the history of India from the earliest period up to 1300 A.D.).

A Comprehensive History of India, in 12 Volumes, planned by the Indian History Congress. Only Vol. II, (The Mauryas & Satavahanas) edited by K. A. Nilakanta Sastri, has so far been published.

BIBLIOGRAPHY

INTRODUCTION

I. For an account of the physical features of the country, *cf. Cambridge History of India*, I, Ch. I and the *History and Culture of the Indian People*. I. Ch. V. For further study of the subject. cf. *Imperial Gazetteer of India* and the District Gazetteers.

II. *History and Culture of the Indian People*, I, Ch. II. The original texts referred to on p. 7 have all been published. The following are available in English version.

Harsha-charita—Translated by Cowell and Thomas.

Rājataraṅgiṇī— „ A. Stein and also by R. S. Pandit.

Rāma-charita— „ R. C. Majumdar and others.

For the Greek and Roman accounts, cf. M'Crindle's translation of the original texts in 6 vols., Schoff's Translation of the *Periplus of the Erythraean Sea*, and *The Classical Accounts of India* by R. C. Majumdar (Culcutta, 1960). For the Chinese accounts cf.

1. *Fa-hien*—Translated by Legge (and also by Giles).
2. *Hiuen Tsang*— „ S. Beal.
„ Watters. (This is a better translation, but is generally in the nature of a summary rather than a running translation).
3. *I-tsing*—Translated by J. Takakusu.

The book of Alberuni has been translated into English by E. Sachau.

As to Archaeology, the more important inscriptions are now published in *Epigraphia India*. a current official Journal exclusively devoted to this purpose. South Indian Inscriptions are published by the Government in two separate series called *South Indian Inscriptions* and *Epigraphia Carnatica*. Another official publication is *Annual Report on South Indian Epigraphy*, An important non-official publication is *The Historical Inscriptions of Southern India*, Edited by S. K. Aiyangar (Madras University, 1932). Important inscriptions have also been edited in the past in antiquarian Journals such as "*Journal of the Royal Asiatic Society of Great Britain and Ireland* (*JRAS*)", "*Journal of the Asiatic Society of Bengal*" (*JASB* or *JRASB*), "*Indian Antiquary* (*Ind. Ant. or IA*)", and "*Journal of the Bihar and Orissa Research Society* (*JBORS*)". Reference may also be made to the numerous publications of the Archaeological Survey of India either in the shape of Annual Reports or special monographs on particular subjects. The Annual Report has recently been replaced by a Journal called *Ancient India* and the *Annual Report on Indian Epigraphy*.

As to coins, they are mainly dealt with in the following

publications, though scattered references in antiquarian Journals are numerous.

Allan, J.—*Catalogue of the Coins in Ancient India* (in the British Museum).

——*Catalogue of the Coins of the Gupta Dynasties* etc. (in the British Museum).

Bhandarkar, D. R.—*Ancient Indian Numismatics* (Carmichael Lectures, 1921).

Cunningham, A.—*Coins of Ancient India.*

————*Coins of Mediaeval India.*

————Series of articles on the coins of the Greeks, Śakas, Kushāṇas and Later Indo-Scythians contributed to *Numismatic Chronicle*, and also published separately.

Gardner, P.—*Catalogue of the Coins of the Greek and Scythic Kings of Bactria and India in the British Museum.*

Rapson, E. J.—*Catalogue of the Coins of the Andhra Dynasty, the Western Kshatrapas etc.* (in the British Museum).

————*Indian Coins.*

Smith, V. A.—*Catalogue of the Coins in the Indian Museum, Calcutta.*

Whitehead, R. B.—*Catalogue* of *Coins in the Punjab Museum, Lahore*, Vol. 1. (This deals with the Coins of the Greeks, Śakas, Parthians and Kushāṇas only.)

The following may be recommended as suitable handbooks for beginners.

Banerji, R. D.—*Prācnīna Mudrā* (In Bengali)

Brown, C. J.—*The Coins of India* (Heritage of India Series.).

Chakravarty, S. K.—*Study of Ancient Indian Numismatics.*

Advanced students may consult "*Bibliography of Indian Coins*, Part I (Non-Muhammadan Series), compiled by C. R. Singhal and published by the Numismatic Society of India, which gives a list of all the articles, published in different periodicals, on Coins.

BOOK I

CHAPTER I

Chakravarty, S. N.—The Prehistoric Periods in India—(*Journal of the University of Bombay*, Vol. X, Part I. (1941).

————An Outline of the Stone Age in India—*JRASB* (L) X. pp. 81-98.

Foote—*Indian Prehistoric and Protohistoric Antiquities, Notes on their Ages and Distribution* (1916).

Piggott, Stuart—*Prehistoric India to* 1000 *B. C.* (1950).

Sankalia, H. D.—*Investigations to Prehistoric Archaeology of Gujarat* (1946).

Wheeler, Sir Mortimer—*Early India and Pakistan* (New York, 1959).

CHAPTER II

Aiyangar, S. K.—*Some Contributions of South India to Indian Culture.*

Anderson, J. D.—*Peoples of India* (1913)

Baines, A.—*Ethnography* (1912)

The Census of India (1901, 1911, 1921, 1931, 1941)

Chanda, R. P.—*The Indo-Aryan Races,* 1916

Chatterji, S. K.—Dravidian Origins and the beginnings of Indian Civilization (*Modern Review,* December, 1924).

Elmore, W. T.—*Dravidian Gods in modern Hinduism* (1915).

Guha, B. S.—*An Outline of the Racial Ethnology of India* (1937).

———*Racial Elements in the Population* (Oxford Pamphlet No. 22).

Iyengar, P. T. S.—*Pre-Aryan Tamil Culture* (1930).

Risley, H. H.—*The people of India* (1915).

CHAPTER III

Hargreaves, H.—*Excavations in Baluchistan.* Memories of the Archaeological Survey of India (*MASI*), No. 35 (1929).

Hevesy, G. De.—On a Writing Oceanique of Neolithic Origin (*JIH,* XIII, 1-17).

Hunter, G. R.—*The Script of Harappa and Mohenjodaro and its connection with other scripts* (1934).

Law, N. N.—Mohenjodaro and the Indus Civilization (*IHQ.* VIII. 121-64).

Mackay, E. J. H.—*Chanhu-daro Excavations* (1943)

———*Further Excavations at Mohenjodaro.*

———*The Indus Civilization* (2nd Edition).

Majumdar, N. G.—*Exploration in Sind* (1939).

Marshall, Sir John—*Mohenjodaro and the Indus Civilization,* 3 Vols. (1931).
(This is the most authoritative and comprehensive work on the subject).

Sarup L.—The Rigveda and Mohenjodaro (*POC.* VIII 1-22 *IC,* IV. 149-68).

Stein, Sir Aurel—*An Archaeological Tour in Waziristan and Northern Baluchistan* (*MASI,* No. 37) (1929).

———*Archaeological Reconnaissances in North-Western India and South-Eastern Iran* (1937).

Vats M. S.—*Excavations at Harappa.*
(The most authoritative and comprehensive work on the subject)
Wheeler R. E. M.—*Harappa* 1946.
(It gives an account of excavations made after the publication of the previous work).

CHAPTER IV

Childe, V. G.—*The Aryans* (1926)
Taylor, I.—*The Origin of the Aryans* (1889).
Tilak, B. G.—*Orion.*
————*The Arctic Home in the Vedas.*

CHAPTER V

For Vedic Literature, the following may be consulted.

Macdonell, A. A.—*History of Sanskrit Literature* (1900).
Winternitz, M.—*History of Indian Literature* (1920).
The original text, in 3 vols, is written in German, Vol. I. dealing with the Vedic Literature, Vol. II, with Buddhist and Jaina Literature and Vol. III with post-Vedic Sanskrit Literature. Vols. I and II have been translated into English by Mrs. S. Ketkar in 1927 and 1933.

CHAPTERS VII VIII and IX.

A. General Works

Dutt, N. K.—*Aryanization of India.*
Iyengar, P. T. S.—*Life in Ancient India.*
Kaegi, A.—*The Rigveda.* Transl. by R. Arrowsmith.
Macdonell, A. A. and Keith A. B.—*Vedic Index.*
(It is a good book for reference).
Muir, J.—*Original Sanskrit Texts.*

B. Political History

Pargiter, F. E.—*Ancient Indian Historical Tradition* (1922).
————*The Purāṇa Text of the Dynasties of the Kali Age* (1913).
Pradhan, S. N.—*Chronology of Ancient India* (1927).

C. Religion

Barth, A.—*The Religions of India* (1882).
Bloomfield, M.—*The Religion of the Veda.*
————*The Atharvaveda.*
Griswold, H. D.—*Religion of the Rigveda.*
Hopkins, E. W.—*The Religions of India* (1895)

Keith, A. B.—*Religion and Philosophy of the Veda and Upanishads* (1925).

Macdonell, A. A.--*Vedic Mythology* (1897).

D. Philosophy

Chatterjee, S. and Datta, D.—*An Introduction to Indian Philosophy* (1950). (Useful for beginners).

Das Gupta, S. N.—*History of Indian Philosophy.*

Radhakrishnan, S.—*History of Indian Philosophy.*

Ranade, R.D.—*Constructive Survey of the Upanishadic Philosophy.*

E. Political and Legal Institutions.

Altekar, A. S.—*State and Government in Ancient India* (1949) (Useful for beginners).

Anjaria, J. J.—The *Nature and grounds of Political obligation in Hindu* State.

Beni Prasad—*Theory of Government in Ancient India* (1927).

Bhandarkar, D. R.—*Some aspects of ancient Indian Polity* (1929).

Ghoshal, U. N.—*A History of Hindu Political Theories* (1923).

————*A History of Hindu Public Life* (1945).

Jayaswal, K. P.—*Hindu polity* (1924). (This book must be used with great caution by the beginners, as it contains many theories and statements not based on proper evidence).

Jolly, J.—*Hindu Law and Custom* (Tr. by Dr. B. K. Ghosh).

Sharma, Ram Sharan—*Aspects of Political Ideas and Institutions in Ancient India* (Motilal Banarsidass, 1959).

F. Social and Economic Condition.

Aiyangar, K. V. R.—*Ancient Indian Economic Thought* (1934).

Altekar, A. S.—*Education in Ancient India*, 4th Ed. (1951).

Altekar, A. S.—*The Position of Women in Hindu Civilization* (1938).

Apte, V. M.—*Social and Religious Life in the Grihya Sutras* (1939).

Das, S. K.—*Economic History of Ancient India* (1925).

Hopkins, E. W.—*Ethics of India* (1924).

Mookerjee, R. K. —*Ancient Indian Education* (1947).

————*Hindu Civilization* (1936).

Sarkar, S. C.—*Some aspects of the Earliest Social History of India.* (1928).

Venkateswara, S. V.—*Indian Culture through the Ages.*

G. The Caste System.

Baines, A.—*Ethnography* (1912).

Dutt, N. K.—*Origin and Development of Caste in India* (1931).

Ketkar, S. V.—*The History of Caste in India* (1911).

Majumdar, R. C.—*Corporate Life in Ancient India* (1922). Ch. V.

Pandey, Raj Bali—*Hindu Saṁskāras* (Banaras, 1949).

BOOK II

CHAPTER I

Bhandarkar, D. R.—*Carmichael Lectures Vol.* II, *Lecture* II.
Davids, Rhys—*Buddhist India.*
Law, B. C.—*Ancient Mid-Indian Kshatriya Tribes* (1924)
————*Kshatriya clans in Buddhist India* (1922).
————*Some Kshatriya Tribes of Ancient India* (1923).
————*Tribes in Ancient India* (1943).

For Alexander's invasion, the most important text is Arrian's "*Alexandri Anabasis*" translated by M'Crindle in "*The Invasion of India by Alexander the Great*" which also gives the other Greek accounts. In addition to Works, cited above, under General Bibliography, one may consult *Cambridge Ancient History*, Vol. VI, Chap. XIII, and Tarn, W. W.—*Alexander the Great.*

CHAPTER II

Megasthenes—*Indika* (Tr. by M'Crindle)
Mookerji, R. K.—*Chandragupta Maurya and his times* (1943).

There is an extensive literature on Aśoka. A few select books only are mentioned below—

Barua, B. M.—*Asoka and his Inscriptions.*
Bhandarkar, D. R.—*Aśoka.*
Hultzsch—*Inscriptions of Asoka* (*Corpus Inscriptionum Indicarum*, Vol. I).
Smith, V. A.—*Aśoka.*

(Our chief sources of information about Aśoka are his inscriptions. These are translated in all the texts mentioned above, which also contain full bibliographical references to numerous critical discussions of various passages in Aśokan inscriptions and other related matters).

CHAPTER III.

Section I

Chattopadhyaya, Sudhakar—*The Śakas in India* (Visvabhārati, 1955).
Konow, Sten—*The Kharoshthi Inscriptions* (*Corpus Inscriptionum Indicarum*, Vol. II.).
Narain, A. K.—*The Indo-Greeks* (Oxford, 1957).
Tarn, W. W.—*The Greeks in Bactria and India, Second Edition*, 1951.

Sections IV—V

Gopalachari, K.—*Early History of the Andhra Country.*

Krishnarao, B. V.—*Early Dynasties of Andhradeśa* (1942).

Sircar, D. C.—*The Successors of the Śātavāhanas.*

For Sections I-V, cf. also the books on coins mentioned above on pp. 535-6 as most of the States dealt with in this chapter are known mainly from the coins.

Section VI

Aiyangar, P. T. S.—*History of the Tamils to 600 A.D.* (1929).

Aiyangar, S. K.—*Beginning of South Indian History* (1918).

Aiyar, K. G. S.—*Chera kings of the Sangam period* (1937).

Pillai, K.—*Tamils* 1800 *years* ago (1904).

CHAPTER IV

Our chief source of information is Kauṭilya's *Arthaśāstra*, It has been edited by R. Shamasastry, Jolly and Schmidt, and T. Ganapati Sastri. There is an English translation by R. Shamasastry and a Bengali translation by Dr. R. G. Basak.

Scholars are divided in their opinion as to the authenticity of the book. Some hold it to be a genuine production of Kauṭilya *alias* Chāṇakya, the prime minister of Maurya Chandragupta, while others deny this claim and regard the book as a later production. An extensive literature has grown up as a result of this discussion.

For the former view cf.

Fleet J. F.—Introductory Note to the English Translation of *Arthaśāstra* by R. Shamasastry.

Jacobi's articles (translated in *Indian Antiquary*, 1918, pp. 157; 187). Jayaswal, K. P.—*Hindu Polity* pp. 203 ff.

Law, N. N.—*Calcutta Review*, 1924, Sept. (512), Nov. (228) and Dec. (466).

Mookerji, R. K.—Introduction to Dr. N. N. Law's *Studies in Ancient Hindu Polity.*

Sastri, T. Ganapati—Introduction to the Edition of the Text.

Shamasastry R.—Preface to English Translation of *Arthaśāstra*; *Calcutta Review*, April, 1925, p. 115.

For the latter view cf.

Jolly—Introduction to the Edition of *Arthaśāstra.*

Keith—*JRAS*, 1916, p. 130; *Ashutosh Memorial Volume published* by J. N. Samaddar (1926-1928), Part I, pp. 8-22.

Raychaudhuri, H. C.—*The History and Culture of the Indian People*, II. 285.

Winternitz—*Calcutta Review*, April, 1924 pp. I ff.

The question must be regarded as open until other evidences come to light.

The study of political theories and public administration in Ancient India has made great progress in recent years. The following books may be recommended for advanced study in addition to those mentioned on p. 504 above.

Bandyopadhyaya, N. C.—*Kauṭilya* (1927).

Banerji, P. N.—*Public Administration in Ancient India* (1920).

Law, N. N.—*Studies in Ancient Hindu Polity* (1914).

————*Inter-State Relations in Ancient India* (1920).

Majumdar, R. C.—*Corporate Life in Ancient India*, (Chaps. II, III).

Sarkar, B. K.—*The Political Institutions and Theories of the Hindus*

Shamasastry R.—*The Evolution of Indian Polity*.

CHAPTER V

Cf. General Works mentioned on p. 504

I. For further studies on Buddhism:

Davids, Rhys.—*Buddhism, its History and Literature*.

————*Buddhism*.

————*Buddhist India*.

————*Indian Buddhism* (Hibbert Lectures, 1881).

Dutta, N.—*Early History of the spread of Buddhism and the Buddhist schools*.

————*Aspects of Mahāyāna Buddhism*.

————*Early Monastic Buddhism*.

Kern—*Manual of Buddhism*.

Oldenberg, H.—*Buddha*. (Tr by W. Hoey, Calcutta, 1927)

On the organisation of the Buddhist Church, cf.

Majumdar R. C.—*Corporate Life in Ancient India*, Ch. IV.

On Buddhist Councils, cf. the article by R. C. Majumdar in "*Buddhistic Studies*" Edited by Dr. B. C. Law (pp. 26-72)

II. The best handbooks on Jainism are:—

Barodia—*History and Literature of Jainism* (1909).

B hler—*On the Indian sect of the Jainas* (1903).

Jagamendra Lal Jaini—*Outlines of Jainism* (mainly philosophical) (1940).

Law, B. C.—*Life of Mahāvīra*.

Shah, C. J.—*Jainism in North India* (1932).

Stevenson, S. (Mrs.)—*The Heart of Jainism* (1915).

Warren, H.—*Jainism*. (1912).

For a complete bibliography cf.

Bibliographie Bouddhique (A. Maisonneuve, Paris, 1937).

"Guerinot—*Essai de Bibliographie Jaina.*

III-IV—For advanced studies on Vaishṇavism and Śaivism.

Bhandarkar R. G.—*Vaishnavism, Saivism and minor religious systems* (1913).

Iyer, C. V. N.—*The Origin and Early history of Śaivism in South* India (1936).

Raychaudhuri, H. C.—*Materials for the study of the Early History of the Vaishnava sect.* 2nd ed. (1936).

V. For general studies on Indian religions cf.

Barnett. L. D.—*Hinduism.*

Elliot—*Hinduism and Buddhism,* Vols. I—III.

Encyclopaedia of Religions and Ethics.

CHAPTER VI

The account of Buddhist literature, as given in the text, is entirely based on "Winternitz—*Geschichte der Indischen Litteratur* Vol. II," the best and most comprehensive work on this subject. Among other authorities may be mentioned:

Davids, Rhys.—(Books mentioned on p. 507).

Law, B. C.—*A History of Pali Literature.*

Oldenberg—*Introduction to Vinaya texts.*

The Pali Canonical Texts have been edited by the Pali text Society, and many of them translated into English.

The "Jātakas" have been edited and translated into English by Fausboll (Cambridge University Press).

For Brāhmaṇical literature see refs. under Vedic Literature (p. 503). The best and most comprehensive treatise on the subject is the monumental work by Dr. P. V. Kane entitled '*History of Dharmaśāstra*' of which 5 volumes (in six parts) have been published so far.

CHAPTER VII

Section 1

The critical study of the Epics has given rise to an extensive literature mostly in German. A good general account will be found in "Winternitz, *History of Indian Literature*" Vol. I, pp. 259-440.

Among English writings on the Epics may be mentioned Hopkins—*The Great Epic of India.*

————The Social and Military position of the Ruling caste (*JAOS* Vol. XIII).
Vaidya, C. V.—*Epic India.*
————*The Mahabharata, a criticism.*
———— *Riddle of the Ramayana.*

The only critical study of the *Rāmāyaṇa* is that by H. Jacobi in his famous book "*Das Rāmāyaṇa.*"

Cf. also a very interesting paper on

"The Ramayana and the Mahabharata—a sociological study" by N. Ghosh in *Ashutosh Jubilee Volume* III, Part II, pp. 361-407.
Puri, B. N.—*India in the Time of Patanjali* (Bombay, 1957).

Section 2

Aiyar Sivaswamy—*Evolution of Hindu Moral Ideals* (1935).
Hopkins—*Ethics of India* (1924).
Jain, J. C.—*Life in Ancient India as depicted in the Jain Canons* (1947).
Mackenzie, John—*Hindu Ethics.*
Maitra, S. K.—*Ethics of the Hindus.*
Patil, D. R.—*Cultural History from the Vayu Purana* (1946).

CHAPTER VIII

For the Aryan conquest of the Deccan:

Bhandarkar, R. G.—*Early History of the Deccan, Chaps.* II-III.
Bhandarkar, D. R.—*Carmichael Lectures* Vol. I, Ch. I.

For the colonial expansion in the Far East:

Chatterji, B. R.—*Indian Cultural Influence in Cambodia.*
Majumdar, R. C.—*Ancient Indian Colonies in the Far East,*
Vol. I. *Champā* (1927).
Vol. II. *Suvarṇadvīpa.* Part I (1936), Part II (1938).
————*Kambujadeśa* (1944).
————*Ancient Indian Colonisation in South-East Asia* (Baroda 1955).
————*Hindu Colonies in the Far East* (1944).
(Useful for the beginners).

The Indian colonisation in Central Asia is dealt with by Sir A. Stein in a number of publications which have all been superseded by his monumental work "*Ser-India*".

P. C. Bagchi—*India and Central Asia* (Calcutta, 1955) gives a good introduction to the subject.

For China.

Bagchi, P. C.—*India and China.*

On the trade and maritime activity:

Chanda, R. P.—Early Indian Seamen (*Ashutosh Jubilee volume III*, part I, p. 105).

Mookerji, R. K.—*A History of Indian Shipping and Maritime activity.*

Rawlinson, G.—*Intercourse between India and the Western World.*

Schoff—*Periplus of the Erythraean Sea.*

Warmington, E. H.—*Commerce between the Roman Empire and India* (1928).

On Trade-Organisations,

Majumdar. R. C.—*Corporate Life in Ancient India*, Ch. I.

On Social and Economic condition in ancient India:

Banerji, N. C.—*Economic Life and Progress in Ancient India.*

Das, S. K.—*The Economic History of Ancient India.*

Fick—*Social Organisation in North-Eastern India in Buddha's time* (Translated into English, by Dr. S. K. Maitra).

Mehta, R.—*Pre-Buddhist India.*

Davids, Rhys.—*Buddhist India*, Chs. III, V, VI.

Samaddar, J. N.—*Economic condition of Ancient India.*

CHAPTER IX

Bachhofer, L.—*Early Indian Sculpture* (1925).

Brown, P.—*Indian Architecture* (1949).

Coomaraswamy, A. K.—*History of Indian and Indonesian Art* (1927).

Fergusson—*History of Indian and Eastern Architecture.* (1910).

Fergusson and Burgess—*Cave Temples of India* (1880).

Havell, E. B.—*A Handbook of Indian Art.*

————*Indian Sculpture and Painting.*

————*The Ideals of Indian Art.*

————*The Ancient and Mediaeval architecture in India.* (Mr. Havell's books, though open to criticism in many respects, give a new interpretation, and bring fresh ideas on the subject.).

Kramrisch, S.—*Indian Sculpture* (1933).

————*The Hindu Temple* (1946).

Ray, Niharranjan—*Maurya and Sunga Art* (1945).

Saraswati, S. K.—*A Survey of Indian Sculpture* (Culcutta, 1957).

Smith, V. A.—*History of fine Art in India and Ceylon* (1930).

For Art associated with Buddhism:—

Foucher, A.—*Beginnings of Buddhist Art* (1918).

Grunwedel—*Buddhist Art in India* (1901).

Vogel—*Buddhist Art in India Ceylon and Java* (1936).

For Gandhāra Art :

Foucher—*L'Art Graeco-bouddhique du Gandhara* (1923).

There exist, besides, a large number of monographs on important buildings, and valuable informations are scattered in the publications of the Archaeological Department.

BOOK III

CHAPTER I

The history of the Guptas is derived mainly from their coins and inscriptions. The inscriptions were edited by Fleet in *Corpus Inscriptionum Indicarum* Vol. III, but some important inscriptions have been discovered since. Many of these are collected in "*Select Inscriptions*" by D. C. Sircar. For the coins cf. "Allan—*Catalogue of the Coins of the Gupta Dynasties* etc. The Introduction to this book gives good resume of historical information.

For the general history of the period:

Banerji, R. D.—*The Age of the Imperial Guptas* (1933). (Somewhat out of date).

Majumdar, R. C. and Altekar, A. S.—*The Vākāṭaka-Gupta Age* (1946). (This book contains a complete list of the Gupta inscriptions with Bibliographical references).

Mookerji, R. K.—*Gupta Empire* (1948).

CHAPTERS II-XIII

(In addition to General Works mentioned on p. 499).

1. *North India*

Barua, K. L.—*Early History of Kāmarūpa.*

Bose, N. S.—*History of the Candellas* (Calcutta, 1956)

Ganguly, D. C.—*History of the Paramāra Dynasty.*

Majumdar, A. K.—*Chaulukyas of Gujarat* (Bombay, 1956).

Majumdar, R. C.—*The Arab Invasion of India.*

————*History of Bengal*, Vol. I. (Edited by R. C. Majumdar).

Mookerjee, R. K.—*Harsha.* (This book has to be used with great caution by the beginners as it contains a number of statements not based on facts).

Niyogi, Roma—*The History of the Gāhaḍavāla Dynasty* (Calcutta, 1959).

Panikkar, M—*Harsha-vardhana.*

Petech, Luciano—*Mediaeval History of Nepal*(Rome, 1958).

Sinha, B. P.—*The Decline of the Kingdom of Magadha* (Patna, 1954).

Tripathi, R. S.—*History of Kanauj.*

2. *Deccan and Southern India*

Altekar, A. S.—*The Rāshṭrakūṭas.*
Banerji, R. D.—*History of Orissa.*
Dubreuil.—*Ancient History of the Deccan.*
————*The Pallavas.*
Ganguly, D. C.—*Eastern Chālukyas.*
Gopalan—*The Pallavas.*
Krishna, M. V.—*The Gangas of Talkad* (1936).
Misra, B.—*Dynasties of Mediaeval Orissa.*
Mukherjee, Prabhat—*The History of the Gajapati Kings of Orisso* (Calcutta, 1953).
Sastri, K. A. N.—*The Colas.*
————*The Pāṇḍyan Kingdom.*
Venkataramanayya—*The Eastern Chālukyas.*

For Muslims Invasion cf:—

Iswari Prasad—*Mediaeval India.*
Nazim, M.—*Sultan Mahmud of Ghazni.*
Habibulla, A. B. M.—*Foundation of Muslim Rule in India.*

CHAPTERS XIV-XX

(In addition to books mentioned in the bibliography to corresponding chapters in Book II).

CHAPTER XIV

Aiyangar, S. K.—*Ancient India* (deals with South India only).
Śukranīti, Translated by B. K. Sarkar.

CHAPTER XV

Majumdar, R. C.—*Corporate Life in Ancient India* (Ch. II.)
Mookerjee, R. K.—*Local Self-Government in Ancient India*

CHAPTER XVI

Chatterji, J. C.—*Kashmir Saivism* (1914).
Farquhar, J. N.—*Religious Literature of India.*
Rajagopalachariyar—*Life of Rāmānujāchārya* (1909).
Subramanian, K. R.—*The Origin of Saivism and its history in the Tamil land* (1929).
Thomas, P.—*Hindu Religion, Customs and Manners.*

CHAPTER XVII

Das Gupta, S. N. and De, S. K.—*History of Classical Sanskrit Literature* (Calcutta University) (1947).
Keith, A. B—*History of Classical Sanskrit Literature* (1928).
————*The Sanskrit Drama* (1924)

CHAPTER XVIII

Altekar, A. S.—*Education in Ancient India*, 4th Ed. (1951).
Mookerjee, R. K.—*Ancient Indian Education* (1947).
Sankalia, H. D.—*The University of Nālandā* (1934).

CHAPTER XIX

Ghoshal, U. N.—*The Agrarian System in Ancient India* (Calcutta, 1930).
Ghoshal U. N.—*Contributions to the History of the Hindu Revenue System* (Calcutta, 1929).
Maity, S. K.—*The Economic Life of Northern India in Gupta Period* (Calcutta, 1957).

CHAPTER XX

In addition to works mentioned on pp. 510-11.

Agrawal, V. S.—*Gupta Art* (1947).
Brown, P.—*Indian Painting* (1930).
Dubreuil, G. J.—*Dravidian Architecture.*
Griffiths—*Ajanta Frescoes.*
Kramrisch, S.—*A Survey of Painting in the Deccan.*
Lady Herringham—*Ajanta Frescoes.*

CHAPTER XXII

See Bibliography under Book II, Ch. VIII.

Identification of ancient places (Places which are identified in the text are not included in this list).

[The following books may be recommended for further study on this subject.

1. Pargiter—*Mārkaṇḍeya Purāṇa* (Eng. Translation)—the chapter entitled "Description of the World."

2. Cunningham—*Ancient Geography of India*—Edited by S. N. Majumdar.

3. Dey, N. L.—*The Geographical Dictionary of Ancient and Mediaeval India.*

Many of the following names indicate both a tribe as well as a country; some, both a city and a country].

Ānartta—Western part of Kathiawar Peninsula. The famous city Dvārakā was its capital.

Aṅga—The modern districts of Bhagalpur and Monghyr, and portion of Purnea.

Avanti—Western Malwa. Sometimes it designated the whole of Malwa.

Chedi—It occupied the country along the south bank of the Yamuna from the Chambal on the N. W. to Karwi on the S. E. Malwa and the hills of Bundelkhand formed its southern limit.

Chera—See page 136.

Chola—See page 136.

Dāhala or *Dabhālā*—Jubbulpore region.

Gandhāra—See p. 284.

Gauda—It originally denoted a part of Bengal but was later used as a designation of the whole province. Karṇa-suvarṇa, the capital of Gauḍa, has been identified with Rāngamati 12 miles south of Murshidabad.

Girivraja—The capital of Magadha. It is now represented by the ruins at Rajgir in the Bihar Sub-division.

Gurjara—The Gurjara tribe gave its name to various places in N. W. India. About the 9th and 10th century A. D. the country, now called Rājputāna, was known as Gurjaratrā-bhūmi. This name corrupted into Gujarat, was applied later to the modern province of that name, probably after its conquest by the Chaulukyas.

Hastināpur.—See under Kuru.

Kaliṅga—It comprised modern Orissa about as far north as the town of Bhadrak in the Balasore District, and the sea-coast south-ward as far as Vizagapatam.

Kāñchī, the capital of the Pallavas, is represented by the modern city of Conjeeveram near Madras.

Kapilavastu—The site of this city has been identified by the discovery of the Rumindei pillar of Aśoka which marks the exact birth-place of Buddha, i.e., the Lumbini Grove, about one mile north of Paderia in Nepal to the north of the Basti District.

Kārushas—The Kārushas originally dwelt in the Shahabad District but later on migrated towards the S. W. and occupied the hilly tract, of which Rewa is the centre, extending from the Ken in the west to the confines of Bihar in the East.

Kāśī, modern Banaras, was the name of the capital as well as the country.

Kauśāmbī, the capital of Vatsas, has been identified with Kośam on the Yamunā, about 30 miles west of Allahabad.

Keralas—Malabar coast.

Kirāta—The Kirātas formed a series of allied yet distinct tribes or clans inhabiting the Himalayan range and its southern slopes from the Panjāb to Assam and Chittagong.

Kośala—roughly corresponds to modern Awadh. Its earlier capital Ayodhyā was about 1 mile from modern Fyzabad. Śrāvastī, the later capital, has been identified with Sahet-Mahet in Bharaich and Gonda districts.

Kuntala—The Kanara Districts and north-western part of Mysore.

Kuru—The kingdom of the Kurus extended from the Sarasvatī to the Gaṅgā. It was divided into three parts, Kurukshetra, the Kuru proper, and Kurujāṅgala (the forest tract). Its southern boundary was Khāṇḍava. Its capital Hastināpura is usually identified with an old town, 22 miles N. E. of Meerut.

Kuśinagara, the place where Buddha died, has been identified with Kasia, 35 miles to the east of Gorakhpur.

Lāṭa—Southern Gujarat.

Madra—see p. 284.

Magadha—It comprised the modern districts of Patna, Gayā and Shahabad.

Mālava—Modern Malwa.

Matsya—Modern Alwar State with portions of Jaipur and Bharatpur.

Mekala—The hilly country round Mekala hills which bound Chattisgarh on the north and west.

Nālandā, the site of the famous University, has been located in the village of Bargaon, 7 miles north of Rajgir. Excavations have unearthed many interesting remains.

Odra or Udra originally comprised N. Orissa, W. Midnapur and probably Manbhum, E. Singhbhum and S. Bankura.

Pañchāla—It roughly corresponded to Budaon, Farrukhabad and the neighbouring districts. It was divided into two kingdoms, N. Panchāla (capital, Ahichchhatra) and S. Panchāla (cap. Kāmpilya). Ahichchhatra has been identified with Ramnagar in Bareilly Dt. and Kāmpilya with Kampil in Farrukhabad district.

Pāṇdya—See p. 136.

Pauṇḍra denoted the same people or country as Puṇḍra, but sometimes it comprised the modern districts of Sāntāl Parganas and Birbhum and the northern portion of the Hazaribagh Dt.

Pāvā—There were at least two cities of this name. One was near Kuśinagara and has been identified by some with the village Padarauana 12 miles to the N.N.E. of Kasia, and by others with Asmanpur and neighbouring villages, about 12 miles to the S. E. of Kasia. The other, still a famous place of pilgrimage for the Jainas, is situated within the Bihar Subdivision.

Puṇḍra comprised the districts of Malda, Purnea, Dinajpur and Rajshahi.

Ramaṭhas—A western people mentioned in the *Mahābhārata*.

Śākambharī—Sambhar in Jaipur.

Sukma—It comprised the modern districts of Hooghly, Howrah, Bankura and Burdwan and the eastern portion of Midnapur.

Takshaśilā—This famous city, the seat of an ancient University, has been identified with the ruins near Sarai-kala 20 miles N. W of Rawalpindi, Excavations have unearthed many interesting monuments.

Tosalī—This has been tentatively identified with Dhaulī, about 7 miles to the south of Bhuvanesvara in Orissa, where a recension of the 14 Rock Edicts of Aśoka has been discovered.

Utkala—denoted the southern portion of Chota Nagpur and the northern part of Orissa.

Vaiśālī—This city, the famous capital of the Lichchhavis, has been identified with the small village of Basarh in the Muzaffarpur district.

Vaḷabhī—The kingdom of Valabhī comprised the Kathiawar peninsula and the districts of Broach and Surat. The capital city of the same name is represented by the ruins at Wala 18 miles N. W. of Bhaunagar.

Vaṅga—It must have comprised a large part of Central, Southern and Eastern Bengal.

Vaṅgāla—South and East Bengal.

Vatsa—The country along the Yamunā, to the west of Allahabad, with Kauśāmbī (q. v.) as its capital.

Vidarbha—It roughly corresponded to modern Berar.

INDEX

(Abbreviation : K=king)

B

N

O

P

T

Plate I

Indus Valley Seals.

Plate II

Male Statue, Harappa.

Asoka Pillar (Lauriya Nandanagarh).

Plate IV

Birth of Buddha (Gandhāra School).

Plate V

Head of Buddha (Gandhāra School).

Plate VI

Karle Cave (p. 225).

Plate VII

Ajanta Cave (General View).

Plate VIII

Facade of Cave No. XIX, Ajanta.

Plate IX

Interior Pillars, Cave No. I, Ajanta.

Plate X

Paintings Cave No XVII Ajanta

Scroll (Gupta Period).

Plate XII

Buddhist Image (Nālandā) (Early Medieval).

Silver Viṣṇu Image (N. Bengal) (Medieval).

Plate XIV

Mother and Child, (Bhuvanesvar) (Medieval).

Mukteśvara Temple (Bhuvanesvar) (Medieval).

Plate XVI

Khajurāho Temple (Medieval).

Plate XVII

Ceiling of Dilwara Temple, Mt. Abu (Medieval).

Plate XVIII

The Great Temple of T

Naṭarāja (South India).